MILITARY and NAVAL SILVER

Treasures of the Mess and Wardroom

MILITARY and NAVAL SILVER

Treasures of the Mess and Wardroom

Roger Perkins

1999

PO Box 29 - Newton Abbot - Devon TQ12 1XU
United Kingdom

Military and Naval Silver
Treasures of the Mess and Wardroom

Copyright, Roger Perkins, 1999

ISBN 0 9506429 4 0

British Library Cataloguing-in-publication Data.
A catalogue record for this book is available from the British Library.

By the same author

(for Kenneth Mason, Havant, Hampshire)
Gunfire in Barbary (with Captain K J Douglas-Morris RN, 1982)

(for Picton Publishing, Chippenham, Wiltshire)
Angels in Blue Jackets (with J W Wilson, 1983)
The Kashmir Gate (1983)
The Punjab Mail Murder (1979 and 1986)
Operation Paraquat - The Battle for South Georgia 1982 (1986)
The Amritsar Legacy (1989)

(privately)
Regiments of the Empire, A Bibliography (1992)
Pathfinder Pilot (1992)
Regiments and Corps of the British Empire and Commonwealth, 1758-1993,
(A Critical Bibliography of their Published Histories) (1994)

Printed on 150 gsm Fineblade manufactured by Townsend Hook Ltd in compliance with American Standard code Z 39.48 (Permanence of Paper and Publications and Documents in Libraries and Archives), and ISO 9706: 1994 (E) - Information and Documentation (Paper for Documents).

Typeset by the author and published privately
Design and origination by Andrew Penny

Printed by Abbey Printers, Salisbury House, Newton Abbot, Devon

Contents

Author's Introduction

Why climb the mountain? Because it's there. Why write a book about military silver? Because nobody has ever done it before. Not in itself a compelling motivation, of course, but it was enough to get me started, three years ago.

Having made a beginning, in 1996, I discovered other reasons to justify the time and effort involved. First was the shock of my early encounters with members of the antiques trade, and in particular with those who deal in second-hand silver. Without exception, they assured me "there's no demand for stuff with army wording engraved on it". So what happens when it comes up for sale at a local auction? "That depends. If the engraving was lightly done, it can be polished off and the piece recycled, as a plain cup, bowl, salver, tankard, cigarette box, or whatever. If the engraver's tool cut deep - too deep to be buffed out - then it goes for scrap".

To someone who had been involved for twenty-odd years in the area of military and naval history - researching and writing - all of this was disturbing and depressing. Dealer after dealer told the same story. "It was a nice enough piece. A pity about all that lettering. Not economic to have it taken off. Binned it".

If this book achieves nothing else, I hope it will sound the alarm. Over many years, thousands of items of military and naval silver have been either melted or had their proof of provenance removed by buffing and re-plating. This is not the fault of the dealing profession. They are in business to earn a livelihood, and they respond to the demands of their market. Conservation of a part of our martial heritage is not their responsibility.

It is important here to distinguish between the major pieces which constitute the bulk of the entries in this book, and the relatively minor items which come to light at provincial auctions and antiques fairs. As will become clear, the former are of museum quality and are most unlikely ever to pass into private hands. The latter are those lesser pieces which, once part of an individual's life and career, became unwanted after he and his immediate family died. This aspect of the subject is pursued in greater detail in Chapter Nine and Appendix "B".

In a much broader context, a primary purpose of the book is to permit everyone interested in silver to see beautiful objects to which normally they have no access. I have stressed, in the narrative and particularly in Chapter One, that they are "the family silver" of the officers and senior non-commissioned officers who have acquired them over a period of one hundred and fifty years and more. Many were made by the most remarkable silversmiths of their day. The craftsmanship incorporated in the great monumental centrepieces illustrated in the following chapters deserves to be viewed by a wider audience, and this can achieved only by the publication of a book.

Hundreds of British Army and associated units, of one period or another, have possessed collections of silver. Regular Army regiments and corps, the Yeomanry, the Volunteers, Militia, Territorials, all have had their own Mess or regimental chattels and treasures. Many are in daily (or at least frequent) use by their original owners. Others have been inherited by successor units, or can be seen in regimental museums, national museums, and the civic museums of counties with which traditionally they are associated. It was never realistic to think of including in this book a representative piece from each and every one. So what has determined its contents?

There are three answers to this question. First and foremost has been the availability of photographs of publishable quality. Certain regiments have good picture archives, the majority do not. Second has been the availability of the required technical descriptions - dimensions, weights, maker's marks and assay marks. For reasons well understood, this information in most cases has never been recorded. Third, obviously, has been the willingness and ability of the custodians to respond to my appeals for assistance. Regimental secretaries and museum curators are busy people, and rarely have all the staff and other resources necessary to deal with the type of demanding enquiry which I was raising.

Those who reacted most positively to my early appeals - mainly through the good offices of The Army Museums Ogilby Trust - did so from a shared enthusiasm for the subject, and a desire to see the history of their regiment and its forebears given an added place in the nation's military bibliography.

In these circumstances, it was evident from the outset that my coverage would appear to be random and unstructured. In compensation, I have attempted to describe the silver of as many different types of collection as possible (both military and maritime), so that they might represent the entire spectrum.

It was never my intention to restrict the coverage solely to the British Army, the Royal Navy and the Royal Marines. Given their shared services in past wars, I aimed also to include some silver of the armed forces of the British Empire and Commonwealth. Thanks to the tremendous interest of The Indian Army Association and its membership, the silver of the old Indian Army receives, in Chapters Four and Five, the attention which it merits. Sadly, despite the best efforts of my many supporters, it has not been possible to unearth any meaningful information in respect of Canada and South Africa, or any of the former Colonies. Only Australia and New Zealand receive some mention (thanks to the efforts of two old and valued friends in those countries).

A few items of aviation interest are described in Chapter Eight. I had hoped to devote as much space to the silver of the

Royal Air Force and the Royal Auxiliary Air Force as to the other services, but the plan came to nothing. Perhaps another writer will one day tackle this interesting area of research.

Apart from the reasons already stated, what message is the book intended to convey? That is simply answered. I have aimed to demonstrate that military and naval silver is unique. It is not just an inanimate alloy, worked into a decorative shape or designed to fulfil a practical function. It is much more than that. Each piece was made to mark a specific event within the framework of the nation's military or maritime history, and each was directly identified with the men engaged in those events. The majority are long dead, but I have told their individual stories as a means of breathing new life into the artefacts which bear their names. Most of them are otherwise forgotten. Here, in their silver, is the permanent record of their years of service and of their passing. It may not be living history, but it is something very close.

Roger Perkins
Haytor, Devon, 1999

Some years ago, a distinguished elder statesman was being interviewed and the talk turned to his life as a young man. In 1944 he had won the Military Cross for a very courageous act during the attempt to reach the besieged airborne forces at Arnhem. Unaware that he was posing an unwise question, the interviewer enquired: "Did you enjoy your time in the army?". His guest visibly stiffened. "The army? I was not in the army, I was with the Grenadier Guards".

While baffling to someone who has never served, his response was understandable to those who have. Central to the story of the British Army and the armies of the British Commonwealth is the concept of pride in one's own regiment or battalion. An elusive quality, *esprit de corps* enables each unit to claim a degree of uniqueness (and, by implication, superiority). It applies to officers and to other ranks in equal measure.

As a full-time establishment, the British Army has always been small when compared with the continental armies against which it has from time to time been pitted. In the world wars of the 20th century, its ranks were thinned severely by the opening battles. British Expeditionary Forces crossed the Channel in 1914 and 1939, but they were almost destroyed at Mons, the Marne and Ypres, and, twenty-six years later, at Calais, St Valery and Dunkirk. For each of the regiments and battalions concerned, the deaths resulting from those early battles caused, at least for a time, a loss of that sense of being a close-knit family which so distinguished their peacetime *ethos*.

The greatly expanded armies which succeeded them were composed largely of volunteers and conscripts, civilians in uniform. The new battalions were commanded by surviving pre-war officers who, promoted away from their parent regiments, prepared to return to battle in the company of comparative strangers. It was their task then to instil a sense of regimental pride in men whose main ambition was to win the war as quickly as possible and, with luck, return intact to their families and peacetime occupations.

That those pre-war officers were generally successful in their aim is a tribute to the strength and permanence of regimental values. Those values were drilled into every young wartime officer and ranker from the earliest days of his basic training. By the time he reached the front line, each was convinced that he and his friends were serving with the finest military unit in the world. This moral ascendancy over the enemy was on many occasions a battle-winning advantage.

The uniqueness of every regiment and battalion has always been reflected in a number of ways, the most obvious outward manifestations being its Colours and Battle Honours, variations in its Dress uniform, the music played by its band, its motto and nickname, its connections with a particular county or city, perhaps its choice of animal as mascot, but, most importantly in the eyes of all ranks, in its helmet plate or cap badge. Over the years, as regiments have been re-titled, amalgamated or assigned to new roles, the loss of a familiar and much-loved cap badge and its replacement by a new creation has caused more

anguished debate than any other topic.

Each unit has tried equally hard to retain its "regimental customs", those family traditions which give it an identity separate from any other. Each custom has its origins in a far-distant time and place, some historic occasion when the regiment distinguished itself in one way or another, or was granted some mark of distinction by the Sovereign.

It has been written that "the British Army is a loose affiliation of regiments which choose to serve together, as and when the need arises". At first glance flippant, the analysis in fact contains more than a grain of truth. There are numerous instances in British military history which demonstrate both the strengths and the weaknesses of this approach, but it is *esprit de corps* which has always been at the heart of the matter. In 1947, Lieutenant General Sir Gordon MacMillan of MacMillan, Colonel of The Argyll and Sutherland Highlanders, made an after-dinner speech in which he summarised the services of each of that regiment's battalions during the recent war. He concluded: "All those chaps have got what we are so blessed with in this regiment, that most priceless regimental spirit. That is the thing we have got to cherish because it is the one thing which makes the soldier fight that little bit longer and little bit harder than the chap on the other side".

There have been many attempts to analyse and describe the essence of the British regimental system and, specifically, the role of silver within that system. Some have come closer to the truth, or at least been more lucid, than others.

In May 1915, an exhibition of regimental silver was held at the premises of the Goldsmiths & Silversmiths Company, at 112 Regent Street, London. It was organised by the British Red Cross and the Order of St John with the purpose of raising funds for the care of the war's sick and injured. The printed catalogue of the items on display was prefaced by an Introduction written by John Fortescue, one of the most erudite of the British Army's many historians. Within the confines of the limited space available to him, he struggled to convey the sentiments and convictions which he felt so profoundly.

"A regiment, even as a College or an Inn of Court, is or tends to become an ancient and honourable Society, to which all its members are, as a rule, most tenderly attached. It has its traditions of great men nurtured and of great services done, and its hallowed memories of suffering manfully endured and of heroic souls who have passed away in glory. In such a Society the officers correspond to Fellows of a College or Benchers of an Inn. It is their duty to uphold the noble traditions they have inherited, and to strive to pass them forward, still more ennobled, to the generations that follow after them. And as Fellows, out of gratitude to the kindly nurse which has reared them, have for ages past rejoiced to enrich their college with endowments and gifts or to adorn it with new and sometimes beautiful buildings; so do officers, according to their means, which are not generally great, seek to enhance the honour of their regiments, occasionally by endowments, but more often by

A photograph which incorporates all the icons of *esprit de corps* and regimental tradition. It was taken at Werl in 1977 when the 1st Battalion, The East Surrey Regiment, displayed its treasures as part of an Anglo-German Week. Dominated by the Queen's Colour and the Regimental Colour, it features the Colour belts, the silver drums, two silver bugles, the Drum Major's silver decorated staff, and all the principal items of Mess table silver. Photo: Lieut Col L M B Wilson MBE.

a present of plate to the officers' mess. Regimental messes, as a general institution in the army, are not much more than a century old; but they are the centres of regimental life, and though possessed of no continuing home, as are Colleges and Inns, carry with them through all their wanderings, except on active service, the household gods which are little less sacred to the regiment than its Colours".

Reading these lines today, some of us might have difficulty with Fortescue's analogous references to Fellows and Benchers, but there is no doubting his intent. He understood full well the function of the regimental Mess, and the role of the silver within it.

There have always been variations in the "Mess rules" and "the customs of the Mess" from one regiment or battalion to another, but particularly from one era to another. The ways in which officers conduct themselves and their daily affairs are firmly rooted in traditions inherited from their predecessors, but they are not immutable. The British Army, as a permanent armed defender of the nation's interests, has existed for three hundred years. Inevitably, as the structure or role of the army has changed, and as the society from which it draws its members has changed, so has the domestic life of the Mess gradually evolved in response to those changes.

The pace of change was at times so slow as to be imperceptible. There have been officers who would have denied strongly that they were conceding one iota of their treasured traditions, who would have responded with suspicion to any

appeal for "progress", and yet they were themselves contributors to the process of change. The beliefs and attitudes of the officer class of the late 19th and early 20th centuries, as an example, were in some ways very different to those of their pre-1870 predecessors. Prior to that year, any eligible young man with money and good connections in society's ruling classes might purchase a commission in the regiment of his choice. If it then proved not to be to his liking, or if it received orders to embark for an overseas station where he did not care to go, he could sell his commission in that regiment and buy another in one of the regiments whose current location was, in terms of his own social and sporting activities, more conveniently located.

All of this depended, of course, upon whether or not there was a vacancy in the regiment, and whether its officers desired his company. It was they who decided whether or not he would "fit in". The applicant needed sufficient private funds not only to acquire the commission but also to then maintain the lifestyle associated with that particular Mess. Each regiment jealously guarded its reputation for dash and courage in pursuit of the fox, for its place in smart society, for its exceptional gallantry in battle, or for whatever other attribute it claimed as peculiarly its own.

Preferred applicants were those whose family background was well known and well regarded. If their fathers, brothers, brothers-in-law and cousins had served with the regiment, and if *they* had "fitted in", then clearly this latest member would be assured of a warm welcome. This is still today a factor in

The British Army's regiments of cavalry, whether horsed or mechanised, have always taken pride in their dash and style. Their standards are reflected in the quality of these pieces, presented to individual officers of the 12th Royal Lancers (Prince of Wales's). The clock on the left was *Presented to Lieutenant R B Wood on the occasion of his marriage. July 1907.* The mounted officer on the right is inscribed *Presented to Captain L Salt MBE by his brother officers on his leaving after 27 years continuous service with the regiment, 14th February 1919 to 7th August 1946.* Photo: Bonhams, Knightsbridge

whether or not a young man entering his profession will be successful when applying to join the regiment or corps of his preference. The same applies to the other ranks. The army is always sympathetic when, for example, a soldier asks if he may join his brother already serving with a particular unit, or if his father had served with it. The policy is sensible, and again ensures continuity of the unit as a family.

Not all commissions and promotions were acquired by purchase. An officer who had won a reputation for bravery or horsemanship or skill-at-arms, but whose chances of promotion within his own regiment were blocked by the number of established officers holding higher rank, might be warmly received if he applied for transfer to another, with or without payment. Similarly, although to a much lesser degree, a non-commissioned officer who had served his regiment well for many years, and was of outstanding character, could be granted a commission even though he had little money and few connections in high places. Lack of financial resources and an unfamiliarity with the social graces were a hindrance but never, in themselves, a barrier to promotion.

There were some officers whose personal wealth permitted them to hold two commissions at the same time. Lord Heathfield, as George August Elliott, was for many years an officer in the Corps of Royal Engineers, but he took the precaution of buying a second commission in the cavalry (in which promotion was faster). Eventually he resigned his Engineer commission, became a cavalry general and was Governor and Commander in Chief of Gibraltar during the great siege of 1779-1782. His portrait by Sir Joshua Reynolds hangs in the National Gallery.

There can have been few officers of the later generations who would have wished to see a return to "purchase". Its abolition, under the Cardwell reforms of 1870-1871, greatly reinforced the concept of the Mess as being a family home rather than, in the worst instances, a club where its members occasionally dined. It also provided an added impetus for the great flowering in military silversmithing which occurred in the

second half of the 19th century.

Presentation and decorative pieces manufactured during the reign of Queen Victoria reflect not only the exuberant, even ostentatious, tastes of her reign, they also mirror the sense of life-time commitment to their regiments felt by their officers. The same applied equally to the members of the Sergeants' Messes. The option of "purchase" never existed for the other ranks, but the impact of being commanded by officers who, after abolition, stayed with them throughout their parallel careers, filtered down and gave the non-commissioned officers a reason and motivation for acquiring Mess treasures of their own.

There were other changes which, in theory at least, might have undermined regimental life. The creation in 1858 of the Staff College, in Camberley, Surrey, was viewed with suspicion by many of "the old and bold". They would have disputed hotly any allegation that their military abilities were amateur but, paradoxically, might have shied away from any claim to professionalism.

A Captain or junior Major who expressed interest in gaining the letters "p.s.c." (passed Staff College) after his name was liable to be treated with amusement or even disdain. To be described as "a clever sort of chap" could be a mixed blessing.

By actively seeking an appointment to the Staff and eventual higher command, the aspirant was in effect stating that his commitment to the army exceeded his commitment to the regiment. For a while, his connection with it was weakened. Later, if he rose to general officer rank, and possibly gained a reputation as a commander of large formations in combat, the regiment proudly claimed him as one of their own. If he was very fortunate, and if the honorary appointment was due to fall vacant, he might be invited to become Colonel of the Regiment. He then once again became intimately involved in its affairs.

The modern British Army is in many respects a very different organisation to that which landed in France in 1914 and its successor which disembarked on that same coast in 1939. Developments in weaponry and methods of communication demand levels of technical competence unknown to former generations of regimental officer. This applies equally to all arms and corps. The current list of officers on the Active List of The Devonshire & Dorset Regiment, as an example, reveals that almost half of them are university graduates. By contrast, W J P Aggett, one of the historians of The Devonshire Regiment, noted that, as late as 1943, there was at that time only one serving officer in the entire regiment who had attended the Staff College (and none had attended a university).

The other ranks also are required to do far more than march and shoot. The impact of modern technology extends to every level.

From all of this it might be assumed that many of the old criteria of military life have been abandoned, or at least altered to such an extent as to have become unrecognisable. However, it is evident that a personal commitment to, first, the regiment (or the battalion), then secondly to the army in general, is still the norm. The terms "brother officer" and "comrade in arms" continue to be more than courtesies, they are a statement of belief.

Officers and soldiers do not *belong* to their regiment, they are *members* of it. They do not serve *in* their unit, they serve *with* it. The intimacy of the relationship is reflected in numerous other subtleties of language. Precisely the same *nuances* are appropriate to membership of an exclusive club, one in which everyone knows everyone else, and in which the rules and customs are tacitly understood and observed.

For nearly three hundred years, every British soldier knew where he stood. His core convictions were based upon service to "God, King and Country". He understood that he was required to fight, and if necessary die, to preserve a national way of life. Much has changed since the end of WWII. Simple certainties have withered under the pressure of political restraint and changing public perceptions.

The greatest influence upon his attitudes has been Northern Ireland. There he may expect to die but not to fight. An entire generation of soldiers have served their time according to "the yellow card rules" which grant the enemy advantages he would never enjoy on the field of battle.

It can be argued that *esprit de corps* rooted in the regimental system is the only thing which has prevented the army from declining into open cynicism and disillusion. No other army in the world could have done what the British Army has been ordered to do in Northern Ireland without losing its way.

That its self-esteem and fighting edge have remained intact, over more than thirty years of "aid to the civil power", was proven in the only two open wars to which the Northern Ireland generation has been committed - the Falklands, and the Gulf. On both occasions the enemy was more numerous and, in the Falklands, better equipped. Were those men fighting for "God, Queen and Country"? Patriotism, certainly, even jingoism, had an enormous influence upon the 1982 conflict in the South Atlantic. For the rest, they seem to have been driven primarily by loyalty to their friends, to their cap badge, and to the traditions which they inherited. This much, at least, they had in common with their forebears.

The number of retired officers who were commissioned before 1939, and who therefore are able to recall army life as it was between the two world wars, diminishes by the year. The following pages will be devoted to the recollections of a number of them. They served with the British Army and the Indian Army, and they have kindly agreed to record their experiences for the purposes of this book. Much of what they will tell us resides only in their individual memories. It is a story of military life, of *domestic* military life, which has not previously attracted the interest of historians.

The events of 1938 were the precursor for five terrible years to come. Hitler made his first armed seizure of a neighbour's territory when his troops marched into the Sudetenland and so set in motion the beginnings of the second world war. During what came to be known as "the Munich Crisis", the British Prime Minister twice flew to Germany to plead for peace. He conferred with the Nazi leader and accepted his assurances that Germany had no further territorial ambitions. The British people wanted desperately to believe that Neville Chamberlain had indeed saved them from the horrors of another European war, but most members of the armed forces were not so sanguine. If ever there was a time for any young man to be entering into the life of a soldier, this surely was one of the most sombre.

Second Lieutenant R P S Erskine-Tulloch passed out of the Royal Military College, Sandhurst, in July, 1938. Granted a commission in The Northamptonshire Regiment, he travelled to Ballykinler Camp, County Down, to join its 2nd Battalion. This had been the 58th (Rutlandshire) Regiment of Foot, and to many it was still known simply as "the 58th". He arrived there in late September, shortly after Chamberlain returned to London and proclaimed "peace in our time".

"A subaltern who had joined the year before said 'I wouldn't unpack if I were you', but he was referring to the Crisis, not the possibility of my being unwelcome in the Battalion. Ballykinler was a remote place, and the camp had originally been built to hold German prisoners during the Great War. It was really three camps: the one occupied by the 58th (as garrison battalion), a second, of wooden huts, near the ranges and occupied for only a few weeks each year by battalions from Belfast firing their annual range course, and a third, of corrugated iron like our own, which had been turned into married quarters for our other ranks. There was a NAAFI shop and store there, the official address of which was 'World's End Camp, Ballykinler', a name which might well have applied to all three.

The building of a permanent barracks had started a year or two before, as part of the Hore Belisha army reforms. By the time I joined, the new buildings included the Orderly Room and Guard Room, the Sergeants' Mess, the NAAFI and Regimental Institutes, and the Officers' Mess, but not the mens' accommodation. This struck me as being the wrong way around, but it was obviously not the battalion's choice. The officers had actually moved into our very well appointed Mess only a week or so before I joined.

There were fifteen of us living in, and I was immediately made to feel at home. I say 'at home' with good reason because, to us, the unmarried officers of all ages and ranks, this *was* our home.

We covered a wide range of experience and rank: two majors with more than twenty years' service (one of whom was the second-in-command, Major J W Hinchcliffe), one Captain (the Adjutant), two Lieutenants with four years' service each, and ten Second Lieutenants with service varying from three years down to one month (in the case of the three of us just joined from the RMC).

I have said that we were made to feel welcome, but obviously there were rules and customs to be observed, just as there had been at prep school, at public school, and at Sandhurst. You kept your mouth reasonably shut, your ears open, and took care not to irritate senior officers who, although always pleasant to us, had nonetheless become very set in their ways after twenty years of Mess life. Much of their service had been spent in bad climates and long before the introduction of air conditioning, refrigerators and Paludrine. They had also, as very young men in the First World War, been through experiences the horror of which we could hardly grasp.

In the 58th we followed the usual custom of presenting an item of silver on joining, but one was not expected to do it immediately. For those of us who joined in 1938 and early 1939, the war caused any presentation to be much postponed. We also often presented something on reaching field rank. I did this in 1955 when I rejoined the 2nd Battalion from the Staff as a substantive Major (after holding the temporary rank for eight years!). I discovered that the Mess had no silver frame to hold the Band programme on Guest Nights and Dinner nights. There had been one years earlier, but it had fallen by the wayside. I had a new one made, with a mounted regimental crest, and it was always placed on the dining table in front of the senior officer and senior guest. I believe it is still used regularly by our

successors, the 2nd Battalion of The Royal Anglian Regiment.

It was not the custom to make a presentation on leaving the battalion, but some Commanding Officers did so on retirement or on promotion. Then, there were occasions when an officer purchased a silver or silver-plated bugle and presented it to the Corps of Drums upon being appointed Adjutant.

Surprisingly quickly we were 'accepted' and, while we were still careful not to 'hog' the Ante Room fire if our seniors were about, we were in no way repressed. Indeed, from the early Spring of 1939, we found ourselves in a much younger Mess. One of the Majors and the Adjutant had left, the new Adjutant being a Lieutenant with six years' service who had come home from India, from the 1st Battalion, to take up the appointment. The Second in Command was still there, but he had always been well disposed to the younger officers anyway. The two Lieutenants had gone, one to India and the other to married life. The Senior Second Lieutenant (an acknowledged position in those days) had achieved his full Lieutenancy and gone to

In contrast with Pat Erskine-Tulloch's account of his otherwise unrecorded initiation into military life, this salver reminds us of an era when senior army officers enjoyed a huge popular following. One who received the greatest public acclaim (during and after the Sudan and South African wars at the turn of the century) was Field Marshal Lord Kitchener. Not surprisingly, his was the face chosen for the 1914 recruiting poster, *Your Country Needs You*. In his lifetime, he received a great many tributes and honours, amongst them the Freedom of several cities. This stunning object is engraved *City of Liverpool. The Right Honourable Charles Petrie, Lord Mayor. This silver tray, together with a silver gilt rose water dish and ewer, was presented with the Freedom of the City to General Viscount Kitchener of Khartoum, the Vaal and Aspinall, GCB OM GCMG, 11 October 1902.* Twenty-seven inches across, it is hallmarked Sheffield 1900, but the name of the maker is not known. It is now in the Museum of the Corps of Royal New Zealand Engineers. Kitchener was lost at sea in 1915. His silver was held by his descendents until the early 1950s. They then gave selected items to various regiments and corps with which he had been associated. There are known references to "the Kitchener plate" in Canada, Kenya and New Zealand, but recent searches have failed to uncover any documentation in those countries or elsewhere. Photo: RNZAF, and RNZE Museum.

Palestine to fill a junior staff appointment.

Two more newly-commissioned officers joined us from the RMC in February. The situation was constantly changing as officers with as little as two years' service went off to take up appointments with newly-formed Territorial Army battalions. I suddenly found myself, after only eight months, understudying the Signals Officer and then, two months later, taking over that post. Normally it was held by a senior Subaltern.

Throughout 1939 we became increasingly a Subaltern's mess. Naturally the married officers came in for a drink and a chat before lunch, but the general tone was less formal than before. We all used Christian names or nicknames for one another, although the Second in Command was usually addressed as 'Sir', also the Adjutant most of the time. As to how we lived, the fact is - comfortably. We were not a well-off regiment. For example, I had my pay of eleven shillings (55 pence) per day, plus another shilling for undrawn rations (the amount which the Messing Officer was able to spend at the NAAFI or elsewhere for each man on the strength of the battalion). I also had a scholarship which I had gained on leaving the RMC, and this helped considerably. Some officers, obviously, had personal allowances from their parents. Others had nothing but their pay and army allowances, but Ulster was a good place to live well at no great cost.

For about four shillings a day we had a four-course breakfast, a four-course lunch, afternoon tea, and then, on ordinary nights, a four-course dinner. On Guest or Band Nights (usually once a month) we had as many as five or six courses. At one period we had a similar dinner on Friday nights, including oysters for those who liked them, because our excellent Mess Sergeant considered that we deserved something special at the end of the week (even though, in those days, Saturday was a working day until lunch time).

We ran our own Messing. Some regiments employed a civilian contractor, but that was a much more expensive way of catering. I must stress that the Mess, being our home, was run as one would run one's own home in civil life. There was no interference in this by any army authority other than the general guidance laid down in The King's Regulations. That, and the wishes of the officers as expressed at our quarterly Mess Meetings, or entered in the Mess Suggestions Book, was what governed the way in which the Mess was run. Indeed, there was no outside interference in any aspect of regimental life as a whole.

There was an authorised 'Peace Establishment for Mess Staff', though I imagine it was sometimes exceeded. Apart from the Mess Sergeant and Mess Corporal (who looked after the wines and the cellar), we had a Lance Corporal silverman and

Traditionally, the staff of every Mess included one man, usually a Lance Corporal or Corporal, personally responsible for the care, maintenance and security of the Mess silver. As the nominated Silverman, he reported any damage to the Silver Member of the Mess Committee. He attended a course of instruction at the premises of whichever firm of silversmiths was his regiment's established supplier. Particular care was taken to teach correct methods of polishing so that heavy-handed cleaning did not result in loss of detail to the decorations, inscriptions and marks. In recent years, financial cutbacks and reductions in manpower have stopped this practice. As a consequence, several pieces are known to have been permanently damaged. Illustrated in this 1930s scene is part of the magnificent collection of The Worcestershire Regiment. Photo: RHQ Worcestershire & Sherwood Foresters Regiment.

two trained Officers' Mess cooks. The latter were regimental soldiers; there was no Army Catering Corps before 1941.

The Mess Corporal also supervised the Mess Waiters, of whom we had three: a Lance Corporal and two private soldiers. The officers' servants were also, as far as possible, trained to take their turn as extra waiters on Guest Nights or Dinner Nights when more help was needed in the Dining Room. One of the Subalterns was in charge of wines and one of messing. We were elected, in turn, at the quarterly Mess Meeting, for a three-month period".

It is worth interrupting Pat Erskine-Tulloch's account to comment, at this point, that the principle of giving Mess responsibilities to even the most junior officer was widespread in the British and Empire armies. It was one way of permitting him, from the earliest stage in his career, to make decisions and be answerable for them. Apart from those mentioned above, and depending upon location and circumstance, other such informal titles were gardens member, library member, entertainments member, and silver member.

In the context of this book, the role of the silver member needs some brief explanation. His duties varied from unit to unit, but they came under three main headings. The first was security, it being the officer's duty to meet each month with the Mess Sergeant or one of his staff and together with them physically check the holdings of silver against the inventory. Over the years, there have been occasions when lapses in security have led to considerable pain for the regiments concerned, and one of these is described in Chapter Seven. The second was maintenance, it being the officer's job to be aware of damage to any particular piece and to arrange for its repair.

His third and most interesting task was that of consulting with the Adjutant and the Second in Command as to the best choice of pieces for the next Guest Night dinner table. Only rarely, if ever, might a regiment or battalion display its entire collection of silver at the same time, so the selection could be tailored to the occasion. For example, the principal guest might be an eminent personage who, in his younger years, had served with the regiment. It would please him to see on display the piece of silver which he had presented to the Mess, many years earlier, "on leaving the regiment". Similarly, the guests might include an officer from another regiment, one with which there were close historical ties and which had in the past been marked by exchanges of commemorative silver. Clearly, any such item needed to be brought out of the strong-room and given prominence on that particular night. The young silver member, still learning the history of his own unit, was well advised to consult the collective memory and knowledge of his seniors on such occasions.

Returning now to 1939 and to Second Lieutenant Erskine-Tulloch: "We paid five pounds, spread over as many months, as a Joining Subscription to the Mess. We also paid a monthly subscription equivalent to one day's pay, plus a maintenance charge of about the same amount. There were regular subscriptions to the Band Fund (Majors and Captains only), to the Corps of Drums (Subalterns only), to the Regimental Sports Fund, and to the Silver Fund. There were also small charges for items such as newspapers and magazines, the rental charge for the Mess telephone, and our collective membership of The Ulster Club, in Belfast. That was a most useful base to have, whenever we were visiting the city.

There was no Wedding Presents Fund as such. It was the custom, when a marriage was forthcoming, for the invitation from the bride's parents to be posted on the Mess notice-board.

With it, from the President of the Mess Committee, would be a notification of the proposed regimental present, and it was on this notice that we wrote our names if we wished to subscribe. I think we each paid seven shillings and sixpence, or about thirty-five pence in today's coinage. With many of the officers of the regiment as a whole contributing, that bought in those days a very nice silver salver, engraved with the signatures of those who had subscribed. The salvers were always made for us by the regiment's silversmiths, the Goldsmiths & Silversmiths Company, in Regent Street.

In all, I suppose one's basic monthly Mess bill (without drinks) was about eight or nine pounds. There was not a great deal left out of a Second Lieutenant's net monthly pay of fifteen pounds by the time he had given his soldier servant eleven shillings 'extra duty pay', and paid for his laundry. That came to about three shillings a week, and was done by the wife of one of the soldiers or NCOs. We also had the use of a Government horse, for which we were charged a nominal ten shillings monthly forage money".

Many years have passed since officers of the British Army each had a batman or personal servant to care for them. Pat Erskine-Tulloch's recollections of his own earliest experiences with these often invaluable guides and mentors are very clear: "They ranged from the young soldier, straight from the Depôt and whom the Company Sergeant Major thought bright enough and clean enough to do the job, to the experienced 'old soldier' like the one whom I inherited when one of our married Majors left the battalion in early 1939. I had three soldier servants during the year before the war. The first, whom I shared with another officer, had a few years' service, and I probably learned a good deal from him about regimental life. The second, a youngster straight from recruit training, went on draft to India after a few months, but I got to know him quite well, talking to him while he did his work in my room in the evenings. The third was Lockwood, a likeable rogue with many years of service in India and at home behind him, and a left sleeve covered in Good Conduct stripes. I would have liked to have taken him to France with me when we left Ballykinler to join the BEF but, like some others amongst our 'old soldiers' who had spent a long time abroad, he was not passed fit.

All our servants saw how we lived, and it was obviously a great deal better than they did, but I do not believe that they grudged it to us. Instead they realised the advantages of their job and enjoyed being, at least for part of the time, out of their Company Sergeant Major's grasp. They could gather in the Batmens' Room (in the Mess building) to gossip and drink tea, undisturbed, while they cleaned and polished our kit. I think they regarded being an officer's servant as a 'perk', and were glad of the opportunity. They were supposed to be trained soldiers with certain military and educational qualifications, as well as being of good conduct, but we were so short of man-power at that time that the first two requirements were often waived.

In 1939 we were well under strength, mustering no more than four hundred. Certainly we were catering in the Cookhouse for only about two hundred, a figure which excluded Sergeants and rank and file living in married quarters. These low manning figures reflected the fact that we had provided drafts of men for our 1st Battalion (the old 48th Regiment of Foot), bringing it up to full war strength for the Waziristan campaign of 1936-1937.

Another visitor to one's quarters in the evenings was the Company Orderly Corporal, with the Company Detail Book. This was the Company's orders for the next day, prepared and signed by the Company Sergeant Major on behalf of the

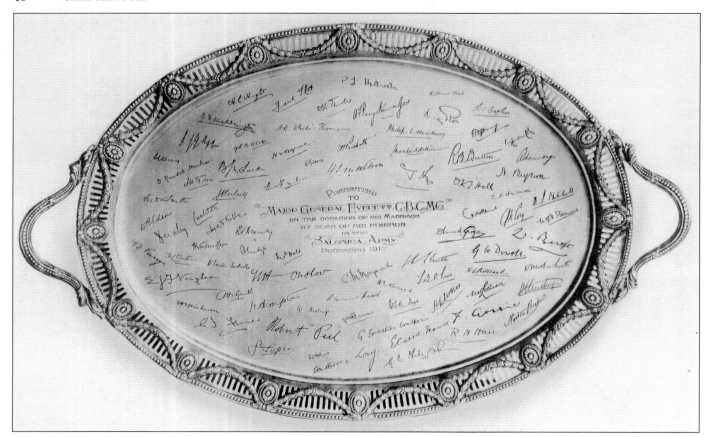

A fine example of an officer's wedding gift, *Presented to Major General Everett CB CMG on the occasion of his marriage, by some of this friends in the Salonika Army, December 1917.* His initials (H J, later Sir Henry) were omitted from the inscription. The National Army Museum has full details of all the officers whose signatures are replicated on the tray. Objects of this type offer an endless source of interest to genealogical researchers. Photo: NAM, Chelsea.

Company commander. All officers living-in had to see and initial it in the evening. I used to take this opportunity to chat with them, and in this way got to know all the junior NCOs.

In the afternoons, most of us were able to play games or ride. Some officers rode with the East Down Hunt or the County Down Staghounds, while others went rough shooting for the abundant snipe (sometimes one could even find snipe within the barracks area, so isolated was Ballykinler in those days). Others, like the Adjutant, still had work to do after lunch (as I did, when I became Signals Officer). After dinner (and incidentally, we dined by candlelight even when the sun was shining outside, that being the custom in the larger private houses in Britain), we managed to amuse ourselves quite successfully with cards or billiards, played for very small stakes.

There was not much social life outside the barracks, although one or two of us did make civilian friends. We were thirty miles from Belfast, quite a distance in those days. Downpatrick was nearby, but its people were somewhat anti-British, to say the least. The town boasted a cinema, where we sometimes went, but the owner did not, for fear of trouble, follow the custom of playing the national anthem or showing the King's picture on the screen at the conclusion of the evening's programme.

So much for who we were, and how we lived, in the days before everything changed for ever".

Pat Erskine-Tulloch's regiment had its origins as the 48th (Northamptonshire) and the 58th (Rutlandshire) Regiments of Foot. They came together in 1881 as the 1st and 2nd Battalions of The Northamptonshire Regiment. The 48th brought with it a Battle Honour which its successor was proud to perpetuate. The Battle of Talavera was fought in northern Portugal on 27 and 28

July 1809. It was the first engagement of the Peninsular campaign where Sir Arthur Wellesley (later the Duke of Wellington) was in command. Over a period of many hours, his force of 16,000 held and beat off a French force of twice that number. At a critical moment, when the enemy were about to gain the upper hand, Wellesley ordered forward the 48th Regiment. It had done well earlier in the day, but its men excelled themselves when they advanced again and, with great coolness and gallantry, restored the situation. In 1909, two silver figures of officers in the uniforms of 1809 and 1909 were purchased by the past and serving officers of the regiment to mark the 100th anniversary of the battle.

It had much earlier become the custom to hold a Talavera Dinner on 27 July every year. In 1877, the officers of the 48th agreed to each forfeit two days' pay for the purchase of the large two-handled cup which has ever since played a central role in that celebration. Every regiment and every battalion of the British Army has in its history one major event which it reveres above all others. The ritual of the Talavera Cup is quoted here as a representative example of comparable special customs maintained in other units over very many years, commemorating important events in their own histories.

Brigadier Erskine-Tulloch describes the ceremony: "Whenever possible, on the anniversary of the battle, a Dinner Night is held at which the guest is the latest joined officer and he sits on the right of the PMC (the President of the Mess Committee) rather than on the right of the Commanding Officer. After the normal toasts, a special toast is drunk to 'The 48th'. It is drunk from the Talavera Cup, which holds about four bottles of Champagne. The cup passes around the table clockwise, each officer standing in turn to call the toast, and each has the officers to his left and to his right standing while he drinks. This continues until the cup completes its circuit and returns to the guest. It may have been replenished along the way, but the guest is required to empty it after calling 'The 48th' for the final time. Normally all the officers play fair by taking a good swig when it is their turn, but this is difficult for the PMC and the other earlier drinkers if they are to avoid spilling Champagne on their Mess Kit. The junior officer, the guest, may find that there is still quite a lot of Champagne to be swallowed, but I don't think any of them have ever complained on that count".

Over the years, most regiments and corps have from time to time sponsored the publication of an account of their past services. Known generically as "regimental histories", these books are a mine of information for everyone wishing to know what a particular unit was doing on a certain date or in a particular battle. If the author did his job well, the narrative includes numerous references to individual officers and men, the acts of gallantry which led to their awards, and the engagements which may have resulted in their deaths.

A conventional element in such books is the inclusion of

Even the most spartan barracks accommodation can be transformed by the unfurling of a battalion's Colours and by a sparkling display of its silver. This is the dining room of the Officers' Mess at Doniford Camp, Watchet (Somerset) in October 1957. The occasion was a visit to The Northamptonshire Regiment by its Colonel in Chief, The Duchess of Kent, and she is seen here (on the right) dining with her officers.
Photo: R Kingsley Taylor, and Brig E P Erskine-Tulloch.

various reference appendices - nominal rolls, statistics, itineraries, citations, and the like. Some authors have taken the opportunity to add a page or two concerning the unit's collection of Mess property and, although these appendices do not contain the fine detail which a specialist in silverware might wish to see, they do help us to understand the huge range of artefacts which comprise "military silver".

Russell Gurney, author of the first volume of the three-volume *The History of the Northamptonshire Regiment*, (printed by Gale & Polden for the regiment) was one of the historians who chose to follow that route. Having commenced with Brigadier Pat Erskine-Tulloch, we may now move forward with Lieutenant Colonel (later Brigadier) Gurney. The following is a selection from some of his entries.

He lists first the possessions of the 48th Regiment (later the 1st Battalion, The Northamptonshire Regiment). Apart from a few single presentation pieces, the officers did not acquire much in the way of working silver until they returned to England from the Peninsular War (1814) and before they embarked for New South Wales (1817). Eighteen years later, returning home from Australia and India, they purchased in 1835 a full range of silver side dishes, soup tureens, knives, forks, spoons, and so forth. The name of the maker is not known but, as most of these pieces are dated 1826, they were presumably bought from his stock rather than being specially commissioned.

In 1858 the regiment completed a tour of duty in Gibraltar and embarked for a return deployment in India. For reasons which Gurney does not explain, it was ordered to leave behind all its heavy baggage (including the Mess silver and furnishings). Presumably the hold in their ship could not accommodate it. As a consequence, when a regular Mess was again established in 1859, at Cawnpore, "the naked appearance of the table, destitute of Mess plate, induced several officers to present silver goblets". Major R Blakeney, Captain J Bedingfield and Captain H F Brooke each gave three, Major J G R Aplin and Surgeon A F Shelton contributed two each, and Lieutenants E Feneran, E G Horne and J Rawlins each provided one. The total of sixteen goblets was augmented by further gifts from other officers in 1860, and it then became a Mess custom for all officers to present a goblet. A halt was called in 1875 when the last presentations were made, by which time the Mess had forty such goblets. We are not told, but presumably the majority were of Indian manufacture.

At that period, silver was normally referred to as "plate" and the table crockery as "Delft". The officers of the 48th did not have a "Plate Fund" until 1860. At their new station, Allahabad, it was proposed "that the old custom of giving Champagne on promotion should cease, and instead, that officers should contribute to a Plate Fund, and that the names of all officers who thus contributed should be recorded on the plate purchased by their contributions, thus permanently associating their names with the material prosperity and traditions of the Mess". It would be hard to find a more concise phrase than this to describe the spirit and purpose of a Mess silver fund, past or present.

The suggestion was adopted, and the fund was started with contributions of twenty pounds from Captains J Farquar and E Feneran (who had just been appointed company commanders), ten pounds from Lieutenant J Rawlins (recently appointed Adjutant), and ten pounds each from Lieutenants C H Chauncy, T Hall and E C Brown (for reasons not recorded). With this money, "two claret jugs were immediately purchased and the names of these officers inscribed upon them".

And so the 48th Regiment began its tradition of building a collection of silver which was directly related to the membership of its Mess, silver which carried their names and which therefore recorded their services both individually and collectively. As previously remarked, no two regiments and no two battalions have ever followed identical routes, but the pattern discernible in the history of the 48th (and as we shall see shortly, of the 58th) can be taken as broadly representative of the practices adopted by a great many others.

By 1866 the 48th was back in England, stationed in the new military town of Aldershot. The Plate Fund had by then grown considerably. It was decided to expend three hundred and fifty pounds for the commissioning of a table centre-piece. The task was given to the firm of London & Ryder, of New Bond Street, London. Made in two parts, a "cup and plateau", its delivery to the regiment was recorded in the *Illustrated London News* of 2 November 1867.

"The chief feature of the design is the appropriate introduction of military emblems and figures. The plateau represents bastions and lines of fortification, and is inscribed with the victories of the Regiment, namely, Toulouse, Vittoria, Peninsula, Douro, Talavera, Albuera, Badajos, Salamanca, Orthes, Pyrenees, Nivelle and Sebastopol. The cup is surmounted by an imposing figure of Victory seated upon a cannon, and holding aloft the 'conqueror's Bays'. The handles are formed of gorgons' heads, intwined with serpents that coil around the cover. On each side are bas reliefs, the one modelled from West's celebrated picture of the 'Death of Wolfe', the other is the Storming of Badajos, in which the Regiment was conspicuously engaged, comprising the assault of 'San Rogue' on 12th April, 1812. The base of the cup is supported by four war dogs, chained, surmounted by shot and shell. Spear heads, gonfalons, banners and military trophies complete the elevation. The total height of the cup and plateau above the table is two feet six inches, and the aggregate weight nearly four hundred and fifty ounces, of silver".

Brigadier Gurney went on to describe some of the possessions of the 58th Regiment. He noted that the onset of the British Army's collecting surge coincided, more or less, with the two major campaigns of the mid-19th century - the Crimean war and the suppression of the Great Sepoy Mutiny in India. They came as an interruption to what were in effect one hundred years of relative calm - the decades which followed the world war of 1793-1815 and preceded the outbreak of the world war of 1914-1918. As Gurney himself wrote, "The year 1851 is the opening of a period of fifty years during which the majority of the silver was collected. It was a period of peace, and the custom of presenting plate to the regiment on joining and on leaving seems to have been well observed".

The earliest recorded presentation of silver to the 58th's Mess was made in 1792, when a Lieutenant Jeffries gave a two-handled cup on which was inscribed: "He joined the 58th with pleasure and left it with regret". This cup, together with a snuff-mull presented by Major John Crongey in 1798, was taken by a thief in Aldershot in 1898 and never recovered.

Probably the oldest piece still in the possession of that regiment's successors, the 2nd Royal Anglians, is a cup presented by Captains Ogle and Sutton in 1799. Sutton was subsequently appointed *aide-de-camp* to General Sir Ralph Abercromby, the officer who commanded the successful expedition of 1801 against the French army of occupation in Egypt.

Brigadier Erskine-Tulloch explains: "I was always attracted by the 58th centrepiece, with its three beautiful figures in the uniforms of different periods between 1760 and 1860. I also liked the silver Sphinx table lighters. They burned methylated spirits from wicks protruding from their heads and were placed on the dining table at the same time as the Port and Madeira. It was during Abercromby's campaign that the 58th, along with several other regiments, gained the Battle Honour 'Egypt'. That is why the cigar lighters were fashioned as they were".

Gurney listed various other items in the 58th's collection, many of them inter-regimental rifle match (shooting) trophies. As expected, these were mainly in the form of cups and shields. He observed: "It is interesting to note that the size and value of the trophy has no relation to the merit of the win".

What particularly shines out from the list of shooting prizes is the geographical spread of their origins. They were won at competitions staged in New Zealand, South Africa, Hong Kong and Malta, in all of which the 58th and other British regiments served extensively in the 19th century. It would have added to the interest of the listings if Gurney had recorded the names of the makers of these pieces and the towns or cities in which they worked. Clearly, to the historian of silverware *per se*, a piece

and usually they carry a small silver plaque engraved with the name of a once-loved but long-forgotten hunter or racehorse. The pair acquired by the 58th in 1882 is in a different league.

The hoofs are relics of a conflict in South Africa which resulted in such a humiliating defeat for the British Army that the War Office subsequently declined to authorise the award of a campaign service medal. One of a series of campaigns fought against the Boers but usually referred to as the First Boer War, it led to the award of the Victoria Cross to Lieutenant Alan Richard Hill (later Hill-Walker), of the 2nd Battalion, The Northamptonshire Regiment. The campaign was reputedly the last in which any British battalion carried its Colours into action.

On 28 January, 1881, at Laing's Nek, Hill and his comrades found themselves under heavy close-range rifle fire. Amongst the casualties was the officer who had been given the honour of carrying the Regimental Colour, Lieutenant L Bailie. When the retreat was ordered, Hill saw that his friend was on the ground, seriously wounded. He galloped back and, having failed to hoist Bailie up into the saddle, started to carry him away in his arms.

Shooting trophies came in many shapes and sizes. Victorian trophies often incorporated views of riflemen at practice on the ranges. This goblet (seen front and rear) was presented in 1861 to the 14th (Worcester) Company, The Worcestershire Rifle Volunteers, by Henry, Earl Beauchamp (shortly after the Volunteer movement was founded and shortly before he died). It was intended for annual competition, and the names of winners are engraved upon it. The maker was S Garrard, of Panton Street, London, and it is hallmarked London 1861. Photo: RHQ The Worcestershire and Sherwood Foresters Regiment.

made by one of the pioneer silversmiths in New Zealand, for example, would be more interesting than a piece routinely sent out from England. The only concessions he makes in this connection are his enthusiastic descriptions of several pieces won by (and purchased by) the regiment during its stay in Hong Kong between 1885 and 1889. They were all made by the Chinese master Wang Hing, and are "of exceptionally beautiful craftsmanship".

In this great welter of silverware, varying from the mundane to the exotic, it comes almost as a relief to find a pair of horse-hoofs, mounted in silver and fashioned as ashtrays. Objects like this are often seen in *bric-a-brac* shops and at country auctions,

Bailie was then hit again, fatally. Hill left him, remounted, returned to the front and this time succeeded in bringing away on his horse a second wounded man. He then rode back and saved another in the same way. Later, having retained the hoofs when his mount died, he presented them to the Mess in the form described.

Another item of this kind is displayed, in a glass case, in the Central Library at the RMA Sandhurst. It is a pair of candlesticks, fourteen inches high with acorn and oak leaf decoration, mounted on a pair of horse's hoofs. The engraved silver plate states: "Hoofs of Charger Ridden by General Sir George Scovell GCB at Waterloo, 1815".

Prizes in silver have always been an integral part of competitive shooting. A typical trophy was "The Lord Lieutenant's Challenge Cup", shot for annually by the Volunteer military units of Gloucestershire. At the County Rifle Meeting of 1899, on the ranges at Bedminster, the winning team represented "C" Company, 2nd Volunteer Battalion, The Gloucestershire Regiment. Standing, left to right: Private G Gorton, Corporal J Webb, Private S H Grist. Seated, left to right: Lieutenant J H Bryan and Bandmaster Knight. Their rifles are the .303 calibre Long Lee Enfield. Private Grist was later promoted Sergeant and continued to shoot competitively for the rest of his life. In 1949, on his 74th birthday and having shot regularly at Bisley for more than fifty years, he beat 400 other marksmen to win The Duke of Gloucester Competition.
Photo: Mr Graham Sacker JP.

Since the end of WWII, the changing role of the army and the constant search for economies in the Defence budget have resulted in a steady erosion of the number of regiments retaining their old (post-1881) county titles. The Northamptonshire Regiment was one of the first to feel the pain of reduction and then amalgamation. In 1948 it was told that its two Regular battalions must form themselves into a single battalion. Apart from the more obvious difficulties of redundancies and reduced promotion prospects for all ranks flowing from this instruction, there was the domestic dilemma of deciding what to do with the two battalions' silver.

The quantity of material was clearly more than the new unified battalion could ever hope to display in its Mess (even less afford to insure and maintain in good order). The problem was considered by the Regimental Council which appointed a board of four officers whose knowledge of the regiment and its history was exceptional. Under the Presidency of the Colonel of the Regiment, Major General G St G Robinson CB DSO MC, the Board made the final decisions. They are described here in some detail because they are representative of the difficulties faced by many other regiments at the time of their amalgamation or disbandment.

All articles "of regimental, historical or sentimental value" were retained and divided between the battalion and the depôt (exactly how the Board could have assessed "sentimental value" in this context is hard to imagine). The "Weallens Bowl",

presented to the 48th in 1906, was handed to the Army Rifle Association on long loan for a competition to be called "The Northamptonshire Cup". Another cup was selected for long loan to the Guildhall, Northampton. Other cups and trophies were handed to the 5th (Territorial) Battalion and to the county's Army Cadet Force. Twenty silver beer-goblets were loaned to the Officers' Mess at the School of Infantry, Warminster. All other surplus items went to the Goldsmiths & Silversmiths Company for melting into bullion. The proceeds of this sale were devoted towards the commissioning and manufacture by that firm of a replica of the Queen Victoria Trophy to commemorate all the past shooting competition successes of both the 48th and 58th Regiments. After the affair at Laing's Nek, they had worked particularly hard at improving their marksmanship and came to be known as "a shooting regiment".

Only twelve years later, in 1960, the past and serving officers of the regiment were obliged to go through the review process all over again when the Northamptons were amalgamated with The Royal Lincolnshire Regiment to form The Second East Anglian Regiment (Duchess of Gloucester's Own Royal Lincolnshire and Northamptonshire). Four years after that they were re-badged again, as 2nd Battalion, The Royal Anglian Regiment.

The story of The Northamptonshire Regiment and its silver has been described here in some detail because Russell Gurney left us with the factual information and because Pat Erskine-

Tulloch has given it a human face. It is time now to turn away from that typical infantry regiment of the Regular Army and to look at one of its counterparts in the Reserve Army.

In November 1901, a part-time volunteer unit was raised from colonials resident in South East England. The first Honorary Colonel was Edward, Prince of Wales, and the unit was designated The King's Colonials. Authorised by the War Office as a Yeomanry Cavalry unit, it had four mounted elements: "A" Squadron (British Asian), "B" Squadron (Canadian), "C" Squadron (Australasian), and "D" Squadron (South African). Each wore the regimental badge, with an additional Squadron badge to distinguish the origins or connections of its members. These latter marks of distinction were discontinued in 1909. Following the succession to the throne of King George V, and his appointment as Colonel-in-Chief, the regiment was renamed King Edward's Horse in memory of his late father. Its secondary title was The King's Overseas Dominions Regiment. Mobilised at the outbreak of war, it fought in France and Flanders in 1915, served in Ireland during "the troubles" of 1916, returned to France in 1918 (suffering great losses at Vieille Chappelle in April), and then moved to Italy (serving as Divisional Cavalry with XI Corps).

The membership of the regiment was unique. To quote from the Preface to its published history: "There was no Dominion, Dependency, Colony, nor portion of the globe where the British tongue is spoken, that had not a representative in the uniform of King Edward's Horse". The officers included men of wealth, experience and influence, and many of the other ranks were "gentlemen troopers". The near destruction of their generation during the war of 1914-1918, followed by the changes in social and military structures which followed it, led to the decision, in 1924, to disband. The regiment was wound up in April of that year.

Although it had existed for only twenty-three years, and although four of those years were devoted to wartime services abroad, the regiment accumulated a sizeable collection of silver. There was no obvious successor to whom it might be handed on. In the event, it was passed to the Governors and Trustees of the Imperial Service College. A public school located in Windsor, the ISC had been formed in 1912 by the amalgamation of three schools, one of which was the United Services College, formerly of Westward Ho!, in the county of Devon.

The USC had been founded in 1863 and one of its most distinguished sons was Rudyard Kipling. As both the USC and ISC titles imply, the boys were given not only a very good education but also a strong sense of duty to the Empire. The membership of King Edward's Horse included many of the school's Old Boys. One of these was Colonel Lionel James DSO, a Militia officer who for a while commanded the regiment during the war and who later became President of the KEH (KODR) Old Comrades Association. His personal connection with the school, plus those of several of his contemporaries, explains the choice of the ISC as a suitable repository for the regiment's silver.

The terms of the hand-over were that the silver should remain the property of the officers of King Edward's Horse, that the College could use it in any way it thought fit but be responsible for its security and insurance, and that it would return it "in the event that the regiment should ever be reconstituted or should be replaced by a regiment of similar imperial standing". To quote a later and admirably succinct archival source: "It seems scarcely probable that this condition will arise for a long period - if ever - so the College may contemplate

having undisturbed possession for a great many years".

Although the ISC had been a thriving school at the time of the 1924 disbandment, its fortunes began to decline in the 1930s. An independent public school, it needed to operate as a commercial enterprise, balancing its books at the end of each month. Instead, very large losses were allowed to accumulate and, by 1942, it was clear that the school could not continue. In March of that year, most of the boys and some of the masters moved from Windsor to Hertford. The College was amalgamated with Haileybury College, a public school founded in 1862 and incorporated by Royal Charter in 1864. Like the ISC, it had a strong tradition of producing candidates for the armed forces and the Colonial services. Renamed Haileybury & Imperial Service College, the school accepted responsibility for the KEH silver on the same terms as those originally agreed with the Trustees of the ISC in 1924.

The College has ensured, particularly in recent years, that the silver should fulfil at least some of its original functions, decorative and practical. Alastair Macpherson, the Honorary Archivist, explains: "It is normal practice for items from the collection to be displayed on special occasions, subject to the approval of the Headmaster. A small selection was displayed at the Speech Day this year (1997), and it attracted a great deal of interest. Some of these items are obviously of considerable value so we do not hold them on public display all the time, but they are a feature at many of the more important functions such as the annual Attlee Memorial Dinner. It is very unlikely that any former members of King Edward's Horse are still alive, but one must hope that the regiment would approve of the way in which its silver is being put to good use".

The silver was not the only tangible evidence of the regiment's short life. By the time it was disbanded it had accumulated some substantial financial reserves. These were consolidated as The King Edward's Horse Endowment Fund which, in July 1930, stood at twenty-eight thousand pounds. Half of this sum was invested with the intention of generating an income to pay for the education of sons of former members of the regiment (or, failing that, the education of "boys from the Dominions"). The other half was used for the construction of a memorial hall, The King Edward's Horse Hall, in Windsor. When the Imperial Service College failed, the building was taken over by the Borough of Windsor. A plaque was fixed to it, explaining the hall's history and the story of the regiment.

King Edward's Horse was able to disband itself gracefully and without any external pressure. The same did not apply to five much older and more famous (Regular Army) regiments. They fell victim, in 1922, to the traumatic events in Ireland.

The British government had introduced, early in 1914, a Home Rule Bill for that historically troubled island. It was a Liberal government, led by Herbert Asquith. The Conservative opposition reacted to the proposal by encouraging the Ulster Protestants to arm themselves and to prepare for war against Catholic domination. The "Ulster Volunteers", led by Sir Edward Carson, are said to have recruited 85,000 men for this purpose. With civil war threatening, various senior army officers were asked whether they were willing to march against the Ulstermen. Given the option, they declined. A large proportion of the British Army's officers were Irish and Anglo-Irish, Protestant and Roman Catholic, with homes or roots in both the south and the north. The army had, and still has, a strong aversion to becoming embroiled in political debates of any kind, but the new proposals were too close to their hearts and loyalties to be ignored.

Silver collections are not exclusive to the fighting regiments. This is the Majuba Cup, an important possession of the Royal Army Medical Corps. Standing two feet nine inches, weighing 140 ounces, it bears London marks for 1893 (maker's mark obscured). Two Victoria Cross actions are depicted on the side *cartouches*. The first winner was Surgeon Anthony Home who, on 26 September 1857 at Lucknow, cared for the wounded in a besieged house. For 22 hours, with a handful of soldiers, he fought off the mutineers and moved the casualties to a nearby shed when the house caught fire. The second was Lance Corporal Joseph Farmer, Army Hospital Corps. On 27 February 1881, at the Battle of Majuba Hill and assisting Surgeon Major Henry Cornish under heavy Boer fire, he took charge when Cornish was hit and severely wounded. Attempting to protect the men in his care, Farmer waved a white cloth. When his arm was shot through, he raised the cloth with his other arm until that too was hit. Farmer survived, but Major Cornish died three days later in hospital. Photo: RHQ RAMC.

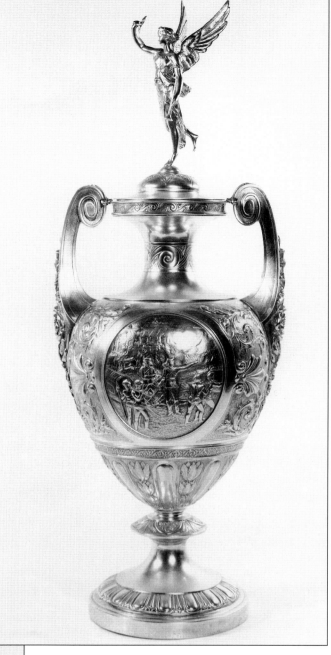

The Forbes Epergne is another great treasure of the Royal Army Medical Corps. Thirty inches in height, it was made in 1848 in electroplate by Elkington & Company, of Regent Street. To quote *The London Illustrated News* of 9 September of that year: *This epergne, after a design by Staff Sergeant D R Dartnell, was purchased with the surplus of a sum subscribed by officers of the Medical Department of the Army for the portrait of the late James Forbes MD, Inspector-General of Hospitals, the Founder of the Medical Staff Mess at Fort Pitt, Chatham, June 1848. Upon the base is a wounded soldier; a medical officer is endeavouring to relieve his sufferings, while a comrade supports the poor fellow.* The intertwined oak and bamboo signify service worldwide. The top of the oak originally supported a shallow fluted dish, but this has been lost. Photo: RHQ, RAMC, Aldershot.

By responding as they did, in what came to be known as "The Curragh Incident", those officers helped to stop Asquith's Home Rule policy in its tracks. The outbreak of war with Germany then pushed the issue into the background for the next two years until, in 1916, the republican leaders launched an insurrection in Dublin. It failed, but they continued to pursue their cause. Between 1919 and 1921, Ireland, and particularly the southern part, became the setting for a full-scale guerilla war between the Irish Republican Army and the forces of the Crown.

Despite the substantial army presence, and the reinforcement of the Royal Irish Constabulary with specially recruited auxiliary units, the British government could not prevail. In 1921, recognising the situation as a stalemate, it offered to the republican representatives a new Irish Free State, with status within the Empire as a Dominion. The offer was accepted and, except for those located within the six partitioned counties of Northern Ireland, the Crown's civil, police and military establishments were quickly dismantled.

The terms of the London agreement, negotiated by Michael Collins, were judged by his more extreme nationalist colleagues to be too much of a compromise. Eamon De Valera's faction wanted a fully independent Ireland, to include all the counties of Ulster, and they wanted no connection of any kind with the British Empire. The quarrel between De Valera's supporters and those who agreed with Collins escalated rapidly into a civil war. It raged throughout most of 1922 and 1923, and Michael Collins was one of hundreds of Irishmen to be murdered by their own people.

The regular British Army regiments caught up in these events were The Royal Dublin Fusiliers, The Connaught Rangers, The Prince of Wales's Leinster Regiment (Royal Canadians), The Royal Irish Regiment, and The Royal Munster Fusiliers. All had long histories of loyal and courageous service to the Crown, but the order was given that they must be disbanded. The same order applied to The South Irish Horse, a Special Reserve regiment.

Along with a multitude of other difficulties flowing from such a decision, there was the essentially domestic dilemma of knowing what should be done with regimental property such as the Mess silver. In the heated social and political climate of the period, there was no place for it within the borders of the new state, and no obvious repository for it elsewhere. The actions of the officers of The Royal Dublin Fusiliers can be taken as representative of what happened in all six of the affected regiments. They reluctantly reached the conclusion that their collection should be broken up and dispersed.

To be fully appreciated, the story of the silver needs to be placed in the context of the regiment's history. Its title, The Royal Dublin Fusiliers, was a relatively modern invention, granted in 1881. The regiment had in fact been an element of the British Army only since 1861. Prior to that date it had always been a unit of the armies of the Honourable East India Company. It had its origins in the Company's construction of Fort St George (its initial foothold on the Coromandel coast of India which later developed into the city of Madras). In 1645 a small force of armed Europeans was raised to guard this installation. A hundred years later, in 1748, Major Stringer Lawrence was given the task of upgrading all such small local units and forming them into some semblance of a professional regular military force.

He commenced the recruitment of Europeans on formal contracts of service. Some he trained as artillerymen for coastal defence, others became infantrymen. The latter, known initially as The Madras European Regiment, went on to gain an outstanding reputation. They fought in several of the great battles of conquest in India (Plassey, Pondicherry, Gujerat, Maheidpore) and in the wars in Burma. By the time of the Great Sepoy Mutiny of 1857, when their title had become the 1st Madras (European) Fusiliers, they and their counterparts in the other Presidencies - Bombay and Bengal - had become a key component in the Company's military forces.

When, in 1861, the British government assumed full control of India's affairs, and when therefore the Honourable East India Company ceased to exist, the regiment was transferred to the British Army as the 102nd (Royal Madras) Fusiliers. In 1881 it amalgamated with the 103rd (Royal Bombay) Fusiliers to form the 1st and 2nd Battalions respectively of The Royal Dublin Fusiliers.

The ranks of their predecessor units had always included a very high proportion of Irishmen, but the RDF later recruited entirely from the population of the southern counties and was therefore almost exclusively Roman Catholic. Many of the men came from the rural communities of County Cork, County Kilkenny, County Kerry and County Limerick, all of which fell under Martial Law during the fighting of 1919-1921. Countless atrocities were committed by both sides. Generations of young Irishmen had volunteered for service in the British Army because it offered three meals a day and the chance to see the world beyond their own shores. For the most part they were not particularly interested in politics. However, when their parents and brothers and sisters back home on the farm began writing to them with accounts of the brutality of British units like the Black and Tans, a division of loyalties and allegiances became inevitable.

To digress briefly from the story of the Royal Dublin Fusiliers, the men of the 1st Battalion of The Connaught Rangers were the worst placed of all because they could receive only fragmented reports of what was happening. The battalion sailed for India in October 1919. By the summer of 1920, it was part of the garrison at Jullundur, in the Punjab, with company detachments at Jutogh and the hill station of Solon. Little more than a year earlier, all of this area had been in turmoil. Just as in Ireland, there was civil unrest in India resulting from disputes with the British concerning the right to self-government. Resentment against British intransigence had resulted in the most dishonourable episode in the history of the Empire.

At Amritsar, on 13 April 1919, Brigadier General Reginald Dyer ordered the shooting in cold blood of 1400 unarmed Indians. Four hundred of them died. Civilians were shot dead by the military and by the police in other cities of the Punjab. At Gujranwala, on 14 April, an unknown number died when aircraft of the Royal Air Force attacked the crowded streets with bombs and machine-guns. These methods succeeded in restoring a sullen calm but, with hindsight, the choice of this particular area of the Punjab as a new home for a Southern Irish regiment such as The Connaught Rangers was, at best, naïve, and at worst, bone-headed.

It is unlikely that the men of The Connaught Rangers felt any particular compassion for the victims of Amritsar or of the other shootings. However, what they could see of the aftermath, all around them in the Punjab, when taken in combination with the spasmodic alarming news from home, had an unsettling effect. The parallels were too close to be ignored. On 28 June, 1920, a substantial number of the Connaughts at Jullundur refused to take orders. They simply no longer wished to serve as soldiers of the British Crown. It was an orderly and passive demonstration, and they had no grievance with their officers.

A more serious chain of events occurred within the company detachment at Solon. As happens so often once the bonds of discipline are broken, violence gained the upper hand. There was a physical confrontation and, sadly, two men died as a consequence.

The story of the subsequent Courts Martial, and the fate of the mutiny's ringleaders, can be found in *The Devil to Pay*, by Judge Tony Babington (Leo Cooper, London, 1991). For the moment, we may return to the story of the Royal Dublin Fusiliers and their silver.

Over the years, both battalions had accumulated the customary assortment of silverware. In 1922, former and serving officers who had at various times donated one or more pieces to their respective Messes were given the opportunity to have those pieces returned to them. Many unclaimed objects were distributed amongst the members of the Royal Dublin Fusiliers Dinner Club. Eleven other pieces of silver were handed to the Royal United Service Institution, in London. The RUSI also became the recipient of four major oil paintings, the regiment's entire collection of medals, a drum carried at the battle for the relief of Lucknow, and some relics from the SS *River Clyde* of Gallipoli fame. However, there were four particular items owned by the 1st Battalion which were selected for much more illustrious permanent homes. What happened next was recorded in some detail by Colonel H C Wylly CB, official historian of the 1st Battalion.

On 23 June 1922, the Commanding Officer of the 1st Battalion of The Royal Dublin Fusiliers, Lieutenant Colonel C N Perreau CMG, wrote to Lord Stamfordham, Private Secretary to His Majesty King George V: "Sir, It is the unanimous wish of the Officers of the Battalion under my command that His Majesty should be asked to honour us by accepting as a memento, a silver two handled cup, presented by the Citizens of Madras, in 1913, on the occasion of the return of the Battalion to the city of its origin, and its home for over two hundred years. As I am unaware of the necessary procedure in this case, I should be most grateful for your advice. I have the honour to be, Sir, your most obedient servant".

Stamfordham replied four days later, stating that Perreau's letter had been "laid before the King" and that His Majesty "will gladly accept this interesting gift and treasure it in remembrance of your distinguished Regiment".

Perreau delivered the cup in person to Buckingham Palace and later received a letter from Lord Stamfordham in which he conveyed "His Majesty's most sincere thanks for this gift which will be treasured among the Royal Plate as a memento of a Regiment whose great and distinguished career has been terminated through circumstances beyond its control".

The last Colonel-in-Chief of the RDF was Field Marshal the Duke of Connaught, the third son of Queen Victoria. Perreau wrote a second letter, to the Comptroller of the Duke's household, Sir Malcolm Murray: "It is the wish of all the Officers of the 'Blue Caps' that His Royal Highness should accept from them some mark of their great admiration and appreciation of all he has done for them during the period he has been their Colonel-in-Chief. The Officers would like His Royal Highness to accept two seven-branch candelabra - one silver, one Sheffield plate - and which have been in possession of the Mess for over 150 years. The Sergeants' Mess are most anxious His Royal Highness should accept a Silver Soup tureen on stand, presented to their Mess by the Citizens of Madras in 1858, in commemoration of the fine achievements of the Battalion, as Madras Fusiliers, during the Mutiny".

Perreau duly delivered these pieces to the Duke's home, Clarence House, St James's, and subsequently received a letter of thanks from Sir Malcolm Murray. It concluded: "Should the Battalion be at any time re-formed as a part of the Imperial Army, His Royal Highness would, of course, be prepared to return the candelabra to the Officers' Mess".

Almost eighty years have passed since that undertaking was given, and it is evident that there will never be another regiment bearing the title Royal Dublin Fusiliers or one having a comparable regimental history which might entitle it to lay claim to the silver. This is in one way fortunate because there is no longer any trace of it.

A recent enquiry (1998) addressed to Buckingham Palace prompted a search through the inventories held by the office of The Surveyor of The Queen's Works of Art. They contain no reference which would explain the subsequent fate of the 1st Battalion's gifts. However, the Royal Archives at Windsor do contain a document which reveals that Lieutenant Colonel Perreau was not alone when he visited London in 1922, and it is quoted here by the gracious permission of Her Majesty The Queen.

The piece of paper shows that Perreau was accompanied by Lieutenant Colonel G S Higginson, commanding officer of the 2nd Battalion of the Royal Dublin Fusiliers, the sister unit which until 1881 had been titled the 103rd (Royal Bombay) Fusiliers. It is apparent that Higginson and the officers of his battalion had come to the same decision to those of the 1st Battalion, and wished to present the King with one of their historic possessions.

The receipt is signed by the Master of His Majesty's Household, Sir Derek Keppel GCVO CMG CIE, and it describes the item as "a centrepiece, almost a replica of that presented by Major General Tapp CB, in 1872, bearing representations in relief of the sieges of Seringapatam and Mooltan". Keppel added a footnote: "The above pieces of plate were handed to the Master of the Household by Lt Colonels Perreau and Higginson and were placed by him in the charge of the 1st Yeoman, Silver Pantry, Buckingham Palace, on the 19th July, 1922". What happened to them thereafter is a matter of conjecture, and seems likely to remain so.

As a footnote to the story of Irish military silver, the fate of the silver once owned by the Royal Irish Constabulary is known with certainty. It was displayed on their table when the Senior Officers held a final dinner shortly before the disbandment of the force in 1922. Its component pieces were given subsequently to individual members of the Mess as a memento of their service. Items from that collection might surface from time to time, in Ireland or elsewhere.

Any survey of the history of the British Army would be incomplete without reference to its bands and their musical instruments. The origins of military music are difficult to trace with accuracy, but it is certain that the soldiers of many empires and many nations have for hundreds of years, even thousands, marched to the beating of drums and the blowing of wind instruments of one kind or another.

Traditionally, the sound made by military musicians has met three basic needs: to encourage the troops on the eve of battle, to give rhythm and swing to their marching, and to convey orders over a distance. Drumbeats and bugle calls have in the past been an efficient method of signalling, both on the battlefield and in camp.

The Colours, silver and other trophies of the 1st Battalion, The Royal Dublin Fusiliers photographed not long before it was disbanded and the collection broken up for dispersal to a variety of new homes. Photo: National Army Museum.

It has always been the custom in the British Army for every infantry regiment to have its own Corps of Drums and its own band. It is important to distinguish between the two. The Corps of Drums consists of drummers, buglers, flautists (fifers), and cymbalists, perhaps fifteen to twenty-five men, all trained to operate as combat soldiers in time of war. Since the 1850s, the cost of their instruments has been paid by the Ministry of Defence (or, earlier, the War Office, or earlier still, by Horse Guards, Whitehall).

The regimental band, on the other hand, has until very recent times been regarded by the authorities as a non-essential appendage to the unit's establishment. It was only in 1994 that the Ministry of Defence agreed to fund the purchase and maintenance of the instruments used by these additional twenty to forty musicians (only one or two of whom are drummers, but all of whom are trained in first aid and casualty evacuation).

Until 1994, their instruments and equipment were purchased by each individual regiment or battalion from its own funds. This, in essence, meant that the officers were required to contribute the money to purchase and maintain all the equipment and uniforms associated with their band and, at one time, to pay the salary of the Bandmaster and of the musicians themselves. From this it can be seen that the most fashionable regiments, having the wealthiest officers, were able to maintain the largest and most magnificent bands, while the less exotic regiments managed with smaller and less flamboyant bands.

Because they were themselves paying the costs, the officers of each regiment could to a considerable extent decide what sort of band they wanted, how the bandsmen should be dressed, and what sort of music they should play.

Just one aspect of this tradition is sufficient to demonstrate the gentle eccentricities of the British Army. In the early 1700s, several regiments began to employ young negro men to play the percussion instruments such as the drums and cymbals,

instruments for which they had a natural affinity. Known as "sable musicians", they were dressed in every style of fantastic uniform: brilliant red pantaloons, cutaway jackets, turbans and fezzes, gold and silver braid, feathers and animal skins. They did not simply play, they performed. On parade, they strutted and posed, swinging their drum sticks high in the air. Two relics of those times can be seen in every modern Corps of Drums - the wearing by bass drummers of leopard or tiger skins, and the exaggerated "swinging of the sticks" by the tenor and side drummers.

The 29th Regiment of Foot, later the 1st Battalion, The Worcestershire Regiment, was particularly committed to the employment of negro musicians. In 1759, the 29th was stationed in Ireland, near Kilkenny. It happened that the commanding officer was the brother of Admiral the Honourable Edward Boscawen, a famous officer of the Royal Navy who had recently forced the French garrison of Guadeloupe into surrender. Boscawen, having there heard the stirring rhythms of Afro-Caribbean music, decided to bring back ten black youths and to present them to his brother in Ireland as musicians.

An officer of the 29th later wrote: "His Majesty's permission was obtained to retain them in that capacity, and when I joined the regiment in 1775 there were three, if not more, of the original blacks in the corps, who were remarkable good drummers. The custom of having black drummers in the regiment was continued for the better part of eighty-five years (the last one died on 15th July 1843)".

Not all of these men came from the Caribbean. It is recorded that more were brought to England in 1820 from West Africa, and the 29th was not alone in following the fashion. The Household Cavalry and the Brigade of Foot Guards employed them also, and they accompanied their respective regiments on the campaigns of the period. Numbers of them served in Wellington's campaign in Spain, and it is probable that some were present at Waterloo in 1815.

Africans and Afro-Caribbeans were recruited throughout the second half of the 18th Century not only as drummers but also as trumpeters. Trumpeters of that period were more than musicians, they acted as messengers and special orderlies to the generals. Regarded as non-combatants, they were symbolically "armed" with swords which had broken-off blades. These men were selected for their intelligence, bearing and fine manners, and were dressed in magnificent uniforms. The Life Guards always had, for many years, several negro trumpeters on their strength, all of them of exceptional height.

The long-running African and Caribbean contribution to British military music ended in the 1840s when Queen Victoria indicated that she did not approve. However, there is a long if limited tradition of men with roots in Africa having served in the British armed forces. The first so recorded was Captain John Perkins, Royal Navy, who commanded a succession of ships between 1782 and 1805 (when he retired). The West India-born surgeon, William Fergusson, served in Sierra Leone in the 1820s with the Royal African Corps and later became that Colony's first black Governor. The first British-born black officer to lead white troops into battle was the professional footballer, Walter Tull. He played for Tottenham Hotspur and Northampton before WWI but was an early volunteer in 1914, joining the 17th (1st Football) Battalion, The Middlesex Regiment. He was killed in action in March of 1918, having been commissioned a year earlier into that regiment's 23rd (2nd Football) Battalion.

The black musicians and their spectacular uniforms were a matter of style. The music itself was a more substantial matter, and it was greatly influenced by the Turks. In the early 1700s, the Ottoman Empire's professional regular regiments of Janissaries each had bands which depended heavily upon percussion instruments unknown elsewhere. The large bass drum, for example, was not seen in continental Europe until 1741. It was then adopted by other armies and, together with increasingly sophisticated types of smaller drum, became central to the sound of western military music. It is not surprising, therefore, that the officers of certain British Army regiments have at times been willing to spend very substantial sums on the purchase of drums.

One of the most expensive sets of drums ever manufactured was produced to the order of Lieutenant Colonel F C King Hunter and his brother officers of the 1st Battalion, The South Wales Borderers, in 1908. A reporter for the Aldershot-based *Sheldrake's Military Gazette* was allowed to view the set while it was being assembled and he described it thus: "(We) have this week been afforded the opportunity of inspecting this beautiful set of Sterling silver drums which are being manufactured by Messrs George Potter & Company, the eminent firm of drum makers, for the 1st Battalion, South Wales Borderers, quartered in Quetta, India. The battalion will soon be the possessors of the set, fifteen in number, consisting of one bass, two tenor, and twelve side drums. (We) were assured that when the elaborate work on the drums is completed they will form the most magnificent and unique set in the whole of the British Army. The heraldry, consisting of Royal arms, title, three badges, and nineteen honours, will all be raised from the Sterling silver shell in *repoussé* work, and there will, Mr George Potter pointed out, be other elaborate and unusual features in carrying out the design of the drums. The set of drum sticks are in ebony relieved with elaborate mounts of silver with raised regimental crests. Old as is the firm (for his forebears were makers of drums carried at Waterloo), he does not remember having executed an order for a full set of drums in Sterling silver (although they have turned out Sterling silver kettle drums, including those belonging to the 5th Lancers). It is a noteworthy fact that the firm were makers of the set of drums belonging to the 24th Regiment which, with the exception of the bass drum, were all lost when the 1st Battalion of the South Wales Borderers, in January 1879, were cut up by a force of 20,000 Zulus".

The *Digest of Services* of the 1st Battalion tells us that the

The silver drums of the 1st Battalion, The South Wales Borderers, displayed at Rawalpindi, N.W. India, in 1936. The drums were used regularly on parades held in Hong Kong in the early 1930s, and again at Rawalpindi between December 1934 and February 1937. They then went into temporary storage when the battalion deployed for active service in Waziristan. Seated, in the front row, left to right, are Drum Major Byrnes, Captain A J Stocker (Adjutant), Lieutenant Colonel A E Williams DSO MC (Commanding Officer), Lieutenant F W Baston (Assistant Adjutant), Regimental Sergeant Major O Theobold, and the Corporal Fifer. Photo: The South Wales Borderers and Monmouthshire Regimental Museum.

recorded that they cost "considerably over one thousand pounds". That 1908 assessment is not surprising because their combined weight in silver is two thousand ounces and the *repoussé* work highly demanding of the craftsmen responsible for it.

The name of Potter had been associated, in London, with the manufacture of musical instruments since the 1750s. Richard Potter specialised in the making of flutes but, in 1810, Samuel Potter wrote and published *The Art of Beating the Drum with Camp, Garrison and Street Duty by Note*. Earlier he had composed and published sheet music for the military fife, drum and bugle horn, and was an acknowledged authority. Samuel was during that period a Sergeant and Drum Major with the Coldstream Guards, a regiment which, in 1786, he had joined as a fourteen year-old drummer boy.

In 1810, following the success of *The Art of Beating the Drum*, he acquired Richard Potter's business and workshops at the sign of The Three Squirrels in Fleet Street, London. The intention was to make drums and other musical instruments for military bands. As a serving soldier, he was not permitted to engage in any kind of trade, and especially not a trade for which the main customer was the soldier's own employer. To get around this obstacle he registered the business in the name of his twelve month-old son, Henry Potter. Samuel was not only astute, he was also very cautious. It was not until seven years later, in 1817, that he retired from the Coldstream Guards and took over the full-time management of his business.

The firm of Henry Potter & Company grew and, when Samuel died in 1837, Henry assumed full control. It had a succession of addresses in London and then, in 1856, an additional branch was opened in the new military town of Aldershot. Henry's own sons followed him into the business and, after various changes in name and location, its traditions and reputation evolved into the firm of George Potter & Company, of Grosvenor Road, Aldershot. The current Managing Director, David Leech, is very aware of the South Wales Borderers' silver drums, made nearly a century ago by his predecessors: "We see them from time to time, perhaps to correct minor damage, that sort of thing. They carry our registered silver mark which, then as now, is 'GP&Co'. The full set was returned to us in 1924 or thereabouts for the Great War battle honours to be added. We had them back again in 1963 for major refurbishment and for conversion to modern rod tensioning".

The reference to "rod tensioning" is of interest. Until sometime around 1960, it was the tradition that military drums (other than kettle drums) were made with wooden barrels and vellum striking surfaces. The vellum was made either from goat skin or calf skin, and it was stretched taut, and tuned, by means of a rope looped around the outside of the barrel. One of the major disadvantages of this arrangement was its vulnerability to dampness. A Corps of Drums could maintain the correct volume and pitch only if the weather was favourable. Heavy rain quickly de-tuned the drums as the vellum lost its required tension. The introduction of synthetic materials, in place of vellum, gave the Corps an all-weather capability. However, it also called for much higher tensions than could be achieved with rope. A new system was designed, replacing rope with metal centre brackets and tuning screws. The drums of the South Wales Borderers were amongst the first to be adapted in this way.

The story of the refurbishment provides an unusual footnote. In the long list of distinguished former officers of the regiment is the name of General Sir A Reade Godwin-Austen

Pipe music is integral to the traditions of Scottish, Irish and Gurkha regiments, and pipers are frequently depicted in military silver. Bearing the words *1915-1955, Forty Years On*, and engraved with their regimental crests, this example was the gift of The Highland Light Infantry to The Worcestershire Regiment. It commemorates the shared services of their 2nd Battalions in WWI. Forming part of 5th Brigade, 2nd Division, British Expeditionary Force, they landed at Boulogne in August 1914 and fought alongside each other for the next twelve months. There was great comradeship and respect between them and, in September 1915, their Officers', Sergeants' and Corporals' Messes exchanged honorary membership. They exchanged gifts, in memory of that friendship, when their 1st Battalions were both stationed at Bulford Camp in 1955. Photo: RHQ The Worcestershire & Sherwood Foresters Regiment.

officers took delivery of their new possessions, at Quetta, on 2 April 1909: "A set of silver drums (15) arrived from George Potter, Aldershot". This single-line entry might have been more effusive if it had not been for the sudden death that day of the officer commanding the Quetta Division, Major General R A P Clements CB DSO. Preparations for his funeral no doubt put a dampener on what otherwise might have been a very good day for the battalion.

Six days later, Colonel King Hunter said goodbye to the battalion on completion of his tour of duty in command. While he and his thirty years of service may have long been forgotten, the drums created as a result of his initiative have not. It was

KCSI CB OBE MC. His father had served with the South Wales Borderers in South Africa in 1877-1878. He followed in his father's footstep by joining the regiment in 1909, and was appointed Colonel in 1950. Between times, while not following his military career, he became a first-class climber. In mountaineering circles he is remembered for having conquered the Himalayan peak, K2, which for many years was known as Mount Godwin-Austen. When he died, his Will bequeathed the sum of one thousand pounds to the regiment and this money was used for the refurbishment.

Ownership of the drums now rests with The Royal Regiment of Wales (24th/41st Foot), the regiment formed in 1969 by the amalgamation of The South Wales Borderers and The Welch Regiment, and they are lodged in the Officers' Mess of the 1st Battalion. A recent valuation (March 1997) of the full set indicated a total worth of one hundred and ten thousand pounds but, in historical terms, the figure has little meaning. To the inheritors of the old 1st/24th's traditions, they are priceless.

In 1996, the battalion was preparing to move from Ballykelly to London for a tour of Public Duties. The Commanding Officer, Lieutenant Colonel Robert Aitken, decided that the time was right for some of the drums to be restored to the standard required for Mounting the Guard ceremonies at Buckingham Palace. A short vigorous fund-raising campaign within the regiment produced sufficient money to pay the cost of refurbishing six side drums, two tenor drums and the bass drum.

The Royal Regiment of Wales inherited not only these silver drums from the South Wales Borderers but also the set of silver-plated steel drums of The Welch Regiment. These had been presented in April 1956 by The Steel Company of Wales (later The British Steel Corporation). They are normally housed in the Sergeants' Mess and they too accompanied the 1st Battalion to London in 1996 (after a short visit to the workshops of George Potter & Company, the cost of their spring-clean being met by The British Steel Corporation). Both sets appeared regularly on State Ceremonial occasions in London, particularly whenever the Commanding Officer was on parade as Captain of the Guard. Their frequent use during that time was not popular with the band's bass drummer, Private "Stretch" Hayward. The silver bass drum and steel bass drum are considerably heavier than modern instruments of conventional construction.

It happened that the steel set had been chosen for the ceremony of Mounting the Guard on the morning of 31 August 1997. The almost unbelievable news of the death, overnight, of Diana, Princess of Wales, had reached the Bandmaster only an hour or so previously. To quote Lieutenant

Colonel Robert Aitken, the 1st Battalion's commanding officer, "It was a very maudlin Queen's Guard which marched, with drum beat but no music, from St James's Palace to a Buckingham Palace already surrounded by a field of flowers".

The story of the music of the South Wales Borderers would be incomplete without mention of a highly unusual artefact on display in the regimental museum. It is a Drum Major's staff, shaped in wood but completely covered with highly decorated silver. Its history is not entirely clear, but it is known that it was made in Birmingham in 1829 to the order of the officers of the regiment (all of whom subscribed to its cost), and was used on a fairly regular basis for the following hundred years. Its weight is not recorded, but it must have required considerable physical strength on the part of the Drum Major.

Over the years, many Corps of Drums have been presented with complete sets of silver bugles. Engraved with their regiments' crests, these appear on the market from time to time as individual instruments. Many have been dispersed through post-WWII regimental silver sales (held by some of the old county regiments at the time of their amalgamations). The number of bugles in regular military use is today far less than in the past, and the older patterns are often replaced by technically improved modern designs. According to David Leech, however, "there are notable exceptions. Last year (1997) we fully repaired twenty bugles for the 2nd Royal Anglians. Some of them were very old, but the Corps of Drums wanted to continue using them on parade. The Light Infantry still use silver bugles only,

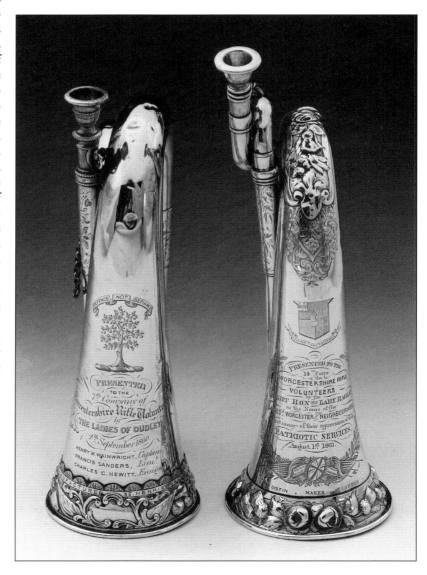

The rapid expansion of the Rifle Volunteer movement in the early 1860s was due partly to a great surge of popular enthusiasm for soldiers and soldiering. The quality of manufacture of these two presentation bugles reflects the degree of civic pride enjoyed by the men of Dudley and Worcester. Photo: RHQ The Worcestershire and Sherwood Foresters Regiment.

and they are regularly repaired in rotation. Their bugles are thus kept in constant good condition. It is interesting to find that some of these instruments date back to the 1920s and early 1930s. I wonder how many other items of military equipment are still in use after seventy-odd years?".

Two silver bugles no longer in use but still in lovely condition are shown here. On the left is an instrument presented to the 7th Company, Worcestershire Rifle Volunteers, by "the ladies of Dudley" on 4 September 1860. It bears the names of the officers of that Company, Captain Henry M Wainwright, Lieutenant Francis Sanders and Ensign Charles C Hewitt, and is hallmarked marked London, 1860. The maker was Kohler, of 35 Henrietta Street, Covent Garden. That on the right was presented to the 14th Corps, Worcestershire Rifle Volunteers, by the Right Honourable Lady Raglan "in the name of the ladies of Worcester and the neighbourhood in testimony of their appreciation of their patriotic services", and is dated 1 August 1861. It is hallmarked London 1861. The maker was Henry Distin.

The Royal Marines possess silver bugles of particular poignancy. In 1920, a fund was raised to purchase thirty-two bugles in memory of officers of the Corps who had died in the war. Made by Boosey, they are of standard service pattern but are entirely of Sterling silver. Embossed with the Corps crest, twenty-one of them are engraved with wording which records the names of individual officers, such as Lieutenant General Adolphus Crosbie, or of particular groups of officers, such as those who did not survive the raid on Zeebrugge.

These bugles have not been used for many years. They are still playable, but they have become fragile and repeated polishing has almost removed the engravings. Originally allocated to the now defunct Chatham, Portsmouth and Plymouth Divisions, they have been split into small groups to form part of the Officers' Mess displays of 40 Commando RM, 42 Commando RM, the RM School of Music, and elsewhere.

And now we must leave the subject of military music and move ourselves back to Ireland. As noted earlier, four other Irish infantry regiments of the British Army were disbanded at the same time as The Royal Dublin Fusiliers. The full story of the disposal of the silver owned by those units has not been researched for the purposes of this book. However, visitors to the National Army Museum, in London, may be interested to know that The Reading Room contains a strange and wonderful relic of The Prince of Wales's Leinster Regiment (Royal Canadians). It is the very large rosewood table upon which visiting researchers are able to spread their documents and the reference books which they have taken down from the nearby shelves. Knowingly or otherwise, they are resting their elbows upon one of the most astonishing of all pieces of Mess furniture.

The 2nd Battalion of The Leinster Regiment came into possession of this table in India, in 1858, during the final stages of the suppression of the Mutiny. More precisely, it was a trophy of war of its forbear, the 3rd Bombay European Regiment. A force of 4500 men, led by Major General Sir Hugh Rose, was one of three columns despatched to deal with the rebel leaders still defying British rule in Central India.

One of Rose's objectives was the fortified city of Jhansi. For reasons which will become apparent, the 11,000 men defending the city were, very unusually, under the command of a woman. After a short siege, Rose launched his attack on 3 April and broke through the city walls. The 3rd Bombay European Regiment took a leading part in the assault and in the severe fighting which followed within the city and the royal Palace. The

attacking force had sixty men killed and 159 wounded. More than 5000 of the defending force died, a figure which by comparison with the British losses suggests that no quarter was given.

As was customary, the victorious troops proceeded to sack whatever treasures they could find. One of the objects which attracted the interest of the officers of the 3rd Bombay European Regiment was a magnificent table in the Palace. It had nineteen leaves, not all of the same size, each supported by four legs, and these sections could be assembled in various combinations according to need and the space available. It was also made in such a way that it was easily dismantled into its component parts, signifying that it was not intended to be left permanently in one place. Presumably it had accompanied the royal entourage, carried on camels or elephants, whenever the Maharajah of Jhansi went on extended tours around his small kingdom. The 3rd Bombay European Regiment did not at the time have a respectable table of their own, so this one became their property. According to legend, it was used in the immediate aftermath of the battle to lay out the bodies of British officers awaiting burial.

In addition to the table, it was at Jhansi that the regiment gained its first Victoria Cross. Private Frederick Conker, serving under the assumed name of James Whirlpool, rescued several wounded men under very heavy fire. While doing so he received seventeen serious wounds, one of which nearly severed his head from his body. He recovered and later emigrated to Australia where he died at Windsor, New South Wales, at the age of seventy.

In 1861 the 3rd Bombay European Regiment became part of the British Army and acquired a new title as the 109th (Bombay Infantry) Regiment. Its officers retained the table for the next nineteen years and it travelled with them to all their stations and on all their campaigns throughout that time. It was used in the Mess at Mhow and Karachi, then went to Aden for the 1865 campaign against the Fudhli Arabs, returned to India (Mooltan, Delhi and Cawnpore) and finally to Jubbulpore. It was here, in 1877, that the 109th handed the table over to their linked regiment, the 100th (Prince of Wales's Royal Canadian) Regiment. Despite its title, this was essentially an Irish-recruited unit which had much in common with the 109th. In fact, only four years later, they were amalgamated to form the 1st and 2nd Battalions respectively of the new Prince of Wales's Leinster Regiment (Royal Canadians).

The 1st Battalion took the table to Sialkot, Umballa, and Fyzabad, and then, in 1895, to Ireland. It was the central piece of furniture in the Messes at, successively, Tipperary, Birr (Parsonstown) and Dublin. The Battalion's next move was to Halifax, Nova Scotia. Purpose-made packing crates were always used during these moves to protect the nineteen main leaves of the table and its thirty-six carved legs, but inevitably it suffered damage from time to time. Close examination reveals that one or two of the leaves may not be original, and there is a later underside reinforcement with stained pine, but it was (and still is) almost completely the same table as that at which the Maharajahs and courtiers of Jhansi once dined.

The 1st Battalion's tour of garrison duty in Nova Scotia ended abruptly in 1899 when conflict erupted in South Africa. It sailed for Cape Town, to fight the Boers, and all excess baggage was shipped back to Ireland. The table went into storage at the depot, at Birr, but it was re-erected two years later in Fermoy Barracks, County Cork, so that the officers could dine from it upon their return from the war.

The Battalion, and the table, were soon on the move once more. After a period in barracks at Shorncliffe, Aldershot and Devonport, the 1st Leinsters were ordered back to India. They served at Bareilly and Fyzabad, but returned at short notice to England when war with Germany was declared in 1914. All Mess furnishings were returned to Birr for the duration of hostilities.

In 1919, the table went back, for the third time, to its original home, India. It travelled extensively around the sub-continent as the battalion was stationed successively at Madras, Wellington and, ultimately, at Calicut (Malabar) during the little-known but horrendous period of sectarian violence known as The Moplah Rebellion. And that was the last time that either battalion of The Leinsters served the Crown. The 1st Battalion was ordered to embark for home and, in 1922, both battalions ceased to exist. They and their forebears had never, in a century and a half, been beaten in the field, but the politicians in London and in their own country had demolished them at the stroke of a pen.

The Leinster table, when fully assembled, is five and half feet wide and, at thirty-six feet, is more than half the length of a cricket pitch. These massive proportions limit the choice of venues in which it can be conveniently housed. At the time of their disbandment, the officers of the regiment, 1st and 2nd Battalions, agreed to present it "on Trust" to the Army Council, at that time the supreme ruling body of the British Army.

The words "on Trust" reflected the written condition "until such time as the Regiment should be re-raised as an Irish Regiment of the Crown". As with the silver of King Edward's Horse and the Royal Dublin Fusiliers mentioned previously, such circumstances have never arisen and never will.

The Army Council kept and used the table for the next twenty-two years. The bulk of it was erected in the Commander-in-Chief's Levee Room at the War Office, with the remainder in an adjoining room. On the initiative of Colonel R A H Orpen-Palmer, silver plaques were made and fitted in 1940 at both ends of the table with the engraved wording: "Presented on Trust to the Army Council by the Officers of The Prince of Wales's Leinster Regiment (Royal Canadians) on Disbandment, July 31st 1922".

Events moved on and, in March 1964, the Army Council itself was disbanded and replaced by the new Ministry of Defence (Army). To mark the occasion, all former and serving members of the Council attended a dinner at the War Office (they had not dined there since 1914), and the Leinster table performed its original function for the last time. Nine years later, on 19 February 1973, it was presented by the MOD to the recently-formed National Army Museum, in Royal Hospital Road, Chelsea, where it now resides in The Reading Room. Even there it is too large to be assembled complete. Eight of the legs and several of the leaves are held in store at the Museum's Study Centre. The table as presently erected is twenty-three feet in length, so the visitor is viewing only two-thirds of its entirety.

There is, hanging in The Reading Room, a large framed photograph which shows the table partly assembled and covered with silver from the 1st Leinster's collection. There are twenty-one large pieces on the table itself, with many more arranged on shelves behind it. The photograph was taken at Fort St George, Madras, in 1922.

The story of the table would not be complete without some reference to its previous owner. The Rani (Regent) was thirty years of age at the time of the Mutiny, a woman who, according to an Englishman who met her, "was fair and handsome, with a noble figure and a dignified and resolute, indeed stern,

expression. On her head she had a small cap of scarlet silk with a string of pearls and rubies encircling and woven into it. Her bodice, freely opened in front, was drawn tightly by a belt worked over and embroidered with gold, and into it were stuck two silver-mounted pistols and a small but elegantly shaped dagger. Instead of the usual petticoat, she wore a pair of loose trousers, from which protruded her small prettily rounded bare feet". Her name was Lakshmibai.

Raised as a tomboy, she had learned from childhood to ride like a Maharatta warrior and to use the weapons of that elite, but at fifteen she was married to the sickly and much older Maharajah of Jhansi. Nine years later she bore him a son. The infant soon died and so, following a recognised Hindu tradition, he adopted a five-year old princely nephew, Damodar Rao. Before he died, the old Maharajah drew up a Will which nominated Damodar Rao as his successor and which also appointed Lakshmibai as Regent until such time as the boy came of age.

The Honourable East Company was informed of these arrangements, and it raised no objection. Jhansi was an independent kingdom with which the East India Company had no immediate quarrel, and indeed both the Maharajah and Lakshmibai admired the British way of conducting diplomatic business. Unfortunately, their trust was not justified.

The Maharajah died in 1853 and Lakshmibai became Regent. The Governor General of India, Lord Dalhousie, then rejected Damodar Rao as the heir apparent and annexed the Kingdom of Jhansi for the Company on the grounds of "the doctrine of lapse". Lakshmabai and the boy moved out of the Palace to a house in the city, a British administrator moved in, and a garrison of Company troops ensured compliance with Dalhousie's ruling.

Over the next three years Lakshmibai corresponded with Dalhousie and with the Directors of the East India Company in London, petitioning them on behalf of her adopted son for a reversal of the annexation. Her appeals were all rejected, but still she did not turn against the British. When the Sepoy Mutiny erupted in May 1857, the locally-stationed Company troops quickly joined it and appealed to Lakshmibai to lead them. Even when threatened, she refused to become involved.

The locally resident European officers and traders and their families took shelter for a while in the Palace but, when offered safe conduct by the mutineers and when they attempted to leave, they were all murdered. Lakshmibai immediately wrote to the Commissioner in Jubbulpore, a Major Erskine, denying any responsibility. Erskine knew her well, and he believed her. He asked her to assume the government of Jhansi until such time as the Company could send more troops and a new administrator. This she agreed to do.

During the following months, she and her followers ejected the mutinous Company troops and fought off attacks by the rulers of three nearby independent states who had ambitions of their own for the future of Jhansi. Then, at the beginning of 1858, Lakshmibai learned that General Rose was assembling his force and that he and the Company had convinced themselves that she was responsible for the earlier murders of the Europeans. At this point she realised that Major Erskine's faith in her was not shared by his superiors. She sent messages to two other rulers, Tantya Tope and Rao Sahib, with whom she had grown up and who were leaders of the rebellion, announcing that her allegiances were now with them.

When General Rose's troops began to smash their way into Jhansi and the end was near, Lakshmibai left the fort at night by jumping her horse down a precipice. She was dressed as a warrior, her hair cropped, and her adopted son strapped to her back. She took with her twenty-five of the best Jhansi *sowars* (cavalrymen) and they headed towards Bhander. Galloping across open country, they ran into one of General Rose's patrols. In the fight which followed, Lakshmibai is described as having plunged into the *mêlée* with a sword in each hand, the reins gripped in her teeth, and the young prince still secured to her back.

She was brought down by a bullet fired from the carbine of a soldier of the 8th Hussars. Before dying a few moments later, she gave orders for the safety of the boy and the disposal of her jewels. A fine bronze statue of this admirable woman, showing her as she was at the time of her attempted escape, was later erected in Gwalior. Sadly, a vandal removed the figure of young Damodar Rao and it has never been restored.

traditions and create the sense of being "at home" no matter where in the world they may be stationed. In years gone by, the logistics of moving a mass of tables, chairs, settees, pictures, ornaments, billiards tables, books, chinaware, cutlery, table linen, bed linen, carpets, and so on and so forth, were very considerable. All of this applied not only to the Officers' Mess but also to the Sergeants' Mess. Their combined crates of silver were only one element in a very much more complex operation.

It has always been the standard procedure, whenever any military unit is moving itself from one place to another, for a number of officers and other ranks to be sent ahead to prepare for the arrival of the main party. This "advance party" ensures, *inter alia*, that there will be sufficient food and accommodation for the troops when they arrive, and the officer in charge signs the numerous bits of paper which acknowledge a correct handover of the buildings and equipment being inherited from

Jhansi was not the only city to be sacked in the 19th century by a vengeful soldiery but, conversely, there were many other groups of citizens who had reason to thank the army for its protection. In 1749, grants of land in Nova Scotia were offered for settlement by ex-servicemen. The British government wanted to establish a permanent town and seaport to counter French domination in the region. The 4000 new settlers were guarded by two British regiments, one of which later became the 29th Regiment of Foot (and later still, 1st Battalion, The Worcestershire Regiment). The soldiers erected fortifications and cleared the site for the new township named Halifax (after the Earl of Halifax, President of the Board of Trade and Plantations). The 29th returned in 1765-1769, and again in 1802-1807. The engraving on this cup states: *Presented to the Officers of His Majesty's 29th Regt of Foot by the Inhabitants of the Town of Halifax in Nova Scotia in Testimony of their High Esteem and Regard.* Photo: Photo: RHQ The Worcestershire & Sherwood Foresters Regiment.

The Leinster's table, if it could speak, could fairly claim to have been on active service on four occasions. The first three were the Central India campaign (1858), Aden (1865), and the Moplah Rebellion (1920-1921). In WWII it came under fire during the London Blitz. On 11 September 1940, a faulty anti-aircraft shell fell and exploded in Horse Guards Avenue. Two soldiers were fatally wounded, and splinters from the shell smashed through the windows of the War Office. Several fragments came to rest in the Army Council Room and were found on the table.

This particular item of furniture is exceptional for its size and its extraordinary provenance, but most regiments possess one or more pieces which, to them, represent their histories and

the "rear party" of the outgoing unit. It is the "rear party" which must maintain its unit's good reputation by not only taking away all of its own property but also leaving the place in immaculate condition for the newcomers.

In times past, and particularly in the more leisurely years before WWII, the quantity of furnishings shipped around the world by some battalions was remarkable when compared with today's standards. It was not unknown for them to inherit a Mess building devoid of all contents (other than, perhaps, the kitchen equipment). Everything else had belonged to the former occupants. The "advance party" might then be obliged to "rough it", or live elsewhere, until such time as the transport arrived with what were, in effect, their household contents.

Unhappy were the officers of the main party if, upon their arrival, they were told that the Mess was not ready for occupation because the transport had been delayed or because everything had been lost in transit. The parallels with domestic house-moving are obvious, and underline the fact that the regiments and battalions of the British and Indian Armies were, and still are, families.

It would be easy, for later generations, to scoff at what might seem an excessive and self-indulgent obsession with inanimate objects. Certainly there must have been instances of particular regiments accumulating so many possessions that their ability to uproot themselves from one place and move to another was impaired. Worse, if there was a sudden emergency, if the regiment or battalion was obliged to quickly change gear and move to a war footing, the responsibility of caring for the furniture and silver was at times an unhelpful distraction from the main aim. Several such instances are cited later in this book. Then again, a critic might point to the diversion of manpower needed to pack and unpack all this stuff, and the cost of transporting it from continent to continent.

Few regimental officers, past or present, would feel obliged to respond to such criticisms. Why should they? Private family matters are precisely that - private. They would not think of criticising the occupant of a civilian domestic dwelling for possessing too much furniture or too many ornaments. It is nobody's business other than the owner's. The War Office civil servants charged the officers of the regiment for their share of the cost of transporting the Mess contents from location to location. Packing and unpacking was often done by civilian Mess staff employed by the officers, or by commercial shipping agents acting on their behalf, and who were not, therefore, a charge upon the public purse. If higher authority suspected that a commanding officer was permitting an excessive commitment to style and comfort in the Officers' Mess to impact upon the fighting efficiency of his unit, he might well have found his career taking an unexpected turn. There were plenty of checks and balances.

In the modern British Army, totally different circumstances prevail and they are largely the consequence of three major changes during the past half century. The first was the sexual revolution of the 1960s. Young people marry earlier in life, they start having families earlier, and therefore they start to create their own homes earlier. Junior officers are no longer willing to observe the long-respected convention that they could take a wife only after they had passed their thirtieth birthday and, even then, only with the approval of their commanding officer. At the end of the working day, they go home to their wives and children. The need for a Mess in the sense that it was the permanent "home" for a bachelor brotherhood, deprived of female company on anything other than a temporary or illicit basis, has largely disappeared.

Such changes are not singular to the British Army. After thirty years as Chief Historian to the United States Marine Corps, Henry "Bud" Shaw Jr recently observed: "The Officers' Mess and Sergeants' Mess syndrome was an actuality in the 19th century but it has pretty well disappeared in many modern bases. Officers' Clubs have a hard time making a go of it most places as there are few bachelors and little disposition to center military social life on base. Most officers and senior NCOs live off base and are wrapped up in civilian pursuits where they make their homes. Also, at least in the USMC, the troops are deployed a good part of the time on board ship or overseas, and when they get back they are preparing to deploy again and trying to catch up with family matters they've missed. Military life nowadays bears little resemblance to the classical profile of the 1800s, or even the first half of this century".

The historical roots and traditions of the American armed forces are different to those of the British but, even so, "Bud" Shaw's comments must strike a chord with British servicemen (especially in those units which have too few personnel trying to cope with too many commitments, at home and abroad).

Continuing cutbacks in manpower since the ending of National Service in the early 1960s have led to the second change in Mess life. Today it centres largely around the bar, and the person serving behind the bar is a civilian. This would have been unthinkable prior to WWII. The concept of the Mess as a comfortable private house or a gentleman's club depended heavily upon the availability of Mess servants who, like domestic servants, were ever ready to respond to the ring of a bell. The soldiers of the Mess staff, who once padded around the Mess ante room, serving drinks, fetching newspapers, exchanging small jokes with their favourite officers, have long departed. The installation of the bar changed the *ethos* substantially. Some Messes, certainly those located within army installations where they are used by the officers of more than regiment or corps, now have more the feel of a hotel than a country house.

The third factor is the greatly reduced scale of the British Army's overseas deployments. In the balmy days preceding the second world war, the Empire and Commonwealth extended to almost every corner of the globe. The army was required to maintain permanent garrison and peace-keeping forces in the Caribbean, in Gibraltar and Malta, in Palestine, in Egypt, in India, in Malaya and Singapore, in Hong Kong and elsewhere.

Earlier, during much of the 19th century, British regiments were sent overseas for tours of duty lasting five, ten or even twenty years. It was important not only to their comfort but also to their efficiency that they should maintain a code of conduct, to recognise a set of values and to hold to them regardless of the environment in which they found themselves. The furniture, the pictures, the silver, and all the rest of it, had a central role in sustaining those standards. One may smile at the old "dinner jackets in the jungle" jokes, but they concealed a deeper need. British soldiers were often called upon to serve in places which were far from civilised society, where they had no natural affinity with the local population, where the climate was unhealthy, where death from disease was a constant risk, where promotion was agonisingly slow, where there was little prospect of winning fame and glory, and where sometimes even the civilian Mess servants were unreliable. There are numerous recorded instances of native cooks or waiters "running amok" with a kitchen knife and killing an officer while he sat at the dinner table.

Written accounts of Mess life, particularly in India and in some of the Colonies, may give the impression that it was excessively comfortable and privileged, but the reality was at times very much harsher. It is not surprising that those officers threw themselves so enthusiastically into whatever activity - pig-sticking, wild-fowling, tiger shooting, hunting, polo, point-to-point racing, cricket, amateur theatricals - would keep at bay the condition known to the French Foreign Legion as the *cafard*. It was not simply a question of preference, it was also a matter of necessity. If the officers of any regiment had allowed their conduct to become lax, or if they had allowed their men to suspect that they were about to "go native" or "go bush", it would have ceased to be a disciplined military unit. In the event, it never happened that way. The bonds of regimental pride and good manners had been forged so strongly, over so many years,

Officers sent to distant corners of the Empire found their off-duty entertainment mainly by using their own initiative and resources. The Fancy Dress Party (above) seems to have been a very serious affair, involving much preparation by husbands and wives alike. It was held near Karachi, in 1892, by the 1st Baluch Light Infantry. The 1956 New Year's Eve celebrations by the officers of the 4th (Uganda) Battalion, The King's African Rifles, reflected the less rigid codes which followed WWII. Photos: National Army Museum and Major Dennis Michell.

that they were never seriously at risk.

It may be argued that these same influences have ensured that, with only a very few exceptions, the British Army has never been guilty of atrocities against helpless civilian populations or against prisoners of war. The soldiers of almost every other nation have from time to time besmirched the reputation of their profession by committing what are today known as "crimes against humanity". The record of the British Army is remarkably unsullied in this regard, and much of the credit must be attributed to the culture of the regimental system.

The process of shedding her Empire began for Great Britain when, in 1947, she withdrew from India. It escalated rapidly in the 1960s when most of the Colonies and Protectorates in Africa were abandoned. Since the 1970s the British Army has had only two major garrison commitments outside the mainland - Germany and Northern Ireland. Both offer good communications for personnel wishing to take home leave. Neither of them normally require them to be overseas for more than a maximum of two years at a time. It is all far removed from the days when a young soldier went with his regiment to India and returned to his home village in Ireland, or Wales, or wherever he had been recruited, ten or twenty years later and without having seen it once in the meantime.

Although they no longer take nearly as much impedimenta with them as in times past, British regiments do still take their silver (or part of it) when they leave the mainland for an extended tour. Units deployed as part of the NATO arrangements in Germany have with them many of their finest pieces. Even for more distant deployments, of shorter duration, it is normal to take a few household possessions in the regimental baggage.

In 1984, the author was briefly the guest of a battalion of the Royal Regiment of Fusiliers, then serving in the Falkland Islands. Its company detachment at Goose Green, setting for the battle in which Lieutenant Colonel "H" Jones gained his posthumous Victoria Cross, was housed in a lonely wind-swept cluster of Portakabins. These sturdy movable structures provide adequate basic living accommodation, but not a great deal more.

The officers of the Fusiliers had inherited the MOD-issue fixtures and fittings, but they also had brought with them to the South Atlantic a dozen or so of their own framed pictures and minor pieces of decorative silver. The effect was to transform an austere box into a Mess. By having a few of their favourite things around them, and even though they were eight thousand miles from England, the Fusiliers were "at home".

The preceding pages are a general survey of the traditions of just a few British Army regiments and battalions. Each possesses (or possessed, in the case of those which have disappeared during the defence retrenchments of the last forty years) Mess silver which can be arranged in three broad categories.

First are the ordinary workaday functional items such as knives, forks and spoons, condiment sets, coffee pots, dishes, tureens, bowls, and salvers.

Second are those trophies and decorative pieces having a relatively modest financial value or historical interest, but which are useful in sustaining a familiar and reassuring *ambience* in the ante-room and dining-room.

Third are the major pieces, often of monumental size and great quality of workmanship, almost always of high monetary value, which are brought out and displayed on special occasions. Amongst them are the table centrepieces, originally conceived and commissioned by the officers of the day as symbols or icons of their regiment's history and achievements. To understand the variety and quality of such objects we may take a look at the possessions of three representative regiments - a Scottish Highland regiment, a cavalry regiment, and an English county infantry regiment.

The Argyll and Sutherland Highlanders

The regiment was formed (under a slightly different title) by the amalgamation in 1881 of the 91st Argyllshire Highlanders and the 93rd Sutherland Highlanders. Officially they became the 1st and 2nd Battalions but, as happened in every other new regiment created by the Cardwell reforms of that year, officers and men alike continued to describe themselves under their old numerical title - "the 91st" and "the 93rd". In some regiments, the habit did not begin to die out until the 1960s, and it is not entirely dead yet.

The 93rd brought to the marriage a centrepiece which it had acquired in 1870, and its sad history is described later, in Chapter Six. A fire in the Officers' Mess in 1980, while the Argylls were serving in Northern Ireland, resulted in its total destruction, and the means have never been available for the manufacture of a replacement.

The 91st Argyllshire Highlanders Centrepiece, on the other hand, travelled the world until 1970 when it was placed on long-term display in the Regimental Museum. The maker was Elkington & Company and it is hallmarked Birmingham 1906.

In 1960, when asked to research its symbolism as a matter of regimental record, Lieutenant Colonel C G Kelway Bamber MBE described it thus: "Purchased by the Officers to commemorate the part taken by the battalion in the South African War, 1899-1902. Description: resting upon a base, Celtic in character, the apex terminates in a group of historical and allegorical significance. At the top, 'Diarmid of the Wild Boar', identifying the 91st with the Clan Campbell or 'Clan Diarmid an Tuirc'; on either side, 'Ossian', the great Highland poet, and the

figure of 'Victory'.

Beneath are two sets of Colours, those carried in the Peninsula and those carried at the present time, while in front, beneath 'Cruachan' (the Campbell war cry), is a representation of the Brooch of Lorn, with an embossed portrait of HRH Princess Louise, and above, her Coronet.

On the base, four statuettes represent General Duncan Campbell of Lochnell (the first Colonel of the 91st, raised in 1794 at Stirling), a soldier of 1794, an officer during the South African War, and an officer in the full uniform of the present day. Four panels resting on bog myrtle (the Campbell Badge) and moss are embossed with the following episodes in the career of the Regiment: Battle of Toulouse, 1814, the Wreck of the *Birkenhead*, 1852, the Battle of Gingindhlovo, 1879, and the Battle of Modder River, 1899. Round the base are the medals earned by the 91st, and the various Battle Honours borne on the Colours, while at each corner is the old 91st cap badge and, above, the Wild Boar, the Campbell crest".

The reference to Her Royal Highness The Princess Louise, mentioned in the above description and nominated within the regiment's title, requires explanation.

In October 1870, Queen Victoria announced that her fourth daughter, Louise, was to marry the Marquis of Lorne, heir to the Duke of Argyll. At that time the 91st (Argyllshire) Highlanders were encamped at Aldershot. Their commanding officer requested permission that the regiment might provide a Guard of Honour for the wedding, at St George's Chapel, Windsor Castle. The Queen agreed, and the regiment was additionally represented on the day, 21 March 1871, by its Band and Pipers.

Subsequently the Queen let it be known that she wished to confer some special mark upon the regiment to commemorate the part it had taken in the wedding. She sent for the commanding officer, Lieutenant Colonel John Sprot, to discuss the matter. He renewed the regiment's persistent and long-standing request for the restoration of the right to wear the kilt. This had been withdrawn in 1809 when it - and the regiment's distinctively Scottish title - were thought to be impediments to recruitment.

The "Highlanders" title and the wearing of the tartan, as trews, were restored in 1864 and 1867. Colonel Sprot was now pressing again for full Highland dress. Her Majesty said "yes", but the Secretary of State for War said "no", and it was not until 1881 that official authority was granted. Having failed to win that concession, Colonel Sprot requested that his regiment should be redesignated "The Princess Louise's Argyllshire Highlanders". This time the War Office could find no objection so, in April 1872, an Army Order was published which confirmed the new title and quoted the Royal Command - "the Regimental Colours shall bear the Princess Louise's coronet and cypher in the three corners". When, in 1881, the 91st amalgamated with the 93rd, the new regiment (including its part-time volunteer units) continued to bear the name of the Princess. She became Colonel

The 91st Highlander's magnificent centrepiece which can be seen in the
Museum of The Argyll and Sutherland Highlanders (Princess Louise's),
at Stirling Castle. The base measures 38 inches by 30, and the overall
height is 46 inches. Photo: RHQ A&SH.

Designed by Boehm in 1869 and made in electro-plated white metal, this equine statuette did not come into the possession of the Argyll & Sutherland Highlanders until 1966, but it relates directly to the regiment's long-standing title. Photo: RHQ A&SH.

say that its turning point was a bayonet charge by a platoon of the Argylls and another by thirty men of the 6/13th. The wedge which had been driven between them was eliminated, and the Germans "were literally thrown off the top of the hill".

Both during the battle and the period of their withdrawal, the Germans were hit hard by mortar fire and by the fire of a Vickers machine gun manned by a Sikh soldier, Havildar Tara Singh. It was his courage which came to symbolise the spirit in which the battle was fought.

In 1947, the Argylls sent to India an officer's full-dress silver cross-belt breastplate. Professionally mounted and fitted with a presentation plaque, it commemorated the shared experiences of the two battalions. The 6/13th paraded to hear their Commanding Officer read a message of greeting from all ranks of the 1st Argylls and an account of the battle. The 6/13th was by now part of the Pakistan Army and entirely Muslim. Every officer and every man filed past the Argyll breastplate and laid a hand upon it. They were honouring the memory of a time when Hindu and Muslim had fought shoulder-to-shoulder, and when soldiers white and brown were brothers-in-arms.

Two years later the 1st Argylls received from the 6/13th a silver statuette of Tara Singh. They were told that the Pakistan silversmith responsible for the work was a direct descendent of a *sepoy* who had fought under Colonel Arthur Wellesley at Seringapatam, in 1799. The wording on the presentation plaque stated simply "In memory of Monte Cerere, Italy 1944". For

in Chief of the Regiment in 1914 and maintained a close involvement in its affairs until her death on 3 December 1939.

The Princess Louise Statuette is an enduring and charming personal memento of her association with the Argylls. The small plaque on its base states simply "HRH Princess Louise on Andrew, 1869". It depicts the young woman as she was, on a favourite horse, two years before her wedding and therefore two years before she began her involvement with the 91st. One of her own personal possessions, it was given to the regiment in 1966 by HRH The Princess Marina.

The Havildar Tara Singh Statuette is a much later piece, and its provenance is an example of the strong historical ties between British and Indian soldiers.

At the close of 1944, the 1st Battalion of the Argylls was serving in Northern Italy. The Allies were attempting to break through the Apennines to reach the plains of the River Po. Blocking them in the mountains was the Gothic Line, a complex of German defensive positions.

On 12 December, the 1st Parachute Regiment - "the toughest, most cunning and resourceful soldiers in Kesselring's army" - launched an attack against a key feature in the hills overlooking Bologna. It was held by "D" Company of the Argylls (Major C G Kelway Bamber) and "C" Company of the 6/13th Royal Battalion (Scinde), The Frontier Force Rifles (Major Bharat Singh). The two battalions had come to know each other well and were great friends at all levels.

The full story of the battle for Monte Cerere appears in the battalion history by Lieutenant Colonel F C C Graham DSO. It is enough here to

Havildar Tara Singh single-handedly manning his Vickers machine gun at the battle of Monte Cerere, 12 December 1944. A curiosity is the choice of unit crest on the presentation plaque. It is that of the 59th Royal Scinde Rifles, Frontier Force. The "Royal" distinction was granted in 1921 in recognition of their services in WWI (at Neuve Chapelle, when all the British officers were killed or wounded, Subadar Major Perbhat Chand took command and later brought the battalion to safety). Only a year after receiving this honour, in the major Indian Army reorganisations of 1922, the 59th were redesignated 6th Royal Battalion (Scinde), 13th Frontier Force Rifles. This engraving, therefore, is the unit crest relevant only to the period 1921-1922. There is no obvious explanation why the "bugle, crown and 13 FFR" crest was not used instead. Photo: Antonia Reeve, and RHQ A&SH.

those who knew the story, it was enough.

The statuette was lost when the Officers' Mess caught fire in 1980. It was one of the pieces which the Museum Committee decided must be replaced. A friend of the regiment, Mrs Rae Campbell, contributed a large part of the cost, and in 1995 the task was given to Hamilton & Inches, of Edinburgh. Including the base, it stands only nine inches high but it records a small infantry battle, one of hundreds fought in WWII, which otherwise might have been long forgotten. In the event, the bond has not been broken. The Argylls are officially affiliated with their wartime comrades who gained a new title after Partition - 1st Battalion (Scinde), The Frontier Force Regiment.

The 91st Argyllshire Highlanders Ram's Head was gifted to the regiment in 1864. The silver plaque between the upper horns is inscribed "For Auld Lang Syne. Presented to the Officers' Mess, 91st Argyllshire Highlanders, by Lieutenants C L Harvey and W Grant, on promotion, Jubbulpore, 30 September

His horns tipped with silver thistles and his head crowned with silver and polished cairngorm stones, this handsome ram was for many years a silent member of the Officers' Mess of the 91st Argyllshire Highlanders. He served as a combined snuff mull and cigar holder. Currently he forms part of the display in the regimental museum at Stirling Castle. Photo: RHQ A&SH.

1864". Below are listed the names of all the officers serving with the regiment at that time.

The heads of sheep, goats and antelope have frequently been adapted, either for military presentation or for the commercial (civilian) market, as mountings for snuff mulls or ink wells. Most of them date from the reign of Queen Victoria and have a distinctly neo-Gothic feel. This fine example is a combined snuff mull and cigar holder. Chased in silver, it is decorated with cairngorms and backed with sheep's wool.

Its width from tip to tip is seventeen inches. Some ram's heads are even larger, a fact which can make them unhandy for display. Those possessing historic significance are usually well preserved in museums, but the few seen on the open market have shown all the signs of hard usage and a lack of interest by dealers and the public alike. The 91st's Ram's Head has retained all its original fittings and exemplifies the style of the period.

The King's Royal Hussars

The silver owned by the regiments of Regular cavalry is

frequently spectacular in its range of styles and historical associations. For the cavalrymen, the process of amalgamation began in 1922 and there have been more mergers since WWII.

One of the newest cavalry titles is that of The King's Royal Hussars. Formed in 1992, it represents and consolidates the history and traditions of what were once the 10th Hussars, the 11th Hussars, the 14th Hussars, and the 20th Hussars, and it has inherited their collections of silver. The following descriptions have been supplied by the regiment, and they exemplify everything which is important in the heritage of military silver.

The St George and the Dragon Centrepiece was a joint presentation to the 11th Prince Albert's Own Hussars by General Sir Crauford Frazer CB VC and Colonel A Lyttleton-Annesley "in remembrance of many happy years in the regiment which they successively commanded as Lieutenant Colonel". Their terms in command covered the period 1861 to 1878.

The knight wears the armour of the 15th century, so he would have retired from active service about three hundred years before the regiment was raised (in Essex, in 1715). The object replicates the Cavalry Memorial in Hyde Park. The allegorical design reflected the popular perception of the cavalry soldier as a "knight in shining armour", a man of superior qualities.

The King George IV Candelabra (page 34) is a stupendous silver gilt object, topped by the figure of George IV dressed as a Roman emperor and once the property of the 10th Royal Hussars. The engraved wording states: "The gift of His Majesty King George IV to the Xth or Prince of Wales's Own Royal Regiment, which he commanded from 1793 until accession to the Throne 1821".

The figures seated at each of the three corners of the central column represent "Courage", "Honour" and "Peace", and a side panel is engraved with the Battle Honours for Benevente, Corunna, Morales de Toro, Vittoria, Orthes, Toulouse and Waterloo. The silversmith was Paul Storr, and this piece is typical of his response to the demand for neo-classical designs in vogue at that period. It was made in 1822, when Storr was working for Rundall & Bridges. The presentation was made by the Marquis of Londonderry, commanding the regiment and acting on behalf of the King, at a sumptuous banquet in St James Square, London. It was attended by the officers of the regiment and all the most distinguished officers of the army. Londonderry made his own contribution to "this joyous day" by giving "two magnificent embossed silver tureens … to form part of a more splendid Service of Plate of the Mess than perhaps any other Corps in the Service possessed".

The Cardigan Group Centrepiece (page 35) stands thirty-four inches high overall and was made in London in 1863 by John S Hunt, of Hunt & Roskell. The central (top) figure is Lord Cardigan, the officer who commanded the Light Brigade in the Crimea and who earlier had commanded the 11th Hussars. At each corner is a mounted trooper representative of 1745, 1838, 1840 and 1862. Two large side panels contain chased scenes of the Battles of Salamanca and the Alma. At one end, below the Sphinx, are some of the regiment's Battle Honours while the main engraving reads: "Presented by Lieut General the Earl of Cardigan KCB and Commander of the Legion of Honour to The 11th Prince Albert's Own Hussars, as a mark of attachment and esteem from their Colonel, who led them in Brigade at Balaclava, after serving with The Regiment for many years and in commemoration of the numerous and distinguished services of the Regiment since it was first raised".

The Lord Cardigan Centrepiece (page 36) also commemorates the 11th Hussars' best remembered officer. It shows him

The St George and the Dragon Centrepiece, 28 inches in height, made for the 11th Hussars in 1878 by Robert Garrard. It is inscribed on the reverse "S Georgius Equitus Patronius" (St George, Patron Saint of Cavalry). Photo: The King's Royal Hussars.

crossing the Russian gun lines at Balaclava on 25 October 1854. Made in London in 1864 by Robert Garrard, it was in the possession of his family until shortly before WWI. In March 1914, Lady Cardigan invited Lieutenant Colonel T T Pitman, the then commanding officer, to tea at her home, Deene Park. During this encounter she revealed that it had always been her late husband's intention to give the centrepiece to the regiment.

There and then, she handed it to him. A month or so later a silver plate was made and fixed to the plinth: "Presented to the 11th Prince Albert's Own Hussars by the widow of the 7th Earl of Cardigan, of Balaclava fame, March 1914".

The Emperor (page 37) takes us from the sublime to the practical, and is the best known trophy of war in the entire British Army. It was acquired by the 14th Light Dragoons (later

Hussars) in 1813, shortly after the Battle of Vittoria, when British cavalry patrols swept forward and overtook the fleeing French baggage train.

The troopers captured the campaign coach of Joseph, King of Spain, brother of Napoleon Buonaparte. Amongst his personal effects was this pot, engraved with the arms of Imperial France and complete with lockable travelling case. The engraving led to the assumption that the object had been given to Joseph by Napoleon, hence it became known as "The Emperor".

As word spread to other units in Wellington's Peninsula army that the 14th Hussars had seized the pot and intended to

keep it, the regiment acquired the nickname "The Emperor's Chambermaids". It gave them much pleasure at the time, and the pot has remained with the regiment and its successors to the present day.

It is still the focus of a Dinner Night ritual. Following the loyal toast and the toast to the Colonel of the Regiment, the Mess Sergeant brings in the chamber pot filled with Champagne. The commanding officer rises and drinks to "The Emperor". The pot then circulates clockwise around the table, each officer and guest rising in turn and drinking the same toast. Guests and others who are taking part for the first time are supported with applause and shouts of encouragement.

Standing 40 inches in height, weighing 1231 ounces, made by one of the most famous of the Regency silversmiths (Paul Storr), this monumental centrepiece was the gift of HM King George IV to the 10th, The Prince of Wales's Own, Royal Hussars. Photo: The King's Royal Hussars.

There was a time when the pot, having completed its first circuit, was refilled and offered to the junior Subaltern or to an officer about to retire. They were invited to try to drink the lot. This custom was abandoned in 1929 after one of the regiment's young gentlemen tried too hard and became unconscious for a worryingly long time.

The foregoing descriptions might give the impression that British cavalrymen are concerned only with horses and long-ago days of glory. The reality is very different. Based in Germany, The King's Royal Hussars are equipped with fifty Challenger main battle tanks, each weighing seventy tons and able to destroy any comparable tank, day or night, at ranges up to two

kilometres. The switch from horse-flesh to horse-power began in the late 1930s, with armoured cars of various types.

The Daimler Armoured Car (page 37) was used mainly as a reconnaissance and patrol vehicle, and was one of the design successes of WWII. Several cavalry regiments used it during and after the war, and replicas in silver were purchased by a number of them. This example was acquired by the officers of the 11th Hussars. Within the plinth is an engraved plate which can be drawn out and read. It states: "This silver Daimler Armoured Car was bought with the proceeds of the sale of a carpet liberated from the Japanese Embassy, Berlin, July 1945. It is dedicated to the memory of Lt Col W Wainman DSO MC and

A figure familiar to everyone who has seen the 1968 film directed by Tony Richardson and starring Trevor Howard in the role of the Earl of Cardigan. This beautiful 1864 centrepiece, by Robert Garrard, shows His Lordship leading The Light Brigade through the Russian gun-line at Balaklava. Photo: The King's Royal Hussars.

all those who served in armoured cars during the Second World War".

A similar pattern of development occurred in the volunteer part-time units known as the Yeomanry. Originally mounted on horses, their role changed (from the 1930s onwards) to artillery and armour. Space does not permit even a superficial account in this book of the complex history of the Yeomanry movement. It is enough to generalise by saying that its regiments have long been associated with certain families and certain social groups in each county, and have roots deep in the soil of their individual territories. Their members have always sustained immensely strong *esprit de corps* and, because financial resources have not been lacking, have each created interesting collections of silver.

Just one representative piece will serve as a mirror for the *ethos* of these splendid groups of dedicated citizens. It is a presentation cup which appeared recently at auction in London and

was hammered at seven hundred pounds. The engraved legend reads: "1878. This cup was Presented by Lieut Genl Wm Parke CB on behalf of 225 Subscribers to Corporal E W Cave of the Blandford Troop of the Queen's Own Regiment of Yeomanry Cavalry, in Token of Admiration of his Success whereby he Upheld the Honour of the Regiment and County, in Competition for the Loyd Lindsay Prize at Wimbledon, in the Years 1876, 1877 and 1878, in Conjunction with Sergeant W Rogers, Private G W Ross and Private R G Cave".

Although not specified in the wording, the county in question is Dorset (Blandford Forum being more or less at its centre). General Sir William Parke, second son of Charles Parke, of Henbury House, Wimborne, was a veteran of the Crimean and Mutiny campaigns. In the former he commanded the 72nd Highlanders and in the second a Field Column in operations in Central India.

"The Emperor", the best known of all regimental trophies and still serving a practical purpose as it approaches its 200th birthday. Photo: The King's Royal Hussars.

The Worcestershire and Sherwood Foresters Regiment

Finally we come to a selection of the best pieces owned by a representative county regiment of heavy infantry. It was formed in 1970 from an amalgamation of The Worcestershire Regiment (formerly the 29th and 36th Regiments of Foot) and The Sherwood Foresters (formerly the 45th and 95th Regiments of Foot). The oldest of these, the 29th, traced its descent from the raising, in 1694, of Colonel Thomas Farrington's Regiment of Foot and gained its first Battle Honour for the War of Spanish Succession, 1701-1715. Their modern (amalgamated) descendent is rooted in the geographical heart of England - Worcestershire, Nottinghamshire, Herefordshire and Derbyshire.

The 11th Hussars' scale model of the Daimler armoured car, seven inches high and mounted on ebonised wood. Photo: The King's Royal Hussars.

The regimental records contain very little information regarding makers and hallmarks, but the wonderful quality of the collection speaks for itself.

The 95th Centrepiece (page 38) was commissioned in 1901 by the officers of the 2nd Battalion, The Derbyshire Regiment, to mark the end of nineteen years of continuous foreign service and to commemorate the campaigns in which the battalion had taken part. The 95th was raised in 1823, too late to serve in the

wars with France, but in their first eighty-five years they saw more active service than any other regiment of the line.

The central column is topped with the winged figure of "Victory", crowned with a laurel wreath, sounding a trumpet and carrying in her right hand a branch of palm. Under this is an ornately decorated cup with the head of Minerva on each handle and the regimental mascot (the Derbyshire ram) on one panel.

The Dorset Yeomanry shooting cup stands 19 inches high and weighs 65 ounces. The name of the maker is not known, the hallmarks are London, 1878. Photo: Sotheby's.

The base of the column depicts scenes from the five campaigns in which the 95th and its successor fought - the Crimea, the Indian Mutiny, Egypt 1882, Sikkim 1888, and the North West Frontier of India 1897-1898.

The four statuettes around the base are - an officer 1823, a Sergeant of the Grenadier Company 1828, a private soldier 1858, and an officer in Field Service Order 1900.

The mounted figure with drawn sword, on the left-hand side, is Major Hume at the Battle of the Alma at the moment his horse "Charlie" was shot from under him. The other mounted figure, on the right, is the Adjutant, Lieutenant MacDonald, being assisted by Private Murphy after he had been wounded at the Battle of Inkerman. Murphy was one of seventeen soldiers of the regiment to be awarded the Distinguished Conduct Medal during the Crimean campaign.

The Alma Memorial (see page 39) is an obelisk draped with the Colours of the 95th Regiment and surrounded at the base by three rams under which are three inscribed panels with lions'

The 95th Centrepiece commemorates the five wars in which The Derbyshire Regiment served in the 19th century. Photo: RHQ The Worcestershire & Sherwood Foresters Regiment.

heads at each corner. Traditionally it is the centrepiece of the silver displayed at the annual Sergeants' Mess Alma Ball, and for this reason is referred to as The Alma Memorial, but in fact it commemorates the names of officers who lost their lives both in the Crimea and, shortly afterwards, in India.

The panels list the names of twelve officers who were killed or died of disease in the Crimea, three during the Indian Mutiny campaign, and eleven between 1860 and 1868. They also record the fact that the regiment lost thirty-one Sergeants and 606 other ranks in the Crimea, and one Sergeant and forty-eight other ranks in the Mutiny.

The 29th Centrepiece (page 40) is a rose bowl mounted on a plinth surrounded by four figures - an officer and a private soldier of the Light Company, and an officer and a private soldier of the Grenadier Company, all dressed in the uniforms of 1847-1849. Three of the panels around the base are decorated with scenes from the Battle of Chillianwallah, 18 January 1849.

The fourth panel is inscribed: "From Gregory Way, to the 29th Regiment, in which he passed the Happiest Nineteen Years of his Life". Gregory Lewis Way was appointed Ensign in the 29th in 1832 and joined the regiment in Mauritius. His uncle, Colonel Sir Gregory Way, had commanded the regiment at the Battle of Bussaco, in 1810.

At the time of the Second Sikh War he was commanding a company and was mentioned in General Sir Walter Gilbert's despatch for his services at Chillianwallah. His commanding officer, Lieutenant Colonel George Congreve, led the regiment through thick jungle towards the sound of the Sikh cannon. Emerging into a clearing, he saw an enemy position ahead of him. Anxious to maintain the momentum of the advance, he called out: "Three hundred rupees to the first man at that gun". He then led the charge himself and, having driven off the Sikh gunners, struck the piece with his sword and shouted: "That's my gun!".

Major Gregory Way retired from the service in 1850 and settled in Brighton. This magnificent piece was his gift to his old regiment a short time before his death, in 1889.

The 36th Centrepiece (page 41) is a design far removed from the norm. The supporting plinth is of ebony, with silver snakes coiled around two of the four supports. The inscription on the top rim states: "Presented to the Officers' Mess by the following officers who were either members of the Regimental Hunt or (were) promoted during the Tour of Service of the Regiment in India, November 1863 to November 1875".

The silver casting represents a mountain crag with four different species of some of the most prized game (trophy) animals found in the Himalaya range of mountains. The topmost figure is *Ovis Ammon*, an animal which lives in the undulating open highlands of Tibet and which can stand twelve hands at the shoulder. Below him, in fighting attitude, are two Markhoor, of which four sub-species are found in the region. The animal on the right-hand side of the scene is an Ibex which, like the *Ovis Ammon* and the Markhoor, carries horns measuring between forty and fifty inches. Two small Tibetan antelope complete this group, these having much shorter and jet black horns. All of these mountain animals are extremely wary and fleet of foot.

The piece is a reflection of a period described in the regimental archive with a telling phrase - "too much rock and sand service". Nothing whatever happened in India between 1863 and 1875. Certain officers of the Indian Army managed to find some adventure on the northern and north western frontiers but, for the vast majority of professional soldiers - British and Indian alike - these were empty wasted years, with no chance to shine and little chance to gain promotion on any basis other than "dead man's shoes".

The regiment served in a succession of seven different locations, all in Northern India. Some, like Lucknow, were healthy and well-sited, but others were not. Of Peshawar it was written that "the fever prevails at all times of the year, and the water supply is impure". Meehan Meer was "drearily situated in an open arid plain … conspicuously unhealthy".

The regiment lost 355 officers and men to disease and the climate during the tour. In one period of five weeks in 1869, during a cholera epidemic at Peshawar, 117 died. To quote a regimental source: "The unhealthiness and tedium of peacetime garrison life and the restricted social round clearly provided a strong incentive for officers to escape when on leave and many were inevitably drawn to pit their wits and skills at fieldcraft and marksmanship against the elusive wild sheep and goats in the remote plateaux and steep slopes of the Himalayas. Though British officers had shot over the plains and jungles of India since the early years of the century, few had penetrated to this region before the 1850s".

The Montagu Tureen (page 42) is a time-capsule of its period, the early 1800s. The elegant simplicity of its Regency design is matched to perfection by the equally elegant lines composed by its donor: "The Officers of the 29th Regt of Foot are requested by Lord Frederick Montagu, their late Lieut Colonel, to accept this terrine as a token of his gratitude for their kind attention to him during the time that he had the good fortune to command the Regiment, and as a sincere though inadequate acknowledgement of the flattering regret they were pleased to express when illness compelled him to resign that honourable situation. 1804".

Lord Frederick Montagu was commissioned as an Ensign in the 1st Foot Guards in 1791. After only eight years he was a Lieutenant Colonel, serving with the 29th Foot in the 1799 expedition to the Low Countries. He retired four years later.

The Rolica Plate (page 42) recalls one of the many bloody clashes which resulted in the saving of Portugal and the liberation of Spain during the world war of 1793 to 1814. At Rolica, on 17 August 1808, the 29th Foot were given the task of forcing one of the steep narrow passes and gaining the heights where the French were established. Colonel G Landman, a Royal Engineer who was there, wrote later: "I was so struck with the marked distinction between the 29th Regiment and all others, there with the Army, that I could not refrain from observing to their commanding officer, 'Well, Colonel, you are dressed as if you were going to be received by the King'. Lake smiled and replied with a dignified air, 'Egad, Sir, if I am killed today, I mean

The Alma Memorial of the 95th or Derbyshire Regiment of Foot is named after its first major battle, the forcing of the Alma river, in the Crimea, on 20 September 1854. Photo: RHQ The Worcestershire & Sherwood Foresters Regiment.

to die like a gentleman'".

Colonel Lake was indeed killed later in the day, along with 183 of his officers and men. Rolica was their first battle of the campaign, a factor which might explain their smartness compared with the raggedy appearance of those around them. Over the following years of hard campaigning they lost a considerable part of their silver and other possessions. This piece, the Rolica Plate, consisting of a tureen and four claw-feet salt cellars made by Paul Storr, was one of the first things they purchased after the war. In 1838, after returning from a tour lasting nearly twelve years on the island of Mauritius, the officers invested heavily in new silver to replace items which were worn out or which had gone missing. The officers serving at that time each received a small piece of the old silver as a memento.

The Mess did acquire one item of interest during the Mauritius tour. The commanding officer throughout those years was Lieutenant Colonel James Simpson, a veteran of the Peninsula and of Waterloo. He decided to donate a snuff mull of the classic ram's horn configuration. To quote the regimental

The evocative 29th Centrepiece, now the property of The Worcestershire & Sherwood Foresters Regiment, was the individual gift to his old regiment of Major Gregory Way, a veteran of the battles of Chillianwallah and Goojerat. Photo: RHQ.

archive: "This mull is a ram's horn with bands and lid of Indian silver and semi-precious stones. The implements attached are - a spoon to remove snuff from the mull, a rake to smooth any lumps in it on the back of the hand, a divider to split the snuff into two piles (one for each nostril), a rabbit's paw to brush off any snuff remaining on the hand after inhalation, and a gavel to tap the lid before passing it on around the table (even if snuff has not been taken)". From this description it is evident that the taking of snuff was part of the dining table ritual, along with the circulation of the decanters and the drinking of toasts.

Colonel Simpson seems to have decided that, after so many years on the island, his officers were becoming a little too relaxed in their ways. He ordered that the Mess rules, which had been drawn up in 1792, should be revised. Under the new rules, which were endorsed by a Mess meeting in 1835, the President of the Mess Committee was given wide powers to levy fines - measured in bottles of wine - on the members.

"If the dog of any member, or that of his servant, comes into the room during Mess, that member shall forfeit one bottle of wine, whether the dog follows him or not. If proved that another member purposely enticed the dog into the room, the owner shall be acquitted and the offender shall forfeit two bottles of wine".

Even the PMC ran the risk of being fined. "Any officer appearing in Mess, in any way unregimentally dressed, shall forfeit one bottle of wine for every deviation, and the President overlooking any such deviation shall himself suffer the penalty as well as the defaulter".

The Howell Davis Bowl (page 43) is inscribed "Presented to the Mess of the 1st Battalion Worcestershire (late 29th) Regiment by Colonel Howell Davis who served in it for twenty five years, on his retirement, at the termination of the five years he had the honour to command it, 2nd March 1883". Information regarding its weight and dimensions, and its hallmarks, is not available. However, the bowl is shown here as a pleasing example of the type of fine silver often given to the officers by a CO who was taking his leave of them (especially if he had commanded for a number of years).

Howell Davis had joined the 29th as an Ensign in 1858, just in time to take part in the final operations against the mutineers in Central India. He remained continuously with the regiment throughout his military life, serving in England, Ireland, Malta, Canada, Jamaica and Barbados.

The Sultan of Johore's Bowl (page 44) is the sort of "thank you" gift which most regiments have from time to time received in respect of "services rendered". During their two years tour in Singapore, from 1904 to 1906, the 1st Battalion, The Sherwood Foresters, were stationed at Tanglin Barracks. This placed them near to the Botanical Gardens which, in turn, were close to the Summer Palace of the Sultan of Johore.

On the night of 11 September 1905, the battalion's main guard sentry reported flames coming from the Palace. The entire unit was immediately turned out, the Foresters assisting the fire brigade and preventing local people from looting the Palace's valuable contents. The bowl itself has no great artistic merit, and its Sheffield 1904 hallmark provides no surprises, but the story is yet another reminder that not all Mess silver has been generated by service on the battlefield, on the shooting range, or in the saddle.

The Royal Marines Statuette is the last of the nine Worcestershire & Sherwood Foresters' pieces listed here as being typical of their *genre*. It shows an officer of the Duke of York and Albany's Maritime Regiment of Foot (known also as The Lord High Admiral's Regiment) in the Dress of 1664. That was the year it was raised on the order of King Charles II, and it is in this long-vanished regiment that today's Royal Marines may claim their origin. A more compelling date is 1755, that being the year when Divisions of Marines were established at Chatham, Portsmouth and Plymouth, under Admiralty administration and with all the officers appointed on merit and qualification ("purchase" being banned in the Corps).

The inscription tells us very little of the statuette's provenance: "Presented to the Officers, 2nd Battalion, the Worcestershire Regiment, by the Officers, Royal Marines, Mediterranean Fleet, 1933". There is no clue, no hint, to tell us

what prompted the Royal Marines officers of a large number of ships (the Mediterranean Fleet of 1933 being nearly as large as today's entire Royal Navy) to subscribe to what is clearly a very nice piece of silver. The Worcesters' records give us the explanation: "During the Battalion's tour in Malta a close liaison grew up with the Royal Marines. The Battalion provided assistance when parties of Marines were training ashore and also invited RM officers to participate in its own officers' training - of particular value to those studying for their promotion examinations. The relationship was further strengthened when detachments of the Battalion were periodically embarked for cruises on naval ships. To mark their appreciation for the assistance and hospitality received, the Royal Marines officers presented this statuette".

The presentation was made by Lieutenant Colonel R D H Lough RM to Lieutenant Colonel B C S Clarke DSO, the 2nd Battalion's CO, at a party given by the Royal Marines officers at the Union Club, Valetta, on 22 August. This was shortly before the Worcester's departure for China after three years in Malta. It would have been a matter for conversation that the Worcesters were themselves no strangers to shipboard life. The regiment's

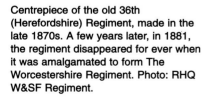

Centrepiece of the old 36th (Herefordshire) Regiment, made in the late 1870s. A few years later, in 1881, the regiment disappeared for ever when it was amalgamated to form The Worcestershire Regiment. Photo: RHQ W&SF Regiment.

The neo-classical Montagu Tureen was given to the 29th of Foot by its commanding officer at his retirement in 1804. Photo: RHQ W&SF Regiment.

Made by Paul Storr, The Rolica Plate of the 29th Regiment of Foot may originally have consisted of several large pieces. These five items - a tureen and four salts - are all engraved "XXIX" and "Roleia" within a wreath and scroll. Photo: RHQ The Worcestershire & Sherwood Foresters Regiment.

The Howell Davis Bowl, presented to 1st Battalion, The Worcestershire Regiment, by an officer who had served with it continuously for a quarter of a century. Photo: RHQ W&SF Regiment.

The ram's horn snuff mull acquired by the 29th Regiment of foot during their nearly twelve years on service on the island of Mauritius, 1826-1838. Photo: RHQ The Worcestershire & Sherwood Foresters Regiment.

1st Battalion - while still the 29th of Foot - had served at sea during the war with Revolutionary France as (effectively) Royal Marines. Detachments of its soldiers were serving in several ships of Admiral Lord Howe's fleet when, on 1 June 1794, he defeated a powerful French fleet off the coast of the Brest peninsula. It was a major action which determined the shape of the war at sea for a long time thereafter. The men of the 29th (especially those who served in the 74 gun ship of the line HMS *Brunswick*) could proudly claim to have played their part.

In 1847-1848, the British government authorised the granting of silver medals to officers and men of the army and navy who had fought in certain specified actions on land and at sea during the previous fifty-four years. Just two former officers and six other ranks of the 29th of Foot were still alive and able to submit their applicatons for the Naval General Service medal with the clasp "1st June 1794". They were Lieutenant C B Egerton, Ensign L A Northey, and Privates Richard S Bamford, Robert Cook, James Kilgrove, William Robinson, Thomas Robson and Thomas Smith.

The Sultan of Johore's Bowl, illustrated here mainly as a cautionary example of the damage which can be done by frequent and excessively heavy polishing.
Photo: RHQ W&SF Regiment.

One of these medals, that awarded to Private Kilgrove, can be seen in the collection of the Worcestershire Regimental Museum, Worcester.

Six other elderly former soldiers received the same medal and clasp, three from the 2nd Regiment of Foot and three from the 25th. They too fought as sea-soldiers in Admiral Lord Howe's fleet.

As an historical footnote, an officer serving as a Master's Mate that day, in HMS *Aquilon*, was Francis Beaufort. Later promoted to the rank of Admiral, he introduced the Beaufort scale for indicating the force of the wind (still used nearly two centuries later, worldwide, by mariners and weather forecasters).

From the Highlanders, the cavalry and the county infantry, we may now move on to the gunners and sappers.

The Royal Marines figurine in the collection of The Worcestershire and Sherwood Foresters Regiment.
Photo: RHQ.

Chapter Three
Gunners and Sappers

Amongst the largest self-contained organisations within the British Army are the Royal Regiment of Artillery and the Corps of Royal Engineers. Each has a central headquarters Mess (Woolwich for the gunners, Chatham for the sappers), with their subsidiary units having their own independent Messes (Regiments and Batteries in the RA, Regiments and Squadrons in the RE). This chapter will describe some of their most significant items of silver and the historical contexts within which they were acquired.

The Royal Regiment of Artillery

Prior to the formation of The Royal Regiment of Artillery, in 1716, the Artillery Trains were activated in time of war by Master Gunners on the Board of Ordnance. They recruited the gunners, and drew whatever guns, powder and shot they needed from central storehouses. In medieval times these were in the Tower of London. At the end of each campaign, the gunners were disbanded and the equipment returned to the Tower. The storehouses were moved to Woolwich, on the south bank of the Thames, at the end of the 17th century.

In 1716, when the first two Regular batteries of Artillery were raised, Woolwich was the obvious place to quarter them because that was where all the guns and other artillery impedimenta were held. Thus began the long association between Woolwich and the Royal Artillery, an association which continues to this day.

As the regiment grew, so did the need for more and more accommodation. New barracks, built away from the river on higher ground, were established between 1758 and 1780. The present Mess building dates from 1783, making it the oldest in the British Army.

Regimental Guest Nights are held twice each year and are known as "The Spring Dinner" and "The Alamein Dinner". The Master Gunner presides, and ten regimental guests, distinguished in all walks of life, are invited. Officers of the regiment and their private guests make up the remainder, a total of one hundred and thirty in all. These are particularly grand candle-lit affairs, with many of the major pieces of silver on the tables and the waiters dressed in livery and knee-breeches. The assembled company is led into the Dining Room with a fanfare of trumpets, officers and guests take their seats at four very large tables, the Royal Artillery Band plays appropriate music, and the beautiful snuff boxes described later are passed after the second round of Port.

His Majesty King George VI was the principal guest in his role as Colonel in Chief at one of these Dinners in 1950. It was the first time he had been able to attend, and he expressed the wish that the name of that appointment should be changed to Captain General. The present Sovereign holds this same title.

It was never appropriate for gunner units to have Colours. In the smoke and confusion of the battlefield, infantry soldiers needed a prominent rallying point. Brightly coloured pieces of fabric, held high by the Ensigns, met that need. For gunners there could be only one such rallying point and that was (and

still is) the guns themselves. For British artillerymen, therefore, their guns *are* their Colours. From this it follows that they have no banners on which to display the names of Battle Honours. In their stead they have the regimental motto - "Ubique". The gunners have indeed served "everywhere", and it is a distinction which they share with the sappers.

Given their proximity to Tilbury and other docks along the Lower Thames, the Woolwich Barracks were an ideal place in which to accommodate regiments of cavalry and infantry waiting to embark for service overseas. During these temporary visits, the officers of such regiments were granted honorary membership of the RA Mess, and they frequently expressed their appreciation for the hospitality received by presenting items of silver. Similarly, regiments sent to London for ceremonial or security duties were often housed at Woolwich, in some instances for quite long periods. They too made presentations of silver, and the first two items described below are typical examples.

The Scots Greys Vase was the gift of the officers of the 2nd Royal North British Dragoons (Scots Greys). During the period 1875-1876 they were stationed, half of the regiment at a time, at

The Scots Greys Vase was made in 1876 by Elkington & Company. It is 17 inches in height, and weighs 118 ounces. Photo: Royal Artillery Institution.

Woolwich. It is considered to be one of the most elegant pieces in the RA Mess collection. It takes the form of a two-handled vase or ewer of classical design standing on a large rose water bowl. This design pre-dated the introduction of the individual finger bowl. Rose water was poured from the vase into the bowl so that officers should rinse their fingers as they left the table.

The Armstrong Gun Centrepiece represents an angel with immense wings seated upon an early breech-loading Armstrong gun. The design is based upon an allegorical poem published in *Punch* in May 1862, the underlying message of which is obscure but basically patriotic. It was presented in 1868 by the officers of the 17th Lancers (Duke of Cambridge's Own) who "enjoyed the hospitality of the RA Mess, Woolwich, June and July, 1868".

The piece demonstrates that things are not always what they might seem. The carriage is made of gun-metal, the barrel of brass, the remainder of Sterling silver. At some stage the entire piece had been silver-plated, and it was only when the plating began to wear thin from polishing that this blend of metals was exposed. It was then restored to its original condition.

The William IV Candelabrum, as its names implies, was the gift of a sovereign. It was given to the Mess in 1833 by King William IV "in testimony of his high approbation of their distinguished services in every part of the globe in which British

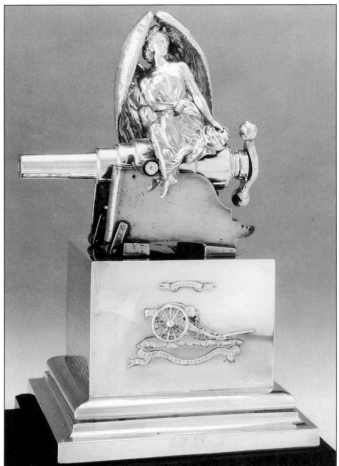

The Armstrong Gun Centrepiece stands little more than 15 inches in height. It was made by Hunt & Roskell, London, in 1868. Photo: RAI.

Arms have been engaged". The inscription lends weight to the regimental motto, "Ubique", granted in the same year.

William paid one thousand pounds for the manufacture of this wonderful object. When he noticed that the design did not incorporate a British lion, he ordered that one should be added. The luckless silversmith, John Bridge, had no choice but to hurriedly make one and place it on top of the foliate finial. There was no other space for it.

The replica weapons mounted on the triangular base are the 6 pounder field gun used by the Royal Horse Artillery in the 1830s, a 12 pounder howitzer of the 1820s, and a 10 inch mortar.

The reign of King William IV was "the golden age of the Mess". The forty years of peace which followed the fall of Napoleon permitted the British Army to devote more time than ever before to its comfort and convenience. More and better barracks were built for the men and their families, and the officers could develop the lifestyle associated with permanent (static) Messes. At Woolwich, it became customary to hold frequent sumptuous dinners and splendid balls. As the cost of these functions rose, so did the complaints by junior and married officers who were being charged at the same rates as those of their much wealthier seniors. It was after the dinner held to mark the arrival of the William IV candelabrum that new tariffs were agreed, with each officer charged according to his means.

The William IV Candelabrum is four and a half feet high, and more than two feet wide across its six branches. This monumental piece was made in London in 1833 by John Bridge. Photo: RAI.

The Willoughby Memorial perpetuates the name of the Bengal Horse Artillery, and of one of its heroic officers in particular. It is 27 inches high, and was made by Storr & Mortimer, London, 1864. Photo: RAI.

were killed in the surrounding streets but, as though by a miracle, Scully was the only European defender to be killed by the blast.

Willoughby, Forrest and Raynor all got away from the city. Forrest and Raynor each received gunshot wounds but survived, and both were awarded the Victoria Cross. The unfortunate Willoughby was caught and murdered by villagers as he tried to escape across country.

There was no provision at that time for posthumous awards of the Victoria Cross and so his services went unrecognised by the authorities, but the officers of the Bengal Artillery claimed him as one of their heroes. They commissioned the manufacture in London of this fine centrepiece "to commemorate the heroic conduct of Lieut G D Willoughby, Bengal Artillery, in defence of the magazine at Delhi on the outbreak of the Mutiny, 11 May 1857". When subsequently the Honourable East India Company was wound up, and the Bengal Artillery ceased to be, the piece was passed to the RA Mess at Woolwich.

It consists of a column supporting a canopy which encloses an urn surmounted by the figure of Victory holding a laurel wreath. On the pedestal are the figures of a Bengal Horse Artillery officer with his horse, and a Bengal Field Artillery gunner with a 6 pounder gun.

The Huthwaite Column is another centrepiece similar to The Willoughby Memorial and typical of its *genre*. The column is topped by a figure representing India and is decorated with a bas-relief of the Battle of Gujrat

The Willoughby Memorial commemorates an act of extraordinary valour. When the Indian Mutiny erupted at Meerut in May 1857, it was quickly evident that the cancer was spreading to other military stations throughout Bengal. Located within the capital city of Delhi were a number of armouries and magazines which, if they fell into the hands of the mutineers, would provide them with the means to conduct a long and bloody campaign against the British. In charge of one of these magazines was a fat and rather shy young officer, Lieutenant George Willoughby, Bengal Artillery, employed there as Deputy Commissary of Ordnance. When disaffected troops from Meerut started to reach Delhi, on 11 May, he immediately understood the importance of denying them access to the weapons and munitions in his care.

With the aid of three principal assistants, Conductor J Scully, and Lieutenants George Forrest and William Raynor of the Bengal Veteran Establishment (both formerly of The Bengal Artillery), he barred the entrance doors and laid demolition charges. He also armed his men and loaded a cannon with grapeshot.

The mutineers started to force their way into the compound, scaling the boundary walls and swarming across the rooftops. His small group of officers and civilian clerks put up a fierce but short-lived resistance before Willoughby gave the order to light the fuse. The resultant explosion was heard in Meerut, nearly fifty miles away. Hundreds of mutineers and Indian civilians

The Huthwaite Column stands 30 inches in height. Made in London by Storr & Mortimer, it preserves the memory of Major General Sir Edward Huthwaite. He served for fifty years with the Bengal Horse Artillery. Photo: RAI.

Snuff mulls (boxes) were at one time as much a feature of the after-dinner formalities as the circulation of the Port and Madeira decanters. These four beautifully crafted examples illustrate the ingenuity of the silversmith in making a statement about the original donor. Full details are given in the accompanying narrative. Photo: RAI.

based upon sketches by a Lieutenant Simmons of The 29th (Worcestershire) Regiment of Foot.

The Battle of Gujrat (Goojerat) was fought on 21 February 1849 and was the concluding major engagement of the Second Sikh War. It was a "gunner's battle", the artillery consisting of elements of Bengal Horse Artillery and Bengal Foot Artillery. The Sikhs capitulated, and in time the magnificent soldiers of this warrior race became staunch allies of the British in countless minor campaigns and in the two world wars of the 20th century.

Edward Huthwaite entered the Bengal Artillery in 1810. He commissioned this piece as his farewell gift to its officers. It is engraved "to the Bengal Horse Artillery Mess as a small token of affectionate regard for the regiment in which he completed a service of half a century on 12 March 1860". An oddity in its design is that the mounted figures on the pedestal are wearing the uniforms of the Royal Horse Artillery, not the Bengal Horse Artillery. Presumably the silversmiths in London (Storr & Mortimer) lacked models or sketches from which they could work, and so did their best in the circumstances.

Snuff boxes (or snuff mulls, to give them their more frequent description) are an outstanding feature of the Woolwich Mess collection. Four of them are illustrated here.

The model of a mortar was presented in 1851 by the 17th Lancers "as a remembrance of a few happy months spent as honorary members". The 17th had been brought to London for the Great Exhibition and, apart from the Royal Marines, were the first to enjoy the facilities of the Woolwich Mess. It was made by Storr & Mortimer and replicates a 10 inch mortar of the type in service between 1750 and 1800. The weapon fired a 93 pounds projectile over a maximum range of 1200 yards. It operated at a fixed elevation of 45 degrees, the range being adjusted by varying the propellant charge.

The upper middle piece is a model of the helmet worn by officers of the 3rd Dragoon Guards (Prince of Wales's). It was made by the Goldsmiths and Silversmiths Company. The wording engraved on the presentation plate states that it was "a slight recognition of the kindness received from the Royal Artillery" during their stay at Shrapnel Barracks between 1896 and 1897.

The lower middle box was presented by the 9th (or Queen's Royal) Lancers in 1872 following a short residence at Woolwich during the summer of that year. In terms of silversmithing skills, it is probably the finest mull in the collection. The box itself was made in 1851 by J Angell of London, but the exquisitely worked lid was commissioned by the 9th Lancers and added to the box in the year of the presentation. It depicts in minute detail, in high relief, an artillery piece in action with an escort of 9th Lancers in the background. The work is so precise and technically accurate that it will stand close inspection through a magnifying glass. The name of the craftsman responsible for this addition is not recorded.

The fourth box, to the right, is a model of a kettle-drummer of the 4th (or Queen's Own) Light Dragoons. It was presented to the Mess by the officers of that regiment "in remembrance of the period during which they enjoyed the privilege of being honorary members" in 1851 and 1852. The two drums are each made to contain snuff. The piece was crafted by Storr & Mortimer, and is hallmarked London 1851.

The Saddlers Trophy is one of those pieces which originated in a civilian context but which today forms part of a military collection. The historical background is to be found in the story of the great City Guilds which once controlled the major crafts and trades in London. The Saddlers Company received its first charter in 1272, from King Edward I. It was incorporated in

The Sadlers Trophy is one of those unusual pieces of commemorative silver which began life within a civilian context but later passed into a military collection. Weighing 62 ounces and standing 13 inches, it was made in London by either Robert Harper or Richard Hennell and bears marks for 1869 and 1872. Photo: RAI.

1395 under a further charter, granted by King Richard II. Five hundred years later, to celebrate that event, the Court members decided to commission the manufacture of a number of replicas of a massive 17th century Carolean tankard in their collection. One of the 1895 recipients was Mr Peter George Laurie.

His tankard was handed down in the family until it came into the possession of his grandson, Major J E C Laurie RA. This officer's active service covered the years from 1928 to 1956, but he was also a member of the Sadlers Company. He was elected Master of the Company in 1964, a fact which explains the otherwise inscrutable wording engraved around the base: "Presented to the Royal Regiment of Artillery by Major John E C Laurie, Master, 1964-1965".

The tankard was handed to the Master Gunner, General Sir Robert Mansergh, at a dinner held at the Sadlers Hall in March 1965. It was for a time used as an award to whichever RA unit was judged to have been the most successful in equestrian matters during the preceding twelve months, but now resides permanently at Woolwich.

The Sudanese Soldier Statuette (page 50) is, according to the regimental records, "shrouded in mystery". In the event, it depicts a West African soldier in the uniform of the period *circa* 1902-1918.

The statuette bears the marks for Frank Hyams, London, 1937. It was given to the Mess in 1951 by Mrs E M Peele, widow of Captain H J J Peele RA, an officer whose early service had been with a part-time unit, the 1st Shropshire & Staffordshire Volunteer Artillery. Presumably Mrs Peele was elderly and unable to provide precise details of her late husband's career when she delivered it to Woolwich.

It is also logical to assume that whoever jotted down Captain Peele's details at that time had hand-writing which could be misinterpreted. The RA arranged for a small silver plaque to be fixed to the base. It reads: "Presented by Captain T T Peele". There is no officer of this name in the Army Lists of the relevant period, but there is a Captain H J J Peele RA. The "J" must have been mis-read as "T", and the "H" omitted. The exact cause of the error will never be known, but there is no doubt that the statuette was once the property of Herbert Joshua John Peele.

Born on 16 May 1879 at Prestfelde, Shrewsbury, he was the son of a Solicitor, the local Town Clerk. He joined the Volunteer Artillery in 1896, age seventeen. He served with it until 12 May 1900 when he was accepted for a Regular commission with the Royal Artillery as a Second Lieutenant. Entrance into the Regular army *via* the Militia was a route followed by many young men of that period, especially those whose parents could not afford to support them at the Royal Military College.

His period of Regular service was very short. He went to South Africa for the Anglo-Boer war but within a few months encountered problems with his vision. Sent back to England, he took residence in Gloucester. He wrote to the Adjutant General "requesting permission to appear before a Medical Board ... my eyesight has recently become so impaired that I am at present temporarily unable properly to perform my duties as an officer of Royal Horse and Royal Field Artillery". Then began several years of medical examinations and correspondence concerning his future. Should he resign his Regular commission or not, and what exactly was wrong with his eyes? After numerous periods of extended sick leave, he was granted permission in May 1906 to resign as a Lieutenant on half-pay of three shillings and twopence (18 pence) per day, back-dated to December 1902. His former Brigade Major expressed his regret - "zealous and would make a good officer, but eyesight not good enough".

While the debate with the army and the medical profession rumbled on, J J Peele needed to earn a living. He moved to London and entered the chambers of Le Brasseur & Oakley, Solicitors, of Carey Street, Lincoln's Inn Court. He intended to follow in his father's footsteps. At the same time, it is clear that he was still keen to return to some form of soldiering. In 1905 a consultant at St Bartholomew's Hospital had found his eyes to be "myopic with astigmatism ... defect caused by strain of excessive gunlaying and anxiety produced thereby ... vision very defective ... unfit for Royal Artillery in any of its branches ... eyes ought to be rested".

Four years later, in August 1909, Peele went back to St Bartholomew's. This time the ophthalmic consultant reported "myopia not increased in past eight years ... unlikely to increase in future ... vision now fairly good ... fit for ordinary occupation". On the strength of this good news, he applied successfully for a Staff Captaincy with the London District Royal Artillery Territorial Force, Special Reserve of Officers.

Known as The Sudanese Soldier, this interesting statuette might perhaps be more accurately catalogued as The West African Soldier. It was donated to the Royal Artillery Mess, Woolwich, by the widow of an officer who battled for years against defective eyesight but then eventually succeeded in getting into action. Photo: RAI.

Having succeeded in three ambitions - recovering his sight, qualifying in 1908 as a Solicitor, and returning to the military fold - he applied for a post in the legal department of the Colonial Office. He was admitted to the rolls of North and South Nigeria, authorised to practice there as a Solicitor, in 1913.

He was working in Nigeria when war with Germany was declared. He immediately volunteered his services and was ordered to join the 1st Light Battery, The Nigeria Regiment. At last, he had a chance to see some active soldiering, an opportunity for which he had been striving since first joining the Volunteers in 1896. The Battery was one of the units ear-marked for the invasion of the neighbouring German Protectorate of Kamerun.

A letter on his file at the Public Record Office (accession No WO/374/53214), sent to the War Office by Major C F S Maclaverty, tells us what happened next. "Lieutenant Peele joined the Expeditionary Force from Nigeria to the Cameroons on 14 August 1914 and joined my Battery. He came under my command on 28 September just before we landed at Duala. He remained with the Battery until invalided home (eyes). He proved a most capable and energetic officer. He displayed great coolness and gallantry on the occasion when I was wounded and out of action. By his handling of the guns, he averted what was very nearly a disaster".

Having taken part in one of the earliest campaigns of the war, Captain Peele qualified for the 1914-15 Star and the British War and Victory Medals. From the French Colonial authorities he received the Order of the Black Star (L'Etoile Noir), 5th Class. It was a decoration which our French allies presented in relatively large numbers to their own officers, but not to the British. After all his earlier frustrations, it must have given him great pleasure.

Arriving back in England in May 1915, Captain Peele returned to the familiar path of Medical Boards and sick leave. Desperate to return to active service, he invoked the support of Field Marshal Sir Evelyn Wood. The distinguished old soldier wrote to the War Office "... to introduce an old friend ... can vouch for him ... would be fit for appointment as Staff Captain in the New Armies". In August he was sent on a course at Shoeburyness to prepare for service in France but, within days, was forced to withdraw because he could not see.

Undeterred, he managed to join the 21st Divisional Ammunition Column, but again went sick. The remaining years of his war were sweated out at Kaduna, Nigeria, on the staff of the Headquarters, The Nigeria Regiment, interspersed with yet more medical examinations in the United Kingdom. His military career ended effectively on 10 October 1919 when the Army Council wrote to him, "... no longer possible that you continue in active employment ... thanks conveyed for valuable services rendered". For administrative purposes, he was transferred to the Regular Army Reserve of Officers, but never again served in uniform.

He is known to have been still working in Northern Nigeria in 1935. He was then fifty-six, and so was presumably preparing to take his retirement in England. The silver figurine is hallmarked 1937, so one may guess that he treated himself to its purchase, as a personal memento, before leaving Africa for the last time. It was one of several cast from the same mould for a variety of customers, private and regimental.

John Peele died on 4 April 1950. His story has been set out in some detail because it demonstrates two points of relevance to any study of military silver. The first is that regimental records are in some instances based upon anecdotal evidence or personal memories which may prove to be faulty. Legends can change in the re-telling, and it can be worthwhile to double-check the facts as stated. The second is the human dimension attaching to such objects. Not all soldiers commemorated in silver were fit and strong. Personal bravery comes in many forms.

The Goodwood Trophy has a curious history. Made in London in 1847, its design was conceived by Frank Howards and modelled by Alfred Brown for the well-known firm Hunt & Roskell. It was made to the order of Lord George Bentinck, a great lover of thoroughbred horses. In 1830 he reconstructed Goodwood Racecourse, improving the turf and creating those distinctive features by which the course is always known, "Glorious Goodwood".

The Goodwood Trophy, of 1847, stands 20 inches high and weighs 545 ounces (including the wooden base). It was made by Hunt & Roskell and is hallmarked London 1847. Photo: Royal Artillery Institution.

Thoroughbreds have been raced at Goodwood, set in the open rolling Sussex Downs, since the first public meeting in 1802. The land was a property of the 3rd Duke of Richmond, and ownership of the course has ever since passed in succession to his descendents.

At the time this trophy was made, the course was owned by the 5th Duke, and Lord George Bentinck was one of his closest friends. Bentinck decided to instruct Hunt & Roskell to make a piece which should incorporate three different themes - well-bred horses, gallantry, and his friendship with the Duke. The chosen scene depicts (on the left) Charles Lennox, 1st Duke of Richmond, riding as ADC to King William III at the 1695 battle of Namur. On the ground is a wounded soldier. The cannon barrel and broken gun-carriage wheel are *motifs* frequently seen in monumental works of this type.

Charles Lennox was an illegitimate son of King Charles II and a lady of the French aristocracy, Louise Renée de Keroualle. His father elevated him to the Dukedom of Richmond in 1675 and it was with this title that he accompanied William on his two major campaigns - the suppression of the Jacobean rebellion in Ireland (1691-1692) and the continental war with Louis XIV and his Catholic allies (1693-1695).

William was defeated at Steinkirk and Landen, but in 1695 he took the powerful fortress of Namur. His victory ended the war. The Peace of Ryswick acknowledged him as the rightful King of England, and his daughter Anne as his successor. With such dashing and romantic historical associations, the Battle of Namur provided an ideal vehicle for Lord George Bentinck to express his sentiments.

The Trophy, valued at three hundred sovereigns, was introduced as the prize for one of the major races run annually at the course, The Goodwood Cup. First past the post that year (July 1847) was the four year-old chestnut colt "The Hero", owned by Mr John Day and ridden by his son, John Junior. The horse was strongly fancied, having won eleven races in the previous year. Apart from being first past the post in 1847 at Goodwood, he won The Gold Vase and The Gold Cup at Ascot that same year.

Having won the Trophy outright, John Day took it home. It then disappeared from view for more than a century until it was acquired in Dublin by a former gunner officer, Sir Desmond Brayley MC JP.

Sir Desmond was commissioned into the Royal Artillery in 1934 and, after transferring to The Parachute Regiment early in WWII, fought in North Africa and with Special Forces in Yugoslavia. In 1968, in a splendid gesture to his old regiment, he presented the Trophy to the RA Mess where it is held on permanent display.

It was the custom in the 19th century for high quality silver to be commissioned as outright prizes for horse races.

Additional prizes in cash were subscribed by the competing owners, but silver was the most valuable recognition of success. Some trophies were in the form of cups (hence the name of this annual race), but they were made in numerous styles.

The RA example is probably unique in having such an overtly martial theme, but there is at least one other Goodwood Trophy in a regimental collection. **The Halt in the Desert** was made by Garrard & Company in 1866 as that year's Goodwood Cup trophy. The identity of the person who commissioned it is not known. The race was won by "The Duke", owned by the Marquess of Hastings.

volunteer colonial units. In June and July a second attempt to conquer the Zulus was more successful and by the end of that year it was all over. Reputations had been lost and won, thousands of men had died, but the Empire had acquired yet another chunk of territory.

The most unexpected participant in all of this was a Frenchman, the first and only son of Emperor Napoleon III and his wife the Empress Eugénie de Montigo. The infant, born on 16 March 1856, was named Louis and his early formative years were geared to the assumption that he would one day wear the crown of France. He was known as the Prince Imperial, a title

The 1866 Goodwood Cup trophy, known as The Halt in the Desert, in the collection of The Princess of Wales's Regiment. The stallion is acknowledged by bloodstock experts to be one of the finest representations ever made in silver of an Arab horse.
Photo: Lieut Col L M B Wilson MBE.

According to their records, the officers of the 70th (Surrey) Regiment of Foot were able to acquire it in 1866, some months after the regiment's return from a long tour of duty in New Zealand and shortly after the race was run. This story raises the question - why would the Marquess part with it so soon after receiving it? Whatever the explanation, the fact remains that it has passed down through the many amalgamations and is today the property of The Princess of Wales's Royal Regiment.

The Empress Eugenie Shield (page 55) also has a very unusual history. The general background circumstances are described in *The Washing of the Spears,* by Donald R Morris, one of the classic accounts of the British Empire and its numerous campaigns of conquest. The scene was southern Africa, and the opponents were the warriors of the Zulu nation.

Having fabricated an excuse to invade the Zulu homeland, the British High Commissioner, Sir Bartle Frere, authorised an expedition in January 1879 under the command of Lord Chelmsford. This mishandled invasion resulted in the famous action at Rorke's Drift and the destruction of the 2/24th Regiment of Foot at Isandhlwana (together with 532 Europeans and Africans of the assorted colonial and native units also massacred that day). The defeat prompted a hurried reinforcement of the British Army's presence in the area with additional regiments brought out from England and by the raising of more

equating to that of the Prince of Wales.

From the day of the birth, Napoleon determined that his son should be trained according to the virtues of the soldier. Before he was twenty-four hours old the baby had been enrolled as a Grenadier and he was commissioned into the 1st Imperial Guard Regiment at nine months. He witnessed his first military review, on horseback, before he had learned to walk. The boyhood years of his education were based upon the military glories of his nation, its uniforms, its flags, and the past achievements of its regiments. An exuberant lad, full of enthusiasm and well liked by everyone who knew him, he became a first class horseman and swordsman.

All of this boyish romanticism ended with the Franco-Prussian War of 1870-1971. Now fourteen years of age, he was caught up in the military chaos following the Prussian victory at Saarbrücken. He was fortunate to escape into the neutral territory of Belgium and, soon afterwards, to England. His father passed into temporary captivity while his mother, Eugénie, disguised herself as a madwoman as a means of getting out of Paris. She too came to England after being rescued by a friendly English yachtsman who, despite a raging storm in the Channel, brought her ashore at Hastings. With the dispersion of the royal Court and the defeat of the Imperial armies came the end of France's Second Empire.

When the Prince Imperial opted to serve with the Royal Artillery, he was joining a regiment which knew how to "put on the style". The Sir Hugh Ross Centrepiece is one of the most spectacular "on leaving" objects ever devised. Made in 1858 by Robert Garrard, London, it stands 20 inches in height. It was given to Field Marshal Sir Hew Dalrymple Ross (the first RA officer to attain that rank) by his brother officers at the time of his departure from active service. It remained in his family until 1927 when his grandson, Colonel H D Ross OBE, gave it to the Woolwich Mess. The gun is a 6 pounder, the standing figure is a gunner of the Royal Artillery, and the mounted officer wears the uniform of the Royal Horse Artillery. Photo: RAI.

The exiled family was soon reunited in rented accommodation near Chislehurst. To their surprise, Napoleon and Eugénie found that they were very popular with the English public and English aristocracy. They and their entourage were happy to join the social round while the adolescent Louis was sent to Kings College London and then, in 1872, to the Royal Military College at Woolwich. It was during his three years at "the Shop" that his father died and he therefore became "the Emperor in waiting". If the people of France ever abandoned their republicanism, he would be Emperor Napoleon IV.

Louis graduated in 1875 with excellent marks and opted for service with the Royal Artillery. His French nationality precluded him from receiving a Queen's commission, but he was assigned to "G" Battery, 24 Brigade, at Aldershot. The next four years were marked by the sort of mild excesses to be expected of a privileged and rather impulsive young man to whom, by virtue of his birth, all doors were open. He travelled widely and lived his life to the full. At the same time he took part in various military manoeuvres with "G" Battery and soon came to be well regarded for his professional competence.

When news of the disaster at Isandhlwana reached England, triggering a great flurry of activity to despatch reinforcements, Louis seized his opportunity. Now twenty-two, maturing fast and still hoping one day to ascend the throne of France, he needed to prove himself in such a way as to overcome the jibes of his republican French critics. Despite the understandable nervousness of Benjamin Disraeli, he enlisted the support of his mother and of Queen Victoria in obtaining

permission to join the field force in Natal.

When he sailed from Southampton on 28 February, he carried with him a letter written by the Duke of Cambridge, Commander in Chief of the British Army, and addressed to Lord Chelmsford. It read: "This letter will be forwarded to you by the Prince Imperial, who is going out on his own account to see as much as he can of the coming campaign in Zululand. He is extremely anxious to go out and wanted to be employed in our army, but the Government did not consider that this could be sanctioned, but have sanctioned me only to you and to Sir Bartle Frere to say that if you shew him kindness and tender him a position to see as much as he can with the columns in the Field I hope you will do so. He is a fine young fellow, full of spirit and pluck, having many old cadet friends in the Artillery, he will undoubtedly find no difficulty in getting on and if you can help him in any other way please do so. My only anxiety on his conduct would be, that he is *too* plucky and go ahead".

The final line in the Duke's letter carried a chilling and prescient note of caution which went unrecognised by its recipient. It is evident that nobody in authority, in England, had imagined that the Prince might be exposed to direct physical danger. In Donald Morris's words, they assumed that "he was only to be a spectator, and the entire British Army was there to protect him". They were mistaken. Within days of coming ashore at Durban - to local public acclaim - the young Prince was taking part in a reconnaissance patrol deep into Zululand. How such a thing could have happened was later a matter of much debate. The fact is that he was allowed to join a scouting party of two hundred men of the Frontier Light Horse. Exalted by the novelty of this wonderful African landscape and the prospect of action, he angered their commander, Colonel Richard Harrison RE, by several times trotting ahead on his own in search of a Zulu to kill.

After that experience, Harrison tried hard to ditch the Prince. He was obliged to keep him on his staff after receiving a written order from Chelmsford, but the order made it clear that Louis should never leave any encampment unless protected by a strong escort.

One of the officers who took part in Harrison's patrol was a subaltern by the name of Jahleel Brenton Carey. Devon-born, educated in France, a graduate of the Staff College, with fourteen years of varied active service under his belt, Lieutenant Carey was an ideal companion for the Prince and they quickly established a personal *rapport*.

Carey's knowledge of France and French politics made him exceptionally aware of the likely consequences in the event of any harm coming to the Prince. In the light of what was about to happen, this insight served little purpose. By a series of command blunders and misunderstandings, the Prince was permitted a second time to go out on a reconnaissance patrol. This time he was accompanied only by Lieutenant Carey and six soldiers and a Zulu guide. With instructions to complete some field sketches which he had started earlier, he and his companions rode out to an area which Colonel Harrison assumed to be safe but which in fact still contained roving parties of the enemy.

For several hours on the morning of 1 June, halting occasionally to correct their maps and sketches, Carey and Louis moved steadily ahead of other British forces. There was no hint of danger. At three in the afternoon they reached a deserted cluster of five grass huts and a stone-built cattle pound, surrounded on three sides by tall grass. Louis wanted to halt and make coffee, and he chose this place because it would provide wood for the fire.

He and Carey then settled into a scenario which can only be described as a picnic. The horses were unsaddled and allowed to wander off in search of grazing. A fire was lit, water was brought up from the nearby stream, and the party settled down to chat and smoke and drink their coffee. Despite evidence of recent occupation, the *kraal* and its surroundings were not searched and no sentries were posted.

After half an hour, the guide, who had been poking around behind the huts, came back to say that he had seen a solitary Zulu nearby. If there was one there could be more, so Louis ordered the party to bring in the horses and saddle up. This took another ten minutes. As he gave the order to mount, the scene changed suddenly and terrifyingly. A smashing volley of rifle fire panicked the horses and thirty or forty Zulu warriors burst out of the grass where they had been hiding.

Carey and those of his men who had managed to reach their saddles galloped flat out towards the shelter of the stream bed, two hundred yards away. Here they reined in and counted heads. Apart from Carey there were just four survivors, and only one of these had retained his carbine. There was no sign of Louis. He had last been seen frantically trying to mount his horse as it dragged him a hundred yards or more away from the *kraal*. One of the troopers had seen him go down and his horse trampling over him.

Carey knew that he could not go back to search for his companion. Zulus could be seen roving around the entire area of the *kraal* and gully, and his only option was an immediate return to camp, ten miles away. Apart from the devastating knowledge that he had failed his young friend, he must have known also that his career as a professional soldier was finished.

The manner of the Prince Imperial's death was later reconstructed from an examination of his body and the evidence of some of the Zulus who participated in it. Having lost his horse, and having injured his right arm, he gripped his revolver in his left hand and ran down into a branch of the stream gully where he turned and faced his pursuers. There were seven of them, and they were determined to kill him. No Prince ever died so alone.

The first spear took him in the thigh. He pulled it out and fired two shots, both of which missed. A second spear went deep into his left shoulder. For a short while he fended off the thrusts of his attackers but then, his body pierced again and again, he became faint from loss of blood and went down in a sitting position. They closed in and ended his life. Seventeen spear wounds were found when his remains were later recovered. They were all to the front of his body.

Granted a Court Martial at his own request, Carey was found not guilty on the charge of "misconduct in the face of the enemy". He consistently denied responsibility for the disaster, publicly placing all blame on Louis for having mishandled the patrol. Privately, however, in a letter which he wrote to his wife, he confessed that he had been in command that day and the fault was therefore his alone. This letter found its way into the hands of the Empress Eugénie. The initial public sympathy for Carey evaporated when the contents of the letter became common knowledge. He retained his commission in the army, but none of his brother officers would have anything to do with him. He became a social outcast and died six years later in Bombay. His immediate superior, Harrison, escaped blame and later became a general. Chelmsford too managed to wash his hands of any personal responsibility.

The exiled Empress had lost her husband and now her only child. The line of succession was broken, France could never again have a Buonaparte on the throne. Queen Victoria rushed to Chislehurst to comfort her. The people of France, even the radical republicans, turned in fury upon the English and the British government. To them (and to many Britons) it was inconceivable that the Prince Imperial could have been exposed to such peril in the first place, and then left to be butchered with no hope of rescue. Allegations of conspiracy flew thick and fast. Surely someone had wanted Louis out of the way and had knowingly engineered his death? There were many bizarre theories and the row rumbled on for years.

Only one person kept her head. Whatever bitterness she may have felt, the Empress Eugénie never expressed it openly. Initially sympathetic to Captain Carey (he received his promotion before the full facts were known), she later coldly refused his appeals that they might meet.

In 1880, some months after her son's death, and to the consternation of the staff, her carriage pulled up at the entrance to the Royal Artillery Mess at Woolwich. There had been no prior notice of her visit and there were no officers in the building at the time. She was received by the Mess Steward, Mr Morris, to whom she explained the reason for her visit. The Prince had many times told her of his affection for the regiment and his many gunner friends. She wished to present the piece of silver which she had brought with her, as a token of remembrance of his service.

As Mr Morris later reported, "I took it over from the Empress on behalf of the regiment". The shield still resides in the silver collection of the RA Mess at Woolwich. Thirty inches

The Empress Eugénie Shield is of a shape which does not lend itself readily to being photographed. Shown here are one of the three illustrative cartouches and the central boss. Originally a symbol of the glories of France, it came to be the memorial to a brutal lonely death in Zululand. Photo: RAI.

The Prince Amoratat Goblet reminds us that many foreign governments have traditionally regarded Great Britain as the best place to send their young future leaders to complete their general and military education. The RMA Sandhurst still puts large numbers of overseas Cadets through its rigorous officer training course each year.

In 1898, a young man arrived at Sandhurst from Siam. Successfully completing the course, he served a year on attachments with the Durham Light Infantry and No 6 Mountain Battery RA, attended the Musketry course at Hythe, and spent a year at Oxford University. He then returned to Bangkok, in 1902, to be crowned Rama VI, King of Siam. Impressed by his experiences in England, he despatched his younger brother to follow a similar path.

Prince Mom Chow Amoratat became a Cadet at the Royal Military Academy, Woolwich, and was made an honorary member of the nearby Royal Artillery Mess. Upon his departure, he presented to its officers the beautiful Siamese silver goblet illustrated here. It is still a prized component of the Mess collection.

There are hundreds of items, major and minor, in the Royal Artillery collection at Woolwich, with hundreds more in the collections of the individual regiments and batteries. Those mentioned here are no more than a random representative listing of some of the most important pieces (or those having the most unusual provenances). A fuller description would underline the fact that, for a gunner, the honour of his

in diameter, it was made to the order of Eugénie's late husband by Leonard Morel-Ladeuil, of Paris, *circa* 1858. That was the period when Napoleon III was preparing the establishment of the Second Empire and it was intended to demonstrate his planned revival of the arts in France.

The design is full of allegorical *motifs* of the new order of affairs. The three surrounding designs show "the flight of anarchy", "the return of prosperity in agriculture, commerce and art", and "a symbolic boat whose rudder is held by the new Chief of State and whose oarsmen are strength, law, prudence, etc". The central boss of the shield carries a design which symbolises "strength threatening anarchy". Within this feature is a man holding an axe. Due to theft, the axe has twice been replaced.

An intriguing aspect of this object is the question of how it came to be in England in the first place. The royal family had arrived in England with little more than the clothes they were wearing. It is unlikely that the new republican government would have felt a need to pack up all their abandoned possessions and forward them to Chislehurst, especially when one of the objects in question was not so much a personal item but an icon of national aspirations. The adventures of the shield, before it reached Woolwich, are an unresolved mystery.

Eugénie maintained a close interest in the Royal Artillery throughout the remaining years of her life. She moved her home to Farnborough, was one of the first to buy a motor car, and enthused over the work of the early aviators at the nearby airfield. A very remarkable lady, she died in 1920 at the age of ninety-four.

The Prince Amoratat Goblet, given to the Woolwich Mess by the brother of the King of Siam as a token of thanks for his honorary membership. Photo: RAI.

unit resides in its guns. The inventory includes a multitude of scale replicas of howitzers, siege guns, field guns, anti-aircraft guns, anti-tank guns and post-WWII rocket-propelled missiles. They are at the heart of the regiment's *esprit de corps*.

The Corps of Royal Engineers

The silver collection of the Corps of Royal Engineers reflects a historical background comparable to that of the Royal Artillery. In medieval times, whenever an English king or queen went to war, he or she called upon the counties to raise the numbers of foot and mounted soldiers required to meet the circumstances. At the end of the campaign, these men were disbanded and sent home. Such *ad hoc* arrangements could not apply to the specialist arms - the artillery and the engineers. Even in times of peace, it was desirable to have some officers in the royal retinue who were responsible for the permanent stores, and who knew how and where to raise and hastily train the men to their particular duties.

The earliest reference to a "King's Engineer" occurs in the records of the Norman Conquest of 1066. When William landed at Hastings he brought with him an officer holding this appointment. It was adopted by many later kings, and persisted through to 1787 when the Royal Engineers received their founding Warrant. The senior serving officer of the Corps is today known as "The Chief Royal Engineer".

Historically, military engineers have been builders of fortifications, entrenchments, roads and bridges. During the centuries when warfare was frequently a matter of laying siege to an opponent's own fortified positions, the engineers built the trenches and earthworks which permitted the artillery to bombard the defences at close range and the infantry to move forward for the final assault. Such works were known as "saps", hence the men were "sappers".

When the Royal Engineers were formed with that title in 1787, they did not at first have a permanent home. During the early years they shared many of the facilities of the Royal Artillery, at Woolwich. Then, in 1812, as a result of early experiences in the Peninsular campaign, the Royal Engineers Establishment was set up at Chatham (in a former artillery barracks) as a training centre. Chatham eventually became the RE headquarters. The Officers' Mess was shared with the gunners until they moved out in 1848.

The silver collections of neither the Royal Artillery nor the Royal Engineers include many items pre-dating the 1840s, and none for the 18th century. Indeed, according to Colonel J M Lambert, author of *The Portraits and Silver of the RE Headquarters Mess, Chatham*, it was not until 1856 that the first notable piece was acquired. By then the sapper officers had occupied the Mess for forty-two years. According to an anonymous contributor to the *Royal Engineers Journal* of June 1872: "Fifteen years ago the Mess dinner table was as bare of ornament as the table of a cadet. One solitary snuff box, presented by an Hon Member, while a fruitful source of jocular conversation and many a bet, served also as a warning against a relapse into utter barbarism. Now the Mess table is not unworthy of the bright uniforms that glitter around it. Surely it is well to be reminded by commemorative plate of scenes of interest gone by, of deeds done by Brothers in arms of whom we may be proud, of kindly faces who have sat with us around the genial board".

There are strong echoes here of the sentiments recorded in the opening pages of Chapter One of this book. The snuff mull to which the writer referred was presented "to Brompton Barracks, the RA & E Mess, from George Sim, Bengal Engineers, an Hon.y Member, Xmas 1844". The mention of "the RA & E Mess" reminds us that, for a long time, gunners and sappers shared the same Mess whenever they found themselves serving together, at home or overseas. This was logical because their Cadets trained together at "the Shop", the Royal Military Academy then located at Woolwich. A classic ram's horn design, with silver chasings, the mull now forms part of the RE Chatham Mess collection.

The Crimean War Centrepiece was the first major acquisition and it is said to be amongst the finest pieces in the Corps' inventory. The year 1856 witnessed the conclusion of the war in the Crimea, and it was then that the Corps began to collect silver on a significant scale. A two-handled fluted cup, with a lid bearing the presentation inscription and topped by an acorn finial, it was made by Stephen Smith, of 35 King Street, Covent Garden.

The ebony pedestal supports three statuettes or figurines - an officer of the Royal Engineers, a soldier of the Royal Sappers & Miners in parade dress, and another such soldier in working gear. During the early decades there had been two related Corps - the Royal Engineers (composed of officers only) and the Royal Sappers & Miners (usually other ranks only but, at times, having a small nucleus of their own officers). This long-standing segregation ended with their amalgamation in 1856.

Also mounted on the triangular pedestal are *cartouches* representing scenes from the siege of Sebastopol. That was the last time Sappers & Miners fought under the command of Royal Engineer officers and, between them, they won eight Victoria Crosses. The actions leading to their awards are described in detail in Colonel Gerald Napier's book, *The Sapper VCs* (The Stationery Office, 1998). This finely produced and fully illustrated publication, which describes fifty-five actions resulting in the award of the Victoria Cross, covers *inter alia* members of The Bengal Engineers, The Bombay Engineers, The Royal Sappers & Miners, and three officers of the Royal Flying Corps who had transferred from the Royal Engineers.

The Crimea cup was given "to the Mess of their Corps by the officers of the Royal Engineers who served in the war against Russia, in 1854-5-6". In most regiments and Corps, it is a custom that the officers who have served in a particular campaign subsequently club together and commission a collective memorial to their own services and those of their fallen comrades-in-arms. This particular cup was the first of its type within the Royal Engineers.

Like the gunners, the Royal Engineers have been represented in every British campaign, large and small, since their formation. It follows, therefore, that the Mess holds many artefacts marking their services from the 1850s through to WWII. Rather than describe any more of the older items, the author has opted to focus instead on much later pieces, made since 1945. They demonstrate the on-going work of the sappers but, of equal importance, they show that the custom of commissioning new pieces of silver was not confined to the "golden age" of the 19th century.

The Frigate Bird commemorates the work of the Royal Engineers on Christmas Island. This lonely feature in the Pacific Ocean was the site of many of the United Kingdom's atomic weapon tests during the 1950s and early 1960s. There are five species of Frigate-bird, known also as "the man-o'-war bird". They are land-bound predators, found in small colonies throughout the tropical and sub-tropical zones and usually associated with ocean islands where they roost and breed.

Curiously for birds so closely associated with it, they will drown if they come down on the sea and become water-logged.

The species *Fregata andrewsi* is specific to Christmas Island. The model measures 24 inches in height and 24 inches in width. It is, thereby, a one-third scale model of the living bird. With a body-weight of no more than three pounds but a wing-span of nearly seven feet, the Frigate-bird can soar for hours at a time in search of flying fish, eggs and chicks from seabird colonies, and baby turtles when they first hatch.

The piece was commissioned by the officers of 25 Engineer Regiment, with financial assistance from Corps funds. The front panel is engraved "Presented to the Officers' Mess, 25th Corps Engineer Regiment, by the officers of the Corps of Royal Engineers to commemorate the first decade of the regiment and its association with Operation Grapple and Christmas Island". The code-word for the deployment is reflected in the grapple mounted on the pedestal. Curiously, this same code-word was used again, nearly fifty years later, for the initial deployment of British troops in Bosnia.

The Frigate Bird was given its formal "dining-in" at the British military base in Osnabrück, Germany, on 6 November 1962.

The Churchill AVRE Centrepiece (page 58) is typical of a great many post-WWII silver scale models of tanks and other armoured fighting vehicles. For obvious reasons, they are usually to be seen in the collections of the cavalry regiments, the

The Frigate Bird was made by Mr Hobson of Walker & Hall, and is hallmarked London 1962. The visible plaque on the base gives a brief summary of the history of 25 Engineer Regiment under its various titles. The regiment was present at Suez, in 1956, then served on Christmas Island in 1957-1958. Photo: HQ RE, Chatham.

Royal Tank Regiment, and infantry units which at various times have been temporarily converted to the mechanised role. The RE pieces, however, represent the very specialised armoured vehicles which evolved, from 1942 onwards, under the inspiration of Major General Sir Percy Hobart. This far-sighted officer anticipated the need for a variety of vehicles which, when the time came to invade Europe, could clear minefields, breach wire entanglements, bridge anti-tank ditches and destroy concrete emplacements, all while under fire.

Known as "Hobart's funnies", these modified tank chassis were grouped under 79th Division, raised and commanded by the General (he was recalled from retirement for the task). His designs were offered to the US Army but rejected. American infantry casualties on D-Day, 6 June 1944, were later judged to have been needlessly high as a consequence.

The acronym "AVRE" signifies "Armoured Vehicle, Royal Engineers", and the engraving on the base states: "Presented to 26 Armoured Engineer Squadron by past and present officers of Armoured Engineers, 1943-1963".

The Aphrodite Statuette (page 58) is an unusual instance of a modern silversmith working to a classic *Rinascimento* design - "The Birth of Venus", painted by the Florentine master, Alessandro Botticelli (1444-1510). The way in which the piece was first conceived is of interest, and the circumstances are described in an article written for the *RE Journal*, December

1964, by Captain C Spottiswoode RE.

Prior to October 1962 there were six different RE units serving in Cyprus. They were then brought together as Headquarters Royal Engineers Cyprus, with a unified Officers' Mess. The idea for a new centrepiece had already been discussed by the officers of 33 Independent Field Squadron, and it was now pursued by the HQ Mess Committee.

Attention focused upon the concept of Aphrodite as being the central *motif*. The Greek goddess of love, fertility and beauty, she was said to have emerged from the foam of the sea at Paphos, on the island's western coast. To the Romans she was Venus, and she is still regarded locally as the goddess of seafarers. As an icon of the natural beauty of Cyprus, she was a logical choice for the new centrepiece.

Three firms of silversmiths were asked to tender. Frustratingly, Captain Spottiswoode does not tell us which firms took part in what were apparently quite protracted negotiations, but he does state that the price finally agreed was two hundred and ninety pounds. In 1996, during an insurance appraisal of the RE silver inventory, the Aphrodite piece was valued at five thousand pounds, a figure which suggests that well-made silver continues to be a sound investment.

One of the presentation plates on the base is worded "To commemorate the services of the Royal Engineers in Cyprus since 1876 *(sic)*". The date (which ought to read 1878) recalls a

The Churchill AVRE Centrepiece is typical of a great many technically precise scale models of tanks and other WWII fighting vehicles. This one was made by Robert Garrard, London, 1962.
Photo: HQ RE.

mainly forgotten episode in European history. Following the Russo-Turkish war of 1877-1878, the British government declared its opposition to the terms of the peace treaty imposed by Russia. It resolved to move a large deterrent force into the region.

A British Army and Indian Army force numbering more than 10,000 men was assembled in Malta under the command of Sir Garnet Wolseley. Designated the Malta Expeditionary Force, it landed in Cyprus in June and July 1878. The island had long formed part of the Ottoman Empire but now, in return for their political support, the Turks ceded it in perpetuity to the British.

Russia and Turkey soon resolved their differences so, within weeks, the bulk of the Malta Expeditionary Force was re-embarked and dispersed. Amongst the officers who stayed behind - to police and administer - was Lieutenant H H Kitchener RE. Over the next four years he conducted a major survey and produced the first accurate maps of the entire island. By 1914 he was Field Marshal the Earl Kitchener of Khartoum, at the pinnacle of his career and building an army of three million men in France and Flanders. Less than a year later he was dead, drowned when HMS *Hampshire* sank off the Orkney Islands.

Sappers continue to serve at the two British Sovereign Bases in Cyprus where the Aphrodite centrepiece is held by 62 Cyprus Support Squadron RE.

The Diving Centrepiece was made in 1988 and it commemorates a century and a half of underwater work by the Royal Engineers and their forebears and affiliated units. Their first venture into diving was a consequence of one of the greatest disasters ever to strike the Royal Navy.

HMS *Royal George,* named in honour of King George II,

The Aphrodite Statuette, based upon Botticelli's famous painting and still gracing the table of the Officers' Mess of 62 Cyprus Support Squadron, Royal Engineers. Photo: HQ RE.

was a first rate of 100 guns. No expense was spared in her building and fitting out which, in total, exceeded the enormous sum of fifteen thousand pounds. Launched in 1756, she was for some years the pride of the Fleet. Corruption and incompetence at the Admiralty then led to a steady deterioration in the state of the Royal Navy which was not corrected until the outbreak of war with Revolutionary France in 1793. By the time she sank, the *Royal George* was inefficiently officered and many of her timbers were rotten.

On 29 August 1782 she was anchored at Spithead, between Southsea and Ryde, Isle of Wight. Admiral Richard Kempenfelt had made her his Channel Fleet flagship and, under orders for Gibraltar, she was preparing to put to sea. With departure imminent, many of the families were allowed aboard to say farewell to their menfolk. Well in excess of one thousand souls were on the ship that day.

The preparations for departure included the renewal of a defective sea-cock, below the water-line. Access could be obtained only by causing the ship to heel over at an angle, and this was done in the usual way by shifting all the main deck guns to one side of the ship. Amazingly, the order to close the lower deck gun ports was not given. Some bulwark timbers to which the heavy cannon had been lashed then gave way. The gun carriages broke loose and so altered the critical angle of heel. The *Royal George* began to roll over, water flooded into the lower deck spaces, and within moments she capsized and sank.

Between 800 and 900 people, including Admiral Kempenfelt, lost their lives. Many of their bodies were recovered and buried in unmarked graves along the seafront at Ryde. No memorial marked their passing for nearly two centuries. The story then came to the attention of Earl Mountbatten of Burma during the period when he was Governor of the Isle of Wight. He directed that a plaque should be erected to mark the tragedy and it was unveiled by him on 31 August 1965. It can be seen in a small garden just to the east of the Ryde Castle Hotel.

The plaque bears a representation of the ship and the following inscription: "In memory of the many officers and men of the Royal Navy and Royal Marines who lost their lives when the *Royal George* sank at Spithead on the 29th August 1782 and who lie buried along this seafront. And here by friends unknown, unmarked, unwept, they rest." The last line is an extract from a contemporary poem by William Cowper.

The fate of those sailors and marines had not in fact been forgotten entirely in the interim. Their ship lay in relatively shallow water. For years she was a hazard to navigation, and her name on the Admiralty chart was a constant reminder to mariners and trawlermen of the perils of going anywhere near her resting place.

Nothing could be done to demolish the wreck before methods had been devised for sending down men and explosive charges. Such technology did not begin to evolve until the late 1830s. One of the pioneers in developing it was an officer of the Royal Engineers, Colonel Charles Pasley. A veteran of Maida, Copenhagen, Corunna and Walcheren, he had an intense interest in military science and, in 1812, founded the Royal Engineer Establishment.

Pasley made it his personal commitment to clear the *Royal George* wreck site. There had been two or three earlier attempts by civilian contractors which had failed, but in 1838 he persuaded the Admiralty to authorise a joint operation. The navy would provide the surface support vessels, the Royal Engineers and Royal Sappers & Miners would handle all aspects of the diving and lifting.

The full technical details of the six years' project were published in Volume II of *The History of the Royal Corps of Sappers & Miners,* by T W J Connolly (Longman, Brown, Green & Longmans, London, 1855). Anyone who has ever been involved in diving - professional or amateur - will find the technical descriptions of the project thoroughly alarming. The

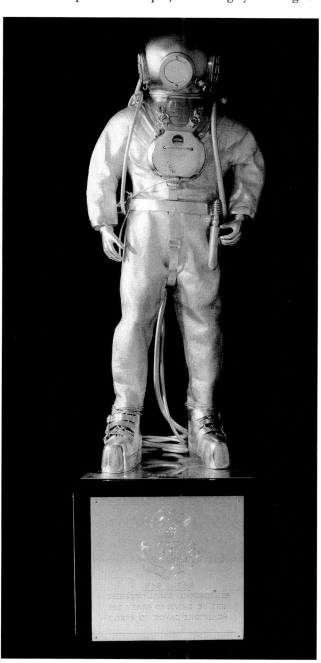

The Diving Centrepiece was made in 1968 by John H Odell, of Gravesend. The silver diver is 15 inches tall, the entire piece stands 23 inches overall. Photo: HQ RE.

basic principles of Boyle's Law - formulated by the Anglo-Irish scientist Robert Boyle in 1662 - were widely understood by educated men such as Pasley, but their practical applications to diving were still being explored the hard way.

Pasley decided that his men would not simply demolish the still largely intact hull, they would first break it up and then bring the pieces to the surface for disposal ashore. Further, he would attempt to salvage the ship's many valuable cannon. Work commenced in the summer of 1839, the first dives being made

Neptune, with his trident and five sea horses, depicted in the Dawn Goodson centrepiece made for 28 Amphibious Engineer Regiment RE. The regiment operated M2 bridging vehicles used for crossing rivers (either as linked sections or as self-propelled ferries). Photo: HQ RE.

with a wood and metal diving bell. Fourteen feet long and four feet wide, it resembled an inverted rowing boat. Heavy and unwieldy, it was soon discarded.

All subsequent dives were made by men wearing the impregnated canvas suit and brass helmet equipment similar to that shown in the centrepiece photograph. Air pumps had been evolving since the 1600s when the first was built by the German inventor Von Guericke. Electrical impulses, for firing the explosive charges from the surface, were generated by "voltaic batteries". These simple devices, which depended upon chemical reaction, had been invented at the turn of the century by the Italian physicist, Count Alessandro Volta.

Dives could be made only at slack tide, and only during the summer months. Underwater visibility was very limited. Cold was a big problem for divers who were working on the bottom for as many as eight hours each day. There were accidents of every kind, from one occasion when a premature explosion caught one of the divers still in the water, to others when they were injured by heavy debris or had their air lines entangled in the lifting year. Bleeding from the ears, nose and lungs were a regular occurrence. Several sappers were permanently disabled but, surprisingly, nobody was killed.

Special rates of pay, as much as four shillings and sixpence (23 pence) per day, were available to the men who made the most dives and brought up the largest pieces of wreckage. Apart from money, the teams were driven by a strongly competitive spirit. Towards the end, when the depth of their dives had progressed

from sixty feet down to one hundred feet, there was rivalry to see who could free and lift a particularly stubborn section of the *Royal George's* keel, embedded in the mud. The two divers working on it became so determined to succeed in getting the lifting slings under this piece that a sea-bed fight broke out between them. Their slow-motion brawl lasted several minutes before they exhausted themselves.

Hundreds of loads were lifted and removed from the site. At the end of the final season, in 1844, only nineteen cannon were still on the bottom, too deep in the soft mud to be recovered. For the rest, the engineers and sappers had cleared away every trace of the original disaster.

The Neptune Centrepiece, by contrast with all the objects recorded so far, was a radical departure from tradition. It was commissioned by 28 Amphibious Engineer Regiment when the unit was formed in 1971. The original concept came from the Adjutant, Captain Suresh Khanna, and the design drawings were produced by Dawn Goodson BA, wife of the first commanding officer, Lieutenant Colonel H J Goodson RE.

A stylised interpretation of King Neptune riding the waves in a sea chariot pulled by five horses, it is mounted on a rosewood base. Around the base is a silver band bearing the names of the officers serving with the unit at its formation. The five horses represent the regimental headquarters, the three Amphibious Squadrons, and the attached REME workshop personnel. Neptune himself emphasises the watermanship skills of the regiment, and is intended to suggest "strength, confidence, speed and victory".

The piece was made by Highley, of Chatham, to a fairly limited budget. The artist herself was disappointed with the end result, but its significance (in silversmithing terms) was that it paved the way for subsequent Royal Engineer pieces of innovative design.

The Northern Ireland Centrepiece records the fact that the Royal Engineers have been deployed in Northern Ireland since 1969. It was decided in the 1980s that a piece of silver should be made to record their services in the Province up to that time. Various suggestions regarding an appropriate design were put forward and examined, but the Corps Committee opted for a modern rather than a traditional approach. Its members agreed to accept the design proposals of Stuart Devlin.

An independent silversmith, Devlin was born in 1931 in Geelong, Australia. After working and studying in his native country for some years, he won scholarships which enabled him to travel to England to study at the Royal College of Art, in London. His abilities thrived under the influence of Professor Robert Goodden. The Worshipful Company of Goldsmiths quickly became aware of this instinctive talent, purchasing for its own collection almost all the of the pieces which he made during his two years at the College. The Company also took at that time the very unusual step of inviting Devlin to design and make a major work - a centrepiece to commemorate the tercentenary of The Royal Society. Such an important commission would normally have been undertaken by an older and more widely recognised artist.

Awarded the highest academic laurels by the Royal College of Art, he travelled to America on a Harkness Fellowship. He studied and worked at Columbia University for two years, then returned to Australia where he designed his native country's first decimal coinage. He has since designed new coinage for more than thirty countries and produced several hundred types of commemorative medallion.

In 1965 he came back to open a small workshop in London, in Clerkenwell, and England has been his home ever since. He soon acquired a following amongst collectors of silver interested in contemporary design and, over the past thirty years, has generated a flow of new concepts in silver and gold, "making rich and romantic pieces while retaining basically simple forms". Over the years he has ventured into the fields of jewellery and

The Northern Ireland Centrepiece, made for the Corps of Royal Engineers by Stuart Devlin. It is hallmarked London 1986, is 26 inches in height, and measures 13 inches across the base. Photo: HQ RE.

The Ubique Centrepiece from conception to completion - a rare glimpse into the mind of the silversmith as creative artist. Above left is a copy of the original watercolour sketch submitted by Stuart Devlin to the Royal Engineers Committee in 1985. The right-hand picture is a photograph of the finished piece delivered to Chatham one year later. Photo: Stuart Devlin CMG.

furniture design, ecclesiastical pieces, and regalia for orders of chivalry (notably the insignia of the Order of Australia).

In 1982 he was appointed Goldsmith and Jeweller to Her Majesty The Queen. In recent years he and his wife Carole have moved to a new home and workshop on the Sussex coast.

Stuart Devlin's pyramid-shaped Northern Ireland centrepiece is much more imposing than a photograph might suggest. Made in gold and silver mounted on a wooden base, it stands more than two feet high and is topped by a Royal Engineers' grenade. A horizontal cross section of the column is at any point an outline of the shape of the Province. The bas-relief side panels - which are almost invisible in this illustration - depict various aspects of the work of sappers in the Province up to the year of its manufacture.

The Ubique Centrepiece was the second commission given to Stuart Devlin by the Royal Engineers. He was asked to submit his ideas for a design which would encapsulate the Corps motto - "Everywhere" - with emphasis on the countries in which sappers had seen active service between 1945 and 1988. He proposed a gimbal-mounted sphere, standing on a vertical column. The accompanying illustrations show the initial design drawing and the finished piece.

Each country outlined on the sphere (a symbolic map of the world) is engraved with its name and the date of the associated campaign. The piece stands nearly two feet high but is only eight inches wide at the base, dimensions which suggest that it may be prone to damage if not handled with caution. The RE records state that the gimbal mountings needed to be re-worked in 1992, by Beeby and Powell. An officer attending a Dinner Night attempted, with adverse results, to spin the sphere. Such incidents are not uncommon with Mess silver of all types and epochs.

Regiments and corps of the British Army which have been disbanded or amalgamated since the end of WWII have left behind them the legacy of their printed records, their memorials, their laid-up Colours, their medals and their memories. Above all, their histories are preserved for posterity in their collections of silver.

The inventories of those collections are now closed, the final lines have been drawn. This is not the case, fortunately, with those regiments and corps which continue to thrive. From time to time, as funds permit and as occasion demands, new acquisitions arrive on the Mess table to join the pieces enjoyed by the officers of former generations. As the army moves forward, adopting new technologies and new philosophies, so is the style of its silver keeping pace with changing tastes. As Stuart Devlin has commented, "these are *living* collections".

By comparison with the British Army, the strength of the Indian Army was in peacetime substantial, and in wartime enormous. The Indian Army of WWII numbered more than two and a half million men, every one of them a volunteer. It has been possible, while compiling this book, to record the experiences of officers who served in the 1930s and who knew what it was like to be a soldier in a world - an Indian world - which has long gone and which will never return. One of them was Major Robert Henderson. His family had sent its sons to serve in India over several generations, and he himself joined the 2nd Royal Battalion (Ludhiana Sikhs), of the 11th Sikh Regiment, in 1937.

"I remember that we had a Mess silver fund to which each officer was required to contribute on joining and when promoted. The amounts involved were quite substantial. Many of the Commanding Officers, at their own expense, presented a piece to the Mess on relinquishing command. Almost all of these items were commissioned from the Goldsmiths & Silversmiths Company, London.

When serving on the Frontier, we would be based in cantonments such as Bannu or Razmak which had permanent perimeter fencing and where we had proper Messes. Our silver would be left there, with suitable security arrangements, whenever we went out for active operations living under canvas. When we were ordered to Iraq, in 1941, the Battalion's silver was sent to the Regimental Centre at Nowshera for safe-keeping.

After the war, at the time of Partition, all of the Battalion's possessions, including our Mess Funds, were left behind for our successors. The Sikh Regiment of the modern Indian Army was expanded greatly, with more than twenty battalions, but my old unit, formerly the 15th Ludhiana Sikhs, still exists. Twice in recent years I have had the pleasure of visiting them and of seeing again all the interesting objects which I remember from my own time with it".

One of these treasures is an item of particular interest to naval historians. Amongst the many steps taken by the British to meet the growing power of the German and Italian fleets in the mid-1930s was the decision to build the new Tribal class of destroyers. Typical of these fine 1870 ton ships, built by Stephen & Sons and launched in late 1937, was HMS *Sikh*. The officers of The Sikh Regiment decided to present to the officers of the new ship a silver statue of a Sikh soldier with which to embellish their Wardroom. Made by the Goldsmiths & Silversmiths Company, it depicted a *jawan* (private soldier) of the period, dressed and equipped in battle order. The design of the statue was based upon a series of photographs, taken in India and despatched to the company in London. The photographer's model was Samund Singh, a strikingly handsome man and *Jemadar* Adjutant of the 2nd Battalion.

The piece was handed over and displayed in the Wardroom but, when HMS *Sikh* went to war in 1939, it was put ashore and left in the Royal Navy's silver repository at Portsmouth. Subsequently, on 14 September 1942, she was sunk by coastal

artillery while engaged in a disastrous Commando-style amphibious assault against the North African port of Tobruk. Her sister ship HMS *Zulu* was lost in the same action. The casualties aboard HMS *Sikh* were particularly severe, with the loss of fifteen officers (including the commanding officer, Captain St J A Micklethwait DSO RN), and two hundred and sixty ratings. A handful of survivors reached the shore and became prisoners of war.

Major Henderson takes up the story: "Early in 1988, together with other former officers, I visited the new Sikh Regimental Centre at Ramgarh Bihar. It includes a museum which impressed me greatly. It contained, amongst other things from later periods, all the mementoes of the hundred years of the Regiment's service to the Crown. An alcove was given over to the story of the ship, with mention of her visits to Haifa and Alexandria when, early in the war, she entertained parties of men from our 2nd and 4th Battalions. This inspired me to contact the Ministry of Defence, to see if the Royal Navy would agree to hand the piece back to the regiment. Approval was soon obtained, but with the reservation that it should be returned to the Navy in the event that there is ever another HMS *Sikh*. In other words, it is on permanent loan. Apart from its associations with our regimental history, it is indirectly a permanent memorial to all those chaps who lost their lives at Tobruk in 1942. Who would remember them otherwise?".

The silver statue was installed as the centre piece of the alcove in the Museum at Ramgarh, and Robert Henderson was able to view it there during a second visit, in 1996. "Several of us had been invited to join in the celebrations of the 150th anniversary of the formation of our forebears, the Regiment of Ludhiana. On our arrival at Meerut we were offered coffee in two silver pots, one presented on promotion in the twenties by my father, Major G B Henderson, the other by me on appointment in 1937. In reply to my challenge that this had been stage-managed, our hosts charmingly insisted that they used these pots every day. Whatever the explanation, it was good to see such items of silver still being put to the use for which they were intended, and some of the old traditions maintained.

One custom which did not survive was the wedding silver fund. This was quite separate from the Mess silver fund. We all paid in so much each month and then, when one of us took the plunge, there was sufficient money to pay for a good piece of presentation silver. This invariably took the form of a fourteen-inch diameter salver on which were engraved the details of the occasion and the signatures of all serving brother officers. I was probably the last to receive one, at my wedding on 11 November 1939. I also have my father's similar inscribed salver, celebrating his wedding in June 1915".

From the era of Queen Victoria through to the Second World War, marriage continued to be a topic as troublesome for the younger officers of the Indian Army as it was for their counterparts in the British Army. There was an unwritten but clearly understood convention: "Lieutenants shall *not* marry, Captains

The young officer joining his regiment needed to start acquiring a variety of uniforms - blue patrol dress, hot weather Mess dress, cold weather Mess dress, hot weather drill order, cold weather drill order, and (until WWI) ceremonial review order. The cost of setting himself up for every occasion was a significant financial burden (especially if he was joining one of the cavalry regiments whose Mess jackets featured intricate and expensive gold braid). The impact could be lessened by taking a long-term loan, or by purchasing the second-hand kit of a retiring officer. Some lucky youngsters inherited the sword of a kinsman who had served in the same regiment but, for the majority, the total outlay inhibited even further any thoughts of early marriage. Seen here, in review order, is Captain Douglas Gray, of the 1st Duke of York's Own Lancers (Skinner's Horse). The picture was taken during the period (1935-1938) when he was ADC to the Governor of Burma. He was the last officer to wear the full saffron yellow coat or jacket of that famous regiment.
Photo: Lieut Col C R D G Gray OBE.

may marry, Majors *must* marry. Further, no engagement shall be announced without the prior approval of the Commanding Officer".

There were several reasons why this should have been the case. One was the monetary consideration. Officers of the Indian Army were financially better off than their contemporaries in the British Army but, even so, the junior officers would have been hard pressed, on their modest pay, to sustain the cost of a wife and children. Worse, until they reached thirty years of age, they could not claim the marriage allowance and did not qualify for access to a married quarter.

Most peacetime stations had a limited number of houses, usually within walking distance of the Mess, built and maintained specifically to accommodate married officers and their families. A young couple seeking a place of their own, and for whom no official quarter was available, would have been obliged to find it on the open market, with a private landlord, at a much higher rent and at a greater distance from the battalion and its activities.

However, the main objection to early marriage was the distraction it would have created from the young officer's primary duty to his regiment and to his professional career. By joining a regiment, he had in effect become married to it. His superiors expected that his thoughts and energies should be devoted exclusively to learning the skills of a soldier, to taking a full part in everything which his unit did and thereby becoming an integral component in it. He could not fulfil these objectives if he left the bachelor brotherhood of the Officers' Mess and moved into married quarters. That, at least, was the thinking of those in authority.

The final barrier faced by every potential bridegroom was the need to seek the permission of his Commanding Officer. Although this was in almost every instance nothing more than a formality, the process did limit the chances of a young man entering into a marriage which was, in the language of those days, "unsuitable". The young lady would be required not only to be a good wife and mother, she would need also a strength of character above the normal.

By marrying an army officer she was joining his regiment. Many of the other wives would be older than her, so inevitably there would be a pecking order to which she must adapt. Her new husband might be absent for long periods, attending courses or on campaign service. Loneliness was something she could face, but she knew in advance that, when her children reached eight or eleven years of age, she would lose all normal contact with them. Depending upon circumstances and the finances available, they would be sent away to a boarding school. Before modern medicine conquered them, India's diseases would probably prevent at least one of her babies from surviving its infancy. Some girls were more gifted than others when challenged by such strains upon their marriages.

It was "the good of the service" which, in the final analysis, determined the way in which all these matters were handled. No single officer, no single marriage, could be permitted to cause a scandal which might damage the reputation of the unit. Any officer cited in a divorce action was required, automatically, to resign his commission. The same fate awaited any officer who had an affair with a brother officer's wife. Wayward wives who were indiscreet in their extra-marital affairs, who attracted gossip, were likely to find themselves on the boat home. It is a tribute to all those thousands of young women who chose to "follow the drum" that the great majority made happy and lasting marriages.

The subject of wedding gifts is described in the recollections of another former officer of the 11th Sikh Regiment, Lieutenant Colonel E Rowland-Jones, who served with the Regiment's 1st Battalion during the 1930s and WWII. "The rule was that one was not permitted to wed before reaching the age of thirty. In my own case the rule was somewhat relaxed because it was wartime, so I obtained my CO's permission at the ripe old age of twenty-six. However, we did have one subaltern before the war, a friend of mine, who ignored the signals coming from our CO and went ahead with his wedding plans anyway. He was told to take himself and his bride elsewhere. He transferred to the Service Corps. It was a pity because it was the loss to us of a fine officer. Later, during the war, he became a Brigadier.

We all made a monthly contribution into the silver fund. The sums were considerable and, over the years, we had accumulated a mass of cutlery, condiment sets, and so forth. We were very well off, and were allowed to borrow money from the fund. In 1935 I was sent on leave to Kashmir and was given a loan of five hundred rupees to help pay for the trip. Amongst the many formal items of silver were three statuettes of Indian Princes who were Honorary Officers of our battalion. They were the Rajahs of Jhind, Nabha, and Faridkot. The latter I knew well because he soldiered with us on a regular basis and even came with us in 1937 for the operations of that year in Waziristan. He knew how to campaign in style, bringing with him his personal servants, his horses, and crates of Champagne.

There were two aspects to our wedding silver arrangements which were unique to the Battalion. The first was a statuette of Eros, very similar to the one which stands in Piccadilly, London, but just twelve inches in height. In 1924 the battalion's eight Subalterns, all bachelors of course, subscribed to its purchase as a sort of private joke amongst themselves. It was made by the Goldsmiths & Silversmiths Company, and was always known as 'The Bachelors Trophy'. Their names were listed on the plinth and the idea was that each officer's name would be scored through with an arrow when he got married. Their names were D W Morell, C A Osborne, H W Dinwiddie, J P L Eustace, H R Swinburn, C W M Morris, D L Clark and R A d'E Ashe. Ownership of the piece would pass to the one who lasted longest. The agreement was kept going right through to 1948 when the sole surviving subscriber, Lieutenant Colonel Arthur Ashe, got married at the age of forty-seven. The silver cupid had become his property in 1938 when Morell succumbed. Arthur and Janet were wed at Exeter Cathedral, and the trophy was given the place of honour on top of their wedding cake. As a matter of interest, two of the subscribers, Osborne and Swinburn, went on to the rank of Major General.

The other aspect was that, as far as formal gifts were concerned, we were allowed to choose from a list of just three specified items, all made by the Goldsmiths & Silversmiths Company. One was a statuette of a Sepoy, another was a salver, and the third was a set of four beer mugs made in the Queen Anne style. I chose the latter, and still have the sole survivor in my home. The figure of the Sepoy, of the 14th King George's Own Ferozepore Sikhs, our predecessors, was made to order from a mould held permanently at the Goldsmiths' workshop.

It was first used in the 1920s when the Battalion decided to commission the manufacture of a table centre piece commemorating the action at Gully Ravine, on Gallipoli, in June 1915. It had been an attack against Turkish trenches which resulted in the deaths of nearly all the Battalion's British officers. They were the Commanding Officer, Lieutenant Colonel F A Jacques, and Captain A W McRae, and Lieutenants L R Fowle, L F Cremen, R J F P Meade and H E Masters, and Second Lieutenants G W

Hornsby, W H Lowry, S V Hasluck and M C G Mathew. The only two surviving British officers, Second Lieutenants Wreford and Savory, were both wounded. The latter rose to be Lieutenant General Sir Reginald Savory KCIE, CB, DSO, MC, the last Adjutant General of the Indian Army before Partition".

As an aside, it should be mentioned that a third survivor from the Gully Ravine disaster was the battalion's Medical Officer, Captain Heerajee Jehangir Manockjee Cursetjee MRCS LRCP. There is no record of his nickname or the name by which he was known to the other officers, but he surely needed something less long-winded. His career demonstrates the excellent quality of the medical men recruited into the Indian Medical Service. A graduate of Gonville and Caius College, Cambridge, he had qualified at The London Hospital and entered the IMS in 1912. Although severely wounded at Gully Ravine, he made a full recovery and, for the last two years of the war, served in Iraq. By 1919 he had twice been mentioned in despatches and admitted to the Distinguished Service Order and the Serbian Order of the White Eagle (5th Class). Between the wars he served in Kurdistan and on the North West Frontier. By the time he retired, in 1946, he had become Major General Sir Heerajee Jehangir Manockjee Cursetjee KCIE CSI DSO. He was appointed a King's Honorary Surgeon in 1941.

Gallipoli, 1915. Frozen in silver for all time, Mohan Singh of the Ferozepore Sikhs prepares to throw a grenade at the Turks. Photo: Lieut Col E Rowland-Jones.

Returning now to the account by "Bones" Rowland-Jones: "The statuette was the figure of a Sepoy named Mohan Singh, caught in the posture of throwing a grenade at the Turks. These grenades were trench made, consisting of gun cotton packed into discarded condensed milk tins. The artist who sculpted the model was very caring with points of detail, and you can even read the name Nestlé on the grenades piled around Mohan

Singh's feet. It is a beautiful piece of work, and the original still has a pride of place in the Officers' Mess at Nabha. In my time it was the principal table centre piece for formal dinners.

It was so interesting and attractive that the unwary were sometimes tempted to reach over and touch it, to read the names of the officers inscribed on the plinth. The custom was that anyone touching the piece was fined a round of port. On a recent visit to the Battalion, in October 1996, I saw that all our old silver was in sparkling condition, and the custom of not allowing any guests to touch Mohan Singh was still maintained. I was watched by my hosts very carefully, to see whether I still remembered. I did!".

the Regiment, I handed it over to the senior member of the Junior Officers Mess, Subadar Major Kunan Singh".

Not every Indian regiment and not every battalion followed the same customs. Much depended upon the composition of the Officers' Mess. In the very early years of British India, the units raised by Robert Clive were officered by only a small nucleus of British (European) officers. The majority of the officer ranks were occupied by Indians, usually of the same clan, class or religion of the men whom they were commanding.

The balance shifted during the period 1796-1804 when, amongst other reorganisations, the establishment of British officers per infantry battalion was increased to twenty-two, and

The decor and layout of the Officers' Messes of the Indian and Pakistan Armies are still much as they were in the last days of the Raj. This is the dining room of Skinner's Horse. At the far entrance is a Mess waiter in full winter uniform. The framed dinner plates on the wall were the property of the 3rd Bengal Cavalry, one of Skinner's pre-1903 forebears. Dominating the table is the figure of "The Charging Sowar" (fully illustrated in Chapter Five). Photo: RHQ Skinner's Horse.

It was during their visit to Ramgarh in 1966 that the former British officers of the 11th Sikhs were able to please their hosts in an unexpected way. Major Henderson resumes his account: "We returned to the regiment an item known as 'The Barstow Statuette'. Consisting of a fine reproduction of a Sikh officer of the 15th Ludhiana Sikhs in pre-1914 uniform, it had been made by the Goldsmiths & Silversmiths Company to the order of our *Indian* officers. The Viceroy's Commissioned Officers were not given to the acquisition of silver for their own Mess, which was always a bit bare, and it was exceptional for them to give silver to any British officer. Remember, the pay of a Subadar was 120 rupees per month (under ten pounds) while a Jemadar was on 70 rupees. However, Major A E Barstow was an exceptional officer, worshipped by the men who had served with him in 1914 and 1915 on the Western Front. When in 1927 his impending marriage was announced, the VCOs decided to spend the equivalent of two months pay each for the purchase of this statuette. It was a remarkable tribute to a remarkable man.

He was killed in January 1942 while commanding the 9th Indian Division in Malaya. The statuette stayed with his widow until she died in 1979. It was then offered for sale at Sotheby's, Pulborough. With the support of General Barstow's nephew, Group Captain Leonard Cheshire VC, our Sikh Brigade Dinner Club raised the money to buy it and it graced the table at our annual reunion dinners in London for the following sixteen years. The 1996 anniversary celebration was the right time to return the piece to its home. On behalf of the Club and in the presence of Lieutenant General Manjit Singh Bhullar, Colonel of

later, twenty-six - one Colonel, one Lieutenant Colonel, one Major, seven Captains, eleven Lieutenants and five Ensigns. There was, logically, a corresponding sharp reduction in the vacancies available for otherwise eligible Indians. There was a similar pattern in the artillery, but the same route was not followed in the cavalry regiments. The basis upon which they recruited their *sowars* was such that they functioned more effectively with a preponderance of their own Indian officers and perhaps no more than four or five British.

It followed that Messing arrangements varied widely between regiments of infantry and regiments of cavalry. With a large number of officers sharing a Mess, the former had a reason for recreating in India the English club or country house accommodation and furnishings with which they were familiar. British cavalry officers were not in the same position. It is unlikely that they acquired much in the way of silver in the early decades. However, even if they did, little of it could have survived the events of 1857 in Northern India. All but three regiments of Bengal cavalry joined the mutineers.

One of the steps taken in 1863, following the transfer to Crown service of the Armies of Madras, Bengal and Bombay, was to reduce to six the number of British officers on the establishment of each infantry regiment. In any given period, one or more of these would be away on a course, on leave, or unavailable by reason of sickness or injury. Command, therefore, was often very much in the hands of the Indian officers. Their ranks did not in each instance have a precise equivalent in the British Army or in those modelled upon it. In cavalry regiments there were three such ranks: *Risaldar Major, Risaldar* (commanding a Squadron) and *Jemadar* (a Troop officer). The infantry officers were: *Subadar Major, Subadar* (commanding a Company) and *Jemadar* (a Company officer). The names of Indians holding these ranks may be found engraved on items of regimental silver, and they should command in full the respect which they deserve.

The *Risaldar Major* and *Subadar Major* were the senior Indian officers in their respective regiments or battalions, directly responsible to the commanding officer (usually known as the Commandant) for all matters relating to discipline and morale. They were the *only* such channel of communication. They were, therefore, always men of immense experience and influence. As with all Indian officers of the pre-1861 period, they held commissions which had been granted by the Governor General of the Presidency to which their regiment happened to belong. The nature of their status changed in 1881 when Victoria assumed the title "Queen Empress of India", thereby changing the title of the Governor General of India to that of "Viceroy". Thereafter, Indian officers became known as VCOs - Viceroy's Commissioned Officers.

The VCOs were officers in every sense of that word, and yet their lives were not the same as their British comrades in arms. They had risen from the ranks, usually after many years of service, and were promoted on merit and proven ability rather than by education or social advantage. Often they were several years older than British officers of similar rank. Many were married and had children before they received their commissions. They were not nearly as well paid. These factors combined to create a gulf made wider by the differences in culture of the two races. VCOs, therefore, did not share the British Officers' Mess but had their own Mess where, apart from any other consideration, they could observe their own dietary rules without any sort of difficulty.

Lieutenant Colonel Robert Going, who was commissioned into the Indian Army before WWII, explains: "In the huge diversity of India, where languages and customs differ so much, the VCOs were a very necessary link in helping the British officer to understand each class and tribe enlisted into his particular regiment. *Urdu* was introduced in the 16th century by the Moguls under their leader Akhbar the Great and it was, by and large, the language of the Indian Army. However, because it was rooted in Northern India, it could not be completely understood in regiments which recruited in some other regions. When written or printed, *Urdu* is in Arabic script, but my own regiment, the 19th Hyderabad, recruited mainly Hindus and only the Nagri script was used. Then, with regard to diet, Hindus are not permitted beef but they do eat chicken, goat and mutton. Muslims on no account consume alcohol or eat pork (although in my experience pork was hardly ever seen in India). Our Hindu soldiers were permitted and enjoyed rum or, in the VCOs' Mess, whiskey and beer. These were just some of the most obvious differences, but there were a great many others, very much more subtle. Only a British officer with a lifetime of service with Indian soldiers could have the same understanding of them all as the VCOs".

It should not be thought that there was no social contact between the British officers and the VCOs. Each were invited from time to time to "drinks" in the other's Mess, and VCOs who did not themselves consume alcohol were happy to supply it in abundance for their guests. The Gurkhas, Garhwalis and Kumaonis have no inhibitions with regard to alcohol, and the VCOs of Gurkha regiments in particular were notorious for testing the capacity of inexperienced young British officers by plying them with a generous flow of one of their favourite tipples, rum.

The years 1921 to 1923 brought the last major restructuring of the old (pre-Partition) Indian Army. A crucial element in the scheme was the commitment to "Indianisation", this being the progressive replacement of British officers by Indian officers. Already, for some years, promising young men from the higher levels of Indian society had been encouraged to follow careers in the army and been given the rigorous basic military training available at the Royal Military College, Sandhurst. Most of these select few had received their earlier education at English public schools or at equivalent establishments in India. With this background they were entirely at home in the surroundings and social atmosphere of a British officers' Mess and so, on passing out of Sandhurst, they received a King Emperor's commission.

In 1923, the instruction was given that two regiments of cavalry and six battalions of infantry should start to "Indianise", with immediate effect. One cavalry regiment and six infantry battalions, plus a number of signals and engineer units, were added to the scheme ten years later. Subsequent progress was slow. The need to bring these young men to England and maintain them here for eighteen months was expensive and cumbersome. There was a clear need for a "Sandhurst in India", and this lead to the opening in 1931 of the Indian Military Academy, at Dehra Dun. Increasing numbers of Indians were sent also to the Indian Staff College, formed in 1905 and established permanently since 1907 at Quetta. From the 1920s onwards, therefore, Briton and Indian alike could share the same Mess on terms of equality, both professional and social.

When Robert Going arrived in India, in 1936, he served the customary year with one of the British garrison battalions, in his case the 1st Battalion, The Duke of Wellington's Regiment, at Nowshera. The purpose of these temporary attachments was that of giving every factory-fresh Second Lieutenant time in which to find his feet before joining the Indian regiment which would be his future permanent home. Robert was destined for the 1st Battalion, 19th Hyderabad Regiment, and he joined it at the sprawling industrial city of Ahmedabad.

"When I arrived there, in 1937, all of the officers were British. Day-to-day life in the Mess was quite relaxed and informal. Majors and above were called 'Sir', at least to their faces, but the rest of us were known by our Christian names; David, Dickie, Don. That was not so easy when, at Razmak, a trickle of newly commissioned Indian officers began to arrive because, obviously, they didn't have the equivalent forenames. Each gained a nickname, usually a corruption of his correct name. Majeed, for example, was a Bengali and was always called Masjid. I don't remember why; it is the word for a Muslim shrine. Then, in the 4th Battalion, there was Thimmaya. He went on to become a General. He was known simply as Timmy.

We did not have a silver fund or a wedding gift fund. There were too few of us for that. The rule about not marrying before the age of thirty was relaxed as the war loomed, and we did have two weddings at that time. The customary gifts were paid for on an individual contribution basis. The girls were very thoroughly vetted by the Commandant before he gave his approval. One was already 'well in with the regiment' because she was the daughter of the local Commissioner of Indian Police and attended many of our functions. The other, Mary Craig, was not well known, so she was invited to come and visit us at our camp at Orhao. That gave the CO and the rest of us a chance to get to know her, to see if she would fit in. She did, splendidly.

Our job at Ahmedabad was to give 'aid to the civil power' in the event of communal unrest. As it happened, there was no rioting while we were there, so our time was taken up with the usual training cycle and preparing for our next move, to the Frontier. However, in the event of serious trouble, we would have been supported by a nearby British battalion and one of their officers was always attached to us for liaison. In my time he was Captain Charles Hoey, of the Lincolns. He joined in all our sports and other efforts, and was an outstanding man in all respects, absolutely dedicated but with a happy helpful nature.

At weekends we would hire a car and go shooting. Charlie was a brilliant shot and would lead through the paddy fields at a fierce pace. He was all the time training himself in the soldierly qualities of finding and memorising the way and moving swiftly. At the outbreak of war, Charlie was given the task of arresting all the German craftsmen and businessmen and their families in

could not invite anyone who was an artisan, but there were traders and businessmen - box *wallahs*, as they were called - who came with their wives and daughters. But there was a desperate dearth of nice young women.

I mention the artisans. There was one such family which lived near our Mess. The father was an ex-Royal Air Force ranker, a very nice chap. He had a pretty daughter and she would come to hear our band practicing. Very soon she was consorting with our young officers. As an artisan's daughter, if she could marry an officer, that would be a big prize for the family. But our young men were not interested in marriage, only in nubile young women. She became a bit of free for all. She was actually a sweet girl, and after we left Ahmedabad, I was so pleased to hear that, in the regiment which replaced us, she found her man.

Later on, after the war started, many of the ex-fishing fleet marriages fell on hard times when husbands were killed in

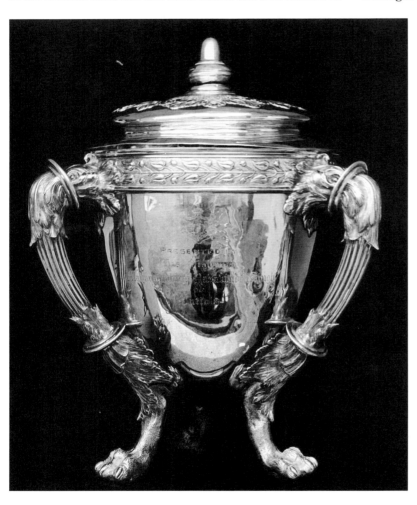

There were not many forms of organised entertainment available in places such as Ahmedabad. One of the "sports" started by the British and continued by their successors is Bicycle Polo. It is a game played with more good-humoured violence than practiced skill, as the slightly battered condition of this trophy might suggest. It was the prize for an inter-unit tournament started in 1956 by His Highness The Maharajah Shri Vadavendra Singh, of Patiala, and is currently held by Skinner's Horse. Photo: RHQ.

the city, a job which he did with kindness and understanding. Four years later he was killed in Burma, under very gallant circumstances, and was awarded a posthumous Victoria Cross.

Every year, in the cold weather season, a lot of girls came out to India in search of a husband. They were known as 'the fishing fleet', and a good proportion of them managed to land their man. When I was with the Duke's, in Nowshera, we held polo competitions, parties, dances, and made trips up to Peshawar and Kashmir. It was all good fun. There were few such attractions at Ahmedabad, so we didn't see much of the fishing fleet girls there. That was not surprising because it really was a hot, dusty, ugly place. From time to time we invited members of the British community to our Mess functions, but they were not a great success. The class system in those days was such that we

action. The young widows, many with children, found themselves alone and a long way from home. Some managed to get back to England, some went to Canada, others seemed to be trapped in India and got themselves jobs. My sister's husband, Major Cecil Caldicott, of the 6th Gurkha Rifles (Frontier Force), died in 1940. Rosamond was left with two young children, so she found herself a job at the Doon School.

In 1944 quite a different 'fleet' of girls started to arrive. These were mainly members of the FANY, sent out from the UK to do the cypher work on Mountbatten's staff, and QA nurses for the military hospitals, all in uniform and all with the same objective as ourselves: to finish off the Japs. They had left cold blitzed war-torn Britain and rejoiced in their new surroundings and new responsibilities. They were the salt of the earth.

A sight familiar to Robert Going and to every other soldier who ever served a tour of duty on the North West Frontier of India. Watch-towers were to be seen in many parts of the Middle East but most particularly in the tribal areas along the border between India and Afghanistan. The sentry gained access by a ladder leading to the door halfway up the tower. Pulling the ladder up behind him, he then kept watch from the high platform. This replica was made for the officers of 106 (Jacob's) Pack Battery RA and is now in the collection Royal Artillery Mess, Woolwich. It stands 12 inches high and was made in 1921 by Garrard & Company, London. Photo: RAI.

But, in 1947, I married one of them, so perhaps I am biased.

The 1st Battalion, which still exists, has a long and interesting history. It began in 1813 when Sir Henry Russell raised The Russell Brigade to help the Nizam of Hyderabad and Berar in dealing with insurgents and freebooters who were causing trouble in his territory. The name of Russell was later incorporated into our title. With such a long history behind us, we had accumulated quite a lot of Mess silver and other possessions. Some silver was permanently displayed in the Mess ante-rooms or used on a daily basis, but the best pieces were brought out for special occasions. Once a week there was a Dining-in Night which all officers were required to attend and when dinner jackets were worn. Guest Nights, when Mess kit was worn, were less frequent.

Dress was a very big thing in those days, and one needed to observe the code very carefully. Of course, after dinner, we quickly lost our smart appearance in the rough and tumble of the usual Mess games. Our guest one evening at Ahmedabad was Sir Roger Lumley, the Governor of Bombay Province. With such a senior and important guest, it was bound to be a more decorous occasion than usual and we adjourned to the Billiards Room to play snooker. Everyone was sweltering, so there was an almost audible sigh of relief and approval when Sir Roger took off his jacket. Standards of dress were maintained when we saw that his braces were made in Old Etonian colours, so that was alright!

Prior to many Mess functions we were told to go out on *shikari* and bring back a mixed bag: hare, partridge, green pigeon, snipe. These were made into a splendid game pie by Abdul, the *khitmagar*, responsible for our food and drink. In 1938 the battalion moved to Razmak, on the Frontier. Some of our silver came with us and we had formal Dinner Nights, toasted the King Emperor, and followed a normal Mess routine. That changed when we moved again, to Secunderabad, to train for Burma. Most of our silver and other possessions then went into store for the duration of the war. In the event we were sent to Iraq as part of Paiforce. There we lived under canvas, with just a few token items of silver in the Mess tent. After that I went to newly-raised wartime battalions, the 9th and the 6th, where of course there was no band and no silver. The CO of the 9th made great efforts to foster a sense of tradition, but we were so busy training for war that there was really neither time nor opportunity for the pre-war ways of doing things.

In 1976 I returned to India, with Colonel Tim Craig, for the Regimental Reunion. Initially we stayed with the 3rd Battalion, in the Red Fort, Delhi. We were treated on arrival to coffee, served from a very nice silver pot. I noted the inscription, 'Presented by Captain J D Holmes, on Promotion'. It happened that I had served with Derek Holmes in Burma, as his second-in-command. After he retired he came to live here in County Wicklow, not far from my own home, and was a great friend and fishing companion. It was pleasing, when I got back from India, to tell him that his coffee pot was still in regular use.

That 1976 visit was remarkable. I was greeted effusively by several men who remembered me, and we were treated royally. During the visit I was given by our hosts several items which have pride of place in my study. One was a silver vase, presented by General Raina, Commander-in-Chief of the Indian Army, and Colonel-in-Chief of the regiment. Another is a silver plated tray, engraved with the insignia of each battalion and with the Russell lion in the centre. The Russell connection is still venerated in the regiment".

The transfer of command from the British to the new armies of Pakistan and India was accomplished, in the main, with remarkably little trouble of any kind. Most units already had a high proportion of Sikh, Hindu and Muslim officers as a result of the "Indianisation" policy of the inter-war years and the huge wartime expansion of India's armed forces. This blending of British and Indian officers in each unit, with a mutual confidence based upon shared service and shared battlefield dangers, meant that the British officers could be withdrawn without rancour and with minimal disturbance to regimental life. But events did not always flow smoothly, as this account by Lieutenant Colonel D M Amoore demonstrates.

"In the autumn of 1947, the months following Partition, I was in Malaya, commanding 3rd Battalion, 9th Gurkha Rifles. Sometime around September we moved back to India with instructions to start handing over to officers of the new Indian Army. We found ourselves camped about thirty miles south of Delhi. Our task was that of organising the movement of some two hundred thousand Muslims who were being transported to the Punjab. We had been there several weeks when a high ranking Indian officer came to see me. After half an hour of general conversation he asked me bluntly what I intended to do with the battalion's Mess silver. He wanted to know which pieces I intended to keep for myself.

I made it quite clear to him that he need have no concern. None of the battalions of the 9th Gurkha Rifles ever took any silver with them on campaign service of any kind. In fact, as Gurkhas, our tradition was that of having regimental silver,

not battalion silver. And, as far as I knew, all of the 9th Gurkhas' silver was still being held, as it always had been, at the Regimental Depôt, at Dehra Dun. My visitor was clearly not impressed by my explanation, and did little to conceal his belief that I was lying. As soon as he had departed I went to GHQ Delhi and reported the conversation. I was there advised that I should pack my belongings and, with my wife, leave India as soon as possible.

A statuette which reminds us that Gurkha soldiers continued to serve the Crown long after WWII, and still do. Rifleman Resambahadur Thapa, of the 2nd Battalion, 2nd Gurkha Rifles, was awarded the Military Medal for his bravery in the "confrontation" with Indonesia. On the evening of 13 June 1964, his platoon was engaged in the jungle of Sarawak by a much larger force. During the fifty minutes fire-fight, he twice broke cover to engage the enemy more closely, killing several of them. The piece was made by Garrard & Company in 1968 and commemorates the 2nd Battalion's service in Sarawak from 1964 to 1966 during which 203 enemy were killed for a loss of 5 killed and 17 wounded. Inscribed on the two side plates are the names of the officers who contributed to its cost. Photo: The Sirmoor Rifles Trust.

This we did, departing from Bombay on 1st January 1948 for a new home in Vancouver. In the event, all of our silver was inherited, with our blessing, by our successors".

David Amoore was a professional soldier who had served nearly twelve years with the Indian Army and been twice decorated for gallantry. In April, 1943, he was commanding "C" Company of 1st/9th Gurkha Rifles at the battle of the Wadi Akrit. When German infantry advanced and fighting began at very close quarters, he climbed an exposed rocky outcrop from which he directed his troops. For this action he was awarded an immediate Military Cross.

Two years later, serving in Italy as Brigade Major, 5th Indian Infantry Brigade, he was awarded a bar to his Military Cross for repeated acts of personal bravery over a period of several weeks during the advances to Pescara and the upper valley of the River Arno. As he said recently: "It had been an honour to serve with Gurkha soldiers. I had a twin brother, Wynyard, and he and I passed out of Sandhurst together in 1936. We both applied for Gurkha service. He went to the 6th Gurkha Rifles and later won a DSO in Italy. All of my service was with the 9th, and I was rather sad to leave them under such sour circumstances".

Unhappy and isolated encounters such as that experienced by David Amoore must be viewed in a wider and much more dramatic context. British India was passing into history, the new nations of India and Pakistan were being born in a welter of innocent blood, and the largest all-volunteer military force the world has ever seen was being split hurriedly into two parts - a new Pakistan Army and a new Indian Army.

The Commander-in-Chief in India at that time was Field Marshal Sir Claude Auchinleck. Known simply and affectionately as "The Auk", he had been commissioned into the Indian Army in 1904. His forty years of service had given him an exceptional understanding of the many races and classes to be found in its ranks. To preside over the break-up of such a magnificent force, particularly at a time when it was still being applauded for its endurance and loyalty during the war, was a necessary but painful duty.

Auckinleck was answerable to the politicians in both London and Delhi for a smooth handover of military authority. His orders required him to do something which he and his predecessors had always avoided. They knew from long experience that it was dangerous to allocate men to any particular unit solely and exclusively on the grounds of their religion. Most units of the old Indian Army were, down to company level, multi-racial and multi-faith, but the two new armies were being built on the premise that its men must be either exclusively Muslim or exclusively Hindu or Sikh. In this distinction could be seen the potential for future conflict. It is to the immense credit of Auchinleck, and to the many who shared his concerns, that the process of division was accomplished with almost no trouble of any kind. The only incidents of religiously motivated unrest occurred in two or three training depôts, amongst young recruits who had not yet absorbed the traditions of their regiments.

Adding to Auckinleck's problems was the fact that the period between the ending of WWII and the commencement of Independence was chaotic for the armies under his command. Two Indian Divisions - the 5th and 23rd - were fighting the nationalist insurgents in Java, and the 20th was policing Indo-China pending the full reinstatement of the French administration. There were elements in Sumatra, Malaya, Burma and

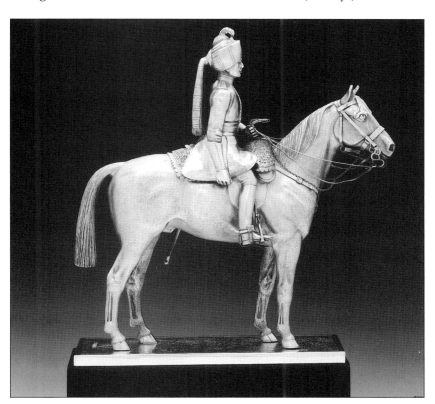

After Partition, British officers who had served in the Indian Army's twenty-one regiments of cavalry resolved to maintain contact by forming The Indian Cavalry Officers' Association (ICOA). Many of them joined Tidworth Polo Club (home of the game for the Services). The ICOA was planning to present a trophy for annual competition between a Combined Services Team and a Visiting International Team when it learned that this statuette was available. It was commissioned early in WWII from the Goldsmiths & Silversmiths Company by the officers of the State Forces of a Maharajah, as their gift to mark his Silver Jubilee. It was never collected. Having languished for forty years in the Goldsmiths' strong-room, it passed to Aspreys who offered it to the ICOA. The money was soon raised, and the statuette (complete with oak and brass travelling case) was named The Indian Cavalry Polo Trophy. It was given to the Tidworth Polo Club in 1988. Photo: Aspreys, and Lieut Col C R D G Gray OBE.

Assam. As they began to trickle back to India they were committed to "aid to the civil power" duties, attempting to stop the widespread sectarian violence. Others were needed for the new Boundary Force, and there was trouble in Kashmir.

As one officer has since observed: "I doubt if there was a single battalion that had settled into a normal garrison state and been able to unpack and open a normal peacetime Mess. It is interesting to speculate that any pre-war regimental silver which found its way to the UK must have come from the functioning regimental centres rather than the individual battalions. The cavalry, being single unit regiments, were able to arrange things more to their satisfaction".

One of Auchinleck's measures, as the day of Partition approached, was his order that all Indian Army regimental silver should remain in its customary place. An officer on his staff, Lieutenant Colonel E W Robinson-Horley MBE, recorded in his memoir (*Last Post*, Leo Cooper with Secker & Warburg, 1985) the reasoning behind the order: "That silver had been donated by British officers, piece by piece, over the years, ever since the regiments had been raised. But as the Auk explained to me, if this heritage had been divided amongst British officers on their departure, it would have had the effect of destroying a large part of the traditions of each regiment. And for what? The silver would have been dissipated far and wide, a piece here and another piece there, with some of it certainly ending up in a saleroom or finding an ignominious resting place in the attic simply because Auntie couldn't be bothered to keep it polished. He was right, of course".

The wisdom of Auchinleck's decision is vindicated by the way in which the modern armies of India and Pakistan have maintained (in many instances expanded) the traditions which they inherited in 1947. However, there was one particular disadvantage to the policy of leaving everything in India and Pakistan. The Regimental Associations, comprising mainly retired officers who had served at one time or another in the pre-1947 Indian Army, continued to organise annual dinners, luncheons, garden parties, and similar social events, where they and their wives could meet and renew old friendships. After Partition, the great majority of these gatherings took place in or near London, usually at one of the capital's well-known clubs, or in the Mess of one of the London-based regiments of the British Army. There was an understandable wish by each Association's membership to have at least a token display of regimental artefacts on these special occasions. In most cases this was simply not possible, but the 5th Maharatta Light Infantry found an interesting solution to the problem.

During the second world war, the silver owned by each battalion of the Maharatta Light Infantry was deposited for safe-keeping at the regimental depôt, at Belgaum. It was a formidable collection. The MLI traced its roots back to 1768 when the East India Company first recruited local men to guard its trading station on the island of Bombay. Over the following century and a half they were succeeded by generations of soldiers recruited from Maharastra, the region stretching eastwards from the Bombay coastal strip to the tableland of the Deccan and the Western Ghats. They served the Company in almost every campaign in India and, later, fought for the Crown in China, Abyssinia, Afghanistan, Burma and British East Africa.

All of the MLI's six immediate forebears (which were brought together under the post-WWI reorganisations) fought with great bravery in the Mesopotamia campaign of 1915-1918. With such a long history of active service in its lineage, it is not surprising that the regiment had acquired many fine and historically interesting pieces of silver. At Partition, the MLI was allotted to India and, being a one-class regiment, did not suffer the break up of sub-units which would have occurred if there had been Muslims in its ranks.

Some years later, the Regimental Association submitted a request to their successors in India, asking whether they might be given, or at least loaned, some of the items from their inventory of silver. The senior officers of the MLI understood the reasons for the request but, while sympathetic, rejected it. Instead they did something which, with hindsight, was eminently sensible. At their own expense, they commissioned the manufacture, by Indian silversmiths, of identical copies of eight of the pieces in their possession. They were presented, as outright gifts, to the Regimental Association.

For many years these reproduction pieces were a focal point to every event at which former MLI officers gathered. By 1996 the passing years had reduced the membership of the Association to a level at which the care and security of the pieces

An item of Mess silver, of Indian manufacture, which surfaced a few years ago in an antiques shop in Sussex. A passing member of The Punjab Frontier Force Association was delighted to acquire it. Depicted is a Lance *Naik* in Field Service Order, and the plate on the pedestal states *Bequeathed to the Officer's Mess, 4th Punjab Infantry (Punjab Frontier Force), by Lt Col Lewis Ernest Cooper who commanded the regiment for two years prior to his death on 9th February 1905.* How and when the piece was brought to England will never be known. A similar (possibly identical) statuette is in the collection of the 9th Battalion (Wilde's), Frontier Force Regiment, Pakistan Army. Photo: Major F W S Taylor.

could no longer be assured. The decision was made to seek a permanent home for them. In June of that year they were donated to the National Army Museum, London, where they now form part of that institution's very large collection of Indian Army artefacts.

Not every unit was willing to obey Auckinleck's instruction. Amongst the minority was The Kumaon Regiment. The officers of its regular battalions decided to send their Mess silver to the United Kingdom. How and why they reached that decision is not recorded, and the officers who made it are no longer alive. However, the emotions of the time can be imagined. They had lived with these treasures since their earliest Subaltern days. Many of their brother officers had died during the recent war. Those of the 4th Battalion had endured the horrors of the disastrous Malaya campaign and the subsequent three and a half years of captivity in Japanese hands. Some lay buried in unmarked jungle graves, a fact which gave added poignancy to any item of silver inscribed with their names. Then, while still in their late twenties, thirties, and early forties, the surviving

The hardy intelligent mule was for decades a key element in Great Britain's ability to wage war in areas inaccessible to horses, camels, elephants, or, later, motorised transport. This finely crafted model was made in 1929 by the Goldsmiths and Silversmiths Company, London, and was once the property of the 17th (Nowshera) Mountain Battery, Royal Artillery. It was one of two pieces selected in 1947 by the new Armies of India and Pakistan as gifts (from the collections which they were inheriting) to the Royal Artillery Mess, Woolwich. The presentations commemorated all of the past shared services of British and Indian gunners. This mule is carrying the wheels and axle of the 2.75 inch screw gun introduced in 1914. The 2.75 required eight mules to transport all the component parts of the gun and its ammunition.
Photo: The Royal Artillery Institution.

officers were being told that their careers in India were finished.

Major Tom Prentice, who was serving with The Kumaon Regiment at the time of Partition, takes up the story. "For a few years these items were on the tables at our (Regimental Association) Dinners and Lunches but, as time went on, the feeling grew that it would have been better to have handed them over to the inheritors of our 'family'. As part of the new Indian Army, our old regiment was expanded to more than twenty battalions and three of our officers - Thimayya, Shrinagesh and Raina - went on to be Chiefs of the Army Staff. They also, in quick succession, were appointed Colonel of the Regiment.

We could take a lot of pride and satisfaction from all of that and so, some years later, the silver was returned to India, to the modern regimental centre at Ranikhet, Uttar Pradesh. In response, the officers of the regiment in India then sent us a centre-piece and some miniature flag-stands which they had had made for us, and these are displayed at our Association Lunches to this day. Though not of the value of the original silver, it is the thought that counts. I have no doubt that our decision to

send everything back was the right one, as the Auk would have agreed.

There was only one thing we did not send back, and that was a Victorian standing salt, on a silver plinth together with a silver spoon bearing the regimental crest. This large centrepiece was the pride of our 1st Battalion (Russell's), and I know that Colonel Trotter, the last British CO, had quite a job in getting HM Customs to release it when it arrived in this country in 1948. For some time it was displayed at The Airborne Club, in Whitehall (the 1st Battalion became a parachute unit in mid-1946), but it is now on loan to the National Army Museum. I cannot recall why this particular piece was retained. I believe it was used for a long time at the ceremony when new recruits were attested and when they 'ate salt' as a symbolic gesture of allegiance to the Queen Empress and, later, the King Emperor. Our soldiers were 'true to their salt'. Perhaps someone felt that the Imperial overtones were too strong for this piece to find a permanent home in modern India. I simply don't know".

Silver was not the only Mess asset to be affected by

Auckinleck's instruction. There were also the various funds under the control or management of each unit's officers. Some related to the welfare of all the men in the regiment or battalion (and their dependent families), but others were associated solely with the running of the Mess. The accumulated sums of money were often substantial. The Maharatta Light Infantry had a British Officers Loan Fund to which each officer made a monthly contribution, and to which he could then apply for financial support whenever he had special need. In 1947 this fund, along with all the others, was left intact for the future benefit of the Indian officers.

Also handed over to their successors by the outgoing British officers were the Polo Funds. Even in pre-war India, Polo was a comparatively expensive sport. Four-man teams were fielded by a great many units and they took part in competitions held throughout India. The cavalry regiments took a leading role, and most cavalry officers personally owned two or more ponies. All ranks followed closely the inter-unit rivalries on the Polo field and the degree of horsemanship displayed by the competitors. A cavalry regiment's reputation depended heavily upon its success in Polo, and this in part justified the high cost of transporting men and ponies from one match or tournament to another. These expenses, and the wages of the civilian *syces* (grooms), were all paid by the British officers.

The Indian cavalry regiments had remarkable histories. Several of them had been formed hurriedly in 1857, as local *ad hoc*

forces, when the Great Sepoy Mutiny erupted. Only later did they become part of the official establishment, but they retained or were granted subsidiary titles which perpetuated the names of the officers who had raised them or first commanded them in action. Probyn's Horse, Hodson's Horse and Watson's Horse are three familiar examples.

Eight years before the Mutiny, Lieutenant Sam Browne raised the 2nd Punjab Cavalry for service on the Punjab frontier. Despite subsequent changes to its numerical designation, the regiment was always titled Sam Browne's Cavalry. In August 1858, in hand-to-hand fighting at Seerporah, he won his Victoria Cross and lost his left arm. The disability caused him to design a belt which allowed him to wear both a sword and a pistol - whether mounted or dismounted - and still have his right hand free. Other officers followed his example and today his name continues to be the familiar description of an item of military kit used throughout the world.

Sam Browne's own belt, which incorporates all the features to be seen in its modern equivalent, can be seen in The Raj Exhibition at the National Army Museum, Chelsea.

Ten or twenty years from now, all personal memories of the pre-1947 Indian Army will have gone forever. Its traditions live on - in the regiments of the two armies which succeeded it - but the tangible record of individual valour, sacrifice and pride is best preserved in its collections of silver.

Chapter Five

Indian Army Silver

The India of the 18th and early 19th centuries produced a number of exceptionally talented young officers. By today's standards, some of their achievements during those early years of conquest were astounding. They were remarkable men, hardy and courageous almost beyond belief. Much has been written of the "romance" of the Indian horsed warrior, and it is a story characterised by the life of one such. His name was James Skinner.

Skinner's Horse (1st Duke of York's Own Cavalry)

His father was a Scot, one of the many adventurers· and soldiers-of-fortune who went to India in the 1700s to seek their fortunes. He entered into a liaison with a fourteen year-old high-born Rajputanee girl, a prisoner of war. Later she bore him six children, two of whom, James and Robert, became professional mercenary soldiers. James took service in the regular army of the Maharajah of Scinde (Scindia), a prince who at that time was allied with the French and with the Maharattas, and was therefore an opponent of the British.

In 1802 the Maharajah declared war on the East India Company and dismissed those of his officers who were of British descent (their loyalty being judged uncertain). James was one of them, and for some months he had no employment. During this time the British forces under Lord Lake fought a series of successful battles which resulted in large numbers of Maharatta soldiers deciding to switch sides.

One of their cavalry groups, of eight hundred horsemen, offered to swear allegiance to the Company but with the proviso that *Sikander Sahib* (their name for Skinner) should also be accepted into British service, as their leader. This posed a problem because he was of mixed race and could not therefore be granted a commission in East India Company service.

A solution was found by the creation of a new unit, additional to the Army of Bengal's standing establishment, and it was given the title Captain Skinner's Corps of Irregular Cavalry. He accepted Lake's offer of command on the condition that he would never be required to draw his sword against his late master, the Maharajah. From this *ad hoc* arrangement emerged one of India's most illustrious regiments.

By 1814 his force had grown to three thousand men, divided equally into three corps. He himself commanded the 1st Corps, his brother Robert the 2nd Corps, and a Major Fraser the third (it was soon disbanded). Every single feature of Skinner's force was the epitome of *esprit de corps*. Following the example of a Rajput Princely legend, they swore "to win or die". Before battle, they smeared saffron on their faces and wrapped themselves in yellow cloaks. These were "the clothes of the dead". They vowed either to die in them or to remove them only after emerging from the fight victorious. Known as "the Yellow Men", they gained a fearsome reputation.

They served in many of the major 19th century wars in India and overseas, mainly under the titles 1st Bengal Lancers and 3rd Bengal Cavalry. Most of the Bengal cavalry regiments

The magnificent Charging Sowar centrepiece was made in 1912 by the Goldsmiths & Silversmiths Company, and stands 23 inches overall. A plate fixed to the hidden side of the pedestal states *Presented to the officers, 1st (Duke of York's Own) Lancers (Skinner's Horse), by the British officers.* The Urdu inscription on the front plate is the regimental motto which translates freely as *With the bravery of man and the help of God.* Silver *cartouches* at each end of the pedestal are engraved with the regiment's crest and its Battle Honours. Skinner's Horse is today fully armoured, but pride in its roots is enshrined in this *sowar* (described as "charging with lance in hand and the look of the Devil in his eyes"). The manufacture is exceptionally skilled, most of the weight of silver being supported only by the horse's hind feet. Photo: RHQ Skinner's Horse.

joined the mutineers when trouble came in 1857, but the fierce loyalties founded by James Skinner held firm.

Through no fault of their own, they saw no serious action in WWI. In 1922, they were unified as a single regiment - 1st Duke of York's Own Skinner's Horse. It was amongst the first to prepare for WWII by converting, in 1939, to the mechanised reconnaissance role (saying goodbye to its horses and learning to operate light trucks). It was ironic, therefore, that the regiment's first action of the war was an engagement in Italian East Africa with Italian-officered colonial cavalry. The Italians bravely charged, but were soon beaten off. The triumphant *sowars* rounded up the loose horses and, for a while, experienced the

Standing 16 inches high and 10 inches wide at its base, this beautiful lidded jug is one of the most prized possessions of Skinner's Horse. Inscribed on the lid are the words *In commemoration of the Afghan campaign 1879-1880 and the march from Kabul to Kandahar, 3rd Bengal Cavalry, by the officers who were on service at the time in the regiment.* The horses are drawing a Roman chariot (matched by another, on the hidden side), and the finial is the allegorical figure of Winged Victory. The piece carries English marks, but details are not available. Photo: RHQ.

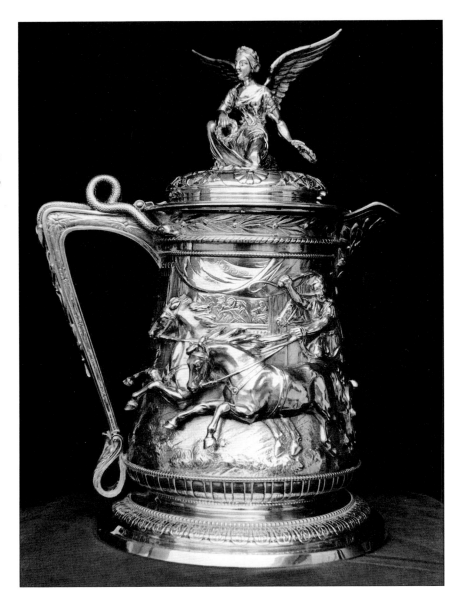

pleasure of being back in the saddle.

The Italian officer in command was Baron Amadeo Guillet. Years later he was appointed his country's Ambassador to the Republic of India. There he was welcomed by all Indian cavalrymen as a fellow spirit, and was made an honorary member of the 4th Indian Division Association (with which Skinner's Horse had served in East Africa).

The full history of the regiment is recorded in *Sworn to Die*, by Lieutenant Colonel M A R Skinner (Lancer International, Delhi, 1984). Nearly two hundred years after its founding, Skinner's Horse is still an integral element in the Indian Army. Based at Gwalior, it is equipped with Russian-made T72 main battle tanks.

In 1947 its Indian officers inherited all of the silver which the regiment had acquired over the preceding decades and, thanks to the present Commanding Officer, Colonel Praveen Bakshi, it is possible to illustrate some of those wonderful pieces in this book.

The Scinde Horse (14th Prince of Wales's Own Cavalry)

Major Donald McIntosh, an officer who was serving in India at the time of Partition, explains what happened in his own regiment. Raised in 1839 as an irregular frontier unit and described as "wild picturesque fellows, very like stage *banditti*", the Scinde Horse came to fame in the 1840s under the aggressive

leadership of another remarkable young officer, Lieutenant John Jacob. His successors retained their Jacob's Horse title until the amalgamations of 1921.

"It was decided that regimental and Mess funds and property would remain with the regiment. This included all our silver. It was also agreed that a part of the Polo Fund should be remitted to England to finance a Regimental Association. In the event, the new Indian Government soon banned the export of all foreign currencies and our first Indian Commandant was frustrated in his attempt to implement this agreement. Other regiments were more successful in their transfer of British Officers' funds and, in many instances, these funds have been set up as Trusts to finance the visits of present-day Indian and Pakistan military personnel to the United Kingdom".

One sad footnote to the great historical events of 1947 was the fate of the animals owned by officers leaving India that year. Whether they were taking an enforced early retirement or making a transfer to British Army service, many officers were faced with the dilemma of what to do with their dogs, their horses and their polo ponies. Rather than abandon them or sell them to local dealers, they chose to have them put down. There are several moving accounts of individuals who, instead of handing the unpleasant task to a third party but as an act of loyalty to an old friend, personally shot their horse or their dog. Leaving India was painful in more ways than one.

The Indian Staff Corps

Items of engraved silver will be seen from time to time which make mention of the Madras, Bengal or Bombay Staff Corps. They were established in 1861, amalgamated in 1891 as the Indian Staff Corps, and disbanded in 1903 under the Kitchener reforms of that year. The officers concerned were not necessarily Staff officers in the usual meaning, that is to say, trained to support a senior commander in matters of planning and administration. Throughout the second half of the 19th century, *every* regimental appointment was treated as a Staff appointment. The system was intended to overcome problems connected with pay and allowances, promotions and seniority.

Its weakness was the inclusion in the Staff Corps of large numbers of officers who had ceased to have any connection with soldiering. They were employed in a variety of administrative posts which otherwise could have been filled equally well by qualified civilians.

At the age of fifty-five, having received automatic "time served" promotions in the meanwhile, they could return to their regiments. As a consequence, elderly and unfit officers of senior rank, who had not soldiered actively for ten or twenty years, could obtain command of troops in the field. The Second Afghan War, 1878-1880, demonstrated the weakness of such arrangements.

By 1 January 1864, when the scheme came into effect, the individual future careers of officers made temporarily or permanently redundant had been settled. Many departed India's shores for ever. The more adventurous spirits went to countries where the discovery of gold, or the opening of new territories, or the raising of local units to fight indigenous native peoples, offered the prospect of adventure and income. The most frequent destinations were Australia (the gold fields), New Zealand (the Maori Land Wars), and North America (the opening of the Midwest).

They did not go gladly. A later account, by General Sir Horace Anderson, gives us a brief impression of what happened to the silver of the 1st Bombay Grenadiers. "The old officers of my regiment allowed a small quantity of plate to be given to the Staff Corps, in their name, under the new organisation. In many other cases, however, the old officers sold their plate, etc, and divided the proceeds amongst themselves. The officers of the original Grenadiers sold theirs. The Government of India tried to stop this, but they had no power. When I was appointed to the 1st Grenadiers, the regiment was very badly off for plate. Only two dozen silver forks and spoons were handed over in 1864 by the old regiment".

It is fair to assume that officers departing for new lives retained one or two items as a memento of their time in India. There is at least one instance of a piece once owned by a pre-Mutiny regiment having surfaced in Australia. The report is sufficient to encourage the belief that other examples of Indian military silver from the first half of the 19th century may still be found in parts of the world where otherwise they might not be expected.

In this context, it is worth noting that unemployed officers had begun to leave India two and three years *before* the reorganisations of 1863-1864. Many went in the immediate aftermath of the Mutiny and sought new employment elsewhere. Several are said to have joined Cavour and Garibaldi and, in company with former officers of the British Army, served in the campaigns to free Italy from French and Austrian occupation. Further research could reveal some intersting personal adventures.

Not all of the pieces in the Skinner's Horse collection were inherited from the British. This attractive casket was presented in the 1950s by the founder's descendents, Lieutenant Colonel & Mrs M A R Skinner and family, on the occasion of the regiment's 150th anniversary. The lion-mask handled drawers in the base contain the regimental history in two volumes. Colonel James Skinner and his first Adjutant, Captain Fraser, are depicted in the left-hand panel. Photo: Skinner's Horse.

Almost certainly of local (Indian) manufacture, this piece is engraved *Commander in Chief's Cup, won by 3rd Bengal Cavalry, 1889.* It is typical of hundreds of such trophies which at one time or another were objects of fierce competition and inter-unit rivalry, but whose origins are now forgotten. It is likely that this example was awarded for tent-pegging or a similar mounted skill. Photo: RHQ Skinner's Horse.

37th Dogras

From time to time there have been instances of regimental silver becoming the subject of contested ownership. One such dispute had its roots in the WWI campaign to eject the Turks from Mesopotamia. The military forces deployed in the field comprised mainly units of the Indian Army, with some British Army units which were already stationed in India when hostilities commenced. They were augmented by units from the United Kingdom, many of them Territorial Army. It often happened that a bond of friendship developed between these units during their shared time in camp or on active service.

One such bond was that between the 37th Dogras and the Territorial soldiers of the 1/5th Battalion of The Buffs (East Kent Regiment). They came together in 1915, at Basra, as elements of the 35th Indian Infantry Brigade. The third and fourth battalions in the Brigade changed from time to time as other units came and went, but the Dogras and the Buffs fought alongside each other through to the end of the war. The cultural differences between them could not have been greater, the Buffs coming from the towns and villages of "the garden of England", the Dogras from the hills and mountain valleys of Jammu and northern Punjab.

In 1919, the officers of the British battalion, commanded by Lieutenant Colonel John Body DSO, presented to the officers of the 37th Dogras a silver statuette of a Buff soldier. To quote an archival source, it commemorated "the very real comradeship which existed between the two units, as strong between rank and file as between the officers, a comradeship tested by many a tough fight on the long road to Baghdad and beyond".

A pretty chutney pot, made by Charles, Nephew & Company, of Calcutta, held privately in Australia. It was presented *circa* 1847 to the Mess of the 69th Regiment of Bengal Native Infantry by Captain G Rankin. The regiment was one of those disarmed and disbanded in May 1857, when its loyalty was questioned. Photo: Mr G K Byrne, Burwood, Victoria.

As a former Dogra officer, Colonel Rex Mace, has recently said, "the episode was a fine example of the friendship which existed between many units of the British and Indian Armies and which was perpetuated by a presentation of silver".

In 1929, the past and serving officers of the 37th Dogras, by then retitled 1st Battalion (Prince of Wales's Own), 17th Dogra Regiment, commissioned the manufacture of a second statuette, this being a figurine of a Dogra soldier in Mesopotamia campaign kit. Purchased for their own Mess, it matched the piece received earlier from Lieutenant Colonel Body and his brother officers. There the matter rested until the great upheavals of 1947.

The rules concerning the treatment of Mess silver at the time of Partition have already been described. However, there are exceptions to every rule. The then Colonel of the 1st/17th Dogras, Major General F L Nicholson CB DSO MC, wrote to the Colonel of The Buffs, Major General The Honourable W P Scarlett CB MC, expressing regret that the granting of Independence might break the tie between their two regiments. He said it was "the wish of his officers that the figure (of the Buffs soldier) should be presented to The Buffs for safe keeping and as a lasting record of a great, memorable and much valued friendship". The statuette was brought to England and delivered to The Buffs, but subsequently it was given to the National Army Museum when the regiment was amalgamated.

In the meantime, the 1st/17th Dogras had given the Dogra statuette to the Dogra Regimental Association (the membership of which comprised mainly former regimental officers resident in the United Kingdom) "in memory of old associations". Thus, by disparate routes, both objects were in the United Kingdom, one in a museum and the other in the custody of the Association's committee.

Years passed until, in 1988, the officers of the 1st/17th Dogras' modern successors, the 7th Battalion, Mechanised Infantry Regiment (1st Dogra), rediscovered the whereabouts of two items of silver which they regarded as rightfully theirs. Correspondence began to flow between the two countries, all of it directed at the question of ownership.

After eight years of discussion between the National Army Museum, the Regiment, and the Regimental Association, it was agreed that both statuettes should be returned to India. One of the Association's members took the opportunity of a planned visit to Delhi to deliver them in person.

The Commanding Officer of the 7th MIR was so delighted with the outcome that he issued a Special Order of the Day. The two metallic soldiers were once again standing shoulder to shoulder in the Officers' Mess.

It seemed that all was sweetness and light. At this point, however, the Association received a letter from the Commanding Officer of another Dogra battalion, the 3rd. Written in "forthright language", it laid claim to two other pieces of Dogra silver still held in England. They consisted of yet another pair of figurines which commemorated periods of high achievement in the regiment's history, and specifically the services of what had once been the 41st Dogras.

Having negotiated for eight years the fate of the 1st Battalion's silver, the members of the Association were now faced with this final decision. It had been their intention to donate these last remaining items to the National Army Museum's superb collection of Indian Army silver where they would provide a permanent memorial in this country to the Dogras' past services. The dilemma was debated at length when, on 20 June 1996, the Association held its Annual General Meeting in London. The result was an almost unanimous vote to return the figurines to their original home in India. That, happily, is where they now reside.

26th Baluchistan Regiment

There has never been any dispute regarding yet another object having an Anglo-Indian military provenance. It is a silver figurine of a Baluch piper in full Parade Dress and is known, simply and logically, as The Baluchistan Piper. It stands nine-and-a-half inches in height and is mounted upon a wooden base to which is fixed a silver plaque inscribed "From The 26th Baluchistan Regiment, To The 1st Battalion, Gordon Highlanders, 1896". Bearing London marks for that same year, it currently resides in Catterick, in the Officers' Mess of the 1st Battalion, The Highlanders.

The inscrutable presentation wording conceals an unusual incident in the story of martial music. The pipes, in one form or another, have been played in India since the earliest times but, in 1894, the officers of the 26th Baluchistan Regiment became aware that their own pipers were not as skilled as those of other units. The cause for concern was that they were due to perform at the great Viceroy's Durbar at Lahore, in November of that year. The 1st Gordons were stationed nearby, and an invitation was extended that their principal musicians might be loaned for instructional purposes.

It seems that Pipe Major Horne and Piper Sanderson worked to good effect in training the Baluch pipers. According to a contemporary report, "they improved so much they now play on route-march, and around the Officers' Mess table (on Dinner Nights)". The Gordons also loaned their Drum Major and senior Drummer Corporal, with equally beneficial results for the Corps of Drums.

Eighteen months later, as a token of their gratitude, the officers of the 26th presented this centrepiece to the officers of the 1st Gordons. For insurance purposes it is presently valued at four thousand pounds, a figure which makes it not only an unusual example of inter-regimental friendship but also one of the most valuable memorials of all time to what was, essentially, a series of music lessons. It accompanies the battalion on all its travels and, in recent decades has been displayed on the Mess table in (amongst other places) Borneo, Cyprus, Northern Ireland and Belize.

34th Sikh Pioneers

Several famous Indian Army regiments were permanently disbanded between WWI and WWII. Amongst those with the longest and most distinguished histories, and therefore the largest accumulations of silver, were the Sikh Pioneers, the Madras Pioneers, and the Bombay Pioneers, all of which disappeared in 1933. A fourth regiment, the Hazara Pioneers, went at the same time, but that was a much younger regiment (having been raised only in 1904).

Pioneers have been described as "a superior kind of infantryman, as expert with the rifle as with the pick and shovel". More formally, they were "trained to carry out those military works requiring for their construction training less expert than Engineers but more skilled than infantry". By 1933, the role of the Pioneer regiments and the regiments of Sappers & Miners had merged to the point at which they were almost identical. The Pioneers were then disbanded and never reactivated.

One very unusual relic of the 3rd Battalion of the 34th Sikh Pioneers is the decorated piece of rock illustrated on page 81. In the closing weeks of 1919 the battalion was part of a force sent

The combination of axe and rifle tell us that this *sepoy* can only be a Pioneer. He is in fact a member of the 34th Sikh Pioneers, a regiment which between 1911 and 1919 served continuously alongside 1st Battalion, The Manchester Regiment. They formed part of the Jullundur Brigade, 3rd (Lahore) Division, and there was a close bond of friendship between them. They fought on the Western Front (1914-1915), in Mesopotamia (1916-1918), and in Palestine at the end of the war. When the Pioneers were disbanded, they presented this statuette to the Manchesters as a farewell gift. Today it is in regular use on Dinner Nights in the Officers' Mess of the 1st Battalion, The King's Regiment. Photo: Museum of the Manchesters, Ashton under Lyne.

into the Mahsud country, Waziristan, to put down a major insurrection. On 18 December the leading brigade of the Derajat column, commanded by Major General Andrew Skeen CMG, pitched camp on the open desolate Palosina plain. It was intended to force a crossing of the Tank Zam river, establish piquets on the far side, and then push deeper into the tribal territory of the Mahsuds.

This plan was abandoned after two days of severe enemy sniping. Skeen decided instead to fortify Black Hill, a feature on his own side of the river, and to use that as his future base. He gave the task to Captain T M Catterson-Smith, 3rd/34th Sikh Pioneers.

Catterson-Smith's two companies began their work on the morning of 21 December. They planned to fortify the peak of the hill with a loop-holed circular *sangar* of stone and sandbags, surrounded by barbed wire. What they could not know was that this was the morning the Mahsud leaders had chosen to make a coordinated attack on the Palosina camp. They hoped to repeat the success of their grandfathers who, in 1860 and at the same spot, had rushed a British camp. Those tribesmen had caused heavy casualties and captured many rifles. Now the Mahsuds had assembled 10,000 riflemen and knifemen, and skilfully hidden them in dead ground all around the camp.

The signal for their attack would be the sight of a second but smaller Mahsud group - a thousand strong - swarming over the top of Black Hill, 1500 yards from the camp. That was where the initial rush was made, and the inexperienced troops assigned to protect the Pioneers quickly ran for their lives. The two hundred Pioneers were on their own, outnumbered five to one by a fanatical enemy who was already getting in amongst them with the knife.

The first attack was driven off but the Mahsuds did not give up. The partly-built *sangar* wall was only knee high, and several times they forced their way inside. For two hours the fight swayed one way and then the other and, in the meantime, the 10,000 men of the enemy's main force waited in vain for the signal to attack the camp. When it did not come, group after group began to disperse and move off in the direction of their various villages. None wanted to rush the main camp and then find themselves isolated and alone.

A relief force from the camp reached Black Hill at three in the afternoon. Catterson-Smith and his three officers (Lieutenants R Wycherley, N Loder, and Australian C R C Lundy MC) were all wounded, and half of their men were casualties. Despite the hazards of getting wounded men down the steep rocky sides of the hill under continuing Mahsud long-range rifle

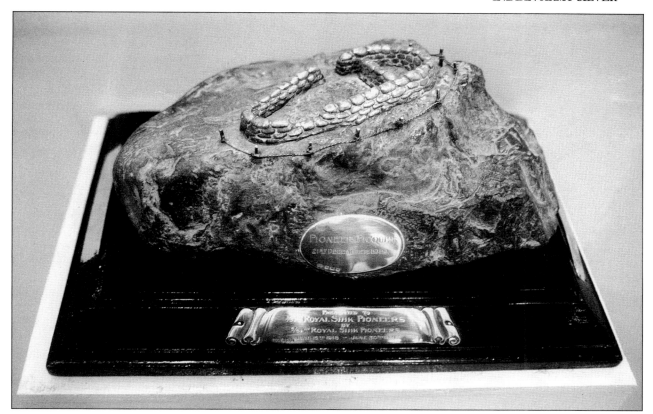

The Pioneer Piquet Centrepiece, simple but emotive memorial to the two companies of Sikh Pioneers who fought their desperate battle, on Black Hill, Waziristan, on 21 December 1919. It was brought to England in 1947, then passed to the National Army Museum where it stayed for some years. Subsequently it was returned to India and is now displayed in the Officers' Mess of the Sikh Light Infantry, at Fategarh. Photo: Major R P Watkin.

fire, they were all brought away safely.

Catterson-Smith died of his wounds some time later, in Rawalpindi hospital, but not before his recommendation for a DSO had been approved. His three subalterns were decorated, Wycherley and Loder receiving the Military Cross and Lundy a bar to his. Twelve Indian officers and other ranks also were granted awards for their gallantry during those few mad hours on Black Hill.

One of the bravest men on the mountain that day was a doctor, Captain B L Gupta. He was seen moving from one casualty to another, outside the *sangar* wall, treating their wounds and ignoring the nearby Mahsuds. He was one of several officers ordered by General Skeen's staff to submit a summary of their actions so that an overall account could be sent to GHQ Delhi. The doctor's report was a masterpiece of candour and brevity.

"To OC 3/34th Sikh Pioneers, Palosina Camp, Waziristan. From Captain B L Gupta, Indian Medical Service. Sir, I have the honour to report that on December 21st, 1919, I did very good work. I have the honour to be, Sir, your obedient servant. B L Gupta, Captain".

Having heard the evidence of eye-witnesses, higher command agreed with this self-assessment and authorised the award of the Military Cross.

On 22 December, the day after the battle, another party of men from the 3rd/34th was able to finish the work of constructing the piquet. They brought down one of the stones from the *sangar*, and this formed the base for the memorial piece illustrated above. When the 3rd/34th was disbanded in June 1921, it was presented to the sister 1st Battalion, 34th Royal Sikh Pioneers.

The Gurkhas

The breaking up of the Indian Army in 1947, forming it into two completely new armies, was further complicated by the dilemma of what should be done with the Gurkha regiments (of which there were at that time ten, each having two regular battalions plus one or two war-raised battalions which had not yet been disbanded). The rank and file were mostly subjects of the King of Nepal, so their status as soldiers employed in the service of the British Crown was unique.

Nepal had embarked, in the early 1800s, on a policy of territorial expansion which brought it into conflict with the East India Company. Three expeditions were mounted by the British between 1814 and 1816, the third being successful in establishing peace between the two nations. The Treaty of Sagauli confirmed the boundaries and other political matters but, most importantly, it established the principle that the Company (and subsequently the Crown) could recruit Nepalese men for military service.

This formal agreement had in fact been anticipated by several months when, in April 1815, Lieutenant Frederick Young was ordered to visit the camps in which Nepalese prisoners of war were being held, at Nahan, in Sirmoor. He called for volunteers to join him in forming the Sirmoor Battalion (much later, the 2nd King Edward VII's Own Gurkha Rifles). Frederick Young remained Commandant throughout the next twenty-eight years.

From this strange beginning, a friendship between the British and the Gurkhas grew and expanded and has endured for nearly two hundred years. The special *ethos* of the Gurkha regiments can be studied elsewhere, it is enough to know that it was (and still is) highly distinctive and always a matter of the fiercest pride. In 1947, therefore, the question of what to do with them was a topic which attracted much forceful comment.

It was decided that six of the ten regiments should be allocated to the new Indian Army. They were the 1st, 3rd, 4th, 5th, 8th and 9th Gurkha Rifles. They retained their former numbers but lost their titles of distinction (the references to Royalty being no longer appropriate). In 1950, the authorities in India introduced a new style for all Sanskrit words. The spelling of Gurkha had been adopted by the British in 1891 (previously it had been Goorkha). Under the new Indian rules it changed again, this time to Gorkha.

The other four regiments were transferred to the British Army on 1 January 1948. They too retained their pre-1948 numbers but, in the case of the three most junior, were later given new titles of distinction. They were the 2nd King Edward VII's Own Gurkha Rifles (The Sirmoor Rifles), the 6th Queen Elizabeth's Own Gurkha Rifles, the 7th Duke of Edinburgh's Own Gurkha Rifles, and the 10th Princess Mary's Own Gurkha Rifles. They have all now been replaced by The Royal Gurkha Rifles, consisting of just two battalions, plus three independent rifle companies serving with British battalions which are short of establishment.

The six regiments which remained in India retained their silver *in situ*, while the four which departed India's shores for ever took theirs to their new stations.

2nd King Edward VII's Own Gurkha Rifles (The Sirmoor Rifles)

To illustrate the history of Gurkha silver, the example of the regiment raised by Lieutenant Young in 1815 may be taken as broadly representative of the whole. The accompanying photographs are reproduced by kind permission of The Trustees of The Sirmoor Rifles Association (UK) Trust.

The Sirmoor Battalion began to demonstrate its fighting qualities in 1826, winning its first Battle Honour at Bhurtpore. Twenty years later it took part in the First Sikh War, making notable contributions to the Battles of Aliwal and Sobraon (where its Commandant, Captain John Fisher, was killed), but it was in the long hot summer of 1857 that its reputation was truly made.

Delhi was in the hands of the mutineers and a scratch force commanded by Colonel Archdale Wilson was ordered to remove them. The operation involved a siege of many weeks, the British forces constantly attempting to improve their positions in preparation for a final assault, the mutineers repeatedly sallying out from the city's walls to drive them away. The attackers fought with the fury of men outraged by the stories of what had been done to European women and children. The defenders fought with the desperation of men who knew what would happen to them if they were captured.

Colonel Wilson lacked the guns and men to surround the city completely. Instead, he concentrated his force against the stretch of wall on the northern perimeter, between the Water Bastion, the Kashmir Gate and the Kabul Gate. A key element was a large property known as Hindu Rao's House, a strongly-built structure which dominated the approaches to the wall. It was occupied by one British Army unit (the 1st Battalion of the 60th Rifles, or King's Royal Rifle Corps), one Indian (the Corps of Guides Infantry), and one Gurkha (The Sirmoor Battalion). During the three months leading up to Wilson's assault, on 14 September, they beat off twenty-six attacks (most of which involved hand-to-hand fighting).

The mutual respect which developed between the British soldiers, the Guides and the Gurkhas during those weeks of shared danger and suffering at Hindu Rao's House was later marked in several ways. The most notable, as far as the Sirmoorees were concerned, was the granting by Queen Victoria of a unique symbol known simply at the time as "The Truncheon". It replaced the privilege of carrying a third Colour which was awarded for their services at Delhi, this distinction being lost in 1858 when the battalion was renamed The Sirmoor Rifle Regiment (Rifle regiments do not have Colours).

The Queen's Truncheon (it was given this extended name in 1953) is a bronze staff embellished with silver bands and motifs, engraved with the Honour "Delhi 1857". Six feet in length, it unscrews into four sections, the original intention being that, in an emergency, each part could be carried in the knapsack of a soldier.

Normally it is kept in a glass case in the Quarter Guard, but on special occasions it is marched to the Officers' Mess where it is handed over to the Adjutant. He unscrews the top half and fits it into a table centrepiece decorated with some of the campaign and gallantry medals earned by members of the regiment. The base of the centrepiece is embellished with four silver figurines of officers and riflemen in the uniforms of different periods. One of the figurines is a Gurkha soldier in the style of uniform worn when the Sirmoor Battalion was raised in 1815, and is illustrated on the facing page. A fifth statuette fits into the top socket of the base when it is not being used to accommodate and support the Truncheon.

The Queen's Truncheon is accorded all the honours of a Queen's Colour, and new recruits lay a hand upon it while swearing their allegiance to the Crown.

Sirmoor was found to be unhealthy as the site for a permanent depôt. It was moved to Dehra Dun, and there it stayed from 1815 to early 1948. An older Mess building was torn down in the 1890s and replaced with accommodation of better quality. The following views (pages 84-85), taken in 1907, illustrate the style of *decor* to be seen in some permanent Indian regimental Messes of that period - part country house, part gentlemen's club, part hunting lodge and part museum.

The Dehra Dun Mess did not alter radically during the following forty years, but the sombre Victorian fabrics and colours were replaced and a generally more comfortable *ambience* created.

The wall display at the end of the dining table (page 85) is of interest. Although at first glance a cabinet, it is in fact part of a long table, fixed vertically and fitted with brackets to support a collection of Indian and Tibetan silver jugs. This table originally formed part of the furnishings in Hindu Rao's House and, according to legend, was used by the surgeons as an operating table during the 1857 battle.

After the siege it was divided between the defending regiments, and all three sections still exist. The 60th's piece, smaller than that shown here but in excellent condition and fitted with legs, is in The Royal Green Jackets Museum at Winchester. The Sirmoor Battalion's piece is also in England, in the office of the Commandant, 1st Battalion, The Royal Gurkha Rifles, awaiting renovation. The Corps of Guides section is thought to be with The Frontier Force Regiment at Abbottabad, Pakistan. The table's original home, Hindu Rao's House, survived the battle and still stands. Much changed and expanded, it is now a hospital.

Troubles on India's North West Frontier at the turn of the century resulted in a series of major campaigns in which soldiers

The fully-assembled Queen's Truncheon and base of the 2nd Gurkha Rifles centrepiece. The second photograph (in close-up, of the Gurkha soldier standing on the right-hand corner of the pedestal, dressed in the uniform and equipment of 1815) provides an excellent indication of the overall quality of workmanship and attention to detail. Photos: The Sirmoor Rifles Trust.

Interior views of the Officers' Mess of the 2nd King Edward VII's Own Gurkha Rifles (The Sirmoor Rifles), at Dehra Dun. The photographs, taken in 1907, show the entrance hall, ante-room and dining room. It is important to distinguish between permanent Mess buildings such as this, and those facilities which are adopted temporarily as a Messing facility when a battalion is on the move. On active service, "the Officers' Mess" might be a tent, the back of a lorry, a dug-out, or simply a designated open space. Wherever and whatever it may be, "the Mess" is the place in which the officers come together to eat and relax while off duty. Precisely the same is true of the Sergeants' Mess. Photos: The Sirmoor Rifles Trust.

of the British Army and the Indian Army once again served side by side. One of these was the Tirah campaign of 1897-1898. At Dargai, the 1st Battalion, 2nd Gurkha Rifles, fought alongside the 1st Battalion, The Gordon Highlanders. After this fiercely contested action, the "Jocks" helped to carry their wounded Gurkha comrades down from the heights. The officers of the Gordons subsequently made the presentation illustrated on page 86 to commemorate that occasion. The piece is still in the possession of The Sirmoor Rifles Association Trust. In 1997 the Trustees loaned it to The Gordon Highlanders Museum, Aberdeen, where it formed part of the display organised to celebrate the centenary of the Dargai battle.

Before we leave the Gurkhas, it may be noted that the Nepal War of 1814-1816 coincided with the onset of a custom which endured for many years. At about that time, British families resident in India began to purchase great numbers of enormous tea services and excessively large trays and salvers. Some of their orders were placed with Indian silversmiths, others with firms in London.

The weight of these sets was of such a magnitude that, complete, they were almost impossible to lift. They were not in fact intended for domestic use, they were instead discreetly disguised forms of currency. In the event of a crisis, they could be melted into bullion bars which would help the family to buy protection as it fled to safety. Quite possibly there were occasions when the ploy was successful.

10th Baluch Regiment

Baluchistan is that sparsely inhabited region of deserts and mountains which forms Pakistan's western border. Although it has no natural resources, its geographical location, adjacent to the valley of the Indus, gave it a significant strategic importance during the period of British administration. It was peopled by nomadic herdsmen, oasis farmers and coastal fishermen, all members of a combative tribal society stretching from Sind (Scinde), in the east, hundreds of miles westwards into Persia (Iran). An important network of camel caravan routes sustained the Baluchi economy and, at times, the business of gun-running. Hardy and virile, the Baluchis made excellent soldiers, and the Honourable East India Company began to enlist them into the Army of Bombay in 1820.

The first such unit was recruited, surprisingly, for service at

The Dargai Centrepiece was made by William Gibson and John Longman, and is hallmarked London 1900. Photo: The Sirmoor Rifles Trust.

sea. It was the 2nd (Marine) Battalion of the 12th Regiment of Bombay Infantry. This was the period when the Company was consolidating its commercial activities in the Arabian Gulf, and it was in and around the Gulf that the new battalion spent the first three years of its existence. In the previous year, a major expedition had been mounted against the Quwasim pirate base at Ras al Khaimah. Consisting of ten Company ships and two of the Royal Navy, carrying three thousand British and Indian troops, it imposed a peace treaty on the Sheikhs of the Pirate Coast. The event laid the foundation for the next one hundred and fifty-one years of British influence and protection in what came to be known as the Trucial States.

More Baluch regiments were formed, and they gave reliable service in the newly acquired territory of Sind (Scinde), conquered by Napier in 1843. This was the first time they served under their own name, as the 1st and 2nd Belooch Regiments.

The Baluch regiment whose silver is illustrated opposite came into existence in 1858, during the Mutiny. The events at

Delhi and Lucknow overshadowed the dozens of other fights, major and minor, which broke out all over northern and central India. Baluchistan and Sind were in an unsettled state, the local peoples sensing that perhaps the British were losing their hold. In response, the officer responsible for the administration of Sind, Major John Jacob, raised an irregular force to "swizzle-stick" the restless tribesmen. Attracted by the prospects of action and good pay, his recruits were enlisted by the *sillidar* system, providing their own clothing, kit and weapons. Known as Jacob's Rifles, they proved their worth in various local clashes and, in 1861, were absorbed into the army's regular establishment as the 30th Regiment of Bombay Native Infantry (later redesignated 30th Baluch Infantry)

This photograph was taken *circa* 1902. The collection is relatively small and details of the individual pieces on display are not available, but the picture serves to confirm that this was a regiment with a fine and proper regard for itself.

Prior to WWI, some of the Baluch battalions began to

recruit men from the Mahsuds. They were known for their independence and fiery temperament, and there was some disquiet in official circles regarding their amenability to military discipline. In the event, when war came, they gave unstintingly loyal service on the Western Front and, later, in the East African campaign.

The historian Major Donovan Jackson states that they worked particularly well as scouts and snipers, situations in which they could use to the full their mountain fighting skills in concealment, silent movement and marksmanship. He tells the story of one Mahsud, a sniper who, in 1915, went out alone into no-man's-land. He found a German outpost and proceeded systematically to pick off its occupants, one by one. He shot the officer, the corporal, the sentry and the bugler before the others fled. Returning to his own lines, he reported himself to his officer and told him what he had done. "And here, Sahib, is the officer's pistol, the corporal's stripes, the sentry's rifle, and the bugler's bugle".

True or not, the tale reflects the pride felt by British officers in the tribal warriors with whom they shared the same cap badge.

The Indian Medical Service

The majority of Britons and other Europeans who went to India in the 18th and 19th centuries were civilians, and they did so in the hope and expectation of making their fortunes. They financed the railways, built the docks and harbours, created the industries and developed the country's financial and judicial structures. Some of them stayed on for five and six generations. There was one profession, however, which uniquely bridged the gulf between them and the army.

British physicians first sailed for the Orient in 1600. They were part of the group of English merchants granted authority by Queen Elizabeth to seek trade in the East Indies and China. They and their successors travelled throughout the Far East, but it was not until 1668 that they first encountered the plethora of unfamiliar diseases which were to occupy the medical profession in India for decades to come. Long after the Dutch, French and Portuguese had established their toe-holds on India's shores, the British planted the seed of their own empire on the island of Bombay.

From the outset, their numbers were depleted by a combination of an enervating climate and those infections against which they had no protection. Amongst the endemic illnesses were malaria, amoebic dysentery, typhus, smallpox and tuberculosis. The Christian cemeteries expanded greatly whenever the settlements were visited by the terrifying epidemic diseases - plague and cholera. Many newly-arrived Europeans had no chance to acquire any natural immunities before they were struck down. Those who did, the "two monsoon men", the men who came through their first two years intact, had every prospect of surviving a normal life span. And if it might be thought that those high rates of attrition prevailed only in the early decades of conquest, it is worth noting that malaria was not fully overcome until 1944. In Burma, at one period in 1942, twenty-five percent of the Allied troops were incapacitated by the disease.

The early medical and hospital arrangements were at best haphazard, at worst non-existent. In the second half of the 18th century, however, each of the three Presidencies in turn established its own regular Medical Service, with staff having fixed grades and defined rules of seniority and promotion. As an example, the Madras Medical Service, established in 1779, began with just eighteen doctors. Throughout the 19th century, they were ranked as Assistant Surgeon, Surgeon and Surgeon Major. These titles were replaced in 1896 by the equivalent ranks of Lieutenant, Captain, Major, and so on, and the three Presidency services were then brought together as the Indian Medical Service.

The IMS had two parts, a Military Branch and a Civil

The principal items of silver in the Officers' Mess collection of the 30th Baluch Regiment, photographed *circa* 1902. A year later it was renamed 130th Baluchis, and then again, under the 1922 reorganisations, as 5th Battalion, 10th Baluch Regiment (King George's Own) (Jacob's Rifles). Photograph: National Army Museum.

Branch. The former provided medical support services to the army. The latter was responsible for the complete range of national health welfare, scientific research, the creation and administration of hospitals and training colleges, and a great deal more. Those in Civil Employment could be recalled to Military Employment whenever the need arose. As Sir Bennett Hance, Director General of the IMS from 1943 to 1946, wrote: "There is no parallel in history of a medical service which is at once military, civil, political, educational, curative and preventative".

Whenever an IMS doctor was attached to a military unit he was granted honorary membership of the Officers' Mess of that unit, but he and his kind had no Messes of their own. Logically, they never acquired any Mess silver. Any item bearing the name of a member of the IMS (or one of its three predecessors) is most likely to have been an individual presentation.

Officially, the life of the IMS ended on 15 August 1947, Independence Day, but it had in effect been shrinking in size and importance for a number of years. Its civilian work had been taken over by a new Ministry of Health and its military work by the new Indian Army Medical Corps, formed in 1944.

There is only one known major piece having an IMS connection, and the names engraved around its plinth serve to indicate the enormous contribution to medical knowledge made by its members. It is a large ornate silver cup, designed and made by Carringtons, of Bond Street, London, and commissioned in 1927 by the Indian Medical Service Dinner Club.

The origins of the cup are explained by Colonel C W A Searle MD: "Unlike the RAMC, we had no Mess in India and there was no Mess in England to which we had any natural affiliation. When the three Presidency services were amalgamated, a Dinner Club was formed in London so that former members of those services could dine together on a regular annual basis. It was open also to serving IMS officers who were home on leave or attending courses.

The Club was founded by Lieutenant Colonel P J Freyer, later knighted for his services to urology, at his house at 46 Harley Street. The date was 27 March 1897, and the first dinner took place a few weeks later at the Café Monaco. Apart from the war years, 1914 to 1919, and apart from King Edward VII's mourning year of 1910, dinners were held annually at The Connaught Rooms and other London venues over the following eighty years.

In 1926 the Committee decided to buy a cup to commemorate the name of the founder, Colonel Freyer, and to record the names of the successive Chairmen and Secretaries. It was displayed as the table centre-piece when we dined, and for the rest of the year it lived in the home of the current Secretary. I had it at my own home for ten years while I was doing that job".

Diminishing membership led to the decision, in 1982, that the Club should close down. On 15 April 1983, the magnificent cup, which at that time was valued at three thousand pounds, was given into the custody of the Officers' Mess at the Royal Army Medical College, Millbank, London. The Mess was the venue that day for the final luncheon of the IMS Dinner Club. The last Chairman, Lieutenant Colonel John Walters, said: "We are delighted that, instead of standing inconspicuously in a museum show-case, it will be cherished among your other Mess silver and, when it appears on a table on Mess Nights, we hope that some of those present may be interested to read the (more than one hundred) names of famous officers of the IMS engraved upon the plinth".

He never served as Chairman or Secretary of the Dinner Club, and therefore is not named on the cup, but the best remembered officer of the Indian Medical Service was Major Ronald Ross. In 1902 he received the Nobel Prize for Medicine in recognition of his work in demonstrating, by experimenting on himself, that malaria is transmitted by mosquito bite. His achievement was ignored by the government when he left India in 1899, but later, when the world came to understand the importance of his discovery, he was showered with honours and distinctions of every kind. As an army doctor, he served in the 1886 campaign in Burma and in WWI in the Middle East.

The Auxiliary Force (India)

Like Great Britain itself, British India had a long tradition of part-time soldiering. One of the consequences of the Mutiny of 1857-1859 was a sharply increased awareness of the great vulnerability of European communities living at a distance from the main garrison towns or cantonments. In the event of another mutiny, they would be totally dependent upon their own resources to defend themselves and their property.

Several groups of armed Europeans had sprung up spontaneously while the events of 1857-1859 were in progress but, from the 1860s onwards, the Government of India gave active support to the raising of permanent part-time Volunteer units in many parts of Bengal, Madras, Bombay, Assam and Burma. The movement became increasingly formalised as the years went by. The authorities encouraged higher standards of training by providing the services of Regular officers (as Adjutants) and experienced British NCOs (as Permanent Instructors).

There was further expansion when the railway operating companies promoted the formation of Railway Battalions and encouraged their employees to attest. It was their primary role to protect India's 28,000 miles of track against sabotage or enemy action. Unlike the majority of volunteer units, the Railway Battalions comprised a high proportion of Indians and Anglo-Indians (Eurasians). This change in composition reflected the fact that, after 1925, several railway companies started to recruit Indians instead of Britons as engineers and managers.

India's tradition of part-time soldiering remained active through to 1947. In the late 18th century, as earlier fears of mutiny gradually subsided, the movement had acquired additional sporting and social strands.

There were many Volunteer units scattered across the sub-continent, but all were subject to the administration and disciplines of a central authority which, following major reforms in 1920, was entitled The Auxiliary Force (India). During both world wars, these units provided large numbers of officer and NCO candidates for the Indian Army. They were also called out, on numerous occasions, to assist the civil police in dealing with local incidents of public disorder.

All of this came to an end with the granting of Independence. The AF(I) was then disbanded. Many of its units could trace their origins back to the 1880s and beyond. During that time they had accumulated the same types of possession as those found in Regular formations - Mess furniture, pictures, ornaments, and silver. Having no natural inheritors of their traditions, they were obliged to arrange for the disposal of these treasures as best they could. This account, by Michael Garnett, tells us what happened in one of the best known of the old AF(I) units.

"I worked for a British tea company for nine years, running an estate in Assam, North East India. In 1962 I was taken ill with malaria and the company sent me to recuperate at the hill station of Shillong, capital of Assam. Shortly before I returned to duty,

The Edney Bowl *(quaiche)* and smaller matching *quaiche* were originally the property of No1 (Calcutta) Field Company RE, an element of the Auxiliary Force (India). Between 1924 and 1929, the Adjutant was Captain A J Edney RE, and he presented this Indian-made set on the expiry of his appointment. Still serving in India in 1947 - when the AF(I) was disbanded - Brigadier Edney retrieved the two pieces and took them with him to his new home in New Zealand. He presented them to the Corps of Royal New Zealand Engineers and they were used for some years as a RNZE inter-unit shooting trophy. It has since been retired from that duty and now resides in the Corps museum. The "Bowl" is 10 inches high and 15 inches wide across the handles. The *quaiche* (Gaelic) is a traditional Scottish vessel for the drinking of toasts in whiskey. Regimental examples are in silver, but they are made also in wood or horn. In this case, the larger *quaiche* would have been passed around the Mess dining table at the conclusion of the meal, the smaller one being offered to the piper after he had finished playing for his officers. Photo: RNZAF, and RNZE Museum.

the locally-based Assam Rifles invited me to dinner at their Officers' Mess. There I was amazed to see the beautiful collection of silver trophies which had been handed to them in 1947 by the Assam Valley Light Horse when it was disbanded. I recall particularly the scenes engraved on some of these pieces which clearly depicted manoeuvres taking place in tea plantations, with the factory buildings in the background. The AVLH consisted mainly of tea planters and employees of the Assam Oil Company, and they would congregate with other volunteer units for rifle shooting competitions, gymkhanas, annual camps, and so forth. I have seen photographs of these gatherings, some of which showed literally hundreds of Volunteers dressed in their khaki britches and pith helmets. They certainly took their duties seriously, and I believe the AVLH alone provided 377 officers for the Indian Army during the second world war.

My grandfather, Major William Garnett MBE, served in India for fifty years, mainly at Cawnpore. In 1886 he helped to form the Cawnpore Volunteer Light Horse. Although commissioned within the Commissariat, he nevertheless joined the Light Horse in the ranks and rose to become Squadron Sergeant Major while still holding that commission. I have a cup which he won, the 'Captain Duckworth Tent Pegging Trophy'. It was made in 1900 by John Round & Son, of Sheffield, and the silver shields on the plinth show the names of ten winners, including my grandfather, between 1903 and 1913. There must have been hundreds of similar Volunteer trophies being competed for, all over India. What happened to them all, I wonder?".

Part of the answer to that question is known with certainty. In 1946 and 1947, the Accounts Officer of the East India Railway Regiment AF(I), based in Calcutta, was Second Lieutenant R E Nissen. He has retained some of his office documents, and they tell us how the two battalions of his own regiment handled the matter.

On the afternoon of Thursday, 1 May 1947, the senior officers and Warrant Officers assembled under their

Commandant, Colonel R B H Whitby ED ADC, in the office of the railway company's General Manager, Khan Bahadur G Faruque CIE OBE. The purpose of the encounter was to hand over to the East India Railway and its Sports Association a large part of the silver which had been acquired since 1869. Several were sports trophies which the regiment had won outright in inter-unit competitions in hockey, athletics, boxing and tug-of-war.

Most of the shooting trophies were set aside for The Bisley Association, India Section, for continuing use as competition prizes. Other items were sold, the money raised being earmarked for the benefit of "the clerical staff and menials". Others again were brought to England so that they could be displayed on those occasions when former members and their guests dined as the East India Railway Officers Dinner Association. This collection included a number of presentation vases, bowls and cups.

The silver was not the only important AF(I) possession looking for a new home. It is known, for example, that another local unit, The Calcutta and Presidency Battalion, arranged for its Colours to be laid up in St Paul's Cathedral, Calcutta, at a ceremonial service held on 7 September 1947. A copy of the Order of Parade shows that the laying up was handled with the same attention to detail and protocol as if these had been the Colours of a battalion of the Brigade of Guards.

Club Silver

Central to social life in British India was "the Club". It was the venue where "the army", "the civil" and "the politicals" could congregate, where they and their families met for a drink, for a meal, and for those peculiarly British pastimes which brought people together in a way not possible within the confines of the Mess or a married quarter. Tea dances, bridge parties, amateur theatricals, tennis competitions, cricket, croquet, these and many other activities provided interest and relaxation.

They also had the civilising effect of permitting young people of both genders to enjoy each other's company and to make friendships which often developed into romance. This was particularly important to junior bachelor officers of the Indian Army whose opportunities for meeting young women of their own race and background were often quite limited. It has been said that the more predatory amongst them regarded the hill stations as ideal venues for "picnics and adultery", and it does seem that, in the heady mountain air, some unaccompanied wives were indeed ready for a discreet adventure.

The hill stations were also a magnet to young widows whose husbands had died prematurely or been killed in action. They and their children were, in many cases, left without adequate means of support, a problem which might be solved by finding a new man and making a new marriage.

Every Club had its own collection of silver and silver plate, pieces which had been presented when, for example, a long-serving Committee member retired from office or, more typically, when a trophy was donated as the prize for an annual competition. There were cups and shields for a wide variety of tournaments and competitions. The winner's name was added to the list of former victors, but the trophy remained in the ownership of the Club and its Committee. With Independence and the British exodus, these objects ceased to have any meaning or purpose. The buildings which housed them became deserted or were put to new uses, and the silver was locked away.

The following account is contributed by a Canadian, Elspeth Cox. "In 1984 I went, with my husband, to live in Dalhousie. We were there for three years. This, like Simla, Mussoorie and Ootacamunde, was one of the hill stations situated on the southern slopes of the Himalayas. Before Independence it had always been very popular with British families during the hot season. They went up there for the healthy cool air. There were usually large numbers of army officers passing through, either on leave or recuperating from illness. The Club building, erected in 1901, is a stone structure with a long glassed-in timber verandah overlooking the surrounding mountains. There is one main room, with a wooden dance floor, and a number of concrete-floored rooms leading off. These are, or were, the billiard and card rooms and the library. Originally Dalhousie was the site chosen for a planned sanatorium, but that was relocated a thousand feet lower when it was found that the access road became impassable during heavy winter snowfalls.

Many of the permanent members of the Club were officers from Lahore who owned or rented houses in Dalhousie and the original names are still to be seen, carved into the walls or gateposts. Rudyard Kipling summered here, and Baden Powell's stepbrother lived in the highest house, at 8000 feet, named 'Snowdon'.

When we first arrived, the Club building was being used as a recreation centre by the officers of the Jammu & Kashmir Rifles. We were guests at one of their dances, and were served with drinks on original Club silver salvers. The waiters were Gurkha soldiers, very smartly dressed in white, with *kukris* tucked into red sashes. However, when Mrs Gandhi was assassinated, a policy of non-fraternisation with foreign nationals was introduced and the place was more or less abandoned.

I did manage to arrange a later visit, in 1987, and the caretaker took me around. He opened a locked cupboard and showed me three shelves of trophies, mostly too dirty and tarnished to read in the short time I was there. The one item which stayed in my memory was a Mappin & Webb silver Cupid awarded for a golf match played in 1910 between 'The Punjab Navy' and 'The Dalhousie Dragoons'. It was a strange sensation, in that cold empty building, to see those relics from so long ago. One could almost hear the voices and the laughter of the people to whom once they had mattered. The banter of the men at the bar, waiters shuffling by with trays of tea, the shrill sound of children, the distant calls of the players on the tennis court, someone playing the latest seventy-eight on the gramophone. Happy days!".

Chapter Six
Silver Lost and Found

Fire, theft, storm and flood, the standard perils familiar to an insurance underwriter are as relevant to military silver as they are to any other category of family treasure. To these four may be added "enemy action" or "the fortunes of war". The following chapter will describe some of the episodes which have, from time to time, temporarily or permanently deprived certain ships and regiments of their possessions.

19th Regiment of Foot

From 1775 to 1783, large tracts of North America were a battlefield. There is just one recorded instance of a British Army regiment having lost any silver as the war swirled back and forth through the virgin forests. The 19th Regiment of Foot (later The Green Howards) was sent from England in 1781 to relieve the garrison at Fort Star, north of Charleston, South Carolina. With them they had their baggage and the payroll for the regiment they were to relieve.

A successful action was fought at Monck's Corner on 16 July but, shortly afterwards and heading for Charleston, they were ambushed. The Americans seized the entire baggage train, including the cash and the officers' personal property. Some of the smaller items were later returned but, logically, they did not include any valuables.

In January 1999, an American researcher acting in the name of the Green Howards Regimental Museum launched an appeal for any items of silver which may still reside in South Carolina. Many local families are descendents of patriot soldiers who fought the British in the War of Independence. It is hoped that a few items of silver may have been handed down over the generations and can still be identified.

If they exist, they cannot properly be described as "regimental silver" in the sense that they carry engraved inscriptions or the regimental crest. Units such as the 19th of Foot had not yet started the custom of making such presentations. Whatever was looted was more likely to have been the personal property of individual officers, items of a practical nature such as plates, beakers and cutlery. However, the South Carolina search would be worthwhile if it revealed any Sterling silver bearing marks for the years preceding 1781. On the balance of probability, it could be concluded that it might well have been part of the proceeds of the ambush.

23rd (Royal Welch Fusiliers) Regiment of Foot

The Americans declared their independence in 1776, and it was formally recognised in 1783. The British were determined that, although they had lost The Thirteen Colonies, they would not lose Canada. From the turn of the century through to 1871, when the last of its regiments were withdrawn, the British Army maintained a large garrison throughout the eastern half of the country. It was in this context that the 23rd Royal Welsh Fusiliers lost a part of their collection of silver.

The regiment's Reserve Battalion had been stationed in Montreal since 1847. In April of 1850 it was ordered to start moving, in three separate contingents, to London, Ontario, where it would relieve another British battalion. One of these parties, Number 8 Company, with wives and children, embarked in the paddle steamer Commerce (Captain John Cochrane) for the long passage up the St Lawrence River and then across Lake Ontario and Lake Erie. Shortly before midnight on 6 May, on the final stage of her voyage, the Commerce came into collision with another lake steamer, the Despatch.

It seems that the Captain of the Commerce did his best to avoid the collision, but there is the suggestion that he and the Captain of the Despatch were engaged in a long-standing rivalry. There may be some truth in this, although poor watch-keeping on the bridge of the Despatch was a more likely explanation for the accident.

As the Commerce gradually flooded and then sank, the Despatch lay, hove to, for thirty minutes before attempting a rescue. When questioned, her Captain explained that he had needed first to deal with his own damage. He fled to the United States before being called to give evidence at the Court of Enquiry and was never traced. Whatever the truth of the matter, the loss of life amongst the Commerce's passengers was higher than might have been expected.

When she went down, she took with her two officers and twenty-two other ranks of the 23rd Regiment. Thirteen of their wives and children, and two other civilians, were also drowned. Three regimental officers survived - Captain F J Phillott, Lieutenant F P R Delmé Radcliffe, and Lieutenant Sir Henry Chamberlain.

Delmé Radcliffe died only four years later, in the Crimea. He was killed thirty yards from a Russian battery while leading a charge to capture it.

All of the Company's baggage was lost in the sinking. Part of the silver was recovered when the wreck of the Commerce was found and raised in June. Some years later, however, one of the missing pieces was found washed up on the beach near Port Maitland. A small salver, it was passed to the officers of the local Canadian Militia unit which later became the 4th Battalion of The Royal Canadian Regiment.

For the next hundred years it held a place of honour in the Officers' Mess. The local community also kept the memory of the tragedy alive. In the Spring of 1914, the local clergy and the Hamilton branch of the Veterans' Association paid for the headstone on the mass grave at Christ Church, Port Maitland, to be refurbished. The grave holds the remains of those victims whose bodies were recovered - Assistant Surgeon Douglas Grantham and twenty-four men, women and children. On 6 May, the sixty-fourth anniversary of the accident, a memorial service was held at the site and a wreath made in the colours of the Royal Welch Fusiliers laid as a token of remembrance.

Over the years, the RWF had become affiliated with the United States Marine Corps and with three Commonwealth regiments. One of these was the famous French-Canadian regiment known always as the "Van Doos" but more accurately

This centrepiece was made long after the *Commerce* disaster. It is an elaborately ornamented cup, with four large and four smaller flexible festoons. Two Welsh dragons and two goat heads oppose each other on the brim. It has four feet and is additionally supported at each end by a Sphinx. Engraved upon the centre panel of the plinth are the words *The Red Dragon Cup, Cymru am Byth*. It was commissioned by the officers of the 1st Battalion, The Royal Welch Fusiliers, in 1903 with funds which had accumulated in the Mess Plate Fund during the Anglo-Boer War of 1899-1902. It was competed for annually in a point-to-point race "of some three or four miles of good hunting country, the horses to be owned and ridden by officers of the regiment". Engraved below the two horses are the names of the runners and riders (first, second and third places) for the events held between 1904-1913, and in 1933-1934. The cup weighs (without the plinth) 437 ounces. The overall height is 24 inches. Photo: The Regimental Museum, Caernarfon.

as the Royal 22e Régiment. The officers of The Royal Canadian Regiment came to the decision that it was more appropriate for the salvaged piece to be held by the officers of the "Van Doos" rather than themselves. At a formal ceremony on 24 February 1973, at the "Van Doos" Regimental Headquarters, La Citadelle, Quebec City, the piece was handed over by Lieutenant Colonel W G Lindsay. Mounted within a glazed frame, it is accompanied by a parchment which explains its history.

The item in question has virtually no intrinsic worth. Its importance is to be found in its historical connections, not its potential sale-room value. It is, in fact, a conventional gadroon-edged salver, approximately fourteen inches in diameter and probably made in the 1820s or 1830s. It was not a presentation piece but simply one of the Mess items of workaday silver. More precisely, it was made as Sheffield plate. The silver plating eroded away during the salver's long immersion in the cold waters of Lake Erie, and all that remains is the original copper base. Engraved upon it is the "*Ich Dien*" device of the Prince of Wales's feathers and the words "Royal Welch Fusiliers".

As a footnote, it should be mentioned that the RWF have had two other unfortunate maritime experiences in their long history. In 1799, returning from the abortive Walcheren campaign, the Grenadier Company and two other Companies were shipwrecked. They were being transported back to England in the Dutch frigate *Valk*. She went down off the Dutch coast

near Ameland and, of the 444 souls on board, only twenty-five were saved. More than half of those who drowned, 265 officers and men, were Royal Welch Fusiliers.

A century and a half later, on 9 September 1943, the Royal Navy's fast mine-laying cruiser HMS *Abdiel*, commanded by Captain D Orr-Ewing DSO, struck a mine in the Bay of Taranto, Southern Italy. Amongst the forty-eight fatal casualties were men of the 6th Battalion (Royal Welch), The Parachute Regiment. No regimental silver was involved in either of these sinkings.

HMS *York*

Another of the many Royal Navy ships lost in WWII was the 8250 ton heavy cruiser HMS *York* (Captain R H Portal RN). Built by Palmer & Company in 1928, capable of 32 knots, she was engaged in 1941 in assisting the British and Anzac forces defending the island of Crete. Writing in 1997, the ship's Royal Marines Instructor of Gunnery, Quartermaster Sergeant F A J Ogilwy, described his experiences as a young man when HMS *York* was attacked in Suda Bay by an Italian one-man explosive speed-boat. It was then that he became the personal custodian of an item of silver from the ship's collection.

"She was hit amidships in the engine room and started to sink. The Captain ordered 'abandon ship'. A destroyer raced to our aid and she was eventually beached in mud and settled with the sea covering the upper deck but not low enough for it to go over the combing around the hatches. As most of the watertight doors were closed, it was possible to get ammunition up from the magazines. With the help of the submarine *Rover*, giving power to the ammunition hoist and to the guns, we could operate the 4.7 anti-aircraft guns. Myself and Petty Officer Storey took two gun crews out to *York* and helped protect Crete from air attacks".

The skeleton crews kept their guns in action for several days. The end came on 29 May when the semi-submerged ship was attacked by Stuka dive-bombers. This happened at a time when two Swedish civilian divers were over the side, attempting to cover the gash in the hull with wood and concrete. Both were killed and later buried at sea with full naval honours.

When Fred Ogilvy left his ship for the last time, he took with him a silver cup which he had been using to hand around tots of rum to the gun crews. "I did not have a mug or cup as my Mess was flooded, so I used this trophy as a mug. I considered it as a trophy of war".

The trophy in question was a Swedish-made silver cup engraved: "A memento of the race, Swedish Navy v British Navy, from Rear Admiral P L H Noble, 30th June 1933, Stockholm, Marine Cutter, HMS *York*". The occasion had been a visit to Stockholm in that year by ships of the 2nd Cruiser Squadron. An inter-ship pulling race between the two navies was won by HMS *York's* Royal Marines detachment. Admiral Noble's cup became thereafter the ship's own annual cutter prize.

Fred Ogilvy used the trophy as a mug during his time on the island, awaiting evacuation, and later took it with him when he emigrated to New Zealand in 1951. For the next thirty-one years it had pride of place on the mantelpiece of his Rotorua house but, in 1982, he decided that it should have a permanent home. The opportunity came with a visit to Auckland by the Swedish cadet training minelayer *Karlskrona*. Having made himself known, he was received by Captain Carl Gustav Frensen. The cup was taken back to Sweden and put on display in the Naval Officers' Club in the Royal Swedish Navy's base at Karlskrona.

That appeared to be the end of the matter. However, the Secretary of the York & District Branch, Royal Naval Association, was on the trail. In 1996, during a visit to New Zealand, Mr G T Miskelly met Fred Ogilvy and heard the story of the Stockholm trophy. Back in England, he wrote to Commander Andrew Moll RN, the officer commanding the current HMS *York*, a Type 42 destroyer built by Swan Hunter in 1982 and the ninth Royal Navy ship to bear that name. A flurry of letters between Moll, the British Embassy and the Royal Swedish Navy brought an immediate agreement that the cup should be handed over.

At the earliest opportunity, when HMS *Iron Duke* was making a courtesy visit to Stockholm, the Swedes delivered it to the ship's officers who, in turn, forwarded it to Commander Moll. The Stockholm Trophy is now a treasured part of the *York's* silver. Not in itself a valuable piece, it is in effect a memorial to the six hundred officers and men of the *York* who fought at Suda Bay, to the two members of the ship's company who died there, and to the two Swedish divers who attempted to save her.

31st (Huntingdonshire) Regiment of Foot

On 1 March 1825, the sea claimed the silver of the officers of the 31st Regiment of Foot while it was on passage from England to India. Their ship, the East Indiaman *Kent*, was crossing the Bay of Biscay when she caught fire. The flames took a rapid hold and the order was given to take to the boats. There were not nearly enough of these to accommodate the people on board, but another vessel saw the fire and came to their aid. At midnight the ship blew up. The 31st lost all its regimental property but, amazingly, there seems to have been no loss of life.

There are three pieces of silver having a direct connection with the sinking. One is a snuff box presented by an officer who had served with the regiment from 1800 to 1808, a Colonel Meade. This was brought away from the ship before she sank. The second is a replica of Colonel Meade's box, presented to the Officers' Mess by a Lieutenant Holford of the North Durham Militia "as a token of their kindness and hospitality during his stay amongst them".

The third, known as The Kent Snuff Box, carries the engraved wording "Presented to Mr Edward Connolly, First Mate of the Brig *Cambria*, by the Officers of The 31st Regt and the Officers and Passengers of the *Kent* East Indiaman, for his valuable assistance in rescuing the 554 persons from the wreck of that vessel during her conflagration on the 1st March 1825".

All three boxes are today displayed in the Regimental Museum of The Queen's Royal Surrey Regiment, at Clandon Park, Surrey.

In 1881, the 31st Regiment was amalgamated with the 70th (Surrey) Regiment of Foot. They became, respectively, the 1st and 2nd Battalions of The East Surrey Regiment. The 70th also had lost the greater part of its silver in earlier years.

70th (Surrey) Regiment of Foot

In 1858 the regiment was in India, stationed at Nowshera, on the banks of the River Cabul. A subaltern serving there at the time wrote this account: "Early in August there had been a landslide far up the Indus, in the hills, and a large body of water formed in a sort of dam. Suddenly heavy rain set in and the temporary dam gave way under the additional pressure. The whole mass of water reached down to Attock, at the confluence of the Indus and Cabul rivers and where the channel is very narrow. Consequently the water rushed *up* the Cabul river, actually making it flow backwards".

Major A E Jones, who was the Mess Sergeant at that time, later recalled that he was woken at four in the morning by one of the native servants. He sent for the President of the Mess Committee and, surrounded by steadily rising water, they hurriedly started to pack up the Mess property. "The water rose in the Barracks about six feet, but where the Mess was, it covered the bungalow".

After the flood subsided, two soup tureens, one sugar bowl and two bread baskets were recovered from the wrecked building. The tureens were gifts of the people of the islands of Antigua and St Thomas in 1806 and 1811, the 70th having been stationed in the West Indies in those years. They too are now on display at Clandon Park. Other objects - silver, glass and crockery - were recovered from the surrounding morass of mud and debris, but much had been lost or damaged.

Several days later a villager walked into the Nowshera barracks carrying a silver Mess hot water dish. He had found it on the banks of the river at Attock, twenty miles down-stream from Nowshera. Then, seventy-two years later, in 1928, a silver tray was recovered. It was found in Rawalpindi - on sale in a bazaar - by an officer of the 1st Battalion, The East Surrey Regiment, who immediately recognised its 70th Regiment engraved crest.

The Bombay Grenadiers

From 1840 onwards, there was a major shift in the employment of India-recruited soldiery. In the early years, these troops were required for the conquest and pacification of territory within the sub-continent itself. As her control over those lands progressively extended, so could Great Britain increasingly call upon her Indian regiments as a tool for expanding her influence in other parts of the world.

One such episode was the 1867-1868 punitive expedition to Abyssinia. The leaders of this multi-ethnic kingdom were amongst the first (in the 4th century AD) to embrace Christianity. Its ruler, Emperor Theodorus, claimed direct descent from Solomon and the Queen of Sheba.

Over several years he courted the British and sought an alliance which would have given parity of status between himself and Queen Victoria. His various advances were either rejected or ignored. In a fit of exasperation and resentment, he seized Her Majesty's representative and other European residents in the kingdom and locked them up. It was to obtain the release of these hostages, and to demonstrate British omnipotence, that Delhi was authorised to mount an invasion of his country.

Theodorus's capital at that time was the mountain fortress of Magdala. After overcoming the logistical problems of transporting 12,000 men and their stores four hundred miles from the Red Sea up to the Abyssinian plateau, 8000 feet above sea level, Lieutenant General Sir Robert Napier launched his attack. The Emperor's men could do little against modern weaponry, and were quickly demoralised when a Royal Navy detachment showered them with explosive rockets.

The fight was soon over. British losses amounted to just two men killed and twenty-seven wounded. With defeat inevitable, Theodorus shot himself through the mouth with a pistol, sent to him some years earlier and bearing an engraved message of goodwill from Queen Victoria. The victors proceeded to plunder the Royal palace and the city's churches.

The thefts were not of the random and destructive type committed, three decades later, in China. In 1900, the Imperial Palace in Peking was aimlessly ransacked by soldiers of the international force employed in suppressing the Boxer Rebellion. Instead, on this occasion, the expedition was accompanied by Richard Holmes, Assistant Keeper of Manuscripts at the British Museum. He was charged with the task of seizing whatever antiquities he might find. Some were sold at auction in Magdala, a week after its capture, others he brought back to England as additions to the Museum's collections.

One of the pieces was a processional cross, made in gold, taken from St Michael's Cathedral. It was acquired by General Napier who presented it to the officers of the 2nd Battalion, The Bombay Grenadiers, as a gesture of appreciation for the battalion's services during the campaign. The Grenadiers did not in fact take part in the fighting but were engaged in the construction of the railway supply line from Zula, on the coast, to Kumavli. The climate was bad, there was a lack of clean drinking water, and all ranks suffered severely from scurvy and other illnesses.

The Grenadiers took the Cross with them when they returned to India in May, 1868, and it was lodged with the Anglican church authorities at St Thomas's Cathedral, Bombay. According to legend, the battalion then began to lose its Indian officers one after another, each of them dying in his prime and for no accountable reason. The number of deaths caused such concern that it was decided to return the Cross to its rightful owners, the Coptic clerics in Magdala. This was done, and it seems that the battalion had no unusual losses thereafter.

Two identical brass replicas were made before the Cross was sent back. One is used to this day at St Thomas's Cathedral, the other is held by the original recipient's successors in the modern Indian Army, 2nd Battalion, The Grenadiers.

Another religious treasure taken from St Michael's Cathedral is also mentioned in some records as "The Magdala Cross". Very similar in design to that briefly owned by the 2nd Battalion, Bombay Grenadiers, it was a silver altar piece. General Napier gave it to the 1st Belooch Battalion, 27th Regiment of Bombay Infantry, in recognition of their leading role in the campaign. Their services were considerable - helping to build the rough mountain track up from the coast in March, beating off an attack at Fahla on 10 April, and then forming part of the force which broke into Magdala three days later.

The Cross was one of the objects removed from the Emperor's palace by Richard Holmes. Apparently the officers of the regiment had no unnerving experiences following its

One of the four Coptic Christian crosses taken from Magdala in 1868 by Richard Holmes and Lieutenant General Sir Robert Napier. Made in silver and gold, they vary slightly in detail but share a common basic design. This example, known as The Abyssinia Cross, is held by the Royal Artillery Mess, Woolwich. Photo: Leslie F Thompson, *The Field*, and the Royal Artillery Institute.

acquisition and removal to India. It remained part of the Officers' Mess collection and was passed on to their successors in 1947. Today it resides with the 27th Regiment's lineal descendents, the 10th Battalion, The Baloch Regiment, in Pakistan, to whom it is a treasure which they regard with due reverence.

Writing in 1948, one of the regiment's historians, Colonel W E Maxwell, described it as "this valuable trophy, a beautiful example of early Christian design and craftsmanship, made of beaten silver, with line drawings on each side of the Madonna and Child and the Twelve Apostles. It is now mounted on a silver pedestal and displayed on special occasions".

There is yet another silver artefact known as "The Magdala Cross", almost identical to those in the possession of the 2nd Grenadiers and the 10th Balochs, and it forms part of the collection of a British Army regiment (which prefers to remain anonymous).

To complete the record, mention must be made of a fourth Christian artefact removed from Magdala. It is held by the Royal Artillery Mess at Woolwich and is listed in the inventory there as "The *Abyssinia* Cross". Of similar or even greater antiquity than the three Crosses already described, it was given by Sir Robert Napier to the officers of "G" Battery, 14th Brigade, Royal Artillery, the only battery of field artillery to participate in the expedition. One of those officers was Lieutenant W G Knox, and he left a written account.

"The guns were carried on elephants for the greater part of 400 miles to the capital over most atrocious roads. The personnel had served in the Crimea, Indian Mutiny and China campaigns, also with (General) Gordon against the Taipings. It was a bit of Battery swagger that on foot parade no man was put in the front rank who had not four medals on his chest. There was a sprinkling of fine old blackguards amongst them and I remember seeing men tied to a gun wheel and receiving fifty lashes from the Provost Marshal for drunkenness on the first march from the coast".

"G" Battery was equipped with 12 pounder RBL Armstrong guns, weapons which completely out-classed those of the Emperor's rag-tag soldiery. The officers presented the Cross to the RA Mess at Woolwich on their return to England in 1870.

The role of Richard Holmes in this affair was rewarded with royal approval. Shortly after his return to England he became the Royal Librarian and later was appointed a Knight Commander of the Victorian Order. It has since emerged that he may not have been entirely candid when reporting his discoveries at Magdala. According to the art historian Martin Bailey, Holmes was one of the first to enter Emperor Theodorus's apartments. Among all the other great treasures he found there was a small oil painting of the head of Christ, an icon which over three centuries had been carried into battle by Abyssinian soldiers as a talisman and upon which the Emperors' officers swore their oaths of allegiance.

It is likely that it had been brought to Abyssinia in the early 16th century by Portuguese Jesuits attempting to win converts to the Church of Rome. They failed, but the picture was adopted as a symbol of military and spiritual power by all successive Emperors. It is not known whether Richard Holmes was aware of its history at that time, but he kept it for himself. When he died, in 1911, it was sold by his widow, passed into the art trade, and disappeared from view.

After five years of research, Martin Bailey has recently (1998) found the picture, known as "the *quarat rasou*", or "the

striking of the head", in a bank in Lisbon. It remains to be seen whether the government of Abyssinia (now Ethiopia) will mount a legal action for its return. Certainly the British government itself had second thoughts regarding one of the most spectacular trophies brought back to London by Richard Holmes - the crown of the Emperors of Abyssinia. It was returned to its rightful owners in 1928 when, as official representative of His Majesty King George V, the Duke of Gloucester travelled to Addis Ababa to attend the coronation of Haile Selassie. We may wonder what alternative arrangements might have been made for that ceremony if the British had *not* returned the crown.

The Connaught Rangers

Fire was a serious hazard in the decades before the invention of electric lighting and in remote military stations where electrical power had not yet arrived. Oil lamps and candles were a constant source of risk. The 88th (Connaught Rangers) Regiment of Foot lost some of its silver when the Mess caught fire in 1848. The regiment was at that time serving in the West Indies, on Grenada and St Vincent.

Only three years later, having moved to Halifax, Nova Scotia, the 88th suffered an even bigger loss when the Mess building burned to the ground. The cutlery and two snuff mulls were saved, but most of the valuable pieces were destroyed in the blaze. The Colonel submitted a claim for one thousand five hundred pounds in damages. The War Office finally agreed to pay twenty percent of this sum, the reason for the reduction being that the items then in use in the Mess were "much too expensive".

The Connaught Rangers did not enjoy the best of luck with their silver. From 1892 to 1893, the 1st Battalion was stationed at Pembroke Dock, and it was there that the Officers' Mess was burgled. In his otherwise very complete three-volume regimental history, Colonel H F N Jourdain devotes just eighteen lines to the battalion's twenty months' service in South Wales, and concludes: "Second Lieutenant G E Payne, to the general regret of the regiment, accidentally shot himself with a revolver. The sojourn at Pembroke Dock was otherwise uneventful". In his (separate) published description of the Mess silver he refers briefly to some of it having been stolen, but gives no details. A discreet veil was drawn over an unhappy episode.

The wish to have it forgotten is understandable. It was later established that the culprit was one of the battalion's own soldiers. Worse, at the time of the theft, he was supposed to be confined to the barrack cells. Thanks to recent research by Stuart Barr, who has trawled through the archives in Wales and examined the original documents, the full story can now be told for the first time.

Private John Fitzwilliam, from Moore, County Roscommon, joined the battalion as a recruit in March 1892. He soon proved to be "a Queen's bad bargain". After only four months he was sentenced by Court Martial to twenty-eight days' detention in the barrack cells for a breach of discipline. He was serving that sentence when, on the night of 10 July, the Officers' Mess was burgled. Suspicion would never have fallen on Private Fitzwilliam if he had not drawn attention to himself with a flamboyant gesture. He had, it was learned later, escaped from his cell, taken a selection of silver from the Mess, chopped up the larger pieces with tailor's shears, passed out of barracks unobserved, hidden his loot, and then returned to the Guardroom at two o'clock in the morning. Presenting himself to the Guard Commander, Sergeant Treacy, he facetiously saluted and asked to be returned to his cell.

There were no witnesses to the theft, but Fitzwilliam was clearly the prime suspect. Given the lack of evidence, it was decided that no formal charges could be laid. Within a week, however, he was brought before a second Court Martial. Found guilty of "desertion whilst undergoing sentence", he was committed on 18 July to twelve months' hard labour and "discharged with ignominy". The officers of the 88th must have been glad to see him go, believing that the author of their troubles had passed out of their lives for ever. But John Fitzwilliam had other plans.

On his release from Carmarthen Gaol in July 1893, he decided to turn his hidden assets into cash. Walking boldly into the barracks, he asked to see the Adjutant, Captain E A Grubbe. He said that he knew where the silver was hidden and, for a consideration of fifty pounds, would reveal the location. Captain Grubbe declined the offer and advised him to talk instead to the police.

Having failed with the Adjutant, Fitzwilliam went to Swansea where he offered the silver to a pawnbroker. The latter did not accept his story that "his sister had brought it back from the Cape" and called a passing policeman. Constable Powell caught up with Fitzwilliam in the street, and having heard that the silver "came from Afghanistan", arrested him.

As they walked to the police station, the Irishman admitted that he had stolen the silver from the regiment and offered to assist the Constable with his investigations. He claimed that he still had two salvers and two cruet stands concealed in a safe place, and offered to show where they were on payment of five pounds. Like his previous suggestion, this too was refused.

Fitzwilliam was charged with "stealing Mess plate to the value of one hundred and fifty pounds, the property of the officers of the Connaught Rangers". In October 1893 he was found guilty of theft at Carmarthen Assizes and sentenced to nine months' hard labour.

Only part of the stolen silver seems to have been recovered intact. The commanding officer, Lieutenant Colonel Sir George de Hochepied Larpent, was quick to arrange for replacements to be made. By June 1893, before Fitzwilliam had even completed his first sentence, the Goldsmiths & Silversmiths Company had been paid two hundred and sixty pounds for new pieces.

The largest was a salver, eighteen inches in diameter, made to match a stolen salver which itself had been a replacement. The original, presented in 1851 by Lieutenant Colonel Sir Horatio Shirley KCB, had been lost in that same year in the Mess fire at Halifax, Nova Scotia.

Other replacement items were three small salvers to match the one remaining, dated 1851, and a new sideboard dish to match three dated 1839 (they had escaped the Halifax fire but not the attentions of John Fitzwilliam).

An imaginative touch was Colonel Larpent's instruction that some of the bullion from the mutilated and non-repairable pieces should be utilised for the making of a four-bottle sauce frame. He designed it himself, and the work was completed in 1895.

The Royal Irish Fusiliers (Princess Victoria's)

Reference has been made in other parts of this book to the silver of the Irish regiments which were disbanded in 1922, but it must be remembered that not all Irish-recruited regiments were affected by the events of that year. The exceptions were those having their depôts north of the border, in Northern Ireland. One such was The Royal Irish Fusiliers (Princess Victoria's). Tracing its origins back to the 87th and 89th Regiments of Foot, its motto was "Faugh-a-Ballagh" (Clear the Way) and for this reason was most commonly known as "The Faughs" (pronounced "Fogs").

In 1939 the 1st Battalion was stationed in Guernsey as the peacetime garrison. There were long-standing local associations. The old 87th was raised in 1793 by Colonel Sir John Doyle, an officer who some years later was Lieutenant Governor of the island during the critical period of the Napoleonic war. Today the Guernsey Museums & Galleries, in St Peter Port, has on display the opulent silver-gilt vase presented to him by the local populace in 1805, and an unusual silver-gilt obelisk presented in 1814 by the officers of The Guernsey Militia. Then, much later, in September 1915, a volunteer company of the Militia was attached to the 7th (Service) Battalion, Royal Irish Fusiliers, for service on the Western Front. A total of 4000 Guernseymen served in that war.

For the 1st Battalion, the gentle pace of peacetime garrison life changed dramatically on 7 August when the battalion was ordered to pack up and immediately embark for England. The War Office was putting into action its plan for sending a British Expeditionary Force to France in the event of a declaration of war. That came soon afterwards, on 3 September. Leaving Guernsey at less than twenty-four hours' notice meant taking a minimum of possessions. The packing and storage of regimental property, which included most of the Officers' Mess and Sergeants' Mess silver, was left in the hands of Major Brian Somerville and RSM "Paddy" Moyne, with a strong rear party.

The silver was carefully packed into eighteen crates and deposited in the vaults of the local branch of Lloyds Bank. All the other items, which included pictures, furniture and ornaments, plus a display of campaign and gallantry medals awarded to former Faughs, were deposited in a local warehouse. It could not be foreseen, at that stage, that the Channel Islands would within a year be German-occupied territory.

At the end of the war, when the Islands were liberated, Brian Somerville went back to St Peter Port to search for any regimental property which might have survived. He had many years' service with the regiment and knew exactly what he was looking for. To his pleasure and surprise, he found that the greater part of the silver was still in the care of Lloyds Bank.

It emerged that the Germans had soon discovered it and, despite fierce protests by the manager, Mr A S Iles, and by the island's Bailiff, Mr Victor Carey, had taken it away for their own use. The German Commandant, Colonel Schumacher, seems then to have had second thoughts because, in March 1941, his staff clumsily repacked most of the major items and returned them to the bank.

The value of this conciliatory gesture was much diminished by a letter addressed to the bank stating that the German authorities still regarded the artefacts as "the property of the Reich". Colonel Schumacher also wrote to the Bailiff, confirming his actions with regard to the historical pieces but insisting that "in accordance with higher orders, the articles of domestic use, i.e. forks, spoons, etc, have to be placed at the disposal of German officers and men's billets in the island and also on the continent". As a consequence, the regiment lost four hundred and sixty-three Georgian silver knives, forks and spoons, thirty crested silver tea and coffee pots, and many similar items of domestic ware (including a set of silver napkin rings, each engraved with an officer's name). None of this material has ever been recovered.

Of much greater importance was the loss of a gold and

jewelled snuff box, presented to King George IV by the Mayor and Corporation of Dublin on the occasion of His Majesty's first visit to that city. For reasons unknown, the box then disappeared until the 1850s when it was found by two officers of the Royal Irish Fusiliers who chanced to see it in the window of a Dublin pawnshop. They bought it and presented it to their Mess. By virtue of its royal and Irish connections, the box came to be regarded as one of the regiment's most important possessions. In 1941 it was removed to Germany where, allegedly, it was given to Herman Goering for his private collection.

Amongst other stolen items of particular value were the last surviving 87th Regiment silver and ivory gaming counters and a small gold eagle commissioned by Major Hugh Gough to commemorate the 1811 battle of Barrossa. The swords of Sir John Doyle, and of his great nephew, Sir Charles Doyle, were also taken, but these were later returned. The Mess pictures and furniture were retrieved intact from the warehouse, also the collection of medals.

The missing snuff box generated a series of events which serve to demonstrate the degree of importance sometimes attributed to such objects. Upon completion of his rescue mission to Guernsey, Lieutenant Colonel Somerville was appointed to the staff of the Military Government in the British Occupation Zone in Germany. The Director of this organisation was Major General Gerald Templer, an officer who had first joined the Faughs in 1916 and who was now Colonel of the Regiment. Templer was known both for his intellect and for his quick temper. Responding with anger to Brian Somerville's account of the thefts, he ordered a year-long search for Colonel Schumacher and for his chief civil administrative officer. In the chaos of divided and devastated 1946 Germany, neither of these individuals could be found, and nor could anyone else having knowledge of the missing Faugh silver and gold.

Abandoning the search, Templer made an application to the Control Commission, on behalf of the regiment, for the award of any German snuff box of comparable intrinsic and historical value "in reparation and restitution". The Commission approved the application and handed over a box, which had belonged to Frederick the Great, from the Hohenzollern collection.

Gerald Templer arranged for this beautiful piece to be housed in a special morocco case lined with velvet, and it was displayed in the Mess on regimental dinner nights during the late 1940s. Then came the bad news. The Hohenzollern family was contesting the legality of the Control Commission's action in giving away something they regarded as rightfully theirs. The family took their case to the International Court at the Hague and won.

Templer refused to concede defeat and attempted to involve the British government's law officers in a challenge to the International Court's ruling. They studied the papers and decided that the case was a lost cause. The Hohenzollern family then threatened to sue Templer personally, in his capacity as Colonel of the Regiment. Faced with the likelihood of an enormous legal bill and little prospect of success, he agreed that the box should be returned to its original owners.

All of this was followed closely by the British High Commissioner in Germany, Sir Ivone Kirkpatrick. He kept the new Chancellor, Conrad Adenauer, informed of developments. Both men were keen to see that the incident did not get out of hand and jeopardise the post-war process of reconciliation between their two countries.

Adenauer had a personal interest in the affair. In 1946,

when he was Burgomeister of Cologne, he and the British general had tried to work together but, after major disagreements, Templer had sacked him from office. There was no lasting animosity, but the Chancellor recognised the saga of the snuff box as an opportunity to oil the diplomatic wheels. He commissioned the manufacture of an entirely new box, to his own design, and presented it to the regiment at the Palais Schaumburg, Bonn, on 9 January 1953. Sadly, his former opponent had by then departed for the Far East and so could not attend the ceremony in person.

Templer went on to gain fame as "The Tiger of Malaya" and completed his active service in the rank of Field Marshal. Conrad Adenauer is best remembered as having steered Western Germany to its post-war recovery and having been one of the founding fathers of the European Union.

In 1968 the three remaining Irish infantry units were amalgamated as The Royal Irish Rangers. This was a logical continuation of their service together during WWII when each had representative battalions in the redoubtable 38th (Irish) Brigade of the 78th (Battleaxe) Division. In 1992 they were retitled again, this time as the Royal Irish Regiment. The successor regiment possesses their combined collections of silver and gold (valued at a figure in excess of two million pounds) and maintains the old motto, "*Faugh-a-Ballagh*".

The Middlesex Regiment (Duke of Cambridge's Own)

For "the Faughs", the war became deadly serious in May 1940 when the Germans made their *blitzkreig* strikes into Holland, Belgium and France. Eighteen months were to pass before British Army units stationed in the Far East were hit by a succession of similar hammer blows.

One of those serving in Hong Kong was the 1st Battalion of The Middlesex Regiment, commanded by Lieutenant Colonel H W M "Monkey" Stewart OBE MC. At that time it was in barracks at Shamshuipo, a dirty suburb of Kowloon, where it had been stationed continuously for five years.

The Imperial Japanese Army had been patrolling mainland China's border with the Colony (just twenty-five miles from Kowloon) since November 1938, and the Imperial Japanese Navy possessed overwhelming strength in the China Sea, but there was little anxiety for the future until September of 1941. The submission of the Vichy French to Japanese territorial demands in Indo-China then exposed a critical potential for direct conflict. It was in this tense situation that Colonel Stewart called a meeting of all the battalion's senior ranks - the officers, the Warrant Officers and the Colour Sergeants. His purpose was to discuss the safety of the silver owned by the Officers' Mess and the Sergeants' Mess, and also the King's Colour and the Regimental Colour. The Adjutant was Captain A G Hewitt, and he describes what happened at that meeting.

"Everyone agreed that the silver should be sent away to a temporary secure home, preferably with one of the Commonwealth units to which we were affiliated. Canada, Australia, India and Singapore were all suggested. I myself pressed for Australia, but the majority vote was for Singapore, thought at that time to be impregnable. It was agreed that the Hong Kong & Shanghai Bank should be given the job, with their people in Singapore responsible for its secure storage. This was done soon afterwards.

The Colours were a different matter. The Second in Command, Major Frank Hedgecoe, argued strongly for their retention. The Regimental Sergeant Major, Bob Challis, was also firmly against parting with them, even on a short-term basis. He

For soldiers stationed in Colonies such as Hong Kong, pre-war life was geared to the grinding repetition of the War Office training pamphlets. Every year, they completed the official twelve-month training cycle which prepared them for the war their fathers had already fought, in 1914-1918. When not on the ranges or route march, they were on the parade ground. Much time was given to rehearsing and performing for events such as the King's Birthday Parade, inspections by senior officers, and visits by assorted dignatories. With hindsight, given their lack of technical equipment and lack of preparation for modern warfare, it is admirable that they fought as well as they did when the Japanese invaded. Here the Pipes and Drums of the 2nd Battalion, The Royal Scots, under Pipe Major D Rankine and Drum Major J Degnan, form up for yet another parade. The setting is Hong Kong Cricket Ground, 1939. Photo: RHQ The Royal Scots.

expressed the conviction that the fighting spirit of the battalion would be that much less if we did not have our Colours with us.

I myself was particularly attached to the Colours because I had joined the battalion straight from Sandhurst, seven years earlier, in Egypt, and throughout my time as a Subaltern had carried a Colour on ceremonial parades. They had been presented to us in England in 1930 by our Colonel in Chief, His Royal Highness The Prince of Wales. From 1931 they went with us, always guarded by an armed Colour Party, to Jerusalem, Cairo, Moascar, Singapore and, lastly, Hong Kong. We all felt strongly about their role in battalion life. It was agreed that they should not be sent to Singapore, and so we had them with us when, later that month, we moved from Shamshuipo to the much nicer Murray Barracks, on Hong Kong island".

The General Officer Commanding all British, Canadian and Indian forces in Hong Kong was Major General C M Maltby MC, with his official residence at Flagstaff House. On the evening of 4 December he was the guest of the 1st Middlesex at a Dinner Night in their Mess at Murray Barracks. The occasion is remembered vividly by Tony Hewitt.

"It was, in effect, our 'last supper'. Thirty-six officers sat down to dinner with the General. Within a month they were all dead, wounded or prisoners of war. There was no silver on the table, of course, but the two Colours were in their usual place on the wall of the dining room. There was reassurance in their lovely blaze of colour and the names of all the campaigns and battles in which our forebears had won fame and glory for the regiment".

The Middlesex was a medium machine-gun battalion, equipped with the Vickers gun and trained to operate in semi-independent sub-units. On 6 December, in response to intelli-

gence reports, "A", "B", "C" and "D" Companies occupied previously prepared strong-points covering all landing beaches except those on the north east corner of the island. Battalion headquarters was formed at Leighton Hill, two miles east of Murray Barracks, and defended by "Z" Company. Everyone was at their appointed post when, in the early hours of 8 December, the invasion began.

The subsequent battle continued without break for the next eighteen days. Colonel Hewitt describes the final hours: "After eleven days of intensive bombing and shelling, the Japanese established a landing at the north east tip of the island and then advanced rapidly. Leighton Hill, governing access to the city, was attacked furiously. Over the next five days the casualties were appalling. When units on our flanks began to be overrun, on 23 December, 'Monkey' moved the Battalion HQ back into the suburb of Wanchai. Here we were visited by His Excellency the Governor, Sir Mark Young. He bravely made his way up through the explosions and gunfire with a message from Churchill: 'A prolonged resistance can win the lasting honour which we are sure will be your due'. The Battle Honour 'Hong Kong' was indeed added to our Regimental Colour, in 1953.

On Christmas Eve I moved the Battalion HQ to the Naval Dockyard, and then, on Christmas afternoon, to Murray Barracks. Thirty-five surviving men of "Z" Company fell back to this position with others from various units, plus some Royal Scots who had fought with great heroism to hold the line.

At three in the afternoon, General Maltby rang to ask Colonel Stewart how much longer we could hold out. The Colonel said 'if the present intensity continues, not more than an hour'. Twenty-three minutes later the General called again, and ordered 'Monkey' to stop the battle.

'Monkey' Stewart was a wonderful soldier and he would have fought on the to the last man and the last round, but there was concern that any further fighting might lead to a Jap massacre of our wounded. We had given the enemy a hard fight and killed a lot of them. We knew their reputation for savagery and what they had done at Nanking.

I was standing beside the Colonel when the instruction to surrender was received. His face was drawn and grey from exhaustion. When he heard that terrible order, he went very white. He insisted on going out alone to talk to the Japs. I fixed a white bed-sheet to a pole, and he went off with it into the roar and stark fury of the battle, bravely walking out through the barrack gate into the Queen's Road. The scene was a horrible shambles of smoke and bodies and firing. I did not really expect to see him again. Some hours later he returned to resume command from Major Hedgecoe. He had been badly handled by the Japs, beaten and kicked, jeered and abused by our despicable enemy. It angered me that this splendid man had been so vilely treated, but he had persuaded them to cease fire, to respect our wounded, and not to enter the Barracks before we had had time to collect our kit and prepare ourselves for our future as prisoners-of-war.

When we first moved to Leighton Hill, on 8 December, the Colours were left behind at Murray Barracks in the charge of our Quartermaster, Major Bob Guscott. The QM Stores and Ration Stores were covered by a strong guard, but they could not protect the barrack blocks when the local Chinese went on the rampage and looted all the furnishings. The looters did not touch the Colours because they were secured in the QM Stores.

When the end came, and while the sounds of firing died down all around the island, the Colours were buried in the grounds of nearby Flagstaff House. Major Guscott had removed their poles and placed them in their black leather jackets together with the two finials. There, on that forlorn Christmas Night, two Middlesex officers, assisted by General Maltby and his ADC, dug a trench in a flower bed and covered the two packages with earth.

Those buried Colours carried the Battle Honours gained by The Middlesex Regiment in almost every British campaign since 1757. At Hong Kong, the 1st Middlesex maintained in full the traditions of the 57th of Foot, the regiment which won its nickname of 'Diehards' at the Battle of Albuhera on 16 May 1811".

Tony Hewitt and the other survivors became prisoners of war on Boxing Day when the Japanese entered Murray Barracks. "They searched us and started knocking us about. During this time the Colonel asked me to write a letter, addressed to all ranks and expressing his admiration for their bravery, discipline and loyalty against a strong enemy supported by air, navy and heavy artillery. Frank Waldron, the Orderly Room Sergeant, a gallant soldier who had given me staunch support in the battle, typed it and distributed copies to everyone who was still with us. Somehow he kept a copy throughout his long imprisonment".

The prisoners were taken off the island *via* the Star Ferry and marched back to Shamshuipo. Here Tony Hewitt quickly decided that he did not wish to remain a prisoner for the duration of the war. "I wanted to escape. I had been seven years in the Battalion. I knew every one of these wonderful Londoners whom I regarded as my mates, and I knew all their families who had been evacuated from Hong Kong in July. Ours was a magnificent battalion, an extended family in which everyone knew each other. All ranks, we had for years boxed together, played rugger together, trained together, had fun

together. I was unmarried, I was the senior Captain, and 'Monkey' considered that I was the most suitable man to tell the relatives what had happened to their men. Also, the authorities would need a first-hand account of the battle.

General Maltby gave me two letters to deliver to the British Embassy in Chungking, capital of Chang Kai-Shek's Free China. On 2 February 1942, after six weeks' captivity, I broke out of Shamshuipo prison camp, escaped through Japanese-occupied China to Free China and then went across to India. General Maltby's letters were delivered in Chungking and relatives were informed from Calcutta. Apart from some alarming experiences it became a wonderful celestial adventure".

Chungking is a thousand miles from Hong Kong. Tony Hewitt's experiences along the way, and his later journey from Chungking to Delhi, were published in his memoirs, *Bridge with Three Men* (Jonathan Cape, 1987). When the Commander-in-Chief in India, General Sir Archibald Wavell, heard the details, he authorised the immediate award of a Military Cross. Hewitt went on to complete a very full military career and rose to the rank of Colonel. Today he and his wife reside in Buderim, in the Australian state of Queensland, still in regular contact with other elderly officers and men who served in "that magnificent battalion".

Not many of the 754 all ranks who went into the battle survived to see the end of the war. Seven months after their victory, the Japanese decided to send the bulk of the captive Middlesex from Shamshuipo to Japan. On 1 October 1942 their transport ship, the *Lisbon Maru*, was torpedoed by the US Navy submarine *Grouper* about one hundred miles off Ningpo. One hundred and thirty-two officers and men of the 1st Middlesex were lost when she sank. Colonel Stewart was rescued and taken to Japan, but later in the war he died from the brutal treatment which he received there.

Major Frank Hedgecoe and Major Henry Marsh were two of the battalion's officers not embarked in the *Lisbon Maru*. In 1945, following their release from local captivity, they went to Flagstaff House to retrieve the Colours from the flower bed. There was almost nothing left. They recovered one finial, but it seemed that white ants or termites had consumed all of the fabric and the two leather jackets. The finial is now laid up in the Middlesex Regimental Chapel in St Paul's Cathedral, London.

The battalion's collection of silver, on the other hand, emerged from the war intact. It had reached Singapore in October 1941, and was deposited in the Hong Kong & Shanghai Bank's wharf-side warehouse. The docks were heavily bombed from December through to February, but the building and its contents escaped serious damage. The silver was soon found by the Japanese.

A curious inter-service dispute then erupted between the local commanders of the Imperial Japanese Navy and the Imperial Japanese Army. The navy claimed possession of all the property in the warehouse on the grounds that it was within the docks and therefore a naval matter. The army claimed possession by right of having captured the island in combat on the ground.

The argument had still not been resolved when, in August 1945, the war ended and the Middlesex silver was recovered and shipped back to England. Only one piece was missing, the gold Albuhera Medal presented to the 57th Regiment, many years after that battle, by Queen Victoria.

Upon its arrival in England the silver was sent to Carringtons for a complete renovation. The collection received its first post-war airing at The Connaught Rooms, in London, on 28 June 1946. The occasion was an Officers' Club Dinner when one hundred and sixty-eight serving and retired officers of The Middlesex Regiment gathered to renew old friendships. Amongst those present was the regiment's most famous living officer, Lieutenant General Sir Brian Horrocks KCB KBE DSO MC, latterly commanding 30 Corps of the British Liberation Army in North West Europe. The 1st Battalion's silver was displayed on the dining tables and, to quote from a contemporary report: "The presence of the silver conjured up memories of the gallant battalion who last used it before the heroic defence of Hong Kong, of Colonel Stewart and his gallantry, and the bravery shown by all those who served under him".

The Royal Scots (The Royal Regiment)

One of the few regiments to have been untouched by the British Army's numerous amalgamations of the past forty years is The Royal Scots. With its headquarters in Edinburgh Castle, it now has just one Regular battalion, but in 1941 it had two and one of them, the 2nd Battalion, was serving in Hong Kong as part of the Colony's peacetime garrison.

In line with other preparations for a possible outbreak of hostilities, the Commanding Officer, Lieutenant Colonel S E H E White MC, gave orders that the Mess silver and other important regimental possessions should be packed and removed to India for safe-keeping. The shipping agents,

McEwan & Younger, were given this task and the crates were sent aboard a ship bound for Singapore. On arrival they were unloaded into the agents' go-down (warehouse) to await transfer to the next ship bound for India. That was the end of their intended journey. The Japanese invaded Malaya, Singapore came under aerial attack, and all routine shipping movements ceased.

The Royal Scots, together with the rest of the British, Indian and Canadian units stationed in Hong Kong and the adjoining mainland New Territories, fought their fierce but hopeless defence and the survivors then became prisoners of war for the next three and a half years. One hundred and seven members of the battalion died in the battle and 230 were wounded. At the time of the surrender only 102 were still in action, and many of these died later in captivity.

The Supreme Allied Commander in South East Asia, Admiral Lord Louis Mountbatten, received the official surrender of all Japanese forces in Malaya at a ceremony at the Municipal Building, Singapore, on 12 September, 1945. Local conditions were chaotic. The Japanese occupation money was worthless, the black market was thriving, thousands of recently released prisoners needed medical care and repatriation, and Mountbatten was so short of troops that he authorised the use of Japanese soldiers to guard public buildings. From all of this emerged a man who was to play a key role in saving an important

The Royal Scots have a fine collection of silver. This centrepiece was made by Hunt & Roskell, for the officers of the 1st Battalion. The steel engraving is taken from the pamphlet produced by the firm to advertise its services to other regiments. Their wording states: "The Trophy, which stands 3 feet, 6 inches high, is designed to illustrate at a glance the history of this, the oldest Regiment of the Line. At the angles of the base are figures, in the uniforms of the times and with weapons then in use, representing different periods of the earlier history of the Regiment, viz: 1625 Pikeman, 1685 Musketeer, 1742 Private, 1813 Colour Sergeant. Between these figures are panels chased in relief representing four battles in which the Regiment won renown, viz: Blenheim, Corunna, Quatre-Bras, and the assault on San Sebastian. At the top is a group representing the brave Sir Robert Douglas, at the Battle of Steenkirke, 1692. This gallant officer, in the face of almost certain death, leapt a hedge to recover a standard which had been lost, and succeeded, single-handedly, in doing so, but was shot dead in returning. At the ends of the tower which support the top group are draped the Regimental Colours, over a Sphinx with the word 'Egypt' to commemorate the Campaign in that Country in 1801, while in front and at the back are grouped Arms and Armour, with a ribbon entwining them engraved with names of battles in which the Regiment was engaged. It is needless to say that in a work of this kind, much antiquarian research has been necessary, and many weeks have been spent in collecting the various details from The Tower of London and the old 'Records' in the libraries of the British Museum and the United Service Institution, in order to obtain the proper authority for the many parts of this important piece. The whole of the work, designing, modelling, etc, has been executed at the Firm's manufactory, 26 Harrison Street, Gray's Inn Road, WC". Source: RHQ The Royal Scots.

Hong Kong, January, 1940. When the officers of the 2nd Battalion, The Royal Scots, posed for the camera, they had no idea of what was to come less than two years later. By then, many of the twenty-four regimental officers seen here had returned to Edinburgh Castle. They were needed to reinforce the new and Territorial Army battalions. The Royal Scots had sixteen officers killed in Hong Kong, but only two of them appear in this picture. In little more than a year there had been an almost complete turnover (the new officers being mainly Reservists and Territorial Army). *Rear row, left to right:* 2nd Lieut K J Campbell (captured), 2nd Lieut D Pinkerton (captured, killed Suez 1956), 2nd Lieut B A Fargus (to 8th RS), 2nd Lieut G D Dunlop (served with Chindits), Lieut K I M Buchanan (to 7th/9th RS), 2nd Lieut D G Gibson, 2nd Lieut N H Cuthbertson (captured, died 17.10.1942), Lieut Niven (not traced). *Centre row:* Lieut J R Pirie (Quartermaster, captured), Lieut A Campbell-Patterson, Lieut J E Ridsdale (Royal Norfolks, attached), Lieut D I H Callendar, Lieut Freeman-Thomas (not traced, possibly padre), Lieut N H M D'Oyly, Lieut J A H Douglass (to 8th RS), Lieut F W A Glossop. *Front row:* Capt D A Duke (to Staff, Singapore, captured, Burma railway), Capt H A C Harland (captured), Major A J Godley, Major S E H E White MC (promoted Lieut Col and CO before the battle), Lieut Col D J McDougall MC (CO in 1940), Major A G Syme MM, Capt S Burn (killed, 16.12.1941), Capt R N Gilbertson (to 8th RS), Capt A C F Drew-Wilkinson (to 1st RS). Photo: RHQ The Royal Scots.

part of Scotland's military heritage. His name was Mervyn Sheppard.

In 1928, having graduated from Magdalene College, Cambridge, he had come to Malaya as a Cadet with the administration of the Federation of Malayan States. A bright star, he moved swiftly up through the various civil service grades and, by 1939, age thirty-four, was a Second Assistant Secretary to the Government. Like most of his colleagues, he was a member of his local part-time military unit (in his case, in the rank of Captain, commanding "C" Company, Perak Battalion, of the Federated Malay States Volunteer Force).

In December 1941, following the Japanese landings, he handed over to his second-in-command and joined the secret group which later evolved as Force 136. This was a covert "stay behind" organisation initially intended to conduct guerilla warfare until such time as reinforcements could move north from Singapore. By March of 1942, having nearly died from typhus contracted during one of these operations, he was captured and later taken to Changi Jail, on Singapore Island. The Japanese knew that he had been engaged in covert operations and they wanted him to reveal the names and hiding places of his comrades. He passed into the hands of the *Kempeitai*, the so-called Military Police. An organisation similar to the Gestapo but much more cruel and sadistic, the *Kempeitai* operated as an

occupation security force and as controllers of prisoner of war camps.

Against all the odds, Mervyn Sheppard survived his period of torture and, at the end of the war, weighing six and a half stone, was freed from the Sime Road camp.

Thousands of people were waiting to return home. Shipping space was limited, priority being given to women, children and married couples. Sheppard's wife and daughter had gone back to England in 1941 and were still there, so his own priority was low. Faced with many tedious weeks of waiting, he applied for a job with the Special Branch "E" Group, created by 14th Army headquarters to investigate war crimes. He was accepted, retaining his rank of Captain.

He had already started to make enquiries of his own. He had learned from a Chinese friend, who held a commission in the Singapore Volunteer Corps, that the Japanese garrisons in the Dutch East Indies were still at liberty. They were deemed to be the responsibility of the Dutch, not of the British 14th Army. The friend had reliable reports, from his contacts in the Chinese community, that hundreds of Japanese had fled to the islands south of Singapore during the final weeks of the war. An unknown but substantial number of these were members of the *Kempeitai*. The nearest islands were the Riau group, specifically Kundur and Singkep.

Mervyn Sheppard later told his daughter that this was "one of several occasions in his life when he had an impulse as sudden and forceful as lightning-strike, he must round up the *Kempeitai* in the Riau Islands". First he needed firm evidence, and this he obtained by tracking down a Formosan named Toh Sween Khoon. This man had been employed as Chief Interpreter to the *Kempeitai* in Singapore throughout the war, and had been present when Sheppard himself went through his interrogation.

Sheppard offered him a deal, promising to speak for him at his trial if he would reveal the names and destinations of senior *Kempeitai* officers who had escaped to Dutch territory. The Formosan quickly agreed and signed a statement which confirmed the earlier rumours. Sheppard then secured an interview with the Army commander, General Sir Miles Dempsey, producing his evidence and requesting authority to mount an operation. He was turned down because the navy already had too many other commitments and the waters to the south were thought to be heavily mined.

Sheppard's Chinese friend produced an alternative solution. He knew a Chinese collaborator who was expecting to be punished when the civil government was restored. He owned two sizeable motor launches which he had been using for black market trading with the Riau Islands, and he was willing to make them available in the hope of acquiring merit with the new administration. Sheppard went back to Dempsey's staff. He told them that he now had his transport but needed some fire-power in case the Japanese were unwilling to surrender. This was agreed, and he was given an Indian officer and two sections of soldiers from a battalion of the 1st Punjab Regiment. Also in his party were a Japanese interpreter and a Dutch fellow prisoner of war, Mr G J A Veling, a pre-war East Indies administrative officer.

Captain Sheppard later wrote an account of his expedition. "I had spent an almost sleepless night making sure that both motor boats were ready. This included gathering the scattered crews, obtaining enough petrol and oil on the black market, and enlisting an expert Malay pilot who knew a safe route to Kundur. It was with a feeling that the age of miracles had not yet passed that I gave the order to sail, from Clifford Pier, only ten minutes after the planned hour of departure.

The mines were either out of our depth or off our course, and though both motor boats had periodic engine trouble, that was soon remedied and we sighted Kundur at 1400 hours on a sunny breezy afternoon. As we moved towards the jetty, with all arms trained on the soldiers who were waiting there, the interpreter shouted through a loud hailer a call to surrender. There was no sign of resistance and we were received by three Japanese army officers and a small guard. Tangjong Batu, the village where we landed, had a garrison of sixty-two, of whom fourteen were *Kempeitai*. Five of these had come from *Kempeitai* headquarters, in Singapore.

A wireless message was sent to Singapore to report our arrival, while the Punjabi officer began collecting all arms and ammunition and confined the Japanese in the local school. Veling and I then checked the stocks of food and petrol, and were astonished to find fifty tons of rice and 1500 gallons of petrol. Evidently Tanjong Batu was a gilt-edged branch of the black market.

By 2300 hours the Japanese commanding officer, a middle-aged Colonel, was insisting that there was nothing more to hand over. It had been a long hot day and the previous night had been almost sleepless, but I noticed a large wooden shed, enclosed by a barbed wire fence which looked quite new, standing a little distance from the road which led to the jetty".

Through his interpreter, Sheppard asked the Colonel what the building contained. He replied that it held nothing of importance but, unconvinced, Sheppard ordered the soldiers to force the door. Entering, he found himself in an outer room which, disappointingly, was empty. Flashing his torch around the walls, he saw another door, heavily padlocked and barred, the entrance to an inner room. This too was forced.

"By the light of my torch we could see rows of packing cases, at least fifty at a quick count. A Punjabi bayonet lifted the lid of the first crate and I picked up a silver spoon with a thistle device engraved on the handle. I recognised it instantly. It was the crest of The Royal Scots, the regiment of my twin brother, Frank".

Mervyn Sheppard knew that this was no ordinary private hoard of Japanese war loot. What he had found was almost all of the 2nd Battalion's silver sent back in 1941 from Hong Kong, plus, as he quickly discovered, a small part of the Mess silver of the 2nd Battalion, The Argyll and Sutherland Highlanders.

There was no room for the crates in the over-loaded launches. When Sheppard and his party departed on the morning of 4 October with his Japanese prisoners, they were left behind in the charge of the Dutchman, Mr Veling. Two weeks later, a naval motor launch, Q851, was sent to Tanjong Batu to collect them and bring them to Singapore. Here the Royal Scots silver was separated from that of The Argyll and Sutherland Highlanders and handed to an officer of the regiment, Captain R M Crockatt. He happened to be serving locally on the staff of the 14th Army, and he arranged for the silver to be shipped back to the United Kingdom and, finally, to Edinburgh Castle.

The success of Mervyn Sheppard's *ad hoc* expedition, mounted on his own initiative, came as a surprise to the army and to the navy. An ex-POW weighing less than seven stone, a Volunteer officer with no staff or even an office, he had organised the liberation of the island and rounded up several wanted *Kempeitai*. The staff at 14th Army headquarters decided to approve a second trip, this time to Singkep. Promoted to Major, he was allocated four Royal Navy launches and a platoon of The Parachute Regiment. Even better, he was put on the official ration strength and started to draw pay (his first since December 1941).

The operation yielded a haul of sixty-five garrison troops and thirty-five *Kempeitai*. It was followed by an even larger expedition, to Bintan, with two destroyers and four assault landing craft, which rounded up seven hundred more Japanese servicemen.

Major Sheppard's final voyage, on 16 October, took him to the island of Rangsang. Here a group of Imperial Japanese Navy personnel had established an armed camp and had already murdered two Indonesian officials sent to investigate. This time he had with him a platoon of West Yorkshires. The Japanese sailors offered no resistance and were brought back to Singapore for investigation. In the space of less than four weeks, starting with Kundur and ending with Rangsang, Mervyn Sheppard had traced and apprehended nearly nine hundred Japanese, many of whom were tried subsequently for war crimes.

The following year he was appointed a Member of the Order of the British Empire. The rescued silver made its way back to the United Kingdom, but he stayed on. During the anti-Communist campaign of 1948 to 1960 he was for a while head of the Food Denial Organisation. His final appointment, in 1957, was Malaya's Director of Museums.

The Royal Scots acknowledged that "the battalion owes to

Major Sheppard its deep gratitude and thanks for his successful recovery of its dearly prized property". The battalion could not know just how close it came to losing that property. In the words of his daughter, Mrs John Buckland: "The price of silver in Singapore after the Japanese surrender was astronomical. At least one or two of the Chinese shopkeepers on Kundur Island must have known of the hoard of silver and, when the Japanese garrison was removed, they would have been in a position to dispose of it. If my father had overlooked the wooden hut that dark night, or accepted the Japanese Colonel's assurance that it was empty and been too tired to investigate thoroughly, several Kundur businessmen would have become very wealthy".

The Argyll and Sutherland Highlanders (Princess Louise's)

The Argyll and Sutherland Highlanders were not quite so lucky. Under the command of Lieutenant Colonel Ian MacA Stewart MC, their 2nd Battalion was, before the war, stationed in Singapore. As the 93rd (Sutherland Highlanders) Regiment of Foot, their forebears had formed the famous "Thin Red Line" at Balaklava. In 1941, following the Japanese invasion, the battalion's women and children were evacuated while their menfolk were rushed to northern Malaya to help stem the tide. They fought the Japanese continuously for nearly three months. Possessing neither anti-tank weapons nor radio equipment, they were driven inexorably down the length of the peninsula. They lost 244 dead in the process, and 184 were to die later in captivity.

Colonel Stewart was unique amongst local unit commanders in having trained his battalion to fight away from the roads - in the jungle and in the rubber plantations - but from the outset he was aware that the odds were stacked against him.

Committed to battle, he and his officers agreed to send the Mess contents to India or, if possible, back to Scotland. Captain D Drummond-Hay was given the task of packing them and delivering them to a firm of shipping agents, William Jacobs & Company. The crates arrived in the agent's go-down at Singapore Docks but, as happened with The Royal Scots' possessions, larger events then intervened.

Who stole the Argyll's silver and what they did with it will never be known with certainty, but it seems likely that much of it was taken to the Riau islands and thereafter traded all around Sumatra as barter on the black market.

Following the reoccupation of Singapore, an Argyll officer on the 14th Army headquarters staff, Lieutenant Colonel J C Cockburn DSO MBE, made it his business to organise a search. In October 1945 he wrote to the regiments' depôt at Stirling Castle, reporting his progress. "The whole business (in the Riau area) is being handled by a Dutch civilian (G J A Veling). He has been quite splendid, taking infinite trouble to collect our stuff, or what he can find of it, from all over the islands. It arrived here in a complete jumble and much of it is in bad condition. There are two of those huge green baize fitted cases and it is pathetic to see the few rather battered pieces inside them. I got a line on a Chinaman the other day and visited his house where, in the attic, he had ten large boxes of silver which he had bought from the Japs. We waded through every box of it with the result that I found four Sergeants' Mess sauce boats, a South Africa football cup, a Rawal Pindi hockey cup, and a cigarette box. The Chink was perfectly open about the whole thing. He had bought from the Japs a job lot of silver, mostly hotel and club plate and cheap sorts of wedding presents, and in which our stuff was included. I've now offered a reward in the Chinese and Malay papers as

The major pieces in the collection of the 2nd Battalion, The Argyll & Sutherland Highlanders, at the turn of the century. The photograph was taken in 1904. Prominent in the middle of the display is the 93rd Centrepiece looted by the Japanese following the fall of Singapore in 1942. Rescued by Lieutenant Colonel J C Cockburn in 1945, it was destroyed by fire in 1980. Few of the other pieces in this display survived the Singapore disaster. Photo: RHQ, A&SH, Stirling Castle.

well as in the English ones, and got them to put over an appeal on the radio, but the devil of it is that there was no distinction made by the Japs between hotel and club stuff and regimental plate, and they are all hopelessly mixed up. I've got back a Sergeants' Mess tankard from Changi Jail, but I fear a lot of it is all over hell's half acre".

Colonel Cockburn was a determined man. He sent messages to the British and Allied authorities as far afield as Saigon, Bangkok and Djakarta, hoping that Japanese soldiers stationed in Singapore in 1942 might have taken their loot with them when they were posted away later in the war. In the end, a greater part of the battalion's silver was never recovered. However, he did succeed in retrieving some of the most important pieces, much of it relating to the period when the 2nd Battalion was still the 93rd (Sutherland Highlanders) Regiment of Foot.

The prize which topped his efforts was the item illustrated here, the massive centrepiece which commemorated the 93rd's services in the Crimea against the Russians and, soon afterwards, in India against the Mutineers. Given everything which happened to it between 1941 and 1945, it was doubly tragic that this regimental treasure should subsequently be destroyed by something as mundane as an accidental fire.

In 1980, the 1st Battalion (by then the regiment's *only* regular battalion), was serving a tour of duty in Northern Ireland, with comfortable accommodation in the permanent barracks at Ballykelly. On 5 June, at one-thirty in the morning, a fire was detected in the Officers' Mess building. The heat was so intense that roof tiles were exploding with the same violence as small arms fire, and the first assumption by the living-in members was that they were under attack by terrorists.

The 93rd Highlanders' Crimea and Indian Mutiny centrepiece, lost and found in Singapore, then lost for ever in Northern Ireland. Photo: Mrs Pauline Ward MBE.

Well-rehearsed battalion fire drills contained the blaze to the ante-room pending the arrival of the local fire brigade. Resolved to get at the seat of the fire, the brigade's leader bravely launched himself at the plate glass entrance door. Failing at the first attempt, he used his helmet to smash a way through. None of the Argylls had the heart to tell him that the door was already unlocked.

Despite the unintended humour, the episode was a disaster for the regiment. Colour Sergeant Crawford and his Mess staff, helped by the living-in officers, moved all the Mess property not inside the burning ante-room to a place of safety, but everything else was lost. The long list of destroyed items included not only the 93rd centrepiece but also a number of important oil paintings and a beautiful set of Orlando Norrie prints of scenes from the Indian Mutiny. To quote the regimental journal: "In all,

some seventeen thousand pounds-worth of regimental history went up in smoke. Of course, our insurers will repay the monetary value, but the history and tradition steeped into the items can never be replaced". When told the next day what had happened, the Colonel of the Regiment said: "We will just have to start collecting all over again".

The centrepiece lost in the fire had been acquired in 1870. It is thought to have been made by Elkington & Company, to an original design by one of the officers, and to have stood about four feet in height. Fortunately, in a letter written in 1960 by Lieutenant Colonel C G Kelway Bamber, we find a precise explanation of its symbolism.

"One side shows the battered wall of an outwork of Sevastopol, where an officer of the 93rd (modelled from Captain A C Nightingale) stands contemplating the dead body of a Russian soldier. Nearby, on the ground, lies a severely wounded private of the 93rd. Above is a life-like figure of the Pipe-Major, represented as playing 'The Gathering'. The other side has an exact reproduction from a photograph of one of the gateway towers of the Sikandarbagh at Lucknow, and an officer (modelled from Lieutenant R Barclay-Allardice) and a private (modelled from Private William Cowie) looking down at a dead Sepoy, emblems of the Mutiny struggle.

Ornamental silver shields on either side of the ebony plinth, surrounded by wreaths of thistle and cat's tail grass (butcher's broom), bear a presentation inscription describing it as a memorial from some of the officers (whose names run round the silver rim on the top of the pedestal) of the part taken by the 93rd in the Crimean War and the Indian Mutiny.

This centrepiece was inspected by Her Majesty Queen Victoria at Windsor Castle in July 1870 when she expressed her approval of both the design and the workmanship. It reproduces exactly the dress and appointments of the 93rd of the period, whilst the uniform and accoutrements of the Russian are copied from one of the regiments opposed to the 93rd at the Alma, and those of the Sepoy from one of the mutinous corps annihilated at the Sikandarbagh".

The Royal Leicestershire Regiment

The 1st Battalion of The Royal Leicestershire Regiment was serving its routine tour of duty on India's North West Frontier when, in September 1939, it was ordered to embark for Malaya. German forces were sweeping across Poland, but the Far East was still a peaceful backwater. The Battalion left some of its best pieces of silver in India, but the move from Razmak to Penang seems to have been arranged on the basis that this was just one more routine change of station. By February of 1940 the Leicesters were settled in northern Malaya, freed from the daily sniping of Frontier tribesmen and beginning to enjoy the relaxed ways of the east. The pace of training increased as the months slipped by, but nobody could imagine the storm to come.

By a quirk of geography, the war which engulfed South East Asia and the Pacific Ocean happened to straddle the International Date Line. At 2.15 a.m. on 8 December 1941 (Tokyo time and date), Japanese assault troops began to come ashore on the beaches at Kota Bahru, on Malaya's eastern seaboard. Waiting for them, having been alerted at the last moment, was the 3rd Battalion of the 17th Dogra Regiment. It was an unknown Dogra soldier who fired the first shot of the Pacific war. One hour and ten minutes later, at 3.25 a.m. (Tokyo time) the first Japanese bomb fell on the US Navy base at Pearl Harbour. Forty-five minutes after that, a Japanese naval force began to put troops ashore at Singora (Siam), and the Crown Colony of Hong Kong came under attack. Yet another major Japanese amphibious force assaulted the American positions on the Philippines. Both the Americans and the British were faced with circumstances for which they made only the poorest preparations. What followed in Malaya has been described as the worst defeat of British arms in modern times.

The Leicesters were ordered to leave their quarters at Penang and to move, in battle order, towards the rapidly advancing Japanese. The regimental baggage, including the Officers' and Sergeants' Mess property, was hastily packed and placed in store. The larger items went into a warehouse while the silver was deposited in the vaults of the Penang branch of the Hong Kong & Shanghai Bank. Many of the officers and men decided, individually, that they too should leave their personal valuables at the bank. Headed for imminent battle, they left behind their silver cigarette cases, their campaign medals, any expensive watches and personal jewellery, and numerous small items of sentimental value.

Within a fortnight, half of the battalion were dead or wounded. Similar losses were suffered by the 2nd Battalion of the East Surrey Regiment, so the survivors of the two depleted units were combined, temporarily, as The British Battalion, 15th Indian Infantry Brigade. Despite a series of rearguard actions, they were driven steadily down the length of the peninsula until, on 15 February 1942, all remaining Allied forces surrendered to the Japanese at Singapore. The captive Leicesters spent the rest of the war in primitive camps around Bangkok.

Word that the war was over reached them on 15 August 1945. Several weeks were needed to deal with the collapse of the Japanese administration and to arrange the evacuation from Bangkok of thousands of former prisoners of war, of several nationalities and all in very poor health. It was not until early October that the commanding officer of The Royal Leicesters, Lieutenant Colonel C E Morrison MC, was able to despatch one of his officers to Penang to discover what had happened to the battalion's property.

Major R G G Harvey was flown south to Penang where he found the town in a state of chaos. The bank vaults and all other commercial premises had been looted, and there was at first no trace of the battalion's possessions. He obtained the assistance of the police in questioning local people and eventually was able to recover a third of the silver. He found the King's Colour, minus its pole and tassels, on a rubbish dump. It was brought home and installed in the Regimental Chapel. All the other items were lost. Sadly, they included not only the band instruments and all personal effects but also the hand-written diary - the *Digest of Services* - which was the battalion's record of its services over the previous one hundred years.

The Gordon Highlanders

There has never been any logical or predictable pattern to the way in which Mess silver might or might not survive the hazards of war or even the perils of peace. The officers of the 2nd Battalion, The Leicestershire Regiment, deposited theirs in 1941 with a bank in Penang and lost almost everything. They fought and died in northern Malaya alongside the 2nd Battalion, The East Surrey Regiment, a unit which lost the majority of its men but whose silver survived the war intact. It had been handed for safe-keeping to The Hong Kong & Shanghai Bank in Singapore. With it was the silver of the 2nd Battalion, The Gordon Highlanders. Their combined possessions were left undisturbed until after the Japanese surrender and were then brought back to the United Kingdom in the battleship HMS *Nelson*.

The Gordon Highlanders were committed to battle, in the defence of southern Malaya and Singapore, in the final stages of that abysmal campaign. They fought with all the courage expected of a proud and ancient Scottish regiment, but lack of equipment, inappropriate training and the general tide of events doomed them to be on the losing side. Their experiences are best summarised by the wall plaque to be seen in Singapore's Presbyterian Church: "To the Glory of God and in Sacred Remembrance of 380 Officers & Men of the 2nd Bn The Gordon Highlanders who, during the Malayan Campaign of 1941-1942 and in the dark days of captivity which followed, made the supreme sacrifice. Their bodies lie scattered on land and sea over almost the whole of South East Asia, but their Name liveth for evermore".

During 1943 and 1944 the Gordons worked in Siam on the infamous Railway of Death but, before being sent there in

Known as "Jock by the Fire", this unusual cigar lighter was *Presented to the 92nd Gordon Highlanders by Lieut Colonel J C Hay, 1881, upon being promoted to Lieutenant Colonel.* They became 2nd Battalion, The Gordon Highlanders, shortly afterwards. Made by S Smith & Son, of 35 King Street, Covent Garden, it measures approximately six inches in height and six inches across the base, and weighs 37 ounces. Within the silver log fire is an oil-fed wick. John Crossland Hay joined the 92nd in 1855 as an Ensign, purchased his Lieutenancy a few months later, then his Captaincy in 1864. His promotions to Major and Lieutenant Colonel followed in 1876 and 1881. By then, "purchase" had been abolished. He commanded the battalion from 1885 to 1887 before retiring with the honorary rank of Major General. The evidence suggests that "Jock by the Fire" did not travel with the battalion to Singapore but instead spent the war elsewhere. He is now on permanent display in The Gordon Highlanders Museum, Aberdeen. Photo: The Regimental Museum.

October 1942, they were imprisoned at Changi, on Singapore's eastern tip. One of the first actions taken at that time by the Commanding Officer, Lieutenant Colonel J H Stitt, was to arrange for a legal document to be prepared so that, in the event of his death in captivity, there would be a group of nominated persons authorised as Trustees to make decisions regarding the security of the battalion's silver. Given the circumstances - the recent shock of battle, the trauma of defeat and imprisonment, the loss of so many comrades in action and (even at that early stage) from disease - it was an extraordinarily pragmatic step. Details of this document appear in Appendix "A".

So the Gordons and the East Surreys were able to recover their silver from the bank, while the Royal Scots and the Argyll and Sutherland Highlanders were blessed with the good fortune of having men like Major Sheppard, Mr Veling and Colonel Cockburn to look after their interests.   Another remarkable rescue at that time was the recovery of a Regimental Colour.

Captain A S Carr, of the Royal Electrical & Mechanical Engineers, was serving with the 36th Division, in Sumatra, when he was granted home leave. He made his way to Singapore where he was delayed for several days, waiting for a berth in a United Kingdom-bound ship. With a friend, Captain B C Young, of the Royal Welch Fusiliers, he was strolling one day in the waterfront area when he noticed some brightly coloured fabric on a street vendor's barrow. Extracting it from the heap of second-hand clothes, he found it to be the Regimental Colour of the 2nd Battalion, The Royal Scots. Evidently it, like the silver, had been looted from the docks in 1942. Captain Carr paid the one dollar asking price and returned it to the regiment on his arrival in the United Kingdom. The King's Colour was never found.

The Royal Hong Kong Police

David Deptford is a retired police officer who began his post-war career with the Northern Rhodesia Police but then served thirty-three years with the Royal Hong Kong Police. He has a long-standing interest in military history, and his experiences help to further explain what happened to regimental silver and other possessions which disappeared during the Japanese occupations.

"I was able to travel widely throughout the Far East and, given my collecting enthusiasms, I always kept an eye open for anything unusual. I never found any Mess silver as such, nor even any pieces of great significance, but I managed to find various bits and pieces in places as far apart as Malaysia, Thailand, Singapore and Hong Kong. A limited number came through agents in various towns and cities in mainland China, which I was myself unable to visit. The silver items were mainly shooting and sporting trophies, and I also rescued a number of British campaign medals. These things could surface almost anywhere - hawker stalls, flea markets or antique shops proper. It seems likely that all manner of things were looted by local people or by the Japanese, and then became barter goods during and after the war. As a result, they were passed from hand to hand and reached destinations far removed from the original British colonial territories".

Prior to WWII, the Gazetted Officers of the Hong Kong Police did not have their own dedicated Mess. It followed, therefore, that they did not own any Mess silver in the usual sense. However, most had in their homes or offices pieces of silver presented to them to mark certain events in their careers. There are several anecdotes which tell of police officers hurriedly burying these valuables in the garden or some other handy plot before going off to fight the Japanese. A hundred Hong Kong policemen, of all ranks, died in the battle or in captivity.

In many instances the surviving officers were delighted to find their silver intact when, armed with a spade or shovel, they went back in August of 1945.

7th Coast Regiment, Royal Artillery

Another group which resorted to burial were the officers of the 7th Coast Regiment, RA. An element in the defence of Singapore Island, the Regiment was deployed on several outlying islands, its guns covering the seaward approaches. The regimental Mess was located on the island of Blakang Mati.

Major P K Higgins RA tells the story: "Whilst I was serving there postwar with the 1st Singapore Regiment RA, in 1959, there was a rumour circulating that some military silver had been buried to hide it from the Japanese Army. No actual place was specified other than it was supposed to be fairly close to the Mess. This was thought to be the location because it was out of sight of the local people, and the two or three officers involved would have had little time anyway. The legend stated that they died while prisoners in Japanese hands.

As inquisitive Subalterns, some of us would from time to time try to predict where it might be buried and have an investigative dig. We did not have metal detectors. We never found anything, so perhaps the silver is still there".

According to the Woolwich records, it is unlikely that the 7th Coast Regiment could have had any major items of silver on Blakang Mati, but there will have been the usual range of decorative pieces and flatware. In 1996, the Royal Artillery Institution received through the mail a silver spoon, engraved with the regimental crest. The covering letter, from a former British gunner, explained that he had taken it from the Mess in 1942, at the time of the surrender. It was his eating implement throughout his years of captivity. He kept it into old age as a *memento*, but then decided to return it to its natural home.

14th Punjab Regiment

One of the units caught up in the tragedy of Hong Kong was the 2nd Battalion of the 14th Punjab Regiment, Indian Army. At the time of the Japanese invasion it was stationed in the New Territories, and was involved in the fighting around Fanling. On the night of 12-13 December 1941, the Mess silver was taken to a quiet corner of the barracks and secretly buried. It remained there, undisturbed, throughout the war. Following the Japanese surrender and the release of their prisoners, a party of the 2nd/14th returned to Kowloon and retrieved it, complete and undamaged

The battalion's 516 survivors were obliged to wait several weeks before shipping space became available to take them home. Also awaiting passage to India in the same draft were 109 men of the Hong Kong-Shanghai Artillery Corps, 153 of the Hong Kong Mule Corps, nineteen of the 5th/7th Rajput Regiment, and a handful of medical staff.

Finally, in early October, they boarded the *Takliwa*, a cargo-liner of 8000 tons owned by the British India Steam Navigation Company. The crated silver of the 2nd/14th Punjab Regiment was safely stowed deep in the hold. The surviving officers and men of the battalion had nothing to do but relax and look forward to their landfall at Madras, but in the event their troubles were not yet over.

Despite having been employed in hazardous duties as a Personnel Ship throughout WWII (taking part in the 1942 evacuation of Singapore, the 1942 and 1943 assault landings in Madagascar and Sicily, and the 1944 reoccupation of the Dodecanese Islands), the *Takliwa* had come through unscathed. However, she was not always the luckiest of ships. In her twenty-one years of voyaging around the Far East she suffered a serious fire in 1924 and ran aground off Japan, in the Saratoga Strait, in 1927. Now, on 15 October of 1945, she steamed into her final misadventure.

Having called at Singapore and passed through the Strait of Malacca, she entered the Bay of Bengal. Here she encountered a powerful south-westerly gale and became stranded on Great

The ill-fated *Takliwa*, wrecked and destroyed by fire on 15 October 1945. There were no human casualties, but the silver of the 2nd/14th Punjab Regiment was lost for ever. Photo: P&O Steam Navigation Co Ltd.

Nikobar, the southernmost of the Andaman Islands. Many of the passengers and 287 crewmen got away by lifeboat or by jumping overboard and swimming ashore.

When she grounded, the ship's fuel tanks ruptured and fire broke out in the engine room. Driven by the gale-force winds, it spread rapidly to other parts of the vessel. HMS *Sainfoin*, a naval assault landing ship on passage from Saigon to Colombo, intercepted her SOS call and two hours later approached the wreck. Her shallow draft permitted her, despite the difficult conditions of weather and smoke, to come alongside and take on board the *Takliwa's* remaining crew and complement of passengers.

On the following day the *Sainfoin* nosed into the beach and rescued those who had got away earlier. No lives were lost in the operation, but the officers and men of the 2nd/14th lost all of the few possessions which they had retained from their years of captivity. The fires continued to burn until the ship was gutted and her back broken. The collection of battalion silver was destroyed, there being no hope of saving even a part of it.

18th Royal Garhwal Rifles

Following their capture of Hong Kong, Malaya, Singapore, and the Dutch East Indies, and their destruction of all major Allied naval units in South East Asian waters, the rampant Japanese swept aside the meagre and ill-prepared defences of Burma. As they pushed westwards towards the border with India, and northwards towards China, the British suffered what was accurately described by the American general most closely involved, Joe Stilwell, as "a hell of a licking". Within four months, the Japanese had taken most of Burma's principal towns and were entering Assam.

Several units of the Indian Army lost all or part of their Mess silver during that period. One of these was The Royal Garhwal Rifles. An officer who served with the regiment was Captain Peter Cashmore. This is his account: "In April 1942 our 1st Battalion was part of 13th Brigade, 1st Burma Division, and they were retreating towards the border with India. They were in the area of the oilfields around Monywa, held up by a Japanese road block. It was the hottest time of the year, and conditions were not improved by the heat from the burning oil installations and by constant sniping. The battalion's transport came under heavy shellfire. It attempted to make a detour around the enemy blocking force, and it was at that stage, it is thought, that all the Mess kit was lost. It included a set of twelve silver goblets, made so that one could drink beer from one end or spirits from the other.

The retreat continued, and none of the kit was salvaged. Three years later, in April 1945, with the tide turned and the Japanese Army now in retreat, a British soldier made a remarkable discovery. Sergeant Morris was serving with 5 Field Company RE, an element of 2nd British Division. His unit had reached the banks of the Irrawaddy. Curled up one night in his blanket, he felt what he thought was a stone pressing into his hip. Rolling back the blanket, he dug out of the ground a blackened object which he recognised as some sort of chalice. Being a good soldier, he put it in his kitbag.

On his return home to England, and after giving it a good wash and polish, he saw that the goblet was engraved with the crest of the Royal Garhwal Rifles and with the name of the 1st Battalion. He wrote to the War Office for a regimental contact address, but received no reply. So time went by until, on 15 September 1991, he saw a notice in the *Sunday Express* mentioning a Garhwali officers' reunion and giving my address.

He contacted me and in due course the goblet arrived. Who knows, perhaps if he had dug deeper, he might have found the other eleven? But the regiment was very grateful to the 87-year old Mr Morris for returning this one to us.

In 1992 I had reason to go to the Regimental Centre at Lansdowne, a pretty military cantonment 6000 feet up in the Himalayas, with a lovely view of Nanda Devi and other surrounding mountains. Here I handed the goblet to the Commandant, and it now rests in the Centre's museum".

1st/6th Rajputana Rifles

Equally strange was the rescue of another piece, an item of silver having a connection with the 6th Rajputana Rifles. The setting for this episode was the border country between western Burma and India's eastern province of Assam. A land of thick jungles and low mountain ranges, it was best known to the outside world for its exports of teak and tea. In the early months of 1942 it became the setting for a human disaster of epic proportions.

Tens of thousands of people had tried, and were still trying, to evade the Japanese invasion by making their way to India. These were not just the survivors from British Army and Indian Army units shattered during the desperate fighting, there were even larger numbers of civilians. Since 1937, when Burma was separated from India and became a Crown Colony, it had had its own administration which employed hundreds of Britons. They and their families were now trapped. The tea, timber and oil industries also employed a great many Europeans and Burmans. There were others, police and customs officers, Burmese civil servants and Indian traders, who knew that they had no future under a Japanese occupation.

Evacuation by sea became impossible when the Royal Navy lost control of the Bay of Bengal, so the only routes out of Burma were through the valley of the Irrawaddy and across the steep-sided jungle hills of Chin and Manipur. For many, especially those escaping Rangoon, this meant a journey of hundreds of miles, mainly on foot.

There is no precise record of the numbers who died on that trail of tears, but it was in the thousands. Men, women and children, civilians and soldiers, Europeans, Indians, Anglo-Burmans and Burmans, they died of exhaustion, starvation and disease. The ill and feeble fell by the wayside with little prospect of rescue. Sick or wounded soldiers were left behind, perhaps with a rifle and a water-bottle, in the slight hope that the Japanese might care for them. Some military units maintained their discipline and managed to get through, others gradually lost cohesion and were never seen again.

One of the steps taken to aid these people was the conversion of a former opium smugglers' path into a jeep road. Tea planters and hundreds of their labourers, supervised by a Royal Engineer, began this stupendous task. As the weeks went by, the number of refugees coming over the mountains slowed to a trickle. It became apparent, however, that thousands were still stranded inside Burma. The arrival of the monsoon had rendered the hill tracks almost impassable, and it was clear that they would die unless something was done to assist them. One of the officers given this task was Major Ramsay Tainsh, MBE, Royal Indian Army Service Corps, formerly of the 16th Punjab Regiment.

"I was a trained Supply and Transport Officer and, although not medically qualified, I had a lifetime interest in fungal diseases and illnesses caused by bad diet. In May 1942 I was ordered from Rawalpindi to Ledo, North Assam. Passing through Calcutta, I spent some days in the library of the Garden Reach Botanical Gardens, learning what edible flora I would find and how the Nagas could live comfortably in jungle at 4000 feet. My initial orders were to install a radio station at Nampong, disarm looters, feed the road workers, and help the estimated 10,000 refugees who had to walk 400 miles through marshes and over five mountain ranges. I had some British medical staff and men of the Assam Rifles, and we built a series of simple camps. Supplies were transported by mule, by Naga porters, and by occasional air drops. I made a total of four trips into Burma. Our methods were very rudimentary, but we lost only nineteen out of the 21,300 people we saw during that time.

In September of 1942, after the monsoon, we built a camp at Nawngyang Hka where refugees rested before climbing the Pangsau Pass. One day a Gurkha soldier came into the camp. He was in rags but still had his rifle and ammunition and some kit in a Naga basket. He had been sheltering throughout the monsoon in a Naga village. Now he was exhausted, having carried a woman eighty miles over the mountains to reach us. I do not know who she was, but he was obviously very devoted to her. She was bloated with oedema, had malaria and pneumonia, and her temperature was 104F.

I treated them in our standard 'first feed' way: hot condensed milk to drink, and some Britannia ration biscuits and Marmite. She was given M&B tablets crushed in milk but, on the second day, she fell asleep and died. The soldier asked for a hoe and quietly carried her into the jungle where he buried her. When he returned the hoe, he handed me a dirty battered silver cup. I saw that it was engraved with the words '104th Wellesley's Rifles'. He told me that he had found it amongst a pile of other trophies thrown down in the moat of the fort at Mandalay. This one he had kept as a drinking vessel during his wanderings of the previous six months. 'I have no more need of this cup. Please, will you find the regiment and return it and explain how it was carried from Mandalay to India'.

The following month, while travelling to Kolhapur, I met an officer of the 1st Battalion (Wellesley's), 6th Rajputana Rifles, the natural successor of the old 104th. He told me that the battalion had never itself served in Burma, so the cup was clearly not its own Mess property. It was more likely to have been abandoned at Mandalay by some unit or individual to which the 104th had years previously made a presentation. Needless to say, I did not at the time make a precise note of the engraved wording. Anyway, I handed the cup over to him and later received a letter from the President of the Mess Committee, acknowledging safe delivery and asking its history. Sadly, I could not tell him the name of the Gurkha soldier, but I hope the cup is still in the regimental collection and that its strange story is remembered".

The Gloucestershire Regiment

One of the few peacetime British Army garrison units in Burma was 1st Battalion, The Gloucestershire Regiment, with its barracks at Mingaladon, near Rangoon. The news from the North African and Russian fronts became ever more serious throughout 1941, but the British administrations in the Far Eastern colonies showed little awareness of any threat to their quiet havens of Empire.

Social and military life continued to amble along at a normal peacetime pace. When Lieutenant Colonel Charles Bagot MC arrived to take command of the battalion, in June of that year, he submitted an "appreciation of the situation" to his superiors. He was fourteen officers and 340 other ranks under establish-

At its extremities, Burma is 1300 hundred miles north to south, and 500 miles east to west. Its hills and mountains - the Chin, Kachin, Shan and Karen - vary between 3000 and 8000 feet. Its three greatest rivers - the Chindwin, Irrawaddy and Salween - drain down to the Bay of Bengal from the snows of Tibet, more than 19,000 feet above the Irrawaddy delta. The British began to gain control of this extraordinary county in 1824, made it a province of India in 1886, and a Crown Colony in 1937. It was garrisoned by the Indian and British Armies long before the Glosters arrived to take their turn in November 1938. One of their predecessors were the Manchesters. This Burmese-made silver Chinthe was *Presented to the 2nd Bn, The Manchester Regiment by the Civil and Military Police of Mandalay District in appreciation of their friendly relations during 1931, and the capture of Saya Sau, leader of the Burma rebellion.* The Chinthe is the mythical dragon which stands guard outside the pagodas of that country. The name was adopted by Order Wingate, and anglicised as "Chindit", when he formed his first deep penetration force in 1943. The 2nd Battalion, equipped with medium machine-guns, returned to Burma in WWII and fought in the pivotal battle of Kohima. Photo: The Museum of the Manchesters, Ashton under Lyne.

ment, he had no radio equipment, hardly any vehicles, very few maps, and little more than token stocks of ammunition. His attempts at jungle warfare training were forbidden because the medical staff believed that it would induce heatstroke and tropical infections.

In desperation, he went to the Army Commander. Some concessions were won, but Bagot realised that he was regarded as an alarmist. He and his Quartermaster subsequently ignored all the usual procedures and, by stealth and barter, extracted from the stores and depôts around Rangoon sufficient ordnance and vehicles to make the battalion fit for combat.

In October, just three months before the Japanese started to bomb Rangoon and Mingaladon airfield, Bagot became so anxious that he asked Army Headquarters for authority to evacuate the battalion's wives and children to India. This was refused on the grounds that it would be "bad for morale". Higher command also refused to provide facilities for the removal to India of the battalion's Colours and silver, suggesting instead that, if the CO was so worried, he should lodge these items with one of the Rangoon banks.

Following the outbreak of hostilities on 8 December, permission was at last given for the battalion's wives and children to be transported five hundred miles north to Maymyo. Under the leadership of the CO's wife, Mrs Finetta Bagot, they eventually reached India without loss. It would be weeks, or in some cases months, before the wives heard anything more of their menfolk. Many then learned that they were widows.

They had been advised to close their family bank accounts before leaving Rangoon and to take their savings with them in body-belts. This precaution enabled them to buy food and clothing when they arrived as refugees at the Indian hill station of Murree and where they were housed for many weeks. The Mess funds and other regimental funds were also turned into cash and given to several officers in waist-belts. Anticipating the chaos which lay ahead, Colonel Bagot planned to use the money to buy food from local people or to pay guides to take his men through the mountains.

The safety of the Colours was secured when Colonel Bagot encountered an air force officer who was about to fly to India. He was entrusted with the two precious pieces of fabric which he deposited subsequently with a bank in Delhi. The silver was a more difficult problem. Bagot was told to abandon it at Mingaladon together with the battalion's collection of campaign medals and Mess furnishings. Instead, he arranged for Captain Charles Fox, of the 1st Battalion, King's Own Yorkshire Light Infantry, to include it in a load of other materiel which he was taking by road to Maymyo. The plan was that later it should be moved on to Monywa and Shwebo, and then up the Chindwin by river steamer to Kalewa and so, eventually, to safety in Assam. In the event, as the fighting intensified and the retreat became a rout, a chronic lack of military transport caused frequent changes of plan.

Rangoon was abandoned in early March, 1942. The Glosters were rearguard for the fighting retreat northward, and casualties began to mount. The Adjutant was killed, and Bagot himself was wounded in action. Confined to hospital in Maymyo, he quickly lost track of his battalion. It was now late April, and the Glosters were far away, being harried through the oilfields and on to Mandalay. However, he discovered that Captain Fox was still in Maymyo and commanding a mixed party of sick and injured Glosters and some men of the King's Own Yorkshire Light Infantry. Fox had been trying to follow his original orders that he should transport towards the Chindwin these men and the Glosters' crates of documents and silver but, every time he had assembled sufficient drivers and vehicles, he had been ordered by the Staff to hand over his trucks to some other unit.

Colonel Bagot discharged himself from hospital and spent several days rounding up an assortment of cars and trucks with which to evacuate all the sick and lost men of various units who had gathered at Maymyo. Three of the eighty vehicles which he foraged in this way, driven by Glosters, were given to Captain Fox who loaded up and set off for Shwebo. He succeeded in finding petrol along the way but, on arrival, all his vehicles were again confiscated by a Staff officer. Fortunately, at this stage, Colonel Bagot and most of the remnants of his battalion also arrived at Shwebo. A fresh plan was made, with the smaller and most valuable pieces of silver being divided between Bagot and two other officers. They carried them in their back packs throughout the remainder of the long march to safety. The Drum Major's staff and one box of silver were transferred to the Battalion HQ truck, and these things also eventually reached India.

There was still the problem of the larger items. One of the packing crates alone weighed nearly five hundred pounds. A friendly British businessman came to the rescue with a car and five trucks, and Fox again got his party on the move towards the Chindwin. Twenty-five miles short of the river he was once more stopped and deprived of his vehicles. This time he had no choice other than to bury the silver, mark the spot with a wooden cross, and set off for the border with his party of walking wounded and medically unfit men. He survived, but most of the men died along the way.

One sad loss to the battalion at about that time was Sergeant George Ransome, the Officers' Mess Sergeant. This legendary soldier had been parted from all the Mess treasures normally in his care, but he amazed everyone by the way he managed to feed and generally care for his remaining officers throughout the long fighting retreat. His end came after the action at Yenanyaung. During the confused aftermath of the defence of the village, he was found to have died from heat exhaustion. Like so many of his fellow Glosters, he has no known grave.

In January 1945, nearly three years later, the Japanese were retreating from Northern Burma and the British 2nd Division was approaching the area where Captain Fox had buried the Gloster's silver. The battalion was now commanded by Lieutenant Colonel Tony Wilkinson MC, and he arranged for a Platoon to be sent to the site with orders to salvage whatever could be found. It soon became clear that local Burmans had found the cache and dug it up. Apart from a few rotten pieces of packing case, there was nothing left. Not surprisingly, there was no trace either of the Mess furniture, pictures, library and photograph albums which Fox had been obliged to abandon.

Colonel Wilkinson ordered the printing of leaflets which were distributed in all the nearby villages, and his patrols carried money and barter goods as reward for any silver handed over by local people. Twenty-four minor pieces of Officers' Mess silver were rescued in this way, but all of the Sergeants' Mess treasures and almost all of the battalion's major pieces were gone forever.

Twenty years later the story gained an unexpected postscript. In 1965, an army officer staying at a hotel in Malaya's Cameron Highlands noticed in the dining room a silver candelabra which was obviously one of a pair formerly owned by the Glosters. It was part of the collection lost in Burma. The proprietor of the hotel had found it in a junk shop in Singapore. Its adventures during the intervening years will never be known, but it may be assumed that the candelabra had made its way from Burma to Singapore in the personal kit of a Japanese officer or soldier. The hotelier agreed to part with it, and it was returned to the regiment in England.

The pieces carried over the mountains in the back packs of Colonel Bagot and Major David Hunter and the Quartermaster, Captain Roland Grist, are now on display at the "Soldiers of Gloucestershire Museum", at Custom House, in the city of Gloucester. During the fighting retreat from Shwebo, they were handed from one officer to another whenever the battalion was in contact with the enemy and depending upon whom between them was judged to be least at risk.

One of the treasures brought out of Burma in this way is "The Waterloo Snuff Box". Made of basalt and gold, with an enamelled interior, its case is decorated with a representation of the Colours and Battle Honours. Other military decorations, on the back, include the names of Peninsular War actions in which the 28th was engaged, and the lid incorporates an allegorical scene from the Battle of Waterloo. The regiment had 557 officers and men under the command of Colonel (later Major

General Sir) Charles Belson when Wellington fought his final battle with Napoleon on Sunday, 18 June 1815. Half of them, 252 all ranks, were killed or wounded that day. Belson later commissioned the manufacture of the box which he presented to the regiment in commemoration of its role in the historic battle. Not surprisingly, it received some damage during its travels in Burma. The minor cracks and chips have not been repaired for, as one veteran of those times has said, "they are honourable scars, received in action".

Despite everything, the Glosters did manage to rescue at least a small part of their historical treasures from the 1942 disaster in Burma. Less fortunate was the Garrison Chaplain at Mingaladon. The Reverend W H S Higginbotham was murdered by scavenging Japanese troops when he tried to stop them from stealing the silver chalices and patens from his church.

The Glosters had come into existence in 1881 when, as part of the great army reforms of that year, the 28th (North Gloucestershire) Regiment of Foot was amalgamated with the 61st (South Gloucestershire) Regiment of Foot. They became, respectively, the 1st and 2nd Battalions of the new Gloucestershire Regiment. Old habits die hard however, and even in WWII, the officers of the 1st Battalion still referred to themselves as "the 28th".

In 1945 they brought a claim against the Government of Burma for compensation in respect of their lost silver and other possessions. Given the events of those immediate post-war years, it is not surprising that the claim was rejected. However, the officers of the 61st Regiment had been more fortunate when, eighty-five years earlier, they lost all of their Mess furnishings in the Great Sepoy Mutiny. They made a claim against the Government of India for two thousand pounds and succeeded, perhaps against the odds, in recovering a third of that sum. The circumstances were later recorded and published by one of the 61st's officers, Captain John Griffiths.

When the Mutiny first erupted, in May 1857, the 61st Regiment was living in barracks at Ferozepore, 190 miles north west from Delhi. The sub-continent was still at that time governed by the Honourable East India Company. It had its own armies based upon the Presidencies of Madras, Bengal and Bombay, but there were in addition considerable numbers of British Army units of various types in India. The 61st was one of these, and all ranks were happy to serve alongside the professional soldiers of the 45th and 57th Regiments of Bengal Native Infantry.

Like most of his brother officers, Griffiths was stunned by the sudden rush of events which had turned their comrades-in-arms into a lawless mob.

"Had he (the Brigadier) shown the smallest aptitude to meet the crisis, there would have been no difficulty, with the ample means at his disposal, in disarming without bloodshed the whole native force at Ferozepore, and so crushing the rebellion at the station. Night came, and we still remained in line under arms without having moved a foot from where we were halted. Officers and men were grieved at the state of inaction in which we had been kept, and an uneasy feeling prevailed that during the night the mutinous sepoys, aided by the *badmashis*, or bad characters, who swarmed in the bazaars and city of Ferozepore, would, under cover of darkness, run riot over the cantonment without our being called on to interfere. And so, unhappily, it came to pass. Suddenly a light was seen in the direction of the cantonment, which quickly turned into a blaze of fire. What new horror was this? Were our houses to be gutted and burnt before our eyes without any attempt to prevent such outrage? The men,

at the first appearance of fire, had sprung to their feet and seized their arms. Surely a detachment would be sent to clear the cantonment of the incendiaries? Even this was not done: the Brigadier was absent, or could not be found, and our Colonel (would) give no orders without the chief's consent".

Captain Griffiths' account continues with the events of the following day, 14 May: "At eight o'clock we were dismissed to barracks, and left the spot where we had stood in line inert and inactive since four o'clock the previous afternoon. Shortly after breakfast I was sent for by the Colonel and informed that I should proceed with my company into the cantonment. I was to patrol the station and search for, and arrest, any *sepoys* or bad characters that might be lurking about. I started without delay with ninety Grenadiers. Not a soul was to be seen. The *sepoys*, after their work of destruction, must have left during the night, and were probably now well on their way to Delhi. The cantonment presented a complete scene of desolation. The church and chapel were a heap of burnt-up and smouldering ruins, our mess-house the same, and numerous bungalows - former residences of the officers - were still on fire".

Four days later, after helping to fight off a half-hearted attack by mutineers, Captain Griffiths was sent back to the cantonment with orders to search for the regimental silver. "We found the mess-house walls still standing, but all inside the building was one mass of ashes and still smouldering embers. After infinite labour by the coolies, lasting some hours, we found portions of the silver. A little lower down we came on more; and here were spoons melted almost out of shape. The large silver dishes, plates and cups - many of the latter of priceless value, for they had been acquired by the regiment during the Peninsular War - were lying one on top of the other just as they had been placed in the chest, but all ruined and disfigured, half melted and blackened from the intense heat. Close by, where they had fallen off a table, were the four massive silver candelabra, the gift of distinguished officers who had formerly served in the corps. These were twisted out of all shape, and beyond hope of repair, of no value but for the bullion. Other articles were there, such as snuff-boxes, drinking-horns, and table ornaments; not one single piece of silver had escaped the action of the fire".

The root causes of the Mutiny of 1857 were diverse and numerous, and there is a great number of published sources which explain precisely what happened. It is important to recognise that the rebellion affected mainly the northern plains of the Ganges valley and those units of the Bengal Army which recruited there or which were stationed there. The men of the Rajput, Gurkha, and Garwhali regiments, together with those composed of Punjabi Sikhs, remained loyal. The Army of Madras and the Army of Bombay were largely unaffected.

Dozens of regiments of Bengal artillery, cavalry and infantry mutinied or, because their loyalty was in doubt, were quietly disarmed and disbanded. As far as silver is concerned, there are few published accounts as detailed as that of Captain Griffiths. He was describing the experiences of his own (British Army) regiment, but it may be assumed that the possessions of a great many Bengal Army units were either stolen or destroyed under similar circumstances at that same time. Even the silver of regiments which stayed "true to their salt" must have been at risk during the campaign's two years of ferocious fighting and almost non-stop marching and counter-marching. Any surviving pieces, manufactured prior to 1857 and having a connection with the Army of Bengal, can therefore be regarded as exceptionally rare. Just two such pieces are recorded in this book, the chutney pot on page 78 and the *attar dan* on page 154.

One of the items of Mess silver which passed the years 1941-1945 in a railway tunnel in Australia. Made in Birmingham in 1872 by Elkington & Company, The Napier Cup was *Presented by Lord Napier of Magdala, Commander in Chief in India, for competition in shooting by the British regiments under His Excellency's immediate command. Won by the 63rd (West Suffolk) Regiment under the command of Colonel Vere H Bowles, January 1873.* Thirty-four regiments were represented in the competition, each producing a team of twenty all ranks. As outright winners, the 63rd kept the cup and, in 1881, it became automatically the property of its successors, 1st Battalion, The Manchester Regiment (now The King's Regiment). Photo: The Museum of the Manchesters.

The Manchester Regiment

The 1st Battalion of The Manchester Regiment was sent to the Far East for a routine tour of duty in 1938, arriving in Singapore on 20 October of that year. It was still there when, in May 1940, the first reports came through that the Germans had launched their *blizkreig* attack into the Low Countries and France. The Manchesters had three battalions - the 2nd, 5th and 9th - fighting with the British Expeditionary Force, and there was great anxiety in the 1st Battalion for the fate of their fellow Manchesters. News of the safe evacuation of the bulk of them from Dunkirk was received in Singapore with thankfulness and relief.

The Commanding Officer of the 1st Battalion, Lieutenant Colonel E B Holmes, did not share the higher command's confidence in the supposed impregnability of Singapore as an island fortress. Early in 1941 he arranged for the Colours, the silver drums and bugles, together with the silver and crockery of the Officers' and Sergeants' Messes, to be sent to Australia for safe-keeping. Responsibility for looking after the battalion's treasures was willingly undertaken by the Manchester's affiliated regiment, The Adelaide Rifles. The latter was part of Australia's Citizen Military Forces, a part-time organisation similar to Britain's Territorial Army.

The Adelaide Rifles provided the bulk of the officers and men who, in WWI, formed the 10th Battalion, Australian Imperial Force, and then again in WWII, the 2/10th Battalion. In 1960, under the major reorganisations of that year, they were disbanded. Some of their records have since disappeared and it is no longer possible to state with certainty the *rationale* for their affiliation with the Manchesters.

One possible (territorial) link is the fact that the 96th Regiment of Foot, which later became 2nd Battalion, The Manchester Regiment, served a tour of garrison duty in Tasmania in the 1830s. During that tour, it sent a company detachment to Adelaide where it remained for nearly five years (before rejoining the regiment at Launceston). A memento of the period is a London-made salver in the collection of the regimental museum (in the Town Hall, Ashton under Lyne). It is engraved "The Turf Club of Van Diemens Land to the officers of HM LXIII Regiment with every good wish, 23rd December 1833".

Whatever the reason for the link, the officers of The Adelaide Rifles immediately agreed to Colonel Holmes' request for help. Initially the crates were held in conventional secure storage but, as the months went by and the Japanese successes on land and at sea followed one after the other, new arrangements were made. Darwin, Derby, Broome, Port Hedland and Townsville were being attacked by Japanese bombers and, in May 1942, their navy's midget submarines successfully penetrated Sydney Harbour. There was real concern that the country was about to be invaded. Together with other important artefacts, the Manchester's silver was moved into an old disused railway tunnel. There it remained until 1946 when it was restored to its owners, in Manchester. Not a single piece was lost or damaged. The battalion's only losses in the war were the paintings and prints left behind in Tanglin Barracks, Singapore, and which were probably destroyed or taken away by the Japanese following the surrender in February 1942.

As a token of thanks, the officers of the Manchesters presented to The Adelaide Rifles one of their early rifle shooting trophies, a cup bearing the boldly engraved numeral "96". This cup is today on permanent display in Adelaide, in the Drill Hall of the 10/27 Royal South Australian Regiment.

In passing, it may be noted that most British Army regiments are or were affiliated in one way or another - formally or informally - with equivalent units in other Commonwealth countries. The most obvious ties are those between the "kilted" regiments. There are, or have been, many such - The Argyll & Sutherland Highlanders of Canada, The 48th Highlanders of Canada, The Queen's Own Cameron Highlanders of Canada, The Cape Town Highlanders, The Sydney Scottish Rifles, and The New Zealand Scottish Regiment, to name only some of them.

Many of these affiliations seem to date from the early 1930s. Ironically, in a number of instances, the units involved in those arrangements have since ceased to exist or been amalgamated beyond easy recognition. Their memories are preserved in the Mess silver inherited by their successors. As an example, the officers of the 5th Infantry Battalion, Australian Army, continue to enjoy a fine table centrepiece presented in 1933 to one of their forebears, The Victorian Scottish Rifles. A detailed statuette of a Gordon Highlander officer in parade dress, it was the gift of the past and serving officers of that regiment.

This photograph was taken in the 1930s and it shows a small part of the USS *Houston's* presentation silver. It consists of a coffee urn with a dozen porcelain cups held in silver stands. The name of the maker is not recorded, but the design and quality of the entire collection was of a very high standard. Photo: University of Houston Libraries, Special Collections & Archives.

USS *Houston*

The Manchesters were fortunate in being affiliated with a unit in Australia, a country to which shipment was relatively simple. Colonel Holmes and his officers took their early decision, and their Adelaide friends stepped into the breech. Similar foresight by the officers of the USS *Houston* did not yield the same happy result. The acquisition of Mess and Wardroom silver is not an established custom in the armed forces of the United States, but this American heavy cruiser was one of the exceptions. Launched at Newport News in 1929, she was named after one of the major cities of the state of Texas. Its proud citizens presented the ship with a fifty-five piece silver service purchased at the very substantial price of $25,000. In early December of 1941, shortly before the Pearl Harbour attack, the US Navy's Asiatic Fleet was ordered to a war footing and all non-essential gear was put ashore for storage.

The *Houston's* silver service was deposited at Cavite, Manila Bay, the principal US Navy base in the Philippine Islands. Shortly afterwards the ship put to sea in search of the Japanese. On 4 February 1942 she was hit by a 200 kg bomb which wrecked her after eight-inch gun turret and killed sixty of her ship's company, but she remained battleworthy.

Her end came three weeks later when, as part of the Allied Squadron commanded by Rear Admiral K Doorman, Royal Netherlands Navy, she was torpedoed and sunk with heavy loss of life in the Sunda Strait. Also lost in what became known as the Battle of the Java Sea were four other cruisers and four destroyers (the entire Allied Squadron). They included the Australian cruiser HMAS *Perth* and the Royal Navy's HMS *Exeter*, a ship which had won fame and glory only fourteen

months earlier against the German pocket battleship *Admiral Graf Spee* in the Battle of the River Plate.

The US Navy's installations at Cavite were bombed heavily during the Japanese invasion. The *Houston's* silver disappeared from view. After the war, the US Navy continued for twenty years to search for it, but the base records no longer existed and most of the *Houston's* people, including her Captain, had gone down with their ship. The silver has never been found. It must be assumed that it was either destroyed in 1942 or taken by soldiers of the Japanese Army occupation force who melted it for its bullion value.

31st Infantry Regiment, US Army

One item of American silver which did survive the Japanese occupation of the Philippines between 1942 and 1945 was The Shanghai Bowl. Its owners were the officers of the US Army's 31st Infantry Regiment, and its story provides an interesting parallel with that of several comparable items of British Army silver.

The 31st was formed in the Philippines in 1916 from elements of other regiments stationed in the islands. It remained there permanently during the 1920s and 1930s, its personnel rotating through from the United States every two years, and came to be known as "Manila's Own".

On Monday, 1 February 1932, the regiment received orders to pack immediately pack and embark in the US Army Transport *Chaumont*. Intelligence sources had concluded correctly that Japanese military forces were about to invade China. The Chinese mainland had been in turmoil for several years. Local warlords were fighting the government of Chiang Kai-Shek (and

The Shanghai Dragon presented in 1930 to 1st Battalion, The Worcestershire Regiment, by the local branch of The Royal Society of St George. The obvious signs of repair confirm how susceptible to damage such pieces were (and are) during their many travels around the world. Photo: RHQ The Worcestershire & Sherwood Foresters Regiment.

each other), and a large multi-national force had been assembled in 1927 to protect foreign nationals living in the Treaty ports. The latest development meant that another such military expedition was required. In company with the 4th Marine Regiment, US Marine Corps, and detachments of troops from other nations, the 31st was sent to guard the Legations and foreign-owned commercial premises in Shanghai.

There followed six weeks of bitter street fighting, between Japanese and Chinese troops, all around the perimeter of the International Settlement. When calm returned, the 31st was told that it would remain in Shanghai for the foreseeable future, so the regiment's families were brought over from Manila by commercial liner. A regular domestic routine soon developed, the men patrolling the perimeter, the children attending the American Mission School, and the wives making the rounds of Chinese craftsmen's workshops where they could buy jade, silver, copper and silk items at very attractive prices.

One craftsman whose skills particularly impressed the ladies of the regiment was a silversmith. The idea emerged that he might be commissioned to manufacture a punch bowl, with a set of matching cups, for use at *despidadas*. These were the dances and drinks parties held at the Officers' Club in Manila on "hail and farewell" occasions. The suggestion was picked up by the regiment's medical officers who, according to the unit's historian, decided that a silver service would be a fitting tribute to the regiment's zero VD rate (apparently something quite extraordinary at that time). The other officers supported the idea (not necessarily for the same reason) and their wives swept into action.

Sixteen hundred silver dollars were raised to pay for the bowl, and each cup was engraved with the name of a contribut-

ing officer. The overall design was heavily influenced by the wives. They also invented an instant "custom", a ceremony to be called "the passing of the cups", and by the time the silversmith had finished his work everyone was familiar with the rules.

The regiment departed Shanghai in June 1932 and returned to Manila in the USAT *Republic*. The Shanghai Bowl continued to perform its intended purpose for the next ten years, and was naturally a focus of attention for guests who were not accustomed to seeing such objects at a US Army base.

The 31st was still serving in the Philippines when the Japanese invaded in December 1941. The only all-white infantry unit in the islands, it was engaged in the defence of the Bataan peninsula, some miles north of Manila City. Most of its survivors took part in the infamous "Bataan Death March" (during which many American prisoners died at the hands of their Japanese captors), but a mixed party of 300 men managed to temporarily evade capture by getting away to the fortified island of Corregidor. One of the things which they took with them was the Shanghai Bowl.

The Americans fought on but, when he realised that he and his men had no hope of rescue, Captain Earl E Short decided to bury it. With two soldiers, he dug a trench and prepared the silver for interment. The bowl and each cup were coated with "Cosmoline", then placed in an iron box packed with sawdust which, in turn, went into a wooden crate. Captain Short and his men were soon after rounded up by the invaders.

In 1945, General Douglas MacArthur kept his famous promise, "I shall return", and ejected the Japanese from the Philippine group of islands. Captain Short had survived the years of imprisonment, and he was sent back to Corregidor with orders to recover the silver. His dilemma, when he arrived, was that the location had changed drastically since his previous visit. Aerial bombardments and ground fighting on the island had damaged or demolished a great many nearby buildings, and the local people had chosen the burial site, unwittingly, as a dumping ground for hundreds of tons of debris. Captain Short remembered the reference points from which he took bearings in April of 1942, but some of those markers also had been destroyed.

Short remained at the site long enough gain an approximate idea of the likely burial location before returning to the United States and having handed the problem to another officer. His workmen needed two months of pick-and-shovel effort to excavate their way through the rubble which, in places, was fifteen feet deep. When the treasure finally came to light, the crate was found to be in good order and the silver intact.

The 31st was reformed in 1946 in Japan as part of the Allied occupation force and the bowl resumed its intended peacetime function. However, in September 1950, the regiment was ordered to take part in the assault landings at Inchon. With the Korean war showing no signs of reaching a rapid conclusion, the Shanghai Bowl was despatched to America for safe-keeping. It rested in a bank vault in Seattle until after the cease-fire. It was then sent to Korea where it was in regular use for the next twenty years. The regiment was steadily reduced in size and, as its battalions were progressively "inactivated", the Bowl travelled through a succession of army bases in the United States. There are strong parallels here with the wanderings of silver owned by units of the British Army which, during the same period, were gradually amalgamated or disbanded or withdrawn from the distant outposts of Empire.

In 1995, the last element of the 31st Infantry Regiment on active duty was inactivated. The Bowl then passed to the Infantry Museum at Fort Benning for a couple of years, forming part of the display there. Since then, the 4th Battalion has been reactivated at Fort Drum, New York, and the Bowl now resides with that unit, a permanent reminder of Shanghai, Manila, Bataan, Corregidor and Korea, and of the men who served in those times and places.

The Worcestershire Regiment

It is has not been possible to obtain a photograph of The Shanghai Bowl, but the piece illustrated here is another reminder of that city. It is the property of a British Army unit, as the engraved plaque confirms - "The Shanghai Dragon, Presented by The Royal Society of St George (Shanghai Branch), to The 1st Battalion, The Worcestershire Regiment as a Memento of their stay in Shanghai, 1929-1930".

During their tour of duty as part of the international peace-keeping force, the Worcesters earned an excellent reputation for their ceremonial and sporting prowess. The highlight was the Trooping The Colour parade on 1 June, the Regimental Day (commemorating the role of the 29th of Foot in Admiral Lord Howe's defeat of a French fleet in 1794).

The Royal Society of St George was founded in 1894 with the aim of fostering a love of England by supporting English traditions and ideals. The Shanghai branch was over one thousand strong and financially healthy. It was active in giving charitable assistance to members of the local English community, in the provision of scholarships, and in organising social and sporting events. The major event of its year was St George's Day when the Society held a church service and wreath-laying ceremony at the British war memorial, with a "grand ball" in the evening. The details are not recorded, but it

seems that the Worcesters took part in some of these events and the Society therefore made this presentation. An identical piece was given to the 2nd Battalion of The Green Howards.

The Shanghai Volunteer Corps

One of the other military units engaged in the security operations in Shanghai between 1929 and 1932, and whose members were a familiar sight to the soldiers of the 31st Infantry Regiment, the Worcesters, and the Green Howards, was the SVC, the Shanghai Volunteer Corps. This was a cosmopolitan part-time Corps recruited from the international community residing in the city and district of Shanghai.

Formed in 1853 at the suggestion of the British Consul, Sir Rutherford Alcock, its membership included Americans, Japanese, Portuguese, Filippinos, émigré Russians, Chinese, Austrians, Germans, Italians, stateless Jews, and the British. They were grouped under separate national, professional and ethnic Company titles. The *raison d'être* of the Corps was to assist in protecting foreign property and personnel in times of strife. It was mobilised on twenty-five widely-spread occasions to deal with riots in Shanghai and North China.

Nothing is known of the major Mess items of silver which the various SVC sub-units (certainly those with a British composition) must have accumulated. However, a unique record of the life of the Corps has survived in the form of a collection of mainly sporting trophies now held privately in the United Kingdom. The majority are stamped with the marks of local Chinese silversmiths. The names of Yee Sing, Zee Wo, Tuk Shang, Zee Sung and Wah Lee have been identified, all of whom were active at various times during the first half of the 20th century. The standards of workmanship are high, with designs frequently including oriental motifs. The standard of silver cannot be determined with certainty in all cases, but at least one Chinese-made piece is stamped "935" so it is likely that, when making pieces for valued local customers such as the SVC, the craftsmen worked with alloy of Sterling or Britannia quality, or similar.

One such item is an eleven inch diameter salver with hammered finish, bamboo edging and three bun feet. It was made by Yee Sing, and is engraved: "Presented to Lieut W G T Howe on the occasion of his departure from Shanghai, 8 March 1941, by the members of the L A (A D) Company SVC". This apparently unremarkable presentation was, in the event, the precursor to three and a half years of horror for the recipient and for tens of thousands of other Allied troops.

Lieutenant William Gordon Theodore Howe, an Anglo-Indian, served part-time from 1927 to 1941 with the Light Automatic (Air Defence) Company of the SVC, hence the acronyms noted on his salver. As a civilian he was employed as an insurance underwriter.

In March 1941 he applied for a commission in the Royal Artillery. He had been commissioned in WWI but, even so, it is perhaps surprising that he was accepted back at the age of forty-three. He was sent to Singapore as a Lieutenant on the strength of the 1st Independent Heavy Anti-Aircraft Battery, RA. Arriving on the island on 5 August 1941, he began to keep a meticulous record of his experiences. Together with his SVC salver, the (as yet) unpublished diary is held in private hands in England. It contains his personal observations of the fight to defend the island, the surrender, and then his years in Changi prisoner of war camp. Documents such as this breathe life into items of silver which otherwise provide no obvious exceptional interest.

Another locally-based part-time unit which existed for many years was the Hong Kong Volunteer Corps (later Defence Force). It is said to have had a fine collection of Mess silver, but protracted enquiries have failed to establish what happened to it when the colony was invaded by Japanese forces in December 1941. Any objects which might surface in the future, having a direct association with the HKVC, should be regarded as rare. Fully researched, they too may reveal tales of courage and fortitude comparable to that of Lieutenant Howe.

The Honourable Artillery Company

The part-time volunteer units of the Empire were a mirror of the long tradition of "citizen soldiering" in the United Kingdom. One of the most colourful of such units is The Honourable Artillery Company, established in 1537 and therefore the oldest in the British Army's order of battle. It is, in fact, the oldest military formation of any kind in the world and, in terms of its membership, amongst the wealthiest.

By reason of its antiquity and its recruiting area at the heart of London, in and around the City, it follows that the HAC was from its earliest years a collector of silver. Apart from any other consideration, its headquarters were located within a short walking distance of the streets in which some of England's finest silversmiths had their workshops.

The Company suffered an early and very unusual major loss, and it happened as a result of the English Civil War of 1642-1649. England was divided between those towns and families which declared for the monarchy, and those who declared for Cromwell and Parliament. Even an armed force such as the Honourable Artillery Company was not immune from the bitter arguments regarding the country's future government. There are no surviving written records, but it seems that the Company's officers were as deeply divided in their loyalties as the rest of the country. Some went off to fight for the royalist cause, others joined Cromwells' New Model army.

The Treasurer of the Company at that time was Lieutenant Colonel William Manby. The Company's assets were entrusted to his care. They included the silver and all the ledgers and records of the preceding hundred years. He was one of those officers whose allegiance was to Oliver Cromwell. When requested, Manby refused to return any part of this property.

It is known to have included "a giult standing Cupp" worth fifty pounds, and "two Silver Flaggons to the valew of fifty pounds".

The officers of the Company pursued him through the courts and submitted petitions to the new Parliament, but without success. In 1661, following his death, they took legal action against his executors, but again failed to recover what was rightfully theirs. There is no way of knowing what other items of silver were involved or even how many, but the loss of the Company's written records has ever since been a major frustration for anyone researching the social and military history of the City of London of the pre-Civil War years.

It might have been expected that the missing HAC silver would have come to light sooner or later. The fact that it never did is most probably explained by the Great Fire. When the capital began to burn, in September 1666, the flames destroyed three-fifths of its buildings and rendered homeless 200,000 of its citizens.

57th (West Middlesex) Regiment of Foot

There have been occasions when Mess silver has deliberately been scrapped. No documents have been traced to verify the following anecdote, but it has been reported from several informed sources and may be taken at face value. It concerns the 57th Regiment of Foot, the forebear of the now defunct 1st Battalion, The Middlesex Regiment. The role of the latter in the Battle of Hong Kong has already been described but, in 1811, the officers and men of the 57th earned the name "Diehards" for the way in which they fought at the equally ferocious Battle of Albuhera. It came from the lips of their Colonel Inglis who, severely wounded, lay in the open in front of the shot-torn Colours. While his regiment courageously stood its ground for four hours against grapeshot and repeated cavalry charges, he could be heard cheering them on and shouting "Die hard, my men, die hard".

With the return of peace, the officers of the 57th decided to commission a table centrepiece to commemorate the regiment's services at Albuhera. This was no ordinary centrepiece. It consisted of several long sections which, when laid end-to-end, showed in dramatic three-dimensional form the role of the regiment in each phase of the battle. It is said that, fully assembled, the display measured eighteen feet in length.

It is not known when this monumental object was commissioned or even who made it. Whoever he was, his skills were greatly admired by everyone saw it, and The Albuhera Centrepiece was for many years a source of great pride for the regiment. As time went by, however, the officers found it to be an increasing burden. It was difficult to maintain, its boxes took up a great deal of space during moves, and there were few occasions when it could be displayed in its entirety. They took what must have been a highly contentious decision to have it scrapped. The bullion value was then spent on the construction of several cottages for the accommodation of deserving old soldiers. All of this seems to have happened sometime around 1850 or 1860. While it is a pity that the full details are not known, it is pleasing to come across such a fine example of officers looking to the welfare of those of their men who, in the language of the period, were "worn out in the service of the regiment".

Albuhera created for the 57th a regimental custom which, unlike that centrepiece, has endured. They had gone into battle six hundred strong. As darkness fell, the one hundred and sixty surviving officers and men gathered together at a Spanish tavern. Weary, smoke-stained, many of them bloody and bandaged, they resolved that the deaths of their comrades should never be forgotten. Silently they toasted the fallen.

Every year since then, on the anniversary of the battle, the 57th and its successors have observed the ritual of "the Silent Toast". In the early evening, before the Albuhera Dinner, the officers, Warrant Officers and Sergeants gather in the Warrant Officers' & Sergeants' Mess. The officers are greeted by the Regimental Sergeant Major, and all those present quietly form a circle. The RSM stands to the left of the Commanding Officer, the junior Sergeant to his right. The remainder of the company are intermingled without regard to rank or seniority.

The Officers' Mess Colour Sergeant hands to the Commanding Officer a piece known as The Albuhera Loving Cup, already charged with Champagne. The CO holds the cup out in front of him and speaks the words "to the immortal memory". There is no response. The cup is then passed in silence around the whole company, right to left, each person taking the cup in both hands, drinking, then turning it and passing it to the next man to his left. When it completes its round, the Junior Sergeant hands it back to the Officers' Mess Colour Sergeant who is the last to drink. The officers then return

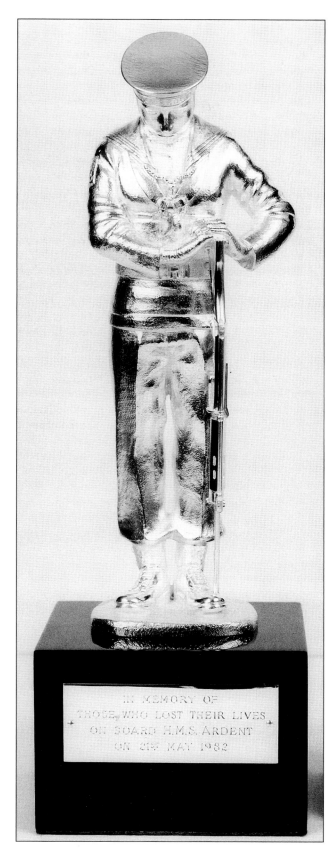

One of Ian Powsey's statuettes of a Royal Navy seaman, standing with rifle reversed and mounted on a hammered finish circular base. Excluding the wooden plinth, it stands 9 inches high and weighs 30 ounces. The plate on this example (one of four) is engraved *In Memory of those who lost their lives on board HMS Ardent on 21st May 1982*. Photo: RN Trophy Centre.

to their own Mess where, after a short interval, they are joined by the Warrant Officers for dinner.

The custom was carried forward into The Queen's Regiment on its formation on 31 December 1966, and is still maintained by its successor, The Princess of Wales's Royal Regiment. To quote a regimental record, "In its modern context the Silent Toast Ceremony serves to reinforce the comradeship that exists between the officers and the Warrant Officers and Sergeants".

HM Ships *Sheffield, Coventry* and *Ardent*

To conclude this chapter, and to demonstrate that military and naval silver continues to be as vulnerable as it ever was in the past, we turn to the year 1982 and the storm-swept waters of the South Atlantic.

On 2 April, Argentine forces landed at Port Stanley, capital of the Falkland Islands. The invasion came as no surprise to the British Embassy in Buenos Aires or to Captain Nick Barker RN, of the ice patrol vessel HMS *Endurance*, but it stunned Downing Street and the Ministry of Defence. Within hours, however, the First Sea Lord, Admiral of the Fleet Sir Henry Leach, had met Prime Minister Thatcher and convinced her that the navy could do what needed to be done. She and her Cabinet colleagues made the almost inevitable decision to eject the Argentines from the lonely British colony, by persuasion if possible but otherwise by force.

Two operations were set in motion, one of them overt, the other extremely secret. The latter was Operation *Paraquat*, a small group of ships commanded by Captain Brian Young RN. His orders were to remove Argentine troops and unauthorised civilians from the island of South Georgia. The very existence of his force and its mission were totally unknown to more than a handful of people in the Ministry of Defence. The ships which instead received such wide coverage on the world's television screens were those which sailed later from Portsmouth and Devonport. They were to form the Task Force for Operation *Corporate*, the planned reoccupation of the Falkland Islands.

Less well reported was the previous despatch of a spearhead battle group commanded by Captain John Coward RN, in the Type 22 destroyer HMS *Brilliant*. His orders were to immediately head down the Atlantic at his best speed, to place his ships in a position three days' sailing north of the Falklands, and if possible bring the Argentine Navy to battle before it could interfere with the main body of the following invasion Task Force. And it was the driving urgency with which Coward's force was sent south which led to the first significant losses of Royal Navy silver since the beginning of WWII.

In late March and early April, the Royal Navy was conducting a major exercise in mid Atlantic, west of Gibraltar. It was code-named Exercise *Springtrain*. In command was Rear Admiral John "Sandy" Woodward, and he had on board his flagship, HMS *Antrim*, the Commander in Chief Fleet, Admiral Sir John Fieldhouse. The two men discussed the problems involved in forming the advance battle group from ships which had been at sea for some time already, and which were running low on fuel and other stores. It was decided to transfer maximum loads of food, oil and ammunition from one half of the ships to the other. The depleted ships then headed for replenishment in the United Kingdom and Gibraltar while those fully stored headed south under the command of Captain Coward.

It is normal practice for all Royal Navy vessels to place their Wardroom silver ashore in safe storage before heading into a war zone. This was impossible in the exceptional circumstances of Exercise *Springtrain*. Three of the ships detached in mid-ocean as part of Captain Coward's advance battle group were HMShips *Sheffield*, *Coventry*, and *Ardent*. All were subsequently sunk. The *Sheffield* was destroyed by an Exocet missile of the Argentine naval air arm, the other two by bombs of the Argentine Air Force. All had their silver still on board, and everything was lost.

To commemorate the officers and men who died in those sinkings, and of those who lost their lives in HMS *Antelope*, the silversmith Ian Powsey was commissioned in 1983 to make four identical figurines of a Royal Navy rating, each mounted on a pedestal bearing a plaque inscribed "In memory of those who lost their lives in HMS ...", followed by the name of the ship and the date she went down. They are currently displayed in successor ships or in shore establishment Wardrooms.

Ministry of Defence Form 441 is one of the thousands of official documents, covering every possible need and contingency, used by the armed forces. Some are more productive than others, but certainly Form 441 has proved its worth whenever a serviceman has been deprived of personal property as a consequence of his duties. Entitled "Claim for Compensation for Loss or Damage to Personal Effects", the form proved its worth to the Royal Navy Trophy Fund in the aftermath of the Falklands campaign.

Because it is uninsurable at normal rates of premium, and because naval silver belongs not to the navy itself but to its charitable Trophy Fund, a Form 441 was submitted on behalf of

the Trustees to the Ministry of Defence in respect of each of the three ex-*Springtrain* ships. The sums claimed were roughly ten thousand pounds for the silver and pictures of the *Sheffield*, eight thousand for the *Coventry*, and five thousand for the smaller *Ardent*.

The Forms were accompanied by detailed inventories, each item having a declared valuation. These individual figures were based upon deemed or declared values at the time of their original acquisition, not their incalculable values at the time of their loss. This meant, in effect, that the Trophy Fund could not recover the sums to which, in other circumstances, it might have laid claim.

The lists of items are not detailed, and they tell us little of the design or provenance of each piece. However, they do serve to confirm that none of them were of outstanding importance in the evolution of silver *per se*. Their value was historical rather than artistic or intrinsic. HMS *Sheffield* carried a centrepiece valued at fifteen hundred pounds, HMS *Coventry* had seven silver fruit and side dishes valued at three thousand six hundred pounds, while HMS *Ardent's* best piece was a two-handled cup at eight hundred pounds. For the rest, the average valuation was approximately two hundred pounds. The claims were settled quickly and in full.

All of these pieces, together with too many of the sailors to whom they were familiar, rest in the depths of the South Atlantic. There they will remain.

Chapter Seven

Silver At Sea

This chapter will be a superficial and very selective pin-hole view of objects associated with the sea, with sea-farers, and with sea-soldiers. To indicate the scale of the subject matter, and the impossibility of more than skimming over its surface, the inventory of silver artefacts owned by the Royal Navy identifies nearly eight thousand different items. The Royal Marines, a relatively small Corps numbering seven thousand officers and men, have four thousand such entries in their records. This figure refers only to items noted in its central Corps inventory. It does not include objects gifted directly to the Messes of individual units such as the Royal Marine Commandos.

Then, in the context of silver associated with the merchant service, there were nearly six hundred autonomous or semi-autonomous shipping companies in *Lloyd's Register* of the 1914-1918 period. As happened again in WWII, these companies had the crucial task of sustaining the British nation and its fighting forces with food, fuel and war supplies. Many of their sea-going officers held commissions in the Royal Naval Reserve and thousands of their vessels were requisitioned or brought under the control of the government (*via* The Shipping Controller in WWI, and the Ministry of War Transport in WWII). Most of them, other than hospital ships, were fitted with defensive armament.

Between 1914 and 1918, the British merchant service had 3305 ships sunk or seriously damaged. Fifteen thousands merchant mariners died in that war.

Twenty years later the losses were even more severe, with 3860 cargo and passenger ships sent to the bottom or seriously damaged. Thirty-two thousand Merchant Navy personnel lost their lives in WWII. More than eight thousand are buried in Commonwealth War Graves Commission cemeteries all over the world. The majority, nearly twenty-four thousand of them, have no grave other than the sea. Their names are recorded on the Tower Hill memorial.

The Boardrooms of the shipping companies, certainly the larger firms, contained (and in many cases still contain) silver which reflects the wartime role of the merchant service. While acknowledging with gratitude the sacrifices of the men who sailed under the Red Ensign, the following pages will focus primarily upon the silver of the Royal Navy and the Royal Marines.

The Royal Navy

We may commence our survey by going back in time to the decades of the sailing navy. If the second half of the 19th century was the "golden age" of collecting for the regiments of the British Army, its equivalent age for the Royal Navy was the period from 1793 to 1814. It was the first truly world war, a conflict fought to the death between Great Britain and her allies, and France and her puppet states.

In the early years, the army was engaged in a number of major but ultimately fruitless campaigns. It was only after 1811, when the rot was stopped at Torres Vedras, that the army under

Arthur Wellesley, Duke of Wellington, was able to launch the campaign which led eventually to the collapse of the Napoleonic empire. In the language of a much later war, his Peninsular campaign was "the Western Front". It was decisive, and some of the commemorative silver generated by that campaign is noted in previous chapters of this book.

For the navy, the Revolutionary and Napoleonic wars began on 18 June 1793 when Captain Edward Pellew RN, commanding the 36 gun frigate HMS *Nymphe*, fought and captured the French 40 gun frigate *La Cléopatre* off Start Point, South Devon. That initial success was followed by hundreds of other actions - single-ship engagements, major fleet battles, coastal raids and cutting-out operations. The naval blockade of the French ports was maintained for twenty years, winter and summer, fair weather and foul, in the harshest service imaginable. The Royal Navy may have been over the horizon and out of sight but, just as happened again in 1914-1918 and 1939-1945, it was at war from the first day to the last.

The senior commanders of the British Army were rewarded for their victories in many ways, especially financial. Honour, glory and accelerated promotion were the only rewards available to their subordinates. Junior officers of the Royal Navy were not so disadvantaged. Every young Commander in Command, detached on his own for patrol duties in distant waters, prayed for the chance to emulate Captain Pellew or to find and seize a valuable enemy merchant ship. The Admiralty's Agents paid for the ships and cargoes brought to harbour by Royal Navy prize crews. Prize money was divided amongst the entire ship's company of the captor ship, but the lion's share went, naturally, to her captain. There were those who, after a few successful cruises, accumulated sufficient wealth to establish themselves ashore with handsome country houses and fine titles.

Their seniors were additionally rewarded in other ways - elevation to the peerage, larger pensions, the Freedom of cities with which they were associated, and presentations in gold and silver. The previously mentioned Edward Pellew, for example, made a great deal of money during the Anglo-French wars. As Admiral Lord Exmouth, he then commanded an expedition in August 1816 which proved to be the pinnacle of his career. It was the Anglo-Dutch assault on the Corsair port of Algiers.

The Corsairs of Tripoli, Tunis and Algiers - the Barbary states - had for nearly three hundred years been the scourge of the Mediterranean. Their profession was kidnap, ransom and slavery. They practiced it by cruising the sea-lanes and taking prize every vessel (not protected by special licence) to come their way. The ships and cargoes were auctioned off and the profits divided amongst shareholders. Crews and passengers were sold into slavery or, if their families possessed the financial resources, were held to ransom. It was a sophisticated industry, driven partly by antipathy towards the infidel Christian but mainly by avarice.

At first restricted to Mediterranean waters by their ships' lateen rig and light construction, the Corsairs learned the skills of surprise attack against small towns along the coasts of Sicily, mainland Italy, southern Spain and southern France. Whole communities were rounded up and taken back to be sold in the slave markets of their home ports. Then, early in the 16th century, they were joined by two renegade European sea captains, John Ward, of Faversham, and a Dutchman, Simon Danser, of Dordrecht.

These men introduced the Corsairs to the square-rigged round ship and taught them how to navigate the cold waters of the north. The slavers of Barbary began to extend their cruises. Corsair raids along the coasts of Madeira, Spain, Portugal, northern France and Denmark became commonplace. In 1627 they raided the coast of Ireland and, in 1654, captured the entire population of a fishing village in Cornwall. Each summer season, between sixty and one hundred of their vessels prowled the Bristol Channel, the English Channel and the Thames estuary. Always known in England as "the Turks", they created for themselves a fearsome and enduring reputation. In Devon and Cornwall, some country people may still describe a troublesome boy as "a proper little Turk".

Beginning in 1541, when an international fleet commanded by Emperor Charles V of Spain made the first attack, Algiers was repeatedly the target for European naval expeditions. On dozens of occasions, warships sailed into the bay, bombarded the fortifications, burned the Corsair ships, extracted promises of future good conduct, signed treaties, then sailed home. On every occasion the Algerines recovered and went back to their old ways. It was only when peace returned to Europe in the wake of the Napoleonic war that the British and Dutch decided to make one final effort. It was this expedition which resulted in the manufacture of several of the finest pieces of silver and gold in Admiral Lord Exmouth's personal collection.

Full details of the battle are to be found in *Gunfire in Barbary* by Perkins and Douglas-Morris (Kenneth Mason, Havant, 1982). It was, by every accepted standard of naval warfare, a most extraordinary affair. Its success in liberating some hundreds of Christian slaves and in subduing the Corsair sea captains was hailed throughout Europe. His Lordship was showered with praise and honours from the heads of nations whose citizens had been set free or whose merchant shipping was once again able to go about its business without fear. Some of those pieces later passed out of the hands of his descendent family, but a number are still to be seen in the ancestral home.

From Pope Pius VII he received an exquisite *Passamonti* cameo, depicting the head of Mars carved in onyx, with a mounting of blue enamel and gold. Many of the Corsairs' victims were Roman Catholic.

The Prince Regent gave him a specially commissioned gold medal. On the obverse is the bust of the Prince and the words "To tame the proud, the fetter'd slave to free. These are imperial arts and worthy thee". On the reverse is a representation of the battle and, in the exergue, "Algiers bombarded, its fleet destroyed, and Christian slavery extinguished, August 27th 1816".

Everyone did indeed believe at the time that Algerine maritime power had been crushed. With hindsight, given their tenacity on previous occasions, it should have come as no surprise that the Algerines once again made good the damage and resumed their traditional way of life. It was brought to an end only when the French invaded in 1829 and created the colony of Algeria.

From the citizens of Marseille, "in testimony of its gratitude", Lord Exmouth received the magnificent piece of

silver illustrated here. Made by Charles Cahier, silversmith to the Emperor of France, it stands three feet in height. The principal *motif* is a scene which shows the Admiral receiving the thanks of a freed woman and child.

The Imperial French silversmith Charles Cahier produced this triumphal piece in 1817 to the order of the city council of Marseille. It was but one of Admiral Lord Exmouth's many rewards for his victory at Algiers. Photo: Christie's.

One year after the battle he was the guest of honour at a banquet arranged by the officers who had served under him that day. They presented him with "a piece of plate of massy size and elegant workmanship as a mark of their admiration for his conduct". The contemporary description does not exaggerate. Designed by Paul Storr and made by Rundell & Company, London, it cost one thousand and four hundred pounds. A table centrepiece of very large proportions, it replicates the lighthouse tower which dominated the entrance to Algiers harbour, surrounded on the pedestal by figures of British sailors fighting with Algerine soldiers and of freed slaves kneeling in gratitude before their liberators. It is an outstanding example of Storr's ability to condense several different themes - tangible and emotional - into a single design.

When the Algiers piece arrived at Exmouth's then family home, Bitton House, Teignmouth, in South Devon, it joined another Storr creation presented to the Admiral two years earlier. That was a silver replica of The Warwick Vase. It was the gift of the officers who had served under him between 1811 and 1814 - his period of tenure as Commander in Chief, Mediterranean

Fleet. When the original Roman Warwick Vase arrived in England, it was seized upon as a model by silversmiths anxious to satisfy the current vogue for pieces having a classical theme. Several replicas were made and given to high ranking officers. Lord Exmouth's example was later sold at Sotheby's and was acquired by a private collector.

Exmouth lived to enjoy his reputation and his rewards. Horatio Nelson did not. The very name of this man evokes everything in which the Royal Navy took and still takes pride. His achievements, like those of Exmouth, were rewarded with presentations of fine craftsmanship shaped in silver and gold, but on a scale which reflected his far greater reputation. The story of his collection of treasures is inextricably tied to that of London's maritime insurance market, Lloyd's.

Before 1793 the insurance of merchant ships and their cargoes was underwritten by a largely unstructured group of men who met daily in the City, at Lloyd's Coffee House. The following twenty years were a dangerous and turbulent period for Great Britain's ship owners and for all merchants whose livelihoods depended upon maritime trade. To the normal hazards of the sea were added the risks of sinking or seizure by enemy warships and privateers (independent sea-raiders operating under licences granted by their governments).

Statistics compiled by John Bennett, Lloyd's first Secretary, show that 3919 British ships were captured by the French between 1793 and 1814. Of these, only 799 were later re-taken or released. Insurance became ever more necessary if the owners were to remain in business, and Lloyd's expanded accordingly. By 1814 the market had developed into a united and powerful society of brokers and underwriters who had played a leading part in supporting the nation's war effort.

Lloyd's links with Nelson date from the first of his three famous victories, the Battle of the Nile, in 1798. Remarkably, in an age when great leaders were hailed as heroes but their men largely ignored, Lloyd's raised a fund of thirty-eight thousand pounds "to relieve the suffering of the wounded and bereaved". Of this sum, five hundred pounds were voted to Nelson himself, "to be laid out in plate as you will be pleased to direct, as a small token of gratitude". The Admiral used this money to acquire a silver dinner service, engraved with his coat of arms. The scale of the service was extended when he purchased more items with additional money voted to him by Lloyd's following his triumph at Copenhagen, in 1801. Part of the service was returned to Lloyd's in 1880, and one of the dishes was at that time engraved with wording which explained the reason for the original (1798) subscription.

Shortly after WWI, items from Nelson's dinner service were presented by The Navy League to Captain N Grant RN, of the armed auxiliary cruiser *Carmania*. On 14 September 1914, off Trinidad, he engaged and sank the German armed liner *Cap Trafalgar*. Some of this silver has been sold in recent years by Spink & Son, of St James's.

A precedent for the Nile fund had been set a few years earlier, in 1794, when news of Admiral Lord Richard Howe's great victory - "the Glorious First of June" - first reached London. Immediately a meeting was convened at Lloyd's and, within an hour, "one thousand guineas had been collected for the relief of the wounded". The fund was swelled by donations from many other sources and finally exceeded twenty-one thousand pounds. The benefits available to crippled sailors and the widows of those who had died were further increased when Howe donated his entire share of the prize money from the battle.

The Nile fund was succeeded by similar charitable money-raising efforts at Lloyd's following Admiral Bridport's action off Brest in 1795, and after Admiral Jervis's battle off Cape St Vincent and Admiral Duncan's defeat of the Dutch fleet, both battles fought in 1797.

The Treaty of Amiens, signed in 1802, brought to an end nine hard-fought years during which the armies of France were as successful on land as the Royal Navy had been at sea. The peace was short-lived. Napoleon Buonaparte, the new dictator of France, was intent upon expansion and war broke out again within a year. In July 1803, a meeting held at Lloyd's resolved to set up a permanent fund to replace the *ad hoc* charitable subscriptions which until then had been raised after each battle. With the name The Patriotic Fund, it invited donations from every level of society throughout the nation and the colonies. As with the previous temporary arrangements, it provided grants and annuities to the disabled and to widows, but part of the money was used for the purchase of silver vases and ornate swords for presentation to army and naval officers who distinguished themselves in action. They were intended as "honourable badges or marks of distinction".

Most of the vases were "of the one hundred pounds value", although a few were more ornate and expensive. The Lloyd's Patriotic Fund swords likewise were valued at one hundred pounds. One of these individually engraved swords was voted to each captain who had served under Nelson at Trafalgar, but some chose instead a silver vase.

In five years, a total of sixty-odd vases and one hundred and fifty swords were awarded. The purpose of the Fund then changed. In 1809, reports of the suffering of the battlefield casualties in Portugal and Spain prompted the Trustees to devote all its future resources to relieving hardship.

The Nelson Collection at Lloyd's holds a remarkable assembly of artefacts associated with the Admiral himself and with officers who received awards from The Patriotic Fund. Amongst the intensely personal possessions is a gold pendant containing a lock of Nelson's hair (worn by Lady Hamilton), and a gold-mounted miniature of her, painted by Samuel Shelley *circa* 1780 (worn by Nelson on a neck chain). One of the many important documents in the Collection is the Log of HMS *Euryalus*. Under the command of Sir Henry Blackwood, this 36 gun frigate accompanied Nelson's fleet at Trafalgar and her Log contains what is said to be the most complete account of the events of that historic day.

Four of the items of silver held at Lloyds' are illustrated here.

The Harvey Tureen, which pre-dates the creation of The Patriotic Fund, is an exquisitely-fashioned sauce tureen presented to Captain John Harvey RN, officer commanding HMS *Brunswick* on "the Glorious First of June".

This was a major fleet action, fought as a series of running engagements between 28-31 May, 1794, and culminating in the great battle of 1 June. The blockading British fleet commanded by Admiral Lord Richard Howe intercepted a French force, under Admiral L T Villaret-Joyeuse, which had broken out of Brest. The French had a convoy laden with foodstuffs coming across the Atlantic from America, and Villaret-Joyeuse planned to join it and escort it into port.

Howe had thirty-six ships of the line, frigates and sloops under command, Villaret-Joyeuse had twenty-six ships of the line. He was forced back to port after losing one sunk and six captured.

This was one of the occasions when British warships had

The superb large tureen given to Captain John Harvey RN. Seventeen inches high and 28 inches long, it weighs 271 ounces and was made by John Schofield. Photo: Lloyd's Collection.

army units serving aboard as marines. Officers and men of three regiments of foot were spread around the fleet as ship's detachments - the 2nd or Queen's Royal, the 29th (Worcestershire), and the 25th (Sussex).

The Burlton Loving Cup also was an early presentation. It is a silver-gilt cup presented "by the underwriters of London" to Captain George Burlton RN, of HMS *Lively*, a fifth rate frigate of 38 guns. The cup, which incorporates several nautical themes in its design, was made by Robert Makepiece.

On 13 March 1795, while on passage off Ushant, Burlton met up with the more heavily armed *Tourterelle*. Like Edward Pellew before him, he fought the Frenchman to a standstill and took him as prize. His professional career and personal finances received a major boost as a consequence.

This beautiful piece is one of the few surviving reminders of his bravery and seamanship. Burlton died before he could claim, in 1847, his retroactive Naval General Service medal. In the event, only four of these medals - bearing the clasp "Lively, 13 March 1795" - were issued to claimants who had served under him. They were a former Midshipman and three elderly ex-ratings. The ship herself sailed on for another fifteen years. She was wrecked off Malta in 1810.

The Hood Wine Coolers were made in 1807 by Digby Scott and Benjamin Smith for Rundell, Bridge & Rundell, London, for presentation by The Patriotic Fund to Commodore Sir Samuel Hood. On 25 September 1806, commanding a squadron off Rochefort, he fought and captured several French ships (losing an arm in the process). His name was given in later years to three ships of the Royal Navy. The third and last in the line was a 41,200 ton battleship. Pride of the British fleet, HMS *Hood* was destroyed in a single shattering blast when she met the *Bismarck* off Greenland in May 1941.

The Backhouse Urn is yet another example of the work of the industrious Paul Storr. He made it in 1806. An imposing piece, its inscription states: "Presented by the Committee on American Captures at Lloyd's Coffee House to Thomas Backhouse, their Chairman, as a token of their esteem and respect for his able, zealous and indefatigable attention to the object of their concerns for the last ten years, London, 10th May 1806". Like several other pieces in the collection, this one appeared years later on the open market. It was purchased by a Member of Lloyds who generously handed it to the successors of its original donors.

The silver-gilt Burlton Loving Cup was made by Robert Makepiece and bears London marks for 1796. It is 28 inches high, 14 inches wide at its widest point, and weighs 227 ounces. Photo: Lloyd's Collection.

The pair of Smith & Scott silver-gilt wine coolers presented by The Patriotic Fund to Sir Samuel Hood. They are 11 inches high, and weigh 272 ounces. Photo: Lloyd's Collection.

The "Committee for American Captures" calls for explanation. After the United States of America won their independence from the British Crown in 1776, relations between their new leaders and the governments of Great Britain and France were relatively peaceful. However, the Anglo-French wars had serious implications for American ship-owners and for those underwriters at Lloyd's who were asked to insure their ships and cargoes. Merchant vessels sailing under American colours were liable to seizure by the Royal Navy if they were suspected of carrying contraband goods destined for France or her allies. They were equally at risk if stopped and searched by French warships, and found to be carrying goods bound for British ports or other proscribed destinations.

Complicating the situation was the tangled web of successive Decrees issued by the French and Orders in Council flowing from London. It is evident that the underwriting of war risks was for many years a difficult and complicated business. In January 1797, as an example, it was reported that no fewer than eighty American merchant ships were being held at Guadaloupe, awaiting the result of French prize court proceedings. The excellent Mr Thomas Backhouse had the almost impossible task of negotiating with all the parties concerned, attempting to protect the interests of Lloyd's policy-holders and, at the same time, ensuring that his Members did not incur unacceptable losses.

The problem eased temporarily when British forces attacked and occupied Guadaloupe in 1779, in 1794 and again in 1810. A significant advance, however, was the

decision by the United States government to send its fledgling navy against the French warships and privateers which were causing such disruption in the Caribbean and Atlantic. Although small, the US Navy was exceptional for the quality of its fast modern frigates and for the competence of the men who commanded them. One of those officers was Captain Thomas Thruxton USN, and his ship was the USS *Constitution*.

Details of the object itself are not available, but it is known that Captain Thruxton was honoured by Lloyd's with a handsome piece of silver inscribed with wording which tells its story: "Presented by the Underwriters and Merchants at Lloyd's Coffee House in London to Captain Thomas Thruxton of the

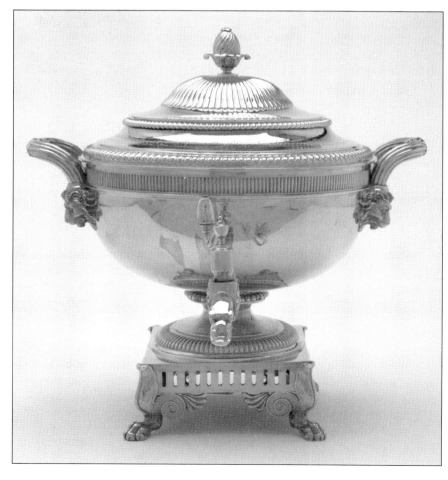

The Backhouse Urn was made by Paul Storr in 1806. Smaller than it seems in the photograph, it is 16 inches high and 11 inches across the handles. It incorporates 210 ounces of silver, suggesting a very solid construction. Photo: Lloyd's Collection.

American frigate *Constitution* as a mark of their sense of his services and admiration of this gallant conduct in taking the *Insurgente*, French frigate of 44 guns, in the West Indies in February 1799". This piece was last reported to be (location unknown) in Washington DC.

Having displayed its mettle against the French, the US Navy went on to even greater success in its dealings with the Deys of the Barbary states - Tripoli, Tunis and Algiers. Between 1804 and 1814, exceptionally talented officers such as Commodore William Bainbridge and Commodore Stephen Decatur forced the Deys into agreeing that they should no longer prey upon American merchant shipping and should release all slaves of American nationality.

The success of their gunboat diplomacy did not endear them to the officers of the Royal Navy. There was jealousy and resentment towards the American upstarts. These emotional overtones were one of the factors which led to the mounting of Admiral Lord Exmouth's expedition to Algiers in 1816.

Feelings ran even higher when they clashed with the Royal Navy during the Anglo-American War of 1812 (precipitated by Great Britain's insistence on the right to stop and search American merchantmen on the high seas). One of their memorable successes was the defeat of HMS *Java* in December of that year. Following a ship-to-ship duel, Commodore Bainbridge captured the British frigate. Despite everything else, he won the grudging admiration of many Royal Navy officers for his professional skill on that occasion and for his chivalry towards his prisoners. By a stroke of irony, the ship which Bainbridge commanded in this engagement was the USS *Constitution* - the same ship which had featured in the Lloyd's presentation of twelve years earlier.

In passing, and to demonstrate how certain people seem repeatedly to have found their way into the pages of history, one of the officers captured by Bainbridge was a General Hislop. He was a passenger in the *Java*, bound for India, and newly appointed as Commander in Chief, Army of Bengal. Emerging uninjured from the battle with the *Constitution*, he was held by the Americans until an exchange could be arranged. Resuming his interrupted journey, he later won fame and glory in the pacification of the sub-continent. His story is told in greater detail in the following chapter.

The name of Paul Storr surfaces time and again in any study of the fine monumental and commemorative silver made in London in the early 19th century. The following entry describes one of his masterpieces which, for reasons which will become apparent, may be unknown to his many admirers in the United Kingdom.

The story is told here in detail because it demonstrates, yet again, how the presentation wording engraved on every piece of military or naval silver can be researched, and the dramatic circumstances which may then be revealed.

The Dawson Tureen was made in 1810 and is engraved on the front of the body: "Presented on the 25th January 1810 to William Dawson Esq, Captain, Royal Navy, by the Merchant Ship Owners and Underwriters of Bombay as an additional mark of the high sense they entertain of his attention to their interests in the protection of the trade of that port".

This impressive piece represents four separate but interrelated stories.

First, Paul Storr. He was one of the most famous goldsmiths and silversmiths of his era, and any work originating in his workshops or made to his design automatically commands keen interest when offered for sale. The two other great masters of his era were Hester Bateman and Paul de Lamerie, and pieces bearing their marks today achieve prices several times higher than those manufactured by their lesser-known competitors. Curiously, neither name has surfaced in the military or naval context during the past three years of research for this book.

Born in 1777, Storr began his career in 1792 in partnership with William Frisbee. Fifteen years later he established his business in Dean Street, Soho, London. He produced a wide range of domestic, ornamental and monumental silver, much of the latter from the designs of the sculptor John Flaxman. They were characterised by their great weight and superlative attention to detail. Many of the more magnificent pieces went to the royal collection at Windsor Castle.

Storr was frequently commissioned by wealthy customers to produce individual pieces recording specific occasions. The inclusion of a family crest in the design of this tureen confirms that it was made for just such a purpose, and the engraved wording tells us that the order originated in India. The event which it commemorates preceded the invention of the telegraph by forty years, hence the customers' written instruction was sent by packet (sea mail) and this explains the two-years gap between the date of the hallmark and the date of the naval action which led to its manufacture. The circumstances explain also why such a high degree of quality and weight of metal were incorporated in its construction. This was, and still is, a very special piece.

In 1808, William Dawson was First Lieutenant in HMS *San Fiorenzo*, a 38-gun frigate of the fifth rate deployed on the East Indies station. She was commanded by Captain Charles Hardinge RN. Originally a French vessel, named *La Minerve*, she had been found sunk in the harbour at San Fiorenzo, Corsica, in February, 1794. The Admiralty had had her raised and refitted, and despatched her to the east as a patrol and convoy protection ship.

On 4 March 1808 she sailed from Pointe de Galle, Ceylon, bound for Bombay. Her course took her northwards through the Gulf of Manaar, the stretch of water which separates Ceylon from the southern tip of India. Shortly after dawn on 6 March 1808, off Cape Comorin, she passed three East India Company merchant ships heading south from Bombay to Columbo. They were the *Charlton* (Captain George Wood), the *Metcalfe* (Captain Matthew Isaake), and the *Devonshire* (Captain James Murray). Like most Company ships of that period, they were armed with a number of cannon, and were well able to defend themselves against pirate vessels and privateers, but they were a tempting and vulnerable target for the heavy French frigates operating from their base at Port Louis, Isle de France (renamed Mauritius by the British after their seizure of the island in 1810).

Shortly after passing the merchantmen, Captain Hardinge sighted one of these predatory French commerce raiders, *La Piemontaise*. Commanded by Captain Epron, she was pursuing the merchantmen with the obvious intention of taking them as prizes. Hardinge set all sail, placed himself between the Frenchman and the Company vessels, and started a cat and mouse series of manouevres which was to continue for the next three days and two nights.

The two frigates tacked back and forth throughout the afternoon and evening. It was nearly midnight before Captain Hardinge succeeded in bringing his opponent to action. *La Piemontaise* was the first to open fire, discharging a full broadside at a range of two hundred yards. The French gunlayers found it difficult to lay their pieces by moonlight, and most of their shots went high. Their aim became even more erratic as the counterblast from the *San Fiorenzo* sent blinding sheets of flame and

The Dawson Tureen was designed by Paul Storr for the serving of soup or other hot food. It has a metal liner, a domed lid with gadroon and shell border, and a finial in the form of a lion holding a rat in its mouth (from the Dawson family bearings). The bowl has a gadroon rim and a continuous band of anthemion and foliate scroll. The handles are each made with lion mask heads and double foliate leaf scrolls decorated with a gadroon border. The base is fluted and raised on four dolphin supports on a circular platform, also decorated with gadroon bordering. The height is 13 inches overall, the width 13 inches, and the weight 252 ounces. The ladle was made much earlier (either 1672-1673 or 1692-1693), but nothing is known of its history. Photo: HMAS *Cresswell*.

smoke into the dark gap separating the two ships.

This first encounter lasted barely ten minutes. The British ship had only three seamen wounded but her sails and rigging were damaged. The French frigate drew ahead, disappearing into the night and seemingly having made good her escape. Captain Epron, however, was a determined man, driven by the prospect of taking three fat East Indiamen and earning enough prize money to keep him and his family in comfort for years to come. He remained in the area throughout the early hours of 7 March.

At first light he was sighted again by the Royal Navy ship, only half a mile away. They closed, and the contest was resumed at a range of four hundred yards. Both ships maintained a steady rate of fire for the next two hours, and it is evident that the *San Fiorenzo* had the worst of it. Eight of her seamen and Royal Marines were killed, and fourteen wounded. More seriously, in terms of her fighting capability, much of her running and standing rigging was cut to pieces and her ability to manouevre, therefore, greatly reduced.

La Piemontaise did not press home her advantage but moved away and was lost to sight over the horizon. The *San Fiorenzo* was not alone in needing time and space in which to lick her wounds and make good the damage incurred during this second clash.

By late afternoon, the British ship had repaired most of the defects and was once again able to go in search of her opponent. There was great anxiety that the French frigate had slipped away to the south and was already overtaking the heavily-laden merchant ships. Captain Hardinge set his course accordingly, and in the late afternoon his opponent's topsails were sighted on the eastern horizon. He gave chase, but *La Piemontaise* turned away to the east and vanished in the quickly descending dusk.

Hardinge was compelled to continue the search and bring his enemy to battle. Apart from a natural desire to emerge as the victor, he knew also that his career would be ruined if the French ship succeeded in evading him and capturing all or any of the East India Company's ships. He drove on and received his reward at midnight when, by the light of the rising moon, his lookouts reported *La Piemontaise* dead ahead.

The two ships passed the night and the morning of 8 March in a succession of moves and counter-moves as Captain Epron attempted unsuccessfully to shake off his pursuer. He tried a familiar but, in the circumstances, futile *ruse de guerre* when he ran up first a Dutch flag and then an English flag. Captain Hardinge pressed on with every sail set and the adversaries joined battle for the third and last time.

Now flying her true colours, *La Piemontaise* fired a full

broadside into the English ship as the two surged past each other, on opposite tacks, at a range of eighty yards. This time the French cannon and carronades were even better served than before, and their gunners quickly discharged a second broadside. It was one of these shots which killed Captain Hardinge. Command of the ship now passed automatically to his First Lieutenant, William Dawson.

Dawson's handling of the *San Fiorenzo* must have been exceptionally skilled because, in less than two hours, his gunners had beaten the enemy into submission. The masts, sails and rigging of *La Piemontaise* were so ruined that she no longer responded to the helm. Captain Epron struck his colours, and a boarding party was sent to accept his surrender. From her crew of 366 Frenchmen and 200 Lascars, she had lost forty-eight killed and 112 wounded. The *San Fiorenzo's* total losses in the three engagements were thirteen killed and twenty-five wounded, a surprisingly light "butcher's bill" in the circumstances.

The armament of the two frigates was very similar, but there was a large discrepancy in their musters. Owing to sickness and the absence of men sent away as prize crews, the effective ship's company aboard the *San Fiorenzo* was only one hundred and eighty-six. It was this factor which made her performance so remarkable. First Hardinge, then Dawson, managed to handle the ship and her guns with less than half of her normal manpower. As the historian William James later wrote, "neither skill nor gallantry would have availed had the *San Fiorenzo* not excelled her antagonist in swiftness of sailing". It was this which determined the outcome of the third and final clash, and which brought such acclaim to William Dawson. He was, clearly, an outstanding ship-handler.

On the morning of 9 March, the French ship's battered masts collapsed and fell over the side. Dawson took her under tow and, three days later, brought her triumphantly into Columbo harbour. She was repaired and taken into Royal Navy service, still as *La Piemontaise*. In 1813, she was sold to a private contractor and broken up at Woolwich. Dawson's own ship, the *San Fiorenzo*, lasted much longer. She was taken out of the line in 1812, laid up in ordinary for harbour service, and eventually broken up in 1837.

William Dawson received the hero's welcome to which he was entitled. He was granted accelerated promotion to Captain, received "the approbation of Their Lordships of the Admiralty", and was paid a very large sum of money by the Admiralty's Prize Agents for their purchase of *La Piemontaise*.

When the European traders in the city of Bombay learned that their ships were safe, they responded in full. Apart from raising a fund to pay Paul Storr for the tureen, they presented the young officer with a sword upon which were engraved the words "To Captain Wm Dawson, the gallant successor of the regretted Captain Hardinge of the *St Fiorenzo*, this sword is presented by the Merchants, Shipowners and Underwriters of Bombay in grateful remembrance of his courage and conduct during the successful action with the French Frigate *La Piedemontese*, IX April MDCCCVIII".

There is a small spelling error in the inscription. The French vessel was *La Piemontaise*, this being the correct French spelling and pronunciation for that part of north west Italy (which at the time was French territory). The error was repeated in the wording engraved upon the blade of a second sword, presented to him by the Lloyd's Patriotic Fund.

Sadly, he did not live long enough to claim his Naval General Service silver medal of the 1793-1840 series. When the terms of eligibility for this retrospective medal were announced in 1847, William Dawson was not one of those former officers and seamen who submitted a claim. However, eighteen of his former shipmates did receive the medal, with the clasp "San Fiorenzo 8 March 1808", when it was issued in 1849.

The tureen remained in the Dawson family until 1966. On 6 December of that year, it was presented to the Royal Australian Naval College, HMAS *Creswell*, by Mrs H H Florance, of Bowral, New South Wales. This lady was the daughter of Rear Admiral Willoughby Pudsey-Dawson and a direct descendent of Captain William Dawson of the *San Fiorenzo*. She felt that the tureen, together with Dawson's soup ladle and his two swords, needed to be given a permanent home in the Wardroom of a naval establishment. With so much valuable silver already held in the United Kingdom, in the possession of the Royal Navy, her choice fell upon the Royal Australian Navy. The silver is now mounted in a display case in the Wardroom at the College, and is brought out for significant occasions such as formal Guest Night dinners.

The Royal Australian Naval College is located ninety miles south of Sydney, New South Wales, on a coastal inlet named Jervis Bay. It was founded in 1913 with the aim of training young men who would enter the newly formed Royal Australian Navy with their own distinctively Australian spirit. The Royal Navy had been responsible for guarding the continent's coastlines up until the turn of the century, but the creation of the Commonwealth of Australia in 1901, with a federal government and national identity, made it increasingly desirable that Australia should have her own professional navy.

In the early years, the College was run on the same lines as the Britannia Royal Naval College, at Dartmouth, Devon. It accepted boys of thirteen, educated them for four years, then sent them to join the Fleet as Midshipmen. In 1958, having for some years been located elsewhere, it returned to Jervis Bay and was commissioned as HMAS *Creswell* (in honour of Vice Admiral Sir William Creswell KCMG KBE RAN, the First Naval Member of the Naval Board when the College was founded). Its role has since changed greatly, and it now provides a wide range of support and training services.

The name of the site, Jervis Bay, has a number of historical connotations. It originated in 1791 when Lieutenant Richard Bowen RN entered the bay while on passage to Botany Bay (Sydney) with the Third Fleet of transported felons. He named the place after John Jervis who, at the time, was a senior naval commander. Jervis entered the realm of naval legend six years later when he comprehensively defeated a Spanish fleet off Cape St Vincent. Elevated to the peerage, he subsequently became Admiral Lord St Vincent, First Lord of the Admiralty.

In 1920, a new class of passenger/cargo ship for the United Kingdom to Australia route was ordered by the Commonwealth Government Line (the shipping company formed by the Australian government in 1916). Five of these 14,000-ton ships were launched and each was named after a well-known bay in Australia. Each bay was in a different State and, when they were launched, each ship was registered in the principal port of the appropriate State. Built by Vickers, in their Barrow yard, the *Jervis Bay* was launched in 1922 and registered in Sydney.

The concept of a national shipping line was not a success. In 1923, the company was reorganised as the Australian Commonwealth Line of Steamers, but it continued to lose money. Five years later, in May 1928, the five *Bay* ships, plus two cargo vessels, were sold to the White Star Line, formerly owners of (amongst many other ships) the SS *Titanic*.

Australia was discovered by the Portuguese in the 15th century and later explored by the Dutch. In 1770, the eastern coastal region was claimed for Great Britain by Captain James Cook RN. Eighteen years later, the First Fleet of convicts and their guards began to settle Botany Bay and New South Wales. This statuette is an attractive example of an explorer being commemorated in silver. Signed "Eusin", it carries a silver plate which simply states *Matthew Flinders, 1774-1814, Captain in the Royal Navy*. It weighs 80 ounces and stands 12 inches in height. Nothing is known of its provenance. Captain Flinders navigated and skillfully charted large stretches of the Australian coastline between 1796 and 1803. Photo: HMAS *Cerberus*, Victoria.

Ownership and management of the *Bay* ships changed repeatedly during the 1930s, but the *Jervis Bay* continued to go peacefully about her business By a strange coincidence, it was during this time that the officer with whom her name will always be associated was appointed to the RAN College, at Jervis Bay, as the Executive Officer. He was Commander E S Fogarty Fegen RN, then age thirty-seven. He held the appointment for two years, 1928-1929, before returning to England. His character was greatly admired by the Australians. He was regarded by everyone who met him as having exceptional qualities of leadership, but ten years later he was still a Commander and the prospect of promotion to Captain was fading fast.

Late in 1939, the SS *Jervis Bay* was taken over by the Admiralty and armed with seven single-mounted six-inch guns and two single three-inch guns. Rated an auxiliary merchant cruiser, HMS *Jervis Bay* went to war as a convoy escort in the North Atlantic. She did so under the command of Commander (Acting Captain) Fogarty Fegen RN.

In November 1940, Fegen's ship was escorting Convoy HX84, a group of thirty-seven merchantmen, homeward-bound from Halifax to British ports. Late in the afternoon of 5 November, one thousand miles east of Newfoundland, they were attacked by the German pocket battleship *Admiral Scheer*. She was heavily armoured, carried six eleven-inch guns, and had a top speed of 27 knots. A contest between the two could have only one outcome.

Fegen turned his ship towards the raider as Rear Admiral H B Maltby, the convoy's Commodore, ordered the merchantmen to scatter. Desperately trying to gain her maximum speed of sixteen knots, the British ship drove forward through the German's shell-falls and attempted to close within a range at which her own armament would be effective. Over the next three hours, the *Jervis Bay* kept herself between the raider and the fleeing merchant ships. The steering gear was damaged and the ship was barely under control. Captain Fegen had an arm blown off, but he stayed on the bridge, directing his battle.

She came to a stop as night fell, burning fiercely and unable to do more. Two hours later she went down with her Colours still flying but taking Fogarty Fegen and thirty-two of his officers with her. One hundred and forty-seven ratings were lost, of whom thirteen were Canadians. Sixty-five officers and ratings were pulled from the water when Captain Sven Olander, commanding the Swedish vessel *Stureholm*, bravely turned back in the darkness to search for them.

The *Admiral Scheer* went in pursuit of the convoy but was able to find and sink only six ships. The German also found and set on fire the tanker *San Demetrio*, owned by the Eagle Oil & Shipping Company. This vessel was carrying 11,800 tons of gasoline. Her crew took to the lifeboats and watched as the abandoned blazing wreck drifted away in the gloom.

Twenty hours later, the men in one of the *San Demetrio's* boats sighted their ship through the mist and rain, still afloat and still burning. The sixteen crew members, commanded by the Second Officer, Arthur G Hawkins, re-boarded and fought the fires for two days and nights. Despite having no charts, no navigating instruments and no radio, they succeeded a week later in bringing her into port unaided.

It was epic seamanship, and the story was made into a commercial film entitled *San Demetrio, London*. It still appears from time to time on the television screen. It has become, in effect, a memorial to the thousands of Merchant Navy seamen who lost their lives in the North Atlantic between 1939 and 1945. The *San Demetrio* did not outlive her fame. Seventeen months later, while on passage to Baltimore, she was sunk east of Chesapeake Bay by the German submarine U-404.

The *London Gazette* of 22 November 1940 carried the announcement that Captain Fegen had been awarded posthumously the Victoria Cross. Publication of the details of his award came at a time when Great Britain was still marveling at what was perceived to be the miracle of Dunkirk and the even greater miracle of the Battle of Britain. The story of Fegen's battle had very great public impact, and HMS *Jervis Bay* became a part of the legend of that momentous year.

Fogarty Fegen's body was not recovered. He is commemorated on the Chatham Naval Memorial and on four other memorials - in Hamilton (Bermuda), in St John (New Brunswick), in Wellington (New Zealand), and on a plaque in the grounds of the Royal Australian Naval College. His memory is kept alive there when, each year, the officers of HMAS *Creswell* hold a special Wardroom Dinner in his name.

It is on such occasions that the Dawson tureen is displayed on the dining table. Captain William Dawson RN and Captain Fogarty Fegen RN commanded ships of very different types, and the actions which brought them glory were separated by one hundred and thirty years. Curiously, though, each was a single-ship action fought in the defence of merchantmen. Thanks to the generosity of Mrs H H Florance, and to the Wardroom custom at HMAS *Creswell*, the two captains are each year brought together, at least in spirit.

For whatever they may be worth, none of the preceding lines would have been written if the tureen described at the beginning had not been engraved with the name and particulars of Captain William Dawson RN. There are collectors of antique silver who would be immensely pleased to own a Georgian piece of this quality, particularly as it bears the mark of Paul Storr. Some, however, would regret the engraving. They would regard it as a defacement on an otherwise desirable example of his work. By good fortune, the tureen remained in private hands for a century and a half, and then passed to a naval institution which understands its provenance. It could have been otherwise. If it had passed out of the family and into the hands of a general silver dealer, it is not unlikely that the engraving would have been removed. It is fortunate that Mrs Florance and her forebears exercised such good stewardship of this historical treasure.

We may now consider some of the other avenues by which ships and officers of the Royal Navy have come into the possession of silver of various categories. A typical example was a ship which joined the Fleet shortly before WWI.

HMS *New Zealand*. In return for the Royal Navy's protection of their coastlines and their merchant shipping, several British Empire countries have at times contributed to the cost of building its ships. Such vessels were then named after the country which had donated the money. Apart from easing the burden on the Admiralty's budget, this custom also emphasised the ties of friendship between Great Britain and the countries concerned, and gave their peoples an interest in the welfare and services of "their ship".

HMS *New Zealand* was built by Fairfields, of Govan, Glasgow, the cost being paid by the government of her namesake country. Launched in July 1911, completed at Devonport in November 1912 and displacing 18,800 tons, she carried eight 12-inch guns as her main armament.

Under the command of Captain Lionel Halsey RN, she joined the 1st Battle Cruiser Squadron but within weeks was detached for a year-long shake down cruise around the world. It was important to let the people of New Zealand see what their taxes had purchased and, given the distance between England and their country, it was an ideal opportunity to "show the flag" at other places *en route*.

After touching at St Vincent, Ascension and St Helena, and after major courtesy visits to Capetown and Durban, the ship arrived in New Zealand waters in April 1913. During her first call, at Wellington, she received 98,170 visitors in the space of just ten days. Thousands more came aboard when she called at the small ports of Napier and Gisborne, but the ship's company must have been almost overwhelmed by the successive welcomes at Auckland and Lyttleton when they entertained 132,365 and then 94,616 visitors

The ship spent nearly three months calling at every New Zealand port that could accommodate her before sailing north to Fiji, across the Pacific to Honolulu, north again to Vancouver, then all the way down the west coasts of the Americas, around

Cape Horn to Argentina, Brazil, the Caribbean, Halifax, and finally home. In all, she had sailed 45,320 miles and been visited by nearly 600,000 people from the forty-six ports at which she called. As a diplomatic and public relations exercise it had been a roaring success, and Captain Halsey was made a Commander of the Order of St Michael & St George in recognition of his services and those of his ship.

Officers and men of the modern Royal Navy can only marvel that this major warship spent most of her first year in service without having had a single opportunity to work in company with other RN ships and without exercising her main armament. In the event, Captain Halsey must have prepared his ship well because, when war came, only months later, she was immediately in action. On 24 August 1914, in the Heligoland Bight and sailing in company with HMShips *Princess Royal*, *Queen Mary*, *Invincible* and *Lion*, she fought in the battle which resulted in the sinking of the Imperial German Navy ships *Mainz* and *Köln*.

HMS *New Zealand* went on to fight at the Battle of the Dogger Bank (24 January 1915) and the Battle of Jutland (31May 1916), and formed part of the escort when the German High Seas Fleet crossed the North Sea to surrender on 21 November 1918. Less than a handful of RN ships could claim to have taken part in all four operations.

Fortunately for readers of this book, the ship's official inventory of silver and pictures has survived. It is instructive in telling us how such items were acquired by a Royal Navy ship of that type and of that era.

In common with every other newly commissioned warship, the officers received from the King and Queen signed photographs of themselves, in Court dress, to hang in the Wardroom. These were followed by similar portraits from the Tsar and Tsarina of Russia. Other pictures were given to the ship during the war, but it is the silver which demonstrates the varied provenances and styles of such pieces.

The first acquisition was the silver ship's bell, named "HMS *New Zealand* 1905" and suspended from a replica of a Maori warrior's head and neck. The date, 1905, reflects the fact that the bell was inherited from the previous (first) HMS *New Zealand*, a battleship built at Portsmouth in that year. She was renamed *Zealandia* in 1911 and relegated to second-line duties before being scrapped in 1921. Ship's bells, made in brass, have for years been highly prized by collectors of maritime artefacts. Examples made in Sterling silver, especially those named to major vessels, are encountered very rarely. Almost always they were presented to the ship by the town, city, county or country which had adopted her as their own, and were not, therefore, standard Admiralty or Ministry of Defence (Navy) issue.

Curiously, when they departed on their world cruise, the officers had no silver in their Wardroom. In later years, builders such as Fairfields would have made a "good luck" presentation of some sort. The Wardroom table began to acquire the expected sparkle when the ship arrived at Durban, in March 1913. There the officers received a cigar box, a punchbowl and two candlesticks "from the people of Natal". They were also given, by the staff of the Pretoria Public Works Department, a silver collar for the ship's dog, Jack.

It is no surprise to find that the majority of the fifty-two principal items listed in the inventory came from sources in New Zealand itself. During her protracted visit from April to June, 1913, the ship acquired the following silver artefacts - a stag's head from a Mr B M Wilson, a boar's head from "the people of Nelson", a claret jug from "some residents of Wellington", a

The Mappin & Webb punch bowl or *quaiche* presented in March 1913 to HMS *New Zealand by the people of Natal* during the ship's visit to Durban. It is now held at the Royal New Zealand Navy base at Devonport, North Island. The purchase was met from public subscriptions organised by the local newspaper, *The Natal Witness*. Photo: RNZN.

salver from Colonel J Allen, a salver from the Wellesley Club of Wellington, a shield from the Canterbury Swimming Association (for competition amongst all the ship's company), a similar shield from the people of Auckland (for the Engine Room Department), a tea service from the Auckland Harbour Board, a loving cup "from the women of New Zealand", a cup from "the women of Timaru", a pair of *timpani* from The Women's Patriotic League of New Zealand, a rose bowl from a Mr Alexander Clark, and a silver globe and plinth purchased by the officers themselves to commemorate their circumnavigation.

The homeward leg of the cruise brought seven tankards "from the New Zealanders in Suva", a *kava* cup from "the New Zealanders of Honolulu", a cup from the Vancouver Rowing Club, a loving cup from "the government and people of Columbia", and a cigar box "from the people of Barbados".

A few more pieces of silver were gifted to the ship during the war from a variety of sources, but the collection reflected mainly the very strong association between the ship and the people of New Zealand. One or two items were kept in the United Kingdom when she was decommissioned and sold to the breakers in 1922, but the bulk of the collection went to the Commodore, New Zealand Division RN, and to the New Zealand Ministry of Internal Affairs. It is believed that most of these mementos are now in store or on display at several locations in their country of origin.

Comparable associations are to be found in the silverware owned by warships named after places in the United Kingdom. The famous three-funnel County-class cruisers were a case in point. Ships so named were "adopted" by the people of those places. There have been many other occasions when silver has been given by citizens to "their ship" and, conversely, when ships have made presentations to local communities.

The four ships successively bearing the name HMS *Sheffield* have been particularly favoured in a different but parallel way. Proud of their world-wide reputation, the steel-makers of that city donated quantities of their high-grade stainless steel for the making of various fittings in the ships' constructions. It is for this reason that all four have always been known as "the Shiny Sheff". The third ship in the series, a Type 42 frigate, was one of the four Royal Navy ships sunk by the Argentines in 1982.

HMS *Nelson* has been the name of three major sea-going ships. Fourth in the line is a "stone frigate", the Royal Navy barracks at Portsmouth. It is here that the navy holds all its items of silver and other treasures while they are not in use or on display elsewhere. One of them is the silver bell, weighing 2692 ounces, given in 1928 to the battleship HMS *Nelson* by the people of Tyneside. It hangs at the main gate, and serves as the establishment's Watch Bell.

Since the early 1980s, when the Devonport and Chatham Divisions were closed, all records have been concentrated under a single roof - The Royal Navy Trophy Centre, HMS *Nelson*. The title of the Centre requires explanation. The Trophy Officer is responsible not only for trophies in the conventional sense of that word but also for every other category of silver held in shore establishments, for the silver of ships no longer in service, for pictures and royal photographs, for historically significant naval cannon, and for certain pieces of important furniture.

In total, the number of items on the Trophy Officer's inventory exceeds twenty-six thousand. Approximately one third of them are silver.

Ownership does not reside with the navy itself but with a registered charity - The Royal Navy Trustee Fund. As described in an earlier chapter (in which the role of Regimental Trusts was discussed) there is great merit in appointing Trustees whose duties are defined under the terms of the Charities Act and its various associated charitable schemes. Apart from ensuring a consistent level of management, this route allows a nominated group of individuals to make decisions promptly. The Trustees of the RN Trophy Fund are senior serving officers.

As with the two other fighting services, the Royal Navy has been much reduced in size since the end of WWII. With fewer ships in commission, there is a great deal more Wardroom silver without a natural home of its own. Much of it is locked away in secure storage at the Trophy Centre, but hundreds of items are still fulfilling their original purpose by enhancing a house or quarter. They are on loan to a wide range of beneficiaries - the Messes of naval shore establishments, the official residences of Flag Officers, the accommodation of Naval Attachés at British Embassies around the world, and the Wardrooms of newly-commissioned ships whose names may not entitle them to lay automatic claim to the silver of earlier ships in the Navy List.

One of the newest ships in the Royal Navy is the amphibious helicopter carrier HMS *Ocean*. There have been five ships of this name before her, the first entering service in 1762 (a 90 gun ship of the line), the last being sold off in 1962 (a war-built aircraft carrier of 13,200 tons). For thirty-odd years, during the time when there was no HMS *Ocean* in the Navy Lists, all silver previously gifted to those ships was held ashore. When the new *Ocean* was commissioned in 1998, the Trophy Centre was able to hand over, on loan and in trust, three silver artefacts from her predecessors with which to embellish her Wardroom and the Warrant Ranks' Mess. They are of minor importance - a cigarette box from 1941, a cup from 1946, and a Spanish bowl (donated by the people of Vigo) from 1956 - but they do at least provide a sense of continuity.

Great emphasis has been placed in earlier chapters of this book on the fact that the Messes of the army are the focal point of a family, a brotherhood. Membership of its Mess is a permanent privilege of every officer in the regiment, and it continues for years, throughout his active service. The navy is in a different position. Even in the first half of the 19th century, ships were normally commissioned for no more than two years at a time. At the end of the commission, the vessel passed into dockyard hands for refit, and her officers and men were dispersed to other ships. The silver was sent ashore for safe-keeping and pending her re-commission.

There can never be the same degree of continuity of customs and traditions in a warship as there are in a regiment or battalion. It is for this reason that every ship's commanding officer works hard during the comparatively short time available to him to work up the efficiency of his ship and, in his officers and men, to develop in her a strong sense of pride. He is creating the naval equivalent of *esprit de corps*. Efficiency and pride are, in practice, inter-dependent and indivisable.

Thrown together for months on end, sharing exactly the same hazards of the sea and of active service, every rank from commanding officer to junior rating must weld themselves into a single cohesive unit. The presence in the officers' Wardroom, and the Warrant Ranks' Mess, of silver which reflects the services of their own ship, and of all the ships of the same name which have gone before her, are potent ingredients in creating "pride in ship". It is no accident that the Royal Navy always refers to "the ship's company", never "the crew".

The following six entries all refer to items of silver in the possession of the Royal Navy Trustee Fund.

HMS *Talbot* was the recipient of an exceptionally interesting gift. When war first broke out between Japan and Imperial Russia, in February 1904, she was one of several warships of different nationalities lying in the neutral Korean harbour of Chemulpo. Two of these vessels were Russian - the lightly armoured cruiser *Variag* (Captain Roudneff), and the gunboat *Korietz*.

On 6 February, Captain Roudneff ordered the *Korietz* to sail for Port Arthur with mail and official despatches. She was quickly intercepted by a flotilla of five Japanese warships which opened fire and forced her to turn back. Despite this hostile act, Roudneff remained inactive, at anchor, because the cable informing him of his government's formal declaration of war had been blocked by Japanese naval intelligence.

One of the warships lying in Chemulpo harbour was the Japanese light cruiser *Kiyoda* (Captain Murakami). At midnight on 7 February she unobtrusively weighed anchor and joined the other Japanese warships patrolling some miles offshore. On the following morning, a Japanese assault force boldly entered the harbour, disembarking troops and supplies without interference from anyone.

Roudneff went to the officer commanding the *Talbot*, Captain L Bayly RN, and asked for his advice as to what action he should now take. He still had no orders from his Admiral in Port Arthur. Bayly was in a difficult position because Great Britain and Japan were at that time allies, and the Imperial Japanese Navy was an important customer for British ship-builders and armament manufacturers. He recommended to the Russian that he should scuttle the antiquated *Korietz* and make a dash for Port Arthur in the *Variag*.

Bayly accepted the personal risk of a backlash from the Foreign Office when he delivered to the Japanese invaders a strongly worded protest at their violation of Korean neutrality.

In the event, Captain Roudneff decided to take both of his ships to sea. In a fine gesture of defiance, he left the harbour with battle ensigns flying, his men standing to their unshielded six inch guns, and the *Variag's* band playing on her quarterdeck.

The one-sided encounter with the waiting Japanese squadron lasted little more than an hour. Heavily damaged above and below the waterline, with all but two of her twelve guns out of action and with nearly half of the ship's complement wounded or dead, the stricken *Variag* was escorted back into the harbour by the *Korietz*.

HMS *Talbot* sent away her boats with her doctor and sickbay attendants to give what help they could. Other foreign ships assisted in removing the wounded and saving the rest of the crew. The *Variag* went down when the last of the Russians to leave their ship opened her sea-cocks. The *Korietz* followed her to the bottom when she was blown up by her crew.

Many of the Russian survivors were accommodated in the *Talbot* pending their repatriation and so were spared the uncertainties of imprisonment by the Japanese. When reports of the episode reached the Tsar, he arranged for the officers of HMS *Talbot* to receive a wonderful punch bowl and ladle made by the House of Fabergé. Engraved around the base are the words: "Presented to *Talbot* by the Emperor of Russia in friendly recognition of the assistance rendered to the crews of the *Variag* and the *Korietz* after the battle of Tchemulpo, Feby 1904".

HMS *Talbot* was sold to the breakers in 1921. During WWI, her valuables were held ashore in secure storage. However, throughout the ten years between Chemulpo and August 1914, her officers were able to enjoy a treasure at that time unmatched in any other Wardroom in the Royal Navy.

Built in Devonport Dockyard in 1898, with a displacement of 5600 tons, she was only a second class cruiser and yet she held a treasure which was exceptionally important then and which today would command the interest of any private collector fortunate enough to see it. Such an opportunity is unlikely to arise. It is currently displayed in a secure environment at the Britannia Royal Naval College, Dartmouth.

Gustave Fabergé began trading as a silversmith and goldsmith in 1842, with premises in St Petersburg. His son Carl, born four years later, assumed control of the firm in 1870 at the

The magnificent House of Fabergé punch bowl and ladle presented in 1904 to HMS *Talbot* by the Tsar of Russia. It measures 15 inches in height, is 22 inches in length, and weighs 263 ounces. The ladle weighs 10.5 ounces. Typically of Fabergé work, the piece is made in the pan-slavic style and is embellished with semi-precious polished stones (in this case, possibly jade). Photo: RN Trophy Centre.

age of twenty-four. In 1882 he was joined, from Dresden, by his twenty year-old brother Agathon, and together they developed their business as the House of Fabergé.

The House won its first Gold Medal that same year when it displayed its wares at the Pan-Russian Exhibition, in Moscow. Its reputation grew rapidly and, in 1884, it received the Warrant as jewellers to the Court of His Imperial Majesty Tsar Alexander III. Shortly before or after this event, the first of the famous Imperial Easter Eggs was presented to the Tsarina Marie Feodorovna.

A branch of the firm was opened in Odessa in 1890, and another in 1903 in London (under the direction of an Englishman, Arthur Bowe). Special pieces were made for the Coronation, in 1894, of Tsar Nicholas II. The Royal Courts of Norway and Sweden granted their Warrants in 1897. By a curious coincidence, the head of the House, Carl Fabergé, was himself visiting the Far East at the time of the *Talbot* incident. He was the guest of King Chulalongkorn of Siam, the monarch wanting to know more about the work of European silver-smiths. The connection led to a thriving export trade to Siam, India and China.

Baron Foelkersam, author of *Inventaire de l'Argenterie*, wrote in 1907: "This firm, which is one of the best and most famous in the world, is renowned above all for its *objets d'art*. Articles made in Fabergé's workshops are known for their technical excellence, especially as regards enamelling, stone polishing and engraving".

The firm's output has been described as "eclectic", and it did indeed reflect the varied tastes of its legendary international clientele. At its core, however, was "the pan-slavic style", also known as "old Russian", with designs heavily dependent upon fine enamelling and decoration with gem-stones. It was the epitome of the Pre-revolutionary grandeur associated with the Russian Court and nobility.

This distinctive medieval tradition was regenerated by many Russian craftsmen in 1913. That was the year which marked the tercentenary of the Romanovs as the rulers of Russia, and all of the arts were stimulated by the celebrations which attended the event. However, the House of Fabergé had always followed the pan-slavic tradition, and the tureen given to HMS *Talbot* was characteristic of its work.

HMS *Lion*, also, was the recipient of an exceptional piece of Russian silver (although the circumstances were much less dramatic than those of the *Talbot*).

June of 1914 was the last tranquil month of that fateful year. There had been a war in the Balkans, but the major

European powers were still at peace with each other. The British government decided to reinforce its cordial relations with Imperial Germany and Imperial Russia by sending two squadrons of her most impressive modern warships to visit both of those countries simultaneously. One squadron went to Wilhelmshaven, where it was inspected by Kaiser Wilhelm II, the other to Krondstadt, naval port of the city of St Petersburg.

The squadron which went to Russia was led by HMS *Lion* (Captain E Chatfield RN), flagship of Vice Admiral Sir David Beatty KCB DSO, commanding the Grand Fleet's 1st Battle Cruiser Squadron. Two years later the name of Beatty was one of those which rang around the world in the wake of the Battle

House of Fabergé creation to be acquired by the Royal Navy (*vide* the accompanying photograph).

It was while these high-level diplomatic visits to Wilhelmshaven and St Petersburg were in progress that news was received of the assassination, in Sarajevo, of the Archduke Ferdinand of Austria-Hungary. As their ships carried them back across the North Sea, the more thoughtful of the Royal Navy's officers must have pondered the implications for themselves and their service. Seven weeks later, the world as they knew it came to an end.

The Brickwood Trophy was commissioned as an annual challenge prize. Everyone reading these lines will be familiar with

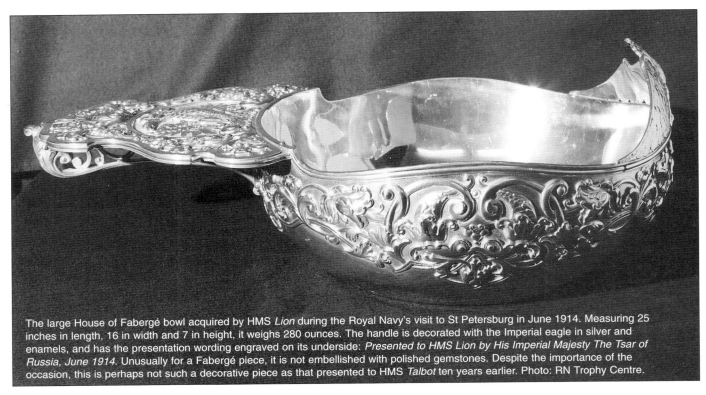

The large House of Fabergé bowl acquired by HMS *Lion* during the Royal Navy's visit to St Petersburg in June 1914. Measuring 25 inches in length, 16 in width and 7 in height, it weighs 280 ounces. The handle is decorated with the Imperial eagle in silver and enamels, and has the presentation wording engraved on its underside: *Presented to HMS Lion by His Imperial Majesty The Tsar of Russia, June 1914*. Unusually for a Fabergé piece, it is not embellished with polished gemstones. Despite the importance of the occasion, this is perhaps not such a decorative piece as that presented to HMS *Talbot* ten years earlier. Photo: RN Trophy Centre.

of Jutland, the biggest battle ever fought at sea.

Also on board the *Lion* was Admiral Prince Louis of Battenberg, the First Sea Lord. As an ADC to King George V, he had the dual role at St Petersburg of representing the Royal Navy and representing the British royal family. He too was to become part of naval history, but for entirely the wrong reasons. Despite having adopted British nationality when a boy, and despite his forty-six years of dedicated service to the navy, he was hounded from office in October 1914 by the British popular press. His Germanic origins and family connections made him an easy target for the hysterical anti-German editorials which characterised the opening months of the war. At St Petersburg he was a very important person. Four months later his career was finished.

The customary round of official visits and receptions began as soon as Beatty's ships arrived at Krondstadt. Rowing and sailing races were arranged between the British sailors and their Russian counterparts, while the officers attended a series of balls and dinners. The highlight was a visit by Nicholas II, Tsar of all the Russias, together with the Tsarina Alexandra and their daughters (including the fabled Anastasia).

Having inspected the visiting ships from the bridge of his yacht, the *Standart*, he and his family and entourage went aboard the *Lion* to be entertained to lunch by her officers. Before leaving, he presented Captain Chatfield with the second silver

the spectacle of the inter-Command Field Gun Competitions which traditionally have featured each year in the programme of the Royal Tournament. It is less well known that Portsmouth Command holds an identical annual competition. The participants are teams from each of its four component shore establishments - HMShips *Collingwood*, *Sultan*, *Dryad* and *Nelson*.

Unlike the Royal Tournament teams, the Portsmouth competitors are unable to devote six months to practice and physical hardening, but they do take the competition very seriously (as they must, given the dangers involved). The encounter takes place at HMS *Collingwood*, and the name of the winning team is then added to the base of the Trophy on a small silver shield. Entry is not restricted to ratings. There have been years when the participants, representing one establishment or another, have consisted entirely of Sub Lieutenants.

Known as The Brickwood Trophy, it was presented to Portsmouth Command in 1931 by the Directors of Brickwoods Limited, a local firm of brewers.

The Haslar Centrepiece recalls a major advance in naval medical care. Built at the tip of the Gosport peninsula, near Portsmouth, Haslar Naval Hospital was opened in 1753. Other naval hospitals were built at Chatham and Plymouth, but Haslar was the first to begin taking in patients. The need was pressing. Until that time, sick and injured men brought ashore from naval vessels received very little care of any kind. A large proportion

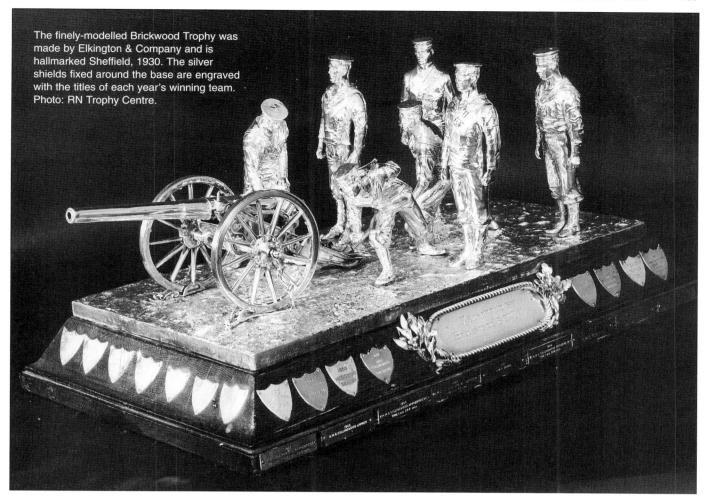

The finely-modelled Brickwood Trophy was made by Elkington & Company and is hallmarked Sheffield, 1930. The silver shields fixed around the base are engraved with the titles of each year's winning team. Photo: RN Trophy Centre.

of seamen were forcibly pressed into the service or were convicted felons taken from county jails. They were regarded as expendable, and for many decades the Admiralty had no interest in them.

Haslar was conceived as an enormous structure. It would have been the largest hospital in Europe if it had been completed to the original design. Even after the plans were modified, it could still accommodate a thousand patients. This figure rose to two thousand when the ailing and frost-bitten remnants of Sir John Moore's army were brought back from Corunna. Haslar then became, temporarily, a military hospital.

The full history of the place is described in *Haslar, The Royal Hospital*, by Surgeon Commander A L Revell RN (The Gosport Society, 1984). It is sufficient to say here that the early rough and ready days of medicine, which were concerned mainly with smallpox, tuberculosis, venereal diseases and "the bloody flux", were succeeded by such improvements that Haslar became one of the best establishments of its kind in the world. Apart from caring for sick seamen and officers, it was a home for naval pensioners and provided training and re-training for naval surgeons (doctors) and the navy's sickberth attendants (nursing staff).

Doctors recruited into the service had already obtained their medical qualifications at the great teaching hospitals in London and elsewhere, but they needed a period of specifically naval training before they could be appointed to a ship. For this they attended a course at Haslar, and it was one such class of newcomers which generated an exceptionally fine piece of silver.

The object shown overleaf is described in the Trophy Centre records as "a silver globe table centrepiece, with embossed scrolls and a rope edge and inscription, supporting an

11-inch silver open wave formation with a 10-inch diameter blue-tinted glass globe inside. The whole supports an 8-inch by 8-inch man-of-war in full sail mounted on a plaited stem depicting waves. The whole on a 16-inch by nine-inch oak stepped and shaped wooden base with two inscribed silver plates. Weight 90 ounces".

The plates inform us that the piece was presented to RNH Haslar "by forty-one newly entered naval surgeons, 1909-1910", with their names listed beneath. Anyone with an interest in such matters could research the subsequent careers of the forty-one named individuals. Some will have gone on to create distinguished careers for themselves, others may have died in the war which came only five years after the presentation. However, for everyone concerned with silver design *per se*, the object's primary interest is to be found in the name of its makers.

The assay marks have been made indistinct through polishing, but the importance of the piece is revealed by the *art nouveau* style lettering engraved along the base: "Omar Ramsden *et* Alwyn Carr *me fecerunt* MCMIX". The Latin "made me" is a pleasing touch, and was a feature of their work.

The creations of Omar Ramsden and Alwyn Carr were rooted in the ideas of the Arts and Crafts Movement. Inspired by the Pre-Raphaelite painter and designer William Morris, the Movement encouraged an interest in objects and materials made by hand rather than by machine. One of its manifestations was the development of the *art nouveau* style. It depended heavily upon sinuous undulating lines which incorporated forms taken from nature, and was exploited with much success by these two men.

Ramsden served his apprenticeship as a silversmith in his home town of Sheffield. In 1898, at the age of twenty-five, he

The unusual Haslar centrepiece made by Omar Ramsden and Alwyn Carr in 1909. The silver content is 90 ounces and the overall height is 21 inches. Photo: RN Trophy Centre.

done by their in-house English, Dutch and French specialists, each of whom became well known in his own field.

The two men were separated by the events of WWI, and they dissolved their partnership in 1919. Ramsden then registered his own mark - "OR *me fecit*" - and his later work was characterised by Celtic themes and a hammered finish.

Research for this book has revealed the existence of two other examples of his work which are probably unknown outside the military sphere. The Worcestershire & Sherwood Foresters Regiment possesses two identical ash trays made by him in 1921. Weighing four ounces, they are five inches in diameter. Commissioned by a Territorial officer who presumably was attached to the regiment in WWI, each has the silvered badge of The Worcestershire Regiment mounted at its centre. Engraved around the rims, in *art nouveau* upper case serif capital letters, are the words "I was wrought for the Officers' Mess of the 7th Worcesters by desire of Capt and Brvt Major G C Edwards (Artists Rifles), 5th Nov: 1921".

As has happened repeatedly over the past three years, the author has been tempted to fly off at a tangent, investigating the life and times of Brevet Major Edwards and possibly discovering the nature of his relationship with Omar Ramsden. The fact that Edwards was first commissioned into The Artists Rifles prompts the thought that he might himself have been involved in the world of the arts. It does not necessarily follow. The Artists Rifles, or 28th (County of London) Regiment, did send a battalion to France in October 1914, but their primary function during WWI was that of finding and training young officers for service with other regiments. Some (initially) were associated with the world of the arts but, as time went on, the majority were not. The author happily leaves it to others to investigate this particular story.

The Monmouth Cup was made by Paul Storr in 1812. It is not known who bought it or where it might have resided during the first thirteen years of its life, but in 1825 it passed into very illustrious ownership.

Engraved within the cup are the words "Auguste, Duchess of Cambridge, to her beloved husband Adolphus Frederick, Duke of Cambridge, a birthday gift, 24th Feb 1825".

Prince Adolphus Frederick, the first Duke of Cambridge, was the seventh son of King George III. In 1818 he married Her Serene Highness Auguste Wilhelmine, daughter of Friedrich, Landgrave of Hesse Cassel. It was their son George whose name became most familiar in military history as (the second) Duke of Cambridge, Field Marshal, Commander in Chief of the British Army from 1856 to 1885 (a remarkably long time by any standard). When he married, he chose a bride from outside the nobility, hence the union was deemed to be morganatic. Their

commenced business in partnership with his friend, Alwyn Carr. Shortly afterwards they moved to London, initially to Battersea, and then to Seymour Place, South Kensington.

Ramsden bought a large house there, which he shared with Carr, and it became their studio-workshop. Public recognition soon followed and, as their business grew, they created a large team of craftsmen - silversmiths, designers, modellers, chasers, engravers, and enamellers. Ramsden did not himself execute any pieces. His role was that of entrepreneur and manager. Carr was the designer and financial supporter.

Production was entirely in the hands of the workshop staff, each having his own role in the manufacturing process. Although the Haslar globe is engraved "Omar Ramsden *et* Alwyn Carr *me fecurunt*", the claim is not strictly true. The practical work was all sons, bearing the surname FitzGeorge, followed distinguished careers in the army and navy but, on the death of the Field Marshal in 1904, the Dukedom became extinct. His possessions were then dispersed and, while it may be assumed that many were inherited by members of his family, it is evident that others found their way onto the open market.

Three years earlier, in 1901, the London & Glasgow Shipbuilding Company launched yet another armoured cruiser

The Monmouth Cup is 20 inches in height (including the base) and incorporates 295 ounces of silver. It has two lids, one resting upon the other. The cup and larger lid are marked for 1812, the top lid (with pine cone finial) for 1814. Presumably the top lid was lost or severely damaged soon after sale, and needed to be replaced. Two basic themes from nature are featured in the design - prominent eagle head handles and heavy embossing with vines, grapes, leaves and flowers. Photo: RN Trophy Centre.

for the rapidly modernising Royal Navy. Displacing 9800 tons, HMS Monmouth carried fourteen six inch guns and had a top speed of twenty-four knots. Given her name, it was natural that she should be "adopted" by the people of Monmouth. When the Paul Storr cup became available in 1904, it was an ideal object for purchase and presentation to "their ship". It was beautiful, it was valuable, and its previous ownership bore an appropriate royal and martial resonance.

The officers of HMS Monmouth had the enjoyment of this piece in their Wardroom for the following ten years. When war was declared, she was in the process of re-commissioning. Her silver was already ashore. Storing and manning were completed rapidly and she sailed to join Rear Admiral Sir Christopher

Cradock's squadron in the South Atlantic.

What happened next is a sad and well known story. Cradock was searching for the German light cruisers Karlsruhe and Dresden. Instead, off Coronel, Chile, he encountered the faster and more heavily armed German East Asiatic Squadron, commanded by Admiral Graf Von Spee.

On the late evening of 1 November, outpaced and outgunned, HMShips Good Hope, Glasgow and Monmouth came under long range fire from the eight-inch guns of the Scharnhorst and Gneisenau. The British flagship, the Good Hope, was hit repeatedly and then exploded. Admiral Cradock and the entire ship's company perished in the blast.

The Glasgow and Monmouth attempted to escape, but were silhouetted against the sunset glow of the western horizon. HMS Monmouth attracted most of the German fire and, when last seen from the Glasgow, was listing heavily and steaming stern-on to the sea. For a while it seemed that she might survive but, when the moon rose, the Germans found her again. Helplessly, the officers on the bridge of the Glasgow counted seventy-five gun flashes on the horizon. Von Spee's ships had gathered around the battered Monmouth and torn her to pieces.

Nothing is known of her final moments. The Germans did not pick up any survivors, and the Glasgow dared not return to search for them at daylight. All six hundred and seventy-eight officers and men of her ship's company were lost.

The Torpedo Trophy is featured (page 136) for two reasons - it is unusual, and it records the names of two Royal Navy cruisers which together won fame and glory in the early months of WWII. It is described as "The 8th Cruiser Squadron Commander-in-Chief's Trophy for Torpedo Efficiency Practice". The first winner, in 1931, was the light cruiser HMS Dragon. There was no competition in the following year, but Dragon then won it again in 1933. Between 1934 and 1939 (apart from 1936 when it was won by HMS York) the trophy was the focus of fierce rivalry each year between HMS Ajax and HMS Exeter. The last holder was the Ajax, in 1939. Only months later, these two ships fought in company in the famous action, known as the Battle of the River Plate, which led to the destruction of the German pocket battleship Admiral Graf Spee.

The four ships named on the base of the trophy experienced very diverse fortunes in the war. HMS Dragon, by then elderly, was for a while deployed with a ship's company of Free Poles, under the ensign of the Polish Navy, before being sunk in June 1944 as one of the blockships off the Normandy beachhead. HMS York, as described in Chapter 6, was severely damaged by an Italian explosive speedboat and abandoned at Suda Bay, Crete, in 1942. HMS Exeter, also mentioned in Chapter 6, was lost in that same year in the disastrous Battle of the Java Sea. Only the Ajax survived, being sold to the breakers in 1949.

HMS Ark Royal is a name familiar to everyone who lived through the early years of WWII. Despite the glories attaching to this name, there have been only five Ark Royals. The first, displacing 700 tons, was little larger than a modern trawler. Launched at Deptford in 1587 as the Ark Raleigh, then renamed, she finished her days as the Anne Royal. There were no more Ark ships until 1914 when the Admiralty purchased a merchant vessel and transformed her into a seaplane carrier.

The most famous in the line was the HMS Ark Royal which entered service in 1939. An aircraft carrier of 22,000 tons, she bore a complement of 1600 officers and men (the largest ship's company of any British warship up to that time) and could deploy up to seventy aircraft (the greatest number of any Royal

Navy carrier). Frequently in the headlines during the first two dark years of the war, she formed part of "Force H" and was engaged in the hunt for the *Bismarck* (one of her Swordfish launching the torpedo which led to the German's later sinking).

The *Ark Royal's* high public profile made her loss an exceptionally severe blow to the nation when she was sunk in 1941. On 13 November, returning to Gibraltar from a patrol in the Mediterranean, she was torpedoed by U81. Listing heavily, she was taken under tow and most of her people transferred to the escorting destroyers. The end came on the following day. She was only twenty-five miles from the safety of Gibraltar

Harrier. One of her well-wishers was the Bernard Sunley Charitable Foundation, and its Trustees commissioned a presentation piece which replicates one of these aircraft. The Sea Harrier design has subsequently evolved as a further series of fighter, ground attack and reconnaissance variants. It is also flown by the Royal Air Force and by the Spanish, Italian and Thai navies, and large numbers have been built in America for the United States Marine Corps.

All of this is a reminder of the Royal Navy's pioneering commitment to aviation from the earliest years of powered flight. Since the end of WWII, the Fleet Air Arm has led the

The Torpedo Trophy is 14 inches long and shows the weapon entering the waves shortly after launch from the deck of a cruiser. It was made by Mappin & Webb and is hallmarked Sheffield, 1930. Photo: RN Trophy Centre.

dockyard. After the rolls were called, it was found that just one man had died.

When he went over the side, Paymaster Commander Richard Steele RN took with him the ship's welfare fund. The ship's company voted to use this money for the making of a silver bell for use by future *Ark Royals*, to commemorate the "bond of friendship". Weighing 3495 ounces (nearly two hundredweight, or 91 kgs), the bell was made by Gillett & Johnston and engraved with the ships' name, crest, and Battle Honours but, for some reason, it was not at the time hallmarked.

The next *Ark Royal*, at 36,800 tons, was an even bigger aircraft carrier. Built by Swan Hunter, at Wallsend on the Tyne, she was launched in 1950 and fitted with the silver bell. She served for nearly thirty years, starred in a major television documentary series, and was then paid off and broken up in 1980. Engraved with the name of every *Ark Royal* commanding officer from 1938 to 1978, the bell was loaned to the Fleet Air Arm Museum, Yeovilton, and put on display.

Five years later, when the latest *Ark Royal* was fitting out, the bell travelled to London. The absence of hallmarks was rectified when it was taken to Goldsmith's Hall. In the presence of the Prime Warden, Mr A G Grimwade, and two officers and two ratings, Mr John Ryder punched the marks for Sterling and London, for the London Assay Office as sponsors, and for the year, 1985. The bell returned to sea and for some years performed its intended duty. Currently it is again on display at the Fleet Air Arm Museum (the ship being out of commission).

The new *Ark Royal* was equipped to operate the Sea

world with a series of revolutionary innovations - the deployment at sea of the pure jet fighter, the steam catapult, mirror landing sights, the angled flight deck, and so forth.

Today's generation of naval aircraft represents but one phase in a continuing story which opened before WWI. The Fleet Air Arm (formerly the Royal Naval Air Service) has since then operated all manner of types and variants, and they are mirrored in the silver collection of the Royal Navy Trophy Fund. Brief mention of a few will suffice to represent the whole.

The first is a scale model of a Short S80 seaplane. It represents an aeroplane built by Shorts in 1913 for a private customer, Mr F K McClean. Powered by a 140 horsepower Gnome engine, it could accommodate the pilot and three passengers. The owner loaned it to the Royal Navy so that they might train their first four service pilots. It was purchased outright by the Admiralty in August 1914 and fitted to carry and launch a torpedo. It was lost only weeks later, on 30 October. The seaplane carrier HMS *Hermes* was torpedoed by a German submarine in the Straits of Dover, a few miles north of Calais. When she sank, she took with her forty-four of the ship's company and Mr McClean's aeroplane.

The second piece commemorates another but much more famous biplane flown by naval aviators. Known as **The Boyd Trophy,** made by the Goldsmiths & Silversmiths Company and weighing 35 ounces, this detailed scale model of a Swordfish was presented in 1946 to Royal Navy Air Command by the Fairey Aviation Company Limited. Designed initially in the 1930s as a torpedo-bomber, the Swordfish operated in a wide variety of roles during WWII, even being fitted with rockets for anti-submarine work. One airworthy example has survived and it flies on special occasions from HMS *Heron*, the Royal Naval Air Station at Yeovilton.

The transition from biplane to monoplane, and from reciprocating engine to turbine engine (in turbo-prop and jet form), is represented in the silver collection by scale replicas of the Seafire, Firefly, Gannet, Hunter, Sea Vixen, Seahawk, and Scimitar. All of these pieces were commissioned by the aircraft manufacturers - firms such as Hawker Siddeley, Armstrong Whitworth, Vickers Armstrong and Fairey Aviation, names which themselves mark the radical changes in the aviation world since the end of WWII.

Matching these examples of fixed wing aircraft is a series of models of helicopters, all supplied over the past five decades by Westlands of Yeovil - the Whirlwind, Wessex, Sea King, Lynx

the Far East in the 1950s and 1960s, and it persists even though these helicopters now spend much of their time in regions having much colder climates.

The working relationship between the Fleet Air Arm and the Royal Marine Commandos is of long standing. The value of the helicopter in the assault was demonstrated, for the first time by any nation's armed forces, when 45 Commando RM was lifted from ship to shore during the invasion at Suez, in 1956. And it is this inter-service dependence which leads us now to look at the silver of Britain's sea-soldiers.

The Corps of Royal Marines

The Royal Navy has from time to time needed to have trained soldiers in its ships. Between 1664 and 1755, regiments of marines were raised for specific campaigns but were then disbanded. The earliest was The Duke of York and Albany's

The Sea Harrier model is precise in every detail. Made by the Goldsmiths & Silversmiths Company, it bears the marks for London, 1986. Twelve inches in length, it is mounted upon a translucent column set in an oval-shaped base of polished granite. Photo: RN Trophy Centre.

and Merlin. Also commemorated is the Wasp, built by Fairey Aviation. It was the tiny Wasp, not much bigger than a family saloon, which helped to cripple the Argentine submarine *Santa Fe* in Cumberland Bay, South Georgia, during the war with Argentina in 1982.

Helicopter units of the Fleet Air Arm are trained and equipped to meet three specific needs. The Small Ships Flights are the airborne eyes, ears and sting of the destroyers and frigates in which they are embarked. The Naval Air Squadrons operate in the anti-submarine role and are known as "pingers". Thirdly, the Naval Air Commando Squadrons provide the lift capability for the Royal Marines, and are known as "jungleys". The nickname originates from the campaigns in the jungles of

Maritime Regiment of Foot, a force of 1200 soldiers authorised on 28 October 1664 for service at sea in His Majesty's fleet during the war with Holland. Many of the recruits were drawn from the Trained Bands of the City of London, men known locally as "Jollies". The nickname passed to the marines, and marine soldiers were called "Jollies" for many decades thereafter.

Other marine regiments came and went during the following decades of turmoil in Europe and in Great Britain itself. In addition and according to need, several regiments of the line were embarked temporarily in Royal Navy ships as a stop-gap substitute for a regular marine force. The first significant year in the evolution of today's Corps of Royal Marines was 1702 when six new marine regiments were raised.

In 1704, elements from this force took part in the capture and heroic defence of Gibraltar against a five months' siege.

Only twelve years later, three of the regiments raised in 1702 were converted to infantry of the line and three disbanded, but the "marine" title was maintained by the establishment of four companies of garrison invalids.

The government once again agreed to the raising of marine front-line regiments, ten of them, for the War of Jenkin's Ear (1740-1748). The position of all those early units was highly anomalous. They were organised and administered on army lines but employed as part of the navy. Too often their command and administration fell between the rudimentary and at times conflicting systems of the two services. Their problems were solved when, at the outbreak of the Seven Years War, 5000 marines were recruited, under Admiralty control, by an Order in Council dated 3 April 1755. It was a seminal date. The regimental organisation was discarded, commissions could no longer be bought and sold, and a Marine Mutiny Act regulated their conduct.

The new force was organised as fifty independent companies divided between three Grand Divisions, each co-located with one of the three principal Royal Navy bases - Chatham, Portsmouth and Plymouth (Devonport). They were not Divisions in the tactical sense, they were administrative structures which provided marine detachments for service in the ships attached to those ports. In peacetime, they provided every naval commander with a highly disciplined and distinctively uniformed force which could perform a wide variety of tasks. In war, they served as landing forces on hostile shores, as boarding parties, and as marksmen (sniping the decks of opposing ships). Later, when improvements in naval gunnery led to battles being fought at much longer ranges, the marines took over the manning of a proportion of the ships' guns.

It was about this time that the term "Bootneck" was born. Soldiers were issued with a leather stock, worn under the jacket collar as a neck protector. Sailors would tease the marines by saying "take my sea boots off your neck", implying that pieces had been cut illicitly from their footwear. The term has persisted and is still in popular usage (although the Royal Navy now usually refers to members of the Corps as "Royal", or "the Royals").

In 1802, King George III granted the distinction "Royal" in recognition of their services during the war with Revolutionary France. At that time there were 30,000 marines, most of them serving at sea.

Two years later, an artillery company was added to each Division to replace the Royal Artillery mortar crews in the navy's bomb ketches. An Order in Council dated 18 August 1804 granted the collective title Royal Marine Artillery to these three artillery companies and to others formed in later years.

A fourth Grand Division was formed in 1805 at Woolwich, also having its own artillery company. This Division was closed in 1869.

In 1855, all the non-artillery elements of the Corps were re-styled as The Royal Marine Light Infantry, and a central marines training depot was opened at Walmer, Kent, in 1861.

In 1859, the Royal Marine Artillery was accorded the status of a separate Division. The companies were concentrated at Fort Cumberland, Southsea, before moving (between 1864 and 1867) into their newly-built barracks at Eastney.

After Waterloo, regiments of the British Army began to have their Colours emblazoned with the names of campaigns and engagements in which they had distinguished themselves -

their Battle Honours. Each of the Royal Marine Divisions also carried Colours. When the time came for them to be replaced, in 1827, the Corps submitted a list of one hundred and six actions in which it had taken a prominent role. It requested that they should all be authorised as Battle Honours, to be shown on the new Colours.

It was an enormous number, far more than any one regiment of the army could earn by itself, and more than the Colours could accommodate. When, therefore, the Duke of Clarence presented the new Colours at Chatham, he stated that "From the difficulty of selecting any number of places to inscribe on these Standards, your Sovereign (King George IV) has been pleased to give them The Great Globe itself".

The new Corps insignia incorporated four elements - the globe (to reflect world-wide service), a laurel wreath (symbolising victory in former battles), the name "Gibraltar" (the earliest campaign in the rejected list of one hundred and six) and, of course, the Imperial Crown. In the same way that "Ubique" represents the world-wide fighting history of the Royal Artillery and the Royal Engineers, so has the Globe and Laurel insignia (crest) since 1827 conveyed the same message - "everywhere".

Throughout the 19th century, the central role of the Corps continued to be that of providing detachments for service at sea. In 1805, Nelson had 3683 marines in his fleet at Trafalgar. His three 100 gun ships of the line (the *Victory*, *Temeraire* and *Britannia*) each had 166 officers and men on board, the other first rates having one hundred and twenty-two. Nearly ten percent of the marines at Trafalgar were killed or wounded. HMS *Victory's* detachment was particularly hard hit, all of her marine officers being casualties.

Apart from such major engagements at sea, the marines' military training and discipline meant that they could be brought together to form much larger units or formations for protracted operations on land. A complete brigade was assembled in England for service in the Second China War, and Royal Marines fought in India during the Mutiny and again in South Africa against the Boers. In 1895, when Kitchener was attempting to reach Khartoum, marines even learned to ride camels, forming part of The Guards Camel Regiment.

In August 1914, a Royal Marine Brigade was despatched in haste to Ostend. Comprising a battalion from each of the Chatham, Portsmouth, Plymouth and RMA Divisions, its orders were to divert the advancing German Army away from Calais and Boulogne - the key disembarkation ports of the British Expeditionary Force. From this small beginning, the Royal Marines' involvement in the land war expanded greatly. Royal Marine Light Infantry battalions fought as infantry with the Royal Naval Division at Antwerp, at Gallipoli, in Salonika, and on the Western Front. Specialist units were formed to meet the particular needs of that war - the RMA Anti-aircraft and Howitzer Brigades, the Royal Marine Engineers, and the Royal Marine Labour Corps At the same time, detachments continued to serve at sea, manning the large calibre gun turrets in the Royal Navy's cruisers and battleships (there were 5832 marines in the British fleet at Jutland).

Some work began in 1924 in developing a Mobile Naval Base Defence Organisation to support the Fleet, and the value of this MNBDO concept came to fruition in WWII. However, the Corps of Royal Marines which we recognise today really began to take shape from 1942 onwards. It was still engaged mainly in its long-established roles - providing ships' detachments, manning coastal batteries, harbour defence, and so forth - but it was clear that sooner or later the Allies would need to invade and liberate the Continent. For this task, men trained to serve both at sea and on shore - *Per Mare Per Terram*, to quote the Corps motto - would be needed in large numbers.

New techniques of amphibious warfare had begun to emerge in 1940. One of Winston Churchill's first decisions after Dunkirk was that the German occupation forces in Europe should not be left to enjoy their victory undisturbed. He ordered the War Office to raise special forces for raids on enemy-held islands and coastlines. Various titles were suggested for these new and unconventional units. No doubt recalling his own experiences as a young man in South Africa (when the British Army was constantly harassed by Boer hit-and-run commandos), he enthusiastically approved the name "Commando" when it was put forward. The Army Commandos gave fine service throughout the rest of the war, but were disbanded at its conclusion.

Soldiers who successfully achieved the Commando standard of fitness and skill were granted the distinction of wearing the green beret. In later years, this emblem of excellence was adopted by the Americans and other nations to identify their *elite* units, and it is still worn by all service personnel who successfully pass the course operated by the Commando Training Centre RM, at Lympstone, Devon.

As the war progressed, and as the need for more raiding forces became apparent, the decision was made to exploit the marines' long-standing familiarity with ships and the sea. In 1940-1941, the Corps formed a conventional infantry division for service wherever it might be required. Then, in 1942, the first two Royal Marine Commandos were raised. Experimental landing craft were tested, new shore assault techniques developed. A year later, six more RM Commandos were raised, and another in 1944. The RM infantry division formed in 1940-1941 was broken up to release manpower for these new Commandos and to provide crews for the landing craft. They served in North Africa, Italy, Burma and North West Europe. The transition from the conventional infantry role to the specialisations of amphibious warfare was a significant event in Royal Marines history.

All Commando personnel - army, marine and navy - received their battle training at Achnacarry, in Scotland. The strength of the Corps in WWII rose, at its peak, to 78,400 officers and men (of whom 16,000 participated in the Normandy operation, ashore and afloat).

The end of the conflict brought many changes. From 1950 onwards, the old Divisions disappeared and the main thrust of training and equipment became directed almost exclusively at amphibious warfare. The Royal Marines Band Service continues to provide bands for the Royal Navy, but at the heart of the Corps today are the three Commandos - 40, 42 and 45 - supported by the Commando Logistic Regiment RM and a helicopter unit (847 Naval Air Squadron). The Special Boat Service RM, with roots in various small units formed for covert operations in WWII, maintains the operational *ethos* of its founders.

Although the modern Corps has become one of the most specialised assault forces of any nation's armed forces, it has not lost its sense of tradition or its concern for the customs of the Mess. When His Majesty King George VI, the Captain General, dined with his Royal Marine officers at the Savoy Hotel, London, on 21 December 1949, it was explained to him that the ten pairs of double-branch candelabra decorating the tables had each been brought there from all the principal Officers' Messes of the Corps. Just before the loyal toast, the electric lighting was doused and the candles lit, creating a pleasing mellow *ambience*. The King liked this so much that he expressed his wish that, at all future Dinner Nights, and after the table had been cleared and the Port passed, the same thing should happen. These pairs of candelabra have ever since been known as "the King's Candles".

On 23 July 1964, to mark the three hundred years which had passed since the raising of The Duke of York and Albany's Regiment of Foot, a dinner was held in the Painted Hall of the Royal Naval College, Greenwich. Again, the officers of the Royal Marines entertained their Sovereign. At the instigation of Admiral of the Fleet the Earl Mountbatten of Burma (at that time Chief of the Defence Staff), Her Majesty The Queen granted to the Royal Marines when in their own Messes the privilege of remaining seated while drinking the loyal toast. This dispensation extends to the members of Sergeants' Messes and Junior Non-commissioned Officers' Messes.

It can be seen from this condensed history that the Royal Marines have generated over the past hundred years a multitude of unit and sub-unit titles, some temporary, some permanent. Each carries or carried its own acronym or abbreviation, easily comprehended by a past or present member of the Corps but possibly bewildering to the outsider. Minor items of silver, such as cups, tankards, salvers, cigarette boxes and cigarette cases, and having an obvious Royal Marines connection, surface from time to time on the open market. The engraved or superimposed "Globe and Laurel" Corps crest is an obvious pointer to their provenance, and usually they are personal presentation pieces - "on joining", "on leaving", "on the occasion of his marriage", "on the occasion of his retirement", and the like - but the acronyms and abbreviations do not always lend themselves to easy decyphering. Breaking the code by other means is part of the challenge of collecting artefacts of this type.

Like the Royal Navy, the Royal Marines decided many years ago to place the ownership of all its historical treasures and other assets into a Charitable Fund (or, rather, a series of Funds). Approximately four thousand items of silver are listed in the inventory of the RM Corps Property Office, Whale Island, Portsmouth, and the following examples demonstrate their range and quality.

The Woolwich Folly is an object which defies precise description. According to the Corps records, it was "cast" in a combination of Sterling silver and electro-plate as an enormous candelabrum for the Officers' Mess of the Woolwich Division. The name of the maker is not stated, but the year of manufacture is thought to have been 1853 or 1854.

The piece depended heavily upon natural themes, consisting of a central representation of an oak tree trunk and foliage. On each side were two branches, continuing the same *motif* and each designed to hold nine large candles. By the time the Woolwich Division was finally closed, in 1869, and most probably under the stress of its own great weight, it had broken into three pieces. Each part was then re-worked and made into a separate free-standing candelabrum. It was the ungainly design of the original which gave the piece its name - The Woolwich Folly.

The largest of the three parts (the trunk) was given to the Officers' Mess of the Plymouth Division. It is now on display at the Royal Marines Museum, Eastney. The two re-structured branches were passed to the Portsmouth and Chatham Divisions. The Portsmouth branch is now in the Officers' Mess at the Royal Marine Barracks, Stonehouse (Plymouth).

The Neptune Centrepiece (page 141) is typical of a great many exuberant monumental pieces ordered by British

The main (central) section of The Woolwich Folly on display at The Royal Marines Museum, Eastney. The ornate pedestal incorporates the figures of Britannia, Neptune and Winged Victory, supported by piled banners and trophies of war. It stands approximately four feet high. Photo: RM Museum.

In the early decades of the 20th century, the wet canteen always featured a great number of pewter tankards on shelves and hooks. Whenever a "three badge" marine came in from the sea, at the conclusion of what might be his last commission before retirement, it was the custom that he should pay for all his friends to drink a "Royal Salute" of twenty-one pints of beer. It is not stated whether there was a time limit to these occasions.

Pagett represented that generation of tough old hands who could drink or fight with equal tenacity. The base of the statuette is engraved "Private Pagett, Reservist, Royal Marines, 1914-1919". The reference to "Reservist" is a reminder that many members of the Corps who served in that war (and in WWII) were well past the first flush of youth when, as pensioners, they were recalled to the Colours.

Colonel Drury's gift is now held by the Commando Forces Officers' Mess at Stonehouse Barracks, Plymouth. When it appears on the table at Dinner Nights, it does so only by special permission of the President of the Mess Committee, and only after the Loyal Toast. The fact that Private Pagett has his Broderick cap tilted to the back of his head, and that he seems to be well on the way to completing his "Royal Salute", makes him questionable company for officers and their guests.

In the event, the appearance of the figurine on the dining table is preceded by a light-hearted ritual. There is a commotion outside the dining-room door, with the sound of raised voices and of empty bottles being kicked around. The Mess Colour Sergeant enters and announces, "Private Pagett wishes to dine with his officers". When permission is granted, he is brought in and placed in front of the Mess President (who can then keep an eye on his behaviour).

In passing, it is unreliably reported that Colonel Drury unearthed the origins of the term "a dead marine". Still used today, it describes an emptied wine or beer bottle. According to his research, the Duke of Clarence (the future King William IV) coined it during a dinner with the officers in the Chatham Mess in the 1820s.

The designer of the statuette was W G Storr-Barber, a sculptor who had himself served as a private in the Royal Marines Light Infantry during WWI. When, after the war, it was decided to erect a memorial to the dead of the Plymouth Division, he offered to design and carve it free of charge. He then took charge of its construction, at cost. Made in Portland stone, it stands on Plymouth Hoe, close to the walls of The Citadel.

The Royal Marine Artillery Howitzer Centrepiece (page 142) is a technically perfect replica of the super-heavy fifteen inch howitzer deployed on the Western Front. It was designed specifically for that theatre of war by Admiral Sir Reginald Bacon KCB KCVO DSO.

When the Germans invaded Belgium, they quickly smashed the frontier fortresses with super-heavy calibre plunging fire. Winston Churchill, First Lord of the Admiralty, told Bacon that he wanted a similar weapon. Admiral Bacon had in fact left the navy in 1909, his final appointment before retirement being Director of Ordnance and Torpedoes. He had then joined the Coventry Ordnance Works as Managing Director, but in the autumn of 1914, Churchill persuaded him to return to the Admiralty where he directed the design team which produced this extraordinary weapon. Bacon was the logical choice because he and the navy's draughtsmen were accustomed to weaponry of far larger calibre than anything normally used by the army, and the navy itself had only recently adopted the fifteen inch gun for service at sea.

regiments and corps in the second half of the 19th century. Their designers showed great skill in bringing together a number of different themes - allegorical, neo-classical, martial and personal. This one begins with the figure of Neptune, mounted on a sea-shell chariot pulled by sea-horses and accompanied by one of his mermaid daughters. Set within the supporting columns and along the sides of the ebony base are silver panels depicting battles in which the Royal Marine Artillery took a notable part. The standing figures on each side are (left) a marine gunner holding a ramrod, and (right) an officer in Parade Dress. Originally the property of the officers of the Royal Marine Artillery, Eastney, it now resides in the Sergeants' Mess at the Commando Training Centre RM, Lympstone.

The Private Pagett Statuette, by comparison with The Woolwich Folly and The Neptune Centrepiece, takes us from one extreme to the other. It stands little more than four inches high (including the base). The piece was made to the order of Colonel W P Drury CBE RM, an author and playwright. One of his fictional characters was Private Pagett, a "three badge man", with three long service chevrons on his sleeve.

The upper half of The Neptune Trophy. The entire piece stands 24 inches high and is 14 inches wide at the base. It was made by Hunt & Roskell and is marked London, 1882. Photo: RM Corps Property Office.

centrepiece in the Officers' Mess at Southsea. An officer who knows it well, Major Alastair Donald RM, explains some of the problems which it caused.

"It is a magnificent thing, with all the elevating and loading parts made to move just like the original. Officers at table could never resist the temptation to fiddle with it, turning the wheels, pulling the chains, that sort of thing. It was damaged from time to time as a result, and needed to be sent to the silversmiths for repair. The stage was reached where several of the smaller components had been lost. The silversmiths then obtained a copy of the original design drawings from the Admiralty archives, just to be completely certain that the silver replacement parts would be technically correct. It is now as it should be, and in a display cabinet where it can be seen by the Museum's visitors but where it is safe from any further fiddling".

The Sergeants' Mess Royal Marines Eastney Silver Jubilee Centrepiece demonstrates once again that not all fine silver is confined to the Officers' Mess, and not all replicas of 19th century weaponry were necessarily made in that period.

The object portrays a siege or bomb ketch mortar of the early 1800s, with ten polished bombs on each side of the oak plinth. Measuring twenty inches by eight inches at its extremities, it was made in 1977 by Damar, of Hatton Garden, London. The inscription reads: "This piece was commissioned by the Warrant Officers and Senior Non-Commissioned Officers of the Sergeants' Mess, Royal Marines, Eastney, to mark the Silver Jubilee of Her Majesty Queen Elizabeth the Second".

The new howitzer fired a 1400 pound shell over a maximum range of 10,800 yards. For transportation, it was broken down into its component parts and moved by five tractors towing eleven trucks (wagons). Each howitzer was served by a detachment of five RMA officers and eighty-three other ranks. Although usually deployed in the field as single weapons, they were administered as a Brigade. Bacon's personal drive and contacts with industry ensured that the first two howitzers reached the Western Front in February 1915. Two more arrived in March and April, with six more in 1916 (in time for the Somme and Passchendaele offensives).

Admiral Bacon was determined to see his project through to the battlefield. Given a commission as Colonel Second Commandant RMA, he went with the RMA Howitzer Brigade to France and Flanders. Having dealt with the early teething problems, he returned to the Royal Navy and commanded the Dover Patrol from 1915 to 1918.

The model was commissioned soon after the war ended. The maker was Elkington & Company, of Birmingham, and the silver plate on the pedestal states that it was "Presented to the officers, non-commissioned officers and men of the Royal Marine Artillery by the temporary officers of the Royal Marine Artillery Howitzer Brigade". It is now displayed at the Royal Marines Museum, Eastney, but for many years it was a table

Pint of beer in one hand, pipe in the other, Private Pagett holds forth in the Wet Canteen. He stands just over 4 inches, weighs 20 ounces, and is marked Birmingham, 1919. Photo: RM Corps Property Office.

The mortar, as a weapon of war, is exceptionally well represented at Eastney Barracks. Several original pieces, with piled bombs, are displayed around the parade ground and mounted on entrance archways. They were all used, for training, in the mid-19th century. The mortar formed part of the design of the unit plaque of the RM Barracks Eastney, and of the unit tie worn by all who have served there.

In common with other corps, the Royal Marines have never ceased to actively acquire new pieces for their collection. The Anglo-Argentine war of 1982 prompted the addition of several new pieces to the inventory. One of these is a statuette of a

The exact scale model of the 15-inch howitzer deployed in limited numbers on the Western Front between 1915 and 1918. When ready for firing, the barrel was elevated at a much higher angle than shown here. Despite the sturdy sectioned steel base plate, the heavy recoil caused the weapon to gradually subside whenever prolonged rain softened the ground. Descending from a great height, its massive high explosive shell was very effective in destroying the Germans' deepest bunkers and fortified strong-points. Photo: RM Corps Property Office.

soldier in the act of aiming a Blowpipe shoulder-held surface-to-air missile. The presentation plate states that it was presented "To Air Defence Troop, 3 Commando Brigade, Royal Marines, from Short Brothers Ltd, Falklands 1982".

An identical piece was given, personally, to Marine Rik Strange. He brought down an Argentine ground attack Pucara aircraft during the battle for Goose Green (where the RM Air Defence Troop was attached temporarily to 3rd Battalion, The Parachute Regiment). It is improbable that Short Brothers, the manufacturers of this weapon, would have ever considered making a similar presentation to the Argentines. They too deployed the Blowpipe in the Falklands in 1982 but, fortunately, without achieving the same success as Marine Strange.

The Falklands Centrepiece is another item dating from the events of 1982. It is a shaped piece of Falklands stone upon which are mounted six silver circular plaques. The finial plaque is a map of the islands, the five surrounding plaques are facsimiles of service badges. Measuring approximately eight inches by eight, it was made by C J Vander Limited, of Hatton Garden, London. The engraving states that this attractive and unusual piece was commissioned "To commemorate those members of the Sergeants' Mess, RM Poole, who participated in the Falkland Islands Campaign, April - July 1982".

The Spean Bridge Centrepiece was commissioned in 1988 by the members of the Commando Forces Sergeants' Mess, Stonehouse Barracks, Plymouth, with assistance from Corps funds. Standing eighteen inches in height, it is a scale replica of the impressive bronze statue erected at Spean Bridge, Achnacarry. More than sixteen thousand army and marine

personnel passed through this Scottish wartime-formed Commando training centre before it was closed in 1946. The senior NCOs at Stonehouse wanted a table piece which would capture those early roots. The Corps Property Warrant Officer at the time was Barry Knight MSM. A veteran with nearly thirty-seven years' service, he had served in the Borneo, Malaya, Southern Arabia, Northern Ireland and Falkland Islands campaigns. Personally involved in the process of bringing the new piece through from conception to completion, he explains the background.

"We were thinking of a design which would epitomise what a Royal Marine Commando should be. The Commando Memorial, at Spean Bridge, was the obvious model in aiming to live up to the standards they achieved. The sculptor of that monument was Scott Sutherland, of the Dundee School of Art. He was no longer alive, so we contacted his next-of-kin to ask permission for a replica to be made. She agreed on the condition that there should be only one casting, the mould then being destroyed. This was agreed and we went to C J Vander, the silversmiths in Hatton Garden who had already made several important pieces for the Corps. Their quotation of twelve thousand pounds was accepted by the Sergeants' Mess and the Corps Committee, and the work went ahead. Vanders, incidentally, ran regular courses for all our Mess silvermen, teaching how them how to care for silver and keep it in good condition. That was done for many years, but was stopped in 1989.

With various other people from the Corps, I went several times to their workshops while they were developing the red clay model. It was important to ensure that every detail of uniform

The Falklands Centrepiece, commissioned and held by the Sergeants' Mess, RM Poole. The stone was brought to England from East Falkland for the specific purpose of commemorating that conflict. Photo: RM Corps Property Office.

and equipment was one hundred percent accurate and complete. While this was happening, I went to Stonehouse where we prized a piece of the local granite from the wall of the Sergeants' Mess. This was sent to Williams & Triggs, stonemasons of Newton Abbot, for cutting and shaping to form part of the pedestal. We also obtained permission to remove a small section of timber from Nelson's HMS *Victory*. She was undergoing repair and renewal at the time, and we were given a discarded piece of her original oak for shaping and fitting to the granite base.

Vanders needed several months to complete the clay model and do the casting in silver. We went up to London again, approved the semi-finished work which needed only the final trimming and polishing, and then witnessed the destruction of the mould. There will never be another Spean Bridge replica, but this one says everything that ever needs to be said about the Commando spirit".

The Mercantile Marine

A great many presentations in silver have been generated by events which occurred at sea but which had no connection of any kind with either the Royal Navy or the Royal Marines. The following three examples serve to represent the *genre*.

The Hindostan Vase perpetuates the name of the first passenger ship on the route to India to be driven by both sail and twin paddle wheels. Ordered by the then still young Peninsular & Oriental Steam Navigation Company, the *Hindostan* was built in timber by Thomas Wilson & Company of Liverpool. Fitted with two-cylinder side lever engines made by Fawcett, Preston & Company, she was completed in September 1842.

The original Commando Memorial was made by H H Martyn & Company, of Cheltenham, Gloucestershire. The casting and finishing of the bronze required twelve months from beginning to end. Seen here in the company's Sunningend works shortly before despatch to Scotland, it receives a final check from Mr Alf Merrett,. He was the welder in the art metal department. A master of his trade, it was said of him that "he could weld paper, if you asked him". Unveiled by HM The Queen Mother on 27 September 1952, the monument stands at the summit of a 600 foot hill, dominating the landscape where the Commandos of WWII learned their profession. Photo: Mr Graham Sacker, from *The Best, A History Of H H Martyn & Company,* by John Whittaker.

The Spean Bridge (Commando Memorial) Centrepiece, encapsulating the spirit and history of all service personnel who have worn the green beret, and especially the men of the Royal Marine Commandos. The recollections of a former Corps Property Officer, Barry Knight MSM, underline the degree of pre-planning devoted to the conception and manufacture of such pieces. Photo: RM Corps Property Office.

Displacing little more than 2000 tons, she could accommodate one hundred and two passengers (and sixty servants) in her sixty cabins. On 24 September she departed Southampton in a blaze of publicity and naval gun salutes for her maiden voyage. The newspapers were lavish in their praise for her facilities, describing them as "superb", "magnificent" and "genteel".

The Suez Canal had yet to be built, and the worldwide chain of coaling stations necessitated by the new age of steam was still being planned. The logistics of reaching India around the Cape of Good Hope were considerable. A fleet of seven colliers had sailed weeks earlier, and they were waiting for the *Hindostan* at Gibraltar, St Vincent, Ascension, Cape Town, Mauritius, Colombo and Calcutta. She arrived in Calcutta after ninety-one days (twenty-eight of which had been spent in ports along the way and re-bunkering).

With her sister ship *Bentinck*, the *Hindostan* served her owners well over the next five years. She operated regularly between Madras and Suez, via Ceylon and Aden. Passengers coming from England travelled by sea to Alexandria, took the train to Suez, then made the second half of the journey in the

Bentinck or *Hindostan*. Their engines were not very efficient but were reliable and needed little maintenance.

By 1847, the *Hindostan* was ready to be brought home for major refit. She made a good return passage *via* the Cape of Good Hope under the command of Captain Samuel Lewis, and it was this voyage which resulted in the presentation of the vase illustrated here. The passengers were so impressed with the ship, with the trouble-free voyage and with the service they received, that they each contributed to its cost. Apart from gratitude, they may also have felt some relief. Voyages around Southern Africa were still hazardous adventures. Violent weather and incomplete charts caused many sinkings. The greatest disaster of the period, in 1852, was the wreck at Algoa Bay of the troopship *Birkenhead* (with the loss of four hundred and forty-five souls).

The *Hindostan* remained in service for twenty years before being reduced to a hulk for harbour employment at Calcutta. Two years later, in the great Calcutta cyclone of October 1864, she was one of the almost two hundred vessels cast up on the shore and wrecked.

The morning of 24 September 1842, and the Peninsular & Oriental passenger steamship *Hindostan* sails proudly down Southampton Water on her maiden voyage to India. Photo: P&O.

Made by Roberts, Edkins & Aston, of Birmingham, The Hindostan Vase is dated 1847 and is described in the P&O records as having "a spreading circular foot, with applied vine leaves and bunches of grapes, with vine tendril and grape stem, the body pierced with scrolls and everted rim chased and applied with trailing vines and engraved with a presentation inscription". Photo: P&O.

The *Appam* Model is a silver replica of a passenger/cargo vessel, the Royal Mail Ship *Appam*. It is 36 inches in length, 13.5 in height, and was made by Walker & Hall. The hallmarks are said to be Sheffield, 1921.

The model replicates the construction of the ship to scale and in fine detail, and incorporates all her fittings and equipment (fourteen lifeboats, anchors, anchor chains, and the like). It is mounted on a hardwood base to which the hull of the vessel is attached by four silver ornate mounts and cross pieces, the former decorated with dolphin, scallop shell and wreath *motifs*. Fixed to the base is a silver and enamel *cartouche*, measuring 9 x

2.25 inches, decorated with crossed tridents, scallop shell and leaf *motifs*, and a pair of enamelled Union and United States shields.

The plate is engraved: "S S *Appam*, Captured by the German raider *Moewe* off the Canary Islands on the 15th of January 1916 and taken to Newport News, United States of America. Released and restored to her owners (British and African Steam Navigation Company Limited) by order of the United States Government in March 1917. This model is presented to Daniel Bacon Esq, New York, by Messrs Elder Dempster & Co Limited and the War Risk Underwriters on the *Appam* and her cargo as a token of their admiration and gratitude for his invaluable advice and untiring assistance which resulted in the vessel being restored to its rightful owners".

Daniel Bacon was the resident agent in New York for the shipping firm Elder Dempster. The model was presented to him at a luncheon aboard the SS *Boutry* in New York harbour on 12 January 1922 by the British Consul General, Captain Gloster Armstrong. It now forms part of the collection of The Museum of America and The Sea, Mystic Port, Connecticut. It was presented to the Museum in 1956 by Mrs Daniel Bacon following the death of her husband.

Built by Harland & Wolff, of Belfast, this 7800 ton ship was launched in 1912 as the *Appam*. She was renamed *Mandingo* in June 1917, reverting to *Appam* on 4 June 1919. Owned by the British & African Steam Navigation Company Limited, she was managed by the Elder Dempster Line. On 15 January 1916, sailing unescorted near the Canary Islands, she encountered the German armed merchant raider *Moewe* (meaning *Seagull*, recorded also as *Mowe*).

The unarmed *Appam* could neither fight nor run, and her Master, Captain H G Harrison, had no option other than to heave to and surrender his ship. The Germans took control of the *Appam* and, given the near impossibility of breaking the Royal Navy's blockade of all German ports, their prize crew set course for neutral America. She docked at Newport News two weeks later, and the diplomatic wrangles then commenced. The Germans were claiming her as a legitimate prize of war, the British were arguing that she was a non-warlike merchant vessel which should be returned to her owners.

The Americans were still strongly against any involvement in the European war, but they were obliged in this case to come down on one side or the other. Whatever ruling might by made in Washington, one of the two claimants would be disappointed.

The Imperial German Navy officer who commanded the armed raider *Moewe*, the imposingly named Captain Nikolaus Graf und Burggraf Dohna-Schlodien. Photo: Hans H Hildebrand, Hamburg, and Mr Richard Cornish.

Daniel Bacon was instrumental in persuading the United States authorities that the British arguments should prevail. A year later, she was released back into the care of an Elder Dempster crew. It was at this time that she was given the temporary name *Mandingo*. Her owners aimed to give her some anonymity and reduce the risk that she might become a special target for other German raiders. She did in fact survive the war and continued in Elder Dempster service under her original name until 1936 when she was sold, for fourteen thousand five hundred pounds, for scrapping by Thomas Ward, of Milford Haven.

Her captor lasted considerably longer. This ship was launched in 1914 with the delightful name of *Pungo*. She was designed for Germany's banana trade with the Cameroons but, following the outbreak of WWI, she was taken over by the Imperial German Navy and equipped as a commerce raider with the new name of *Moewe*.

Her task was that of hunting along shipping lanes frequented by Allied ships sailing alone rather than in convoy. Her main armament consisted of four 6-inch guns, and they gave her a weight of fire-power comparable with that of a light cruiser. Even though British merchantmen carried one or two guns for self-defence (mainly against surfaced U-boats), their range and impact was much less than that of raiders such as the *Moewe*. Allied merchant captains sailing unescorted usually followed the Germans' instruction to stop and take to their lifeboats. Helplessly, they then watched as the raider fired a few shells into the waterline of their ship and sent her to the bottom.

One merchant captain who was unwilling to strike his colours was Archibald Bissett Smith. Despite his name, he was a Scot, born in Cults, Aberdeenshire, in 1878. He was commanding the New Zealand Shipping Company's 9600 ton liner the SS *Otaki* when, on 10 March 1917, she was found by the *Moewe*.

The following encounter led to one of the only two awards of the Victoria Cross ever made to members of the merchant service. Although his ship was armed with no more than a single four-inch gun, Smith decided to fight. The *Otaki* was carrying no cargo and no passengers, a factor which may have influenced his decision.

After exchanging fire for twenty minutes, both ships were seriously damaged. The *Moewe* had five men killed and was so badly hit that she developed a heavy list and caught fire. She needed three days to get under way again. Most of the *Otaki's* crew got away in their lifeboats. When she went down, four hundred miles south west of Lisbon, she took with her five men killed by gunfire. Also lost were Captain Smith and his Chief Steward. It seems that the gallant captain decided to follow the custom of the sea, remaining on his bridge until the end. His

The meticulous Walker & Hall scale replica of the SS *Appam*. Silversmiths are accustomed to making models of warships or major ocean liners, but rarely a piece for which the subject was an unremarkable merchant vessel. Photo: Mystic Seaport Museums, Connecticut.

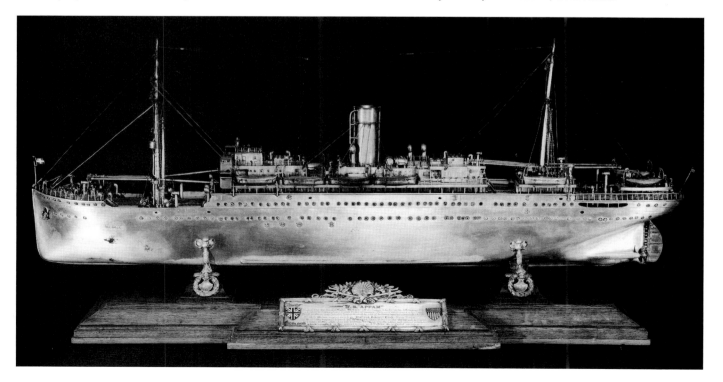

award of the Victoria Cross was announced in the *London Gazette* on 24 May 1919. The Admiralty had granted him a posthumous commission as Lieutenant, Royal Naval Reserve, thereby qualifying him for the award under the terms of the Royal Warrant (the VC not being available to civilians).

The *Moewe* survived the war and was returned to her German owners in January 1919. She was then, in May 1920, seized by the British under the terms of the war reparations and handed to the banana importers, Fyffes. For the next thirteen years she sailed back and forth between the Caribbean and Avonmouth as the *Greenbriar*, doing the job for which she had been constructed.

In 1933 the ship went back to German ownership and was again renamed, this time as the *Oldenburg*. Her end came on 7 April 1945 when, taking part in Germany's desperate effort to evacuate her troops from Norway, she was found by the Royal Air Force in the Sognefjorden. Like dozens of other German vessels caught in Norwegian and Baltic waters during those closing weeks of the war, she was bombed and rocketed and became a total loss.

Neither the *Hindostan* nor the *Appam* episodes involved any high drama or personal sacrifice, but each was rewarded with silver of great quality and workmanship. The final entry in this chapter confirms that the value of presentation silver does not always reflect the value of the service rendered.

The SS *Wiltshire* Rescue Tankard recalls an incident off the coast of New Zealand in 1922. On the night of 1 June, the 12,160 ton merchant ship *Wiltshire* was on the final stage of her passage from Liverpool to Auckland. The weather was foul, with a big sea, poor visibility, and the wind gusting to storm force. Despite the conditions, her Master did not reduce speed. Captain G B Hayward was familiar with these waters and was confident of his position.

Auckland is situated deep within Hauraki Gulf, the approaches to which are guarded by the thirty miles-long Great Barrier Island. There are many inlets and headlands along this stretch of North Island's coastline, and it is well provided with navigational markers and lights. Hayward had expected to see the first of these lights, marking the approaches to the Colville Channel, at ten in the evening. It did not appear on time, but he still maintained the same speed and course. Shortly after eleven, the *Wiltshire* drove onto the rocks at Rosalie Bay, three miles up from Great Barrier Island's southern tip.

Her SOS call was picked up in Wellington and Auckland, and passed to the Royal New Zealand Navy's depôt ship *Philomel*. She was berthed in Wellington harbour. Orders were given to raise a rescue party of local naval reservists, and they were rushed by train to Auckland. There they departed for Great Barrier Island aboard a vessel named *Moeraki*. At the same time, two Union Steamship Company vessels, the *Katoa* and the *Arahura*, responded by changing course and sailing towards Rosalie Bay. There they found the conditions of wind and sea to be so violent that they could not approach the stranded ship.

The Master of the *Katoa* decided to sail around to the leeward side of Great Barrier Island where he put a party ashore at the settlement of Tryphena. They were joined by the rescue party from the *Philomel*, also equipped with ropes, rockets and other tackle needed for a ship-to-shore rescue. Word of the wreck had spread to the townspeople and local farmers, and they turned out with pack-horses and hurricane lamps. Then began a nightmare journey of several hours across the island, through thick scrub, flooded creeks and driving rain, to Rosalie Bay.

The cliffs overlooking the wreck were one hundred feet high, but the rescuers managed to descend to a point at which they could start to rig a breeches buoy. The *Wiltshire's* crew were now in mortal danger. Because she was lodged bows-on to the shore, with waves bursting over her stern, they had gathered on the forecastle. This saved their lives when, only half an hour after the stranding, her back broke "with a noise like an explosion" and the after part of the ship sank into deeper water.

Repeated attempts were made throughout the following day by those on shore to rig a line, but their rockets were swept away in the wind. Success came at four in the afternoon when the people in the ship threw a wooden grating into the sea with a long rope attached.

The waves carried it in towards to the rocks, but not close enough for the rescuers to take a hold. This was the critical moment. The light was beginning to fade and the gale blowing as strongly as ever. On his own initiative, Able Seaman Wilfred Kehoe, of the *Katoa*, waded into the surf and clambered over the rocks to reach the grating. After several minutes of struggle with its weight and with the surge of the sea, he pulled it within the grasp of waiting hands. Kehoe himself was dragged ashore, more dead than alive.

The breeches buoy was rigged and four men brought off the ship before darkness fell. The second night was equally wretched for the rescuers and for the men on the *Wiltshire*. Exposed and hungry, they waited for the bleary dawn. When it came, with improving conditions, the business of rescue went forward at a brisk pace. By the end of the afternoon, one hundred and three crew members had made the journey to shore. Also rescued were one stowaway and the ship's cat.

Wilfred Kehoe received a silver pint tankard with the inscription "Presented by the Chairman and Directors of the New Zealand Shipping Co Ltd to Able Seaman W Kehoe in recognition of his bravery in the rescue of the crew of the SS *Wiltshire* at Rosalie Bay, Great Barrier Island, June 1, 1922". He was also given a sum of money. The tankard has remained in family hands, in New Zealand.

The Directors presented a small silver cigarette case to each member of the Royal New Zealand Naval Reserve - one officer and sixteen ratings - who made the emergency train journey and sea passage from Wellington. The wording engraved on these cases was a very condensed version of the event: "From owners, *Wiltshire*, Wrecked G Barrier, 31/5/22, to ......, HMS (*sic*) *Philomel*", with the name of the recipient. There was no mention of his rank or service. One example is known to have survived. Given to "A G Sandy", it is held at the Auckland Institute and Museum.

With wording as obscure as this, only someone with knowledge of the wreck and the gallant rescue would understand its significance. It is probable that, like so many items of minor presentation silver, some of the other sixteen cigarette cases have been scrapped for their modest value as bullion.

Chapter Eight
Objects Great and Small

The reader who has persisted thus far will have concluded, rightly, that the story of military and naval silver is enormous in its scope and impossible to describe comprehensively within the covers of a single volume. He or she will have concluded also, it is hoped, that each piece has a provenance, a *raison d'être* for which it was originally manufactured or ordered. Unlike domestic or purely ornamental silverware, the category of object recorded here is integral to the history of a regiment or ship or individual, and almost always commemorates a specific event or period in human experience. It is this intensely personalised aspect of the silver of the armed forces which generates its fascination.

The following pages will describe several more pieces which encapsulate those sentiments. They have been selected at random and are listed in no particular sequence. They have been chosen for any one of three reasons (or for any combination of the three) - they have been suggested by the book's knowledgeable and very helpful contributors, they can be illustrated by photographs of suitable quality, or they simply appeal to the author by virtue of the people and events attaching to them.

27th (Inniskilling) Regiment

The first is a small rectangular silver box containing a misshapen lead musket ball (attached to the interior of the box by a silver chain). It was made by Rebecca Ames and Edward Barnard, and is dated 1819. Engraved upon the lid is the explanation: "The ball which caused the death of John Pring, Esquire, of Ivedon, Devon, Captain in the 27th Enniskellen Regt of Infantry. He was wounded by it at the seige (*sic*) of Badajos, 1811. After 9 years it was extracted by Sir Astley Cooper but he did not long survive the operation and died 2nd May 1820 aged 37 years".

This macabre object surfaced at a local auction in Somerset in 1998. The vendor could not explain where it had been hiding for the best part of two centuries, but it represents to perfection the type of collectable military silver which would entertain a researcher for a long time. Sir Astley Cooper is stated to have been one of the most famous surgeons of his day. The location of Ivedon has not been identified, but John Pring is thought to be buried at Awliscombe (Devon). His own military career can, with time, be unravelled. The role of the 27th Regiment in the famous assault on the Spanish city of Badajoz is easy to research but, for the rest, the story is full of intriguing challenges.

The Hislop Box

It is a round screw-capped box, three inches in diameter and three inches in height. It weighs six ounces, was made by John Daniel of London, and is hallmarked London, 1817. The lid is engraved: "Presented by Lord Moira, Governor General of India, in testimony of the honourable and courageous conduct of his duties at the Battle of Mehidpur on the 21st December 1817, that he, General Sir Thomas Hislop, did defeat the Pindaris at the said battle. Presented this year of our Lord, 1818".

The Pindaris were outlaws and renegades who terrorised large parts of India from the end of the 17th century until they were finally suppressed by the British. The accounts of their activities make sombre reading. In gangs numbering as many as 10,000 men, they roamed at will in search of loot of every kind. On countless occasions they descended upon some luckless town or group of villages and remained there until their taste for rape, theft and destruction was exhausted. There were few boundaries to the territory which they dominated, and they owed allegiance to nobody but themselves. In 1817, with the connivance of some Maharatta rulers who viewed them as a means of damaging the Honourable East India Company, they started to raid into British-controlled territory.

On the orders of Lord Moira, the Governor General, a punitive field force was assembled under Lieutenant General Sir Thomas Hislop, Baronet, Knight Commander of the Order of the Bath. His adventures in HMS *Java* were mentioned in Chapter Seven.

It was Hislop's column, of 9000 British Army and Company troops, which met and defeated 35,000 Pindaris, under the command of the Holkar of Indore, at Mehidpur (Maheidpoor) on 21 December of that year. The Pindaris lost all of their artillery and baggage trains in the battle. The survivors were scattered far and wide and, although some attempted to make a recovery, they were a spent force. The bravest and most resolute leaders, with a handful of followers, skulked in the hills for a year or so, but then surrendered themselves and pleaded for clemency. The British granted them pardon and small pensions. Thereafter, the Pindaris disappeared into the pages of history and were never again the cause of terror and cruelty with which their name is still associated.

Hislop's role in the defeat of the Pindaris was widely recognised and applauded. On 5 September 1818 he was elevated to the Grand Cross of the Order of the Bath. The outcome of the battle clearly came as a relief to the East India Company, and the honour bestowed upon him was commensurate, in the context of that age, with the achievement.

The reference to the name of Moira, in the engraving, is intriguing. It has its origins in the Irish rebellion of 1641 when the English suppressed the people of that island in a campaign of greed and brutality which still today sours the relationship between the two countries. One of the Englishmen who took part was George Rawdon. He was rewarded for his efforts by the grant of confiscated land and by elevation to the English peerage as Baron Rawdon, of Moira, County Down. A series of judicious marriages produced a line of able sons who played leading roles in the affairs of England and Ireland. They were honoured by the granting of increasingly elevated levels of title within the aristocracies of Ireland, England and Scotland until, by the year recorded on The Hislop Box, his descendent, Francis, was Viscount Loudon, Earl of Rawdon and Marquis of Hastings.

Francis is described (*Burke's Peerage*) as "a gallant soldier, an eloquent senator and a popular statesman". He made his

The screw-top box presented by Lord Moira to Sir Thomas Hislop following his successful campaign against the Pindaris. Photo: Asprey, London, and Steppes Hill Farm Antiques.

name as a soldier in the American War of Independence. In 1812 he was appointed Governor General and Commander in Chief of the forces in India. It would seem that, at the time of the presentation, he preferred to be known as Lord Moira. The majority of the published sources which describe him and his role in India refer to him as Lord Hastings.

One other aspect of this box is of interest. The air-tight screw top ensured that the contents (most probably snuff) were protected from excessive variations in humidity. It was made in London in 1817 and presented sometime in 1818. Voyages between England and India at that period lasted between three and four months. It is unlikely that Moira could have sent a written order to London for the box to be made and engraved and then sent out to India within such a narrow time scale. It is more probable that the box had, with other such items, been made by John Daniel and shipped out to India by an agent for the general enjoyment of the gentry there.

It would not at that time have carried the lettering referred to earlier. When the need arose for a presentation to General Hislop, it may be supposed that it was selected from stock as being a suitable gift and was then passed to an English engraver living and working in Madras or Bombay (there were many such). He will have inscribed it with the wording ordered by his Lordship.

The Royal Scots (The Royal Regiment)

This is a silver snuff-box, hallmarked Dublin 1837, with maker's mark "RS" (presumably Richard Sawyer, a Freeman of the Guild of Silversmiths of Dublin at that time). The plain box stands on four ball feet with a two-part hinged lid, the first engraved on the outside with the crest of The Royal Scots, the second engraved on the inside with the names of seven officers of the regiment killed in the Waterloo campaign, thus: "Officers killed at Quatre Bras and Waterloo on the 16th and 18th June 1815". The front of the box carries the legend: "This box was made from the breast plates of the officers of The Royal Scots

who were killed at Waterloo".

A fine example of the style of Irish silver made in the final year of the reign of King William IV, the box is of interest in two particular connections. First, it was made from the silver breast plates (cross-belt buckles) of those Royal Scots officers who died in the battle which resulted in Napoleon's exile to St Helena and which heralded "The Forty Years' Peace" in Europe.

The official reports of the battle stated that the battalion which represented the regiment - its 3rd Battalion - lost eight officers killed and twenty-six wounded. There are in fact only seven names engraved within the half-lid. The reason for the apparent discrepancy is not known with certainty, but it is said that an officer first reported to be dead was later found recovering from his wounds in Brussels. The officers commemorated on the box were Captain W Buckley, Lieutenants J Armstrong, J E O'Neil and W Y Younge, and Ensigns A Robertson, J G Kennedy and W Anderson.

The other and remarkable point of interest is that the survivors of the battle were able to organise a search for the bodies and to retrieve at least some of the silver breast plates. The battalion had lost more than half its strength by the end of that day. The survivors were exhausted, darkness was falling, and the battlefield was half hidden by drifting smoke and carpeted with the corpses of 15,000 British, 7000 Prussians and 30,000 French. As the firing faded away, hundreds of scavenging Belgian peasants began to carry away everything of value, real or imagined. It is unlikely that the battalion's surviving officers were able to find every one of their brother officers' remains before these civilians got to them, but that is of little importance in the larger context. The box now resides in the Regimental Museum, at Edinburgh Castle, where it is a permanent reminder of those events of nearly two centuries ago.

The Royal Irish Fusiliers

A minor piece with historical connections is a silver table spoon engraved "Cavan Regt" in two *cartouches*. It bears the maker's mark "JP" (John Power) and is hallmarked Dublin 1797/98.

County Cavan is in the historic province of Ulster, but in 1922 its people expressed their wish to join the Irish Free State and it is now in the Republic of Ireland. This spoon represents one of the many milestones along the long and difficult road which culminated in the emergence of the Republic as an independent state.

From the earliest times, the territories of Ireland each had its own means of defence which was organised on much the same lines as those of Saxon England. To quote the chronicler Litton Falkiner: "By an old law, the Septs and men in (each) Town or County were formed into armed associations, choosing their chief head or Captain as most fit to defend them". In 1641, with the onset of the Great Rebellion, armed service for all males between 18 and 60 years of age became compulsory. The local *ad hoc* arrangements of earlier decades were replaced by a more formal system. The men of each Royalist town or district were attested in Regiments of Militia which trained on a part-time basis during periods of peace but which could be mobilised for full-time campaign service whenever the need arose. The latter occurred three times, the Irish Militia taking part in the wars of King James II (1685) and of King William III (1690), and being called out by Queen Anne in 1702.

By the end of the 18th century, revolution was in the air. The Americans had obtained their independence from the Crown, and the French too had followed the republican path. There were other peoples who were becoming restless, and prominent amongst them were the Irish. In 1793, the Irish Parliament consolidated all the existing legislation into a new Militia Act. It required each County to maintain its own regiment (or equivalent force), their combined strength being 21,660 armed men. The records of the Royal Longford Militia describe the scene: "The State of Ireland in 1792 was most disturbed. Midnight marauding to obtain arms, and local uprisings, etc., openly usurped the freedom of the Government, whilst in 1793 the outbreak of war with France, and with the Country stripped of regular soldiers though in a state of rebellion, brought about a reorganisation of the Irish Militia to stop the tide of anarchy".

Two events were soon to demonstrate the wisdom of these changes. In 1796 the French attempted to invade the island. Fierce storms scattered the ships of their expeditionary force and the project was abandoned. However, there was a continuing threat that they might try again.

Then, in May 1798, a major rebellion erupted throughout the island and much of the burden of suppressing it again fell upon the Militia. The Cavan Regiment, commemorated on this spoon, had six men killed at the Battle of Arklow on 9 June, and formed part of the army which faced the rebels again a few days later at Vinegar Hill, County Wicklow. On 22 August a French force, said to be 1200 strong, landed at Killala Bay, County Mayo, with orders to support the rebellion. It had some initial success, but was then forced to surrender at Ballinamuck, County Mayo. The French survivors were marched off to the prison hulks while their rebel Irish supporters drew lots to decide whom amongst them should hang.

The severity of the 1798 crisis can be judged by the decision of the British government to raise more than forty Corps of Fencibles in England and Scotland and despatch them to the disturbed areas in Ireland. In total, the number of troops deployed in the face of the rebellion exceeded forty-four thousand (of whom the majority were Militiamen and Fencibles).

The spoon's hallmark date, 1797-98, is of interest. Law and order were restored after the 1798 rebellion, but it was evident to the authorities that a recurrence could be avoided only by maintaining a strong military presence. The British Army could spare few of its Regular units to police the turbulent Irish. It was fully engaged in fighting France and her allies, and would be struggling to meet that commitment for years to come. Not until 1815 and Napoleon's defeat at Waterloo would the burden be lifted and, thereafter, Treasury economies caused major reductions in military establishments. The total impact of these events was to attach greatly increased importance to the Irish Militia as the internal security force. Its men were given better and more frequent training, improved scales of equipment and weaponry, and were expected to meet higher standards of discipline.

This increased level of formality in its activities led the officers of the Militia to acquire possessions of a more permanent quality than anything which had gone before. Coming together more frequently and holding regular Dinner Nights, they had both the need and the motivation to acquire respectable furnishings and tableware for their Messes. The officers of the Cavan Regiment probably needed a year or so in which to debate the matter, to decide what silver should be purchased, and to raise the money to cover the cost, so we may

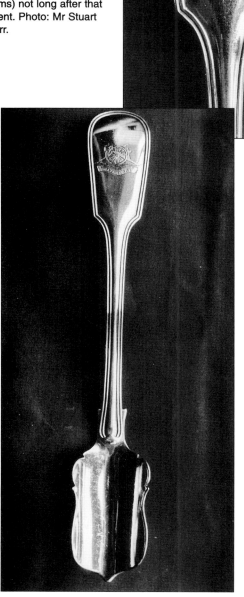

Another example of flatware originally owned by a regiment of Irish Militia. This electroplated cheese scoop was made by Elkington & Company in 1853 and was used in the Officers' Mess of the Waterford Militia Artillery. The Waterford regiment was converted from the infantry role to artillery in December 1854, so the field gun crest suggests that it was purchased and engraved (with other such items) not long after that event. Photo: Mr Stuart Barr.

assume that the order was placed sometime around 1800. And there the matter rested for the next eight decades.

The 1881 major reorganisations of the British Army and its ancillary units brought changes for Militia units everywhere. Under the new Territorial system, they were redesignated as Reserve battalions for those Regular regiments which were given a new County or regional title (in place of the old system of regimental numbering). In the case of the Cavan Regiment, it was assigned to the Princess Victoria's (Royal Irish Fusiliers) as its 4th Battalion. At the same time, the Armagh Militia Regiment became the Fusiliers' 3rd Battalion and the Monaghan Militia Regiment became its 5th Battalion.

In 1968, the three regiments which previously had formed the North Irish Brigade, including the Royal Irish Fusiliers, were amalgamated as the Royal Irish Rangers. It was then that some of the silver formerly owned by predecessor units such as the Cavan Militia Regiment was sold off. This spoon, plus two others like it, are now in the possession of Mrs Judy Chatterton Dickson. Her father, Lieutenant Colonel Maurice French, was killed in 1943 while commanding 2nd Battalion, The Royal Irish Fusiliers, on the island of Leros during the abortive Aegean campaign. His widow subsequently married Lieutenant Colonel George French OBE, her late husband's elder brother. He had commanded the regiment's 1st Battalion and, after the war, its 4th Battalion. It was the latter, it will be remembered, which had its origins in the volunteer soldiers of County Cavan. These facts demonstrate not only the historical strands to be found in apparently mundane items of tableware, but also the role of family links in sustaining the regimental system.

The Devonshire Regiment

Here is an example of a Militia piece with an English provenance. It is a silver cigar lighter, with maker's mark "HWD", dated London, 1835. Shaped as an Aladdin's lamp with wick and oil reserve, it has a serpent handle and lion finial. Incorporated in the design is a silver medallion, one inch in diameter, with the struck wording "South Devon Militia, in Testimony of Merit". Engraved upon the body of the piece is the legend: "The above medal is one of those presented by the City of Waterford to the officers and soldiers of the South Devon Militia for services in 1798-1799".

The preceding entry (the Cavan Regiment spoon) describes the role of the Irish Militia in maintaining Crown rule during one of the major insurrections in their country. A measure of the British government's anxiety at that time was its decision, as previously stated, to mobilise some forty-odd English Militia and Fencible regiments and send them to the aid of their Irish coun-terparts. The South Devon Militia was one such unit, and it would appear that its services in and around Waterford were appreciated by the Royalist community in that city. Nothing is known of the circumstances leading to the design and manufacture of the small (approximately one inch diameter) medallion incorporated in the item of Mess silver described above, but it may be assumed that sufficient were struck for a presentation to be made to every officer and man who took part in the operation. Following the custom of the day, it is probable that the medallions given to officers were struck in silver, with the other ranks receiving an identical piece struck in bronze or some similar alloy. No other examples have been sighted, and it is likely that this one has survived only because the officers later decided to incorporate it in the design of their cigar lighter.

The South Devon Militia had its roots in the "great muster of armed men of the Counties in England and Wales" ordered by Henry VIII in 1539. The King needed to know exactly how many men could be mobilised, and the weaponry available to them, at a time of national peril. His daughter had even greater need of such intelligence when she learned of the imminent arrival of the Spanish Armada. The mobilisation ordered by Elizabeth in 1588 produced, in Devon, a force of 3661 trained men.

It was not until 1763 that the County's Militia units were formally organised into three regiments - the North Devon, the East Devon and the South Devon. In 1853 the North Devon Regiment was converted to the artillery role, and the other two redesignated as the 1st and 2nd Regiments of Devon Militia. Finally, under the reforms of 1881, they became respectively the 4th and 3rd Battalions of The Devonshire Regiment. The cigar lighter has survived all those moves and subsequent changes in organisation and is today displayed in the Officers' Mess at Wyvern Barracks, Exeter.

77th Regiment of Foot

Illustrated here is a silver wine label, of triple-reeded rectangular shape with cut corners, approximately two inches by one inch, and weighing half an ounce (very light gauge, with thin suspension chain). Engraved "Madeira", with three plumes (only) and the numeral "77", it was made by Francis Powell, and is hallmarked London 1818.

The Francis Powell wine label (bottle ticket), once the property of the 77th Regiment of Foot. Photo: Mr Kevin A Barrington.

The 77th Regiment of Foot was raised in 1787, being granted the title 77th (East Middlesex) Regiment in 1807. It was one of four new regiments formed in that same year and in direct response to a crisis in India. For several years, the Honourable East India Company had been in conflict with the rulers of Mysore, the large Muslim state in Southern India. The most recent outbreak, known as the Third Mysore War, had been fought three years earlier, in 1784. A short-lived peace was breaking down and there was an urgent need for more troops. The previous ruler, Haidar Ali, had been succeeded by an even more ferocious leader, his son, Tippu Sultan, and British trading stations were again under attack. The discovery that Tippu's people were putting to death with unusual cruelty all Europeans who fell into their hands made it certain that a Fourth Mysore War was about to unfold.

The British Government agreed to help the Company by raising four new British Army regiments, but with the condition that the Company should pay the expense of transporting them to India and paying the costs of maintaining them after their arrival. This was agreed, and the 77th Regiment of Foot was speedily recruited and embarked. It is unlikely that its officers had time in which to acquire a great deal of silver (if any) before their departure. However, once arrived, and despite being so often on active service, it is probable that from time to time they sent orders to the English, Scottish and Indian silversmiths in Madras, Calcutta or Bombay. The manufacture of silverware to the European taste had commenced in India some decades before, from the early 1700s onwards.

The 77th campaigned almost continuously between 1788, when it arrived in India, and 1807, when it embarked for the voyage back to England. It was engaged in numerous actions during those years, but the most telling were the battles in 1799 at Seedaseer and Seringapatam (the latter resulting in the death of Tippu Sultan). These places became the regiment's first official Battle Honours.

It appears that, after coming home, the officers of the regiment decided to start acquiring English hall-marked silver, and to do so on a significant scale. The following account was written in 1808 by a young officer who had just joined the regiment, at Winchester. In a letter to his mother, dated 20 November, Ensign William Keep told her: "The furniture of the table is entirely (like the band instruments) the property of the officers, and by continual contributions is very sumptuous (the Paymaster has deducted from my pay for the purpose six pounds and ten shillings). Grand silver candelabras and choice plate with all the other things necessary are provided by this means".

William Keep joined the 77th Regiment at a time when the British Army was commencing operations to save Portugal from French occupation (and eventually to liberate Spain). However, only a few months after he wrote his account, he and his comrades were despatched to the Low Countries. The regiment formed part of a major expedition which had as its objective the destruction of a French invasion fleet being built in the port of Antwerp. The mishandled enterprise was a disaster. Of the 40,000 British troops involved, one tenth died of disease.

Ensign Keep later wrote a memoir of his experiences at Walcheren and Flushing and, subsequently, in the Peninsula campaign under Wellington, but sadly made no further reference to the Mess silver. It is not possible, therefore, to state whether it accompanied the regiment on all these travels or, if it did, whether it survived those five years of marching and fighting. However, the recent (1997) appearance on the London silver market of the wine label described above might indicate that at least some pieces did need replacing after the war.

Silver wine labels first came into common use in the early part of the 18th Century, and their original purpose was essentially functional. They were designed to be suspended, by a chain, from the necks of bottles (the contents of which might not otherwise have been apparent). Their common name at that time was "bottle ticket". Beginning in the 1770s, they became larger and more ornate and were intended for attachment around the necks of glass decanters. They were made in various sizes and shapes according to changing fashion throughout the 1700s and early 1800s, and were engraved with the names of the beverages popular during those decades - "Port", "Lisbon", "Tenerriffe", "Barsac", "Marsala", "Champagne", "Hock", "Sherry", "Claret" and, simply, "White Wine".

Before the 1790s, all such labels were cast or wrought by hand. This began to change when Matthew Linwood, of Birmingham, introduced a process of die-stamping. The piece described here, from the workshop of Francis Powell, is a good example of the items being commissioned after the war by prestigious customers such as the 77th Regiment.

Powell was not a prolific maker of labels. According to Sir Thomas Barlow, Secretary of the Wine Label Circle, only two other surviving examples of his output have been identified (neither having a military connotation). This was one of the first items of silver to bear his registered mark and was made during his brief partnership with Robert Coates. Their workshop was in

A regimental wine label for Port, made in 1855 by Rawlings & Summers. The reverse is engraved *22nd Foot*, an abbreviation for the 22nd (The Cheshire) Regiment of Foot. The oak leaf *motif* originated at the Battle of Dettingen, in 1743, when French cavalry broke through to the oak tree where King George II and his staff were directing the battle. A detachment of the 22nd ran up and quickly formed a ring around them. The French were driven off after a brisk fight. The King took a leaf from the tree and, handing it to the officer commanding the detachment, requested that the regiment should henceforth treat it as a symbol of his gratitude. The Cheshire Regiment still adorns its Colours and head-gear with oak leaves every year on the anniversary of the battle. Photo: Phillips, Knightsbridge.

the City of London, at 4 Fann Street, Aldersgate. Powell set up in business on his own account only a few months later and thereafter worked from a succession of addresses in and near the City. He seems to have retired sometime around 1850, by which time he had returned to his original location in Fann Street.

In 1860, the new Licensing Act made it illegal for bottles to be sold without having a descriptive paper label. This meant that bottles could be purchased singly instead of by the case, and could be brought directly to the table. Demand for silver labels marked with the names of ordinary table wines declined as a consequence of the Act, but there was a continuing demand for the labels named "Port" and other types of fortified wine because these were decanted and stayed for a while on the sideboard. The same applied to drinks such as Whiskey and Brandy (or Cognac), and very much later, after it ceased to have a purely working class association, Gin.

The example cited here, "Madeira", will have been one of a set of four or five or more. The fortified wine of Madeira was widely drunk by the British, partly because they liked it but also because it was consistently available. A possession of England's oldest ally, Portugal, the island could continue freely to export its produce while continental Europe was suffering the disruptions of the Revolutionary and Napoleonic wars. Indeed, during the crucial years of 1801 and 1807-1814, Madeira was garrisoned and directly governed by the British. Whenever they had the chance to do so, ships of the Royal Navy and the armed merchant vessels of the East India Company called at the island so that, apart from loading victuals and fresh water, the officers could "buy a couple of dozen pipes" for themselves.

It was not until the return of peace that the vintners of Spain were able to re-establish their products permanently on the British market and gradually to oust Madeira wine from its recent temporary dominance. Indeed, it can be argued that the wine growers of Madeira had enjoyed a near monopoly of the British market throughout those twenty years of conflict. The vineyards of Jerez and Oporto, and all the associated wine producing infrastructure of the region, were devastated by the armies which swept over them.

It is known that French merchants continued to ship wine and brandy to England and Scotland (London and Leith) by clandestine routes through Madeira, the Azores and the Channel Islands. Forged ship's papers and manifests enabled them to claim neutrality and so pass through the Royal Navy's blockade of France's coastlines.

The German producers of Hock must surely at times have had similar difficulties in getting their produce down the Rhine to the Low Countries and across the North Sea. The records at Lloyd's, the London insurance market, indicate that some trade was maintained by the use of "simulated papers" or by shipping indirectly through neutral ports

Further research might reveal a connection between the impact of the conflict and the style and types of wine label being manufactured by English silversmiths during those troubled years.

As far as examples with a demonstrable military or naval origin are concerned, the evidence indicates that they may be very rare. Kevin Barrington, a collector with an interest in such matters, has searched through the *Journal* of the Wine Label Circle for the years from 1952 to 1986. He has found just ten such references, and only two to these specify the names of the owners - the 8th (The King's Regiment) and the 22nd (The Cheshire) Regiment of Foot. An old Phillips catalogue mentions an 1890 Claret label made by Charles Stuart Harris for the 9th Bengal Native Infantry but, for the rest, this is barren ground.

The rarity factor was confirmed when the John Beecroft Collection was auctioned by Phillips, at their New Bond Street rooms, in November 1998. John Beecroft was for half a century an active collector of early wine labels. Of the one hundred and sixty Lots in the Phillips catalogue, only one had a regimental provenance (the 22nd of Foot, as noted above and illustrated).

The St Helena Artillery

This object is an ornamental silver trowel with a (rare) St Helena ebony handle, 11 inches long overall, weighing 4.5 ounces (including the handle). It has no marks of any kind, but was almost certainly made by Joseph Saunders, a local silversmith, and is finely engraved in running script: *Hoc lapidem primum aedificii ad Astronomicas res promovendas apud Insulam Sanctam Helenam constituti Uxor Gubernatoris Alexandri Walker posuit, Id: Sept: AD MDCCCXXVI.*

The inscription translates (freely) as "The wife of Governor Alexander Walker laid this first stone of the building established for promoting matters astronomical on St Helena Island, Ides September 1826".

The Observatory (the building referred to above), became operational in November 1829. It was an extension to The Military Institution founded by the Governor, Brigadier General Alexander Walker, and opened on 7 October 1823 "for the pursuit of science amongst …. the youth of any branch of the service". The Branch which he had most particularly in mind was the St Helena Artillery. Its young officers had received their

earlier instruction at Addiscombe, the Honourable East India Company's military college near Croydon, Surrey, but the Institution provided the continuing acquisition of knowledge which the isolation of the island might otherwise have denied them.

Alexander Walker had an adventurous and distinguished career before being recalled from retirement to become Governor of St Helena from 1823 to 1828. Born in 1764, he joined the Bombay Establishment and was very shortly caught up in the campaign against Tippu Sultan. Barely twenty years of age, he volunteered himself as a hostage at Mangalore, survived that affair, then went to Canada to set up the Company's fur trading station at Nootka, Vancouver Island. He returned to India to serve under Sir Arthur Wellesley in the final and successful battle with Tippu at Seringapatam, and was then appointed Quarter Master General and Auditor General of the Bombay Army. However, his Indian reputation rests mainly upon his pacification of Baroda and Gujerat and the social reforms which he set in motion there. Notable amongst these was the suppression of female infanticide. He died in Edinburgh, in 1831, at the age of sixty-six.

Mess silver relating to the island dates from 1820, when the officers of the St Helena Corps of Artillery, the St Helena Regiment (infantry) and The Medical Department decided to form a combined Mess in Main Street, Jamestown (it is now the Post Office). The island, previously uninhabited, had become a British possession in 1659. It provided water and temporary haven for East India Company ships on their voyages to and from India. Over the decades, it became a fortress and was more heavily defended than either Gibraltar or Malta.

By the India Act of 1833, St Helena was transferred from the Company to the Crown. Three years later, on 24 February 1836, the first Colonial Governor, Major General George Middlemore, arrived with strong detachments of Royal Artillery and the 91st (Argyllshire) Regiment of Foot. He caused outrage by marching into Jamestown "as if he was invading some hostile shore".

His first action was to disband - "without thanks or ceremony" - the local gunner, infantry and medical units. Their officers responded by promptly stripping their Mess of all its silver, china and glass, and dividing it amongst themselves. There were thirty-eight members at that time. Stranded without pay or prospects, most departed for the Cape or other Colonies, or returned to make new homes in Great Britain. The silver was therefore dispersed from Australia to the Americas, but most of it going to South Africa.

Trevor Hearl, who has made a detailed study of St Helena's history, has located some of the silver which went to the Cape. Several items are held in the Beaufort West Municipal Museum, other pieces are still in South Africa in private hands. There were as many as four silversmiths working on the island at one period, but the difficulties of time, distance and transport prevented them from submitting their work for assay in England or Scotland. The pre-1836 items (salvers, wine coolers, flatware) are engraved with the lion *motif* of the East India Company and can be identified by the name or initials of the St Helena units which once owned them. Given their excellent quality, it is probable that a significant number have survived, and could surface almost anywhere in the world.

13th (1st Somersetshire Light Infantry) Regiment

In 1839, the British entered and occupied part of Afghanistan. They replaced the Afghan leader with their own puppet, Shah Shuja, and the capital Kabul soon settled down to be one more East India Company station. The Afghans were unhappy with this intrusion and, in 1841, they mounted a revolt. Kabul was surrounded, Shah Shuja and the British Political Agent were murdered, and the garrison food stores destroyed. The elderly officer commanding the garrison, who had failed to make any preparations against such a scenario, now agreed to withdraw the bulk of his force to India. The Afghans offered them safe passage on condition that the British left behind their treasury, their artillery pieces, some of the officers and their wives, and a large number of other military and civilian personnel - men, women and children.

Having effectively divided the British force into a depleted garrison at Kabul and a retreating column in the mountains, the Afghans broke their word and attacked both. Some of the hostages in Kabul were spared and later rescued but, from the column, only one officer reached safety. He was a military surgeon, Dr William Brydon. A few dozen British and Gurkha soldiers hid in the hills and evaded their pursuers, but the bodies of all of the others - 690 European troops, 3910 Indian and Nepalese troops, and 12,000 camp followers - lay scattered through the mountain passes.

There were still British and Indian troops inside Afghanistan, isolated and ripe for piecemeal destruction. One such force held the fortress of Jellalabad, roughly midway between Kabul and the Khyber Pass. It comprised a mixed bag of Indian artillery, cavalry and sappers together with two regiments of infantry - the 13th of Foot (with 774 all ranks) and the 35th Bengal Native Infantry (with 846). Throughout the opening months of 1842, and until a relief force arrived from India, they held off a besieging force many times their own number. The walls and towers were badly damaged when the fort was struck by an earthquake. There were shortages of food and medicines, and the half-starved defenders were frequently under fire. By the time the relief force arrived the newspapers were calling them "The Illustrious Garrison".

An officer serving with the 35th BNI was Thomas Seaton, later Major General and Knight Commander of the Order of the Bath. Many years afterwards, describing his recollections of the siege, he wrote: "Great numbers of soldiers had friends among the *sepoys* with whom they were always talking, and I have more than once known a soldier, when he lay dying, send for his *sepoy* friend to be with him in his last moments".

The seeds of the friendships forged at Jellalabad had taken root when, for a while, both regiments formed part of the garrison in Kabul. Quartered in the same group of buildings, they quickly came to know each other well, sharing the garrison guard and ceremonial duties. There were occasions when Quarter Guards were provided by the 13th under the command of *havildars* (sergeants) of the 35th. Such an arrangement was unprecedented at that time. In later years, it was accepted that British troops be placed under the command of Indians whenever it was appropriate.

With the ending of the siege the two regiments marched back into India and camped at Ferozepore. The Indian officers of the 35th BNI presented themselves to their Commanding Officer and made a submission: "Sir, we shall soon be separated from our brothers, the 13th Light Infantry, and our whole regiment wishes to give them a farewell dinner. We will buy everything for our brothers but pig's flesh, and will take over their guard on that day so that every man may be present".

Having enjoyed the feast, the British soldiers and their officers reciprocated by subscribing to a fund which paid for a second dinner, this time entertaining their Indian comrades. The soldiers subscribed so liberally that there was a large cash surplus. The money was sent to a firm of silversmiths in Calcutta with orders that they should make a piece of silver for presentation to all ranks of the 35th BNI.

The design is of interest because it is a departure from the customary run of cups, salvers, statuettes and candelabra. Described as an *attar-dan*, it is an ornate globe standing on a wide round pedestal. The globe and its lid are heavily encrusted with a mass of flowers and fruit worked in matt and bright silver. Within the globe are six small vessels which, when used at an Indian feast, are filled with *attar* of roses. In fact, translated literally, *attar-dan* means "rose bowl". Dismantled into all its components, the piece consists of twenty-six parts.

A *cartouche* mounted on the side of the globe, supported by the figures of a soldier of the 13th Regiment of Foot and a *sepoy* of the 35th BNI, is engraved with a legend, in English, Urdu and Hindi - "Presented to the 35th Bengal Native Infantry by their Comrades of the 13th of Prince Albert's Light Infantry".

The base plate carries a later engraved legend: "Presented to Major Genl Sir Thomas Seaton KCB, from his Brother Officers of the late 35th Regt Bengal N.I."

The 35th was first raised, in 1799, as the 2nd/17th Regiment (being renumbered in 1824). The first commanding officer was Lieutenant Colonel James Noke, and for the rest of its time the unit was known as *Noke-ki-Paltan*, or "Noke's Regiment". In the event, he led it for only four years, being then promoted away as full Colonel. Two years later, in 1805, while he was still in his forties, one of India's numerous maladies took him, at Cawnpore, to an early grave. It is a reflection of those times that he was unmarried, but his Will made provision for one dependent in particular. His papers tell us that he "kept a native woman", a common practice in India in those days.

The regiment gave efficient and loyal service throughout the first half of the 19th century. Sadly, when the Mutiny broke out in 1857, it was judged to be unreliable. To the great distress of the officers and the majority of the other ranks, the *sepoys* were disarmed and sent back to their homes. It is possible that some may have made their way to Delhi and joined the mutineers, such was the confusion and anger resulting from the mismanagement of the British authorities.

The British officers kept the *attar-dan* safe throughout the Mutiny, perhaps hoping that one day the regiment might be reconstituted. In 1863, however, they were dispersed to other regiments and their silver then needed a new home. They voted to give the *attar dan* to Sir Thomas Seaton as a memento of his thirty-seven years of service in India, almost all of them with the 35th.

Over the next hundred years it was held by descendent members of the Seaton family, and the Somersets lost track of it. A Royal Welch Fusiliers officer, Lieutenant Colonel P R Butler DSO, then became interested in the story and, in 1943, he wrote an article for *Blackwoods Magazine* in which he questioned whether or not it still existed. His interest derived from the fact that his artist mother, Lady Butler, had painted the famous depiction of Dr Brydon approaching the walls of Jellalabad on his dying pony and titled *The Remnants of an Army* (owned by the Tate Gallery and since loaned to the Regimental Museum in Taunton).

Publication of the *Blackwoods* article prompted a letter from the general's grand-daughter, Lady Agnew, assuring him that it was safe and stored in her Oxford home. And there the matter rested until 1953 when the Curator of the Museum,

The exuberant table centrepiece presented by the 13th (1st Somersetshire) Regiment of Foot to the 35th Regiment of Bengal Native Infantry in 1842. Weighing 185 ounces, it measures 14 inches in height. The maker was the important firm of Hamilton & Company, of 8 Old Court House, Calcutta (the partners being William Remfry, George Remfry, Henry Woolaston and Robert Dring). The company had additional branches in Simla and Bombay. Like many other India-based silversmiths, Hamiltons were to experience a significant reduction in orders from military customers following the departure of the British in 1947. Photo: National Army Museum, Chelsea.

Lieutenant Colonel A Hunt, renewed the contact and requested that the *attar-dan* might be given or loaned to the regiment. By that time it had disappeared. Lady Agnew's home had been requisitioned in 1942 as an army billet and then as a lodging for refugees. All of the contents had been moved around or placed in storage. Lady Agnew had no idea where it might be.

Believing that it must have been stolen by these temporary visitors, Colonel Hunt launched a vigorous campaign to trace it. Appeals for information were published in magazines and journals read by antiques collectors and dealers. The Oxford City Police visited all the antiques and bric-a-brac shops in the force area and talked to their contacts in the local criminal fraternity.

Two years later it emerged that it was safe, and in the possession of another member of the family, Captain J A M Seaton. In 1959, Captain Seaton and his two sisters decided to present it to the RMA Sandhurst (the Somerset Light Infantry having by then been amalgamated with the Duke of Cornwall's Light Infantry). It is now on display at the National Army Museum, Chelsea.

The King's German Legion

Great Britain's world-wide commitments in the opening years of the 19th century were such that her army was severely over-extended. The shortage of manpower was met, at least in part, by the creation of regiments recruited from a wide variety of non-British populations. Their short-lived titles reflect the extent to which the British were obliged to scrape the barrel - The Albanian Regiment, The Corsican Regiment, The Corsican Light Dragoons, Charmilly's Uhlans Britannique de St Domingo, The French Emigrant Artillery, The Minorca Light Dragoons, La Tour's Loyal Foreigners, The Sicilian Light Infantry, and so forth.

By far the best was the King's German Legion. Initially a Hanoverian force, its ranks were gradually diluted with recruits of lesser quality from other countries as the war progressed. It was in fact a complete corps, with eight light infantry battalions, two regiments of Dragoons, two of Light Dragoons, and its own artillery and engineer units. They served in England, Ireland and the Low Countries, but their most important role was in Wellington's campaign in Spain.

A number of British Army officers were detached for service with the Legion, and one of these was Major F R N Ludlow Beamish. After the war he set himself the task of compiling a monumental history of the KGL and it was published in two parts by Thomas & William Boone, London (Volume I in 1818, Volume II in 1832).

The return of peace had removed the need for such a force and it was disbanded, but the following details indicate that its surviving officers formed a large and influential Regimental Association.

Seven years after he completed his Volume II, Ludlow Beamish was the recipient of a truly massive silver centrepiece. Weighing 876 ounces, it consisted of an ornate vase and cover mounted on a base and supported by ten figures (thought to have been representations of soldiers and officers in the Legion's various constituent regiments). The engraved wording was: "Presented on 6th May 1839 by the late officers of the King's German Legion in token of their remembrance from the Corps. To Major N Ludlow Beamish FRS KH, from the Officers of the King's German Legion, MDCCXXXIX". This was then repeated in German.

The subsequent fate of the piece is not known. It was made by the German silversmith G Drerves to a design by E von

Brendel, and some details of its manufacture are held by the *Historisches Museum von Hanover*, but the piece itself has disappeared (possibly into a private collection). If it still exists, and if it ever emerges into public gaze, it will serve as an impressive reminder of a very remarkable military force.

50th (Queen's Own) Regiment

The Anglo-German connection was renewed nine years later when the 50th (Queen's Own) Regiment was the recipient of a commemorative cup from His Royal Highness Prince Waldemar of Prussia. For reasons which the records do not explain, the Prince decided to travel from Europe to India. In 1845, he and his ADCs were permitted to attach themselves to the army commanded by General Sir Hugh Gough during the series of battles which came to be known as The First Sikh War.

The East India Company had been expanding its influence north west towards the Punjab, the "land of the five rivers" and home of the mighty warrior race, the Sikhs. Their leader, Ranjit

The gold cup presented to the 50th (Queen's Own) Regiment by His Royal Highness The Prince Waldemar of Prussia as a memento of his time with the regiment in India. Source: the regimental history, by Fyler.

Singh, died in 1839 and the Punjab then slid into a state of near anarchy. Its military leaders, who were hostile to the British, gained control and conflict became inevitable.

On 11 December 1845, the Sikh army crossed the Sutlej river into British controlled territory. It consisted of 60,000 soldiers trained to European standards, 200 cannon, and several groups of irregulars. Gough had 35,000 British and Indian troops with one hundred cannon. The following ten weeks witnessed four major engagement between the two sides, with Gough emerging victorious at the fourth, at Sobraon, on 12 February 1846. The uneasy peace which followed this campaign lasted little more than two years and was then followed by the Second Sikh War, but that is another story.

It was at the Sobraon battle that the men of the 50th Regiment particularly distinguished themselves. They charged a fortified field-work, planted their Regimental Colour on the summit, and captured the battle flag of their opponents. This event is portrayed on one side of the cup while the other shows the action at Ferozeshah, a few weeks earlier. After an action fought throughout the night of 21-22 December and the following day, the British killed 10,000 Sikhs and captured seventy-four guns. And it was during this battle that the Prince won the admiration of his British comrades. His personal physician, Dr Hoffmeister, had been attending in open ground to the wounded of the 50th when he was seen to fall. Prince Waldemar galloped over to rescue him, dismounted, found the doctor to be dead and then returned to the British line under heavy Sikh musket fire.

The Prince returned to Prussia, and his cup was handed to the regiment on his behalf two years later by General Viscount Hardinge GCB (who had served as second in command at Sobraon). It was engraved: "This goblet is presented by His Royal Highness Prince Waldemar of Prussia, as a token of remembrance of the happy days spent amongst the officers of the 50th Regiment at Loodiana, and the following glorious campaign of the Sutlej".

The presentation was made at a Mess Dinner at Dover Castle in December 1848. The Prince was unable to attend in person, but General Hardinge read the following letter: "My Lord, as you are a soldier, you must know that the tie of friendship between fellow officers will last for ever. I shall keep, therefore, always the warmest interest to one of the regiments of the Sutlej Army in particular, in considering myself as a kind of fellow soldier of the officers of Her Majesty's 50th Foot. It is impossible to forget the happy days which I have spent among those officers at Loodiana, who obliged me greatly by the kindness and hospitality which they bestowed upon me. I consider the most obliging of all their attentions, that they had elected myself and the gentlemen of my suite to be honorary members of their Mess.

So your Lordship will understand that, after having received so many proofs of kindness from the officers of Her Majesty's 50th Foot, I am anxious to express to them my thankful feelings and highest esteem, as this regiment must be regarded as one of the bravest which fought on the Sutlej.

I beg, therefore, your Lordship to deliver the accompanying goblet, which I have ordered purposely to be decorated with some sceneries of the different battles after my own drawings, to the officers of Her Majesty's 50th Foot. I believe it will be most gratifying to them, who

deserve such a distinction, and give still a greater value to the goblet if it is presented under these circumstances".

Allowing for the effusive language of the period, the letter makes two points of particular interest. The first is that the Prince acknowledged that his membership of the regiment's Mess was by the consent of its established officers. The principle is as sound today as it was then. In the same way that one cannot walk into a private house without an invitation from the owner, nobody can enter a Mess and make use of its facilities without the approval, tacit or otherwise, of those to whom it belongs. Officers attached to a unit on a temporary basis may normally expect to be made honorary members of that unit's Mess, but they enjoy the privilege by consent and not by right.

Secondly, the battle scenes depicted on the cup were based upon sketches prepared personally by the Prince. This was not unusual in years gone by. It was part of the curriculum of young officers under instruction, in all of the European armies, to be taught "field sketching". Royal Engineer officers in particular were encouraged to develop a skill in drawing landscapes and topographical features. In the decades preceding other forms of surveillance and intelligence gathering, an accurate sketch was

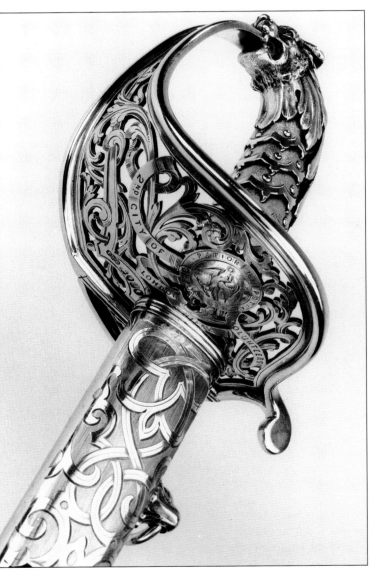

The City of London Rifles presentation sword, an object of equal appeal to collectors of silver and of edged weapons. Photo: Sotheby's, London.

often the best way of conveying to a senior officer and his staff the nature of the terrain being viewed by the army's forward elements.

According to a contemporary description, the cup stood two feet in height. In recent years the ornate lid has (at least at the time of writing) been lost. However, the main body of this magnificent silver-gilt piece has survived and is displayed in the museum of The Queen's Own Royal West Kent Regiment (which forms part of the Maidstone Museum and Art Gallery).

Apart from the two battle scenes already described, its design incorporates various features specific to the Sobraon campaign. The missing lid was surmounted by a reproduction of the chain armour, shield, lance, surcoat and helmet worn by a captured *sirdar*, together with more Sikh lances and banners. Apparently this part of the design was executed in exquisite detail, but it was so delicate that it suffered damage over the years following the presentation. Also on the lid were two "sleeping lions of the Punjab". The Curator of the regimental museum will be delighted to hear from anyone having knowledge of the lid and of where it might be.

The City of London Rifles

Here is a fine Victorian officer's presentation sword, with 32.5 inches blade, constructed by Widdowson & Veal, goldsmiths, of 75 The Strand, London. The guard and fittings are worked in Sterling silver by Thomas William Dee and bear his mark, London 1862. It is engraved "To Major G A Spottiswoode, Commanding 2nd City of London Rifle Volunteer Corps, from the Officers, Non Commissioned Officers and Privates, April 1862".

Firearms and swords are the soldier's workaday tools and therefore do not often bear researchable inscriptions. However, weapons with an identifiable provenance do come along from time to time, and they provide an interesting contrast to the customary range of cups, bowls, salvers and the like. This example bears the emblems of the 2nd City of London Rifle Volunteers, a unit with a well recorded and accessible history.

It was raised in 1860, its early members being mainly members of the printing and newspaper industries in and around Little New Street and Fleet Street. Two complete companies of men were employees of the *Daily Mail*. In 1881 it became a Volunteer battalion of the King's Royal Rifle Corps and then, when the Territorial Army was formed in 1908, was re-assigned as the 6th (City of London) Battalion, The London Regiment. Its part-time citizen soldiers mobilised in 1914, crossed the Channel in 1915, and fought for the next three years on the Western Front.

The recipient of this handsome sword, George Andrew Spottiswoode, resided at 3 Cadogan Square, London SW, and was evidently a man of substance. His wife was the daughter of a Baronet, and no doubt a researcher could uncover in his life an interesting *vignette* of Victorian society.

The Manchester Regiment

The subject of this entry is a Sterling silver pocket watch. In contrast with the preceding story, it provides us with a *vignette* of the social structures and attitudes of the Edwardian period. Described as a "Doctor's" pattern, with three-quarters lever movement and stop/start second hand, it was made by "TPH", and is hallmarked Chester, 1896. The fine ornate engraving states: "Presented to Corpl M Rowan, 1st V B Manchester Regt, By his comrades on his Return from the South African War, June 1901".

Corporal Rowan was a member of the 1st Volunteer Battalion of the Manchester Regiment. It had its headquarters in the town of Wigan, and its thirteen local companies were based throughout that area of Lancashire which comprises Wigan, Swinton, Leigh, Worsley and Flixton. He himself was a resident of Wigan.

Martin Rowan was born on 20 August 1877, received his education at St Joseph's Roman Catholic School, then took employment with a local leather trading company as a shop assistant. He joined the battalion on 16 April 1895, and was

Another presentation pocket watch, made by Mappin & Webb in 9 ct gold in 1910. It was won, in 1911, by Lieutenant J Betts for swordsmanship at The Royal Naval & Military Tournament (it evolved later as The Royal Tournament). Unusually, the engraving is on the exterior. In most instances, it appears on the inside of the casing (where it is protected from wear or damage). Photo: Spink & Son, London.

promoted to the rank of Corporal in 1898. Two years later he responded, together with nine of his comrades, to the call for reinforcements for service in South Africa with The Manchester Regiment's Regular battalions. It happened that the regiment had three of its four Regular battalions currently engaged in the war.

On 20 February 1900, the Wigan "Active Service Men" formed up and soon after departed for their twelve months tour of duty overseas. With them sailed a number of similar parties of men from other Lancashire towns where the five other Volunteer Battalions were based. Their subsequent adventures on active service have not been researched but, whatever they were, they have less interest in the context of this book than their experiences when they returned to England.

As stated previously, the Boer War was a popular war. Even the long casualty lists generated by disasters such as Spion Kop and other bungled battles did not dampen the British public's enthusiasm. When the soldiers began to arrive back in their home towns and villages, they were greeted as heroes.

Throughout the land there were civic receptions, rallies, parades, street parties and the like. Local Mayors and Aldermen took the lead in raising funds to pay for a wide variety of items which, with due pomp and celebration, were presented to the men who had volunteered and who now were reunited with their neighbours and families. The style of gift was frequently a medal, especially commissioned and designed to reflect local connections and pride, and paid for by public subscription. They were not "official issue" and could not be worn in uniform, but they seem to have been appreciated by the recipients and large numbers have survived the wastage of the passing years. Known today as "Boer War Tribute Medals", they provide a specialist collecting field in their own right.

Wigan honoured its local heroes with much more than a medal. When the Active Service Men returned to their home town, they were met on the railway platform by the Wigan Volunteers Band & Patriotic Concert Committee. Carriages were waiting to take them along the crowd-lined streets to the Borough Courts where they were received by His Worship the Mayor, Thomas Fyans, and the Borough officers and councillors. Each man was presented with a silver casket, made in the form of a book, engraved on the front with the crest of the 1st Volunteer Battalion, and on the reverse with the coat of arms of Wigan Borough. Fixed inside the left cover was a group photograph of the ten men, taken in a local studio shortly before their departure for South Africa. Inside the right cover was an illuminated address of welcome: "Presented to (the recipient's rank and name) of the 1st Vol Batt, Manchester Regiment, by the townspeople of Wigan on his return from active service in South Africa, as a small token of their appreciation of his loyalty and devotion to Queen and Country, in responding to the call for Volunteers at a time of national emergency, and of the courage he has displayed during the long and arduous campaign".

It is not known whether any of the ten Wigan Borough silver caskets have survived, but at least the story of their origins is clear enough. What is less certain is the story of the silver watch described at the head of this entry. The engraved wording suggests that the officers and men of the entire 1st Volunteer Battalion contributed to a fund for the purchase and engraving of silver watches for presentation to every one of their comrades who had served in South Africa. Admittedly, public enthusiasm for the war was great and pride in the soldiery high, but silver watches have never been cheap and the quality of the engraving on Corporal Rowan's watch is exceptionally fine. The contributors must have been willing to dig deep into their pockets to pay for all of this. No other comparable watch (same style, same date, same unit) has so far been sighted, so it is reasonable to assume that only the ten Wigan men were honoured in this way.

The sparse surviving records suggest that the Volunteer Band & Patriotic Concert Committee took charge of the arrangements and organised a Smoking Concert for the Active Service Section when the battalion returned from that year's annual camp. It would have provided an appropriate setting for the formal presentation of the watches. The Committee also planned to commemorate the event by installing an embossed tablet in the Wigan Drill Hall, but no other details of this have been traced.

It is for a particular purpose that the story of Martin Rowan's watch has been set out here in some detail. A nice enough piece, it does not in itself have any great intrinsic value. It contains a standard type of commercial movement which, as is often the case with pieces of this age, no longer functions. What instead makes the watch interesting are the attitudes and convictions of the society from which it emerged.

In the reigns of Victoria and of Edward VII, it was normal to see young men in the street and in public places wearing uniforms of one kind of another. Soldiers had their off-duty "walking out" dress, smart and colourful, even dandified, as an expression of regimental and personal pride. Pillbox hats tipped over one eye, moustaches long and well waxed, jacket and trousers as trim and taut as decency allowed, silver-headed swagger sticks at the ready, they sauntered through town on a Saturday evening to the delight of the girls and the envy of lesser men. It is hardly surprising that the Volunteers were never short of applicants for membership. Military service was an integral strand in the nation's social fabric, and there was respect for those who served. It was in this context that the people of Wigan were moved to spend a considerable sum of money on the purchase of the silver "welcome home" caskets, and the members of the battalion to spend even more on the commissioning of the engraved pocket watches. It was all part of the ebb and flow of military silver which so distinguished that era.

One hundred years later, the circumstances of Martin Rowan's life and times seem ever more remote. To avoid attack by terrorists or abuse from local drunks, servicemen no longer wear uniform while off-duty. Apart from annual events such as the Edinburgh Tattoo, the Royal Tournament and the Queen's Birthday Parade, the army has largely disappeared from public view. The abolition of National Service in 1962, combined with a subsequent shrinkage in the establishments of the armed forces, has had the effect of creating a society in which only a small minority has ever served in uniform. Apart from the currently serving Regulars, the majority of those who *have* served are the men and women who, now in their seventies and eighties, fought in the war of 1939-1945, and the men who, now in their sixties and seventies, served in Korea, Malaya, Cyprus, Kenya and elsewhere as National Service soldiers in the 1950s.

Ten or at most twenty years into the 21st century, there will probably be only a very small number of people who will know anything at all about military life and, therefore, about the nation's military history. It was in part with the hope of stimulating a sense of curiosity about that history, as represented by its silver icons, that the author chose to write this book.

1st Newfoundland Regiment

This is a piece with strong emotive overtones. It is a silver salver, 14.5 inches diameter, weighing 43.5 ounces, with gadroon edge and four plain feet, with marks for Mappin & Webb, London 1915. Engraved centrally with the Caribou crest of The Newfoundland Regiment, it has twenty-eight facsimile signatures surrounding the central crest and the legend: "Presented to Lieut Col & Mrs Hadow by the Officers of the 1st Newfoundland Regiment on the occasion of their marriage, April 1916".

Arthur Hadow was nearly forty years of age. Educated at Repton and Oriel College, Oxford, his career to that time provided an interesting contrast between Empire building and conventional regimental soldiering. His medals tell their own story (like the salver, they have remained in the family). His first was the India Medal (King Edward VII issue) with clasp "Waziristan 1901-02". A scarce award to British Army personnel, it resulted from his detached services as a Transport Officer during that essentially Indian Army campaign. His second medal came two years later when, still a Lieutenant, he commanded a Machine Gun Detachment of seventeen other ranks of The Norfolk Regiment during the Tibet campaign. It was a strange little mountain war, caused by disputes between the British and the Dalai Lama and was fought, uniquely, at altitudes up to 14,000 feet. The Tibet 1904 medal is not in itself rare, but this example (complete with "Gyantse" clasp) is thought to be unique to an officer of The Norfolk Regiment. His three other medals, which came later, were the 1914-15 Star, the British War Medal and the Victory Medal.

Having managed twice to obtain Extra-Regimental (detached) employment while the Norfolks were in India, Hadow may have been dismayed by the prospect of returning to routine garrison duties. He succeeded in avoiding them. In 1905

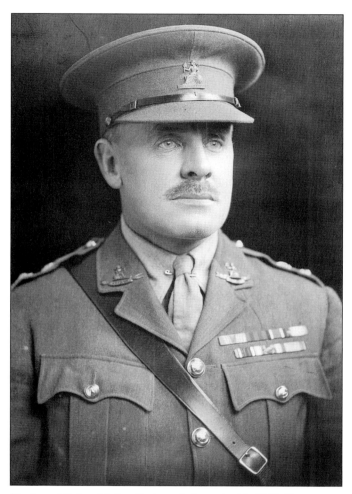

Lieutenant Colonel Arthur Hadow, photographed in 1919. He was one of dozens of commanding officers who saw their carefully trained battalions torn to pieces when they attempted to go "over the top" on the morning of 1 July 1916. His Newfoundlanders did everything asked of them, but few ever saw their homes again.
Photo: Major E A Hadow.

he was in South Africa, but then obtained a transfer to the Egyptian Army. The Sudan had been administered since 1899 under an Anglo-Egyptian Condominium, its turbulent tribes controlled by Egyptian troops commanded by British officers. He arrived in Khartoum in 1905. For his subsequent services he received, from the Khedive of Egypt, the Order of the Nile, 4th Class.

Hadow next comes to notice in Gallipoli during the ill-fated expedition to gain control of the Dardanelles. According to his unpublished memoirs, he and all his fellow British officers then serving with the Egyptian Army were desperately anxious to leave the Sudan. As professional soldiers they wanted to get into the European conflict where fame, glory and promotion beckoned. In August 1915 he finally obtained his release under a curious ruling that officers who had served a long time in the

Sudan's enervating climate could leave the country "for a period of rest and recovery on Gallipoli". Presumably the authorities in Khartoum were unaware of the conditions prevailing there.

Hadow quickly made his way north to Alexandria and took passage to Suvla. He was appointed a Brigade Major in the 29th Division and then, in November, in the 11th Division. Prior to participating in both phases of the Allied evacuation from the Gallipoli peninsula, he was given command of the 1st Newfoundland Regiment. It was the first time he had encountered Colonial soldiers who, to a man, were wartime volunteers with plenty of dedication but no previous military experience or tradition. The Newfoundlanders, like their counterparts from Australia and New Zealand, were sent into their first battles against a very tough enemy in a nightmare terrain. Their bravery was not enough, and the Allies were forced to admit defeat.

After refitting and reinforcement in Egypt with new drafts of volunteers, the Newfoundlanders were ordered to the Western Front. Hadow drove them hard, earning their respect if not their affection. Under his leadership, the Battalion achieved high standards of physical fitness, built up its endurance for marching long distances, and greatly improved its shooting skills. As he often said: "There are twenty-four hours in the day, and they are all available for musketry". In the event, none of this intensive preparation could save them from the carnage which was being planned by Haig and his generals in the summer of 1916.

The full story of the disastrous Battle of the Somme can be studied elsewhere, as can the role of the Newfoundlanders. It is enough to know that, in one hour on the morning of 1 July, they were destroyed as a fighting unit. After the war Hadow wrote: "Our part in that battle can be described in a very few lines. Our approach began at dusk the previous evening. We occupied trenches we knew well. We went into the attack with twenty-five officers and 776 other ranks. By evening I was able to collect sixty-eight unwounded men. Myself and the Adjutant were the only officers of the Regiment who were not killed or wounded".

The short stretch of frontline where they fell, at Beaumont Hamel, has been preserved by the people of Newfoundland as a shrine to their memory. Dominating it is the magnificent bronze statue of a Caribou, the emblem incorporated in their cap badge. As a senior officer later said: "Their assault failed because dead men could advance no further".

The Battalion was rebuilt with yet more volunteers, and fought on for the remainder of the war on the Western Front. Hadow commanded it in eight of its major battles, including Cambrai and Third Ypres in 1917 (operations in which the Regiment's losses were almost as severe as those suffered at Beaumont Hamel). It was after Ypres, and in recognition of its valour there, that King George V bestowed upon the Newfoundland Regiment the "Royal" prefix. In the whole history of British arms, only two previous instances are recorded of this distinction being conferred while the nation was still at war. One was in the year 1665, to the Royal Regiment of Foot of Ireland, the other in 1885, to the Princess Charlotte of Wales's Royal Berkshire Regiment.

Hadow's contribution was recognised by three Mentions in Despatches and by his appointment as a Companion of the Order of St Michael & St George. By Christmas of 1917 he was physically worn out and was ordered to relinquish his command. He returned to England, survived the rest of the war, commanded 2nd Battalion, The Norfolk Regiment from 1922 to 1925, then retired a year later. In WWII he served in the Home

Guard in Kemsing, near Sevenoaks, Kent.

At the end of WWI, Colonel Hadow decided to record the fate of some of his wartime officers in a very unusual and personal way. Twenty-seven of those named on the salver can be identified with certainty. It was they who subscribed to the cost of the wedding gift and whose signatures were so skilfully reproduced upon it by the engraver. Some but not all of these officers were serving with the 1st Battalion when it met catastrophe at Beaumont Hamel only three months later. Several died that day, others succumbed in the following weeks and months. Hadow traced their dates of death and then instructed an engraver to add these details under the signatures of the individuals concerned. The names of the identified signatories as seen on the salver, are: Captains A E Bernard, Conn Alexander, J A Ledingham (killed 9.10.1917), J W March, Augustus O'Brien (died of wounds 18.10.1916), L Paterson (Medical Officer), Arthur Raley (Adjutant), R S Rowsell (killed 14.4.1917), H A Timewell (Paymaster), Lieutenants B Butler, James Donnelly (killed 12.10.1916), J Nunns, Wilfred Pippy, H Rendell (killed 29.9.1918), Frank Summers (Quartermaster, died of wounds 16.7.1916), Second Lieutenants R W Bartlett (killed 30.11.1917) Cecil Clift (killed 12.10.1916), Gerald Harvey, H C Herder (killed 1.7.1916), Frank Knight, R G Patterson, Bruce Reid (killed 1.7.1916), R A Shortall (killed 1.7.1916), O W Steele (died of wounds 8.7.1916), R Stick, C S Strong (died of wounds 13.4.1918), George Taylor (killed 1.7.1916).

In total, 1294 members of the Royal Newfoundland Regiment lost their lives in the war of 1914-1918. Hundreds more were so physically or mentally damaged that they never fully recovered. The impact of these losses on such a small and close-knit community was particularly severe. Not only did many families suffer grievous personal loss, the economic future of the Colony itself was jeopardised. Fortunately, in the second world war, the mistake of concentrating so many of the best young men in one place and at one time, as at Beaumont Hamel, was not repeated. The Newfoundlanders who volunteered in 1939 were widely dispersed in the Royal Air Force, the Royal Navy, and the Merchant Marine, and they provided the personnel for two regiments of Royal Artillery. There was also a specialist forestry unit which crossed over to Scotland in 1940. When not working in the mills and forests, its men served as the 3rd Inverness (Newfoundland) Battalion of the Home Guard. It was unique in being the only Home Guard unit composed exclusively of colonials.

129th Duke of Connaught's Own Baluchis, Indian Army

The opening months of the Great War witnessed many outstanding acts of bravery and self-sacrifice. The British Expeditionary Force was fighting for its very existence. The Indian Corps came to its aid, and had a key role in preventing the Germans from breaking through to the Channel ports.

The Corps included regiments from many parts of India and Nepal. Amongst them was the 129th Duke of Connaught's Own Baluchis, and one of their men was *Sepoy* Khuda Dad Khan. Born in the Jhelum district of the Punjab, twenty-six years of age, he became the first Indian to win the Victoria Cross.

On 31 October 1914, at Hollebeke, the Baluchis came under severe pressure from advancing masses of German infantry. Khuda Dad Khan was working one of the regiment's two machine guns. The British officer commanding the machine gun detachment was wounded, a shell destroyed one gun, and then all the other men in the detachment were killed. Alone, himself wounded, he continued to fire at the enemy until his

position was overrun and he was bayoneted. Left for dead, he managed hours later to crawl back to rejoin his regiment. He survived the war and rose to the rank of *Subedar*.

The 129th was later retitled the 4th (Duke of Connaught's Own) Battalion, 10th Baluch Regiment. Today its direct successor is the 11th Battalion, The Baloch Regiment, Pakistan Army, and to its officers the name of Ypres is a source of immense pride. Their predecessors were amongst the first to fight in the defence of that Belgian city, and they took part in the second great battle of the following year. The 11th Battalion is unique in carrying on its Colours the Battle Honours for both battles, "Ypres 1914" and "Ypres 1915".

After the war, the officers subscribed to the manufacture of a silver memorial commemorating the regiment's role in the two battles. Mounted on a wooden stand, it is topped by a replica of the Ypres (Menin Gate) Memorial, perhaps the best known of the Commonwealth War Graves Commission's memorials and a source of reverence to the people of the city. Carved into the stonework are the names of 54,375 British, Indian, Canadian, Australian and South African soldiers. They died in what came to be known as The Ypres Salient during the first three years of the war, and have no known grave. Each evening at eight o'clock, traffic in the adjacent streets is brought to a halt and buglers sound "Last Post".

On the front panel of the Baluchi memorial is a silver representation of the Ypres Cloth Hall as it was during the war. The Hall was almost totally destroyed by German shell fire but later was meticulously rebuilt to the original plans. This beautiful centrepiece (of which no photograph is available) resides in the Officers' Mess of the 11th Battalion in Pakistan, where it holds the place of honour.

The Machine Gun Corps Font, RMA Sandhurst

Here is a striking instance of military silver being re-worked and acquiring a new purpose. It is an octagonal christening font with silver cover and plug, mounted on a silver embellished ebonised stand, the whole approximately four feet in height, the font and cover being 17 inches in width at its widest point and 17 inches high, engraved with the crest of the Machine Gun Corps. It was made by the Goldsmiths & Silversmiths Company, and is hallmarked London 1919.

The cover (lid) is engraved with the words *"In Manus Tuas.* Presented to the Officers, NCOs and men of the Machine Gun Corps by the Officers, NCOs and men of the two Training Brigades of the Machine Gun Corps in proud memory of those passing from the Brigades into the Corps who fell or died for King and Country, 1914-1919. *Dulce et Decorum est Pro Patria Mori".*

Accompanying the font and its cover are a ewer, 17 inches high, and a silver handled baptismal shell. The ewer is engraved with the words: "This font and ewer, originally placed in the Machine Gun Corps Chapel at Grantham, were presented to the Royal Military College Chapel by the Machine Gun Corps, May 4th 1921".

The finely executed font is located in The Royal Memorial Chapel, RMA Sandhurst. The original Sandhurst chapel was built in 1813. It now serves as the Indian Army Memorial Room. A new chapel - the origins of the present structure - was built in 1879. Much enlarged immediately after WWI, it was reconsecrated by the Archbishop of Canterbury in May 1921 and completed in 1937.

Details of precisely how and why the font came to be made, and then presented to the RMC, cannot be established with certainty due to the absence of College records for that period. However, the engraved wording itself, when combined with other evidence, gives a broad picture of a series of events between 1914 and 1922.

At the outbreak of WWI, each battalion of line infantry was equipped with just two medium machine-guns, the .303 Vickers model. The general view was that machine-guns were a useful adjunct to a unit's firepower, but that individual musketry skills were much more important. The personal weapon of the British soldier was the excellent bolt-action SMLE .303 rifle which, fitted with a ten-round magazine, enabled a trained soldier to discharge fifteen aimed rounds per minute. When the British Expeditionary Force landed in France in August and September of 1914, most of its men had reached this standard (some could fire double that number). At Mons, when the advancing masses of German infantry felt the weight of their firepower for the first time, suffering enormous casualties in the process, they were convinced that they were under attack from great numbers of machine-guns, not riflemen.

A year later it was decided that machine-gunners could no longer be trained adequately at battalion level but should instead receive specialist instruction and status as members of their own Corps. The Mons scenario, where they had fired by line of sight directly into formations of men moving about in the open, had long gone. Machine gun were now being used in vastly greater numbers and frequently were engaged in providing indirect barrage fire (intended to deny the enemy the use of designated stretches of the battlefield). The way in which the weapon was deployed had become much more sophisticated.

The new Machine Gun Corps was formed by Royal Warrant on 14 October 1915. Its main training establishment was located in a pair of linked temporary wartime camps at Grantham, in the county of Lincolnshire. It had several branches - infantry, cavalry, armoured car - with other depots at Clipstone, Bisley and Mansfield. As indicated by the engraved wording on the font, the Grantham centre grew to the equivalent of two Brigades. One hundred and sixty thousand officers and men passed through it, on their way to the Western Front and the Middle East.

The Armistice brought a rapid winding-down in the need for such men. The Grantham Officers' Mess had acquired some silver during the previous two years, and it was decided to have it melted for the manufacture of the font. It was installed in the centre's Chapel (a converted wooden hut). Eight months later, in July 1919 and at only a few days notice, the entire establishment (which at full capacity could accommodate 20,000 men) was closed down.

It seems likely that the font went into storage for the next year or so. Then, when the War Office announced its intention of disbanding the Machine Gun Corps entirely, its senior officers made the decision to hand it over to a new and permanent home, the RMC Sandhurst. It has been in regular use there ever since.

The evidence suggests that not all of the Mess silver was melted for the production of the font and ewer. Following the pattern of events seen elsewhere, when a unit was disbanded permanently, a number of pieces were given to (or perhaps purchased by) senior officers at that time employed in the Corps or associated with it. In 1996, a large salver engraved with the facsimile signatures of seven such officers appeared on the London market. It surfaced at a routine auction of second-hand pieces, and now forms part of the author's collection (see following entry).

The Reverend W B Paine, of the Royal Army Chaplains Department, with the Machine Gun Corps font in the Royal Memorial Chapel, RMA Sandhurst (where he is the Assistant Chaplain). The font, ewer and baptismal shell are in excellent repair and regular use. Photo: Jim Farrar.

The Machine Gun Corps Salver

It is a silver salver, weighing 44 ounces, 18 inches in diameter, with gadroon edge, three ornate curled leaf feet, and made by Walker & Hall, Birmingham 1919. Engraved around the central MGC crest are seven facsimile signatures. The latter are all legible and have been identified as follows:

Colonel L F Renny CMG DSO, born 1877, educated Brighton College and RMC Sandhurst, commissioned into the Royal Dublin Fusiliers, he served on the Staff in the Boer War, with the

West African Frontier Force in 1904, and in WWI in various commands and appointments (ultimately as Inspector of Machine Gun Units GHQ and, post-war, as Commandant of the Machine Gun School).

Colonel J H J Phillips, born 1878, commissioned into the Coldstream Guards in 1900, he served with the Mounted Infantry in the Boer War. He embarked for France with the BEF in 1914 and served on the Western Front throughout the war. His involvement with the MGC is not known.

Colonel W J Lockett DSO, born 1873, commissioned into the 11th Hussars in 1893, he saw much action between 1899 and 1902 as a Captain in South Africa (where he gained his DSO). He too went to France with the BEF in 1914. After being twice wounded in action, he was appointed Machine Gun Officer of 18 Corps in 1917.

Brigadier E Pearce-Serocold CMG, educated at Eton and the RMC Sandhurst, commissioned into the King's Royal Rifle Corps in 1889, he served in Malta, India and South Africa (the siege of Ladysmith). Second-in-command of his regiment's 2nd Battalion, he was wounded at the battle for Hooge in October 1914. Later in the war he was a Brigade Commander, still on the Western Front. Between 1918 and 1920 (when he retired) he commanded the Prees Heath Camp, Shropshire.

Colonel A G Bayley CBE DSO, born 1878, educated Shrewsbury and the RMC Sandhurst, commissioned into the Oxfordshire & Buckinghamshire Light Infantry, he served in South Africa, India and Burma. In WWI he was mainly in France, on the Staff. In 1918 he became Superintendent of Training at the Machine Gun Training Centre, Grantham. Retiring from the army in 1935, he became Director of Military Studies, London University, where he stayed until 1948. For much of WWII he also served as Librarian at the Staff College, Camberley.

Colonel R F Pearson TD, originally commissioned into the Buffs (Royal East Kent Regiment), he saw pre-WWI service in India (the Relief of Chitral, 1895) and the Tirah campaign (1897-1898), and then in South Africa against the Boers. Retiring on full pay in 1910, he joined the Territorial Force as a Major and was given command of Cheltenham College Officer Training Corps. Shortly after the outbreak of war he went to France with the BEF, but it is not known in what way he was involved with the Machine Gun Corps.

Major General R O Kellett CB CMG, an Irishman, born in 1864 in County Tipperary, commissioned into the Royal Irish Regiment Militia in 1882, he served in India (Hazara Expedition, 1886), became an Instructor of Musketry in India and at Hythe, then retired on full pay in 1913. In 1914 he returned to service, commanded an Infantry Brigade on the Western Front (1915-1918) and a machine gun training unit (1918-1919).

These condensed biographical notes, which represent only a small proportion of the records available, serve to give some idea of the almost limitless volume of information which can be extracted from an otherwise unremarkable item of silver. The salver carries no self-explanatory wording. Only the MGC crest provides the basic clue that it is "military silver". Thereafter, identifying the signatories in the Army Lists and other publications such as *Who's Who*, was a fairly straightforward piece of detective work.

The Australian Tank Corps

As may be seen from the photograph, the object is an accurately detailed silver model of a WWI tank, scale one half-inch to the foot, mounted on a mahogany stand (the carved surface of which represents the shell-pitted surface of a battlefield). It was built in 1934 by Mr Paul Fripp, of Bath, each part being made and fitted together by hand.

In the autumn of 1914, the all-volunteer 1st Australian Division embarked for Europe in company with the leading elements of a New Zealand Expeditionary Force. Together they and others who followed them were to win fame and glory as the Anzacs - the Australian and New Zealand Army Corps. Their first battles were fought on Gallipoli. Despite the greatest dash and gallantry, they and their British, Indian, Gurkha, and French comrades were withdrawn after eight months.

Regrouping in Egypt, they were divided into two parts. The Light Horse regiments reverted to the mounted role for service against the Turks in Sinai, Gaza and Palestine, and the infantry units, now expanded to five Divisions, moved to the great killing ground of the Western Front. On arrival, and despite protests from their commanders and their home government, they were separated and assigned piece-meal to various Corps of the British Army. It was not a happy arrangement.

In 1917, at the Battle of Bullecourt, twelve miles south of Vimy Ridge, Australian troops went into battle with the promise of British tanks to support them. In the early hours of 10 April, in driving snow, they formed up to attack the formidable Hindenburg Line. The assault was called off at the last moment when the tanks failed to arrive. On the following night they formed up again, but now against a thoroughly alert enemy. Three tanks did cross the start-line on time but were quickly disabled. Despite this, and despite the failure of the British artillery fire plan, the Australian infantrymen forced their way bodily through the German wire and, in savage hand-to-hand fighting, reached the second line of enemy trenches. After six hours, lacking armoured support and protective shellfire, the few survivors were forced to withdraw.

In the later words of Lieutenant General Sir Hugh Elles, Colonel Commandant of the Royal Tank Corps: "We attempted to assist you with our earlier and rather primitive machines but, owing to an unfortunate chapter of accidents, we were not successful. Failure, with its accompanying casualties, ensued, and the final impression left was not good. When, therefore, fifteen months later, further cooperation was suggested, it is not surprising that you were a little coy". The latter comment was a massive understatement. By 1918 the Australian people and their troops at the front had become profoundly disenchanted with the way in which the British high command was conducting the war. At Bullecourt, of the 5000 officers and men who went over the top on the morning of 11 April, 3289 were killed, or wounded and left behind in German hands.

The scale of the slaughter was such that the Germans deliberately held their fire for much of the afternoon (after the attack had failed) so that Lieutenant J H Julin, of the 52nd Battalion, AIF, could take fifty stretcher-bearers up to the German line to rescue some of the wounded. The Germans at this time mercifully shot a number of Australian casualties who were so badly injured that they had no prospect of recovery.

Despite the objections of their own generals, the British politicians were persuaded eventually to agree that all Australian units on the Western Front should be brought together as a unified Australian Army Corps under the command of their own general, John Monash.

Monash was an intellectual, holding degrees in Law and the Arts. A qualified civil engineer, he had learned his soldiering with the Australian Militia. This background did nothing to endear him to the close-knit fraternity of the British General Staff.

A fine example of silver having been given by the armed forces of one Commonwealth country to another. The inscription reads *Presented by the officers, Royal Tank Corps, to the officers, Australian Tank Corps, on its formation and in memory of comradeship and co-operation in the Great War, 1914-1918. This model is of the Mark V tank, sixty of which went into action for the first time at Hamel on 4th July 1918 in co-operation with three Brigades of Australian infantry. In this brilliant action, the enemy defences were penetrated on a frontage of 6000 yards to a maximum depth of 2000 yards, 400 prisoners being taken with a loss to our troops of about 600 officers and men and 5 tanks.* Photo: School of Armour, Puckapunyal, Victoria.

Even more damning, in their eyes, was the fact that he was a Jew, of German descent, his parents having emigrated to Australia from Prussia. British feathers were even more ruffled when this Colonial amateur soldier proved to be a superb Corps commander. His men captured more ground for less casualties than any other Corps, and took a leading role in driving the Germans back during the final months of the war.

The wording engraved on the piece illustrated here suggests that command and control procedures had changed considerably by the time the battle for Hamel was fought. The design and efficiency of the machines themselves was much improved. The battle, contrasting so positively with the failure at Bullecourt, provided a suitable point of reference for the presentation.

It was made in London on 25 January 1935 by General Elles to the High Commissioner for Australia, the Right Honourable S M Bruce PC CH MC, who accepted the piece on behalf of the Australian Tank Corps. Also present was Brigadier A C Courage DSO MC, the officer who commanded the 5th Tank Brigade at Hamel and at a number of subsequent actions when his tanks cooperated successfully with Australian infantry.

High Commissioner Bruce made the expected gracious response, but one of his comments is of interest to students of early armoured warfare: "My own experience during the war with tanks and the kind of vehicles which preceded them was confined to Gallipoli. There, the armoured cars had a habit of falling into trenches and drawing enemy fire from the whole of the peninsula, and causing us to curse their presence".

It was not until 15 December 1926 that authority was granted for the establishment of an Australian Tank Corps. The success of British tanks at Cambrai in November 1917 had demonstrated their potential, and the success at Hamel in July 1918 convinced the Australians that tanks had an important role in modern warfare. However, both they and the British continued to believe that the tank was essentially a mobile pillbox, useful for supporting infantry in the attack but little

more. It was the brilliant success of the German *blitzkreig* campaigns in WWII - in Poland, France and Russia - which brought about a radical and long-overdue change of heart.

The silver tank is always used as a table centrepiece during formal Dinner Nights in the Royal Australian Armoured Corps Officers' Mess at Puckapunyal, in the State of Victoria.

The Royal Fusiliers (City of London Regiment)

A small memento of times past is a round silver medallion, with ring suspender, one inch diameter, and weighing approximately half of one ounce. It was designed by Mappin & Webb, and is hallmarked Birmingham, 1914. A quality piece, it is well struck on both sides. The obverse has two crests (one being the regimental crest of The Royal Fusiliers and "The Sportsman's Battalion", the other being the Cunliffe-Owen family crest), plus the engraved number "3363". The reverse has the facsimile hand-written text "From E Cunliffe-Owen, Jan 1915, God Guard You"

The 23rd and 24th Battalions of The Royal Fusiliers were raised, as the 1st and 2nd Sportsman's Battalions of the New Armies, on 25.9.1914 and 20.11.1914 respectively, by Edward Cunliffe-Owen CMG. Men volunteering for attestation into the 1st Battalion were enrolled at the Hotel Cecil, in the Strand, London, which their sponsor had hired for the occasion. The place of enrolment for the 2nd Battalion, two months later, is not known.

Edward Cunliffe-Owen was the son of a Royal Engineers officer, but he himself seems not to have had a military background. He was educated at Wellington and Trinity College, Cambridge, and resided at 16 Stratford Place, London W. By profession he was Secretary of the Metropolitan Electric Supply Company, and presumably was a major share-holder in that company. At the outbreak of war he was fifty-seven years old and therefore over-age for military service. He was one of the men of wealth and influence who responded to Kitchener's

The obverse and reverse of the E Cunliffe-Owen medallion. Approximately 2000 are presumed to have been made, to his order, by Mappin & Webb. It is hallmarked Birmingham, 1914, and must have been commissioned shortly after he decided, in response to the Kitchener appeal, to sponsor the raising of two "Sportsman's Battalions" for The Royal Fusiliers (City of London Regiment). Each medallion was hand engraved with the individual soldier's service number. To date, no records have been traced, but presumably they paraded for Cunliffe-Owen in January 1915 and each man then received his medallion. The raising of Kitchener's New Armies was a strange and, in some ways, chaotic episode (the War Office did not officially assume responsibility for the Sportsmen until 1 July 1915). Further research may reveal more precise details regarding this emotive small piece of silver. Photo: Alan Cooper.

appeal for volunteer recruits by sponsoring the formation of new battalions which, in due course, were taken over by the War Office and absorbed into the New Armies. As their sub-titles imply, the appeal of the 23rd and 24th Battalions, Royal Fusiliers, was that they aimed (at least initially) to recruit well-known figures from various sports such as football, rugby, rowing and cricket. The membership became much more cosmopolitan after both battalions joined the 2nd Division on the Western Front in late 1915 and began to suffer the inevitable casualties.

They remained on the Western Front throughout the war. Few of the men who joined in 1914 were still serving with them in November 1918. The great majority were dead or permanently disabled.

The date on the medal, "Jan 1915", is significant. The eager volunteers had reached the stage in their training at which the two battalions could parade for their sponsor, each man being presented with a medallion as a keepsake and as the equivalent of a St Christopher good luck charm.

It may be assumed that many of the Sportsman's medallions were taken to France and now rest, together with their owners, in the fields of Flanders. Others were left behind, with wives and sweethearts, before the men embarked for France.

Mappin & Webb were recognised as designers and makers of high quality silverware, and Cunliffe-Owen evidently went to considerable trouble and personal expense in commissioning the manufacture and distribution of these medallions. Fortunately, for the researcher of such matters, he went to the additional expense of instructing Mappin & Webb to engrave each medallion with the Service number of the man to whom it was to be presented.

The number "3363", engraved on the example recorded here, is that of Charles Henry Crowle, a Cornishman, the bachelor son of Charles and Mary Crowle of Trelissick Terrace, Hayle. This area was, and still is, one of the strongholds of Cornish rugby union. It might have been expected that he and his pals would enlist into their county regiment, The Duke of Cornwall's Light Infantry. The fact that he chose instead to volunteer for the Sportsman's Battalions of the London-based Royal Fusiliers suggests that perhaps he was himself a rugby player. It is even possible that his entire local team signed up "to beat Kaiser Bill". The fact that Private Crowle's Cunliffe-Owen medallion has surfaced in a West Country flea market makes it almost certain that he gave it to his parents on his last home leave before embarking with his friends for their great adventure.

He went to France with the 24th (Sportsman's) Battalion, The Royal Fusiliers, and lost his life on 3 August 1916. The tragic Battle of the Somme was in its fifth disastrous week, and the 24th were engaged in the fighting at Delville Wood. Three German regiments were wiped out when the British attacked in July, and the woods were reduced to a wilderness of shattered trunks, fallen branches and shell-smashed ground. Every dip and hollow was packed with the bodies of the dead when the Germans were finally evicted on 28 July. "C" Company of the 24th Battalion took over the front-line trench between the southern edge of the wood and Waterlot Farm.

On 30 July they attempted a further advance, but were quickly counter-attacked by enemy troops using flame-throwers. Charles Crowle was mortally injured during this encounter. He died three days later at an advanced dressing station near Montauban, six miles east of Albert. Like so many of his comrades who were evacuated from the front-line only to die later at this station, he was buried in what became later the Commonwealth War Graves Commission's "Quarry Cemetery". He was twenty-four years of age.

The British Legation Medal (Addis Ababa)

Here is another very small piece of silver of little intrinsic worth but having a remarkably strong association with the lives of otherwise unknown soldiers. The setting for the story is again Abyssinia, a country mentioned in another context in Chapter Four but now renamed Ethiopia. The year is 1935. Mussolini's troops are poised in Eritrea and Somaliland, about to strike south and west and determined to add this wild mountainous country to the ramshackle Italian colonial empire. Emperor Haile Selassie will fly to Geneva to make a dignified appeal for international support before the general assembly of the League of Nations. He is jeered from the podium, and fascism will march on unopposed towards the disasters of the second world war.

In this climate of rising tensions, the status of the foreign Legations began to cause concern. Apart from the American Embassy, all the diplomatic missions were located several miles north of the capital, Addis Ababa. The British Legation sat in a parkland of one square mile, surrounded by feeble fencing and dominated by a steep-sided hill. The eight-man guard of Indian Army soldiers was totally inadequate to protect its staff in the event of trouble.

After much indecision in Whitehall, and despite the nervousness of the Emperor at having foreign troops on his soil, the order was given for a much larger defence force to be deployed. It was the Sikh company of the 5th Battalion (40th Pathans), 14th Punjab Regiment. In command was Major W F Charter MC, his officers being Captain G A E Keene of the 1st/16th Punjab Regiment, Lieutenant C W Pearson of the 1st/12th Frontier Force Regiment, and Captain T E Palmer of the Indian Medical Service.

The Italians opened their offensive in October 1935 but, even though they made free use of poison gas and aerial bombardment, made only slow progress against the Emperor's barefoot tribesmen. It was not until January 1936 that they started to advance rapidly. The Emperor fled his capital, leaving orders that the contents of his palace and government storehouses be given to the people. The following free-for-all led to a swift breakdown in law and order, with large armed gangs roaming freely throughout Addis Ababa and the surrounding countryside. They included policemen and soldiers whose officers had fled with the Emperor.

Major Charter had spent the previous weeks preparing for this scenario. Trenches were dug around the British Legation buildings, fields of fire cleared of vegetation, and arms and ammunition distributed to the staff of the almost defenceless American, Japanese and German Legations. The crisis came on 2 May. When frightened European, Indian and Somali civilians came flooding into the British compound, his men had already prepared a temporary refugee camp, with cooking facilities, water supplies and latrines, for three thousand people.

Active patrolling helped to keep the marauders at bay for much of the time, but all of the Legations came under sporadic

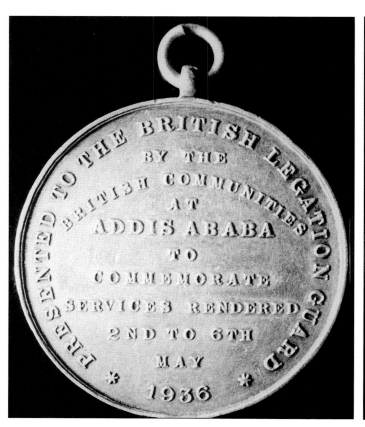

The obverse and reverse (much enlarged) of the silver medal presented to approximately 140 officers, men and followers engaged in the defence of the British Legation at Addis Ababa, May 1936. Very few of these (unofficial) medals have survived the passing years. Two are known to be in England, two others are in the USA in a private collection. A fifth, the example shown here, was sold at auction some years ago by Glendinnings, London. It was purchased by a private buyer for £600. Photo: Lieut Col Patric Emerson OBE.

assault and constant sniping. The most serious incident was an attack on the Belgian Legation by a large body of the leaderless Abyssinian Imperial Guard. Lieutenant Pearson and a platoon of Sikhs rushed to their aid by lorry. A short furious action followed, the Guard was driven off , and not a single *jawan* was injured. Pearson was awarded the Military Cross for his leadership and personal bravery in this affair.

By 6 May, Major Charter's force was close to exhaustion and running out of supplies. It was saved by the arrival in the city of 25,000 Italian troops who swiftly quelled the rioters and looters. They did this so effectively that most of the refugees in the British compound soon returned to their homes and businesses.

Armed guerilla groups still roamed the countryside, harassing the Italian invaders. At the end of July, one of their leaders, Ras Kassa, launched a well-planned attack with the aim of driving them out of the city. It culminated in a full-scale battle, lasting forty hours, in a wooded area on the periphery of the British compound. The Sikhs were "stood to" throughout this time, watching the fight but cautious of the stray shots coming their way from both sides. In the event, they had only one casualty, a Lance *Naik* slightly wounded in the head.

Throughout these weeks, Major Charter and his men received extensive coverage in the world press. The British Prime Minister and Foreign Secretary praised their work in the House of Commons, and the national governments whose Legations were being helped during the crisis were generous with their messages of support and gratitude. When Charter marched to the railway station to return to India, he and his company were received there by Marshal Rudolfo Graziani and a Guard of Honour of Italian *askari*. Graziani made an effusive speech, praising what had been achieved. Ironically, only four years later, he would lead his country's army against British and Commonwealth forces in the opening stages of the Western Desert campaign. A handsome heavily bearded man, he was known to the British and his own troops alike as "old electric whiskers". At the end of the war he was sentenced as a collaborationist to nineteen years imprisonment.

The medal illustrated here was commissioned by the British expatriates in Addis Ababa as a token of their appreciation. Two inches in diameter, struck in silver, it is worded on one side "Presented to the British Legation Guard, 1936", and on the other "By the British Communities at Addis Ababa to commemorate services rendered 2nd to 6th May". The medal was given without distinction to everyone who served under Major Charter - officers, soldiers, medical orderlies and followers alike. Each was engraved with the name of the recipient, and it is thought that the total number presented was one hundred and forty.

These medals are now extremely rare. Five are known to be in private hands. There may be two or three still unrecorded, but most collectors and dealers are unlikely ever to encounter them. The sole reason for listing the British Legation Guard medal in this book is to give point to one of the author's primary aims - to emphasise that military silver, of every kind, monumental or mundane, is directly related to individuals and the circumstances in which at various times they have found themselves.

1st Battalion, The Somerset Light Infantry (Prince Albert's)

British India came to an end on 15 August 1947. Many British Army and Royal Air Force units stationed in Pakistan and the new Republic of India still awaited repatriation. The logistics of handover and withdrawal were complicated by the chaotic conditions in areas overwhelmed by millions of Hindu and Muslim refugees. Despite the difficulties, by early 1948 only a handful of British units remained. Concentrated around the port cities of Karachi (West Pakistan) and Bombay (India), they waited for the troopships which would take them home. It was time to go.

On 26 February, the 2nd Battalion, The Black Watch, made its ceremonial departure from Karachi. It embarked, appropriately, in the troopship *Empress of Scotland*.

On the following day, at Bombay docks, the 1st Battalion, The Somerset Light Infantry (Prince Albert's), boarded the *Empress of Australia*. She then moved out to anchor overnight in the harbour. As dawn broke on 28 February, seven of the battalion's officers and fifty other ranks prepared to return ashore for a busy and well-rehearsed programme of inspections, presentations and speeches. They were to form a Colour Party and Escort. The Indian military and civil authorities were determined to see them off in style, the Somersets equally determined to match the occasion. The regiment was in its two hundred and sixty-third year, many of them spent in India. The Somersets' record and reputation had made them prime candidates for the honour of being the last to leave.

Under the command of Major F M DeButts MBE, the officers and men chosen to parade at the farewell ceremonies were ferried ashore and treated to morning tea at the Royal Bombay Yacht Club. Then, after changing into stiffly starched jungle greens and blanco-white belt and gaiters, they marched to The Gateway of India. A huge masonry archway, it had been for generations of Britons their first and last view of India as the great ocean liners carried them to and from this, the country's principal passenger port.

Guards of Honour were provided by detachments of the Royal Indian Navy, the Maharatta Light Infantry, the Indian Grenadiers, the 11th Sikh Regiment and the 5th Royal Gurkha Rifles (Frontier Force). Distinguished guests took their seats, the band played, flags fluttered in the warm breeze of a fine morning, enthusiasm was high. When the Somerset's Colours and Escort took their place on the parade ground, they were greeted with the Royal Salute by the Indian Guards of Honour and an emotional burst of applause by the thousands of Indian spectators.

Speeches and presentations followed, one of the latter being the acceptance by Lieutenant Colonel John Platt DSO, the battalion's commanding officer, of a specially commissioned silver replica of The Gateway of India. It was handed to him by Major General D R E R Bateman CIE DSO, the last commander of British forces, Bombay Area. On the polished wooden base of the model was a plate inscribed "28th February 1948. To commemorate the comradeship of the soldiers of the British and Indian Armies, this model of The Gateway to India is presented by the soldiers of the Army of India in the Bombay Area to 1st Bn The Somerset Light Infantry (PA) on the occasion of the departure of the last British unit to serve in India - September 1754 to August 1947 - *Ultimus in Indis*".

Colonel Platt made a speech of thanks and farewell before presenting a Union flag to the local Indian Army commander. Both national anthems were played and then the Somersets slow-marched through the Gateway to the tune of "Auld Lang Syne". As Colonel Platt later wrote: "Never can an occupying army have had such a send-off".

The Colour Party and Escort boarded the waiting launches for the short run out to the troopship. It was perhaps only then that those watching and those participating realised the full

Above, the fine Indian-made silver replica of The Gateway to India presented to 1st Battalion, The Somerset Light Infantry, and now on permanent public display in the Somerset Military Museum, Taunton. It is 9 inches in height (excluding the base), and 22 inches in length. Below, the Colour Party at the moment of its departure from the quayside on the morning of 28 February 1948. The King's Colour is carried by Captain P N Pearson, the Regimental Colour by Captain M J Ryall. On the extreme left is Regimental Sergeant Major K E Bartlett. Photos: The Trustees, Somerset Military Museum.

implications of the occasion. Some of them, and their successors, were reminded of it exactly fifty years later. The Gateway of India Centrepiece took pride of place at a Regimental Dinner, held on 28 February 1998, to mark the fiftieth anniversary of the Somerset's departure from India.

As a footnote, readers unfamiliar with the history of British India may wonder why the presentation plate concludes with the Latin phrase *Ultimus in Indis*. It is a play on words, a reference to the regimental motto of The Dorsetshire Regiment. As the 39th Regiment of Foot, the Dorsets had gone out to India in 1754 and they later incorporated the words *Primus in Indis* into their crest.

While it is true that the 39th was the first British Army *infantry* unit to reach India, it was preceded six years earlier by Goodyer's Company, Royal Artillery. The task of reorganising and upgrading the Honourable East India Company's ramshackle local defence forces had been given to Major Stringer Lawrence. Hard pressed, he desperately needed a stiffening of trained gunners. The despatch from Woolwich of Goodyer's Company was Whitehall's response to his appeal for help. The British gunners arrived just in time to take part in one of his battles with the French, the Siege of Pondicherry. It was fought in August of 1748, almost exactly two hundred years before the Somersets sailed away from Bombay.

The China Challenge Cup

We have looked, in the preceding pages and chapters, at many strange and wonderful objects. Some of them are almost heroic in their design, size and weight. We come now to the largest of them all - the China Challenge Cup. It is a shooting trophy, and the name by which it is known is explained by its oriental provenance.

Major Frederick Brine, of the Hong Kong Volunteer Corps, decided that it would be a friendly and pleasing gesture to send a shooting trophy to England for annual competition amongst the Volunteer units of the United Kingdom. He contacted his fellow commanding officers of the Shanghai Volunteer Corps, Edward Webb and Robert Antrobus, and they agreed to join with him in raising the necessary funds. The European grip on commerce in the region, particularly the trade in opium, had tightened greatly in the wake of the Anglo-French punitive expeditions between 1856 and 1863, and there was money aplenty for lavish gestures of this kind. The Cantonese master silversmith Lee Ching was commissioned to design and make the cup, and he was instructed to work to a budget of six thousand pounds. It was a huge sum of money, and he responded in kind.

Lee Wing and his craftsmen needed many months to make the cup, and it was not yet finished when The China Challenge Cup competition was shot, for the first time, in 1865. Ten Volunteer marksmen from each county met under National Rifle Association auspices at Wimbledon, firing five shots each at 200 and 500 yards. The winning team returned in triumph to their home county of Somerset, but it was not until the following year that the tangible evidence of their victory was delivered to Wentworth, the ancestral home of Earl Fitzwilliam, Somerset's Lord Lieutenant.

Even the Victorian nobility, accustomed as they were to ostentation, must have been impressed. The cup, for which Territorial Army soldiers still compete each year at Bisley, weighs more than 2000 ounces (52.08 kilograms). It stands four and half

Bisley, 1962. The winning China Challenge Cup team that year came from the Territorial Army and was drawn, with one exception, from the membership of 123 Field Engineer Regiment, an element of the 42nd (Lancashire) Division (TA). The victors were (standing, left to right) Lance Corporal M Whelan, Lieutenant J O Kennedy RE, Sergeant J Brogden, Sergeant A Hebron, Sapper A H Goring, and (seated, left to right) Lance Bombardier J E Crocker of the 5th Bn, The King's (Liverpool) Regiment, Major F R G Rose RE, Captain A C R Brasher RE, and Corporal J Edge. They competed with the infantry weapons familiar to every soldier who served in the second world war and the 1950's, the .303 No4 Lee-Enfield rifle and the .303 Bren light machine gun. Photo: Gale & Polden, and Mr Jack Brogden.

African colonial forces did not possess silver as magnificent as the China Cup, but they did have many fine Mess, regimental and inter-unit competition pieces. This was the shooting team of the 4th (Uganda) Battalion, The King's African Rifles, shortly after its return from the East Africa Command Rifle Meet held in Nairobi, 1958. Competing against fourteen other battalions (eight British Army, six East African), they made a clean sweep of the trophies displayed in this picture. Seated, left to right, are Captain Ian Graham of Claverhouse, Major Adrian Rouse, Major John Dent, Lieutenant Colonel John Peddie MC, Captain A J "Sandy" Ward, and the battalion armourer, Sergeant Clare (REME). The figure standing on the extreme left is Company Sergeant Major Idi Amin (later to gain infamy as dictator of his unfortunate country).
Photo: Mr Alastair Ward.

feet in height, and is two and a half feet wide at its widest point. It is reputed to hold sixty-four pints of Champagne.

It was brought from Hong Kong to England in a ship of the Peninsular & Oriental Steam Navigation Company. As a goodwill gesture to the Volunteers, the Directors of P&O made no charge for its transport. Her Majesty's Customs took a less kindly view. They impounded the cup pending payment of one hundred and twenty-five pounds in import duty. The National Rifle Association invoked powerful friends in Westminster to convince the Customs people that, because it was a competition trophy, not intended for private use or resale, the charge could be waived.

There is an interesting element in the design of this piece. It incorporates several depictions of five-clawed dragons. Traditionally a symbol of power exclusive to the Emperors of China, any improper portrayal of the beast was an offence punishable by death. The story circulated in English shooting circles that Lee Ching had been beheaded for having breached the rule. It was not until 1896, thirty years later, that the story was quashed. A knowledgeable visitor from China assured the NRA that, while the five-clawed dragon had indeed been protected stringently by Imperial law until the early years of the 18th century, the restriction was later relaxed. Lee Wing lived for many years, continuing to craft beautiful silver and enjoying his fame.

The China Cup is an exceptional piece, but cups and shields of conventional design and quality are still the focus of shooting competitions of every kind.

The Caterpillar Club Lapel Pin

After the enormous China Challenge Cup, the contrast provided by the next entry could not be sharper. With a length of only three-quarters of an inch (20 millimetres), it is indeed tiny. The object in question is the lapel pin of the Caterpillar Club, the unique and exclusive fellowship sponsored in 1922 by the American aviator, Leslie Leroy Irvin. His full story is told in the book *Sky High Irvin*, by Peter Hearn.

In 1919, at McCook Airfield, he gave his first demonstration to the American public and Press that it is possible to fall freely through the air without losing consciousness, to open a parachute manually, and to make a safe descent. A few months later he teamed up with a silk garment manufacturer, George Waite. They formed the Irvin Air Chute Company and began making safety parachutes for customers in America and overseas. The business expanded rapidly, and a subsidiary was established in England. Owing to a spelling error in the legal documents, the new company was mistakenly registered as Irving Air Chute of Great Britain Limited. The terminal "g" was retained until the company was restructured, in the 1960s.

The first aviators to use Irvin parachutes to save their lives, in 1922, were Lieutenants Harris and Tyndall, of the US Army Air Corps. Irvin was an astute businessman, and he exploited the attendant publicity to form the Caterpillar Club. There were two reasons for its name - the parachutes of that period were made from silk (woven by the silkworm but referred to by Irvin as a caterpillar), while the silkworm (caterpillar) spins a silken thread when it needs to descend gently to the ground. In combination, these facts gave the Club its motto, "Life depends on a silken thread".

The Club is still thriving. To qualify for membership, the applicant needs to have saved his or her life by using an Irvin-designed or manufactured parachute when jumping from an aircraft in an emergency. Membership is, and always has been, open to civilians and service personnel of all nationalities. Upon being accepted, the new member is presented with a gold pin in the shape of a caterpillar, made in 9 ct gold with two ruby-coloured glass eyes, and engraved on the back with his or her name (and, for servicemen, rank).

Harris and Tyndall were the first recipients. Membership increased steadily throughout the 1920s and 1930s and, by the outbreak of WWII, more than 4000 people owed their lives to

commenced their massive bombardment of North West Europe. Most of the bombers that went down took their crews with them, but nearly twenty percent of the Allied airmen managed to jump before their aircraft exploded, broke up, or hit the ground. At the peak, the Irvin company was receiving each day, through the International Red Cross, up to one hundred and fifty cards and letters from aircrew who had become prisoners of war. Just a few are enough to capture their gratitude and the spirit of the period.

"Dear Sir, will you please enrol me as a Member of the Caterpillar Club. I baled out over Holland on August 15th from a blazing kite and made a wizard landing".

"God bless you, Brother Leslie, on behalf of my wife and children, as yet unknown".

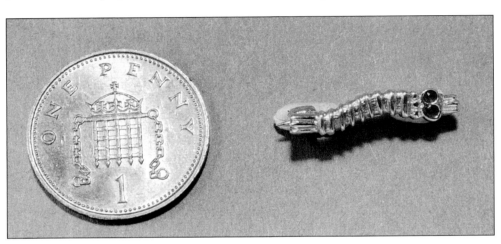

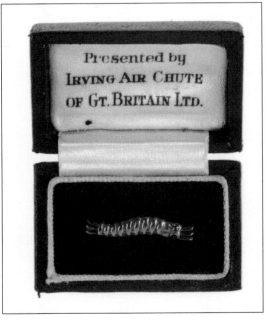

In its original box of issue is the Caterpillar Club lapel pin given to Pilot Officer Saunders following his dramatic escape from a stricken Spitfire during the Battle of Britain. More than 100,000 of these pins have been sent by the Irving (Irvin) company to aviators who owe their lives to its parachutes. Being so small and inconspicuous, it is probable that a great many have been lost, or passed later into the hands of people who did not recognise their significance. Photos: Sotheby's, and Irving Aerospace.

Irvin parachutes. They included some of the most illustrious names in aviation history. Colonel Charles Lindbergh, the first trans-Atlantic soloist, jumped four times in two years. John Cunningham and Geoffrey de Havilland abandoned their Moth Minor when it went out of control in April 1939. Ernst Udet, the WWI fighter ace and pioneer of the Luftwaffe's Stuka dive-bombing technique, parted company with his Curtiss Hawk when, during a test flight over Berlin in 1934, the tailplane broke off. Letters of application from these and other famous aviators form part of the priceless Irvin records at Letchworth.

The archive expanded hugely during WWII, especially after the RAF's Bomber Command and the US Army Air Corps

"Dear Leslie, I'd like to thank you for the sweetest moment in all my life, when my parachute opened and I realised I was not going to die. Your 'chutes are so good I am going to name my son (when I have one) Irvin as it was due to one in particular that I am alive enough to woo, marry, and get me a son".

The number of people who have used an Irvin parachute to save their lives, baling out from an aircraft which they had no intention of abandoning when it first took to the air, is today well in excess of one hundred thousand.

The author's interest in the Lelsie L Irvin story was triggered by the discovery, at an antiques fair, of one of these Caterpillar Club pins in a tray of cheap second-hand jewellery.

Still (pleasingly) in its original presentation box, it was engraved on the reverse *P/O C H Saunders*. As remarked elsewhere in this book, the wording engraved on any item of military, naval and aviation silver rarely explains itself at first glance. Only time and research will tell whether it has an interesting provenance.

A great number of Caterpillar Club pins were given to aviators who left their aircraft under fairly unremarkable circumstances. For example, a pin might have been claimed by a WWII tail gunner who jumped when his Wellington suffered an engine fire during a routine training flight over Scotland. It was daylight, the weather was good, he had plenty of time to obey his pilot's instructions, and he floated down into the waiting arms of a sympathetic crofter. On the other hand, a Lancaster pilot might have been attacked by a night fighter over Berlin, had his aircraft badly damaged, told his crew to jump, then single-handedly nursed his aircraft back as far as the Belgian coast before himself "taking to the silk". Evading capture, he was picked up by the resistance movement and, six months later, made his way back to England. Clearly, the second of these two pins is a great deal more interesting than the first because the circumstances (invented to demonstrate a point, but in no way untypical) were so much more dramatic.

In recent years, two authors have compiled books which are based upon the company's letter archive. They are *Into the Silk*, by Ian Mackersey, and *The Silken Canopy*, by John Lucas. They are an exciting record of sometimes terrifying events which resulted in awards of the Irvin company's pin.

All of which brings us to Pilot Officer C H Saunders. Who was he, and why and when did he apply for membership of the Caterpillar Club? In this instance, the company was able to confirm that Caterpillar Club pins and membership cards were sent, simultaneously, in December 1940, to Saunders and to his friend, Pilot Officer Bill Watling. Spitfire pilots, both had been shot down on 9 September while operating from RAF Biggin Hill with 92 Squadron. With so much published information available regarding that period, the task of researching the story was then very simple. Of particular relevance is *Men of the Battle of Britain*, by Kenneth G Wynn.

Cecil Henry Saunders joined the Royal Air Force with a Short Service commission in August 1939. At the relatively advanced age of twenty-eight, he learned to fly at the Civil Training School, Derby, and at 14 Fighter Training School, Kinloss. Posted in April 1940 to RAF Croydon, he began flying the Spitfire Mark I with 92 Squadron. It was in the process of converting from the twin-engined Blenheim Mark If, and did not become operational with its new aircraft until 9 May. Its first sortie over the French coast came two weeks later, a patrol which resulted in the shooting down of six Bf 109s.

After operating successively from Northolt and Hornchurch (flying sorties over the Dunkirk evacuation beaches and the English Channel), 92 Squadron moved to RAF Pembrey, South Wales, for a rest period and to provide air cover for shipping in the Bristol Channel. The Luftwaffe was becoming active in the area and, on 4 July, Pilot Officer Saunders destroyed a He 111 bomber, claimed a second as probably destroyed, and shared in the destruction of a third. For the rest, the summer passed quietly.

All of that changed in September. The Battle of Britain was approaching its climax, with the Luftwaffe sending mass formations of bombers and fighters against London and the key RAF stations in Kent, Sussex and Hampshire. On 9 September, 92 Squadron flew from South Wales to RAF Biggin Hill and was immediately ordered into the cauldron of the skies over South East England. In the afternoon, they tangled with a swarm of Bf 109s approaching their station at high altitude. Saunders' aircraft was hit, and he started to spiral down from 24,000 feet. When it descended to 15,000 feet, still not responding to the controls, he decided that it was time to go. He came down on Romney Marsh and was taken to the RAMC hospital at Brooklands for an operation to remove shrapnel from his legs. His Spitfire, L 1077, crashed at Midley, near Rye.

Shot down in the same engagement was Pilot Officer W C Watling. A Channel Islander, from St Jacques, Guernsey, he had entered the service as a cadet at RAF Cranwell in August 1939. Completing the shortened wartime course, he received a Permanent Commission and was posted directly to 92 Squadron, at Pembrey, in July 1940. He claimed his first success with the shared destruction of a Ju 88 bomber on 13 August.

Like Saunders, his first major battle was the high altitude fight over Biggin Hill on 9 September. His Spitfire, P 9372, was hit and set on fire at 24,000 feet. Watling baled out as quickly as he could, but not before being badly burned on his face and hands. Within weeks he rejoined the squadron and claimed a Bf 109 as probably destroyed on 2 November (and another, damaged, on 1 December). It was at this time that Cecil Saunders sent his letter to the Irvin company. It was written on their joint behalf, so it may be assumed that Watling was still having difficulty with his partially healed hands.

The applications were accepted and the two pins despatched to Biggin Hill in late December. Watling was still with 92 Squadron when, a few weeks later, on 7 February 1941, he was shot down and killed during a combat over Kent. He was buried, age twenty, in St Mary Cray Cemetery, Orpington.

Cecil Saunders survived the war. He retired in 1958 as a Wing Commander, DFC, having scored further victories with 92 Squadron in October and November 1940, and later moving to the Middle East where he commanded 154 Squadron (operating with Spitfires from bases in Corsica and Southern Italy).

The Caterpillar pin may be very small, but it represents a vast range of human experiences. The Club continues to receive, on average, between 150 and 200 applications each year. Some are from former aviators whose original pins have been lost or damaged. The majority are from serving aircrew who, like tens of thousands before them, owe their lives to Leslie Irvin and his 1922 invention.

The Sabre Trophy

The next item also is a part of the history of 92 Squadron. It had been formed in 1917 as a Canadian unit and operated over the Western Front in the fighter and ground attack role. Disbanded after the war, it was reformed in October 1939. During the Battle of Britain it claimed 127 enemy aircraft destroyed. By 1945, it was the top-scoring RAF fighter squadron, with 317 victories to its credit. Amongst its most successful members was the legendary post-war test pilot, Squadron Leader Neville Duke DSO, OBE, DFC, AFC.

Between January 1954 and early 1956, 92 Squadron was one of twelve equipped with the North American Sabre F1 and F4 (built under licence in Canada).This was an aircraft which had shown its worth during the air war over Korea, and could fly higher, faster and further than the RAF's other fighter aircraft of that period. The decision to purchase the American design was influenced by the need for a high performance interceptor pending the arrival in squadron service of the greatly superior English Electric Lightning.

In April 1956, the Sabres of 92 Squadron were replaced by

The Canadair presentation scale model, mounted on a sheathed sabre. No hallmarks are recorded, and it is possible that this is one of several cast from the same mould by a Canadian silversmith. Photo: Air Commodore G R Pitchfork MBE.

the Hawker Hunter F4. It was at this time that the technical representative of Canadair, contractors for North American, presented the model illustrated here. The wording on the base states: "Presented to No 92 Squadron, Royal Air Force, by Gordon Eldridge, Canadair technical representative, to commemorate the last Sabre jet squadron in service with Fighter Command".

The Squadron came to public prominence when, in 1961, it became the official RAF aerobatic display team, "The Blue Diamonds". After service in Germany, it was disbanded in the early 1990s. The silver trophy was last reported at the Joint Services Command & Staff College, Bracknell.

The Kinkead Trophy, Royal Air Force College Cranwell

It has been difficult to assemble any comprehensive information concerning the silver of the Royal Air Force. From small beginnings in 1912, followed by its enormous expansion during WWI as the Royal Flying Corps, the RAF was formalised as a completely separate service on 1 April 1918. Its opportunities for acquiring silver were limited by the economic climate of the 1920s and 1930s, and by the dispersion of its squadrons on "policing" duties in the Middle East and on the North West Frontier of India. Only the fashionable part-time Royal Auxiliary Air Force squadrons had the sort of wealthy membership which could sponsor decorative silver of significant quality, but information concerning that silver has proved elusive.

Probably the most interesting items are those relating to the RAF's involvement, between the wars, in various speed, endurance and altitude attempts. The following example is illustrative of the whole category.

It is a silver centrepiece consisting of four sections, the topmost being a replica of the Supermarine S5 floatplane. With a wingspan of ten inches, it is mounted upon a circular plinth supported by four stylised dolphins. Below is the globe, fixed to the pedestal by four "wings of the winds of the earth". The whole is mounted, in turn, upon a shaped ebonised wood pedestal bearing inscribed plates on each of its four sides. The overall height is 18 inches. It bears marks for the Goldsmiths & Silversmiths Company, London 1929, and in 1931 was valued at eighty-five pounds.

When Orville and Wilbur Wright made their first powered flight in 1903, at Kitty Hawk, North Carolina, they opened a new age. From that day forward, man has never ceased striving to fly higher, faster and further. Aviation achieved its greatest advances under the pressures of the two world conflicts, but early progress was stimulated also by a variety of peacetime challenges and competitions. The most famous was the series of annual international Schneider Trophy competitions, initiated in 1913.

Dominated at first by France, it was nearly won outright after WWI by the Italians. The nation which could achieve three wins in five years would retain the Trophy in perpetuity. Italy was overtaken in 1923 by a well-prepared American military team, flying the biplane Curtiss racer. The Italians fought back in 1925 with a completely new monoplane design by Macchi and Fiat. Not until 1926 did the Royal Air Force produce a winning combination, at Venice, so bringing the venue for the competition back to England for the first time in six years.

In that following year, 1927, the RAF team aircraft were fitted with Rolls Royce engines, and they won again. One of the victorious pilots was Flight Lieutenant Samuel Marcus Kinkead DSO DSC and bar, DFC and bar. A South African, credited with more than forty "kills" while a fighter pilot over the Western Front and Russia, he was retained as a member of the next (1928) team.

The Kinkead Trophy, commemorating a Royal Air Force officer killed in 1928 while practicing for the world high-speed record. The Trophy is held in the Daedalus Mess, RAF College Cranwell. Photo: Cranwell, and Air Commodore G R Pitchfork MBE.

Trial flights began in February and early March from the seaplane base at Calshot, Southampton Water. The target speed was 300 miles per hour, a figure almost achieved a few months earlier by the Italian aviator, Mario de Bernardi.

On the afternoon of 12 March, Kinkead took off from Calshot in a specially tuned S5 floatplane. Poor weather had prevented any high speed flights for several days. Conditions were still not good, but there was an urgent need to demonstrate the capabilities of the latest configuration. The team was convinced that Kinkead could beat the 300 mph barrier, and probably by a wide margin.

It was late in the day by the time he began his high-speed run, and mist had formed over the still water. There was no horizon, making it virtually impossible for the pilot to assess his altitude. The aircraft hit the sea and he was killed instantly.

In the following year, his family and friends presented to Cranwell the trophy described here. He had been an instructor at the College between 1920 and 1924, and it was their wish to perpetuate his memory in this way. One of the plates on the pedestal is inscribed "Presented to the Cadets of the Royal Air Force College Cranwell in memory of the late Flight Lieutenant S M Kinkead DSO DSC DFC, to be held successively by the

Squadron producing the R M Groves Memorial Flying Prize Winner". The terms of eligibility for receiving the award have changed over the years but, in essence, it recognises excellence of performance in the air and in the classroom.

The names of the young winners, each July and December, are inscribed on silver plates and they cover the period from July 1929 to December 1955. Many rose to high rank, were highly decorated and, in some cases, became legends. Detailed research of their engraved names would generate enough material for a book, indeed several books.

The full story of the Schneider Trophy races held in the

Objects made in silver were given to aviators who took part in endurance and long distance flights, opening new air routes in the years between the two world wars. The Kingsford-Smith Trophy (above) perpetuates the name of a pilot who, with his navigator, C T P Ulm, made a number of pioneerng flights around the Pacific rim in the 1920s and early 1930s. Their aircraft was "Southern Cross", a Fokker tri-motor monoplane. On 11 September 1928, they made the first crossing of the Tasman Sea. In 1934, the Royal Aero Club organised a race from England to Australia. This cigarette box (below) was given to one of the participants, Flight Lieutenant A F Franks, RAF. Photos: RNZAF, Mr H E Chamberlain, and Sotheby's.

Another piece with a strong aviation resonance is the King's Cup trophy commissioned in 1933 by the Royal Aero Club. The winner of the air race that year was Captain Geoffrey de Havilland, and he received it from the hands of HM King George VI. Photo: Sotheby's, London.

years following the 1928 tragedy is well recorded in print and on film. The Royal Air Force's later successes were due in part to the skills and courage of its pilots, but mainly to three civilians. One was the legendary R J Mitchell, chief designer for Supermarine Aviation. His ideas created the RAF's Schneider Trophy competition aircraft from 1922 to 1931. They evolved in the mid-1930s as the Spitfire. The second was Sir Henry Royce. He ensured that his company was closely associated with the work of Mitchell and Supermarine, a collaboration which produced the Rolls Royce Merlin, greatest of all WWII aero engines. The third, by contrast, was the vivacious and slightly eccentric philanthropist, Dame Fanny Houston. When she heard that the Air Ministry lacked the funds to finance the RAF's 1931 team, she donated one hundred thousand pounds from her personal fortune to ensure that Great Britain should not fall behind the other nations. Without her wealth and patriotism, and without the genius of Reginald Mitchell and Henry Royce, the Battle of Britain might have had a different outcome.

Chapter Nine

Collecting Military Silver

This chapter is written specifically for those readers who previously have never sought to acquire items of military silver but, possibly encouraged by what they have read so far, may be thinking of becoming active collectors.

The sort of monumental treasures illustrated in earlier parts of this book are at the heart of every great Mess collection. They are very unlikely ever to pass into private ownership, but this should not be a deterrent to acquiring examples of a lesser order.

The first and most obvious question must be - where does the private individual find these things? How can they (legitimately) be obtained?

There is no simple answer. Silver is unlike every other strand in the story of the nation's military heritage because it is the *only* one which has so far failed to attract any substantial interest outside the boundaries of the armed forces themselves. There are clubs and societies, and commercially published magazines, which cater for people involved in collecting *everything* from military buttons and cap badges through to uniforms and vintage armoured fighting vehicles. The hobby of collecting campaign and gallantry medals commenced a century ago and has since developed into a multi-million pound business. People are happy to spend very considerable sums when seeking to add to their collections of classic firearms and edged weapons. Out-of-print reference books, particularly regimental histories, command ever higher prices as more and more dedicated enthusiasts seek to add them to their own private libraries.

All of these specialised collecting activities are thriving. They bring a great deal of pleasure to the tens of thousands of individuals who buy, and they sustain the hundreds of businesses which sell. What is generally known as "militaria" enjoys a well-established and clearly recognisable infrastructure, and the entire edifice rests upon a network of auctioneers and dealers who earn their livings by finding the objects which the collecting fraternity considers desirable.

At the present time there are no dealers specialising in military silver. There are no dedicated sales catalogues which the aspiring collector can study. Until now, there has not been a single printed source of reference. It is not surprising, therefore, that members of the silver dealing trade - when asked if they have any "military silver" for sale - will invariably reply, "sorry, I never touch the stuff, there's no demand". It is for this reason, as described in the Author's Introduction, that so much interesting or even historically important silver has been scrapped or buffed smooth and recycled.

Dealers deal to make money. They do so by seeking to satisfy the *existing* demands of their customers, not by attempting to create new fields of collecting. They quite certainly cannot be expected to practice an idealistic "duty of care". Further, because the British have not been committed to a major war since 1945, comparatively few of them have been required to don a uniform. Therefore, and as a sweeping generalisation, there is within the dealing profession no wide understanding of military and naval life.

It is evident that many thousands of pieces have already been lost, but this does not mean that it is too late to start collecting. Agreed, this is not the easiest of militaria fields in which to make a cold start, but the rewards more than compensate the effort involved. The thrill of the chase is, after all, a large part of the pleasure in acquiring antiques of any kind.

The author can do no better than describe how he himself found a way of building a collection. It may not be a route which everyone would find to their liking, but it has been agreeably successful and instructive. Others will find their own ways forward.

The first step, beginning in 1995, was to start visiting local antique fairs, *bric-a-brac* shops and car boot sales. The second was to make contact with local auction houses, asking for prior notice of any likely Lots. The third was to seek out and establish a friendly working relationship with people engaged in the various branches of the silver trade - auctioneers, dealers, retailers, valuers and restorers.

In general terms, antique and *bric-a-brac* shops have proven to be the least productive source. Contact with local auction houses has from time to time been fruitful, most often on those occasions when they have been instructed by executors to clear all the contents from a house formerly owned by a retired officer. On a rising scale of productivity, medium- and large-sized antiques fairs are consistently good venues for the type of object sought. Two very good pieces were purchased at London (general catalogue) auctions conducted by Bonhams and by Sothebys. By far the most successful source, however, has been direct contact with professional silver dealers who earn their livings by travelling constantly between one fair and another, or one auction and another, and who therefore each week view hundreds of pieces of silver of every kind. They have become good friends. They quickly understood what was needed, and now bid for items which previously they would have disregarded (or "avoided like the plague", as one of them expressed it).

Military silver does not appear on the market in a constant even flow. That is not in the nature of things. Even during the lean periods, however, the professionals have been unfailingly generous with their knowledge of silver in general, guiding this neophyte into their own specialised world.

Asking people to "scout" for you means that you are morally obliged to take everything they have bought on your behalf. In any other collecting field, where people like to pick and choose, this would be a dismaying prospect. With silver it is not a problem because it is only *after* the engraved wording has been investigated in depth that the object's historical significance or desirability (in the military collecting context) becomes apparent. Even though the piece may be a run-of-the-mill tankard or salver or cup, and even though its presentation wording may seem uninspiring, time and effort spent on research may reveal an exciting story. By the same token, of course, an attractive and apparently very promising piece may fail to reveal a provenance of any profound interest. Things are rarely what they seem to be and this, perhaps, is the true fascination of military silver. It is often a gamble, a lucky dip.

At the end of the day, even if an object proves to possess little or no historical merit, it still has value in more obvious ways - its weight in silver, its quality of craftsmanship, or its utility as an item of decorative or practical metal-ware (tankards, salvers, vases, *epergnes*, rose bowls, boxes, and so forth, being common examples).

The following pages describe some of the pieces which the author has been able to acquire over a period of little more than four years. There are (currently) one hundred and sixty such objects in the collection, ranging from the mundane to the extraordinary, and they are listed here for three reasons - to illustrate the types of military silver which appear on the open market, to show that they are still available in sufficient numbers to justify the effort of seeking them out, and to demonstrate their research potential. The latter is a theme which has been emphasised repeatedly in the preceding chapters.

The prices paid for each piece are not recorded because there would be no purpose in so doing. This collection has been acquired by the author, piece-meal, from a variety of sources in rural south west England at a time when he has been the only person buying such artefacts. There has been no competition. Indeed, several items were ear-marked for the melting pot or the buffing machine when, at the last moment, they were rescued by kindly dealers willing to indulge the obscure and eccentric tastes of this lonely crusader.

It may be helpful to state that the lowest price paid was fifty pence, the highest fifteen hundred pounds. It was only in the third year of collecting that sufficient courage and understanding of the subject had been acquired to permit such a major outlay. At the outset, anything more than a hundred pounds was considered brave. Overall, and ignoring the single recent purchase at fifteen hundred pounds, the average cost of these items has been approximately sixty pounds. By comparison with most established areas of militaria collecting, this is modest.

Excluding those pieces which by virtue of their age qualify as "antiques", a primary factor in determining a price for each object has been its weight. The current (1999) scrap value of Sterling silver is no more than £3.00 per ounce, so any piece weighing (say) ten ounces must be worth £30.00 as a minimum. This simple and rather brutal calculation provides a benchmark by which to commence a calculation of value.

Other and much more compelling factors forming the equation are condition, artistic merit, the fame or reputation of the maker, the wording of the inscription, the quality of the engraving, and competition from other categories of collector. The latter applies to vestas, inkstands, claret jugs, casters, condiment sets, and similar specialised areas of interest. Such things have for long been regarded as collectable in their own right, hence those who seek them may in certain instances overcome their dislike of "military writing" (or, when deciding how much to pay, allow for the cost of having it removed).

In general, the military silver described in this chapter was made in the 20th century and is, therefore, of minimal interest to many collectors of silver *per se*. For them, antiquity can be a major factor in determining desirability and value. To someone like the author, it is irrelevant.

The preceding comments must be qualified by two considerations. There will always be a gap, sometimes a large one, between "provincial price" and "London price". The implications of these terms are best learned by experience. Then, secondly, publication of this book may stir interest and

awareness to a higher degree than has existed in the past. If that proves to be the case, the law of supply and demand will come into play.

It will be seen that not all the items in the collection are Sterling silver. Some were made by silversmiths in China, India, Egypt, and in other countries where the British have at one time or another maintained a military presence. Silver collectors in general tend to steer away from non-Sterling pieces on the grounds that the degree of purity is unknown or questionable. This is understandable, but it does ignore the fact that many of those smiths worked in silver of a purity equal to the .925 Sterling standard.

It will be seen also that the list includes items which were not even made in silver. Some are pewter, many are electro-plate. The diversity of metals reflects the author's personal interest in researching the stories attaching to them rather than the shape, form or quality of the objects themselves. While such a liberal interpretation of the term "military silver" will not appeal to everyone, these entries do at least serve to demonstrate the range of material to be found on the open market.

Tankards (often described as mugs) are by far the most frequently encountered examples of the *genre*, and they provide an ideal point of entry for anyone who is starting to feel his or her way into the hobby. They cost comparatively little, and usually carry sufficient detail in their engraved presentation wording for a start to be made on research. Some are of quart capacity, some of half-pint, but the majority are pint-sized. They are made in three metals - pewter, electro-plate and silver. The commonest are modern pewter, containing a high percentage of tin and therefore lacking the satisfying substance and warmth associated with silver. The quality of manufacture is frequently disappointing. Old pewter, made in the 19th century, is much more solid and should have a pleasing patina of oxidation.

Pint tankard with lid, pewter, made by James Dixon & Sons, engraved with the crest of the School of Musketry, Hythe, *June 1864, Best Shot No 4 Section, Lieut C Pigou, 104th Regiment.* Later promoted Lieutenant Colonel, Clement Pigou served throughout the Indian Mutiny with the 3rd Bengal European Regiment. His medal appeared at auction in London in 1988.

Quart tankard with lid, pewter, by James Dixon & Sons, retailed by Powell, Oxford, engraved with the Prince of Wales's plumes, and crossed rifles, *Brasenose Company, Scratch Shooting, O.U.V.R. May 1867. Corpl R H Rodgers, Privt A Macmillan, Privt W B Brown, Privt G T Popkin.* They were undergraduates serving with the Oxford University Volunteer Rifles. None of them became professional soldiers.

Pint tankard, electro-plate, Elkington & Company, *Presented by Lieut Twogood of the Duke of Manchester's Light Horse, Shot for by Seventeen Members of the St Neot's Detachment of the 1st Hunts RV and Won by Sergeant Plum, June 25th 1867.* This is another typical prize for a Rifle Volunteers shooting competition.

Pint tankard, pewter, *James Ainslie Johnston, The Royal Naval Armoured Car Old Boys Association, 1919-1938.* It seems to have been presented to him at the time of his retirement as Honorary Secretary.

Half-pint tankard, electro-plate, made by Mappin & Webb, with the crest of The Devonshire Regiment, and *Sergt J Davey, 29.5.05.* John Davey came from Teignmouth, Devon. He served in the Boer War as a Corporal with his regiment's 2nd Battalion and in WWI with its 8th Battalion. He was killed in action on the Western Front on 8 December 1915.

Half-pint tankard identical to the above, both being Sergeants' Mess tankards presumably presented on promotion, engraved *Sergt W Woolacott, 24.6.02.* He and Sergeant Davey must have known each other well. He too was killed in action, on 18 December 1914.

Half-pint tankard, electro-plate, engraved with the crest of the Staffordshire Regiment, *80th S.M. 1908, Best Score 500 yds.*

Pint tankard, good quality pewter, made by Manor. Engraved with the crest of The Durham Light Infantry, and *Capt H E B Daniell 1914 - Hooge 1915.* An Officers' Mess tankard, one of a batch ordered for each member (as indicated by the numeral "12" engraved on the handle).

Half-pint tankard, electro-plate, made by Unity. Engraved with the crest of The Devonshire Regiment, *5th Battalion, Lieut Col R Bastard DSO.* He served in the Boer War and WWI, and was twice admitted to the Distinguished Service Order.

Two matching half-pint tankards, electro-plate, named to the Hampshire (Fortress) Royal Engineers. The first engraved *R Emmett T.D., Surgeon Lieut 24.4.97, Surgeon Capt 23.4.00, Major R.A.M.C. 23.10.08, Lt Col 1916, retired 15.19,* the second engraved *R H Emmett T.D., 2nd Lt 8.8.14, Lieut 22.2.15, Capt 30.3.24, Major 14.4.30, Bt Lt Col 1.1.38, retired 15.8.38, Hon Col 1947-53.* Presumably they were father and son.

Pint tankard, electro-plate, *Past Officers Cups, 1924, Winners, "D" Coy, Sergt C H Charlesworth.* Charles Harry Charlesworth enlisted as a Private in the Royal Army Medical Corps in July 1915 and was invalided out of the service only six months later. It is not known with which unit he was serving when, eight years later, he won this cup.

Pint tankard, hammered-finish pewter, *1939, L/C B Bradford, Presented by "A" Coy, 8th Devons.*

Pint tankard, electro-plate, engraved *Sgt/Pilot F E Denston (754398), 19(F) Squadron Duxford, 1940-41.* It is the Sergeants' Mess bar tankard of a Spitfire pilot of the Battle of Britain period. He has not been traced as having flown operationally in the battle. There is an anecdote which states that he fell off his motor-cycle just before the battle commenced, and did not recover until after it was over.

Pint tankard, silver, 16 ounces, made by the Goldsmiths & Silversmiths Company, London 1943. Engraved with the crest of the Royal Devon Yeomanry Artillery, and *Capt F B McGuire, from the Officers, 96th (RDY) Field Regiment, 19th March 1944.*

Pint tankard, pewter, made by Bentley and bearing his touches, finely engraved under the base *To Lieut A C Mann from No 2 Ptn A Coy 6th Bn (Leatherhead) Surrey Home Guard.* An excellent piece of antique pewter, presumably given to him by his men at the time when the Home Guard was stood down, in 1944. It demonstrates the need to check for wording underneath an object, not simply on its sides or lid.

Pint tankard, electro-plate, engraved *Det Inspr G Crosbie-Hill, The Flying Squad, New Scotland Yard, 9.7.1956.* Presumably an "on retirement" piece, this is an unusual reminder of "the sweeney".

Pint tankard, electro-plate, part engraved, part impressed, *Presented to CQMS Furmedge F J, by WO's and Sgt's Mess, 1st Bn The Queen's Royal Regiment.*

Pint tankard, electro-plate, engraved with two police force badges (of The Sabah Police Force pre-Independence, and of the same force post-Independence), *Presented to J E Fairbairn OBE, Asst Commr of Police, 15th November 1947 to 31st August 1965. From Officers and Other Ranks of the Sabah Component, Royal Malaysia Police.* Fairbairn is reported to have been an outstanding police officer and commander. It would have been

pleasing if, after seventeen years continuous service, he could have received from his brother officers a tankard made in Sterling silver rather than EPNS.

Cigarette cases made in silver were one of the personal possessions carried by most men when smoking was commonplace. The number manufactured between the 1870s and the 1960s must have been enormous, and a great many had a "military" provenance. After WWII, the practice of transferring cigarettes from the manufacturers' packaging into a silver pocket case died away, and the cases themselves ceased to be a stylish accessory. When the price of bullion rose, thousands (probably tens of thousands) were scrapped. Even so, a great many have survived and are seen frequently at antiques fairs. It is always worthwhile to open them and to check whether there is any interesting wording engraved inside (where it is normally found). The following examples are all Sterling silver unless otherwise stated.

3 ounces, made by Hassett & Harper Limited, Birmingham 1919. Engraved within *Presented to L/Cpl J Jefford, by members of Cpl's Mess, 3rd Dragoon Gds, Sialkot, 1922.*

The cigarette case of Regimental Sergeant Major F H Young, AVC, presented in 1918. It demonstrates the skills of the engravers of that period, and the care taken even with minor pieces of this nature.

3 ounces, made by C.C., Chester 1925. Engraved within *Presented to Sgt Charlwood, by members of (the) R.A.S.C. Mess, Malta.*

3.5 ounces, made by Deakin & Francis, Birmingham, 1918. Engraved within *4th Bn, The King's Own Royal Regiment, Battalion Rifle Meeting, July 7th and 8th, 1928. Officers' individual shoot, Capt C G Lowden.*

4 ounces, made by L Feigenbaum, Birmingham, 1932. Ornately engraved on the cover *S.J.C.,* engraved within *Commissioned 3/17th Bn, London Regt, 17.6.16. Winchester 22.6.16-10.11.16. Havre 11.11.16. Hill 60 1/17th Bn London Regt, 20.11.16-21.1.17. Joined Tank Corps 4th Batt, Blangy-sur-Ternoise 22.1.17. Arras "Push" April 1917. Passchendale 24.6.17-23.10.17. Cambrai Novr 1917. The Great Retreat (5 Army)*

March 1918. Asst Adj 4th Tank Bn 4.18. The Great "Push" 8/18, 9/18, 10/18. 4th Tank Brigade 10.18.Armistice, Bretencourt, 11.11.18. 2nd Tank Group Asst E.O. 11/18. Demobilised 21.3.19. The case came from a house clearance, so it was easy to identify S.J.C. He was Captain S J Ching, and his decision to record his services in this way (thirteen years after leaving the army) enables us to follow him almost step by step during his two years and five months on the Western Front. The details are all confirmed in the unit War Diaries.

5.3 ounces, made by C.C., Chester 1917. Engraved within *To Regimental Sergt Major F H Young, from (the) officers, A.V.C., Woolwich, October 1918.* This is one of two items found with an Army Veterinary Corps connection.

4.25 ounces, made by J Gloster Limited, Birmingham 1923. Engraved *S.J.S.* on the cover, engraved within *Presented to Captain S J Smith OBE by the members of his Department, 21st May 1925* (followed by the names of five men (Messrs) and seventeen women (Misses). Captain (Quartermaster) Sydney James Smith served in WWI with the Labour Corps and with the 7th Battalion, The Norfolk Regiment.

6.2 ounces, made by H C Davis, Birmingham 1917. Engraved within *Presented to Capt H T Smith, The Lancashire Fusiliers, by officers and N.C.O.s, 1920.*

4 ounces, made by Elkington & Company, Birmingham 1910. Engraved on the front cover *F.W.C.* Engraved inside the front cover *Whirlwinds, Hurricanes, Typhoons*, then, inside the back cover, the Royal Air Force crest and *486 (N.Z.) - 137 Sqns,*

Cardington, Skegness, Cosford, Tangmere, Manston, Southend, Lympne, Colerne, Fairwood, Lympne. Despite its 1910 assay mark, this is a record of service for the period 1942-1945. An aviation enthusiast would be able to identify F.W.C. and trace his activities in detail. The year mark indicates that the owner purchased a second-hand case rather than one from a retailer's new stock.

3 ounces, made by F Howard, Birmingham 1931. Engraved within *Presented to C.S.M. W H Kelly by "B" Coy, 5th Devon Regt, 1933.*

Cigarette Boxes (and occasionally cigar boxes) were for a long time regarded as a very acceptable form of gift or presentation. A great many have been scrapped since smoking started to become unfashionable, especially the cheaper sorts or those in distressed condition. However, because they can be used for other purposes (as jewellery boxes, for example), they were not consigned to the melting pot quite so quickly as cigarette cases. The designs are usually very simple, but the overall quality of manufacture does vary greatly (mainly with regard to the gauge of metal, some boxes being much stronger and heavier than others, and with more robust hinges). All of the following examples are Sterling silver unless otherwise stated.

20 ounces, made by Joseph Rodgers & Sons Ltd, Birmingham 1898. The lid is engraved with the crest of The First East Surrey Rifles, and *Capt B Bridges, from his Brother Officers, July 17th 1906.* Bertram Bridges, a pre-war Territorial,

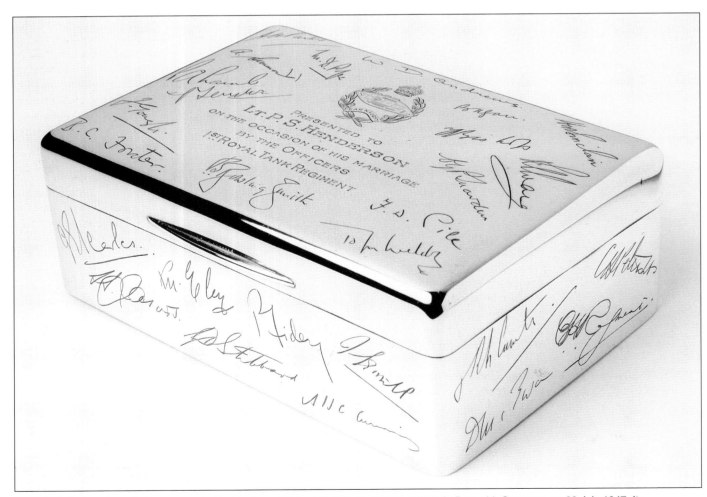

A particularly fine cigarette box, presented to Lieutenant Peter Henderson at his marriage in Detmold, Germany, on 28 July 1947. Its exceptional condition is due to him and his wife being non-smokers. He fought with 1st Royal Tank Regiment in the North West Europe campaign from February 1943, and the signatures of most of his brother officers can be decyphered by reference to the April 1947 Army List. He fell ill two months after the wedding and never returned to active service. His subsequent involvement in motor racing is described in *Tribute to Trophy,* by Rex Hays.

The beautifully decorated cigarette box presented to Field Marshal Sir John Harding. The lid is a fine example of niello work.

served in WWI in India, from January 1916, presumably as a Staff officer.

9 ounces, maker's mark illegible, Birmingham 1914. Engraved *Hon.ble Louis Johnstone, From Central Association VTC Executive Committee, Lord Desborough, General Sir O'Moore Creagh, C J Stewart, Percy A Harris, W G Everitt, 1.7.15.* These gentlemen were amongst the great and the good of their generation and, in 1914, were prime movers in establishing the London-based Volunteer Training Corps.

38 ounces, made by Charles & Richard Comyns, London 1921. Engraved *Presented to Colonel A F U Green CMG DSO on his Departure from Malta by the Members of the Malta Racing Club, 19th March 1924.* Arthur Greene had a long and interesting military career, amassing a variety of medals and decorations and retiring in the rank of Brigadier. His entry in *Who was Who, 1961-1970* includes the intriguing fact that he joined the Home Guard in 1940, became a Battalion Commander in 1941, and reverted to Private in 1943.

8 ounces, maker's mark illegible, Birmingham 1933, with retailer's mark "Page, Keen & Page, Plymouth". Engraved *From the Officers, HMS Grimsby, 1934.* This is a ship's commissioning piece. She was a 990 ton sloop, built at Devonport Dockyard and launched in 1933. When some months later she was accepted into Royal Navy service, the ceremony was attended by the Superintendent of the Dockyard, the Dockyard Admiral, and various civic dignitaries. The ship's officers paid the cost of presenting to each of the most important guests one of these boxes as a souvenir of the occasion. Under the command of Commander K J D'Arcy RN, HMS Grimsby was bombed and sunk off Tobruk on 25 May 1941.

9.2 ounces, maker's mark illegible, Birmingham 1941. Engraved *Presented to Captain W P Worden by the Officers of the 5th Devon Regt, Sept 1941.*

13 ounces, made by Walker & Hall, Sheffield 1939. Engraved *Presented to Sub Lieutenant J K Noakes RNVR, by the Officers of HMS Royal Arthur, 18.5.40.* The mention of a specific date suggests that this was probably an "on the occasion of his marriage" piece. The *Royal Arthur* was a shore training establishment.

6 ounces, made by Robert Pringle & Sons, London 1916. Engraved *Capt W J Spencer, from the Officers of the Military Hospital, Gibraltar, 1917.* This officer has so far defied all efforts to identify him.

13 ounces, made by the Goldsmiths & Silversmiths Company, London 1930. Engraved *Capt A G Ralston, From the Stewards, Simla Races, 1932.* A veterinary surgeon and keen horseman, he served in India from 1929 to 1934. He returned there in 1939 and, in WWII, was a pioneer in treating Surra, a disease of mules (an animal vital to the war in Burma). He rose to become Director, Army Veterinary and Remount Services, in which appointment in the 1950s he led the successful campaign against proposals to disband the Royal Army Veterinary Corps.

10.2 ounces, maker's mark illegible, Birmingham 1927. Engraved on the front *Presented to Capt Langford by the Bridlington and Dist L V Assn, 1936,* and his initials *V.H.E.L.* At first glance, this box holds no great interest. It was given to Valentine Langford when he retired as Secretary to a local Licenced Victuallers Association. Research then revealed that he was one of those very rare men who successively held commissions in all three services. A pre-WWI Territorial officer, he won the Military Cross in 1917 while serving with The Sherwood Foresters, transferred to the Royal Air Force in April 1918 as a Captain, then retired. In June 1940 he volunteered to take his pleasure boat to France and helped to extract the British Expeditionary Force from Dunkirk. He was granted a commission in the Royal Naval Volunteer Reserve in July 1940, back-dated to 21 June 1940. It seems that he continued to command small craft throughout WWII.

25 ounces, made by Richard & Company (in India, no other marks), engraved *Presented to Major H K Rich RA by the Officers, WOs, NCOs and Men of 201st HAA Battery RA, as a Token of their Esteem and Appreciation of his Five Years Command, India Nov 1944.*

12 ounces, made the Goldsmiths & Silversmiths Company, London 1949. Engraved with the crest of The East Yorkshire Regiment, and *Major A L R H Thresher, from Brother Officers, 1st Bn, on the Occasion of his Marriage.*

21.2 ounces, made by Walker & Hall, Sheffield, 1935.

Engraved *Capt F W Mace CBE RNR (Retd), MD & HB, 1902-1937.* With six facsimile signatures of his fellow members of the Mersey Docks and Harbour Board.

8.2 ounces, three marks, identified as a local silversmith in Alexandria, Egypt, *circa* 1945, engraved on the base, *Lt Col R L Moss RA (acting Lt QM), from "Q" Staff, 381 POW Camp.* He was commissioned into the 4th Queen's (Royal West Surrey) Regiment in December 1914, and seems to have spent all of WWI in India. He surfaces again in 1940 as a Staff Officer, most probably with the BEF in France, and then went to the Middle East. He served on the administration of a camp, in Egypt, holding German or Italian prisoners of war.

12 ounces, maker's mark illegible, Birmingham 1946. Engraved *Presented to Air Commodore C L Falconer CBE by his Brother Officers on his Marriage, 1st Jan 1947. Air Headquarters and 16 Works Area, RAF Northern Ireland.* A pilot, he flew with 14 Squadron in Palestine and Jordan in the 1920s. His WWII services are not known, but his age and seniority probably kept him away from operational flying.

19 ounces, made by The Inman Manufacturing Company, Birmingham, 1945, *Presented to Lt (E) J.S. Northcott R.N. on the occasion of his marriage, by Officers of HMS Gambia, 3-4-48.* The (E) indicates that he was an officer of the navy's Engineer Branch.

22 ounces, stamped on the base "Sterling Thainakon Thailand", very finely decorated in the niello technique and incorporating the allegorical figure of a Chinthe (the mythical figure which guards Buddhist temples). Engraved *To Field Marshal Sir John Harding, a Token of Remembrance of the First Meeting of SEATO in Bangkok, Thailand. Field Marshal P Pibilronggur, President of the Council of Ministers. Government Residence, Bangkok, February 25, B.E. 2498 (1955).* One of the most famous fighting soldiers of his generation, John Harding was a Grammar School boy whose first job was bank clerk. He joined The Finsbury Rifles before WWI as a ranker and subsequently, in 1952, became Chief of the Imperial General Staff. It was in this capacity that he attended the inaugural meeting of the South East Asia Treaty Organisation in 1955. The B.E. 2498 cypher is from the Buddhist calendar, dated from the time of Buddha's enlightenment.

Smoker's Paraphernalia extends beyond cigarette cases and cigarette boxes. Earlier pages in this book carry details of several Mess cigar lighters, usually very ornate and of high value. At the other end of the scale are the following pieces.

Vesta case, 1.5 ounces, no hallmarks but seemingly of good quality silver, *Tug of War, 1907, Won by Woodstock Squadron, Sergt F Whitlock.* This pretty but minor prize was most probably funded by the officers of a Yeomanry Cavalry unit for those of their men who competed in an annual regimental sports meeting.

Table-top combined cigarette and match holder with striker, electro-plate, no marks, engraved *Sergt Major Chesshire, 2nd North Staffs Regt, 16 Dec 1914.*

Silver ashtray, 2 ounces, made by EV, Sheffield 1960. Impressed in plain non-serif capitals, *Presented to Brigadier D G H Mackie OBE, CRA 53 (W) Division (TA), By the Officers of 282 (Glamorgan & Monmouthshire) Regt RA (TA).* Douglas Mackie served from 1934 to 1962, receiving his OBE while commanding 48 Field Regiment RA in Malaya (1956-1958).

Silver ashtray, 2 ounces, made by W H Leather & Son, Birmingham 1924. Engraved only with the crest of The Royal Sussex Regiment. This is not a presentation or commemorative piece, it is simply an example of the small items of silver manu-factured on behalf of almost every regiment at one time or another. They were intended either for Mess use or as a gift from a member of the regiment to a friend or relative.

Chrome-plated steel table-top patent cigarette dispenser, in art deco style, stamped "U.S.A.". Engraved *To Col Marsh, with best wishes, from Col Lusniak, Eugen, Polish Army, 1941.* By far the ugliest object in the collection, it has one of the most emotive stories. Colonel E B Marsh was a surgeon in the Royal Army Medical Corps (he retired in 1949 as a Major General). Colonel E Lusniak escaped from Poland after commanding the divisional artillery of the 55th Infantry Division, an element of the Army "Krakow". He was wounded in action, and presumably Colonel Marsh operated on him when he arrived in Scotland. The Free Polish Army had proportionately more officers than troops to command, and only the youngest and fittest were sent to front-line units. Born in 1892, Lusniak was too old. He stayed in Scotland, commanding FPA artillery regiments under training. Repatriated in 1946, he disappears from the records. In common with many other FPA officers who had been "tainted" with Western values, it is likely that he was shot by the hard-line Communist regime in the early 1950s.

Cups and goblets are the commonest forms of trophy or prize for shooting, sporting and other types of competition. They vary enormously in size, quality and researchability. The following are typical. All are Sterling silver unless otherwise stated.

Plain cup (goblet), 5.5 ounces, 7.5 inches, made by Charles Stuart Harris, London 1885. Engraved *Q.O.O.H., Corpl W T Morris, "B" Troop Prize, 1886.* The regiment (a Yeomanry Cavalry unit) was the Queen's Own Oxfordshire Hussars. The reason for the award will probably never be known.

Double-handled cup, electro-plate, 7.5 inches, Yorkshire P.W.O. Hussars, *Presented to Sgt Jepson for good turn out, 1901.* And another, 9 inches, *Yorkshire "A" P.W.O. Hussars, Presented to S.Q.M. Sergeant Jepson, by his officers for efficiency, 1905.* James Sykes Jepson went on to serve in WWI, being commissioned into the Army Service Corps in October 1915.

Double-handled cup, 6 ounces, 6 inches high, made by Deakin & Francis Limited, Birmingham 1926. Engraved *Shanghai Defence Force, RAMC Golf Tournament 1927, Winner Major R H Lucas.* Reginald Lucas qualified as a doctor in 1913 and entered the army in December 1914. By the end of the war he had been wounded, twice mentioned in despatches, awarded the Military Cross, and admitted as an Officer of both the Order of the British Empire and the Order of the Crown of Italy. Promoted to Major in 1919, he was a surgical specialist in Hong Kong and with the international force sent to Shanghai during the troubles of 1927. He retired from the RAMC in 1930 but rejoined in September 1939, serving in France with the British Expeditionary Force. After evacuation from Dunkirk, he served in the Middle East, in the North West Europe campaign, and then in India before retiring again in 1946. In WWII he was again mentioned in despatches and elevated to Commander of the Order of the British Empire.

Double-handled cup, 3.2 ounces, 3.5 inches, made by Deakin & Francis Limited, Birmingham, 1927. Engraved *Presented by Major the Hon.ble R Graham Murray, 1928, won by A Woodstock.* The donor of this cup was a Territorial Army officer. He served in WWI with the 4th/5th Battalion, The Royal Scots.

Double handled quaiche, 4.5 ounces, 4.5 inches, made by Mappin & Webb, Birmingham 1937. Engraved *HMS Dolphin,*

An unremarkable cup of the type sold by every silver retailer. What brings it to life is the engraved wording. A golf trophy won in China by Major R H Lucas RAMC, it is a reminder of a long and distinguished career.

Victor Ludorum 1938, Presented by Rear Admiral R H T Raikes CB CVO DSO. This was an annual sports trophy for which personnel serving in the Royal Navy's submarine service shore establishment competed. Admiral Raikes was a submarine captain in WWI and was twice awarded the DSO (he torpedoed and sank the German submarines UC10 and U81).

Plain cup (goblet), 9 ounces, 7.5 inches, made by W Adams Limited, Birmingham 1935, engraved with the unit crest and motto of the 10th Battalion, County of London Regiment, *Justitia Torris Nostra. Presented to the officers of the Tenth London Regiment by the Misses F.G. & E.L.Claydon in memory of their nephew, Capt A.W.Scrivener MC, Gaza 1917.* He was killed by machine-gun fire in the early hours of 2 November while leading "C" Company against Turkish entrenchments at Rafa.

Plain cup (goblet), 9 ounces, 7.5 inches, all marks illegible. *Vide* the preceding entry, this cup is likewise engraved with the crest and motto of the 10th Battalion, The London Regiment, *Presented to the officers, The Tenth London Regiment, by 2/Lieutenant H A Moorley, 1929.* It is a typical "on joining" piece. The engraved wording is clear and legible but the assay marks are polished smooth, so this is possibly an early example of recycling. Henry Moorley had served on the Western Front as a private soldier, and then as a Subaltern with the Nottinghamshire & Derbyshire Regiment, in the final weeks of the war.

Plain cup (goblet), electro-plate, 3 inches, *2nd Battalion, The Norfolk Regiment, Sports 1933, 1 Mile, 1st, Pte W H Suffolk.* This soldier is well recorded in the regimental journals of the 1930s as a track athlete and boxer. He was killed during the fighting retreat to the Channel coast in May 1940 and has no known grave. His cup was the first such item purchased by the author. Discovered on a junk stall at a vintage car rally, it cost fifty pence (plus, later, four pounds for replating). Of no intrinsic value, it is probably now the only tangible evidence that he ever lived.

Plain cup (goblet), electro-plate, 3 inches, identical to that described above, *2nd Battalion, The Norfolk Regiment, Regtl Novices Boxing Competition 1930, Feather Weight Winner, L Cpl*

Another conventional cup, this example demonstrates not only the skill of the engraver but also the *ethos* of the turn-of-the-century Yeomanry Cavalry.

E Harrison. He and Private Suffolk no doubt trained and boxed together. Both of their trophies surfaced (separately) in the area of Plymouth. The Norfolks were stationed there during the 1930s, and several men married local girls. Privates Harrison and Suffolk probably left the cups with their wives when they moved on, or went to war.

Plain cup (goblet), electro-plate, 4 inches, engraved with the crest of The Argyll & Sutherland Highlanders, *C Stout, 1st, 440 yds, Allahabad, India 1923*. He was a Lance Bombardier in the Royal Field Artillery.

Double-handled cup, 15 ounces, 9 inches, maker's mark illegible, Birmingham 1928. *Y.M.C.A. Bagatelle Cup, Presented by Major F G Sellwood OBE MC, 1930*. Frank Sellwood served throughout WWI with the Army Service Corps (Gallipoli and Mesopotamia) and again in WWII (the Somaliland and Abyssinia campaigns). Between the wars he was an estate agent in Cullompton, Devon.

Double-handled cup, 5.3 ounces, 6 inches, made by W Neale & Sons Limited, Birmingham 1936. Engraved *Commandant's Challenge Cup, Presented to the Larkhill Artisans Club by Brigadier Lord D Malise Graham CB DSO MC* (with three winners named on the silver base plate, 1937, 1938 and 1939). This was a golf trophy for the civilians employed on the Royal Artillery ranges at Larkhill. In 1914, Lord Douglas Malise Graham was ADC to Major General Sir Charles Fergusson, commanding the 5th Division, BEF. At the defence of Le Cateau, with swords drawn, the two of them trotted their horses under fire along the Divisional front, chatting to the soldiers and steadying them as they awaited the German assault. Like so many of the people listed here, it would easy to write a complete chapter about this officer.

Double-handled cup, 2 ounces, 4 inches, made by Robert Pringle & Sons, London, 1928. Engraved *376th (D.Y.) Battery R.A., Challenge Cup, Won by Bdr L A Wills, 1927*.

Double-handled cup, 17 ounces, six inches, made by W Adams Limited, Birmingham, 1908. Engraved *Stevenstone Hunt, Point to Point, March 29th 1911. Yeomanry Cup. Presented by (the) Colonel & Officers of Royal Devon Hussars. Won by Sergt T Cleverdon*. He was a farmer, at Westacott, North Devon. He was a member of the Royal Devon Hussars Yeomanry for at least ten years before WWI, and rode regularly with the Stevenstone Hunt, in the area of Torrington.

Double-handled cup, 14 ounces (with wood base), 8 inches, made by Turner & Simpson Limited, Birmingham 1937. Engraved *Presented to "D" Coy, 34th County of London Battalion, by Major E Thomas MC, for the most efficient platoon*. This was a Home Guard unit.

Double-handled cup, 16 ounces (stamped .900), 6 inches, made by Francis Meli, Malta. Engraved *Presented by Captain C J Briggs and the officers, HMS Revenge, won by Guy Howell Parsons, Midshipman, cutter's sailing and pulling race, May 1899*. Parsons retired as a Lieutenant Commander, but Briggs went on to become Controller of the Navy (1910-1912), and Vice Admiral commanding 4th Squadron, Home Fleet (1912-1914). This is the only piece seen so far which was made in Malta, and yet a great many must have been commissioned by ships of the Mediterranean Fleet and by military units stationed on the island. The use by local silversmiths of .900 alloy may have condemned much of their output to the melting pot in later years.

Double-handled cup with lid, 20 ounces, 10.5 inches, made by Mappin & Webb, Sheffield 1906. With ornate solid cast handles on ram's head mounts, the cup and lid both decorated with *repoussé* oak leaves and neo-Gothic floral edging, the lid

having an acorn finial. Engraved on one side *Presented by the officers of HMS Exmouth to Lieutenant F C Dreyer, Gunnery Lieutenant, 19.5.04 - 7.1.07*, and on the other side *HMS Exmouth, Channel Fleet, Flagship of Admiral Sir A K Wilson V.C. &c, First in Gunlayers' Tests and Battle Practice, 1904, 1905, 1906*. Dreyer had a brilliant naval career and was prominent in the Battle of Jutland. His name, combined with that of Wilson VC, is yet another instance of a piece of silver generating far more historical and biographical information than can be recorded here.

Beakers are vessels having no handle or lid. From the two examples seen, it is likely that they were customarily presented as shooting prizes. Both are Sterling silver.

5 ounces, 4 inches, made by Elkington & Company, Birmingham 1904. Embossed with the figures of a Plantagenet archer and a rifleman of 1860. Engraved *Lieut Col R Sandeman, 10th Prize, Handsworth Compn* (competition), *Bisley 1905*. Colonel Sandeman commanded The Royal Gloucestershire Hussars Yeomanry.

The beaker given to Colonel Sandeman, of the Royal Gloucestershire Hussars, following his success at Bisley in 1905.

5 ounces, 4 inches, maker's mark illegible, London 1902. Also embossed with an archer and rifleman, the dates 1300-1500-1860, and a motto *Sit Pertetuum* (the motto of the National Rifle Association). Engraved *Lieut W M Huntbach, 2 V.B. Shropre L.I., Winner of the 143rd Prize in The Graphic Compn, Bisley 1902*. It is thought the competition was sponsored by one

of the newspapers of the day, *The Graphic*. This officer received a silver beaker even though he was 143rd in the tally of scores. The explanation may be that (say) 2000 or more entrants were whittled down in stages to a final field of two hundred. If that was the case, 143rd place would have been an admirable achievement.

Salvers vary greatly in size, but are normally of good workmanship and gauge of metal. They are traditionally a form of silverware given to an officer, by his brother officers, at the time of his marriage. As the following examples demonstrate, there are exceptions to that general rule.

6 ounces, 6 inches diameter, pierced border with beaded

centrally *Captain F B Newport-Tinley M.C., 20th Deccan Horse, on the occasion of his marriage*, with nine surrounding facsimile signatures. The fact that only nine brother officers are named on this salver is a reflection of the small European establishments of Indian cavalry (as discussed in Chapter Four).

21 ounces, 10 inches diameter, plain edge, four plain feet, also made by Harrison Brothers & Howson, Sheffield 1917. Engraved *From the officers of the 3rd Rifle Brigade, to 2nd Lieut W A Houghton, March 23rd 1918*.

19 ozs, 10 inches diameter, gadroon edge, three pedestal feet, manufactured by Ollivant & Botsford (Manchester), London 1923. Engraved centrally with the *fleur de lys* crest of the Manchester Regiment and *6th/7th Battalion, The Manchester*

The pretty little Victorian salver presented by Captain T Merthyr Guest. Like the Stevenstone Hunt cup, it recalls the glory days of the mounted Yeomanry.

edging, three foliate shell feet, made by Edward Hutton, London 1883. Engraved centrally *1861-1891 Q.O.D.Y.C.*, and below *Quarter Master of The Blackmoor Vale Troop, R English, 1878-1891, From Capt Merthyr Guest, B.V. Troop*. The regiment was The Queen's Own Dorset Yeomanry, and the Blackmoor Vale is traditionally fox hunting country. Thomas Merthyr Guest was "County gentry", married into the nobility. He served with the Dorset Yeomanry from 1877 to 1889.

44 ounces, 15 inches diameter, gadroon edge, three curled ornate leaf feet, made by Walker & Hall, Sheffield 1918. Engraved centrally with the crest of the Machine Gun Corps, surrounded by seven facsimile signatures. Originally in the headquarters Mess of the MGC, this piece is described in detail in Chapter Eight.

30 ounces, 11.5 inches, gadroon edge, 3 plain feet, made by Harrison Brothers & Howson, Sheffield 1916. Engraved

Regiment. Presented to Captain W Carter DSO MC on his Retirement from the Service and as a token of appreciation of his services as Adjutant, March 31st 1925. Surrounding the central wording are the facsimile signatures of fifteen persons, presumably all the Territorial Army officers of the battalion. This salver was intercepted when it was already on its way to a silversmith's workshop for buffing and recycling.

18 ounces, 10 inches diameter, gadroon edging, three plain feet, made by Carrington & Company, London 1924. Engraved centrally with the crest of the Royal Air Force and, below, *Presented to Flying Officer C D Spiers by the officers of No.12 Squadron, Royal Air Force, on his marriage, 5th July 1924.*

10 ounces, 9 inches diameter, plain edging, three half-ball feet, Chinese marks and "HC". Mounted at the centre is a silvered unit badge consisting of St George and the Dragon, and the motto *Pro Aris et Focis*. Engraved *E.H.Browne Esq., from the*

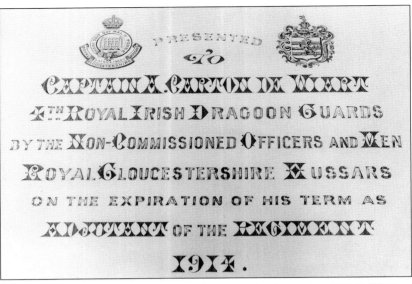

PRESENTED TO CAPTAIN A. CARTON DE WIART 4TH ROYAL IRISH DRAGOON GUARDS BY THE NON-COMMISSIONED OFFICERS AND MEN ROYAL GLOUCESTERSHIRE HUSSARS ON THE EXPIRATION OF HIS TERM AS ADJUTANT OF THE REGIMENT 1914.

Although the craftsman took great pains when engraving the centre of the de Wiart salver, especially with the unit crest and the recipient's family bearings, his choice of lettering is one of the least attractive so far seen. Possibly it was regarded at the time as very fashionable.

design, made by Walker & Hall, Sheffield 1920. Engraved upon the underside of the bowl, *Lieut P W Tregillis R.N., for highest score with pistol at Northern Command Rifle Meeting held at Penrose, N.Z., 23-24th March 1923.*

Table spoon, electro-plate, 8.5 inches, made by Mappin & Webb. Engraved upon the finial with the (Victoria crown) crest of The Grenadier Guards and *Sergeants' Mess, 3rd Battalion.* A spoon which is not in itself researchable, but nonetheless worth rescuing as a reminder of a bygone age of soldiering. In a distressed condition when first found (in a box of discarded cutlery at a junk sale), it has been beautifully restored by a Devon-based silversmith.

Table fork, electro-plate, 7.5 inches, made by Elkington, Mason & Company (c.1854). The handle is engraved with the Prince of Wales's plumes and *Ich Dien* motto, and the name of the regiment, Longford Militia. The story of the Mess silver of the former Militia units of Ireland is told in Chapter Eight.

officers and members, Shanghai Light Horse, on the occasion of his marriage, 10.11.38. The background story of the Shanghai volunteer units is described in Chapter Six. The Light Horse gained their name in 1880 (having been first raised as the Mounted Rangers Troop in 1860).

86 ounces, 19 inches, gadroon and foliate shell edging, four plain feet, made by William Hutton & Sons Limited, Sheffield, 1912. Engraved with the crest of the Royal Gloucestershire Hussars and the armorial bearings of the recipient, with the wording *Presented to Captain A Carton de Wiart, 4th Royal Irish Dragoon Guards, by the Non-commissioned officers and men, Royal Gloucestershire Hussars, on the expiration of his term as Adjutant of the Regiment, 1914.* The life and military adventures of this extraordinary soldier are delightfully recorded in his popular autobiography, *Happy Odyssey.* He won his Victoria Cross at La Boiselle on 2/3 July 1916.

Flatware is a generic description for knives, forks, spoons and similar items. Such things might seem an unpromising field for military or naval research but, perhaps surprisingly, various bits and pieces do come along from time to time which carry an historical resonance. They offer some scope for research, and at modest cost.

Table spoon, silver, 2 ounces, 5 inches in length, made by Mappin & Webb, London 1917. Exquisitely engraved on the upper side of the handle with the crest of The Royal Fusiliers and, in very small lettering, *No.3 Company, 6th Bn, The Royal Fusiliers, miniature range shooting competition, best shot in the company, won by L/Cpl A Tucker.*

Tea spoon, silver, 1 ounce, 5 inches in length, made by The Alexander Clark Company Limited, Birmingham, 1924. The upper side of the finial being the crest of the Malay States Volunteer Rifles. Engraved upon the reverse *B.R.A., Kuala Lumpur.* It was probably one of a set of six, but the provenance has not been traced. The R.A. acronym possibly signifies Rifle Association. Engraved or enamelled tea spoons have been awarded frequently in connection with shooting competitions (especially small bore indoor events), and one collector specialising in the field has accumulated (over many years) more than four hundred.

Table spoon, silver, 2.5 ounces, 7 inches in length, rat-tail

Tableware is a term which serves to describe some of the other objects encountered.

Napkin ring, silver, one ounce, made by Thomas Bradbury & Sons Limited, Sheffield 1927. Engraved *D V Jesseman*, with

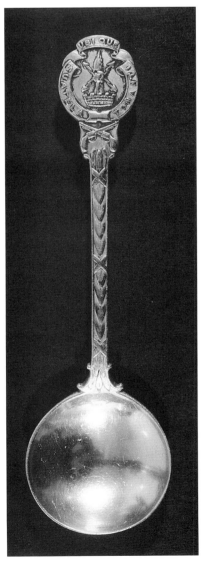

Spoons presented as shooting prizes can provide interesting avenues of research. This example (not in the author's collection) carries the crest and motto of the Royal Military Academy, Woolwich, and on the reverse the words *Revolver Club.* Engraved on the shaft is a name and date, *J C D'Arcy, May 1913.* It is still in the possession of his family but, even if their records were not available, reference to the Army Lists would reveal an unusually successful career. When Gentleman Cadet John Conyers D'Arcy passed out of Woolwich he was commissioned into the Royal Artillery, served on the Western Front (twice wounded, awarded the Military Cross), served on the North West Frontier of India in the 1930-1931 campaign (again wounded), formed the 1st East Africa Light Battery in 1939, rose rapidly to command the 9th Armoured Division, and became General Officer Commanding troops in Palestine and Transjordan, 1944-1946. He retired as Lieutenant General J C D'Arcy CB CBE MC. Photo: Major Michael D'Arcy.

Once in a while, something truly unusual will appear at an otherwise unremarkable auction of old silver. The salver presented in 1914 to Captain Adrian Carton de Wiart is described on the facing page. In the normal run of events, it would today attract little attention (other than by virtue of its great size and weight). Its interest is to be found in this officer's subsequent career. Two years after the presentation, he was commanding the 8th Battalion, The Gloucestershire Regiment, as a Temporary Lieutenant Colonel. On 2-3 July, at La Boiselle, he took command of three other battalions and forced home the British attack with a complete disregard for his own safety. His inspiring leadership led to the award of the Victoria Cross. During the course of the war he was wounded eight times, losing an eye and his left hand. In WWII, he served with the Free Polish Army in Norway, was sent to Yugoslavia to liaise with Marshal Tito, negotiated the surrender of Italy, and then went to China as Churchill's representative with Chiang Kai-Shek. Knighted for his wartime services, he was decorated by the governments of Belgium, France and Poland. Picture: The Attack at La Boiselle (after the painting by J H Valda, *Illustrated London News*).

the names of eleven Royal Navy ships in which he served - as Paymaster Lieutenant RN to Commander (S) RN - between 1935 and 1957. He was aboard HMS *Durban* when, in the early weeks of 1942, she was engaged in the reinforcement of Singapore and the evacuation of civilians and casualties. The ship was severely damaged at sea when attacked by Japanese dive bombers.

Napkin ring, electro-plate, made by Elkington & Company. Engraved *Douglas Watts, Cadet, Cambridge O.T.C., 2nd Lt Jan 18th 1918, joined 55 Division for France, April 11th 1918*. This is another instance of an officer utilising a personal possession to record his travels. Lieutenant Watts served on the Western Front, with the Royal Field Artillery, for the last seven months of the war.

Cocktail shaker, electro-plate, 8 inches, no marks. Engraved *Presented by the Sick Berth Staff of HMS Drake to Wardmaster Lieutenant R E M Pryce, Royal Navy*. His rank is unusual and interesting.

Muffin warmer, electro-plate, no marks, engraved *Presented to Mrs Thomas, July 7th 1915, in appreciation of services rendered to the Army Service Corps at the Y.M.C.A., Wells, 1915*. From Somerset, this piece stirs the imagination of anyone with knowledge of the way in which the New Armies were raised and

the enthusiastic voluntary work of local communities in caring for "the boys".

Pickle jar holder with fork, silver, no marks but almost certainly of Indian manufacture, *circa* 1918, mounted with a small engraved plate *Madras & S Mahratta Ry Rifles*. Also bearing the unit "bugle and 1"crest and *32 Indian Defence Force*. The story of the railway company Volunteer regiments is told in Chapter Five. The pedigree of the 1st Battalion, 32nd Madras & Southern Mahratta Railway Rifles, appears in John Gaylor's excellent book, *Sons of John Company*.

Tea caddy, silver, 6 ounces, 3.5 inches, made by A & J Zimmerman, Birmingham, 1910. Delicately engraved on the cap (lid) with the figure of a Jenny Wren and the crest of the Royal Navy, then *J P Tudgey, from the Wrens (sic) Sailing Club, 1943-45, Kittiwake*. The full story is likely to be unresearchable, but Mr Tudgey was presumably the club boatman at a Women's Royal Naval Service shore training base. This very pretty piece of Edwardian silver comes under one of the established "collectable" categories, tea caddies being much sought after. The engraving condemned it. It was retrieved (literally) from under the heel of a dealer who was about to crush it and throw it in the scrap bin. In passing, it was the Honourable East India Company's representative in Japan, Mr R L Wickham, who first

A nice example of a naval officer using his personal napkin ring as a means of recording the names of the ships in which he served.

reported the existence of tea. That was in 1615, the period when London was the coffee-drinking capital of the world. It was not until 1657 that the first commercial consignment of tea was offered to the British public.

Table pepper mill, 4 inches (including steel interior parts), made by Hukin & Heath Limited, Birmingham 1907. Engraved with the crest of The Scots Guards and *Guy Nevill, on leaving the regiment, August 1906*. Like other silver mills of mediocre quality, this one was found in a distressed condition. The 3rd

A typical small piece of regimental tableware, this menu card holder was once the property of the officers of the 2nd Volunteer Battalion, The Devonshire Regiment. The additional title "Prince of Wales's Own" was conferred on the 2nd VBDR in 1880, hence the three plumes and Ich Dien device incorporated in the design. The holder was made in Birmingham in 1905 by G W Harvey & Co. Photo: Mr Dennis Lee and Mr Stuart Barr.

Battalion of The Scots Guards were probably glad to part with it when, after inevitable hard usage, the light gauge silver began to crack. An Old Etonian, Guy Temple Montacute Nevill was the son of Lord George Montacute, head of a wealthy Sussex family. He served with the Guards from 1903 to 1906, resigned his Regular commission, joined the 2nd Battalion, Sussex Yeomanry, and became a member of the London Stock Exchange. In WWI he commanded an administrative centre in England and then went to France as a Staff Captain.

Spill vase, silver, 21 ounces (much of the weight will be a lead filler in the base, giving stability to the piece), 10.5 inches, made by Goldsmiths & Silversmiths Company, London 1905. Engraved upon the base *Presented by Major Quentin Agnew MVO DSO, on leaving the regiment, 27.4.06*. In contrast with the previous entry, this piece represents a wonderfully challenging opportunity for any military researcher. From 1885 to 1920, from Burma to the North West Frontier of India, from South Africa to Egypt and Serbia, he went everywhere and did everything. He made his presentation in 1906 when retiring after twenty years with the Royal Scots Fusiliers, but then returned to active command on the Western Front in WWI.

Trinket tray (also known as a pin tray), 2 ounces, 5.25 inches in length, made by The Alexander Clark Company Limited, Birmingham 1919. Engraved *Capt H Walker, 3rd Vol Bn, Hertfordshire Regt, 1914-1919*.

Entrée dish, oval, with lid and detachable handle, electro-plate, 12 inches, made by "L&W". Engraved *Presented to Captain J B Anderson R.A. by the officers, 662 Sqn, 22.5.54*. A typical post-WWII wedding gift, and the only piece seen which relates to the Army Air Corps.

Wine cooler, electro-plate, made (in Belgium) by Schoup Coppn Déeg. Engraved *Souvenir to Major Dodds from the officers of No.1 A. Tps. Coy (Belg), 5th Feb - 30th Apr, 1945*. An object of no consequence, it does at least remind us of the Belgian Free Forces and of the British officers attached to them.

Candle holder, silver, 10.5 ounces (which presumably includes a pitch filler), 4 inches, made by Ollivant & Bottisford, London 1906. Engraved upon the base *Iraq Autumn Tournament, Baghdad, Novr 1927, Winners Subsidiary Tournament, Capt P Mumford 1. Capt Crawford Clarke 2. F/Lt P Foster 3. Lieut C E Lewin Harris 4.* This is a polo trophy, won by an inter-services team at a time when the British were creating and governing Iraq. Like so many of these objects, and for collectors interested in such things, it provides the fun of researching four careers for the price of one. There is an unusually long gap between the year of manufacture and the year of the award.

Hot water jug, silver, 13.4 ounces, 8 inches, made by Atkin Brothers, Sheffield 1907. Engraved *Lieut J H Bateson, Royal Artillery, from the officers, 23rd Peshawar Mountain Battery (F.F.), 10th Sept 1908.* This is a relic of the days of the *elite* mountain gunners, and Bateson was a well-known member of that small band of brothers. By the end of WWI, as a Lieutenant Colonel, he held the DSO, the CMG and the French Croix de Guerre. The pot was given to him at the time of his first marriage.

Pocket Watches, usually in silver but sometimes in gold, were frequently the gift to a non-commissioned officer at the time of his retirement from the service. One such piece has been described in detail, in Chapter Eight. It is worthwhile to maintain contact with dealers specialising in timepieces because, by virtue of the volume of material passing through their hands, they are the most likely to produce something of interest to the military collector. The items seen have had casings of a sound quality but were fitted with standard commercial movements which ceased to function long ago. The cost of repair or renewal is usually more than can be justified by their limited horological interest. It is their finely engraved wording which provides any stimulation to the researcher.

Pocket watch, made by Richard Oliver, London 1863. Engraved within *Presented by the members of the 6th Herts Rifle Volunteers to their Drill Instructor, Sergt Beard, as a mark of respect on his leaving the Corps, 10th Oct 1863.*

Pocket watch, "Stokes of Dublin". Engraved within *Presented to C.S.M. A Charlwood by members of (the) Sergts' Mess, 4th Bn, The Worcestershire Regt, on his retirement to*

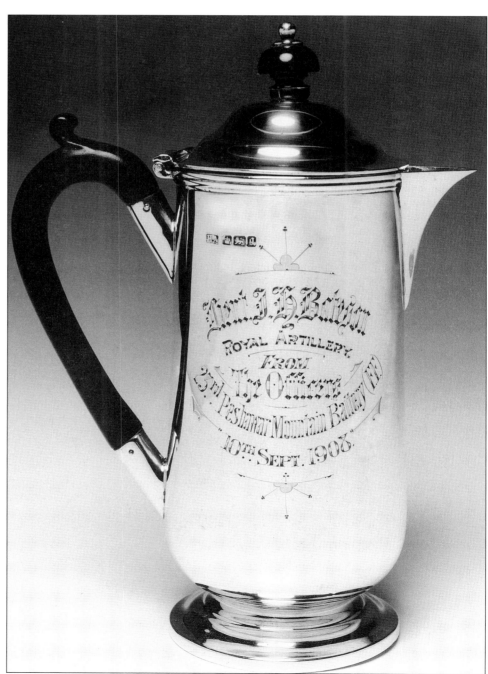

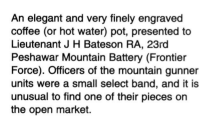

An elegant and very finely engraved coffee (or hot water) pot, presented to Lieutenant J H Bateson RA, 23rd Peshawar Mountain Battery (Frontier Force). Officers of the mountain gunner units were a small select band, and it is unusual to find one of their pieces on the open market.

pension, 1921. Albert Charlwood served with the battalion at Gallipoli and on the Western Front. At the time of his retirement, it was stationed in Ireland (Phoenix Park), hence the name of the retailer.

Tribute medals received a brief mention in Chapter Eight. They were the silver medals sponsored by local authorities in various towns and cities across the nation and given to local men, as tokens of regard, when they came home at the end of the Anglo-Boer War of 1899-1902. They are usually of fine quality and attractive design, and represent a narrow but interesting field of collecting. What has come to light over the past three or four years is the fact that local community "tribute" presentations were not restricted to medals, and did not begin and end with the Anglo-Boer War. The ten valuable silver caskets given by the Borough of Wigan to Martin Rowan and his friends of the 1st Volunteer Battalion, The Manchester Regiment, were described earlier, in Chapter Eight. The following examples are not of that quality, but they demonstrate a concern for "all our local lads" which continued through to the conclusion of WWII. They are as much social history as military.

A small double-handled cup, silver, 2.5 inches, 2 ounces, made by The Alexander Clark Company Limited, London, year mark illegible. Engraved *Presented to the sailors & soldiers of Kenton who served in the Great War, 1914-1919, by their grateful fellow parishioners.* Kenton is a village situated on the estuary of the river Exe, near Exeter. The cup is not individually named, so the identity of the recipient will never be known.

Pint tankard, electro-plate. Machine engraved, *Presented to Albert G Down, by the people of Wambrook, Somerset, in appreciation of services rendered to King and Country, 1939-1945.* An enquiry addressed to Wambrook failed to generate a response, but it may be supposed that every man and woman of the village who went off to serve in the war was given one of these well-made tankards *circa* 1946.

Canes and sticks were once part of the "walking out" dress of every soldier and of the service dress of officers. The term "swagger stick" describes their purpose to perfection. They were (and still are, depending upon circumstance) useful for slapping the thigh or riding boot, pointing at things, scratching a tactical plan in the sand, or simply occupying the hands in moments of repose. Collectable examples are those having a silver toe and finial, the latter being stamped with a regimental crest. Desirability depends upon the antiquity and size of the regiment or corps depicted in this way. Few of them are hallmarked, and even fewer can be attributed to an original

owner. However, unusual examples of "swagger sticks" and walking sticks can be found from time to time.

Walking stick, Malacca cane, 38 inches, unmarked silver finial with the (cast) regimental "Death or Glory" crest of the 17th Lancers (Duke of Cambridge's Own). Professionally engraved *Lieut H F Parbury, 17th Lancers.* He was commissioned into the regiment as a Second Lieutenant in 1907. His subsequent promotions were Lieutenant 1908, Captain 1915, and Major 1922, commanding "B" Squadron. He resigned three years later. In early October 1918, during the British forcing of the Hindenburg Line near Le Cateau, the regiment was operating in the mounted role as part of 6th Brigade, 3rd Cavalry Division. The Germans were beginning to crack, but they fought desperately to prevent the British cavalry from breaking through to the rear areas. Their machine-gunners stuck to the task and held the line for several days. Despite casualties, the 17th Lancers continued to probe. From 9 October to 14 October, they were commanded by Captain Parbury (the most senior officer still in action). For his leadership during that week he was awarded the Military Cross.

Conclusions

Having read through these compressed entries, each reader will have formed his or her own opinions. On the one hand, it might be thought that none of the objects are of any importance in terms of design or craftsmanship. By comparison with the magnificent pieces described in earlier chapters, this is beyond dispute. On the other hand, it is self-evident that every piece has a story to tell. There is surely much here to interest the military historian, the social historian and the genealogist. But is it enough to justify the effort of becoming involved in the first place?

The answer to that question relates directly to the personal enthusiasms of the individual reader, obviously. However, as a broad principle, it is hard to exaggerate the "surprise element" in this field of collecting. Nothing is ever quite what it seems to be at first glance. There are few (if any) other hobbies which offer the same opportunities for satisfying one's sense of curiosity - examining the clues, assembling the evidence, and attempting to prove the case.

The outcome is sometimes disappointing, occasionally stimulating, often deeply satisfying. At least half of the items in the author's collection may fairly be described as run-of-the-mill, but the other half have taken him into areas of British history where otherwise he would never have ventured. There is much pleasure in these voyages of discovery, and some of them are described in the following chapter.

Chapter Ten

Some Vagaries of Fortune

By the law of averages, it is inevitable that sooner or later the collector will encounter an item of exceptional interest. A rough-and-ready assessment indicates that, depending upon personal intuition and the vagaries of fortune, at least one in ten come within this category. The following entries describe eight of the pieces which, as research projects, have provided the author with particular interest.

Lieutenant Colonel Sir Harry Darell, 7th (The Princess Royal's) Dragoon Guards

Chapter Two included a description of a ram's head snuff mull acquired by the 91st Argyllshire Highlanders in 1864. The following notes describe the central part of what was once a comparable object but which today survives only by virtue of its silver content. This is not in itself a major cause for regret. It is, after all, the engraved wording on the lid of the mull itself which stirs the imagination.

Weighing little more than 5 ounces, it bears marks for Sheffield 1850. The maker's mark is indistinct, but is thought to have been that of Martin Hall & Company. The engraving states:

"A souvenir of the Cape, presented to the officers of the 7th Dragoon Guards by their brother officer, Lieut Col Sir Harry Darell, Bart". This bland and conventional statement conceals a story which must appeal to anyone interested in the early conquest of Southern Africa.

First, the regiment. The 7th Dragoon Guards traced their origins to 1688. They acquired a numeric designation in 1746 as the 4th (or "Black") Irish Horse, but were retitled as the 7th (Princess Royal's) Dragoon Guards in 1788. With minor amendments, this was their title through to April 1922. The regiment then amalgamated with the 4th Royal Irish Dragoons to form the 4th/7th Royal Dragoon Guards. It is likely that some of the Mess silver, including this mull, was dispersed at that time.

The piece reappeared in 1996 when it was offered for sale at a general auction in Parr, Cornwall. The original ram or antelope head, doubtless by then much battered and moth-eaten, had been discarded somewhere along the line, but the silver element survived. Fortunately, the auctioneer recognised its historical interest and catalogued it correctly. It was purchased

The central part of the Mess snuff mull presented by Colonel Sir Harry Darrell. The original ram's head mount has long gone, so the underlying bowl is now protected by being set into a recessed base of polished oak. The exquisite engraving is a strong feature of this piece.

for the author by a local dealer, Elizabeth Nicolson, "with the hope that you will like it".

Sir Harry Francis Colville Darell was born on 17 November 1817. He inherited his title in 1828 on the death of his father, a senior merchant on the Bengal establishment and Commercial Resident of the Honourable East India Company at Eatwah and Calpu. The baronetcy had been created by King Charles I when he knighted one of his treasurers, Marmaduke Darell.

Nothing is known of Harry's early years but, in view of his father's place of residence, it seems likely that he was educated partly in India and partly in England. In 1832, at the age of eighteen, he obtained a commission as Ensign in the 18th (Royal Irish) Regiment of Foot. He first comes to attention in the First China War. The British were attempting to develop their trading establishments at Canton and elsewhere on mainland China. Specifically, they sought to import and market on a large scale their supplies of opium. The Chinese wanted neither the British nor their opium, and a confused series of campaigns ensued during the years 1839 to 1842. Harry was an excellent horseman and he was attached to the staff of Brigadier General Burrell as a "galloper" (officially, *aide-de-camp*). In this appointment he took part in the assault on the city of Chusan on 19 October 1842. Its 300,000 inhabitants were fanatically defended by its garrison, and the fighting was severe. Losses on both sides were heavy but, as was customary with the British Army during that period, battle casualties were far exceeded by deaths resulting from disease, bad food and lack of medical facilities.

Returning from China, Harry transferred to the elite 7th Dragoon Guards, a regiment of heavy cavalry. It may be supposed that, like many other officers who served in China, he brought back to England various valuable trophies. If that was so, he turned the loot to good account by purchasing a vacant Captaincy in the Dragoons and then sustaining the life style associated with such regiments. The move from infantry to cavalry meant that he could indulge to the full his passion for horses.

In 1843, the regiment was ordered to South Africa as part of the permanent garrison. For many years there had been trouble in the Cape region. The indigenous tribes resented the European invasion of their lands, and the long-established Dutch communities objected to the authority imposed by the English administrators. In 1839-1840, these Dutch (Boer) families made the epic "Great Trek" to the north-east where they established their independent republics of Natal, the Orange Free State and the Transvaal.

The British would not leave them alone. In 1842, they invaded and attempted to occupy Natal. They were stopped in their tracks by the Boers at Congella. More troops arrived from England and a second attack was launched, this time into the Orange Free State. The Boers were defeated at Zwartkopjes, where Harry commanded a troop of his regiment, and an uneasy peace was imposed upon them.

With the Boers suppressed, the 7th Dragoon Guards settled during the mid-1840s to routine garrison duties. They established their headquarters at Fort Beaufort, on the Cape's eastern frontier. Here they were joined by a civilian huntsman and a pack of foxhounds which the officers had purchased in England. Kennels were constructed, and a series of regular meets organised. Together with local English farmers and land-owners, dressed in traditional pink, they pursued jackals. Over two seasons they killed forty-six and half brace of these animals.

Dragoons were of necessity recruited for their physique. A trooper with all his accoutrements weighed nineteen stone (112 kgs), so the horses were selected for their size and stamina. Harry is recorded as having weighed fourteen stone, and he must have been a powerfully built man. In August 1848 he wagered that he could ride from Fort Beaufort to Tomlinson's Inn in a faster time than one of his brother officers (who had covered the twenty-five miles in one hour and fifty minutes). Backing himself for fifty pounds Sterling, he rose from the dinner table and, still dressed in Mess kit, covered the distance by starlight in one hour and twenty-four minutes. Later, after training for the ride, he repeated the performance, this time for a wager of one hundred pounds, in one hour and seventeen minutes. The fate of his horse is not recorded.

Friction with the Xhosa nation continued throughout this time. Labelled "Kaffirs" by the Europeans, they consisted of several major tribes. One of their chieftains, Sandile, was held responsible for numerous raids on white settlements resulting in the theft of cattle. The Governor, Sir Peregrine Maitland, authorised a punitive expedition consisting of 2600 British Army personnel - five regiments of infantry, one of cavalry (the 7th DG), and detachments of Royal Artillery and Royal Engineers. Also included in the force were the Cape Mounted Rifles and a number of locally-recruited levies. In overall command was Colonel Henry Somerset.

Full details of the campaign can be studied elsewere. It came to be known as The War of the Axe, and was the seventh of the Kaffir Wars which had started many years earlier. These notes will concentrate upon the engagements in which Sir Harry Darrell is known to have taken part and for which eyewitness accounts are available.

The scale of the fighting escalated sharply during the (southern hemisphere) winter of 1846, and quickly involved far more than the simple theft of cattle. Settler farmsteads were raided and burned, European families murdered, military convoys ambushed and looted, and attempts made to assault and seize British military outposts. The total strength of the 7th Dragoon Guards is not known, but Captain Darell's troop consisted of just thirty-eight men, a figure which suggests that the regiment was much under strength. The tribes they were facing could field hundreds, on occasion thousands, of warriors armed with the *assegai* (throwing spear) and with muzzle-loading muskets and rifles. Many were horse-mounted and highly mobile.

The country was rolling *veldt*, with outcrops of rock and frequent patches of dense scrub. The tribes were expert in moving rapidly through this country, making sudden attacks and then swiftly dispersing. The British, on the other hand, had poor intelligence of their opponent's moves and rarely used scouts or reconnaissance patrols. Heavy cavalry regiments were trained for the mass charge, riding knee-to-knee into the set-piece battle with the sabre. The correspondent of *The London Illustrated News* reported: "The 7th Dragoon Guards are a brave set of men, but are not up to bush work against an unseen foe. They keep together and are regular targets for (the) Kaffirs".

Harry Darell and his troop had been chasing their elusive enemy for several weeks when, in late May, he had a chance to "display the cavalry spirit". He was ordered to search for a body of Kaffirs near Fort Peddie. Breasting a low hill, he saw 2000 tribesmen in the valley ahead of him. Dismounting, his men opened fire with their carbines. A small field gun also was brought into action. He kept the tribesmen at bay until a detachment of infantry, from the 91st of Foot, arrived on the scene. Seeing the size of the enemy force, the Major in command ordered a withdrawal. Darell ignored him and called to his men "Draw swords, charge". The little band of horsemen galloped into the astonished Kaffirs and scattered them (killing and wounding a number with their sabres). The only Dragoon casualty was the Troop Sergeant Major, slightly wounded. This was the first time the 7th DG were able to employ cold steel at close quarters.

Harry Darell was in action again two weeks later when, with detachments of Cape Mounted Rifles and some friendly Boers, he attacked and scattered a party of Kaffirs on the Keiskamma River. Later that day, 8 June 1846, Colonel Somerset moved his force across a series of hills and approached the valley of the Gwanga River. As usual, no scouts were sent ahead, so the British were surprised to find themselves facing a column of 3000 warriors moving along the river bank. Somerset immediately ordered his artillery into action. This consisted of two 6-pounders and two 12-pounder howitzers. Fortunately for the Kaffirs, the ammunition for these pieces had been in store for ten years and was virtually useless. A couple of shots were discharged, but the guns then spluttered into silence. For the same reason, an attempt to launch explosive rockets was a fiasco.

Somerset had found his enemy in an unusually vulnerable position. The terrain was completely open, free from natural obstacles and ideal for mounted action. The river was not an impediment because at this point it was shallow, with low banks on each side. He ordered Darell to charge. According to an eyewitness, his men followed him in a compact group, punching solidly through the mass of panicking natives. Behind them came a troop of the Cape Mounted Rifles, armed with carbines.

Yelling, hacking, slashing, the Dragoons swept on across the plain. There was nowhere for the Kaffirs to hide. Some ran until they were cut down, others stood their ground. As his troop gradually broke up, Darell's men plunged into a chaotic series of individual combats. The accounts of these man-to-man fights make sombre reading. They reflect credit on both sides - the courage of the cavalrymen who were outnumbered by at least forty to one, and the bravery of the tribesmen who chose to stand, fight and die. Four hundred of them were killed, many others injured.

The losses suffered by Darell's small force were eight men wounded (one of whom later died), two horses killed and six wounded. Darell's horse was speared several times, and he himself received two *assegai* wounds. Together with the other casualties, he was taken to Fort Peddie for treatment and later made a full recovery.

Their defeat at the Battle of Gwanga River was a shattering blow to the morale of the chieftains. It did not end the war at a stroke, but it marked the end of any serious resistance. Colonel Somerset's force was heavily reinforced from England during the following months, and the conflict came to an end with a parley at King William's Town in January 1847.

Sir Harry Darell continued to serve with the regiment until its return to England in June 1847. His promotion to Major came three months later, and he was granted a Brevet Lieutenant Colonelcy in September of the following year. This distinction was presumably a recognition of his services in South Africa. It carried with it a higher level of pension, and he took the opportunity to retire.

Little is known of his travels during the next five years. An accomplished amateur artist, he produced a series of lithographs of the recent campaign (including a depiction of the Gwanga battle in which he had taken such a leading part). He then surfaces in Sardinia, at the end of 1853. There is no way of knowing why he should have been there. He was not yet forty

years of age, in his prime and an experienced soldier. It is possible that he had taken service with this independent kingdom as some sort of military advisor or, if his old wounds were still troubling him, he may simply have gone to the island for a rest. Whatever the explanation, it is known that he went north from Cagliari into the Agliastra mountains for a shooting expedition with his friend, Captain Payne Gallway. The weather was harsh, and he contracted a chill which turned into pneumonia. He was taken down to Cagliari and there he died, six days later, on 31 December.

He had never married, so the title passed to his brother, the Reverend William Lionell Darell MA, Rector of Frethorne, in the county of Gloucestershire. Despite a recent search through local archives by the British Consul in Cagliari, Harry's place of burial has not been established.

Lieutenant Colonel Sir Harry Darell was the product of his class and era, a brave hard-riding cavalryman who knew instinctively what needed to be done whenever the call to action came. Less typically, there was an artistic streak in his nature. Unlike his regiment and the baronetcy, some of his prints have (along with this mull) survived the passing years. They are his only enduring memorials. He left no medals. Authority for the issue of a retrospective South Africa medal was approved by Queen Victoria in 1854. It was given to officers and men who had served in the various Kaffir campaigns, and who were still alive. Harry did not live long enough to submit a claim.

His Highness The Maharajah Chandra Sham Sher Jang Bahadur Rana, GCSI, GCMG, GCVO, GCIE, Prime Minister of Nepal

Silver frames fall into two categories - picture frames and band programme frames (the latter being used alternatively to display menus). It would be unusual to find, on the open market, a frame engraved with individual presentation wording. Judging by those seen at antiques fairs, their military provenance is normally identifiable only by the engraving of a regimental or service crest on the top cross-piece, or by the mounting of a cast silver badge. The desirability of such objects, from the military collector's perspective, is then determined by the name of the unit itself. As an example, a frame which once stood in the Mess of a small and long-defunct Colonial unit would be more attractive than one bearing the crest of a very large Corps or service such as the Royal Engineers or the Royal Air Force. With this type of artefact, the "rarity factor" comes into play.

One example which surfaced in 1998, in a Newton Abbot flea-market, is illustrated here. It had been purchased by a dealer, a week earlier, at a general auction in Torquay. The previous owner was an elderly gentleman who, for forty years, bought and stored any bits and pieces which happened to catch his fancy. His random collection of silver formed part of the auctioneer's catalogue.

The portrait is signed "Chandra Sham Sher, 1911", and this, combined with the crossed *kukris*, was the first clue in identifying him. The country of origin was almost certainly Nepal, and the object was most probably associated with the great Delhi Durbar. It was in 1911 that King George V and Queen Mary visited India and received, in circumstances of the greatest pomp and splendour, all the Maharajahs of British India and of the independent Princely States, and numerous dignatories of the Raj.

The King of Nepal could not himself attend the Durbar. He and his forebears and successors were, from the early 1800s through to 1950, confined in the royal palace at Katmandu. They

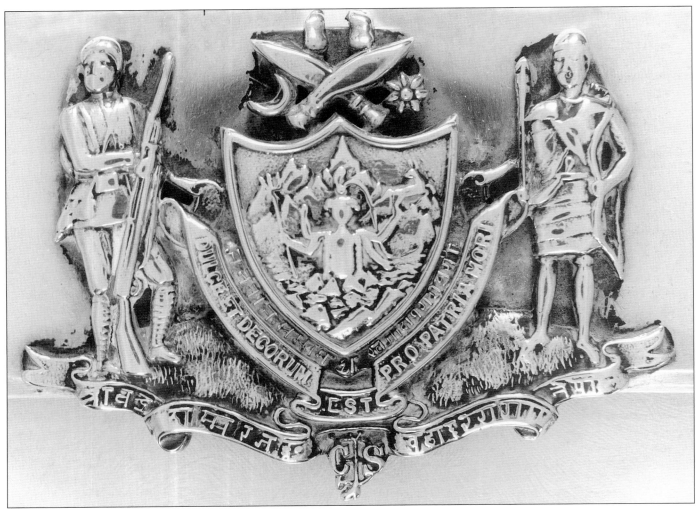

The coat of arms is full of interest and symbolism. The sun, moon and wandering feet surrounding the crossed *kukris* are auspicious omens to take one through life. The supporting figures are a soldier of the Royal Nepalese Army of the 1900s and a Nepalese warrior armed with bow and arrow and kukri. The central shield shows Siva (Shiva), the Hindu god of destruction and rebirth, against a background of Himalayan mountains. The Nepali motto, in Deva-Nagri script, translates as *Glory to the Ruling Monarchy*. The classic Latin tag, *It is sweet and becoming to die for one's country*, is thought to have been adopted by Chandra Sham Sher's grandfather following his visit to England to meet Queen Victoria. Photos: Alan Cooper, Newton Abbot.

were no more than revered figure-heads. The country was governed by the Rana family, a group which passed from generation to generation the title of Prime Minister. It was they who held the true power, and it was their current incumbent, Chandra Sham Sher, who represented Nepal at the Durbar.

It is safe to assume that some months earlier he had sent an order to London for the manufacture of a number of silver frames and arranged to be photographed in Court dress. Arriving at Delhi, and in the same way as all the other assembled Maharajahs, he and his entourage and servants took up residence in their own magnificent tented enclave on the outskirts of the city. There he entertained HM King George V to a sumptuous luncheon and no doubt gave him one of these framed photographs. Chandra Sham Sher and the King's father, Edward VII, had been personal friends. After the Durbar, King George and Chandra went off together for a memorable shooting expedition in the Terai (where the English visitor shot, amongst other animals, twenty-one tigers).

It is impossible to say how many of these framed portraits he presented to other notables, but it is likely that the number was not large.

It is worth noting that before it was intercepted *en route*, the picture was destined for "re-cycling". The photograph itself was to be discarded, the armorial bearings removed and scrapped, and the basic frame then made good and sold on as an excep-

The Maharajah Chandra Sham Sher Jang Bahadur Rana, wearing the cloak and breast emblem of the Grand Cross of the Star of India and the collar chain of the Grand Cross of the Royal Victorian Order. In later years he received the Grand Crosses of the Order of St Michael & St George and the Order of the Indian Empire. He was made an Honorary General of the British Army, and the President of France appointed him a Grand Commander of the Legion of Honour. His support for the Allied cause during WWI was particularly valued.

The silver frame which houses Sham Sher's portrait is of exceptional proportions. Seventeen inches high and 11 inches wide, it was made by William Comyns and is hallmarked London 1910.

tionally large and collectable Edwardian frame. Picture frames of this size and quality are very desirable in their own right.

Does such an object qualify as "military silver"? In the opinion of the author, yes, it does. The Kings of Nepal were nominally the heads of the Royal Nepalese Army, units of which served alongside the British and Indian Armies in both world wars and in several lesser campaigns. It was the hereditary Prime Ministers such as Chandra Sham Sher who authorised these deployments and, despite their limited national treasury, made donations to British war funds. Most importantly of all, they sustained the friendship with Great Britain which had begun in 1816 and, throughout all those years, continued to approve the enlistment of Gurkha soldiers into regiments of the East India Company and the Indian Army. Chandra's own friendship with the British was reflected in the many high honours bestowed upon him Apart from his decorations, he was appointed an Honorary Lieutenant General in the British Army in 1915, and full Honorary General in 1919.

He followed closely the movements and campaigns of the Gurkha regiments in British service, maintaining regular contact with them and occasionally presenting their Messes with valuable artefacts. One such is the exquisitely carved ebony fireplace overmantle which now stands in the ante-room of the Officers' Mess at Church Crookham. It was given by Chandra to the Sirmoor Rifles who, for many years, had it in their Mess at Dehra Dun.

The relationship changed in the early 1950s. The leading members of the Rana family then lost their hereditary Prime Ministerial privileges, and the king finally achieved full sovereign power.

Surgeon Commander G Murray Levick, RN, FRGS, FZS

Chapter 7, *Silver at Sea*, included a reference to Haslar Naval Hospital and the work of naval surgeons. In 1996, at an auction held in Exmouth, South Devon, the personal effects of one of the most remarkable of those doctors were seen by the public for the first time. The sale attracted bids from institutions and collectors all over the world.

The name of George Murray Levick is forever associated with that of Captain Robert Scott RN, the pioneer Antarctic explorer. Scott had led the first expedition in *Discovery* in 1901-1904, and he was determined to go back and be the first to reach the South Pole. The Admiralty was willing to assist him with men and other resources, but Scott himself was responsible for all aspects of funding and organisation. It was not until 1910 that he could depart, in the *Terra Nova*, for his greatest and final adventure.

A key factor in determining who would join him was the question of money. Some selected officers paid Scott as much as a thousand pounds for the privilege of joining him as "gentlemen adventurers". Murray Levick was a bachelor of comfortable means, and it is likely that he too contributed. The Admiralty agreed to grant him leave of absence, and he joined Scott as expedition doctor and zoologist.

The full story of the heroic but flawed (and ultimately fatal) attempt by Scott and his companions to walk to the South Pole is well recorded in print and on film. Murray Levick did not participate in that part of the expedition. Instead, and once Scott had established his main base at Hut Point, he and five other men were taken by the *Terra Nova* to a point several hundred miles north. Led by Victor Campbell and known as "the northern party", this small group planned to devote the Antarctic summer to making various scientific observations. They were put ashore on the ice shelf with a tent and sufficient stores to carry them through to the planned date of re-embarkation.

Murray Levick had a particular interest in penguins, birds which previously had not been studied scientifically. He devoted the following weeks to collecting data and keeping himself busy with his notebooks (his findings were later published as *The Social Habits of Antarctic Penguins* and *A Monograph on Adelie Penguins*). As the summer approached its end, however, it became evident that the weather was deteriorating rapidly and the pack ice accumulating much faster than expected. Campbell and his five companions realised that the *Terra Nova* would be unable to force a passage, and that they were stranded. Facing the prospect of certain death if they did not act quickly, they spent three days killing penguins and seals, cleaning them and making a *cache* in the ice. They then excavated with ice picks a hole in the side of a glacier, creating a cavern measuring twelve feet in diameter. This refrigerator was their home for the following six months.

The remaining stocks of tinned food and hard-tack biscuits were stringently rationed (with one biscuit per man each day). Heat and light were generated by burning the blubber of the frozen penguin and seal carcasses. When eventually they were rescued, the six men were hardly recognisable. They had six months' growth of hair and beard, and their skin was so ingrained with soot from the lamp and cooker that their hands, faces and clothes had merged into a uniform blackness.

Surgeon Commander G Murray Levick RN, photographed at Scott's Antarctic base during the *Terra Nova* expedition. The doctor kept extensive notes of his observations, particularly with regard to the species of penguins in that area. They attracted great interest in the zoological world when he returned to England. His other notes and papers prompted even greater enthusiasm when they appeared at auction in 1996.
Photo: Frank Debenham, and Scott Polar Research Institute, Cambridge.

founded and managed the Public Schools Exploring Society (taking parties of boys to Greenland, Norway and Finland).

He had a life-time interest in personal fitness, physical training and the treatment of sports injuries. Recalled by the Admiralty in 1939, he served first with Naval Intelligence and was then responsible for the preparation of training programmes for the new Commando forces. After the war he retired to Budleigh Salterton, on the South Devon coast, and died there on 30 May 1956.

His possessions were later crated and placed in store, and there they remained until offered at the 1996 auction. It was attended by more than three hundred people, and telephone bids were received from Australia, Japan, Italy and Sweden. Items connected directly with the *Terra Nova* expedition attracted the greatest interest, with Murray Levick's medals being hammered at £6500 and his two Antarctic diaries at £6000. A single letter addressed to him and signed by Captain Scott was sold for £4300. Ten percent buyer's premium was added to each hammer price.

The item now in the author's collection was not included in that catalogue. It is a heavy (20 ounces) silver cigarette box, made by S Clifford & Company, London 1909. Engraved upon the lid, in very ornate lettering, is the wording: "Presented to Surgeon G Murray Levick RN by the Royal Navy Rugby Union in grateful recognition of his zealous work as Hon Secretary, Dec 18 1907 - May 27 1910". The Union, which is still thriving, was in fact founded by him and he was the first Secretary. He resigned from that post when Scott accepted him as a member of the *Terra Nova* team.

Instead of being included in the main catalogue, the box was held back for sale in a subsequent specialist auction of silver. There it was seen by Peter Brand, a professional dealer and one of the author's most valued guides and mentors in the complex world of second-hand silver and plate. By then, the Polar exploration collectors had long departed. Peter was unaware of Murray Levick's adventures, but his intuition told him that here was something of interest, and he bought it.

From the collector's perspective, two lessons emerge from this story. The first underlines a point made earlier - that there is much to be gained by having friends in the silver trade who are aware of your specific interests. The second is that not all desirable objects are precisely described in important catalogues. For one reason or another, an auctioneer's staff may decide to feature the (obviously) most important items in a high profile catalogue, and then dispose of the (seemingly) lesser items in a follow-up sale. It can be worthwhile to check the Lots due to be sold in the later sale, or to ask the auctioneer whether there is anything further in the pipe-line.

The episode is described in great detail in *Antarctic Adventure*, by Raymond Priestley, and it records one of the most remarkable examples of man's determination to survive against all the odds. The strains and uncertainties of their situation are hard to imagine. Only one episode of (unintended) humour is recorded. There are no "days" in the usual sense during the Antarctic winter, but cooking and cleaning duties were assigned according to a twenty-four hour rota. On one occasion, it was Murray Levick's turn to prepare and cook the daily meal. Thinking to break the monotony of seal and penguin flesh, he added to the stew several pharmaceutical mustard poultices from his medical supplies. He should have studied the label. The poultices contained no mustard but were instead made from a linseed oil extract. This had a disastrous effect upon the party's bowels, and Murray Levick was not its most popular member for the next day or two.

Rescue came in the following early summer. Surprisingly, when weather conditions began to improve, they were fit enough to starting walking across the ice towards Cape Evans. There they were found by a search party moving up from Hut Point.

Murray Levick returned to regular naval duties in late 1913 and was subsequently appointed to ships serving in the North Sea and the Mediterranean. His WWI services have not yet been researched, but there are references to him having taken part in the Gallipoli campaign as surgeon aboard a hospital ship. Between the wars, amongst a great many other involvements, he

Lieutenant Colonel H C Uniacke, CB, The Gordon Highlanders

Here we revert to the area of silver goblets, but this one is special. It stands 7.5 inches in height, is 3.5 inches in diameter, weighs 16 ounces, and is stamped with the marks for Hancocks

& Company, London 1914. Embossed upon one side is the crest of the 92nd (Gordon Highlanders) Regiment of Foot, the regiment which in 1881 became 2nd Battalion, The Gordon Highlanders. This piece, a christening cup, surfaced in 1996 at an antiques fair in Exeter.

Engraved around the lip of the goblet are the words: "U.G.L.H. (born in the Regt), from his godfather, Lt Col H.P.Uniacke, 1913". It was immediately clear that at least three lives were represented in this wording - the recipient (the then unknown infant "UGLH"), the donor (most probably the officer commanding the regiment depicted in the crest), and the infant's father.

Following an introduction by the dealer involved in the transaction, the identity of the recipient was soon established. Very much alive and thriving at the age of eighty-two, he was Lieutenant Commander (retired) Ulric Gilbert Lang Huggins RNVR, of Heathfield, East Sussex. Having no descendents interested in such matters, he had decided to dispose of the goblet with the hope that someone, somewhere, would care for it. We shall take first the story of his father.

Major Charles Gilbert Dingwall Huggins was born at Whyteleaf, Surrey, on 6 August 1882. He was educated at Wellington College and, from the school, was commissioned directly into The Gordon Highlanders at the age of eighteen. Within months he was in South Africa, serving in the Anglo-Boer war. By 1913 he had attained the rank of Captain, commanding a company of the 2nd Battalion in Egypt. He and his wife had a house at Ghezira, and their son Ulric was born there on 6 November of that year. The name "Ulric" had no precedent in the Huggins family. It was his mother's choice. She was acquainted with an officer named Captain Ulric Oliver Thynne DSO, an adventurous horseman and Yeomanry officer whom Mrs Huggins described as "having a good leg for a boot". Evidently she had some admiration for him but, as Ulric said recently, "my father didn't seem to mind". Thynne had a remarkable career, and it is tempting to write several pages about this one officer alone.

Following Ulric's birth, his father asked his commanding officer if he would be the boy's godfather. Colonel Uniacke agreed, and in due course arranged for the purchase and naming of the goblet. Presumably it was handed over at some time during the first half of 1914, before the battalion embarked for England on 13 September. Within days, it had absorbed the Reservists needed to bring it up to full strength and sailed for Zeebrugge. Two weeks later, on the morning of 30 October at Zandvoorde, Captain Huggins was severely wounded in the arm. He rejoined after several months of treatment, but was then blown up. Severely shell-shocked, he was medically down-graded and given a Staff job at the War Office where he remained for the final years of the war.

After the war he commanded the regimental depôt at Aberdeen for three years. In 1932 he was appointed Adjutant of The Royal Hospital, Chelsea, responsible for the day-to-day welfare of the famous Chelsea Pensioners. Retiring from uniformed service in 1937, he acquired The Wilderness, Hadlow Down, Sussex, which he farmed for many years. He died in March 1964.

Young Ulric was sent, like his father before him, to Wellington College, and seemed destined for a career in the army. The words on his christening cup - "born in the regiment" - were almost a portent. Instead, and "having endured enough square bashing in the Wellington OTC to last a lifetime", he entered The Royal School of Mines, London University, with a

view to making a career in mining engineering. Illness prevented him from completing the full degree course but, in 1937, he began work in the Lancashire coal industry.

With war looming, he applied for and obtained a commission in the Royal Naval Volunteer Reserve. He was attached, for training and administrative purposes, to a shore base in Liverpool, HMS *Eaglet*. Mobilised in August 1939, as a Sub Lieutenant, he was appointed to the Devonport-based light cruiser, HMS *Caradoc*. A "C" class ship armed with 6-inch guns, she had been built in 1916 and was unfit for service in home waters. She lacked any anti-aircraft defences and had no de-gaussing (anti-magnetic mine) gear. She was sent Canada with her magazines full of gold bullion from the Bank of England, and was then deployed in the search for blockade runners in the Atlantic. Several German merchantmen were intercepted and their crews put ashore on the island of Bermuda. She was involved also in the hunt for the *Admiral Graf Spee* but, to quote Ulric, "luckily we never found her".

Captain C G D Huggins, The Gordon Highlanders, seen here shortly before the outbreak of WWI. Photo: Regimental Museum.

He parted company with the *Caradoc* in October 1940 and was sent to the naval gunnery school, HMS *Excellent*, at Whale Island, Portsmouth. The peacetime course lasted two years but, under wartime conditions, the students were rushed through in six months. Having qualified, he was appointed Gunnery Officer on the staff of the Captain "D", First Destroyer Flotilla, based at Portsmouth. He received his first sea-going appointment in December 1941 as Gunnery Officer, HMS *Aurora*. A modern (launched 1936) cruiser with a displacement of 5270 tons, armed with six-inch guns, she was the tenth Royal Navy ship to bear that name. At the time Ulric joined her (and he was always known in the navy as Peter), she had already seen much action in the Atlantic, off Norway, and in the Mediterranean. She was currently under repair at Liverpool, having struck a mine off Tripoli.

The next two years were packed with action - attacks on Axis supply routes, and the Allied landings in Algeria, Sicily and Salerno, A highlight was a night-time action off Bizerta which resulted in the almost total destruction of an enemy convoy. Two enemy destroyers, a large landing craft, and a troopship of 7000 tons were sunk, with other vessels damaged. The fire of HMS *Aurora* was judged to have been "devastatingly accurate", and Ulric's work was recognised by a Mention in Despatches.

Colonel Henry Uniacke's "92nd" christening goblet, his gift to a godson who outlived him by more than eighty years. Uniacke was killed by a German sniper within a few months of attending the baptism and making the presentation.

The ship's luck ran out in 1943 when, operating from Alexandria, she took part in the abortive attempt to evict the Germans from Rhodes and other Aegean islands. On 27 October, she was attacked by Ju87 Stuka dive-bombers which succeeded in hitting the anti-aircraft gun deck. Fifty-five men were killed and many injured, but she managed to reach the safe haven of Taranto.

With the *Aurora* dry-docked for extensive repair, Ulric was sent to Devonport Gunnery School as an Instructor, then to the Admiralty Signals Department for secret work on the new "chaff" systems (designed to protect Royal Navy ships from radar-equipped enemy ships and aircraft). After demobilisation in 1945 he worked for Shell International Petroleum for twenty years, then, like his father before him, became a farmer in Sussex.

So much for the baby Ulric and his father. Who was the godfather? A great deal is known about this officer. Henry Percy Uniacke was the son of Captain Henry Uniacke, 19th Regiment of Foot, of Laywell, Devon. Born in 1862, he obtained a commission in the Militia and was then accepted into the Regular Army. He joined the 1st Battalion, The Gordon Highlanders, in May 1884. He took part in the Tirah expedition (the North West Frontier of India, 1897-1898) and fought in the actions at Chagru Khotal and Dargai (where he was slightly wounded). He was at the capture of the Sampagha and Arhanga Passes, and the operations in the Bara Valley. He was Mentioned in Despatches and received the campaign medal with two clasps.

A minor but stirring incident took place during the march down the Bara Valley. On the night of 11 December 1897, Captain Uniacke (as he now was) came under fire from a building occupied by hostile tribesmen. Taking four riflemen with him, he instantly rushed forward and cleared the house with the bayonet. He then held it until the battalion's scattered rearguard was contacted, rallied, and brought in to fortify the place. This affair was later quoted in military textbooks to illustrate the value of boldness and bluff.

He was promoted Major in November 1903. From 1899 to 1904, he was Adjutant to a Volunteer unit, The Queen's Edinburgh Rifles (and, additionally, Inspector of Musketry for Scotland). Then, after three years commanding the regimental depôt in Aberdeen, he assumed command on 13 September 1912 of the 2nd Battalion in Cawnpore. Shortly afterwards he took it to Egypt, and it was stationed at Ghezira when war broke out in Europe.

An element of the 7th Division, BEF, the 2nd Gordons arrived in that area of Flanders which, over the next four years, came to be known as the Ypres Salient. Severe fighting around Gheluvelt on 28 October 1914 caused heavy casualties in the battalion. It was during this action that Lieutenant J A O Brooke was killed while leading an attack to recover a line of trench. On the recommendation of Colonel Uniacke, he was awarded the Victoria Cross.

The Germans continued their advance towards Ypres and, two days later, the 2nd Gordons were marched hurriedly to Zandvoorde to help plug the gaps in the British line. Heavy shell and small arms fire inflicted more casualties and two of the evacuated officers were Colonel Uniacke and Captain Huggins (with his arm injury). Both rejoined the battalion some months later.

The scene now moves to the battles around Neuve Chappelle and Hill 60. On 12 March 1915, the battalion was waiting in reserve near German positions at the hamlet of Moulin du Piétre. Orders arrived during the night to move forward and prepare to make a bayonet charge, the next day, across open ground.

At first light, Colonel Uniacke went up to the front to see what needed to be done. Crawling along a shallow trench and intending to observe the terrain, he cautiously raised his head above the parapet. Instantly he was seen by a German sniper who shot him dead.

Command of the battalion now passed to Major Stansfield. Under constant shellfire, and steadily losing more and more men, he cancelled the bayonet charge and kept the survivors under cover until evening. A party then went forward and recovered their Colonel's body. They buried him that night in the civil cemetery beside the church at Estaire.

For his services during the opening months of the war, he was appointed a Companion of the Order of the Bath, this honour being announced in the *London Gazette* of 2 March 1915 (just eleven days before his death). He had a cousin, only a few years younger than himself, who was similarly honoured and who died at almost the same time. Lieutenant Colonel Robie Fitz-Gerald Uniacke, Royal Inniskilling Fusiliers, was a French-speaking Divisional staff officer who was admitted to the Distinguished Service Order before dying in an accident behind the lines on 28 May 1915. The cream of the professional soldiers of the Allied armies and the Imperial German Army were killed in those opening months of the conflict. These two men were amongst the thousands of their generation who could never entirely be replaced.

After the war, Henry Uniacke's widow presented his medals and memorial plaque to the Regimental Museum in Aberdeen. She also donated two of his silver trophies (a challenge shield and a statuette). All these items are still to be seen there, and it is to the museum that we turn for the final strand in the story.

Why did Colonel Uniacke choose, as his christening gift, a goblet bearing the numeral "92"? The old 92nd of Foot title had ceased to exist when, in 1881, that regiment was amalgamated with the 75th. The wording - "born in the regiment" - seems incongruous for a presentation made in 1913. The puzzle was solved by correspondence with a former Curator of the museum, Stuart Allan. He explained, first of all, that goblets of this pattern were for many years presented to the Mess by individual officers to mark special occasions ("on joining", and so forth). The custom began in the 1870s and continued through to at least 1994 (the time of the latest amalgamation). The Museum's collection alone has more than forty examples in its inventory, and others are held by 1st Battalion, The Highlanders (Seaforths, Gordons and Camerons). For a long time after the 1881 reorganisations, the 75th and 92nd badges continued to be incorporated in their design. That was certainly still the practice when Colonel Uniacke placed his order. The numeric *motif* was then gradually abandoned and replaced by the "sporran" badge. Interestingly, the "Ulric Cup" is the only one not in the immediate possession of the regiment and the museum.

Apart from the human drama which it represents, this goblet demonstrates the importance of raising enquiries - in respect of provenance - as soon as possible after making an acquisition. Henry Uniacke was a well-known officer, frequently mentioned in the history and archives of his regiment. Researching his career was always going to be easy. The "UGLH" element in the engraving, on the other hand, would very probably have remained an enigma if the intermediary had not been contacted. Thanks to the cooperation of Henry Willis, the Sherborne dealer in antique silver, it was possible to make direct contact with the original owner. The missing pieces of the jigsaw then fell into place.

Brigadier General R T I Ridgway, CB, Indian Army

Again, we are looking at a goblet, but of much simpler design than the previous entry. Standing 7 inches, it weighs 10.6 ounces and bears marks for London 1891. The maker's mark has been made illegible from heavy polishing. Engraved on one side is the regimental crest of the 40th Pathans and, on the other, "Lieut R Ridgway, presented on appointment". In other words, it was once part of the Mess silver of one of the best known infantry regiments of the Indian Army. Combined with their (unique) early policy of recruiting only Pathan hill tribesmen, their numeric designation made it inevitable that they were known as "the Forty Thieves" or the "Ali Babas".

The following is a condensed version of the ample information available. Richard Thomas Incledon Ridgway was born on 17 August 1868. He was the son of Captain Poltimore Ridgway, of the 94th Foot, and was educated at Wellington School (1880-1886) and the Royal Military College Sandhurst (1886-1887). He was commissioned first into The Connaught Rangers but then, two years later, transferred to the Indian Army. After brief service with the 26th Punjab Infantry, he was appointed in May 1891 to the 40th (Pathan) Regiment of Bengal Native Infantry and was made Adjutant. His first campaign was the Tirah expedition of 1897. Temporarily detached from his regiment, he served in that campaign with the Nabha Imperial Service Infantry (a unit on loan from their Maharajah).

In 1900, he was sent as recruiting officer into the Pathan tribal areas. This was a task which called not only for advanced linguistic skills but also an exceptional understanding of the quick-silver Pathan temperament and complex clan society. The published regimental history contains several references to his adventures during that period (including an incident when he was obliged, personally, to hang a convicted murderer). Six years later he was second in command of his regiment when it took part in the Mohmand expedition.

Major Ridgway's next move came in 1912. After twenty-one years with the 40th Pathans, he went to their linked battalion, the 33rd Punjabis, of which he assumed command on 22 March 1913. When war was declared, he took them to Egypt. They were involved in several minor engagements with the Turks in Sinai before moving to the Western Front in September 1915 as part of the Indian Corps. Here they were plunged into the mayhem of the Battle of Loos, a style of warfare for which Indian troops were totally unprepared either materially or mentally. Colonel Ridgway was wounded in the attack at Moulin du Piétre (the place where Henry Uniacke was killed, as described in the preceding entry).

There is an anecdote, uncorroborated but persistent, which states that Ridgway was hit in the chest, and that the bullet was deflected away from his heart by his silver cigarette case. Whatever the truth of the matter, he recovered and was able to resume command of his regiment before its next move. His men had fought bravely and well in the Loos battle but, together with all the other Indian Army infantry regiments, they were withdrawn in 1916 and sent to the Middle East.

After a brief spell in Aden, the 33rd were committed to the campaign against the Germans in Tanganyika and Portuguese East Africa. Promoted Brevet Colonel, Ridgway was given command of Number Two "Han" Column during the last eighteen months of bush warfare. Later he wrote an account of this period for the *Army Quarterly*.

After the German surrender, and returning to India, he went directly into his final campaign, commanding the Kohat-Kurram Field Force in the short-lived Third Afghan War of 1919. He retired as a Brigadier General in December 1920. He was made a Companion of the Order of the Bath in 1916, and during the war was four times Mentioned in Despatches. Leaving India for the last time, he retired to Campden Hill, Kensington. He wrote three local history books, served on the Council, and in the 1930s helped to organise the Borough for the coming war.

Under the reorganisations of 1922, the 33rd Punjabis were redesignated as the 3rd Battalion, 16th Punjab Regiment, but the "old and bold" amongst their officers and senior NCOs continued for the next twenty years to speak of themselves as "the 33rd". Then, early in 1942, all of that came suddenly to an end. The 3rd/16th was one of the unfortunate battalions committed to the defence of Malaya, the survivors being forced to surrender at Singapore. Richard Ridgway was spared the pain of hearing that news. He died on Armistice Day, 11 November 1939, at the age of seventy-one.

Colonel J H S Gibb DSO, The Worcestershire Regiment

Previous chapters of this book have included descriptions of the beautiful rose bowls presented to the Royal Artillery and to The Somerset Light Infantry. At the other end of the scale, but designed to meet the same practical need, are simple finger bowls of the type illustrated here. It was "Presented to the officers, 1st Battn, The Worcestershire Regiment, by Lieut Colonel J.H.S Gibb, D.S.O., 2nd March 1903".

It is one of a matching set of twelve. Eleven are still in the possession of The Worcestershire & Sherwood Foresters Regiment, and one has been acquired by the author *via* a recent regimental dispersal sale. At the time of writing, this is the only example to have been released. It is possible, even probable, that the remaining eleven bowls also will be sold into private hands at a later date. In that case, as many as twelve fortunate collectors (or members of the regimental association) will have the pleasure of caring for a part of Colonel Gibb's remarkable career.

The Colonel Gibbs finger bowl weighs 8.5 ounces, is 5 inches in diameter, and was made in 1902 by John Bodman Carrington, of 130 Regent Street, London.

John Hassard Stewart Gibb was born on 13 February 1859 and received his commission with the 29th (Worcestershire) Regiment of Foot on 13 August 1879. Promoted to Lieutenant after only eight months, he transferred to the "linked" regiment, the 36th (Herefordshire) Regiment of Foot (shortly before the two were merged as 1st and 2nd Battalions, The Worcestershire Regiment).

The next four years were devoted to learning his profession. This was not a good time for adventurous young men such as John Gibb. Most of the world was at peace. For many of the British Army's regiments, at home and overseas, life revolved around the predictable routine of garrison life. Only Egypt offered any prospect of action, and that was where Lieutenant Gibb decided to go. He requested a secondment to the Egyptian Army, and this was granted in May 1884.

Formerly an integral part of the decaying Ottoman Empire, Egypt had acquired a new importance with the opening, in 1869, of the Suez Canal. When the country became bankrupt, the British and French had strong financial and strategic reasons for ensuring its security. They backed the Khedive, Tewfik Mohammad, and took an increasing part in the management of Egypt's affairs. This caused resentment amongst fervent nationalists and, in 1881, a revolt led by Arabi Pasha was supported by the Egyptian Army. Within weeks, London had authorised a major expedition to crush the mutiny and to take over the affairs of the country. This was more easily said than done.

Between 1882 and 1889, the British Army (with contingents from Canada and Australia) fought a succession of campaigns to gain control not only of the Nile Delta region but also the up-country areas and the Sudan. They are remembered best for the individual roles of men such as Gordon, Kitchener, Winston Churchill, and others who in diverse ways came to public attention during those years.

Many British regiments were involved, but they needed the support of the reconstituted Egyptian Army, trained and commanded by officers such as John Gibb. He was appointed to its 9th Battalion and served with it as a company commander in the Nile Expedition of 1884-1885 (the abortive attempt to rescue General Gordon from the besieged city of Khartoum). During this campaign, on 27 June 1884, Gibb jumped into the Nile to rescue an Egyptian interpreter who had fallen into the water and was, literally, going down for the third time. Subsequently he received the Bronze Medal of the Royal Humane Society.

Given command of the 9th Battalion in 1885, he saw a great deal of action over the next twelve months with the Frontier Field Force. Conditions in the border areas between Egypt and the Sudan were chaotic, with various tribal groups warring with the infidel British and against each other. He led his battalion at the major engagement at Ginnis, on 29 December 1885, when 4500 British and Egyptian troops fought and defeated 6000 Sudanese. The Khedive rewarded his services with the Order of the Osmanieh, 4th Class.

All of this high adventure came to an end in September 1886. He rejoined the 1st Battalion of his parent regiment, at that time stationed in India. Two years later he returned to Worcester on his appointment as Adjutant of the part-time 4th (Militia) Battalion, an experience which led to another bout of itchy feet.

This time he managed to obtain a job in Uganda. A beautiful and fertile region, its history was scarred by centuries of inter-tribal warfare and the cruelties of the Arab slave traders. Both the French and the Germans had for a while held ambitions to occupy it and bring it within their rapidly expanding African empires. The British East India Company established trading posts but, lacking adequate finance, failed to exploit their toehold. The task of imposing British control was given to Major Frederick Lugard, one of the great Empire builders. In December 1890, with one Maxim gun and a small force of Sudanese and Swahili (Kenya coast) soldiers, he signed a peace treaty at Kampala with the King of Buganda. This gave him a firm base from which to operate deeper into the hinterland, but he lacked sufficient troops and experienced officers to command them.

By chance, Lugard encountered a force of Egyptian Army (Sudanese) troops. In the aftermath of the chaos in the Sudan, cut off from their paymaster and sources of supply, they had wandered south into Uganda and were living off the land.

To Lugard, any officer with experience of commanding Egyptian/Sudanese troops in battle was worth his weight in gold. John Gibb was an ideal choice to take them in hand, and he arrived from England in September 1893. By the end of the year he was in action, as second in command to Colonel M Colville, of the Grenadier Guards. Their orders were to enter the neighbouring kingdom of Unyoro, the pastures and forests of which reach up to the foothills of the fabled Mountains of the Moon. Buganda and Unyoro had long been in conflict with each other, and the time had come to impose *pax Britannica*.

Following his return from Uganda, Major J H S Gibb poses for the camera *circa* 1898. It is remarkable how closely the officers of that period resembled each other. It is possible that the effect was enhanced by the heavy moustaches favoured by Kitchener and other senior commanders. Photo: RHQ The Worcestershire and Sherwood Foresters Regiment.

Colville's column consisted of 200 Egyptian (Sudanese) troops and 5000 Bugandan Levies. A confused series of actions culminated in an expedition to Mruli which, for a time, brought a temporary peace. The Sultan of Zanzibar was an ally of the British, with a strong interest in affairs on the mainland, and Captain Gibb subsequently received from him the Order of the Brilliant Star, 3rd Class.

Captain Gibb was involved for a while in the work of the Uganda Boundary Commission before returning to regimental soldiering in March 1895. He saw no further action over the next five years (a long time by his standards), serving with the 1st Worcesters in Rangoon (1895), Aden (1896) and Plymouth (1897-1899). The next call to battle came with the outbreak of the war in South Africa. Now a Major commanding a company, he embarked in the S.S. *Braemar Castle* at Tilbury Docks on 18 March 1900.

The full story of the Worcesters' participation in the Anglo-Boer War can be followed elsewhere. It enough here to say that Gibb emerged from it with two more campaign medals, a Mention in Despatches, and admission to the Distinguished Service Order. He was by now reaching the peak of his career. The crowning event, in 1903, was his appointment as Commanding Officer of his regiment's 1st Battalion. It was that which prompted the presentation of the set of finger bowls described earlier.

In 1906 he was made a Brevet Colonel (which helped his pension), and in 1907 retired to Christchurch, Dorset. After twenty-eight years' service, it seemed that his time in uniform had run its course. But it was not to be. In 1915, he was recalled and sent to France as a Divisional Base Commandant. This appointment lasted no more than a year. He was now fifty-eight years of age, and the War Office decided to release him. An obituary, recording his death in August 1933, tells us only that his retirement years were spent very quietly. Some of his many memories - of fighting "Fuzzy Wuzzies" in the Sudan, Unyoro tribesmen in Uganda, and the Boers in South Africa - are recorded in his diaries and letters held in the archives of the National Army Museum.

Major J T Carpenter-Garnier, The Scots Guards

This item is featured here because it is different to the norm. It is a finely decorated baluster-shaped silver teapot with the mark of the Edinburgh assay office and the year mark for 1855. It is one of only two (military) items of Scottish silver to have been recorded so far by the author, and the fact that it is a collectable antique in its own right meant that the price was higher than that of a corresponding piece of later date. The attraction, as always, was the additional engraving. Within a *cartouche* on one side is the regimental crest of The Scots Guards, while on the other is a matching *cartouche* in which this wording appears: "To Sergeant Major Superintending Clerk D Kinlay. On his selection for promotion to commissioned rank, by Major J T Carpenter-Garnier, Regimental Adjutant, April 1909".

Some explanation is needed. The Brigade of Guards is, in numerous ways, a law unto itself. Only the Guards refer to the senior non-commissioned officer in charge of the Regimental Orderly Room as the Superintending Clerk. Almost by definition, he has many years of service and knows by heart the correct administrative procedures but, most importantly, he is wise in the ways of his regiment and its battalions. He is an oracle, and every prudent officer will seek his advice from time to time.

Likewise, only the Guards have an appointment known as the Regimental Adjutant. Its meaning is simple and logical - he is a Major who fulfils the duties of Adjutant to the entire regiment and is thereby senior to the Adjutants (normally Captains) of the individual battalions of that regiment. We shall look first at the donor of this teapot, Major John Trefusis Carpenter-Garnier.

In early August of 1914, the 1st Battalion of The Scots Guards was stationed in Aldershot. The Commanding Officer was Lieutenant Colonel H C Lowther, CB, CVO, CMG, DSO, and Carpenter-Garnier was his second in command. Mobilisation was completed on 13 August, and the battalion embarked at Southampton on the following morning in the SS *Dunvegan Castle*. Landing at Le Havre, they marched to a camp near Harfleur. Enthusiasm ran high, the guardsmen glittered magnificently, and everyone was spoiling for the fight which "would all be over by Christmas". The awakening came when they were committed to the Battle of the Aisne, the successful

Garnier's Superintending Clerk, he was now his brother officer.

Little more than a year later, following the Battle of Loos, Kinlay was the only remaining battalion officer of the twenty-eight who had sailed from Southampton. All of the others had been posted away, killed, or wounded and invalided home. When the Armistice came, on 11 November 1918, he was still there. His services were recognised by the award of the Military Cross.

Given time and effort, a great deal more information could be generated with regard to these two officers. Their story has been told here, in compressed form, because they are named on an item of silver which is attractive not only to students of

The elegant Carpenter-Garnier teapot was made in Edinburgh, in 1855, by James Howden & Son. It weighs 22 ounces. The engraved regimental crest of The Scots Guards appears in a matching *cartouche* of the reverse side.

blocking action which diverted the Germans away from Paris, their intended objective. The trench warfare of later years had yet to develop. This was still the textbook scenario of massed formations of infantry moving through a largely undamaged landscape of fields, hedgerows and woodland. What was not in the training manuals was the full impact of artillery and machine guns. On 13 September, only days after going into battle, Major Carpenter-Garnier was hit in the head by a shell splinter. He died the following day.

Sergeant Major Kinlay duly received his commission as a Lieutenant Quartermaster and, in normal circumstances, would have expected to soldier on for a few more years before taking his retirement. In the event, he too sailed for France on 14 August with the 1st Battalion. He was no longer Carpenter-

military history but also to collectors specialising in antique teapots. The "military silver" collector must accept the fact that he or she will on occasion need to invest more money than they would wish in order to "buy a story" which interests them.

Wing Commander C R Hancock OBE DFC, RAF

Here, by contrast, is a very ordinary handled cup, 4.5 inches high and standing on a wood base. It bears marks for London 1931, and is engraved "Flight Lieutenant C R Hancock, for the best air firing score, No.25 Squadron, 1931". As an item of silverware, it is of little consequence. It is the provenance which gives it meaning.

Charles Ronald Hancock commenced his flying training in January 1925. Sent to India, he served with 20 Squadron through to 1931. Equipped with Bristol fighters, it was based at Peshawar. It took part in air operations over the border areas of Afghanistan during "the Red Shirt rebellion". He qualified for the India General Service medal with the appropriate clasp, and was awarded the Distinguished Flying Cross "for distinguished services on the North West Frontier between 23.4.30 and 12.9.30". Only two other pilots were similarly decorated.

Flying over the tribal areas in a single-engined aircraft, dropping leaflets and bombing the hill villages, carried risks exceptional to that area. The greatest was engine failure. A forced landing and capture by hostile tribesmen could lead to very unpleasant experiences. All RAF aircrew engaged in these operations carried a document known as a "gooly chit". It offered a handsome reward if the bearer was returned intact. Usually the offer was accepted, but not always.

Promoted Squadron Leader in 1936, Hancock joined 25 Squadron at Hawkinge, Kent, flying Siskin fighters (soon replaced by the Hawker Fury). Later, after attending RAF Staff College, he moved to the Air Ministry (in the Directorate of Staff Duties).

His career during the next year or two is hard to define. He was promoted Wing Commander in January 1940, and can then be traced with certainty to the small RAF station at Ballyherbert, Northern Ireland, in 1943. It was occupied at that time by 303 (Polish) Squadron, equipped with the Spitfire Mark IX and commanded by Squadron Leader Jan Falkowski VM KW DFC (a high scoring ace of the Battle of Britain and of recent operations from Northolt). His squadron was in Ulster for a period of rest and to give air cover to shipping in the Firth of Clyde and the Irish Sea. Hancock was there as the Station Commander and presumably to gain the experience of piloting a modern high-speed fighter which he had missed while working at the Air Ministry.

At 1510 on 29 December, in the gathering gloom of a winter's afternoon, he took off in Spitfire AD 457 for a local familiarisation flight. Fatally, he decided to fly alone, without a wingman. This meant that he was totally dependent upon his engine and his radio. If either failed, he would be in trouble. The evidence suggests that he lost first his radio and then, thoroughly lost in low cloud, ran out of petrol. Nothing was heard from him after take off, and he was never seen again.

The squadron launched several pairs of aircraft at first light on the following morning, looking for flares, wreckage or a dinghy. The search ranged from the Mull of Kintyre all the way south to the Isle of Man. Visibility was very limited and nothing was found. Hancock had presumably exhausted his fuel and gone down in the sea. Alternatively, if disoriented, he might have flown south west over Ireland and crashed in a bog. Wartime aircraft and their aircrew have been found in recent years in isolated areas of Irish peat bog and, for all we know, that is where one day he might be discovered. For the time-being, his name is recorded on Panel 118 of the Commonwealth War Graves Commission's memorial, at Runnymede, to aircrew who have no known grave.

Like so much of the silver described in this chapter, this cup is probably the only relic of his life and times.

Some Lessons Learned

The author does not in any way pretend to understand all the intricacies of silver, or even a meaningful proportion of them. Like gold, it has for thousands of years been used by man as a form of decoration, a symbol of power, and a unit of commercial exchange. All of this is described in the published bibliography available to everyone wishing to study its history, or to understand the manufacturing processes which generate the many shapes and forms in which it is seen.

While interested in a general way in that background, the author has been drawn primarily to the regimental and maritime connotations discussed in this and the preceding chapters. That was inevitable, given his background. Others must approach the subject from their own perspectives. The concluding lines of this chapter will be limited to those practicalities of collecting silver which have formed part of the learning process of just one individual.

The point has been made already that it is productive to establish personal contacts within the various *strata* of the trade. By the time a piece has reached the highest levels, possibly the rooms of a major auction house or show-room, it may have passed through many hands. Each of the dealers involved in the chain will have needed, understandably, to turn a profit. In a perfect world, therefore, it is financially beneficial to identify the existence of a piece before it travels far up the commercial tree. The disadvantage with this approach is that it imposes certain demands in time and effort, and not everyone has time to spare. This need not be a cause for dismay. Auctioneers are always glad to give early notice of choice Lots to potential bidders, before the catalogue is published, and *if* they have been told what type of material is being sought.

Even more relevant are those instances when an auctioneer has been asked to value a piece and to find a buyer by private treaty. The descendants of the original recipient may not wish it to be widely known that they are selling great-grandfather's silver trophy, especially if it is engraved with the family name. As with so many things in life, "who you know" is often more important than "what you know".

The case has also been made in this book, probably to the point of over-exposure, that the early interception of a piece will ensure that it does not pass unrecognised for what it is (with the result that it is consigned at an early stage to re-cycling or the scrap bin).

Even when an interesting piece does reach the top branch of the tree, offered for sale in a major sales room, it may not be accurately or completely catalogued. Not many years ago, a much respected international house listed a silver trophy as being "of massive proportions". The engraved presentation wording was quoted in full, and there were some explanatory notes concerning the recipient and his regiment, but the essential technical information - height, weight, maker, assay office, year mark - received no mention. Such shortcomings will no doubt be corrected in the future but, for the time being, the prospective purchaser may at times find it appropriate to raise his or her own enquiries before placing a bid.

Reference has been made to the varying qualities of metal on offer. Sterling silver, Indian silver, Burmese silver, Chinese silver, St Helena silver, these and others have been mentioned. In addition, items with a military provenance were made in Sheffield plate, electro-plate, and pewter (of varying qualities). The meaning of these terms is explained briefly in the Glossary, but the budding collector is advised to indulge in some background reading (in other published sources) so that he may better comprehend what he is looking at when deciding whether or not to buy.

The term "solid silver" will make an appearance from time to time. It needs to be treated with caution. Pure silver is fundamentally too soft to be crafted or wrought. Copper is added to give it strength and hardness. It is true that pure silver might be cast and applied as an embellishment or decoration to a larger (Sterling silver) object, but this is not the norm. Apart from any other consideration, pure silver applied in this way is more vulnerable to wear from usage and polishing than the (harder) alloy.

The words "solid silver" are on occasion used in connection with objects which are in fact hollow or which contain a filler. Candelabra and candlesticks, as examples, are built up from sections of silver alloy and then filled with a material which gives them weight and balance. Pitch is the substance usually employed for this purpose. The base of the piece is sealed off with plaster of Paris and covered with, say, green or scarlet baize. The manufacturer had no intention to deceive, he was simply ensuring that the piece would be stable and secure when loaded with candles and placed on the table. However, this traditional technique does need to be kept in mind if a buyer is using weight as a key factor in calculating how much he wishes to pay.

Likewise, "plate" or "plated" can cause confusion if the collector has not done his homework. The *Glossary* provides further explanation but, in the context of this book, it is enough to say that the majority of modern silver artefacts are plated in one way or another (certainly those of the type likely to be found by the military collector, and made since the mid-19th century). In order to shape his material, and to fix one part to another, the silversmith needs to apply heat until it is, literally, red hot. Known as "firing", this annealing process may cause an unsightly discolouration of the alloy and is described as "fire stain". Sometimes it is eliminated by special workshop techniques during the final stages of manufacture, but usually it is concealed when a thin final layer of pure silver is added to the piece after all other work has been completed. Since the introduction of electro-plating, in 1843, this has been done by electrolysis. In earlier years it was done by a process known as "sweating", but that was in times when manufacturing processes were quite different.

While interesting in itself, knowledge of the technical methods employed by the silversmith in creating a beautiful end product is not essential for its enjoyment by the collector. The subject of plating has been raised here for one reason only, and it relates to the condition in which items of old silver may be found. With time, if silver is carefully housed and handled, it will acquire a uniform pale golden tone. This is "patina", and many collectors of antique silver find it attractive and desirable. However, some pieces will have been subjected to heavy polishing over many years, an obvious sign being the exposure of the "fire stain". This gives the object an ugly appearance, and may lead to its rejection as a potential purchase. In the event, the problem can easily be overcome by replating.

Straightforward plating or replating is not, in relative terms, expensive. Any qualified silversmith or silver restorer can give advice with regard to repairs and renovation, and quote the cost of the work. By law, he is obliged to submit the piece for further assay if (a) he makes a structural addition of more than five grams in weight, or (b) the new plating exceeds two microns in thickness. In the case of (a), the addition must be made in metal of the same standard of purity as the original. In practice, it would be unusual for a repair or renovation to involve a new assay.

Much of the silver seen at minor antiques fairs and similar venues is in a distressed condition. Having been several times dropped, or badly packed during its moves from place to place, it has acquired various "dinks", bruises and scratches. Pieces made with light gauge metal may have splits or tears. Cigarette boxes in particular seem to have adventurous lives. It is rare to find one in pristine condition, and the steel hinges are usually rusty or in some way damaged. There is no cause to be deterred by any of this, almost everything is repairable. Indeed, one of the pleasures of buying them is to later arrange for their restoration to the sort of condition in which they were once seen on a Mess table or on a retired officer's sideboard.

Over very many decades, antique silver has attracted the unwelcome attention of forgers. This has nothing to do with Mess or Wardroom silver. Instead, we are considering here what might be described as (for lack of a better word) "civilian" silver. These are very old and beautiful pieces which, if genuine, command high prices, and which a dishonest silversmith may attempt to replicate. Every year, a "Fakes and Forgeries of Silver Seminar" is held in London, at Goldsmiths' Hall, Foster Lane, in the City of London. Organised by The Goldsmiths' Company, it provides its membership with an opportunity to understand the ingenuity of generations of fakers and learn how to recognise their handiwork.

The legal penalties for malpractice are severe, but there has always been someone, somewhere, ready to chance their luck. Some of their methods are very simple, such as cutting the hallmarks from a severely damaged but once very valuable piece, and re-fixing them into a less important piece. By such means, they hope to bestow upon the latter an antiquity which it does not possess, or an attribution to a famous maker who was never involved in its design or manufacture. We need not concern ourselves here with that field of study because it is not, for the time being at least, relevant to the examples of military silver which are likely to come the way of private collectors.

However, and assuming that pieces with a military or naval provenance might start to attract more interest than they have in the past, there is one aspect of the forger's "art" which could conceivably cause anxiety in future years. Clearly, the criminal element will ponder the possibilities of taking a perfectly genuine piece of Georgian, Victorian or Edwardian silver and having it engraved with presentation wording which relates to a particularly famous officer, regiment, ship or event. It is unlikely that they will pursue the idea very far.

There are too many variables which would need to be brought together in the one piece. They would need to have a good knowledge of silver *per se*, and a quite profound knowledge of military and naval customs and records. They would need access to an engraver possessing the skills required for the replication of styles of lettering fashionable at different periods over the past two centuries (and willing to participate in the deception).

Finally, they would need to find a way of giving to that lettering the "rub" which comes only from many decades of regular polishing by the housemaid or Mess silverman. Having examined, with a powerful glass, the lettering on dozens of genuine pieces, the author is of the view that the forger will either fail to deceive or will choose some easier way of earning a living.

Any other lessons the author may have learned over the past three or four years are described in earlier chapters. What is certain is that there are a great many more still awaiting his attention. Military and naval silver, and everything associated with it, offers a limitless challenge for the acquisition of knowledge. Even more importantly, it provides the private individual with an opportunity to exercise good stewardship in preserving a part of the nation's military and naval heritage.

Appendix A

Trust Document of 2nd Battalion, The Gordon Highlanders, Changi 1942

The document is quoted by kind permission of the Trustees of The Gordon Highlanders Museum, Aberdeen. The circumstances are described in Chapter Six.

"To all to whom these presents shall come I, John Heslop **Stitt**, of Kitchener Barracks, Changi, Singapore, in the Colony of the Straits Settlements, a Lieutenant Colonel in His Majesty's Army, send greetings.

Whereas I am the officer commanding the Second Battalion, The Gordon Highlanders, now prisoners of war at Changi aforesaid and as such Commanding Officer all regimental property of the officers and men of the said Battalion vests in me,

And Whereas in the uncertainty which arises as to the movements of myself and the whole of the said Battalion I am desirous of appointing attorneys to act for me and for the President of the Officers' and Sergeants' Messes in respect of all the property and in particular the silver, plate, china, glass, books, pictures, prints, Colours, Banners, decorations, medals, souvenirs and other articles belonging to the Officers' Mess or the Sergeants' Mess or to the Second Battalion, The Gordon Highlanders (hereinafter called "Regimental Property"),

Now hereby nominate, constitute and appoint Lieutenant Colonel Donald Gordon **MacLeod** OBE, c/o Mercantile Bank of India, Singapore. Lieutenant Colonel William Maurice **James** MC MM, of No.193 Ampang Road, Kuala Lumpur. Major Charles Herbert **Withers-Rayne**, of No.10 Collyer Quay, Singapore. Captain George Reginald **Roper-Coldbeck**, of Union Buildings, Singapore. Captain Duncan F **Hutton**, of Bukit Dorah Estate, Sungei Buloh in the State of Selangor. Philip Stewart **Gordon**, c/o The Straits Settlements Police, Singapore. Charles **Thornton**, of No.198 Ampang Road, Kuala Lumpur. And William **Munro**, of Raffles Place, Singapore, Advocate and Solicitor, all at present prisoners of war in Singapore aforesaid, and any two of them jointly, to be my true and lawful attorneys for me and on my behalf and on the behalf of the Second Battalion, The Gordon Highlanders, and in my or its name or otherwise with the powers following exercisable in the Colony of the Straits Settlements and the Federated and Unfederated Malay States, the Empire of Japan, and in any other State whatsoever where any Regimental Property shall be situate, that is to say …."

The second page of the document then specified the "powers following". They were, "To apply and sue for, claim, demand …. To prosecute, defend and take any legal proceedings …. To compound, compromise and settle any claim …. To pay any monies …. To sign and endorse any cheques …. To insure any regimental property …. To make any arrangements as may seem proper for the custody or forwarding or shipment of any Regimental Property to Great Britain or elsewhere …. To sign or execute any document …. To substitute and appoint and at pleasure to remove one or more attorney or attorneys …."

All of this was carefully typed on foolscap flimsy paper, under conditions which can only be imagined. Attached to it were meticulously detailed descriptions of the property of the Officers' Mess and Sergeants' Mess, plus a great many other items such as the Drum Major's Staff, sets of regimental bagpipes, an historical Big Drum, and numerous oil paintings and prints. More than two hundred items were specified. Everything had been packed in twenty-six brass-bound fitted teak chests. Those containing the silver were stored in the vaults of the Hong Kong & Shanghai Banking Corporation, the pictures and lesser items in the warehouse of the Singapore Cold Storage Company. Both locations were ransacked by the Japanese.

The sole surviving (carbon) copy of this document is in the archives of The Gordon Highlanders Museum, Aberdeen. It is undated and unsigned. Nothing is known of the original (top) copy. All the officers nominated as attorneys (trustees) were either civilians or Reserve and Volunteer officers (rather than Regular regimental officers). This seems strange, but there is no ready explanation. Colonel Stitt had, presumably, been separated from his officers and men by the Japanese. From the perspective of more than half a century later, it is extraordinary that this group of men, facing an unknown future in circumstances totally alien to them, so studiously accepted the responsibility to which they set their hands. In the event, the records of the Commonwealth War Graves Commission indicate that they all survived their three and half years in Japanese hands. Colonel Stitt and Captain Roper-Coldbeck (a Reserve officer of the Gordons) are known to have been released from a camp near Bangkok in early September 1945.

Appendix B
The Battle of the Sittang River Bridge

The following story appears as a separate appendix because it underlines, in the most dramatic and poignant way imaginable, the significance of military silver as a permanent record of human endeavour.

The 1st Battalion of the 3rd Queen Alexandra's Own Gurkha Rifles was raised, as the Kumaon Battalion, in 1815. It served in many wars and battles but, in 1941, it was on the threshold of the strangest campaign of all. The jungle war in Burma would last three and half years, and eventually absorbed the energies of two million men. One of them was a professional soldier, Captain Bruce Kinloch. In February 1942, he and his company of the 1st/3rd Gurkha Rifles were an element of the hastily-assembled 17th Division, charged with the responsibility of defending Burma's southern frontier with Thailand.

All of Burma's great rivers run north to south, and they provide a natural obstacle to lateral movement of any kind. For an army, with its "tail" of logistical support services, possession of the bridges across these rivers is of crucial importance. The Divisional Commander, Major General Sir John Smyth VC MC, was fully aware of this and he deployed his forces accordingly. There were three rivers in particular which occupied his thoughts - the Salween, the Bilin and the Sittang. The former was the first obstacle encountered by the Japanese. Despite fierce resistance by British forces, especially the 1st and 3rd Battalions of the 7th Gurkha Rifles, they forced a crossing and pushed rapidly westward. This brought them into full contact with the main body of the 17th Division, deployed in the sixty miles of jungle which separates the Salween from its westerly sister, the Sittang. What followed has been forgotten for its heroism and remembered only for its failures.

Bruce Kinloch takes up the story. "If ever a battle epitomised the phrase 'the fog of war', it was the battle for the Sittang River bridge. The root cause of this tragic disaster was the almost complete failure of communications between Division and Brigades, between Brigades and Battalions, and finally between Battalions and their infantry companies locked in close combat, in dense jungle, with a determined, well trained and fanatical enemy". In his unpublished account of those turbulent days, he describes the strain and losses caused not only by the inadequacies of the radio equipment but also the frequent misdirected attacks by the Royal Air Force and the lack of any conditioning of the troops and their officers for jungle warfare. Only three weeks had passed since the battalion arrived in Burma, and it was still not acclimatised. They and the other British forces were soon driven back to the Sittang, to the combined road and rail bridge which was their only route to comparative safety.

Early on the morning of 22 February, hungry and tired, the 1st/3rd Gurkha Rifles reached the village of Mokpalin, situated near the eastern bank of the river and a few hundred yards south of the bridge. With them were the two other battalions of the 48th Gurkha Brigade, the 1st/4th and 2nd/5th Gurkha Rifles. Between this force and its objective were two jungle-covered features, Pagoda Hill and Buddha Hill, already occupied by the Japanese.

It was quickly decided that 1st/3rd Gurkha Rifles should launch an attack against these positions and so gain access to the bridge. Supported by the mule-packed 3.7 inch howitzers of 21 Mountain Battery, the leading companies stormed up the slopes. Both sides suffered heavy casualties in the savage hand-to-hand fighting with kukri and bayonet which followed. The Commanding Officer of 1st/3rd Gurkha Rifles, Lieutenant Colonel G A Ballinger, almost immediately lost contact with those companies. Going forward to see for himself what was happening, he and several others were treacherously shot dead by a party of enemy soldiers who were pretending to surrender. One of the handful of survivors from this encounter was the battalion's senior Gurkha officer, Subedar Major Gagan Sing Thapa.

While fighting continued on Pagoda Hill and Buddha Hill, the Japanese began to infiltrate the perimeter established by the Gurkhas around Mokpalin village and its railway station. The order was given to concentrate the defences on the nearby OP Hill. When night came it brought no rest for the defenders. The Japanese made a series of attacks, casualties mounted, and ammunition could be replaced only by daring forays to the abandoned and burning vehicles in no-mansland. During one such sortie, Bruce Kinloch found a Thompson sub-machine gun with a number of 50 round drum magazines.

"During intermittent lulls we could hear sounds of desultory fighting from where 'C' and 'D' Companies were isolated on Buddha and Pagoda Hills. Altogether it was a very noisy night, with heavy shelling and mortaring and streams of red tracer and Verey lights providing a dazzling firework display, but, lying prone on the lip of the sunken road and cuddling my tommy-gun, I felt comparatively safe. Then, at five-thirty in the morning, at the first hint of dawn, it happened. From the direction of the river, beyond Pagoda Hill, came the roar of three enormous explosions. We realised that the bridge over the Sittang had been prematurely blown by our engineers and our life-line cut.

As the echoes of the explosions died away there was an utter silence. All firing had ceased abruptly and every living thing seemed to be holding its breath. Then, suddenly, the Japanese, sounding like a troop of excited monkeys, broke into a shrill chattering. On OP Hill, believing that everyone else had got away and that we had been abandoned to our fate, we were filled with mounting anger. For a while there was a lull, then at 0730 hours, to our astonished eyes, some thirty Japs appeared, in close formation, marching along the railway line and only about 150 yards away. They were singing and laughing and carrying a large flag, obviously unaware of our presence and presumably convinced that the battle was over.

It was a target we could hardly miss and our light machine-guns opened on them to good effect. The survivors rolled down the railway embankment into the jungle. Soon after, a Jap reconnaissance aircraft appeared from the north, coming low over OP Hill. It was flying slowly, only about 100 feet above us. Everyone who had a weapon opened fire, I even gave it a full drum with my tommy-gun. It suddenly banked and dived into the ground, exploding in a ball of fire. A great cheer went up over the whole area. Despite our predicament, the Japs were not having it all their own way".

Captain Kinloch had been appointed Adjutant early in the battle. He was the third in almost as many days, his predecessors having been successively killed or wounded. He and the battalion's second-in-command, Major F K Bradford, organised the evacuation of OP Hill and set up a new position in a ravine at the river's edge. Here they had their first sight of the shattered bridge. The ends of the fallen central spans, resting in the water, were only a few feet apart. This gave Kinloch the idea that men could still be got across to the other side, providing that the Japs did not control the bridgehead. Having obtained the second-in-command's agreement, he decided to make a one-man reconnaissance. He took with him his revolver and, in his binocular case, two hand grenades with the pins straightened for instant use.

"I didn't know the ground and I knew nothing about any enemy forces between me and the bridge, but it seemed sensible to go alone. More men make more noise, and there was no point in risking even more casualties. By that stage we were all bone-tired, but sight of the bridge had boosted our morale and fired me up to see what could be done. I moved warily along the river bank, but everything was eerily quiet. I came across a few Indian *sepoys*, wandering like lost sheep with dazed looks on their faces, while in the shallows by the river's edge corpses rolled lazily in the ripples, but there was no sign of the enemy. I came across a sand-bagged trench but it was unoccupied. Mounting a steep track, I reached a high point about a hundred yards from the end of the bridge.

There was an unusually large tree, a real jungle giant, casting a deep shadow. I saw movement, and the outline of what looked like a British-pattern steel helmet. I challenged, then leapt forward. Crouching beside the enormous trunk, I peered cautiously around it to find myself looking into the eyes of a Japanese officer. Black leather knee boots, breeches, soft khaki peaked cap and traditional Samurai sword, they were all there".

The British officer ducked back, removed a grenade from the binocular case, released the pin and lever, then rolled it around the base of the tree. "I heard a gasp, a shuffle of feet, and a shattering explosion. In an instant the air was full of flying bullets, and it was evident that I had bumped into an ambush. I then came close to equalling the Olympic record for the hundred yards sprint".

Having heard Kinloch's report, Major Bradford conferred with Major Jack Robinson. He had joined the Gurkhas with his "B" Company, 2nd Battalion, The Duke of Wellington's Regiment, only recently arrived in Burma from India. They had been training for desert warfare at Peshawar, North West Frontier. They were unprepared for jungle fighting but were much fresher than the Gurkhas. It was agreed that Kinloch should lead two of Robinson's platoons in an attempt to secure the eastern end of the bridge. The enemy were ready for them, and the attack failed after hand-to-hand fighting and further heavy casualties.

As the sun dipped towards the horizon, the British trapped on the wrong side of the river assessed their increasingly serious situation. They now had only two choices - give themselves up to the surrounding Japanese, or somehow cross the Sittang

which, at that point, was a thousand yards in width. Bruce Kinloch volunteered to test its depth and rate of flow, and to search the far bank for boats of any kind.

With two other officers, Captain "Barney" Darley (Quartermaster of the 1st/3rd Gurkha Rifles) and Captain J Mackenzie (attached to the battalion from 21 Mountain Battery), he stripped off and launched himself into the river. They needed an hour to make the journey, pushing ahead of them a makeshift raft on which they had piled their clothes and weapons.

The western bank at this point was deserted, but they found a sampan and this was used during the remainder of the night to make five journeys back and forth, bringing away all the wounded men of different units who had gathered in the Gurkhas' ravine The rescued casualties were then loaded onto bullock carts commandeered from a native village, and were sent off, westward, in the care of the battalion Medical Officer, Lieutenant Sundaram, of the Indian Medical Service.

There was still the problem of evacuating the rest of the battalion, or whatever remained of it and whenever it could be found and assembled. Early on the following morning, 24 February, the bootless and near naked Kinloch and Darley conferred with Major Bradford and agreed to cross the river again, this time in broad daylight, to see whether they could find more boats.

"This plan was set in motion, and Darley and I were searching along the west bank when we heard firing from the opposite shore. We saw Japanese soldiers swarming out of the jungle down to the beach, and then a number of Gurkhas swimming the river under fire. Some were shot or drowned, but eventually the survivors reached us on the western shore. They included a handful of 'C' and 'D' Company men who had held

Eighteen months after the Sittang battle, and after reforming at Kohima, the 1st/3rd Gurkha Rifles went back into action in the Fort White area of the Chin Hills. Six thousand feet up on the Ngalzang ridge, Major Bruce Kinloch MC, finds a rare quiet moment in September 1943 to pose for the camera. Photo: BK.

on to Pagoda and Buddha Hills until long after their ammunition had run out. Most of their comrades had been killed or taken prisoner, but these few had managed to find the rest of the battalion in the river-edge ravine. And it was there that the last sad episode of those two days of battle took place. We watched it all through our binoculars and, from what we saw, and from what we heard from the men who had just crawled ashore, we pieced the story together.

When the Japs found the remnants of the battalion in the ravine, they opened fire and it was returned by the Gurkhas and the Dukes. However, Major Bradford decided to end what was becoming a pointless loss of life and ordered the men to surrender. It was not part of the soldier's code of Subedar Major Gagan Sing Thapa, a veteran of several campaigns, to surrender to anyone, let alone a Japanese. As a Japanese officer approached him, he shouted a scornful Nepalese expletive, drew his revolver and fired at him. His shot missed but, without trying again, he shot himself through the heart. The Jap officer, who had received Major Bradford's revolver as a token of surrender, turned and shot Bradford dead. An enraged Gurkha naik (corporal) then shot the Jap officer through the head. Eventually all firing ceased and the remainder of the battalion was rounded up and marched off".

Kinloch and Darley collected all the stragglers they could find along the west bank. They were soldiers from his own battalion and a few men of The Burma Rifles. Ragged, bare-foot, and totally exhausted, they marched due west across open paddy country in intense heat in the hope of finding a friendly

face. Hours later, having been bitten along the way by a snake, Kinloch was relieved to hear in the darkness a challenge in a broad Scots accent. He and his party were taken under the wing of The Cameronians (Scottish Rifles) who plied them with whisky before sending them on to the town of Pegu. Here the 17th Division was re-grouping and preparing fresh lines of defence.

The Japanese, as it transpired, had suffered such heavy losses on the Salween and the Sittang that they too needed a respite. There was plenty of fighting and marching ahead, and nearly four months would pass before the British were finally ejected from Burma but, for a while, both sides paused to lick their wounds. Bruce Kinloch was appointed Divisional Liaison Officer and sent south to Rangoon with orders to beg, borrow or steal all the provisions and equipment which the 17th so badly needed.

"I made the rounds of the local depôts and warehouses and collected a lot of stuff. Rangoon was being regularly bombed, so the usual lengthy paperwork could be ignored. One of the trophies I transported back up to Pegu was a case of Moët et Chandon champagne. I felt I had earned it. One evening I met up with the four other British officers of my battalion who were still alive and still free. They were our former Adjutatant, Captain Robin Bishop, who had been injured and hospitalised in Rangoon shortly after we landed there, our Motor Transport Officer, Lieutenant W D McQueen, the Signals Officer, Lieutenant A H Mann, and "Barney" Darley. We were all that was left of the British officers of our battalion. Most of the

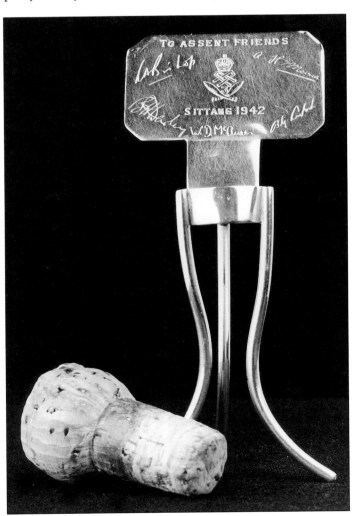

The Kinloch menu-holder. Of little intrinsic value, it preserves the memory of the Gurkha soldiers and their British officers lost at the tragic battle for the Sittang River bridge in February 1942. The Indian silversmith was unfamiliar with English spelling, hence the inscription is to "assent" friends. Photo: BK.

Gurkha VCOs were gone, and a great many of the other ranks. In fact, for the remainder of the withdrawal, they were amalgamated with the survivors of the 2nd/5th Royal Gurkha Rifles to form a temporary composite battalion with the title 5th/3rd Gurkha Rifles.

We sat and looked at each other. It was a very emotional and private occasion. The bottles of champagne were opened and we drank a toast to absent friends, to our missing friends of both races and all ranks. The 1st/3rd would in the fullness of time be rebuilt and retrained for the battles ahead, but that evening was the time to remember times past. I kept one of the champagne corks as a memento and used it as the stopper in my field service water bottle throughout the long march and many battles that lay ahead of us before we reached Manipur and the Indian border.

Later in the year I was in Calcutta. I went to an Indian silversmith and asked him to make a small table piece, a menu-card holder, engraved with the battalion crest and with the facsimile signatures of myself and my four brother officers. Most particularly, I told him to incorporate into the design the cork from my water bottle. I still have the result of his work here in my home, a constant reminder of the Sittang, of Pegu, and of brave men I once knew and fought alongside".

Bruce Kinloch received an immediate award of the Military Cross for his services in the Sittang battle and was later promoted to the rank of Major. A number of personal accounts have been woven into the narrative of this book, accounts intended to demonstrate that military silver has greater signifi-cance, in terms of human experience, than any other category of silverware. Bruce Kinloch's story has been quoted in detail because it meets two separate but equally important criteria. First, in terms purely of military history, it is one of the very few recorded eyewitness descriptions of the Sittang disaster. Secondly, it may help to convince everyone engaged in the silver trade that they should never condemn to the melting pot or the buffing machine any item which comes into their hands simply because they do not understand it.

The Kinloch piece, in the unlikely event that it was ever to pass out of the family and into the trade, would be a prime candidate for instant scrapping. It is undistinguished "native work", of little interest to a silver collector. The metal is "Indian grade", not of the desirable Sterling standard. It is only a small light-weight menu-card holder, of which there are many on the market. There is a cork built into it, and this is strange and unsettling. Worst of all, there is an unknown crest and some writing on it. To research its meaning would involve time and, therefore, expense. On the other hand, removal of the engraving would cost more than the object's potential recycled market value.

The fate of the piece would be sealed. The cork would be ripped out and the metal thrown in the bin to await, along with dozens of other bits and pieces of old unwanted silver, the next visit by the scrap dealer. If it achieves nothing else, perhaps the story of the Sittang battle and its strange little silver memorial will cause some dealers to pause and reflect.

Appendix C
Suggested Further Reading

The military and naval material for this book was drawn from a very wide range of sources - published, unpublished and personal. The latter are noted in the Acknowledgements section. With regard to the printed sources, it would not be helpful to list them all because they would not necessarily assist a future researcher concerned with his or her own particular lines of enquiry:

The History of the Armed Forces

There are two previously published books which relate directly to regimental life. Both are suggested as supplementary reading:

Officers' Mess - Life and customs in the regiments, by Lieutenant Colonel R J Dickinson (published privately, 1973 and 1977). This is a light-hearted collection of yarns and incidents based upon the recollections of officers from several different regiments. It also explains the rules (or absence of rules) for the various after-dinner Mess games which can be so ruinous for Mess kit and Mess furniture (and which oblige the Mess staff to remove all silver to a place of safety before mayhem commences).

Military Customs, by Major T J Edwards MBE (Gale & Polden, Aldershot, 1948) is a more academic work. It is a compendium of facts and legends drawn from the records of a cross-section of British Army units, and is helpful to an understanding of their *esprit de corps.*

There are five publications which deal either wholly or in part with regimental silver. They are:

A History of the Mess Plate of the 88th, The Connaught Rangers, by Captain H F N Jourdain FRGS FHSL (The Ballantyne Press, Edinburgh, for the Regiment, London, 1904). It includes pictures of the regiments' most important possessions, with accompanying notes concerning the officers with which they were associated. As far as can be determined, this was the first illustrated account of Mess silver available to a general readership. The author, as Colonel Jourdain, later compiled (separately) the complete authoritative campaign history of The Connaughts (published in three volumes, 1924, 1926 and 1928).

The Pictures and Plate of the Royal Engineers Headquarters Mess, Chatham, by Lieutenant Colonel B R Ward RE ("for private circulation", The Royal Engineers Institute, 1909). Principally a narrative account of the lives of famous officers of the Corps, it includes a few photographs of major pieces of Mess silver.

The Portraits & The Silver of the RE Headquarters Mess, Chatham, by Colonel J M Lambert (The Institution of Royal Engineers, Chatham, 1963). This is an updated and improved version of Ward's book, with many more photographs of the Corps' silver.

The Silver Room, The Royal Artillery Mess, Woolwich, by Lieutenant Colonel P R S Jackson OBE RA (no imprint, 1976). It contains ninety photographs of major pieces held

permanently at Woolwich, with some accompanying historical information.

Regimental Heritage - A pictorial record of the paintings and silver of the Royal Regiment of Artillery, compiled by Colonel D Evans RA, designed by Malcolm Harvey Young (published for the Royal Regiment of Artillery by Europa Publications Limited, London, 1984). This is an exemplary book, stunningly produced, with hundreds of high definition photographs of historical artefacts of every kind (many of them silver).

It should be noted that the first three titles listed above, by Jourdain, Ward and Lambert, contain little or no information regarding assay marks, makers' marks, weights and dimensions.

In the context of military history in general, there are literally hundreds of books which, depending upon circumstance, the reader might find useful. The following are just a few of those which have assisted the author:

A History of the Regiments & Uniforms of the British Army, by Major R Money Barnes (Seeley Service & Company Limited, London, 6th edition 1967). His book is highly regarded for its colour plates of uniforms, but his narrative contains all manner of useful commentary (not always objective) regarding 18th and 19th century battles and campaigns.

History of the British Army, by Brigadier Peter Young and Lieutenant Colonel J P Lawford (Arthur Barker Limited, London, 1970). A clear broad brush narrative, it tells the story in general terms.

A Register of the Regiments and Corps of the British Army - The ancestry of the regiments and corps of the Regular establishments, by Arthur Swinson (The Archive Press, London, 1972). An admirably succinct publication, it has been one of the author's constant and valued companions over many years.

British Regiments, 1914-1918, by Brigadier E A James OBE TD (Samson Books, London, 1978). As the title implies, it locates each regiment and battalion at the outbreak of hostilities and at their conclusion.

Battle Honours of the British and Commonwealth Armies, by Anthony Baker, (Ian Allan Limited, London, 1986). This is a book which may fill gaps left by other accounts.

British Battles and Medals, by E C Joslin, A R Litherland and B T Simpkin (Spink & Son Limited, London, 1988). The contents are devoted mainly to medallic awards, but the book is helpful in establishing which regiments fought where and when.

The Register of the Victoria Cross, by Nora Buzzell (This England Books, Cheltenham, 1988). It is a compendium of biographical entries for each of the 1530 recipients of the highest award for valour. Any item of silver named to a VC winner, or even related to an event or person associated with such an award, is clearly of outstanding interest.

Sources helpful to an understanding of the Indian Army are:

India's Army, by Major Donovan Jackson (Sampson, Low, Marston & Company Limited, London, 1940). Jackson compiled this fat little volume in the late 1930s as an easy way of tracking

Indian Army units and their many changes of title.

A Matter of Honour - An account of the Indian Army, its officers and men, by Philip Mason (Purnell Book Services Limited, with Jonathan Cape, London, 1974). Mason's is one of the most respected books on the subject.

The Indian Army, by Boris Mollo (Blandford Press, 1981) is devoted mainly to uniforms and unit titles. It can be used to complement Jackson's work, especially for the early years of British India.

Sons of John Company - The Indian and Pakistan Armies, 1903-1991, by John Gaylor (Spellmount Limited, Tunbridge Wells, 1992). As the sub-title suggests, this excellent book identifies movements, services and changes of title during the 20th century.

Every regiment and corps has produced, from time to time, a history of its past services. They are a goldmine for anyone seeking to trace the movements of a particular battalion (and therefore of an officer or soldier of that battalion whose name is engraved upon an item of presentation silver). There are two bibliographies which list all the regimental histories ever published:

A Bibliography of the Regimental Histories of the British Army, by Arthur S White (Military History Society, 1965, updated by Naval & Military Press, London, 1992). Compiled according to the traditional bibliographic format, White's is a very comprehensive listing which tells us that a book exists, but not what it contains.

Regiments - Regiments and Corps of the British Empire and Commonwealth, 1758-1993, A Critical Bibliography of their Published Histories, by Roger Perkins (published privately, Newton Abbot, 1994). The sub-title - "Critical Bibliography" - makes it plain that each listed title is described in great detail. However, it does not cover the British Army. Its main value, for the collector of military silver, is probably the "India" section (comprising one quarter of the whole).

An alternative route in tracing the services of a named individual is to write to the Curator of the regimental museum. Their addresses are listed in:

A Guide to Military Museums and Other Places of Military Interest, by Terence and Shirley Wise (published privately, Knighton, Powys, 8th edition, 1994). It contains telephone numbers, opening hours, the names of the Curators, and so forth, and is a valuable point of entry into the regimental system.

It is important to understand that the Curators and their staff (if they have one) are constrained by tight budgets, and are usually over-loaded with requests for information. All enquiries should be phrased in clear and concise terms, should not be submitted before they have been double-checked for accuracy, and ideally should be accompanied by a donation to the Museum funds.

The most relevant accounts of the history of the Royal Marines, especially for the period when major items of silver were being acquired, are:

Britain's Sea Soldiers - A record of the Royal Marines during the war, 1914-1919, by General Sir H Blumberg KCB RM (Swift & Company, Devonport, 1927).

The Royal Marines Artillery, 1804-1923, by Edward Fraser and L G Carr-Laughton (Royal United Service Institution, London, 1930).

Some of the information for the naval and merchant service entries has been drawn from:

A Naval Biographical Dictionary - Comprising the life and services of every living officer in HM Navy from the rank of *Admiral of the Fleet to that of Lieutenant inclusive, compiled from authentic and family documents,* by William O'Byrne (John Murray, London, 1849, republished by Naval & Military Press, 1997 and 1998).

England's Sea Officers - The story of the naval profession, by Michael Lewis (George, Allen & Unwin Limited, London, 1948).

Dictionary of Disasters at Sea During the Age of Steam, 1824-1962, Volumes I and II, by Charles Hocking (Lloyd's Register of Shipping, London, 1969).

Ships of the Royal Navy, Volumes I and II, by J J Colledge (Greenhill Books, London, 1989)

Britain's Sea War - A diary of ship losses, 1939-1945, by John M Young (Patrick Stevens Limited, Wellingborough, 1989)

With regard to the Royal Flying Corps, the Royal Air Force and the Royal Auxiliary Air Force, the following titles are highly recommended as starting points for research:

Bomber Squadrons of the RAF and their Aircraft, by Philip Moyes (Macdonald & Company, London. 1964)

Fighter Squadrons of the RAF and their Aircraft, by John Rawlings (same publisher, 1969)

Coastal Support and Special Squadrons of the RAF and their Aircraft, by John Rawlings (Jane's Publishing Company Limited, London, 1982)

Above the Trenches - A Complete Record of the Fighter Aces and Units of the British Empire Air Forces, 1915-1920, by Christopher Shores, Norman Franks and Russell Guest (Grub Street, London, 1990)

Men of the Battle of Britain - A Who was Who of the pilots and aircrew, British, Commonwealth and Allied, who flew with Royal Air Force Fighter Command, July 10 to October 31, 1940, by Kenneth G Wynn (Gliddon Books, Norwich, 1989).

Other reference sources useful to the collector of military silver are the same as those familiar to every genealogist. To investigate the personal career and family roots of a man named in an engraving, the researcher has recourse to a wide range of publications. Depending upon the person's social standing, he might (with luck) be found in works such as:

Burke's Peerage, Baronetage & Knightage,
Burke's Landed Gentry
Debrett's Peerage, Baronetage, Knightage and Companionage
Kelly's Handbook to the Titled, Landed and Official Classes
Whitaker's Peerage, Baronetage, Knightage and
Companionage

most of which have been published in various editions over the past hundred years and more.

Lesser mortals may be found in successive editions of:
Who's Who
Who was Who
The Concise Dictionary of National Biography

and the obituary columns in back copies of *The Times, The Daily Telegraph,* and other major newspapers (accessible through most county library services).

Officers who served as army, naval or air force padres should appear in:
Crockford's Clerical Directory
The Church Directory and Almanack

both of which have been republished in updated editions over many years.

Doctors who served as army, navy or air force medical officers are listed in:
The Medical Register
Butterworth's Medical Directory

old copies of which can sometimes be found in second-hand

book shops at modest cost.

Commissioned officers and Warrant Officers not listed in any of the preceding types of publication will be found in the quarterly, half-yearly and annual Official Lists produced by the Admiralty, the War Office, and the Air Ministry (all combined since 1962 as the Ministry of Defence). They are titled, logically, as *Navy Lists*, *Army Lists* and *Air Force Lists*. To obtain a complete picture of an officer's career, it may be necessary to pursue him through a succession of editions. Complete "runs" are accessible only in central regional libraries or in specialist libraries such as that held by the National Army Museum (for which a Reader's Ticket must be requested before entry is granted).

Amongst the numerous other available archives, relevant to any investigation into servicemen named on military, naval or air force silver, are the Public Record Office, Kew, and the India & Oriental Collections of The British Library. The private collector who lacks the time and the endurance required to enter such establishments is well advised to divide his detective efforts into two stages. The first is to carry out as much research as he can, exploiting his own resources and initiative and by consulting the categories of publication described above. Having exhausted all those avenues, he might then pass his accumulated notes to a professional researcher with the request that he should attempt to fill the gaps. Most large libraries will supply on request a list of recognised research agents who are familiar with their holdings. These experts charge professional fees for their time and effort but, as with most things in life, the knowledge and experience of the specialist can be invaluable.

The History of Silver

We may now turn to the second category of publication having relevance to the study of military silver. These are books which deal with the subject of silver *per se*. They are numerous, and they deal with every aspect - history, styles and fashions, manufacturing processes, makers, assay marks, valuations, and so forth. As stated previously, it is the author's personal view that a deep understanding of these matters is not essential to an appreciation of silver having a military or naval provenance. However, all knowledge breeds a thirst for yet more knowledge, and it is better to understand than to not understand.

The author has found the following publications to be particularly helpful in finding a way into the world of silver:

Phaidon Guide to Silver, by Margaret Holland (Phaidon Press Limited, Oxford, 1978) is helpful to an understanding of the diversity of the silversmith's skills. Of great value are the simple line drawings which explain the meaning of many of the technical terms associated with design and decoration.

Silver - A practical guide to collecting silverware and identifying hallmarks, by Joel Langford (The Apple Press, London, 1991). This is a lovely book, beautifully illustrated, and packed with condensed but understandable information.

Lyle Price Guide, Silver, by Tony Curtis (Lyle Publications, Galashiels, 1995, currently out of print). Its principal value is to be found in its hundreds of photographs and accompanying explanatory notes.

Knowledge of the marks punched into every item of Sterling silver is very important, even to the collector who is interested primarily in the "military and naval history" aspect of the hobby. The year marks are particularly relevant in confirming that there is nothing amiss. For example, a collector would need to think twice if he or she encountered a salver with the typical engraving "Presented to Captain A Brown …. On the Occasion

of his Marriage, 10 March 1889", but the piece being punched (stamped) with the year mark for 1922.

Conversely, it would be perfectly acceptable if the dates were reversed. Chapter Nine gives several instances of gifts having been made with antique silver or antique pewter, manufactured long before the piece was passed to an engraver for the addition of presentation wording.

Amongst the many publications which recount the history of the Assay Offices, their marks, and the marks of the silversmiths, are:

Discovering Hall Marks on English Silver, by John Bly (Shire Publications Limited, Aylesbury, seventh edition 1986) is a pocket-sized ready-reckoner (handy when wandering around an antiques fair). The tables of year marks refer to the Assay Offices in London, Birmingham, Exeter and Sheffield. The opening half of the booklet contains useful condensed notes on, *inter alia*, the history of English silversmithing, traditions, styles, and famous makers.

Jackson's Silver and Gold Marks of England, Scotland and Ireland, by Sir Charles Jackson (first published in 1905, subsequently revised and reprinted, currently available, 1996 edition, under the editorship of Ian Pickford, published by The Antique Collectors' Club Limited, Woodbridge). This is a massive work, an essential reference source for the professional dealer or valuer, and for the dedicated student of antique gold and silver. For collectors of military silver, however, it probably contains more information than they are likely to need. A *précis* edition, *Jackson's Hallmarks*, also edited by Ian Pickford, was published by The Antique Collectors' Club in 1991.

Bradbury's Book of Hallmarks - A guide to marks of origin on English, Scottish and Irish silver, gold and platinum, and on foreign imported silver and gold plate 1544 to 1994: Old Sheffield plate makers' marks 1734-1860, by Frederick Bradbury (J W Northend Limited, Sheffield, first published 1927, revised edition 1993). This also is a handy pocket-sized guide, concise and comprehensive.

English Silver Hallmarks, by Judith Banister (W Foulsham & Company Limited, London, new edition 1995). This is another pocket-sized instant reference source. It describes the marks of the principal Assay Offices and of three hundred makers' marks registered between 1697 and 1900.

There are three major accounts - by John Culme, Arthur G Grimwade and Sir Ambrose Heal - which describe the lives and works of London-based goldsmiths, silversmith, jewellers and traders. Excellent in themselves, they tend to focus on the centuries which preceded the "golden age" when the majority of British Army regiments began to collect silver on a large scale. Their practical value to the military silver collector may, therefore, be limited.

Comparable books describe the work of silversmiths based in and around provincial centres such as Birmingham, Chester, Newcastle, Norwich and York. In the event, the author has found, over the past four years, that at least ninety percent of the pieces coming to his attention bear the marks for London, Birmingham or Sheffield. Some important items of Mess silver were made in Dublin, but they are rare exceptions. In the author's own collection are two minor items assayed in Chester, and a solitary Edinburgh-marked item (the Carpenter-Garnier teapot). Given the antiquity and territorial roots of famous Scottish regiments such as The Royal Scots, The Black Watch and The Argyll & Sutherland Highlanders, it is perhaps surprising that their officers seem to have ordered their silver mainly from English rather than Scottish makers.

For information regarding pieces made in Sheffield plate, electro-plate and old pewter, the following sources have been found helpful:

The Silver and Sheffield Plate Collector - A guide to domestic metal work in old Silver and old Sheffield Plate, by "W.A.Y." (not identified), (published by Herbert Jenkins Limited, London, no date, *circa* 1910). A strange and intriguing little book, and long out of print, it traces the evolution of table and decorative metalware over many centuries. If found in a second-hand bookshop, it should be bought.

Phaidon Guide to Pewter, by Vanessa Brett (Phaidon Press Limited, Oxford, 1981). A finely illustrated guide to pewter objects of every kind, it covers the work of pewterers throughout the British Isles, Europe and America. It is most unlikely that artefacts of this quality and range of styles would ever have been the subject of a military or naval presentation, but the book is helpful to an understanding of the alloy in its many wrought forms.

A Dictionary of Marks, Ceramics, Metalwork, Furniture, Tapestry, edited by Margaret Macdonald-Taylor (Antique Collectors' Guides, published by Barrie & Jenkins Limited, London, current edition 1993). As the title indicates, this is a useful quick source of reference for a wide range of collectable items.

The Identification and Dating of Sheffield Electroplated Wares, 1843-1943, by E R Matheau-Raven (Foulsham, Chippenham, 1997). Pieces made for the Mess or Wardroom are almost always made in Sterling silver. However, individual or team prizes (especially sports and shooting trophies) are frequently marked "E.P.N.S." (electro-plated nickel silver), or may carry other marks which make it clear that the metal is not Sterling silver. They are of no interest to the dedicated collector of silver. However, for the military collector, it is their engraved wording which makes them desirable. Part of their attraction lies in the fact that they can be researched and enjoyed at less cost. That said, it should be noted that good quality *Victorian* electro-plate has itself become "collectable" in recent years (on occasion achieving prices even higher than those of equivalent pieces made in Sterling silver). This book is an excellent introduction to the subject.

As remarked earlier, British soldiers were stationed all over the world as garrison troops, their officers having permanent Mess buildings in almost every quarter of the globe. India was the army's principal commitment. The circumstances under which the Union flag was first flown there, and then finally lowered in 1947, have already been described in detail. Less well known is the fact that the army maintained powerful garrisons in several other territories which subsequently grew to nationhood and are today valued co-members of the Commonwealth. Canada was a regular posting until the last regiment was withdrawn in 1871. South Africa saw many regiments of cavalry and infantry come and go between the early 1800s and the early 1900s. The colonies in Australia and Tasmania saw the last British soldier depart in 1870. In that same year, New Zealand bade farewell to the British Army when the 18th (The Royal Irish) Regiment of Foot set sail.

From all of this, it would be reasonable to assume that at least a few pieces of Mess silver must have been commissioned from local silversmiths. There were plenty of them - immigrants and settlers from England, Scotland, Germany, France, and other European countries. The high quality of their work is well recorded, and several examples of pieces made in India are noted in this book. Silver made by smiths resident in other Empire countries has, unfortunately, proved elusive. The author, and two people in particular who tried hard to support him in his aim, strove to identify items of British Army silver manufactured in Canada, South Africa, Australia and New Zealand. It all came to nothing, and this has been a cause for disappointment. Others may be more successful, and the following publications will be of immense assistance to them in identifying and understanding any such pieces which they may encounter:

Pièces Honorifiques de la Collection Henry Birks d'orfevrerie Canadienne, by Ross Fox (Musée des Beaux-Arts du Canada, Ottawa, 1985). The only copy seen is this, the French language edition, although it seems to have been published also in English. It deals with Canadian makers during the period 1850-1899, and describes many of their pieces. Several are engraved with "military" presentation wordings, and Ross Fox ensured that they are clearly legible in the high definition photographs. The accompanying captions confirm their military provenances. This, in the experience of the present author, is an exceptional state of affairs. Whenever a silver artefact of an obviously military or naval association is illustrated in a British reference work, the caption almost always totally ignores its existence. British authors and cataloguers dispose of the subject by stating "with engraving", or something equally unhelpful. This disinterest is symptomatic of the *malaise* highlighted in the Author's Introduction.

19th Century Australian Silver, Volumes I and II, by J B Hawkins (The Antique Collectors' Club, Woodbridge, 1990). Two highly detailed and well-illustrated books, they give full details of Australian makers and their output (which expanded greatly with the discovery of gold in Victoria and with the wealth created thereby).

Gold and Silversmithing in Nineteenth and Twentieth Century New Zealand, by Winsome Shepherd (The Museum of New Zealand, and David Ling Publishing Limited, Auckland, 1995). Another large (A4) format volume, it is packed with high definition photographs of New Zealand marks and the characteristic pieces made by that nation's silversmiths.

Students of silver made in India are particularly well served by the many years of research of Wynyard Wilkinson. His two monumental works are:

The Makers of Indian Colonial Silver - A register of European goldsmiths, silversmiths, jewellers, watchmakers and clockmakers in India, and their marks, 1760-1860 (privately, London, 1987), and

Indian Silver, 1858-1947 - Silver from the Indian sub-continent and Burma during ninety years of British rule (privately, London, 1999).

In conclusion, it is not suggested that, in order to enjoy the hobby, the potential collector of military silver will need to acquire all of the titles listed here, or even a significant proportion of them. Time and experience will reveal which are most likely to suit the needs of the individual. When in doubt, it is helpful to seek the advice of book-dealers specialising in new and second-hand military books, or those having knowledge of silver.

Appendix D
The Care of Silver

The following appendix is based upon guidelines originally compiled by Colonel R L Wallis, of the Royal Corps of Transport, and subsequently published by The Regimental Association of The Royal Logistic Corps. They were intended to assist military personnel involved in the handling and safe custody of Mess and regimental silver. In practice, they provide a helpful set of rules for everyone - serving officers, Mess silvermen, regimental museum Curators, traders and collectors alike.

The author is indebted to Colonel Wallis for his wise counsel, and to the RLC Regimental Association for its permission to reproduce a large part of his work.

Introduction

Items made in silver, usually referred to as "pieces", are both valuable and vulnerable, hence the need for caution in their handling, cleaning, storage and transportation. These notes provide guidelines to those having responsibility for such pieces. The aim is to ensure that they will always be displayed and enjoyed to the full.

The term "silver", as used here, refers to items made in Sterling hallmarked silver. However, the same basic advice for good care and maintenance applies equally to foreign silver and to all items which are silver-plated.

Values

Silver has value based upon four main considerations:

a. The intrinsic value of the metal. The heavier the piece, the more valuable it is likely to be.

b. The "singularity" of the piece. Regimental silver falls into two categories - mass produced items (for example, flatware, ashtrays and picture frames), and individually made pieces which were hand-crafted for a particular reason. Given their uniqueness, the latter are likely to possess the greatest financial value.

c. The aesthetic consideration, i.e. the quality of design.

d. Rarity. As with any other antique, old silver is usually the most rare and therefore, in general terms, the most valuable.

e. The marks punched into the base or on some other part of the piece (and into any accompanying or component part, such as a lid). They confirm its age, the town or city where it was submitted for assay, the fact that it conforms with the Sterling or Britannia standards, and the name of the maker. The latter is important if the mark is that of a silversmith whose work is more highly regarded than others.

Vulnerability

Silver is essentially a soft metal. Because it is expensive, many pieces tend to have been made as thin as possible (within the constraints of structural integrity). Frequent use and polishing can make them even thinner. For these reasons, they are extremely vulnerable to accidental damage. The principle causes are:

a. Scratching, grazing or digging, from contact with anything harder than silver itself. Most things are, especially other metals.

b. Denting, by being dropped or knocked against any hard object.

c. Rubbing against another piece of silver while in transit, or against any abrasive surface.

d. Chemical reaction, particularly when the plating comes into contact with salt, sea air, acid foodstuffs such as vinegar, and with the natural acidity of the human skin.

Handling

In the light of its value and vulnerability, the less it is handled the better. However, Mess silver is unlike that in private homes. It is moved more frequently, is more regularly used or displayed, and may be exposed to greater hazards. The following recommendations should, therefore, be observed by all Mess staff (and officers holding the appointment of Mess silver member).

Cotton gloves should be used whenever they are available. This eliminates the risk of finger marks and the unsightly tarnish caused by human sweat. White cotton gloves (mitts) impregnated with silver preservative are available commercially.

All dusters used for either handling or polishing must be 100% free of grit or anything in the least abrasive. Even when a duster is dropped briefly on the floor, it can acquire minute particles of dirt. Invisible to the eye, this *detritus* acts as a sanding agent when reapplied to the surface of the silver, and causes "hazing".

Access to awkward corners can be gained with a small brush. Silver brushes can be purchased from stockists, but an old toothbrush is an acceptable substitute (provided that it is natural bristle, never nylon).

If neither gloves nor dusters are available, use acid free tissue paper - "silver paper".

When a number of small objects are being carried from one place to another on a tray, remember to first place a clean dry cloth on the tray (to prevent the silver from sliding off).

Cleaning

Silver looks its best when it is bright and shining. Paradoxically, excessive or incorrect cleaning causes damage. The following points should be kept in mind:

The work must be done in a clean working environment. The table top should be covered with a clean sheet, an old blanket, or a piece of baize. Alternatively, wear an apron and hold the piece in your lap.

Never use any cleaning or polishing materials which have not been produced specifically for silver. Some domestic cleaning agents are acid, or alkali, and can cause damage. When in doubt, take the expert advice of a qualified jeweller, silversmith or silver restorer.

Pieces held for a long time in storage may have become not

simply tarnished but also dirty. The cold metal attracts moisture which, if there is a kitchen in the vicinity, condenses as a greasy film. A similar problem arises with silver exposed to tobacco smoke. Before polishing, therefore, wash the piece in warm soapy water (using natural soap, not a detergent). Wash off the suds with clean warm water, then immediately wipe dry with a chamois leather. If it is not possible to remove all the droplets from the crevices, leave the piece in an airing cupboard for an hour or so before polishing.

If the piece is fixed permanently to a wooden base, protect the colour and surface of the wood by tying or taping a plastic bag around it before commencing work on the silver.

Silver-handled knives with steel blades must be washed and polished separately. The steel will mark the plating on the spoons and forks if they come into contact.

Grease is removed from candlesticks by immersing and rinsing the encrusted area (the socket and sconce) in very hot water. The grease should then float off. Never immerse the entire piece in the water, and never attempt to scrape off the spilled grease with any sort of metal instrument.

When buffing with a cloth or duster, never apply heavy pressure. Let the polish and the material do the job for you. Light small circular movements with the duster will remove the residue of the polish and produce a uniform finish.

There are various proprietary brands of polish on the market. Some are intended for light regular use, others for treating pieces which have become heavily tarnished. There are products which are intended to give "long life" or "permanence" to the shine. It can be preserved also by coating (lacquering) with a compound based upon cellulose or silicone. Depending upon the nature of the collection and its condition, and the end result required, it is advisable to invite the opinion of someone who handles silver as a full-time occupation before selecting any of these products.

It may not be necessary to use a proprietary polish every time the piece is cleaned. Often it is enough to give it a light buffing with a fluffy (clean) duster.

No attempt should be made to polish items made in silver-gilt. The surface layer of gold is extremely thin, and there is the risk than it will wear away. Cleaning should be restricted to warm soapy water, wiping with a *chamois* leather, and a very light final buffing with a duster. In most cases, silver-gilt is probably best left alone.

Damage and repairs

All Mess silver in regular use is damaged from time to time. It is important to deal with damage as soon as possible after it has occurred. Component parts which have broken off are too easily misplaced. Even if the nature of the injury is comparatively minor - perhaps a dent in a cup - subsequent polishing will quickly wear through the silver plating around the lip of the indentation. Repairs should be undertaken only by qualified silversmiths or professional restorers. Examples have been seen which were mended by people lacking the necessary skills and equipment. It then became necessary to repair the repair.

Storage and transport

Major pieces such as large centrepieces are usually packed in purpose-made wooden boxes or crates, lined with baize or padding, and shaped internally to accommodate them. Smaller objects will be packed together in boxes which may not be tailor-made for the job. The basic rules of common sense apply here. Each piece must be completely wrapped in acid-free tissue, given

its own space within the box, and separated from its neighbours with wads or layers of acid-free bubble-wrap or similar. Old newspapers should **not** be used for wrapping (the ink, and the paper itself, are injurious to silver).

Strong wooden crates can be stacked, but not cardboard boxes. The weight of the higher boxes may crush those at a lower lever.

Each crate or box should be clearly labelled. This avoids the turmoil of disturbing the entire collection whenever there is a need to retrieve one particular piece.

Most permanent Mess buildings have a strong-room where the silver is stored on purpose-built shelving. Proprietory tarnish-inhibiting capsules can be placed on the shelves, their purpose being to reduce the need for frequent polishing.

When knives, forks and spoons (flatware) are being packed, they must **never** be bundled together with elastic bands. The rubber will burn a black mark into the plating. It cannot be polished out, so all the afflicted pieces will need to be replated.

Summary

So much for the (slightly edited) guidelines originally drawn up by Colonel Wallis. It might be thought that some of them are so self-evident, so obvious, that they are not worth listing. The evidence suggests that this is not the case. The author has been privileged to hear the experiences of a professional restorer who repairs the silver of a branch of the armed forces (the identity of which is best not revealed).

Cigar or cigarette boxes are a handy size to be used as the "ball" in a game of Mess rugby. Box and lid soon part company. This has happened several times.

A presentation salver was the target for a young officers' impromptu after-dinner shooting competition with a high-powered air rifle.

Following a Guest Night, the Mess staff washed the Georgian cutlery in a sink fitted with a waste disposal unit. Several pieces fell into it, with disastrous results.

A Georgian candelabra was placed in a dish-washing machine. It collected numerous scuffs and scratches but, worst of all, the very hot water dissolved the plaster of Paris base and melted the pitch filling. The latter spread itself far and wide.

During redecorations in the Mess, some of the silver was splashed with paint. It was later removed with a knife and wire wool. Much of the silver plating and engraved wording was removed with it.

Entrée dishes made in Sheffield plate are often placed in ovens to keep the food hot. The excessive heat melts the lead mounts, and the piece disintegrates. Such dishes were designed for *serving* hot food, but never for prolonged exposure to high temperatures.

Britannia metal teapots (see the *Glossary*) have at times been placed on very hot metal surfaces (such as the top of an Aga). They have melted.

Bleach has a ruinous effect on all silver plating - Sterling, Sheffield or EPNS. Pieces have frequently been left overnight to soak in bleach or bleach-type products. The silver turns black. This can be corrected only by having the piece completely replated.

Kitchen staff commonly resort to the use of scouring powders and scouring pads made from nylon or wire wool. Even if they do not remove the silver plate, they will leave its surface with a dull haze (which necessitates prolonged and probably professional re-polishing, or even replating).

Multi-branch candelabra seem to be the most frequent

sufferers from inept handling. When staff are loading the candles, they often hold the piece by its main column or trunk. They then press the candle firmly down into the socket. As a consequence, the branch, having no support, bends or breaks off. The correct technique is to place one hand under each socket in turn, inserting the candle with the other. For the larger and heavier pieces, it is best to have two people engaged in the operation (the first to hold the main column steady, the second free to devote both hands to inserting the candles in the branch sockets).

The removal of old candle stubs from their sockets is a regular source of trouble. Faced with the problem, people resort to the use of screwdrivers to prize them out, or grip the sconce (drip pan) and try to wrench the stub out by brute force. Either way, they inflict severe damage. If hot water fails, a gentle flame can be applied to the under surface of the socket (thus melting the old stub).

Condiment sets, in particular the salts, are by far the greatest victims of incorrect storage. Being hygroscopic, salt quickly attracts moisture. The mineral then attacks not only the silver plating but also the underlying alloy and the surrounding joints. In very little time, the piece is ruined. Most salts are fitted with a glass liner. This ought always to be used. However, at the end of the meal, the liner should be taken out so that any grains which have fallen down between it and the silver outer can be removed. Even a single grain of salt will cause "black spot", a serious type of damage.

Some conclusions

For very many years, it was the practice that all service personnel directly engaged in caring for silver were sent on residential courses, lasting a week or more. These were operated by firms which specialised in the making of Mess and Wardroom silver. Each regiment tended to place its orders with one particular company, and it was logically to that same company's premises that new Mess silvermen were sent. The system ensured that good silver would be treated properly after it had left the workroom and, in modern terminology, it was good "after sales service". It seems that firms such as Carrington, Elkington, the Goldsmiths & Silversmiths Company, Hunt & Roskell, Mappin & Webb, and probably others, provided it to all their customers, both service and private. The same training facility was available, of course, to the owners of the great houses who sent their silver pantrymen and aspiring butlers to attend the same courses.

In more recent years, the routine has changed. The companies themselves have been subject to market pressures and have altered some of their working practices. The landed gentry no longer order silver on the same scale as they once did. Civic authorities gear their budgets to social amenities and services rather than decorative or presentation silver. The number of British Army regiments and corps has shrivelled by comparison with those serving in "the golden age" of Victoria and Edward. The Royal Navy is a great deal smaller than it was before WWII.

In sum, the nature of the silver trade has evolved away from its traditional patterns. Most significantly, the practice of sending trainee Mess staff to London, Birmingham or Sheffield, to receive expert tuition from silver craftsmen, appears largely to have been abandoned. The reasons are not hard to find. They spring from the modern philosophy of cutting expenditure and reducing manning levels to the bone. Running costs have undoubtedly been reduced.

The reverse side of the coin is the risk of long-term diminishing standards of expertise. This is partly offset by the relatively new practice of appointing a qualified silversmith who visits the regiment or corps every few months, and is asked by the Trustees to quote the cost of repairing damaged pieces. Having negotiated a price, he takes them back to his workshop for restoration. This system provides an element of good maintenance but, naturally, its efficacy is restricted to the funds available to meet his bill.

The new system, it can be argued, is based upon a philosophy of "cure" rather than "prevention". The cost of repairing severe damage to just one valuable centrepiece can equate to several months' wages for a single trained silverman. The nub of the problem is, of course, the fact that the costs of repair are paid by the Trustees and so are not a burden upon public funds. The traditional Mess silverman was a serving soldier, and therefore part of the nation's defence expenditure. The basic principles of conservation and care are largely determined, therefore, by the question, "who pays?".

Aggravating the problem is the modern practice of competitive tendering for Mess catering services. This also, it may be argued, has saved some money in the short term. However, it means that silver worth thousands (even many tens of thousands) of pounds, is being handled by part-time civilian employees. It is a task for which they have little (if any) training. They cannot reasonably be expected to comprehend the true significance of the artefacts which they are required to clean or pack, or to move from one part of the Mess to another.

By no means all blame for the damage inflicted upon historical silver can be placed at the door of well-meaning but untrained civilian staff. There is ample evidence to support the view that some of it is caused by exuberant young officers. Still learning the ways of their profession, and possibly having wined and dined too well, they can in a moment of foolhardy high spirits inflict damage costing a great deal of money to rectify.

It may be that the RMA Sandhurst, and the Britannia Royal Naval College Dartmouth, have something to learn here. Cadets should be given to understand, at the outset of their careers, that they are about to inherit not just the honour of the service into which shortly they will be commissioned. They are entering also into a responsibility of care for its silver. They will inherit collections which embody the services of generations of officers who have gone before them, and whose valour and devotion they may be hard pressed to emulate. Such instruction would, at an early stage, allow them the opportunity of understanding the deeper meaning of Mess and Wardroom silver, and to respect it accordingly.

It is impossible to estimate the monetary value of the collections of silver held by the armed forces. Its significance is, in any case, essentially historical. However, to judge by the insurance valuations seen by the author, it is reasonable to state that the total runs into many tens of millions of pounds, probably several hundreds of millions. There must surely be some concern for the future well-being of this unique element in the nation's history.

Appendix E
Glossary of Terms and Titles

This glossary is arranged in two parts. The first deals with terms having a military or naval connotation. These are the words or titles which may be found engraved on items of silver (or encountered during related research). The second deals with words or terms relating directly to the manufacture and design of silver artefacts of all kinds.

Military

Adjutant - a regimental officer appointed by his commanding officer to plan and execute all aspects of the day-to-day management of the Orderly room (the regimental or battalion office), the orders issued by that office, the forward planning of the unit's activities, and the maintenance of the unit's standards of discipline.

Army - there are two alternative meanings. First, generically, a nation's military forces. Secondly, a military formation consisting of two or more corps (q.v.) and commanded by a General.

Battalion - a unit consisting of 500-1150 all ranks (depending upon the period in question), comprising between four and eight companies (q.v.), and commanded by a Lieutenant Colonel.

Battery - a unit of artillery comprising 80-150 all ranks, equating to a company of infantry, and commanded by a Major.

Brigade - most commonly used to describe a grouping of three or four battalions of infantry, and commanded by a Brigadier General (shortened to Brigadier since WWI).

Colonel in Chief - an honorary appointment accepted by a royal personage with the approval of the Sovereign. The person so appointed may be a member of the British royal family or may be of foreign royalty. There is always some connection between the appointed person and the regiment or corps in question. The tie may be historical, territorial or personal (for example, he at some time served with it). Not all regiments and corps are able to claim such a connection. In the case of the Royal Artillery and the Royal Marines, the appointment is replaced by that of Captain General, and is held by the sovereign.

Colonel of the Regiment - an honorary appointment conferred upon a senior officer (serving or retired) who has normally (but not necessarily) served with the regiment concerned. The appointment requires the approval of the Colonel in Chief (q.v.) or the Sovereign, and of the MOD (Army). It is normally for a period of five years, but can be extended. The Colonel of the Regiment is kept informed of all happenings within the regiment. If so requested by the Commanding Officer (q.v.), he will give advice on matters concerning the overall welfare of the regiment and its institutions. He accompanies the Colonel in Chief (q.v.) during the visits which he or she may make to the regiment. He also makes regular visits of his own, not only to the Regular battalion(s) but also its affiliated Territorial Army and Army Cadet Force units. The appointment ensures a continuing strand in the regiment's

esprit de corps, and provides a channel of communication (formal and informal) to other elements of the army.

Colour Sergeant - originally the title of the Sergeants responsible for the safe custody of the unit's Colours. In modern practice, it has widened to include senior Sergeants having special responsibilities, or awaiting promotion to Warrant rank, or as a mark of distinction for a long-serving Sergeant approaching retirement.

Commandant - most likely to be encountered as the title of the Commanding Officer (q.v.) of a unit of the Indian Army.

Commanding Officer (CO) - a Lieutenant Colonel in command of a regiment (cavalry, artillery or engineer), and/or of a battalion of infantry (a regiment may have one or more active battalions). These are known generically as "units". Sub-units (squadrons and companies) are under the command of Majors, and they are known as Officers Commanding (OC). Larger formations are under the command of a Commander (for example, a Brigadier commanding a Brigade), or a General Officer Commanding in Chief (for example, a Lieutenant General or General commanding an Army (q.v.).

Corps - two alternative meanings. As a tactical unit, it consists of two, three, four or five Divisions (q.v.). As an organisation, it provides support services to the front-line units. Examples are the Royal Corps of Engineers, Royal Logistic Corps, Royal Army Veterinary Corps, and Royal Corps of Signals.

Division - a military formation consisting of three or possibly four brigades, with ancillary units, and commanded by a Major General. See Chapter Seven for a definition specific to the Royal Marines.

Group - for the army, a tactical assembly of elements of various regiments and corps for a temporary battlefield need, as in "battle group". For the RAF, it is the administration and command of several squadrons and the airfields from which they operate.

Non-commissioned officer - literally, it describes any soldier who does not hold a Queen's commission. In practice, it is applied only to Lance-Corporals, Corporals, Sergeants, Staff Sergeants and Colour Sergeants (q.v.). The Warrant Officers are usually referred to under their own distinctive designation.

Officer Commanding - an officer in command of a military sub-unit (q.v.), or an officer commanding a ship of the Royal Navy. Major ships are commanded by Captains RN. Lesser ships, those having a smaller ship's company, are commanded by officers holding the rank of Commander (with three rings on this sleeve). They hold the *appointment* of Captain, but are more precisely described as Commanders in Command.

Other ranks - all members of the army other than the commissioned officers. Thus, the term covers Warrant Officers, Non-commissioned officers and private soldiers alike.

Platoon - an infantry sub-unit, comprising 15-40 all ranks, commanded by a Sergeant or Subaltern (q.v.).

President of the Mess Committee (PMC) - a senior officer

within a unit, appointed by his Commanding Officer to oversee the management of the Officers' Mess. He is usually a Major or senior Captain. The term of his appointment is initially for three months, but often this is extended. He is assisted by three, four or five other (junior) officers, each of whom may have specific responsibilities (as the Messing Member, Wines Member, Silver Member, and so forth). The PMC is responsible also for the Mess Accounts.

President of the Regimental Institute (PRI) - a senior officer (usually a Major) appointed by the Commanding Officer (q.v.) to manage and administer all aspects of the messing and welfare of the other ranks (q.v.). The PRI's responsibilities include the accounts of the Sergeants' and Corporals' Messes, the NAAFI and Regimental Institute, the recreational funds, and so forth. He also holds a central bank through which holders of minor funds are able to transfer money and settle accounts with civilian contractors.

Regiment - a military unit having its own distinctive designation or title, its own identity as demonstrated in its cap badge, Battle Honours, Colours or Guidon, and its own unique "family" or regimental spirit. It is a component part of all the main arms - cavalry, artillery, engineers, signals and infantry. A regiment of infantry might have only one Regular battalion (q.v.) or, in time of war, it might have several more.

Squadron - a sub-unit within a regiment of cavalry, engineers or signals, with a strength of 60-150 all ranks and commanded by a Major. A squadron equates to a company of infantry. In the context of the RAF, the Fleet Air Arm and the Army Air Corps, it describes a self-contained unit which operates aircraft or support equipment/services.

Station - a permanent military or air force base, accommodating one or more units. Normally it has barracks accommodation, married quarters, recreational buildings, rifle ranges, and permanent Mess buildings. In India, they were known as cantonments.

Subaltern - neither a rank nor an appointment, but a general description of army officers holding the rank of Second Lieutenant or Lieutenant.

Troop - a military sub-unit within a squadron (q.v.), comprising 20-70 all ranks, and commanded by a Sergeant or Subaltern (q.v.). A troop equates to a platoon of infantry.

Unit - most commonly used to describe a regiment or battalion, but generally convenient as describing any type of military, naval or air force formation.

Warrant Officer - a senior non-commissioned officer who has been granted a warrant rather than a commission. He will be a man of exceptional abilities and many years of service. If he is in regimental employment, he will be the Regimental Sergeant Major (Warrant Officer Class I), or Company (or Squadron) Sergeant Major (Warrant Officer Class II). If he is not currently in regimental employment, he is addressed as Mister.

Silver

Assay Office - the place to which most objects made in gold, silver or platinum must be sent for testing before they can (legally) be offered for sale as such.

Britannia metal - an alloy consisting of 90% tin with 10% antimony, copper, zinc or lead, and can be described as a form of pewter. It has a relatively low melting point and therefore, like Sheffield plate (q.v.) must never be exposed to excessive heat. It will take a polish of sorts, and was essentially a means of satisfying the demand for metal tableware at very low cost.

Britannia silver - an alloy of 95.8% silver and 4.2% copper,

known as "the higher standard". Between 1697 and 1720, it was the only standard of purity permitted for English silversmiths. See Appendix F for details.

Cartouche - a square, oval, or round area on the surface of a piece, or sometimes made separately and mounted on its wood base. It is surrounded by decorative scroll work, and is frequently occupied by engraved presentation wording.

Centrepiece - any artefact made in gold, silver or silver-gilt, and designed for display on the dining table on selected occasions. Normally they are kept in the strongroom or in a purpose-made crate or box. They were (and still are) commissioned to mark important events, and the designs are therefore almost always unique. Some have a practical use (as candelabra, for example), but the design themes of the majority are centred upon a specific campaign or battle or event, and the people who took part. In general terms, they are the largest and most valuable pieces in the Mess or Wardroom collection.

Electro-plating - the application of a pure silver coating to otherwise finished pieces made in Sterling silver, nickel steel, and other suitable alloys. The process was perfected in Birmingham, by the firm of Elkington, sometime around 1843.

Embossing - the creation of a pattern on the surface of a piece by striking it from behind with a variety of rounded punches. The pattern can be augmented with indentations embossed from the front.

Engraving - words, lines or decorative *motifs* cut into the surface of the piece from the front. Presentation wording, as seen on minor items of military and naval silver, may have been engraved mechanically, and this is easily identified by examination with a magnifying glass. Hand-tooled engravings (of presentation wording) can be beautiful in their own right, reflecting great caligraphic skill and artistry by the craftsman. Almost all military and naval silver is hand-engraved.

Finial - the top-most feature of a lid or cover, or of any piece made with a top (terminal) point. Traditionally, they are shaped as pineapples, acorns, pine cones, urns, and so forth. Pieces made for military and naval customers are more likely to have finials shaped as a "flaming grenade", as a fouled anchor, a mounted cavalryman, a rifleman, or whatever *motif* is appropriate to the unit and to the circumstances of the presentation.

Flatware - a generic word for knives, forks and spoons, and similar implements.

Gilding - the application of a very thin coating of pure gold on an otherwise finished piece made in silver. It can be achieved by chemical reaction, but pieces made since the 1840s are likely to have been coated by electrolysis. They are catalogued as "silver gilt".

Hallmarks - the set of icons punched or stamped into a piece (and any detachable component parts) when it is submitted to analysis at an Assay Office (q.v.), and is found to meet the required standard of purity. Prior to 1 January 1999, there were normally four - the registered mark of the maker, the mark for Sterling silver (or its equivalent for gold and platinum), the mark of the Assay Office, and a mark denoting the year in which the assay was made. Further details appear in Appendix F.

Hollow ware - a term used generically to describe objects which are to a greater or lesser degree hollow, *vice* flatware (q.v.). Cups, goblets, bowls, tureens, *entrée* dishes, pots, tankards and beakers all come within this category.

Moulding - a border or rim, added to give the piece strength and as a decoration. The metal may be cast, or may be hammered into the required shape. Salvers, typically, have prominent mouldings around their rims, and they conform to numerous styles - Chippendale, foliate shell, gadroon, foliate shell and gadrooning, shell and scroll, and so forth.

Niello - a black alloy of silver, copper, lead and sulphur set into surfaces which have previously been engraved or etched with acid. It produces an effect of in-laying, and is distinctive of silver made in Siam. One such piece is illustrated in Chapter Nine (the cigarette box of Field Marshal Sir John Harding).

Parcel gilt - the surface of the piece has been partially but not entirely gilded (q.v.).

Pewter - an alloy consisting traditionally of approximately 95% tin, 3% lead, and 2% copper, antimony or bismuth. Cheap qualities contained up to 40% lead and were known as "black metal". Lead has been banned in the United Kingdom since 1969. Modern pewter is usually 94% tin, 4% antimony and 2% copper or bismuth.

Pierced - the design includes decorative patterns which have been achieved by cutting or stamping spaces through the metal.

Plate - in this book, the term is used to describe the (usually oblong) pieces of flat silver riveted or pinned to the wood base of a presentation piece or trophy (q.v.), and upon which the appropriate wording is engraved. The plate (with or without engraving) was usually supplied by the maker of the main piece at the time of delivery, but not always. It may have been added later, in which case it will have a later year mark and may even bear the mark of a different maker. An alternative word for such plates is "plaque".

In a totally different context, "plate" was in the past the generic description for all flatware (q.v.) and hollow ware (q.v.), regardless of its manufacture. It comprised objects made in Sterling and Britannia silver, Sheffield plate, electro-plate, gold, silver gilt and parcel gilt. On occasion, in the records of old Indian Army regiments, it applied also to Mess possessions made by Indian silversmiths. Researchers consulting regimental records compiled in the 19th century, or even some of later date, will encounter this word frequently. Since the early part of the 20th century, the phrase "Mess plate" has given way to the current "Mess silver".

Repoussé - a form of embossing (q.v.). Decorative or illustrative effects are achieved by punching from the front. On individual high value pieces, it is done by hand. Similar effects are obtained with mass-produced pieces which are annealed (heated and softened) and then stamped with the required design or *motif*.

Sheffield plate - a compound metal invented in 1743 by a Sheffield cutler, Thomas Bolsover. He fused (by heating) a thin sheet of copper with a thinner sheet of silver. After several passes through heavy steel rollers, it was cut or stamped into any desired shape. A variation on his method was to sandwich an ingot of copper between two ingots of silver (the rolled sheets then having a thin layer of silver on both sides). When articles were made from Sheffield plate, the edges and joins of the component parts were often soldered together with a lead-based compound (which is the main reason for ensuring that items made in Sheffield plate are never exposed to high temperatures, as in a stove or on a kitchen hot-plate). The process was adopted as a means of producing attractive objects at less cost than those made in Britannia or Sterling silver. It was abandoned in the 1840s with the arrival of the electro-plating method (q.v.).

Silver paper - a quality of tissue paper which is ph negative (neither acid nor alkali). It is designed for wrapping objects which are plated in silver (and gold), and is available from most jewellers or trade stockists.

Stamping - the manufacture of mass-produced parts such as borders and edgings, decorative features, or even complete (small and simple) pieces. The silver is annealed to a high temperature and then mechanically struck with hard steel dies. Such decorations are soldered to the main body of the piece, the whole being then given its final plating in pure silver.

Trophy - has a number of connotations, depending upon the context. The most frequent military and naval examples are "trophy of war" (an object taken from the enemy) and "shooting trophy" (the prize awarded for a shooting competition, or equally, the prize given for sailing, rowing, athletics and equestrian events).

Historically, "trophies" have been adopted by architects and silversmiths as a design *motif* consisting of shields, spears, standards, plumed helmets, cannon, and so on. The word has also at times been used generically to describe *all* of the silver owned by a regiment or ship. Those owned by the naval Trusts, as an example, are administered by the Royal Navy Trophy Centre.

The story of hallmarking is long and complicated. It is described in detail in numerous works of historical reference, and the titles of several are noted in Appendix C. The following is a condensed and simplified summary.

King John (1167-1216) was the first monarch to understand the need to standardise the purity or "fineness" of his coinage. To assist the English coiners, he brought to London a group of European silversmiths. It was they who established the alloy of 92.5% silver and 7.5% copper as the English standard for coins and plate. They came from the region which later evolved as Germany. Because they came from the east, their English counterparts referred to them as "Easterlings". According to legend, this nickname was gradually shortened until it became Sterling, a word which has ever since described objects and people of worth and reliability.

The English system of applying hallmarks to objects made in gold and silver has its origins in a Statute of King Edward I, signed by him in 1300. It had two intended purposes. The first was to protect honest goldsmiths and silversmiths from unfair competition. It was too easy for a dishonest smith to undercut them by using alloys containing higher levels of base metals and proportionately less of the expensive precious metals. The second was to protect the buyer. He needed an assurance, when buying an artefact styled as "gold" or "silver", that it conformed to a recognised standard of purity. Edward's Statute was, therefore, the earliest form of consumer protection.

The guardians of the standards were the Wardens of what is now titled the Worshipful Company of Goldsmiths of London. Formed under the Charter granted by Edward, the Company (the Guild) attempted to ensure that the alloy used for every English manufactured article should be "good and true". Having satisfactorily subjected the piece to assay, they struck it with a (single) distinctive mark. Initially it was called "the King's mark", and it signified that the alloy was of "good Sterling silver". The chosen *motif* was the face or mask of a lion, the heraldic device which in Old French was the *leopart*. At the time of these events, the language imported by William the Conqueror was still in common usage by the educated classes. The mark has since become known as "the leopard's head".

In 1363 it was decreed that there should be a second mark, a symbol or icon signifying the name of the maker. It permitted the Wardens to identify a silversmith who, when his past work was melted for re-use, was found to have employed an inferior metal. In the early years, when few people could read, the marks were symbols which reflected the maker's name (a bell, if that was his surname) or perhaps a ship (if his workshop was behind a tavern which carried that sign). Over the centuries, many thousands of them have been registered with the Company. The study of these marks, and of the variations registered when business partnerships changed, provides an absorbing field of research in its own right.

The day-to-day business of assaying, and the maintaining of records, was conducted in the City of London, at the Goldsmiths' Hall. It is for this reason that the group of marks found on every piece of Sterling silver is known commonly and collectively as "the hallmarks".

The term "assay mark", which is only one of the hallmarks, derives from the Old French word *assai* (meaning examination).

In the reign of Henry VI, sometime around 1423, it was ordained that assay offices should be established in York, Newcastle, Lincoln, Norwich, Bristol, Salisbury and Coventry. Each had its own distinctive touch or mark, and each held a register of local makers' marks. Other Offices were opened later in Edinburgh, Exeter, Dublin, Glasgow, Chester, Birmingham, Sheffield and elsewhere.

The practice of adding a third mark - denoting the year in which the piece was assayed - began at the end of the 15th century. It had a very practical purpose. The Wardens of the Assay Office were appointed every twelve months, usually in April or May. A letter from the alphabet was allocated to each twelve months period. In the event that the Wardens of that year failed in their duty - by approving a piece later shown to be deficient - the year mark ensured that they could be identified and punished.

When the alphabetical sequence was exhausted, the background shape of the mark (the escutcheon) was changed and a new shape or style given to the letters of the next cycle. The following tables demonstrate the ingenuity of the Wardens of the various Assay Offices in finding an almost limitless permutation of letters (upper case, lower case, serif, non-serif, ornate, plain) and escutcheons (circles, squares, pointed shields, baluster shields, shapes with "cut" upper corners, others without).

Control of the craft was considerably tightened, by a Statute of King Henry VII, in 1504. He ordered that officers of the Crown be involved in the conduct of the Company and of the Assay Offices, and granted powers to fine or imprison silversmiths who broke the rules. The new law also permitted the Wardens to destroy any pieces submitted for assay which did not meet the official requirements of purity.

In the medieval period, tableware in the homes of prosperous merchants and land-owners consisted of earthenware, wooden platters, jugs and bowls in pewter, and items made in silver. The most important symbol of wealth and prestige was the silver, particularly the standing salt. When the master took his place to dine with his guests, the salt was set before him at the centre of the single long table (placed facing the fire, with everyone sat along one side). His wife sat to his left. The other members of his family and household, in decreasing seniority, were seated to her left. To the master's right were his guests, carefully placed in diminishing order of rank, wealth and importance. From this careful observance of *etiquette* we have inherited the phrases "right hand man" and "worth his salt". The same customs can be seen, in greatly modified form, in the seating arrangements at regimental Guest Nights and other important Mess dinners.

The symbolism of the standing salt, often crafted in beautiful and ornate form, was much later reflected in the acquisition by regimental officers of magnificent decorative table centrepieces. Not only did they commemorate great events, they were a statement of the regiment's prosperity and social standing.

The next important event was the introduction of a fourth mark, the "lion *passant*", the Sterling mark. Over many years, the coinage of the realm had been steadily debased. By the reign of King Henry VIII, the intrinsic value of silver coins was only half of their face value. Wrought or manufactured silver, on the other hand, continued to be made to the Sterling standard. In 1544, the Wardens of the Goldsmiths' Company decided that all such silver, irrespective of its place of assay, would in future carry this new Sterling mark. It was a continuing guarantee that their output, at least, had not been debased. The "leopard's head" then ceased to be "the king's mark". It became the assay mark for London.

Henry's daughter, Elizabeth, restored the value of English coinage, and it was thereafter made to the Sterling standard.

Until the reign of King Charles II, all English coins were struck by hand (hammered). To make them more or less round, the coiners clipped the outer rough edges before issue into public circulation. This made it easy for people to clip a bit more every time a silver coin passed through their hands. Having accumulated enough clippings, they sold them to forgers who (with a fake die and stamp) made more coins. This went on for years, despite the severe punishments of hanging or branding. The problem reached epidemic proportions in the aftermath of the English Civil War and Cromwell's Commonwealth. The restoration of the monachy led to a great upsurge in demand for decorative and working silverware. Partly it was needed to replace the huge quantities which had been melted as bullion to pay for the cost of that war, and partly because the nation was celebrating the end of Puritanism. Beauty and the arts were back in fashion. Clipping reached fever pitch as silversmiths, struggling to meet the demand, offered ever higher prices for scrap silver. Hundreds of men and women involved in the illicit trade were carted to Holborn Hill and publicly hanged.

New technology ended all of that. In 1697, the Treasury opened a horse-powered mechanised mint in Whitehall which produced perfectly round coins. They were immune to clipping because any interference to their rims was immediately obvious. However, the process of calling in all the old coinage and replacing it with the new took a long time, and clippings continued for a while to be a major source of raw material for the silversmiths. The law was therefore changed, it being ordained by the King and the English Parliament that the Sterling standard of fineness (92.5% pure) be replaced by a higher "Britannia standard" (95.8%). At a stroke, the new law stopped the trade in clippings. Thereafter, old coins and old scrap silver were sent to the smelters for the recovery of the pure silver and its re-alloying to the new standard. These events pre-dated the Act of Union (1707) and so did not apply to Scottish silversmiths.

Between 1697 and 1720, all English pieces made to the new (only) standard were stamped with the seated figure of Britannia, complete with helmet, shield and trident. The "lion *passant*" mark disappeared during those years. The higher grade alloy was, of course, softer and more difficult to work. As soon as national economic conditions permitted, it was agreed that the Sterling standard be reintroduced. From 1720 onwards, English and Scottish silversmiths have been free to work with alloys of both standards of purity, Sterling and Britannia, their work being marked accordingly.

In the event, and for the reasons stated, most of the silver made since 1720 has been Sterling. This means that, in the context of military and naval collections, the Britannia mark is unlikely ever be seen. However, it is always possible that a generous 19th century (or even 20th century) benefactor might have presented to a regiment a piece of very old (1697-1720) silver as a special token of his regard. The slight possibility of the Britannia mark appearing in a regimental inventory should therefore be kept in mind.

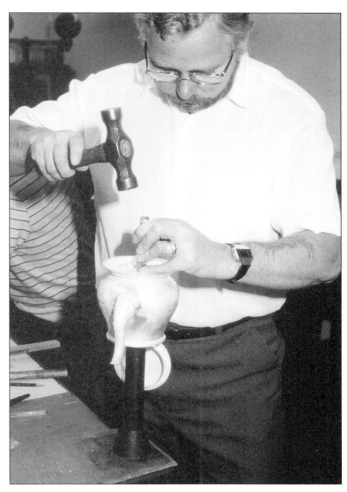

The process of hallmarking. Here Mr John Ryder applies the London mark to a piece which has met the legal test for purity. Photo: London Assay Office.

The year 1784 saw the introduction of yet another mark, the fifth in the hallmarking series. The government began in that year to impose a tax on all new artefacts made in Sterling and Britannia silver. The duty money was collected by the Commissioners of Stamps (later the Inland Revenue) working in conjunction with the Assay Offices. To show that the silversmith responsible for each piece had paid the tax, his work was stamped with a depiction of the monarch (at that time King George III). Known as "the sovereign's head mark" or "duty mark", it will be found on all Sterling and Britannia silver made during the next one hundred and six years (1890 was the last in which the silver tax was levied).

The practice was briefly revived in later years to celebrate three royal events (having no connection with tax). The "Jubilee mark" was stamped on all pieces made in 1933, 1934 and 1935 to commemorate the twenty-fifth anniversary of the accession to the throne of King George V and Queen Mary. It shows their conjoined heads in profile. The "Coronation mark" appears on all pieces made in 1952 and 1953 and is the head of Queen Elizabeth II. Then, in 1977, all pieces weighing more than fifteen grams were again stamped with the present sovereign's head, this being the "Silver Jubilee mark".

A few words regarding methods of assay may be of interest. When a piece is almost complete, it is sent to the Assay Office for examination. At this stage, it still has rough or unfinished edges. A sample of the metal is clipped or scraped from these extraneous parts and tested. In the early years, it was a colour test. The sample was rubbed on a piece of slate (a "touchstone") and a comparison then made between the colour of pure silver and that of the streaks left by the rubbing. It was not accurate and was overtaken in the early 14th century by the fire assay method. This depended upon a careful weighing and heating of the sample, and a calculation of the amount of pure silver driven out of the alloy when melted in combination with other substances. Later still, chemical analysis replaced the fire method. Today, the laboratories of the four remaining Assay Offices operate sophisticated equipment unimaginable to the craftsmen of former centuries. Despite such advances, the basic principles remain unaltered. Semi-finished work is examined for purity, the marks are punched only when it has passed the test, and it is then returned to the maker for finishing.

Although it is unlikely to concern the current generation of collectors and regimental museum curators, it may be noted that the British system of hallmarking has, since 1976, been going through a period of radical revision. It culminated on 1 January 1999. Changes to the Hallmarking Act have altered the way articles made of precious metals are marked, and they allow the sale to the public of pieces having a lower standard of purity. These changes have brought United Kingdom law into line with European law, and ensure that UK manufacturers can compete on equal terms with their European counterparts. Further information is available from the Department of Trade and Industry, 1 Victoria Street, London SW1H 0ET, or locally from retail outlets.

Requests for information specific to the work of each of the four Assay Offices may be submitted to:

The Deputy Warden
The Assay Office
Goldsmiths' Hall
Gutter Lane
London EC2V

The Assay Master
The Assay Office
Newhall Street
Birmingham B3 1SB

The Assay Master
The Assay Office
137 Portobello Street
Sheffield S1 4DR

The Assay Master
The Assay Office
39 Manor Place
Edinburgh EH3

The reader interested in identifying hallmarks has access to a wide variety of published sources (several are listed in Appendix C). The following tables of year marks are devoted to those of the four remaining Assay Offices. As a generalisation, the majority of pieces commissioned by the armed forces were made during the hundred years *circa* 1850 to 1950. It was a period when the competitive business of testing and marking was dominated by the Offices in London, Sheffield, Birmingham and Edinburgh. With both factors in mind, these tables are restricted to that "golden age".

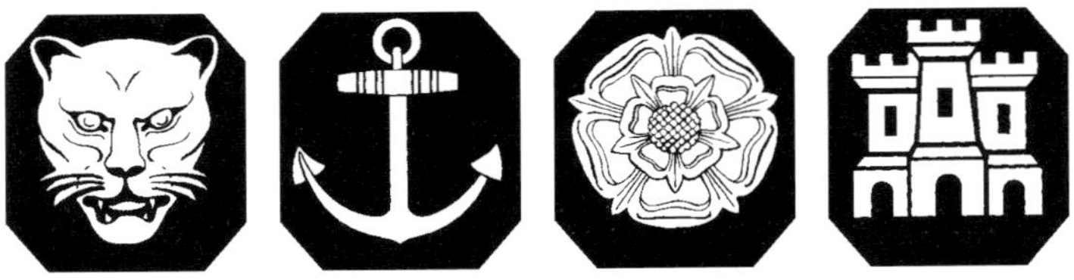

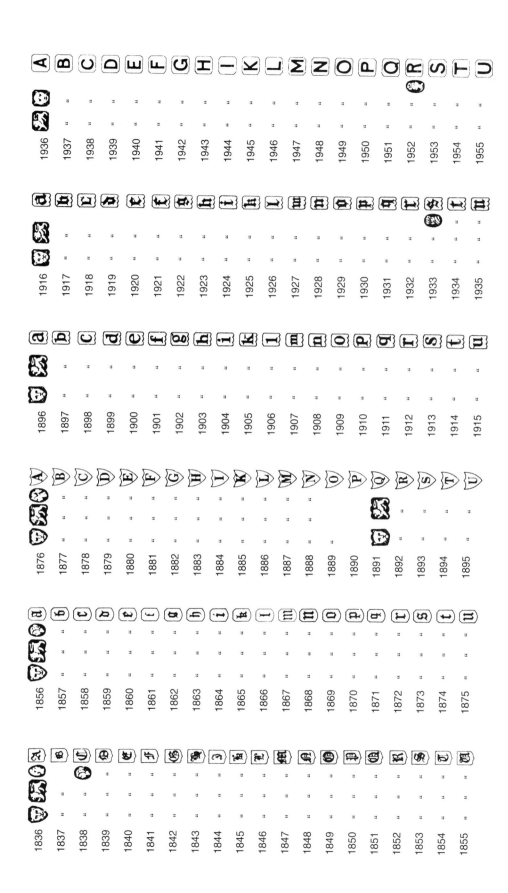

A B C D E F G H I K L M N O P Q R S T U

1936 1937 1938 1939 1940 1941 1942 1943 1944 1945 1946 1947 1948 1949 1950 1951 1952 1953 1954 1955

1916 1917 1918 1919 1920 1921 1922 1923 1924 1925 1926 1927 1928 1929 1930 1931 1932 1933 1934 1935

1896 1897 1898 1899 1900 1901 1902 1903 1904 1905 1906 1907 1908 1909 1910 1911 1912 1913 1914 1915

A B C D E F G H I K L M N O P Q R S T U

1876 1877 1878 1879 1880 1881 1882 1883 1884 1885 1886 1887 1888 1889 1890 1891 1892 1893 1894 1895

1856 1857 1858 1859 1860 1861 1862 1863 1864 1865 1866 1867 1868 1869 1870 1871 1872 1873 1874 1875

1836 1837 1838 1839 1840 1841 1842 1843 1844 1845 1846 1847 1848 1849 1850 1851 1852 1853 1854 1855

LONDON

BIRMINGHAM

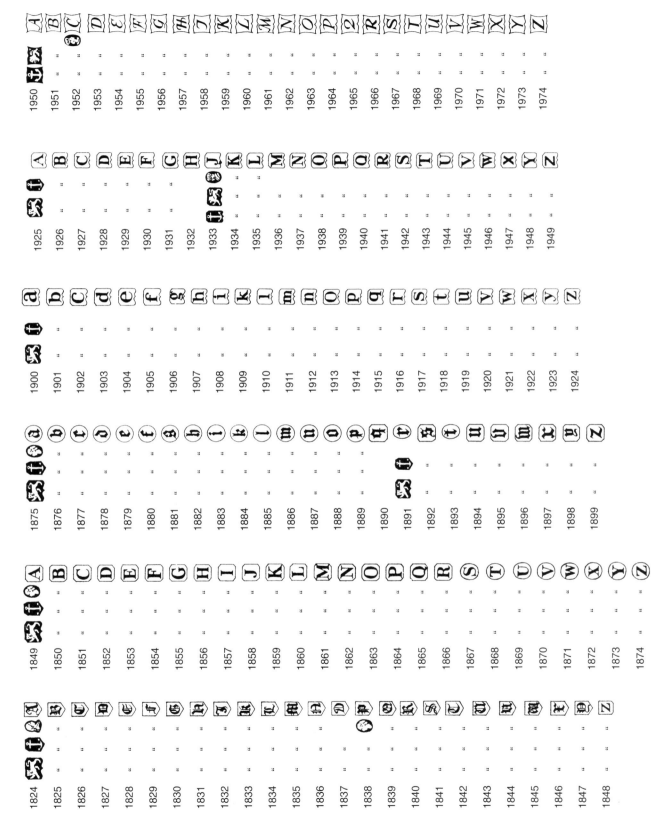

SHEFFIELD

The mark for Sheffield was, until 1975, a crown. It was then changed to a rose.
In the same year, all United Kingdom Assay Offices adopted a common date letter.

a	1824
b	1825
c	1826
d	1827
e	1828
f	1829
g	1830
h	1831
k	1832
l	1833
m	1834
p	1835
q	1836
r	1837
s	1838
t	1839
u	1840
v	1841
x	1842
z	1843

A	1844
B	1845
C	1846
D	1847
E	1848
F	1849
G	1850
H	1851
I	1852
K	1853
L	1854
M	1855
N	1856
O	1857
P	1858
R	1859
S	1860
T	1861
U	1862
V	1863
W	1864
X	1865
Y	1866
Z	1867

A	1868
B	1869
C	1870
D	1871
E	1872
F	1873
G	1874
H	1875
J	1876
K	1877
L	1878
M	1879
N	1880
O	1881
P	1882
Q	1883
R	1884
S	1885
T	1886
U	1887
V	1888
W	1889
X	1890
Y	1891
Z	1892

a	1893
b	1894
c	1895
d	1896
e	1897
f	1898
g	1899
h	1900
i	1901
k	1902
l	1903
m	1904
n	1905
o	1906
p	1907
q	1908
r	1909
s	1910
t	1911
u	1912
w	1913
x	1914
y	1915
z	1916
—	1917

a	1918
b	1919
c	1920
d	1921
e	1922
f	1923
g	1924
h	1925
i	1926
k	1927
l	1928
m	1929
n	1930
o	1931
p	1932
q	1933
r	1934
s	1935
t	1936
u	1937
v	1938
w	1939
x	1940
y	1941
z	1942

A	1943
B	1944
C	1945
D	1946
E	1947
F	1948
G	1949
H	1950
I	1951
K	1952
L	1953
M	1954
N	1955
O	1956
P	1957
Q	1958
R	1959
S	1960
T	1961
U	1962
V	1963
W	1964
X	1965
Y	1966
Z	1967

EDINBURGH

The Jubilee and Coronation marks used by the other offices were adopted also by Edinburgh.

1832	1833	1834	1835	1836	1837	1838	1839	1840	1841	1842	1843	1844	1845	1846	1847	1848	1849	1850	1851	1852	1853	1854	1855	1856

1857	1858	1859	1860	1861	1862	1863	1864	1865	1866	1867	1868	1869	1870	1871	1872	1873	1874	1875	1876	1877	1878	1879	1880	1881

1882	1883	1884	1885	1886	1887	1888	1889	1890	1891	1892	1893	1894	1895	1896	1897	1898	1899	1900	1901	1902	1903	1904	1905	

1906	1907	1908	1909	1910	1911	1912	1913	1914	1915	1916	1917	1918	1919	1920	1921	1922	1923	1924	1925	1926	1927	1928	1929	1930

1931	1932	1933	1934	1935	1936	1937	1938	1939	1940	1941	1942	1943	1944	1945	1946	1947	1948	1949	1950	1951	1952	1953	1954	1955

1956	1957	1958	1959	1960	1961	1962	1963	1964	1965	1966	1967	1968	1969	1970	1971	1972	1973-4

Acknowledgements

This book would never have been written without the generous support of a great many people. Some were responding to the author's requests for information in their private capacity, others as representatives of a wide variety of official, service or commercial organisations. Despite the already heavy burdens upon their time and resources, all have been unstinting in their support for the author's aims and objectives.

It was always the hope that this would be a very "visual" book. In order to illustrate the great range of artefacts which qualify as military and naval silver, it was essential to incorporate as many photographs as practicable. Prints of the required quality are not easy to obtain. In the main, they are available only from archives held by regimental and other service institutions. The author is profoundly grateful to the custodians of several such collections, as named in the captions, for having entrusted him with the temporary loan of their pictures, and for having granted authority to reproduce them.

Some of the pictures have been donated by important London auction houses (Bonhams, Phillips, Sotheby's, and Spinks). Again, their generosity has been invaluable.

Most of the photographs appearing in Chapters Nine and Ten were produced by Alan Cooper Colour Laboratories, of Newton Abbot, Devon. The skill of their photographer, Colin Riley, is self-evident in those pages.

Whenever an author has the seeds of an idea for a new book, he may wonder whether they will ever grow to maturity. This is certainly the case when the concept involves a great deal of research, and particularly when there is no precedent. The subject of military and naval silver has never previously been investigated in depth and committed to print. It is during those early stages, therefore, that words of encouragement are most needed.

In this case, the initial moral and practical support of six long-standing and valued friends was crucial. They were Howard Chamberlain MSM, Richard Cornish MIMarEng, Major Michael D'Arcy, Lieutenant Colonel Patric Emerson OBE, Lieutenant Colonel Maxwell Macfarlane RA, and Graham Sacker JP. If the reader has enjoyed this book, he or she owes to them the same debt of gratitude as the author.

The first step was to ask the Editors of various publications (newsletter and journals) to publish an appeal for contacts. In this context, the author is greatly obliged to Mrs Lesley Castell (Scottish Museums Council), Lieutenant Colonel Richard Corkran OBE (King's African Rifles & East African Forces Dinner Club), Major Alastair Donald RM (Royal Marines Historical Society), Lieutenant Colonel Patric Emerson OBE (Indian Army Association), Major General A J Makepeace-Warne CB CBE BA (Army Museums Ogilby Trust), Lieutenant Colonel Sam Pope OBE RM (British Commonwealth Ex-Services League), and Theon Wilkinson MBE (British Association for Cemeteries in South Asia).

It had been hoped to dedicate a chapter to the silver of the former Colonial forces, military and police. In the event, it proved impossible to gather the desired quality and quantity of information and photographs. It was not from want of effort. Several people tried hard to meet the requirement in respect of the Far East, namely Colin Bellingham, Chris Bilham, David Deptford, David Mahoney, and G A R Wright-Nooth. There were even greater problems with East and West Africa, where so much unit silver seems to have disappeared without trace since the former British colonies became independent. Correspondents having knowledge of the King's African Rifles and the Royal West African Frontier Force were Major Peter D'Buisson, Lieutenant Colonel John Dent OBE, John Hamilton MA, Eric Lanning MBE FSA, Colonel A F Mackain-Bremner, Major A E D Michell, Brigadier Malcolm Page, the late Lieutenant Colonel John Peddie MC, Keith Steward, Alastair Ward and Mrs Pauline Ward MBE. Sadly, it was all in vain.

The references to Australia and New Zealand are the result of much hard work by Major Michael D'Arcy and his many contacts within the Australian armed forces, and by Howard Chamberlain, with his own extensive knowledge of the armed forces of New Zealand. Through them, contacts were made with Miss Thérèse Angelo (Royal New Zealand Air Force Museum, Christchurch), Lieutenant P D Barnes RAN (HMAS *Kuttabul*), Major Peter Branagan (Australian School of Armour), Flying Officer T V Coromandel (Air Command, Royal New Zealand Air Force), Commander J A P Graham CSM RAN (HMAS *Cresswell*), Warrant Officer Anne Hayward (HMAS *Albatross*), Commander P K Naughton RAN (HMAS *Cerberus*), and Malcolm Orchard (Army Museum of South Australia).

Canada did not produce any publishable results, but Captain Mark Reid (Canadian War Museum, Ottawa) did try to stir some interest. Useful additional information regarding the *Commerce* disaster (Chapter Six) came from Kyle McIntyre (Access Research Associates).

Amongst many others who kindly gave their support to the project in one way or another were Mrs Judy Adams (Irvin Aerospace), Mrs Rosemary Andreae and Miss Kathryn Bellamy (Goodwood House), Captain Timothy Ash MBE (India and the Gulf), Bill Ashley and Mrs Katherine E Fox (University of Houston, USA), Carl J Austrian Jr (United States Marine Corps), Sir Thomas Barlow, Kevin A Barrington and John Rocyn-Jones (regimental wine labels), Stuart Barr (the disbanded Irish regiments), Malcolm Baxter (Machine Gun Corps), Mrs Margaret Bidmead (Royal Navy Submarine Museum), Captain Alan Brocklehurst (Yeomanry units), Jack Brogden (Royal Engineers), Philip L Budlong (Mystic Seaport Museum, USA), Gordon K Byrne (India), Christopher Carnaghan (Indian Police), Captain W W F Chatterton-Dickson RN (the East India Company and Ireland), Mrs Patricia Cooke (Goodwood Racecourse), Mrs Elspeth Cox (India), Stuart Devlin AO CMG (designer), Michael Garnett (India), Gordon Everson (South Africa), Mrs Dawn Goodson BA (designer), Andrew M Graham (HM Honorary Consul General, Cagliari), Major E A Hadow RE (Newfoundland), Mrs Marion Harding (National Army

Museum), Trevor Hearl (the history of St Helena), Peter Helmore (Devonshire Regiment), Mrs Pat Henderson (Royal Tank Regiment), Miss D Hillier (Central Library, RMA Sandhurst), Lieutenant Commander Ulric Huggins RNVR RD (Gordon Highlanders), David Leech (George Potter & Company), John Liffiton (North Yorkshire Hussars), Dr A L Lloyd OBE KStJ (the medical services), Timothy J McCann (West Sussex Record Office), Alastair Macpherson (King Edward's Horse), Jonathan Marsden (The Royal Collection Trust), Dr Richard B Meixsel (Philippines), H J H Nelson (British in India Museum), the Revd W B Paine CF (Memorial Chapel, RMA Sandhurst), Cliff Parrett MA (India), Stephen Rabson and Mrs Lynn Palmer (Peninsular & Oriental Steam Navigation Company), Wing Commander Jim Routledge RAF (Royal Air Force), John Rowe (Devon Militia), Major Jack St Aubyn (bibliography), Henry I Shaw Jr (United States Marine Corps), David Scheeres (Antarctic exploration), Mrs Philippa Smith (Scott Polar Research Institute), Kenneth L Smith-Christmas (United States Marine Corps), Andrzej Suchcitz (Polish Institute & Sikorski Museum), Victor Sutcliffe (bibliography), John Tamplin MBE TD (in numerous ways), Dr P J Thwaites MA MSc (The Sandhurst Collection), Ray Westlake (bibliography), Major General John Whitelaw (Australia), and Lieutenant Colonel R J Wyatt (bibliography).

Documents held at the PRO, Kew, are quoted by permission of The Keeper of Public Records.

The bulk of the entries refer to regiments and corps of the British Army and Indian Army. Here the author is deeply indebted to a very large number of people who have contributed information or personal memories, or who have on many occasions attempted to steer him along the path towards truth and accuracy. To take the British Army first, they are Brigadier P J F Painter, his successor Colonel M J N Richards, and their colleagues (Royal Artillery Institution, Woolwich), and Major R L Smallman RE (Royal Engineers, Chatham). Guiding lights throughout the past three years have been, for the gunners, Lieutenant Colonel Maxwell Macfarlane RA, and for the sappers, Colonel Gerald Napier.

Three British Army corps are featured in the book, and thanks are extended to Colonel Geoffrey Banks (Royal Army Medical Corps), Lieutenant Colonel J G Hambleton MBE (Royal Logistic Corps), and Lieutenant Colonel P A Roffey DL (Royal Army Veterinary Corps).

Silver of The King's Royal Hussars is beautifully illustrated in Chapter Two by courtesy of Major P J C Beresford (KRH Home Headquarters, South). Other fine photographs and historical information have been provided most generously by Stuart W Allan and Miss Melanie Brooker (Gordon Highlanders Museum), Captain R A Bonner (Manchester Regiment), David Bownes BA MPhil (Royal Welch Fusiliers Museum), Lieutenant Colonel A M Cumming OBE (The Highlanders), Brigadier Pat Erskine-Tulloch (Northamptonshire Regiment), Major J Etherington and Major N P R Woodward (4th/7th Royal Dragoon Guards), Major M Everett TD (South Wales Borderers Museum), Brigadier A I H Fyfe DL (Somerset Light Infantry), Major E Green (Staffordshire Regiment), Colonel Anthony Hewitt MBE MC (Middlesex Regiment), Major P K Higgins RA (Royal Artillery), Mrs Sally Hoffman and Richard Parsons (Honourable Artillery Company), Captain J M Holtby (Queen's Royal Lancers), Colonel J H C Horsfall DSO MC and Lieutenant Colonel T Illingworth (Royal Irish Fusiliers), Major N J Lock (Royal Welch Fusiliers), Colonel John Lowles CBE (Worcestershire & Sherwood Foresters Regiment), Major R P Mason (Royal Scots), Major R E B Morris MBE (Middlesex Regiment), William Norman (Duke of Wellington's Regiment), Major W H Reeve (Royal Norfolk Regiment), Colonel N O Roberts (Royal Regiment of Wales), Brigadier A G Ross OBE (The Royal Hospital Chelsea), Lieutenant Colonel A W Scott Elliott (Argyll & Sutherland Highlanders), Captain I G Spence (Royal Gloucestershire, Berkshire and Wiltshire Regiment), Major Robin White (Scots Guards), Colonel H B H Waring OBE (Queen's Own Royal West Kent Regiment), and Lieutenant Colonel L M B Wilson MBE (Queen's Royal Surrey Regiment).

Several other British Army regiments offered their support but, for one reason or another (usually the lack of suitable photographs), are not mentioned in the book. However, their interest was at the time most welcome.

Amongst the most enthusiastic responses were those of former officers of the pre-1947 Indian Army. With the passage of time, their regimental associations have in most cases diminished to very small memberships, and in some cases have disbanded. Those who remain are, however, remarkable for their drive and energy. The author is greatly indebted to them. They are Major Ron Allen (7th Rajput Regiment), Mrs Janet Ashe (11th Sikh Regiment), Major R J Bentley (Probyn's Horse), Captain Peter Cashmore (18th Royal Garhwal Rifles), Lieutenant Colonel P M W Doyle MC (5th Mahratta Light Infantry), Sir Charles Frossard KBE (Frontier Scouts), Lieutenant Colonel Robert Going (Kumaon Regiment), Lieutenant Colonel C R D Gray OBE (Skinners' Horse), Colonel D F Hefill (8th KGO Light Cavalry), the late Major Robert Henderson (11th Sikh Regiment), Major John Hookway (Sikh Light Infantry), Brigadier F H B Ingall DSO OBE (6th DCO Lancers), Major D F Kerr (13th DCO Lancers), Captain R C Loadsman (14th Punjab Regiment), Major D C McIntosh (Scinde Horse), Colonel Rex Mace (17th Dogra Regiment), Lieutenant General Stanley Menezes PVSM SC (in numerous ways), Major James Mottram (4th Bombay Grenadiers), R E Nissen (Auxiliary Force India), Captain S D M Ottowell (7th Rajput Regiment), Colonel Praveen Bakshi (Skinnner's Horse), Major T A E Prentice (Kumaon Regiment), Captain Terence Rochford (10th Baluch Regiment), Lieutenant Colonel E Roland-Jones (11th Sikh Regiment), Lord Sandberg of Passfield CBE (6th DCO Lancers), Colonel C W A Searle (Indian Medical Service), Colonel J M Singh (2nd Grenadiers), Lieutenant Colonel Surinder Singh (2nd Guards Mechanised, 1st Grenadiers), Major A Ramsay Tainsh MBE (Royal Indian Army Service Corps), Major F W S Taylor (Punjab Frontier Force), Major R P Watkin (Sikh Light Infantry), and Major D G Williams (17th Dogra Regiment).

Mess silver of the Gurkhas is represented in this book by the collection of the 2nd King Edward's Own Goorkha Rifles (The Sirmoor Rifles). The author is greatly indebted to the Trustees of The Sirmoor Rifles Association (UK) Trust for permission to reproduce their photographs. In particular, he wishes to thank Colonel Denis Wood for his unfailing support over the past three years. The assistance of Lieutenant Colonel C N Fraser, Regimental Secretary of The Royal Gurkha Rifles, is gladly acknowledged also. Unique personal recollections came from Lieutenant Colonel David Amoore (9th Gurkha Rifles), Major Bruce Kinloch MC (3rd Gurkha Rifles), and Lieutenant Colonel A A Mains (9th Gurkha Rifles).

Chapter Seven, "Silver at Sea", is based largely upon photographs and background information received from Geoffrey Buck (Trophy Officer, Royal Navy), John Curtis and his successor Richard Keane (The Nelson Collection, Lloyd's), Kieran McCarthy (Wartski, London), Matthew Little (Royal

Marines Museum), Lt Col A J F Noyes RM (Royal Marines Corps Secretary), Warrant Officer Philip Shuttleworth RM (Royal Marines Corps Property Officer), and Barry Knight MSM (Royal Marines). The author is most grateful to Major Mark Bailey RM and Major Alastair Donald RM for having generated, in that chapter, the condensed history of the Royal Marines.

The references to the mercantile marine have come from a stalwart ally and friend, Richard Cornish. He, like Graham Sacker, has been a fount of knowledge and wise counsel since the earliest days of the project.

The representative entries for the Royal Air Force have kindly been contributed by Air Commodore Graham Pitchfork MBE BA FRAeS RAF, and by Mrs Jean Buckberry (Librarian and Archivist, RAF Cranwell, by permission of the AOC and Commandant).

Permission to reproduce hallmarks and tables of year marks has generously been granted by David Evans, Deputy Warden of the London Assay Office, and the Assay Masters of the Birmingham, Sheffield and Edinburgh Assay Offices, namely, Michael Allchin, Ashley M Carson and Scott Walter. Much valuable information has been provided by their colleagues Miss Geraldene Mitchell and Mark Grimwade (London), Mrs Phyllis Benedikz (Birmingham), Mrs Jackie Richardson (Sheffield), and by Henry Fotheringham. To each of them, the author extends his heartfelt thanks for their swift and expert guidance whenever it was requested. Other very helpful advice was received from David Beasley (Librarian, The Goldsmiths' Company).

The process of learning about silver at the grass-roots level has come from regular contact with people who depend upon it as their livelihood. The hurly-burly of the second-hand market teaches many lessons. The author is indebted to his mentors, namely Hugh Baigent, Billy Buck, Peter Brand, Viv Goode, Rupert Huddy, Graham Morris, Elizabeth Nicolson, Paul Robinson, Chris Spaull and Henry Willis. Other valued counsellors, over many years and in a wider context, have been David Erskine-Hill, Andrew Litherland and Michael Naxton.

It can be seen that more than two hundred people were involved in the compilation of this book. Whenever relevant, they were asked to proof-read the drafts of the material which they had contributed (or of which they had expert knowledge). They did everything possible to ensure historical and technical accuracy. In the final analysis, however, the words committed to print are essentially those of the author, and he accepts full responsibility for any errors of interpretation or emphasis which the reader may identify.

Finally, the author must thank his designer and printer, Andrew Penny, of Abbey Printers, Newton Abbot. His patience and painstaking attention to detail have been at all times a source of great reassurance.

Indexes